LEXIS®-NEXIS®

LEXIS®-NEXIS® At A Glance

Finding a Single Document

THE LEXSEE® FEATURE

Use the LEXSEE feature when you have the citation for a case, law review or ALR® article, Private Letter Ruling, Revenue Ruling, Revenue Procedure, *Federal Register* document, or certain administrative documents.

LEXSEE Search Examples:

TO FIND	ENTER
Case	***lxe 490 us 462***
Public law	***lxe 101 pl 73***
Federal Register	***lxe 58 fr 45495***

THE LEXSTAT® FEATURE

Use the LEXSTAT feature when you have the citation for a state or federal statute section, *Code of Federal Regulations* section, U.S. Constitutional provisions, or certain states' administrative codes.

LEXSTAT Search Examples:

TO FIND	ENTER
State code	***lxt oh code 4582.30***
United States Code Service	***lxt 11 uscs 101***

To return to the screen where you entered the LEXSEE or LEXSTAT feature,
ENTER: ***resume***

NOTE: To see a list of LEXSEE and LEXSTAT formats for different reporter series or states, access the HELP mode by typing **h [ENTER]**.

USE THE NAME

To find a case when you know the names of the parties but don't have the citation, select the appropriate library and file and use the NAME segment in your search request. For example,
ENTER: **name (cipollone AND liggett)**

THE LINK™ FEATURE

The LINK feature lets you move directly to a document cited within the document you are viewing. If you see a symbol like **<=1>** next to a cited document, the LINK feature is available. To see a cited document which has a corresponding LINK marker, double-click on the LINK marker or enter the marker number (e.g., ***=1***).

To return to your original research,
ENTER: ***resume***

Searching for Documents

1. DEFINE your issue – What is it you need to know?
2. SELECT a LEXIS-NEXIS library and file.
3. DEVELOP a search request using the traditional Boolean method or the revolutionary FREESTYLE™ feature.
4. VIEW documents in any display format.

BOOLEAN SEARCH LOGIC

A Boolean search request, the traditional and original method used to perform online research with the LEXIS-NEXIS services, uses proximity connectors, special characters, and precision search commands. For example, to find federal U.S. Courts of Appeals case law that deals with the issue of employment discrimination against physically challenged individuals,

LIBRARY: GENFED
FILE: USAPP
ENTER: **atleast5 (handicap! OR disab! OR physical! challeng!) W/5 discriminat! W/25 employ!**

THE FREESTYLE™ FEATURE SEARCH ALTERNATIVE

The FREESTYLE feature offers you a search logic alternative to Boolean, allowing you to use "natural language" (as in plain English) to construct your search query. For example, to find case law from all federal courts online with the LEXIS-NEXIS services that discuss the admissibility of evidence obtained from DNA testing,

LIBRARY: GENFED
FILE: COURTS
ENTER: **.fr** (to invoke the FREESTYLE feature)
ENTER: **is evidence obtained from dna testing admissible in court**

Options with the FREESTYLE feature

The WHERE screen (location of terms) helps you to decide which documents to view first. At the document retrieval screen, type *=2* and press the ENTER key. If you are are viewing documents, type *.where* and press the ENTER key. To view a specific document you want to see, type the number assigned to the document and press the ENTER key.

The WHY screen (number of documents) summarizes your search results. At the document retrieval screen, type *=3* and press the ENTER key. If you are already viewing documents, type *.why* and press the ENTER key.

Refine Results

The .MORE feature finds more documents similar to a document that you found and consider to be a close match to your research needs.
ENTER: **.more**

The FOCUS™ feature lets you spotlight words within the documents in your search results (Boolean and FREESTYLE) even if those words are not part of your original search request. For example, to a display the word *forbidden* within your retrieved documents, ENTER*: .fo forbidden*
To exit the FOCUS feature,
ENTER: **.ef**

Modify a Boolean search request when your answer set is too large (add terms that will narrow results) or when your answer set is too small (add terms that will expand results). At the search result screen,
ENTER: **m**

Then enter the appropriate connector (all modifications must begin with a connector) followed by the additional word(s) you want to add to your search request.

Checking a Citation

SHEPARD'S® CITATIONS SERVICE

To SHEPARDIZE® a case, e.g., *Sony Corp. of America v. Universal Studios, Inc., 464 U.S. 417,*
ENTER: ***shep 464 us 417***

THE AUTO-CITE® SERVICE

To check a case in Auto-Cite, e.g., *United States v. Leon,* 468 U.S. 897,
ENTER: **ac 468 us 897**

THE LEXCITE® FEATURE

To find references to a case, e.g., *488 U.S. 469,*

LIBRARY: GENFED
FILE: CURRNT
ENTER: **lexcite (488 us 469)**

LEXIS®-NEXIS®

LEXIS®-NEXIS® At A Glance

Dot commands

Search

.cf	Change file
.cl	Change library
.ca	CITES assistant
.cm	Change menu
.ns	New search
easy	Go to Easy Search™
.so	Sign off

View

.ci	CITE Citations list
.fu	FULL Full text
.kw	KWIC™ 25 words either side of search terms
.vk	VAR KWIC 50 words either side of search terms
.se	SEGMTS Specified portions (segments) displayed
.le	LEAD
.sk	SuperKWIC™ (the FREESTYLE feature only)

Review

.dl	Display different level
.fd	First document retrieved
.fp	First page current document
.np	Next page of current document
.pp	Previous page of current document
.nd	Next document
.pd	Previous document
.up	Move up through text
.down	Move down through text
s	Sort documents (not in all files)
resume	Resume options screen

Refine

.fo	Enter FOCUS™ feature
.ef	Exit FOCUS feature
.more	Enter .more
.em	Exit .more
m	Modify search request
.rank	Rank documents

Display

.linkon	Display LINK™ markers
.linkoff	Erase LINK markers
.con	Turn on display commands
.coff	Turn off display commands

Print

.gd	Go docs
.pa	PRINT ALL (MAIL IT)
.pr	PRINT DOC
.sp	Print displayed screen
.pm	Print manager
.pn	Print now
.le, p	Print LEAD paragraph

Store

.keep	Store search request in LOG
.log	Display LOG
.delall	Delete LOG contents

Select Service

.ss	Enter select service
.es	Exit select service

ECLIPSE™ feature

sav	Save search to ECLIPSE
rec	Recall ECLIPSE search

FREESTYLE feature

.fr	Switch to FREESTYLE feature from Boolean
.bool	Switch to Boolean from FREESTYLE feature
.where	Display WHERE screen
.why	Display WHY screen
.sk	SuperKWIC display

Online Information

h	Help
t	Time elapsed current session
p	Number of screens in current document format
r	Display current search request
c	Client screen
.cost	Display cost estimate screen

Special Characters

litigat!	= litigate, litigator, litigated, litigation, litigating
bank***	= bank, banker, banking (word cannot begin with an *)
judg*ment	= judgement but not judgment

Connectors

OR	*stock OR share*
W/n	*john W/3 doe*
W/s	*sanction W/s frivolous*
W/p	*rule W/p sanction*
AND	*capital gain AND fraud!*
PRE/n	*cable PRE/3 television*

Precision Search Commands

atleast	*atleast10 (cercla)*
allcaps	*allcaps (aids)*
nocaps	*nocaps (aids)*
singular	*singular (aid)*
plural	*plural (aids)*

LEXIS®-NEXIS® For Law Students

Steven L. Emanuel

Author, Emanuel Law Outlines Series
Member of the New York Bar

Third Edition

Emanuel Publishing Corp.
1865 Palmer Avenue
Larchmont NY 10538

Library of Congress Cataloging-in-Publication Data

Emanuel, Steven.
LEXIS-NEXIS for Law Students / Steven L. Emanuel. — 3rd ed.
p. cm.
Includes bibliographical references and index.
ISBN 1-56542-002-0 (pbk.)
1. LEXIS (Information retrieval system) 2. Information storage and retrieval systems — Law — United States. 3. Legal research — United States — Data processing. I. Title.
KF242.A1E454 1997
025.06'34'0024375—dc21 97-25610
CIP

ISBN 1-56542-002-0

Preface

This is a book about how to use the LEXIS®-NEXIS® services, which I believe to be the best method available today for doing legal and law-related research. I have written this volume specifically to assist law students, whose needs are of course different from those of practitioners.

This book is being paid for by LEXIS-NEXIS, a member of the Reed Elsevier plc group. That is, LEXIS-NEXIS has paid for the printing of the book, and has also paid a writing fee to Emanuel Publishing Corp. Nonetheless, the ideas and opinions expressed in this book are my own, and the manuscript has been subjected to virtually no editorial control by LEXIS-NEXIS except for matters of copy-editing, trademark protection, and the like.

In particular, I would like to emphasize that I do indeed believe that LEXIS-NEXIS represents the best research solution for most lawyers. Long before I approached LEXIS-NEXIS with the idea for this book, I used the LEXIS service as my only Computer Assisted Legal Research (CALR) tool. To this day, LEXIS remains the sole CALR system in use at Emanuel Publishing Corp., and we use it most extensively in the preparation and updating of our outlines.

You can use this book either as a "tutorial" or as a "reference." I suggest you do both. That is, you should first read it — or at least skim it — from front to back, so you get at least a general sense of how the LEXIS service works and what you can do with it; you should try many of the examples yourself as you read. Then, consult the book for more specific help when you have a particular research problem that you think might benefit from CALR.

The information in this book is, in general, accurate as of about May, 1997. When the number of cases or documents retrieved from searches is stated, the results are those received by running the search during the spring of 1997. By the time you read this, more documents are likely to have been added to the file you are searching, so the number retrieved may be higher.

You may wish to pay special attention to Chapter 12, covering the *LEXIS-NEXIS Office for Legal Education*. This is an exciting package of PC software that assists law students in performing many different law-school tasks.

(continued on next page)

This is the third edition of this book, and I expect to prepare still further editions. Therefore, I would most appreciate it if you would send me your questions, comments and suggestions. You can write to me at Emanuel Publishing Corp., 1865 Palmer Ave., Larchmont NY 10538; or, better still, E-mail me at semanuel@pobox.com.

Steven Emanuel

Larchmont, NY

June, 1997

Acknowledgments

Many people helped bring this book about.

LEXIS-NEXIS devoted substantial resources of both people and money to this project. For reasons of space, I can list here only people (and not even all of them) who worked on this Third Edition. Some of the many LN'ers who either answered my questions, or reviewed the manuscript and made suggestions, are: Peter Adams, Valerie Akerson, Lisa Allemang, Dave Beals, Kim Buchanan, Phyllis Clark, Missy Cottongim, Mary Ann Dean, Eileen Donnelly, John Driggers, Susan Ebert, Gayle Farmer, Jen Harding, Chuck Havener, Tom Heferle, Crystal Henderson, Scott Hindenlang, Rob Holbrook, Greg Horner, Kurt Horner, John Hourigan, Tyler Howes, Esther Judson, Scott Koorndyk, Tony Latessa, Linda Leiwig, Vanessa Lloyd, Teresa MacGregor, Lynn Menard, Lisa Mohnsam, Erin Murray, Sharon Murray, Mariann Penska, Pam Rath, Mark Rickert, Martha Schroeder, Sharon Southam, Leslie Sprigg, Missy Thomas, Shari Townsend, Fran Warren, Kristi Weaver, and Linda Wesner. Special thanks to Lisa McDonough and Pat Cassidy, for their yeoman service in editing, critiquing and assembling the final manuscript.

Thanks as well to the dozens of other people at LEXIS-NEXIS, many of them people whose names I still don't know, who worked to ensure the accuracy of this book. Needless to say, any errors are mine alone.

Also, thanks to Eric Lambert, Associate General Counsel of Emanuel Publishing Corp., who has helped with many of the editorial and technical details. Lastly, my deepest thanks to my father, Lazar, and my wife, Marilyn, both of whom have been unceasingly supportive during what has been an intense and sometimes difficult process.

Table of Contents

CHAPTER 1

INTRODUCTION

CHAPTER 2

BASICS OF SEARCHING, DISPLAYING & PRINTING

CHAPTER 3

USING SECONDARY LEGAL AUTHORITIES

CHAPTER 4

FINDING CASES

CHAPTER 5

STATUTORY LAW

CHAPTER 6

ADMINISTRATIVE LAW

CHAPTER 7

SPECIALIZED LEGAL RESEARCH

CHAPTER 8

NEXIS® AND OTHER LAW-RELATED INFORMATION

CHAPTER 9

CITATORS

CHAPTER 10

CheckCite™ , CiteRite™ , CompareRite™ , and FullAuthority™

CHAPTER 11

JOB PROSPECTING

CHAPTER 12

THE LEXIS®-NEXIS® OFFICE FOR LEGAL EDUCATION

APPENDICES AND INDEX

Chapter 1

Introduction

I. WHAT IS LEXIS®-NEXIS®?

A. Introduction: The LEXIS®-NEXIS® services are the leading full-text computer-assisted legal research (CALR) services. The LEXIS service contains (among other things):

- the full text of reported cases from the last 50 years (plus a lot of cases decided before then, including some from the 1700's);
- the full text of federal and state statutes;
- a vast array of federal and state administrative and regulatory materials;
- a large collection of secondary legal authorities (e.g., legal encyclopedias, the Restatements, over 100 law reviews, etc.).

A companion service to LEXIS, the NEXIS® service, is the world's largest database of full-text news and business publications. Other files on the LEXIS-NEXIS services give you full-text documents for finance, accounting, medicine, geopolitics, etc. In total, the LEXIS-NEXIS services are probably the world's largest single collection of full-text-searchable materials.

The LEXIS and NEXIS online services represent just a portion of the law-related products available from LEXIS-NEXIS. Some of the other products are:

- Michie Books and CD-ROMs, from the Michie Company, a unit of LEXIS-NEXIS.
- A set of software packages to do law-related tasks (e.g., CompareRite™, which lets you compare two versions of a document; CheckCite™, which lets you automatically cite-check and download the full text of a case, etc.)[1]

B. History: The LEXIS service began its life in the late 1960s as a project of the Ohio State Bar Association, which wanted to put the case law of Ohio and other states onto a centralized computer, so that remote users could search it by any word or phrase. The OSBA contracted with Data Corporation, a small Ohio high-tech company, to build a system to do this. In 1968, before the project got underway, Data Corporation was acquired by The Mead Corporation, a large paper and printing manufacturer located in Dayton, Ohio.[2]

---

1. This collection of software is discussed extensively in Chapter 10.

2. Surprisingly, at the time the Mead Corporation acquired Data Corp., Mead wasn't interested in (or even aware of) the OSBA contract, but was instead after Data Corp.'s ink-jet printing technology. Mead didn't discover the OSBA contract until several months after the acquisition.

Mead formed a division, Mead Data Central, to develop the service. Under the name LEXIS, Mead Data Central launched the service nationally in 1973. At its outset, the system contained the case law of two states (New York and Ohio), federal case law, and federal statutes. (As you undoubtedly know, and as I explain in detail below, it's a bit bigger today.)

Mead sold the LEXIS-NEXIS services, and other law-related businesses, in late 1994 to Reed Elsevier Inc., a member of the Reed Elsevier plc group. The Reed Elsevier plc group is one of the world's largest publishers, with annual revenues of over $5 billion, much of it in the legal area (e.g., Butterworths, the largest legal publisher in the U.K.) The LEXIS-NEXIS services are run as a division (called simply "LEXIS-NEXIS") within Reed Elsevier.

C. **Today:** From the modest beginnings described above, materials have been added to the LEXIS-NEXIS services year by year, until they contain today virtually all useful case law and statutes, and a lot more besides.

1. **Size:** The LEXIS-NEXIS services contain more than ***1,100 gigabytes*** of information. If you're a computer hacker, you know that a gigabyte is one thousand megabytes (or one billion characters), so this would make the LEXIS-NEXIS services 1,100 billion characters worth of searchable information. At 2,000 characters per page (the amount of text on a typical single-spaced typewritten page), this comes to over 550 million pages of information.

   To wow you with some additional numbers:

   - The LEXIS-NEXIS services contain nearly 7,300 different databases (actually, they're called "files");
   - More than 9.5 million documents are added each week to the approximately one billion documents already online;
   - The services have 816,000 active subscribers.

D. **How full-text searching on the LEXIS service works:** Every database on the LEXIS-NEXIS services is "full text searchable." This means, in essence, that you can search for ***any word or any phrase***, and almost instantly find every document containing that word or phrase. How do the services do this? Today's computers may be fast, but they're clearly not fast enough to search through 1,100 billion characters worth of information in a few seconds, to find the documents containing the word or phrase you are looking for.

The secret lies in the use of an ***"inverted list,"*** basically a master dictionary of every word in the database. For every word in the database, the inverted list contains not only the number of the document that the word occurs in, but also information about the ***position*** in which that word falls in the document. Suppose that you are looking for every case, from anywhere in the U.S., in which the phrase "comparative negligence" occurs within 10 words of the word "pedestrian." You would probably select the *MEGA*™ file in which to do this search.[3] Here are

3. I'll be talking soon about what a "file" is. For now, assume that it is equivalent to what is commonly called a "database," that is, a single mass of information that can be searched by a single query. The largest file on the LEXIS service is the *MEGA* file (in the *MEGA* library), which consists of the full text of every state and federal court case collected by LEXIS-NEXIS from around the nation.

the steps that the LEXIS service would take to resolve this search:

Step 1: The service looks in the *MEGA* file's inverted list, under the entry for the word "comparative." From this list, it collects the document number for every document (i.e., case) containing this word. It also stores the position(s) that the word occupies in each of these documents. (*Example:* In document 45847, "comparative" occurs as the 359th and the 842nd words.) It does the same for the words "negligence" and "pedestrian."

Step 2: The computer now compares the entries for the various words, to satisfy the search. (*Example:* Since "comparative" occurs in document 45847, the service looks to see whether this document number is among the listings for "negligence" and "pedestrian" as well. If it appears on all three lists, this document is marked as a potential hit.)

Step 3: Since our search specifies "proximity" — that is, it specifies a precise positional relation that must occur among the various words — any document number that remains on our list as being one containing all three search words must now be checked for proximity. (*Example:* The service knows that "comparative" occurs at word position 359 in document 45847. It now checks to see whether "negligence," when it occurs in document 45847, occurs at position 360, i.e., one word later than the first occurrence of "comparative.") After all the cross-matching of positions, the service comes up with a final list of documents that satisfy our search request.

Step 4: Only when we want to see parts of a document does the service go to the actual text of the document. Thus if we press the [CITE] key (or type `.ci`), only now does the service go out to the disk to read the actual text of the underlying documents necessary to display their citations.

II. THE STRUCTURE OF THE LEXIS-NEXIS SERVICES

A. Libraries and files: Information on the LEXIS-NEXIS services is organized at the highest level into ***"libraries,"*** and then within each library into ***"files."***

1. **Libraries:** You don't actually search in a library. Instead, you select a library as a means of narrowing down the files in which you will be searching. Examples of important libraries on the LEXIS service include *GENFED* (files containing federal cases and other federal materials), *MEGA* (many files, each containing case law from a different jurisdiction), *CODES* (many files, each containing the statutes of a particular jurisdiction), and *STATES* (many files, each containing cases and other materials from a particular state).

2. **Files:** Once you have selected a library, you then select one or more "files." A file is the smallest grouping of documents on the LEXIS service. There is a separate inverted list for each file. For instance, within the *GENFED* library, there is a file called *US*, which consists of all U.S. Supreme Court cases; there is a single inverted list, or master dictionary, of every word contained in all of these Supreme Court cases, making it easy to search, say, for the phrase "freedom of speech" wherever it occurs in a Supreme Court case. In many

libraries, you are able to ***combine*** multiple files together for a single search, as long as all of the files are in a single library.[4] When you combine files, the service has to look in the separate inverted list for each file, but it is able to do this quickly and, from your perspective, "transparently."[5] This is also true of a "group file" (i.e., a pre-defined collection of files set up by LEXIS-NEXIS).

You can think of a filing cabinet as being a metaphor for the library/file/case structure of the LEXIS service; the library is a file drawer, the file is a Manila folder containing numerous stapled documents, and each case is one or more sheets stapled together and placed in the Manila folder:

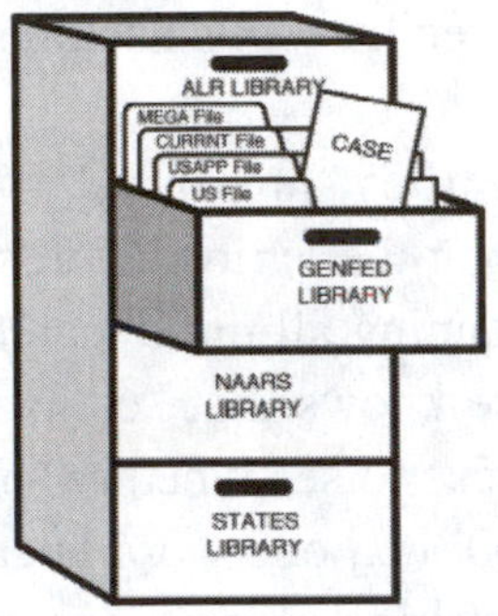

To get a better feel for how libraries and cases fit together, you may want to glance ahead to the listings of libraries,[6] and the listings of the files within some of the more important libraries.[7]

III. ACCESSING THE LEXIS-NEXIS SERVICES

A. Your choice of systems: You can access the LEXIS-NEXIS services from three different types of computers: (1) IBM PC-compatibles running MS-DOS®; (2) IBM PC-compatibles running Microsoft® Windows®; and (3) Apple Macintosh® computers.

B. Hardware and operating system requirements: Here's a brief summary of hardware and operating system requirements:

1. **Communications:** For all systems, you will of course need a modem, which can be internal or external. You will want at least a 9600-baud modem, because virtually every city

4. This process of combining multiple files for a single search is called ***"custom file selection,"*** and is discussed more fully on p. 1-29.

5. In computer jargon, an operation is said to be "transparent" to the user when it is performed quickly and easily enough that the user is not made aware of the fancy stuff going on behind the scenes.

6. See pp. 4-26 and 4-27.

7. See, e.g., Appendix F-1 for a listing of some of the files in the *MEGA* library, p. 4-28 for some of the files in the *GENFED* library, and p. 4-29 for some of the files in the *STATES* library.

containing an ABA-accredited law school is now served by one or more 9600-baud access numbers for the LEXIS-NEXIS telecommunications network.[8] In general, any modem supporting the industry-standard Hayes Command Set should work.

2. **Printer:** You will also find it highly desirable, though not essential, to have a printer.

3. **DOS requirements:** For MS-DOS machines, you will need the following:

   - A computer running MS-DOS version 3.3 or higher.
   - A hard disk with at least 1.5MB of available disk space. (You'll need at least 6 MB if you want both the LEXIS-NEXIS and CheckCite packages.)
   - At least 512K of RAM, of which at least 367K is available at the time you start up the LEXIS-NEXIS Research Software.
   - One 3-1/2 inch floppy disk drive.
   - A monitor (monochrome, CGA, EGA or VGA).

4. **Windows requirements:** For computers running the Microsoft Windows or Windows 95 operating system, you will need the following:

   - 386 or higher processor (Windows 3.1), 486 or higher processor (Windows 95).
   - Microsoft Windows 3.1 or higher, or Windows 95.
   - At least 4 MB of RAM (16 MB is recommended for Windows 95 users).
   - A hard disk with at least 5MB of available disk space. (Research Manager 7.0 needs at least 8MB of available disk space; The Windows 95 version needs at least 8MB of available RAM.)
   - One 3-1/2 inch high-density floppy disk drive.
   - A mouse supported by Windows (not required, but highly recommended).
   - A CD-ROM drive is required for LEXIS-NEXIS Research Manager 7.0.

5. **Macintosh requirements:** For Macintosh-based systems, you will need the following:

   - A Macintosh computer or compatible.
   - Macintosh System software version 7.0 or later, or MacOS. (The latest version of the research software for Macintosh, Version 2.9, will not work on Macintosh computers running any version of the System software earlier than version 7.0.)

C. **Installation and setup:** When you receive a copy of the LEXIS-NEXIS Research Software to install on your home computer, you'll also receive a copy of the installation guide for the type of software you're installing (MS-DOS, MS-Windows or Macintosh). If you need further installation instructions, call LEXIS-NEXIS Customer Service at 1-800-45LEXIS (available

8. The LEXIS-NEXIS Telecommunications Network is LEXIS-NEXIS's network for connecting hundreds of cities to the main LEXIS-NEXIS computers in Dayton, Ohio. When you configure your LEXIS-NEXIS communications software, you will typically tell it to connect to the services via the LEXIS-NEXIS Telecommunications Network, which lets you make just a local telephone call rather than a long distance call.

around-the-clock except 2:00 a.m. Sunday-10:00 a.m. Sunday, EST). The rest of this book assumes that you have a working installation that enables you to dial into the LEXIS-NEXIS computer and get to the point where you are asked to sign on.

D. Research software: For each of the three types of computers with which you can access the LEXIS-NEXIS services, LEXIS-NEXIS supplies a different version of the software you run to do so, called "Research Software." In general, there is no variation among the three packages in terms of what you can do. The principal difference among the packages is that the software used on the two Graphical User Interface (GUI) systems (Windows and Macintosh) makes extensive use of the mouse, and lets you control functions by clicking on-screen "keys," whereas the MS-DOS version for the most part requires you to press actual function keys on the keyboard.[9]

The similarities among the three versions of the Sessions Software are greater than the differences. In all three, for instance, the LEXIS service computer sends its information to you in a central region of your PC's computer screen, and this central region contains exactly the same information regardless of which Session Software you are using. For instance, when you first sign on, you are given a list of libraries. Here is how two of the packages, the MS-DOS package and the Windows package, compare as to this opening screen:

LIBRARIES -- PAGE 1 of 2
Please ENTER the NAME (only one) of the library you want to search.
- For more information about a library, ENTER its page (PG) number.
- To see a list of additional libraries, press the NEXT PAGE key.

NAME	PG	NAME	PG	NAME	PG	NAME	PG	NAME	PG	NAME	PG	NAME	PG	NAME	PG
General Legal						Public Records				Helps		Financial		Nexis	
MEGA	1	2NDARY	2	LAWREV	3	ALLREC	4	INSOLV	5	EASY	6	COMPNY	7	NEWS	22
GENFED	1	ALR	2	MARHUB	3	ASSETS	4	LEXDOC	5	GUIDE	6	INVEST	7	REGNWS	22
STATES	1	BNA	2	LEXREF	3	DOCKET	4	LIENS	5	PRACT	6	NAARS	7	TOPNWS	22
CODES	1	ABA	2	HOTTOP	3	FINDER	4	VERDCT	5	TERMS	6	QUOTE	7	LEGNEW	22
CITES	1	CAREER	2			INCORP	4			CATLOG	6	D&B	7	CMPGN	22
LEGIS	1	CLE	2							CUSTOM	6	BLMBRG	7	WORLD	22
Area of Law														Medical	
ACCTG	8	CORP	9	ETHICS	10	HEALTH	11	LEXPAT	12	PUBHW	13	TORTS	14	GENMED	15
ADMRTY	8	CRIME	9	FAMILY	10	IMMIG	11	M&A	12	REALTY	13	TRADE	14	EMBASE	15
ADR	8	EMPLOY	9	FEDCOM	10	INSURE	11	MILTRY	12	STSEC	13	TRANS	14	MEDLNE	15
BANKNG	8	ENERGY	9	FEDSEC	10	INTLAW	11	PATENT	12	STTAX	13	TRDMRK	14		
BKRTCY	8	ENVIRN	9	FEDTAX	10	ITRADE	11	PENBEN	12	TAXANA	13	UCC	14		
COPYRT	8	ESTATE	9			LABOR	11	PUBCON	12	TAXRIA	13				

Enter .NP for Individual States, International Law and more News information

Library Menu Screen, p. 1, under MS-DOS

9. The MS-DOS version, beginning with version 2.7, does have some limited mouse support.

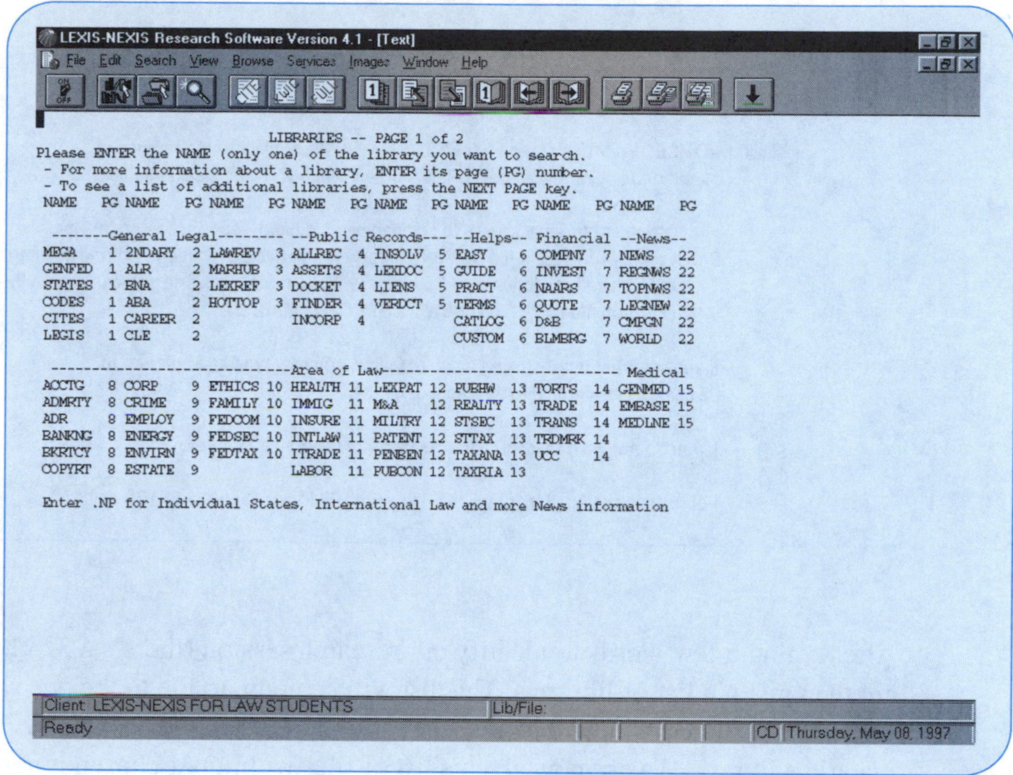

Library Menu Screen, p. 1, under MS-WINDOWS

Observe that except for the menu items at the top of the Windows screen, and the on-screen "keys" in that version, the two versions are identical. This would also be true of the Macintosh version of this first screen. For simplicity's sake, in the rest of this manual, when I generally show you a sample screen, I do so using the DOS version, mostly because this can be done in the smallest space.

IV. A BRIEF TOUR OF THE LEXIS®-NEXIS® SERVICES

A. The tour: Let's now take a quick "introductory tour" of the LEXIS service. My purpose is to give you just the flavor of the service, and a sense of the kinds of things you can do with it — the detailed "how to do it" instructions will come later.

1. Sign on: First, we sign onto the service. Using whatever Session Software (MS-DOS, Windows or Macintosh) we have on our system, we tell it to dial the LEXIS service in Dayton, Ohio.[10] The first time we will actually type anything is when we see a screen somewhat like the following one, which typically tells us about some new feature or file that has been recently introduced to the service, then prompts us to identify our research:

10. You will probably have loaded the Session Software with your personal I.D., so it can log you in automatically. The remaining instructions assume that you have done so.

1...5...10...15...20...25...30..

NOTICE: Your use of the LEXIS-NEXIS services is subject to the terms and conditions appearing in the TERMS library, which you may view at no charge.

For cost effective, easy access to company and industry reports, search the Investext Preview file (INVPRE) in the COMPNY library. 12 Intertec publications expand coverage of the Media and Telecommunications Industries! Coverage is from March 1996, and you can search them now in the new Intertec group file (INTRTC) in NEWS, CMPCOM or MARKET.

If you want to identify the research to follow, you may type and enter up to 32 characters identifying the client or matter.

If you do not wish to identify the research, press the ENTER key.

For further explanation, press the H key (for HELP) and then the ENTER key.

After typing a few words to identify our research session (there's a 32-character limit), we are then given a list of libraries. This list will be comparable to the one shown above on p. 1-6. Let's assume for now that we select the *GENFED* library, which is the basic federal-materials library. We are now given a list of files within our chosen library:

Please ENTER, separated by commas, the NAMES of the files you want to search. You may select as many files as you want, including files that do not appear below, but you must enter them all at one time. To see a description of a file, ENTER its page (PG) number.

FILES - PAGE 1 of 10 (NEXT PAGE for additional files)

NAME	PG	DESCRIP	NAME	PG	DESCRIP	NAME	PG	DESCRIP
-----COURTS GROUP FILES--			---------SUPREME COURT---------			--------------RULES--------------		
MEGA	11	Fed & State Cts	US	1	US Supreme Court	RULES	24	Federal Rules
OMNI	1	Fed Cases & ALR	USPLUS	12	US,BRIEFS,PRE-VU	----ADMINISTRATIVE-----		
COURTS	1	Fed Cases	BRIEFS	12	Argued from 9/79	ALLREG	16	FEDREG & CFR
CURRNT	1	Cases w/in 2yrs	USTRAN	12	Sup.Ct Transcripts	FEDREG	16	Fed. Register
NEWER	3	Cases from1944	USLIST	12	Sup.Ct Summaries	CFR	16	Code of Fed.Reg
SUPCIR	1	US,USAPP & CAFC	USLW	12	US Law Week	COMGEN	14	Comp.Gen.Decs.
FED	8	CAFC,CCPA,CIT.	----------LEGISLATIVE---------			-----SECONDARY SOURCES----		
--------U.S. COURT FILES------			RECORD	19	CongRec frm 1985	SSMEGA	33	All Secondary
US	1	US Supreme Ct	BILLS	27	All Bills Files	ALR	33	ALR &L.Ed.Annos
USAPP	1	Cts of Appeal	PUBLAW	15	US Public Laws	RESTAT	33	Restatements
DIST	1	District Courts	USCODE	15	USCS & PUBLAW	EXTRA	11	In the News...
CLAIMS	2	Ct. Fed. Claims				PUBS	38	Legal Pubs

To search by Circuits press NEXT PAGE. NOTE: Only court files can be combined.

Let's now select the *MEGA* file, which contains all federal and state case law. We're now asked to type our search request. Assume that we've got a torts problem: we want to find out whether, where a bystander watches another person be killed or injured in an accident, the bystander may recover against the tortfeasor for negligent infliction of emotional distress. We would identify several critical words or phrases (e.g., "bystander," "liable" and "emotional distress"), and would link them together with various "search connectors" to specify the logical relation that must occur between or among the various words or phrases. In this case, assuming that we want all cases where the word "bystander" occurs within 10 words of the word "liable," and the word "liable" occurs within 10 words of the phrase "emotional distress," we would type our search request into the service as follows:

Library: **GENFED**
File: **MEGA**
Enter: **bystander w/10 liable w/10 emotional distress**

On the service, the screen will look like this when you're typing in your search statement:

```
bystander w/10 liable w/10 emotional distress

Please type your search request then press the ENTER key.
What you enter will be Search Level 1.

Type .fr to enter a FREESTYLE (TM) search.

For further explanation, press the H key (for HELP) and then the ENTER key.
```

The service then tells us that it has found 84 cases that satisfy this search request. We could then press the [CITE] key (F7 on PC keyboards, or type **.ci**), to get the caption, court, citation and date for each of these cases:

```
LEVEL 1 - 84 CASES

1. BLINZLER v. MARRIOTT INT'L, INC., No. 95-2108, No. 95-2199, UNITED STATES
COURT OF APPEALS FOR THE FIRST CIRCUIT, 81 F.3d 1148; 1996 U.S. App. LEXIS 7575,
  April 12, 1996, Decided

2. GOTTSHALL v. CONRAIL, No. 91-1926, UNITED STATES COURT OF APPEALS FOR THE
THIRD CIRCUIT, 988 F.2d 355; 1993 U.S. App. LEXIS 1940,    May 7, 1992, Argued,
  February 8, 1993, Filed, Petition for Rehearing Denied March 11, 1993,
Reported at 1993 U.S. App. LEXIS 4622.

3. MARTIN v. UNITED STATES, Nos. 92-15322, 92-15611, No. 92-15593, UNITED STATES
COURT OF APPEALS FOR THE NINTH CIRCUIT, 984 F.2d 1033; 1993 U.S. App. LEXIS
1267; 93 Cal. Daily Op. Service 647; 93 Daily Journal DAR 1297,    December 15,
1992, Argued, Submitted, San Francisco, California,    January 28, 1993, Filed

4. In re AIR CRASH DISASTER NEAR CERRITOS, CALIFORNIA, AUGUST 31, 1986, No.
90-55224, UNITED STATES COURT OF APPEALS FOR THE NINTH CIRCUIT, 973 F.2d 1490;
1992 U.S. App. LEXIS 20459; 92 Cal. Daily Op. Service 7467; 92 Daily Journal DAR
12119,    December 5, 1991, Argued and Submitted, Pasadena, California,
September 1, 1992, Filed
```

Now, we would probably take a look at these cases. We would probably start by looking at the cases in the KWIC™ (Key Word In Context) format, which will show us just that portion of each opinion surrounding our "hits." To do this, we would press the [KWIC] key (F5, or type `.kw`). For one of those cases (it happens to be the 46th of the 84), here's what the first screen of the KWIC format looks like:

```
LEVEL 1 - 46 OF 84 CASES

      STRICKLAND et al. v. HODGES
      No. 50330

  Court of Appeals of Georgia

  134 Ga. App. 909; 216 S.E.2d 706

      March 10, 1975, Argued
      May 29, 1975, Decided

DISPOSITION: Judgment affirmed.

OPINION:

 ... [*909] [**707]  In an excellent and learned brief citing both foreign
and Georgia decisions appellant's able and articulate advocate seeks to persuade
this court to create such right of action.  He points out that in dealing with
negligent infliction of  emotional distress  the various jurisdictions have
devised three theories under which defendants have  [*910]  been held  liable
 to  bystanders.  These carry the appropriately descriptive names of "impact,"

Press Alt-H for Help  or  .SO to End Session  or  Alt-Q to Quit Software.
```

Observe that in addition to the portion of text surrounding the hits, we are also given the basic citation information (name of parties, name of court, cite, date). If we want to take a look at the full opinion, rather than this abridged form, we would press the [FULL] key (F6, or type `.fu`). The FULL format will show us the full text from the portion of the document that contains the search words:

134 Ga. App. 909, *909; 216 S.E.2d 706, **707

of emotional distress the various jurisdictions have devised three theories under which defendants have [*910] been held liable to bystanders. These carry the appropriately descriptive names of "impact," "zone of danger," and "fear for another" rules.

As the nomenclature indicates, the "impact rule" required that defendant's negligent conduct result in actual bodily contact to the plaintiff. Excepting for special situations discussed hereafter, Georgia follows this doctrine. <=1> Blanchard v. Reliable Transfer Co., 71 Ga. App. 843 (2) (32 SE2d 420); <=2> Kuhr Bros., Inc. v. Spahos, 89 Ga. App. 885, 890 (4) (81 SE2d 491). Thus, in <=3> Southern R. Co. v. Jackson, 146 Ga. 243 (91 SE 28), a mother crossing railroad tracks was permitted to sue for her personal injuries sustained in a fall while avoiding the approaching engine operated in a grossly negligent manner, but in the second headnote our Supreme Court held that "the fact that she witnessed the mangling of the child and became frightened and suffered a severe nervous shock therefrom would not entitle her to a recovery." See the annotation on this subject in <=4> 29 ALR3d 1337 where the writer at page 1344 comments that on this subject "the authorities are in a state of dissension probably unequaled in the law of torts."

While recognizing these Georgia authorities to be controlling in a "negligence" situation appellants'

At this point, we can continue to peruse the various cases retrieved directly by our search. We can move around within a case by using the [NEXT PAGE] (F1, or type **.np**), [PREV PAGE] (F2, or type **.pp**), and [FIRST PAGE] (Shift-F6, or type **.fp**) keys; this is true whether we are in KWIC format (in which case [NEXT PAGE] and [PREV PAGE] move us from hit to hit) or FULL format. We can move several pages ahead or behind in the document by using a number after the move command (e.g., **.np10** to move 10 pages forward.) We can skip from document to document by using the [NEXT DOC] (F3, or type **.nd**), [PREV DOC] (F4, or type **.pd**) and [FIRST DOC] (Shift-F7, or type **.fd**) keys.

At any point, if we find a document that is especially relevant to our issue, we can use the **.more** command to find more cases similar to this especially-relevant one.[11]

At any time, if we are looking at a document that we would like to print, we can do so by pressing the [PRINT DOC] (Shift-F3, or type **.pr**) key. This is true whether we are looking at a case, a statutory section, or some other kind of document (e.g., an administrative regulation, law review article, newspaper article, etc.). We can arrange for our document to be printed not just in FULL format, but in one of the other formats if this would be more efficient (e.g., a printout in KWIC format will just show the citation of the document plus those portions containing hits). After we press [PRINT DOC] while looking at a document, the system acknowledges our request and shows us how that request will be interpreted:[12]

11. **.more** is discussed more fully on p. 2-67, *infra*.

12. If your ID is set up so that your printouts are routed to a Stand Alone Printer (described *infra*, p. 2-82), you'll see a "Delivery Options" screen before you get to the screen reproduced here.

```
Confirming Your Document Delivery Order
                  Document:  1ST
              Print Format:  FULL
  Number of Printed Pages:   5        (approximate for dual column)
   NOTE: You may change the print format by using the format commands.

          ENTER:        Y        To confirm your order.

                        N        To cancel your order.

  Check Options        OPT       To view or change print options.

                       PAG       To print selected pages.

--> Your destination is the attached printer or disk.
-----------------------------------------------------------------------------
For further explanation, press the H key (for HELP) and then the TRANSMIT key.
```

At this point, we'll enter **Y** to confirm the print order, or **N** to cancel it. Then, we'll press the [ENTER] key to return to the document we were viewing.

Apart from looking through the retrieved cases, we might also range further afield. In fact, we can do this without "losing our place." For instance, suppose in reading the *Strickland v. Hodges* case shown above, we saw a citation to another case, and decided we would like to see that case. We can do this very easily, by use of the LEXIS service's LINK™ feature: each time a case is cited in another case on the LEXIS service, a LINK marker like **=1** is presented next to the cite. Assuming we have a mouse, we can simply click on this special symbol, and see the cited case. If we did not have a mouse, we would type **=1** [ENTER]. Thus to view *Blanchard v. Reliable Transfer* (shown in the screen on p. 1-11 with the symbol **[=1]** next to it), we would simply click on the **[=1]** (or type **=1** [ENTER]), and we would immediately be shown the full text of the *Blanchard* case.

We can also use the LEXIS service to show us ***statutes***. For instance, suppose that we have a cite to California Civil Code §1624, the California Statute of Frauds. No matter what library and file we were logged into, we could immediately see this section by using the LEXSTAT® feature. We would press the LEXSTAT key (or type **LEXSTAT** or **LXSTAT**), and then type **cal civ code 1624**[13]. We would then be shown the relevant section:

13. Not all states name their statutes in this way. For an Ohio statute, for instance, you'd type merely **lexstat oh code 1701.95**.

```
To be able to browse preceding or succeeding code sections, enter B.  The
first page of the document you are currently viewing will be displayed in FULL.
----------------------------------------------------------------------------------
         DEERING'S CALIFORNIA CODES ANNOTATED
       Copyright (c) 1996, by Bancroft-Whitney, a division of
              Thomson Information Services, Inc.

*** THIS SECTION IS CURRENT THROUGH THE 1997 SUPPLEMENT (1996 SESSION) ***
    *** INCLUDING URGENCY LEGISLATION THROUGH CHAPTER 3, 3/4/97 ***

                    CIVIL CODE
                 DIVISION 3. Obligations
                   PART 2. Contracts
             TITLE 2. Manner of Creating Contracts
                 Cal Civ Code @ 1624 (1996)

@ 1624.  Statute of frauds

The following contracts are invalid, unless they, or some note or memorandum
thereof, are in writing and subscribed by the party to be charged or by the
party's agent:
```

We could then browse among adjoining sections of the statute by typing **B**, then using the [PREV DOC] and [NEXT DOC] keys. When we are finished with looking at the statutory materials, we can go back to wherever we were when we first used the LEXSTAT feature, by pressing the [EXIT SERV] (Shift-F2, or type **.es**) key.

When we are ready to conclude our research session, we press the [SIGN OFF] key (Alt-F9, or type **.so**). The system summarizes our search session, and tells us how to save our research for reuse later in the day:

```
           DATE:  May 5, 1997
         CLIENT:  LEXIS MANUAL
        LIBRARY:  GENFED
           FILE:  MEGA

Your search request is:
BYSTANDER W/10 LIABLE W/10 EMOTIONAL DISTRESS

Number of CASES found with your search request through:
  LEVEL  1...    9

Enter:      Y  To save your research (until 2:00 A.M. Eastern Time)
            N  If you do not want to save your research

If you do not want to end this research session, press the SIGN OFF key again.

For further explanation, press the H key (for HELP) and then the ENTER key.
```

Once we tell the service that we do or do not want to save our research, we are automatically disconnected, and returned to the control of our local Research Software.

That's it for our brief "intro tour" of the LEXIS service. In the sections below, we'll take a more in-depth look at certain aspects of the service.

V. SOME BASICS

A. Signing on: The precise way you will dial into the LEXIS service and sign on depends on which Session Software you are using. For details on how to sign in, consult the manual accompanying your software. You should have been assigned an individual I.D. that you can use to access the LEXIS service from either home or school.

For home access, you will probably want to pre-store your personal I.D. in your Session Software, so that you will not have to manually key the I.D. in each time you log on. If you are like most law students, you're extremely busy, and saving those few seconds each time you log into the LEXIS service, multiplied by the dozens or hundreds of times you will use the service each year, makes for a substantial time savings.[14]

B. Identifying your research: Once you have entered your I.D., you will see a screen like the one on p. 1-8, asking you if you want to "identify your research." You will usually want to accept this invitation. There are two main benefits to identifying your research:

- If you save your research, and come back to it later in the day, you'll have a nice named session to remind you what you were doing; and
- It's a habit you should develop; when you begin working in the real world, your monthly bill will identify each session, so your employer can track its CALR costs.

The ability to track usage costs is only a hypothetical advantage when you are accessing the LEXIS service at no charge as a law student, but it will become critical if you go into private practice and need to turn your use of the LEXIS service from a law firm "cost center" into a "revenue center" by re-billing clients for charges incurred in using the service.[15]

C. Typing commands and editing them: No matter what you want to do in the LEXIS service, you will need to type things: search statements, search connectors, library names, directions to the system, etc. All of this typing gets done at the upper part of your screen, on what we can

14. It's almost in the same class as the time you would save by not brushing your teeth for a year, but with less impact on your social life.

15. In the cruel economic climate of the late '90s, you are more likely than ever before to be judged as much by your ability to bring in a net inflow of dollars as by the sheer excellence of your work. Being good at things like tracking LEXIS charges, however mundane it seems, is part of that skill. If you went to law school under the belief that it was preparation for a "high profession" — in contrast to, say, something more worldly like being a plumber — you'll be surprised at how grittily mercantile the practice of law is today. Like your plumber (or at least like my plumber, judging by last month's $1200 bill for a new hot water heater), the modern lawyer charges for both time and materials, and marks up the latter. The LEXIS-NEXIS services will constitute some of your most important "materials."

loosely call the "command line." Here are a few things to remember about typing things onto the command line:

- After you have typed something, you may ***edit it*** by using the [LEFT ARROW] and [RIGHT ARROW] keys, and by overtyping what's already there. (In word processing terms, you are by default in "typeover" mode rather than in "insert" mode, if your cursor is on top of a character you've already typed. You can shift to "insert" mode by pressing the Insert key on your keyboard, which on IBM PC's is the key marked "Ins" on the numeric keypad.)
- After you have made an editing change, it is very important that you move your cursor past the ***last character you wish to transmit,*** before you press [ENTER]. The reason is that everything to the right of the cursor is ignored. For instance, suppose you type, as the name of the library you wish to use, "GINFED." If you use the left arrow to correct the "I" to an "E," and then immediately press [ENTER] without first returning your cursor to the end of your search request, the service would interpret you as having typed "GE" rather than "GENFED."
- Once you have finished typing whatever you need to type, and wish to signal the service that you are finished, you do this by pressing [ENTER], that is, the large key labelled "Enter" or "Return" on your computer. (In general, when in this book I give you instructions about what to type, I omit the [ENTER] instruction.)

D. Introduction to LEXIS-NEXIS keys: In most instances, when you want to tell the LEXIS service to do something, you accomplish this by pressing a special "key" assigned to that function. For instance, to change from one library to another, you press the [CHANGE LIBRARY] key (F10, or type `.cl`).

If you're accessing the LEXIS service from an MS-DOS system, the "keys" are literally function keys; you should have received a template as part of your LEXIS service materials, showing you what physical key to press for each function (e.g., Shift-F4 for the "PRINT ALL" function).

If you're using MS-Windows, you can choose between using the physical function keys and using on-screen "virtual" keys. Thus in the following screen taken from a Windows session, you can see that individual functions are available either by clicking a virtual key at the bottom of the screen, a menu item at the top of the screen, or both:[16]

16. Your screen may look slightly different, depending on which version of the LEXIS-NEXIS Windows-based Session Manager software you're using.

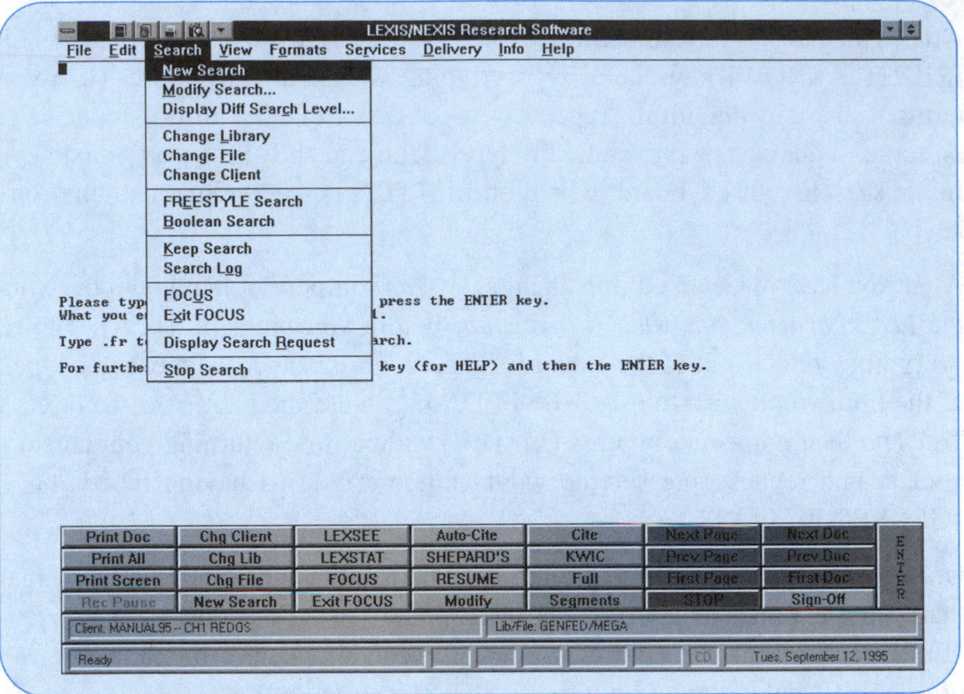

Thus in the above screen, you can see that you could issue a [CHANGE LIBRARY] command either by clicking the virtual key marked [Chg Lib] at the bottom of the screen, or by clicking on the menu item at the top of the screen called "Search," and selecting the sub-item called "Change Library."

The Macintosh version behaves similarly to the Windows version: you can select a function either by pressing the appropriate function key, or by clicking an on-screen representation of a key. Some functions are shown by an on-screen key, and others are shown as menu options.

1. **Dot commands:** Apart from "keys" (whether actual function keys or on-screen "virtual" keys), the LEXIS service provides you with an entirely distinct, alternative method of telling the service what you want to do. This is by means of so-called ***"dot commands."*** The advantage of using dot commands is that they can be used the same way on any PC, regardless of its type or its keyboard. When you use a dot command, you actually type out each command, using the regular alphanumeric keys on the keyboard. For instance, in lieu of pressing the [NEXT DOC] key, you can type **`.nd`** and then [ENTER]. Beginning on the next page is a list of dot commands and other short-cut commands.

   Observe that in the chart, most but not all commands begin with a ".", hence the name "dot commands." For the two-letter dot commands, you can basically remember what letters to use by the following rule: if the command has two words, use the first letter of each word (e.g., **`.ns`** for new search, **`.cl`** for change library, etc.);[17] if the command has one word, use the first two letters (e.g., **`.fo`** for FOCUS™). (There are numerous commands, how-

17. But Print Document is **`.pr`**.

ever, that do not follow this rule, such as **`.more`**, **`.keep`** and **`.bool`**.)

Dot commands may seem like a very old fashion and cumbersome way of entering data. However, very experienced LEXIS users frequently prefer to use dot commands rather than function keys, because: (1) your fingers don't have to leave the alphanumeric keys, and you don't have to hunt around for the right function key or the right place on the screen to click; and (2) if you frequently shift computing environments (e.g., you're on an MS-DOS machine one day and a Macintosh the next), you don't have to make any adjustment. Furthermore, there is one type of operation for which you *must* use dot commands: if you want to use the SHORT CUT feature, by which you use semicolons in order to bypass menu screens, you have no choice but to use dot commands. For instance, if you did a search in one library/file and wished to repeat the same search in another library/file with a minimum of typing, you could type the following:

```
.cl;states;omni;;.kw [ENTER]
```

This SHORT CUT method (discussed further on p. 2-48 below) would change library and file for you, repeat the search, and then display the results in the KWIC format.

"Dot" & Other Short-cut Commands

Searching:

.ns	=	New search
.cf	=	Change file
.cl	=	Change library
.so	=	Sign off
.ca	=	CITES Assistant
.easy	=	Return to EASY searching

Viewing Formats:

.fu	=	FULL
.kw	=	KWIC™
.sk	=	SuperKWIC™ [a]
.vk	=	Variable KWIC (.vk*n* for Var-KWIC within *n* words, where *n*=1-999)
.ci	=	CITE
.se	=	SEGMTS
.le	=	LEAD

Reviewing Results:

.np	=	Next page of current document
.np#[b]	=	Skip 1-999 pages forward
.pp	=	Previous page of current document
.pp#[b]	=	Skip 1-999 pages backward

Display Commands

.con/.kon	=	Turn display commands on
.coff/.koff	=	Turn display commands off
.linkon	=	Display LINK™ markers
.linkoff	=	Erase LINK™ markers

Printing:

.sp	=	Print displayed screen
.pr	=	PRINT DOC
.pa	=	PRINT ALL (MAIL IT)
.gd	=	Go docs
.pm	=	Print Manager

Using SELECT SERVICE:

.ss	=	Enter select service
.es	=	Exit select service

Finding Online Information:

h	=	Help
t	=	Time (elapsed time in current research session)
p	=	Number of screens in current document format
r	=	Display current search request
c	=	Display client screen

Continued on Next Page; Footnotes a & b are also on next page

"Dot" & Other Short-cut Commands

Reviewing Results: (Cont.)			**Finding Online Information: (Cont.)**		
.fp	=	First page of current doc.	.cost	=	Display cost estimate screen
.nd	=	Next document	.se	=	Display search charges for files just after entering library
.nd#[b]	=	Skip 1-999 documents forward			
.pd	=	Previous document			
.pd#[b]	=	Skip 1-999 documents backward	**ECLIPSE™:**		
.fd	=	Display first document retrieved	sav	=	Save search
			rec	=	Recall search
.dl#[b]	=	Display different level 1-255			
s	=	Sort documents (not in all files)	**Storing Results**		
			.keep	=	Store search request in LOG
resume=		Display resume options screen	.log	=	Display LOG
.down	=	Move down through large segment	.delall	=	Remove all saved requests and results from log
.up	=	Move up through large segment			
Refining Results			**FREESTYLE Commands**		
m	=	Modify search	.fr	=	Switch to FREESTYLE™ feature
.fo	=	Enter FOCUS™ feature			
.ef	=	Exit FOCUS feature	.bool	=	Switch to Boolean
.more	=	MORE like this	.where	=	Display WHERE screen
.em	=	Exit MORE	.why	=	Display WHY screen
			.sk	=	SuperKWIC display format

a. Available only when using the FREESTYLE feature.
b. # = the specific number of documents or levels desired.

E. Sign off: When you have finished a research session or need to pause in your research, press the [SIGN OFF] key (Alt-F9, or type `.so`). Now the LEXIS service displays a screen asking you if you wish to save your research:

```
        DATE:  May 5, 1997
      CLIENT:  LEXIS MANUAL
     LIBRARY:  GENFED
        FILE:  MEGA

Your search request is:
BYSTANDER W/10 LIABLE W/10 EMOTIONAL DISTRESS

Number of CASES found with your search request through:
  LEVEL  1...    9

Enter:       Y  To save your research (until 2:00 A.M. Eastern Time)
             N  If you do not want to save your research

If you do not want to end this research session, press the SIGN OFF key again.

For further explanation, press the H key (for HELP) and then the ENTER key.
```

If you choose to save your research, your last search request and the documents it retrieved will be saved. (Only searches performed in a particular library and file can be saved. Thus requests to special LEXIS features like LEXSEE®, LEXSTAT, AUTO-CITE® and SHEPARD'S® cannot be saved.) If you save your research, the saved session will be kept until the end of the day (2:00 a.m. Eastern Time).

If you have saved your search, and sign on later that same day, you will see a screen like the following:

```
A new research session begins each time you enter your personal LEXIS number.
Each research session is timed separately.  Your last research session today
ended at 9:43 P.M. Eastern Time and took 3 MINUTES, 18 SECONDS.
The number of searches executed during the session was 1.

        DATE:  May 5, 1997
      CLIENT:  LEXIS MANUAL
     LIBRARY:  GENFED
        FILE:  MEGA

Your search request is:
BYSTANDER W/10 LIABLE W/10 EMOTIONAL DISTRESS

Number of CASES found with your search request through:
  LEVEL   1...    9

Additional CASES were added to this file while your research was stored. If you
want to continue this research, press the Y key (for YES) and then the ENTER key
and LEXIS will rerun your search request in the updated file at no extra charge. If
If you do not want to continue this research, press the N key (for NO) and then the
ENTER key.

For further explanation, press the H key (for HELP) and then the ENTER key.
```

VI. PRICING OF LEXIS-NEXIS SERVICES

A. Introduction: When you are using your Educational Subscription, your use of the LEXIS service is, of course, free of charge to you as a student. However, there will come a time — at least, I hope there will — when you will be in practice, and will be using the LEXIS service on a pay-for-it basis. Since you will have a fair amount of discretion in exactly ***how*** you use the LEXIS service — for instance, Do you use large files or small ones? Do you read cases online, print them to read offline, or read them from hard-copy sources? Do you use [NEW SEARCH] or [MODIFY]? — you should have some idea how LEXIS-NEXIS prices its services, so that you can search in a cost-effective way. Here, then, is an overview of pricing for the LEXIS-NEXIS services.[18]

1. **Various choices:** The LEXIS service has a number of pricing options for firms to choose from. The main ones, and the ones I summarize here, are: (1) Transactional; (2) Hourly; and (3) the LEXIS®-NEXIS® ADVANTAGE Program. Ordinarily, the user's law firm selects either Transactional or Hourly. However, depending on the size of the firm, it may be possible to combine Transaction or Hourly pricing with the ADVANTAGE program.

B. Transactional ("Pay-as-You-Go") pricing: The standard, most frequently-selected pricing plan on the LEXIS service is the ***Transactional*** method. The essence of the Transactional method is that you pay ***only a per-search charge*** to do work in a file — you pay nothing extra for connect time, or for examining the text of a document once you've retrieved it as part of your answer set. So in a very real sense, with this plan LEXIS-NEXIS has "turned off the clock" — you can take as much time as you want to do a given amount of research, without increasing your bill.

1. **Searches:** You pay a charge for each individual ***search*** which you tell the service to execute. The amount charged per search varies considerably depending on which file you are accessing. You can discover current search charges using the system itself, by the following method: choose the library in which you want to search; then, while looking at the list of files within that library, press the [SEGMTS] key (Shift-F10, or type `.se`). You will see a listing of files with search charges, such as the following (which is the first page of listings for the *GENFED* library):

18. These statements are accurate as of Spring, 1997. There are some small charges that I do not mention (e.g., charges for training at the beginning of a subscription), and some pricing methods that I do not consider.

Please ENTER, separated by commas, the NAMES of the files you want to search. You may select as many files as you want, including files that do not appear below, but you must enter them all at one time. Some files have access charges as well as searching charges. Searching charges appear below.

FILES - PAGE 1 of 10 (NEXT PAGE for additional files)

NAME	$	NAME	$	NAME	$
MEGA	105			RULES	29
OMNI	65	USPLUS	65		
COURTS	60	BRIEFS	29	ALLREG	35
CURRNT	42	USTRAN	29	FEDREG	32
NEWER	42	USLIST	0	CFR	32
SUPCIR	38	USLW	32	COMGEN	29
		RECORD	42	SSMEGA	90
US	27			ALR	42
USAPP	38			RESTAT	0
DIST	38	USCODE	42	EXTRA	9
CLAIMS	29				

There are literally thousands of files on the LEXIS-NEXIS services, so I can give you only a small sense of search charges. In general, charges run between $20 and $59, though extremely small files can be less and a few very large multi-jurisdiction files are more. Here are some representative charges:

Library & File Name	Description	Charge Per Search
GENFED Library:	General Federal	
COURTS	All federal court cases, back as far as the LEXIS service goes	$60
NEWER	All federal court cases, but generally only from 1945 to present	$42
SUPCIR	All Supreme Court and federal Court of Appeals cases, as far back as the LEXIS service goes	$38
1ST, 2ND, etc.	Federal Court of Appeals and District Court cases from a given Circuit, from 1912 to present	$32
1CIR, 2CIR, etc.	Federal Court of Appeals cases from a given Circuit, from 1912 to present	$29
USCS	United States Code Service (U.S. Code plus annotations)	$32
CFR	Code of Federal Regulations (current)	$32
Custom File	Two or more *GENFED* files specified by the user for simultaneous searching	$65

Library & File Name	Description	Charge Per Search
STATES Library:		
OMNI	All state case law available on the LEXIS service, plus ALR® materials	$65
COURTS	All state case law available on the LEXIS service (but not ALR material)	$60
HIGHCT	All case law available from the court of last resort in each state	$32
AKCTS, ALCTS, etc.	Case law from a single state	$29
MECTS, MSCTS, NECTS, SDCTS, VTCTS, WVCTS	Case law from the 6 low-population states	$27
Custom File	Two or more *STATES* files specified by the user for simultaneous searching	$65
CODES library:		
ALLCDE	All state statutes together	$65
ALCODE AKCODE, AZCODE, etc.	Statutes of a particular state	$42
Custom File	Two or more *CODES* files specified by the user for simultaneous searching	$65

Special Purpose Libraries:

Library & File Name	Description	Charge Per Search
FEDTAX library:	Federal Tax Library	
MEGA	All federal and state tax cases on the LEXIS service	$105
RIAFTC	RIA Federal Tax Coordinator	$42
CORP. Library	Corporate Law Library	
MEGA	Corporate cases from all states, ALR articles on corporate law, and federal cases construing Delaware corporation law	$105
OMNI	Corporate cases from all states and all ALR articles	$42
ALCTS, AKCTS, etc.	Corporate law cases, etc. from a single state	$29

Library & File Name	Description	Charge Per Search
NEWS library:	General news and business library	
CURNWS	All full-text *NEWS* stories from the last 2-3 years	$50
ARCNWS	All full-text *NEWS* stories dated prior to the last 2-3 years	$50
ALLNWS	All full-text *NEWS* stories regardless of date	$60
MAJPAP	All stories from 20 major newspapers	$32
PAPERS	All stories from all newspapers	$32
MAGS	All magazine stories	$27
NWLTRS	All newsletters	$27
WIRES	All wire-service stories	$27
SCRIPT	All transcripts	$27
Custom File	Two or more *NEWS* files specified by the user for simultaneous searching	$50

2. **Connect time:** As I noted, there's no charge for connect time under Transactional Pricing. This is a big benefit, if you structure your search techniques to take advantage of it. Here are some of the implications:
   - You can browse through your results as long as you like, without paying an extra cent.
   - You don't have to worry about getting a large answer set, because time is not a factor.
   - You can literally use FOCUS and MODIFY for free.
   - You can use GUIDE and other help features for free. This means, in turn, that you can spend as much time as you wish deciding on the right library and file to use, without incurring any extra charge.

3. **Printing and saving to disk:** There is a separate charge for Printing. This charge applies when you use the [PRINT DOC] or [PRINT ALL] commands.[19] It applies whether you have the system print to paper or instead have it save to your hard disk. Under Transactional Pricing, there is a flat charge of $3.00 per document for the vast majority of documents.[20] This $3.00 charge per document applies for any display format in which you choose to print; thus if you print in KWIC it will cost you the same amount as if you print

19. See *infra*, pp. 2-83 and 2-85 for an explanation of these commands.

20. The main exceptions to the $3.00-per-document rule are: Public Records (*ALLREC, ASSETS, DOCKET, INCORP, INSOLV, LIENS, VERDCT* AND *FINDER*), $1.00 per document; SEC filings or *COMPNY* group-file documents, $25 per document; Investext, $50 per document. Also, printing or downloading documents from SHEPARD's and Auto-Cite is free.

in FULL. (But if you print a CITE list, you are ***not*** charged $3.00 for every document in the list; instead, you're charged $3.00 for the ***entire list***.)

If you use the Print-Screen key to print the current screen to your attached printer, there's no charge.

4. **Charges for special features:** There is a separate charge for use of some special features. Often, you will pay less than you expect with these features, because they are similar to a search, yet are priced at less than the per-search charges. The main special-feature charges are:

Feature	Charge Per Item Checked
LEXSEE	$5.00
LEXSTAT	$5.00
Auto-Cite	$3.50
SHEPARD'S	$3.50; $5 per SHEPARD'S jump (from SHEPARD'S to the text of the citing case)
ECLIPSE	Price depends on frequency: Daily: $14/search Ea. bus. day: $18/search Weekly: $21/search Monthly: $27/search Printing results: $3.00/document View results online: FREE
FOCUS	FREE
MODIFY	FREE

5. **Monthly subscription charge:** In addition to the above "variable" charges (that is, charges that vary with the amount of work you do), there is a fixed monthly subscription charge. Normally, this charge is $125 per firm.

C. Hourly pricing: Many searchers are accustomed to paying for their research on the basis of a flat hourly charge, regardless of how that time is used. For these users, LEXIS-NEXIS has developed the ***Hourly*** pricing structure. Essentially, this pricing structure replaces the per-search charge component of Transactional pricing with a per-minute database-access charge that varies depending on the size of the file accessed. This database-access charge ranges from $0 to $885 per hour.

Usually, the Hourly charges[21] are between 6.5 and 10 times the per-search charge assessed in the Transactional scheme. Thus *MEGA/NEWER* costs $595 per hour (compared with $84 per search); *GENFED/COURTS* costs $480 an hour (compared with $60 per search); *GENFED/*

21. By "Hourly charges," I mean the database-access charges.

USCS costs $245 per hour (compared with $32 per search); *GENFED/CFR* costs $245 ($32 per search); *STATES/OMNI* costs $480 per hour ($65 per search); *STATES/HIGHCT* costs $245 per hour ($32 per search); individual state-law files in the *STATES* library cost $245 per hour ($29 per search generally); individual state codes cost $245 per hour ($42 per search); and *NEWS/ALLNWS* costs $480 per hour ($60 per search).

Charges for Printing and Storing to Disk are $3.00 per document (the same as in Transactional). The special research features (LEXSEE, LEXSTAT, Auto-Cite and SHEPARD'S) are also the same as they are in Transactional.

There is the monthly subscription charge—normally $125 per firm—in the Hourly structure as in the Transactional structure.

The Hourly structure obviously gives you an incentive to do the maximum number of searches per hour, and the minimum of online browsing.

D. Choosing between the methods: Which method should you use? Transactional pricing remains overwhelmingly the most popular LEXIS service option. I would say that you should use Transactional pricing unless you have a clear reason for using Hourly pricing.

You should choose Hourly pricing only if you tend to do a lot of searches in a given hour, relatively little browsing or reading of materials, and relatively little printing/storing-to-disk of materials. Since Hourly pricing is on average about eight times the cost of a single search under the Transactional method, you will do better with Hourly only if you tend to do ***nine or more searches*** an hour.[22] In computing this, keep in mind that use of MODIFY, FOCUS, LEXSEE, LEXSTAT, Auto-Cite and SHEPARD'S do not represent additional searches — it's only when you either press the [NEW SEARCH] key, "Back Modify" a search level, or change the file and/or library that you will be deemed to be doing a "new search."

Furthermore, I believe that using the "lots of searches per hour" technique — the one scenario where Hourly pricing will be cheaper for you than Transactional — will cause you to lose a lot of the benefits of CALR. To understand why, you'll have to bear with a brief digression on the "theory of searching."

Academics who theorize about full-text searching note that there are two different objectives that a searcher tries to achieve; they've named these ***"precision"*** and ***"recall."*** "Precision" means keeping "false hits" to a minimum; thus if you retrieve 10 documents, and they turn out all to be relevant, you've had "high precision." "Recall" means not missing relevant docu-

---

22. My sense is that a fairly rapid searcher — in the sense of one who doesn't spend a lot of time looking at the materials, and concentrates mostly on locating citations — will frequently do more than one new search every seven or so minutes, and will thus be a candidate for Hourly pricing. Also, people who spend a lot of time in very large files (like the *MEGA* combined state and federal case law file in the *MEGA* library, where the hourly charge is less than five times the per-search charge) may benefit more from Hourly pricing than do people who spend a lot of time researching the case law of one state at a time (since in single state case law files, the hourly charge is more than nine times the per-search charge); however, this is at least partially offset by the likelihood that a big file will typically yield larger answer sets that will take longer to browse through.

The LEXIS service's research suggests that the average searcher who is using Transactional pricing makes from 7-8 searches per hour; the average searcher using Hourly pricing does 9-10 searches per hour.

ments; thus if there are in reality 20 relevant documents out there, and your search finds them all, you've had "high recall" (even if you retrieved 200 documents and had to plow through them all to find the good 20.)

To some extent these two objectives are at odds with each other — if it's very important to have high recall, you're likely to achieve this goal only by sacrificing high precision.

Which of these objectives should you be trying hardest to achieve in your CALR, precision or recall? Almost anyone who's practiced law would tell you, "high recall." *The consequences of missing a key case, statute or other document are much worse than the consequences of retrieving a lot of irrelevant documents along with the relevant ones.* In fact, many expert searchers believe that if your first search on a topic doesn't yield a pile of documents at least half of which are irrelevant, you haven't defined your search broadly enough (i.e., you're getting too much precision and too little recall.)

So how does this tie in to pricing? Well, two key aspects of LEXIS-NEXIS Transactional pricing today are that: (1) the only item of cost, the per-search cost, is the same whether your search retrieves a lot of documents or a few; and (2) because there's no connect-time component, you can spend as long as you want scanning the retrieved cases on screen without increasing your bill one cent. This means that you can pursue the "high recall, (relatively) low precision strategy" very cheaply using Transactional pricing. With Hourly Pricing, you can't — you're paying much more for scanning through a large number of cases online than you would for scanning through a small number.

The LEXIS service's tools for scanning cases quickly online also push you towards Transactional rather than Hourly pricing. Tools like FOCUS[23] and SuperKWIC[24] are designed to let you scan documents online quickly to determine their relevance. Transactional pricing lets you use these tools at zero incremental cost. Hourly pricing, by contrast, is designed for a strategy of "do lots of searches per hour, print (or read from the printed reporters), and read offline." This strategy throws away the benefit of the scanning tools. I believe that it's much more efficient to scan cases online looking for keywords than to read the full text of each retrieved case offline. If you agree with me, you'll inevitably use Transactional pricing.

When you're deciding whether to use Transactional or Hourly (and deciding whether to scan cases online or read them offline), you should take into the *value of your own time*. Let's assume that if you scan cases online you can scan 20% more cases per hour than if you search online but read offline. If your time is billed out at $150/hour, you should add an extra $30/hour as the "imputed cost" of reading offline rather than scanning online.

E. The LEXIS-NEXIS ADVANTAGE Program for Small Law Firms: The LEXIS-NEXIS services were long viewed as mostly the province of large, well-heeled private law firms. In particular, many solo practitioners and practitioners in small groups felt that the system was too expensive for them. LEXIS-NEXIS responded by introducing what I consider to be a very major innovation, now called the LEXIS-NEXIS ADVANTAGE Program for Small Law

23. FOCUS is discussed *infra*, p. 2-75.

24. SuperKWIC is discussed *infra*, pp. 2-35, 2-61.

Firms. The essence of the ADVANTAGE plan is that if you do most of your research in the law of a single state, you can make ***unlimited use*** of the LEXIS service for what I think is an amazingly low flat monthly fee.

The ADVANTAGE program is now available for each of the 50 states and the District of Columbia.[25] Normally, you would choose the state in which you practice.[26] Here is what ADVANTAGE pricing looks like; the following chart assumes that we're talking about New York, but it is the same for the vast majority of states.[27]

New York ADVANTAGE Pricing

Type of ADVANTAGE Product	Monthly Minimum[a] (1 attorney)	Additional Monthly Rate Per Attorney	Capability
New York ADVANTAGE Program	$75	$75	Unlimited searching and online printing of materials in the New York ADVANTAGE library
New York ADVANTAGE Program with Second Circuit Caselaw and USCS	$95	$95	Unlimited searching and online printing of the materials in the New York and Second Circuit ADVANTAGE libraries, as well as U.S. Supreme Court cases and United States Code Service (federal statutes).

a. Does not include any applicable subscription charges.

By the way, your firm must pay the additional per-attorney monthly rate (shown in the above chart, second column from the right) for *every attorney in the firm*, regardless of whether each attorney plans to use the LEXIS service. For this reason, the ADVANTAGE program is usually only sensible for firms having 10 or fewer lawyers; for firms beyond that size, other flat-rate subscription plans (or negotiated plans) are available that simulate some of the flat-fee effect of ADVANTAGE.

When you take the ADVANTAGE program for a state, you get a surprisingly large variety of materials. For New York, for instance, here is just some of what you get:

- All New York State case law as far back as the LEXIS service goes (Court of Appeals, Appellate Division and Miscellaneous.)
- New York State tax-related materials.

---

25. You can also use it for particular subjects, covered nationwide, as discussed on p. 1-28.

26. However, you may select more than one state, or a state different from your state of practice. You pay a separate flat monthly rate for each state.

27. The prices in the chart apply to all states except AK, FL, IL, PA and TX. In these five states, the Monthly Minimum (1 attorney) for state law (without federal law) is less than shown in the chart.

- New York Statutory materials (including the New York Code and Constitution).
- Materials from New York public agencies (e.g., Public Service Commission decisions, Department of Environmental Conservation materials, etc.).
- Files relating to current legislation (e.g., New York bill tracking).
- The *New York Law Journal.*
- The full text of law reviews from New York law schools.

Some very simple arithmetic can show you what a significant development the ADVANTAGE program represents. Suppose, for instance, that you are a solo practitioner, who practices solely in New York and does most of her research on New York materials. For a flat fee of just $75 per month[28] you can have unlimited use of all the New York materials, plus unlimited printing of those materials. By contrast, if you were an Hourly subscriber, and used only the New York case law file, this would cost you $285 per hour.

Even if you do most of your searching in your own state library, but occasionally need to access other libraries on the service, you can do this in connection with the ADVANTAGE plan. You just switch back and forth from your home-state library to the other libraries; when you are in the other libraries, you will pay the LEXIS service's standard charges in addition to your flat monthly fee.

1. **Single-subject ADVANTAGE libraries:** If you do a lot of work in a particular subject or specialty, but need nationwide cases in that subject, there are now ***single-subject*** ADVANTAGE libraries that may fill the bill. Each of these libraries contains federal and state caselaw, statutes, and more.

ADVANTAGE Single-Subject Libraries

Specialty	Monthly Minimum Per Attorney
Bankruptcy	$100
Energy	$150
Environmental	$150
Family Law	$ 90
Business & Financial	$150
International Law	$130
Labor & Employment	$110
Public Contracts	$ 90
Securities	$140
Tax	$150

28. Plus a monthly subscription charge that will never be more than $125, and will typically be $25 if you are a member of a bar association group that has a group ADVANTAGE arrangement with LEXIS-NEXIS, such as the ABA.

ADVANTAGE Single-Subject Libraries

Specialty	Monthly Minimum Per Attorney
Torts and Insurance	$110

F. **Some tips on cost-effective searching:** Assuming that you or your firm are paying for usage on one of the two "traditional" methods (Transactional or Hourly), here are some tips to help you work more cost-effectively:

- Most important of all, ***choose the SMALLEST FILE that will retrieve the materials you need.*** Larger files have higher, often significantly higher, search charges than smaller files. Here are a few examples of how you can save by using a smaller file:
  - In the *MEGA* library, the *MEGA* file (all federal and state case law without regard to date) costs $105 per search. The *NEWER* file is all federal and state case law, but only after 1944; it costs $84. If you're not going to need pre-1945 cases, you can save more than 25% by using *NEWER*.
  - In the *STATES* library, the *COURTS* file is $5 per search cheaper than the *OMNI* library; the only difference is that *OMNI* includes ALR materials.
  - Also in the *STATES* library, the *COURTS* file costs $60 per search, whereas the *HIGHCT* file costs $32 per search. The only difference is that *HIGHCT* does not have the intermediate-level state courts. So if you just want a good sampling of state law from around the country, taking the 47% discount by using *HIGHCT* is worthwhile.
- Notwithstanding the statement made just above, do ***not*** count on getting much of a savings by using the ***special-subject*** libraries. You get some savings, but usually less than you might expect. This is especially true where you are looking at a single state's law in one of these special-subject libraries. For instance, looking at all cases from a particular state in the *STATES* library costs $29 per search. Looking at the cases from a single state in a special-purpose library like *CORP* (corporate law) or *EMPLOY* (state employment law) costs the same $29. On the other hand, the large group files in these special-purpose libraries are a better bargain; for instance, the *OMNI* file in both the *CORP* and *EMPLOY* libraries (covering cases from all states, plus ALR articles) costs $42 per search, versus $65 for the *OMNI* file (all state case law plus ALR articles) in the general-purpose *STATES* library.
- Use ***custom file selection***[29] cautiously, and only when a pre-defined group file won't do. In general, the price for custom file selection in a library is the same as the price of the most expensive file that you can use for custom file selection in that library (even if that file is not one that you are in fact using for your custom selection). For instance, in the *STATES* library, the most expensive file (*OMNI*) costs $65, and so does custom file selection.

29. Custom file selection consists of selecting two or more individual files and searching on them simultaneously. You do this by listing the files you want, separated by commas, when the system prompts for your choice of file after you change libraries.

This means that you must be fairly careful before you use custom file selection. For instance, let's suppose that you want to look at New York and New Jersey case law in the *STATES* library. The two individual case law files (files *NY* and *NJ*) would cost $29 apiece, or $58 total, if you searched them separately. If you used custom file selection, you would pay $65, a clear net loss. On the other hand, if you use the *COURTS* group file, and then use the *COURT* segment to restrict yourself to New York and New Jersey courts, you would pay $60 per search, and save the effort of doing your searches in two separate individual state batches.

In general, custom file selection makes sense only if: (1) you are using more than three files; and (2) there is no pre-defined group file that meets your needs well. But two other situations where I've noticed that custom files seem to produce at least some net economic benefit are: (1) in the *MEGA* (combined federal and state case law) library, where most individual files cost $20 to $70 per search, and custom file selection is only $105; and (2) in the *NEWS* library, if you want to look at certain newspapers and magazines together (since custom file selection is $50, and just looking at newspapers alone or magazines alone is $27).

- Make extensive use of the MODIFY, FOCUS, LEXSEE and LEXSTAT features. MODIFY and FOCUS do not incur any extra search charges (though "Back Modifying" a previous level does incur a new search charge). LEXSEE and LEXSTAT can find you an individual case or statute for far less than the cost of doing a conventional search.

- Plan carefully before using the [NEW SEARCH] key. If you use a well-thought-out search that then needs to be narrowed down, MODIFY and FOCUS will work well. But if you use a poorly-thought-out search (one that uses inappropriate search words), you may find it impossible to correct the problem with MODIFY or FOCUS, and you will have to use [NEW SEARCH] again, doubling the cost.

- When you're using Transactional pricing, take your time online to be sure that you're using the most efficient files in which to do your research. A good way to do this is to use online GUIDE[30] to find out more about the files you have available to you. Since you're charged only when you perform a search, not when you use GUIDE (or otherwise browse), you should spend a fair amount of time ensuring that you're using the right sources.

- If you can, get two IDs (one for Transactional and one for Hourly); then, use each one as the situation requires, assuming you can determine in advance which will be cheaper on a given occasion. (Most of the time, Transactional pricing will be more cost effective.)

VII. YOUR EDUCATIONAL SUBSCRIPTION

A. Limits to the educational subscription: Your Educational Subscription gives you access, at no charge to you as a student, to the vast majority of materials on the LEXIS-NEXIS services. However, for contractual reasons a few materials are eliminated from the Educational Sub-

30. See infra, p. 2-76 for a discussion of GUIDE.

scription. When this occurs, you will simply not see the library or file in question on your menus. Examples of omissions include the *EXPERT* file in *LEXREF*, which lists expert witnesses; the Associated Press wire service (file *AP* in the *NEWS* library); real-time quote and market information (file *RT* in library *QUOTE*); and most brokerage reports on companies (in the *COMPNY* library).

When I discuss a file or library that you do not have access to under your Educational Subscription, I have tried to note this fact. So if you don't see any such caution, you can generally assume that you do have access to a given file or library that I discuss.

Chapter 2

Basics of Searching, Displaying & Printing

I. FULL-TEXT SEARCHING

A. How full-text searching works: The LEXIS-NEXIS services are a ***full-text-search system***. That is, for every single document (case, statutory provision, article, etc.) on the services, you can search for any word, word-combination or phrase to be found anywhere within that document.[1]

1. Case insensitivity: The LEXIS service is normally entirely ***case insensitive*** from the searcher's point of view. That is, the service generally ignores whether a given word in a given underlying document appears in all lower case, initial capitals or all upper case; similarly, the service ignores the case of anything you type unless you tell it to the contrary.

a. Advantage: For the most part, this ignoring of case is to your advantage. Assume, for instance, that you're interested in cases using the phrase "First Amendment." You don't want to have to worry whether the underlying document says "first amendment" or "First Amendment." And on the LEXIS service, you don't have to worry about this — you can type your search as: **`FIRST AMENDMENT`** or **`First Amendment`** or **`first amendment`**. Any of these formulations will find all documents where the phrase occurs as either "FIRST AMENDMENT," "First Amendment," or "first amendment."

b. Occasionally a disadvantage: Occasionally, the lack of case sensitivity can be a disadvantage. Suppose, for instance, that you want to find references to "Xerox," meaning references to Xerox Corporation. You do not want to find documents that use the word "xerox" as a generic term, as in, "Please make me a xerox of this letter." The absence of case sensitivity prevents you from doing exactly what you want.

Fortunately, there is now a way to ***override*** this "case-independence." The LEXIS service now supports the following three search commands:

`CAPS` — retrieves words with at least one capital letter

`ALLCAPS` — retrieves only words that are all capital letters

1. This is true, by the way, whether you're using Boolean or FREESTYLE searching. Most of Part I (p. 2-1 - 2-31) of this Chapter, however, applies only to Boolean searching.

NOCAPS — retrieves words with no capital letters

Thus if you want to find documents containing the word "aids" used as a verb meaning "to assist," and do not want to get documents using the capitalized abbreviation "AIDS" (which, of course, stands for Acquired Immune Deficiency Syndrome), you would search for:

nocaps(aids) or assists

Conversely, if you want to get all documents with "AIDS," and not "aids," you would search for:

allcaps(aids) or acquired immune deficiency syndrome

B. **The connectors:** In the vast majority of searches, you will want to use one or more ***"connectors,"*** (**AND**, **OR**, **W/n** etc.) to link the words you are looking for in the underlying document

1. **Single-word searches:** You do not absolutely *have* to use a connector in a search statement. For instance, you can search for a single word simply by typing that word, and then pressing [ENTER]. Thus to find all cases involving the Rule Against Perpetuities, an over-inclusive but mostly-successful way to do what you want would probably be to search (perhaps in the *STATES* library, *COURTS* file) simply for:

   perpetuities [ENTER]

   But even in this instance, you may get cases that aren't what you want. For instance, the LEXIS service automatically pluralizes the singular, as I discuss *infra*, p. 2-19. Thus your search for "perpetuities" will also find documents containing the singular form "perpetuity." Therefore you will find documents containing phrases like, "Testator left the property to the American Red Cross in perpetuity. . . ." *It will be a rare situation where a single-word search is the optimal search.*

2. **Phrases:** You can also search without using a connector if you are looking for a particular ***phrase***. To search for a phrase, you simply type the phrase as you would expect it to occur in the underlying document. Thus to find cases using the phrase "federal question jurisdiction," you would type the following search (perhaps in the *GENFED* Library, *NEWER* file):

   federal question jurisdiction

   The LEXIS service treats certain very common words as "noise words," i.e., words that are not placed into the master dictionary.[2] Therefore, it is a good idea to omit noise words from any phrase. However, keeping the noise words in your phrase search will generally not do any actual harm; you will just get a warning from the system that it is ignoring the noise word. For instance, if you are looking for all documents that contain the phrase "justice of the peace," the best way to do this is to search for:

   justice peace

2. Noise words are discussed more extensively *infra*, p. 2-18.

However, no harm would come if you searched for:

justice of the peace

The service would give you a warning that it was ignoring "of the", but would then interpret your search safely, as a search for any document in which the word "justice" occurs just before the word "peace," disregarding any noise words that may come between the two.

There are two exceptions to the rule that no real harm is done by including noise words in a phrase search: the words **AND** and **OR** are simultaneously noise words and "***reserved words***," i.e., words having a special meaning to the LEXIS service. Therefore, you must be careful not to use "and" and "or" as part of a phrase search, because the system will interpret these two words as being search connectors. Thus if, in a constitutional law research problem, you search for:

necessary and proper

the service will interpret this search as requesting all documents in which the word "necessary" occurs and in which the word "proper" also occurs (including documents where the two words are far from each other). Therefore, the closest you can come to getting the documents you really want will be to search for:

necessary proper

which will find all documents in which the word "necessary" occurs immediately before "proper," except for any noise words that may separate the two.

3. **The connectors:** Now, let's take a detailed look at each of the connectors that can be used to link together the words or phrases you use in your search. Connectors specify what the ***logical relationship*** should be among search words. There are seven main connectors[3] that can be used in the LEXIS service:

   OR
   AND
   W/P
   W/S
   W/n
   PRE/n
   W/SEG

   Of these ten, you should probably use three — **OR**, **AND** and **W/n** — more frequently than the others. We'll take an in-depth look at each of the seven.

   a. **OR:** The **OR** connector tells the LEXIS service to find documents in which ***either*** or ***both*** of the words or phrases linked by **OR** occur. For instance, if we want cases discussing wrongful killings, we could search (perhaps in the *STATES* library, *COURTS* file) for:

3. In addition to these seven "affirmative" connectors, there are "negative" connectors corresponding to most of these seven: **NOT W/P, NOT W/S, NOT W/n, NOT W/SEG** and **AND NOT**.

murder or homicide or manslaughter or wrongful killing

This will find us documents in which ***any*** of our four search words are used, including documents that use two or more of these words.

Here are some of the types of situations in which you will want to use the **OR** connector:

- **Synonyms:** You may want to find documents using any of two or more words that are ***synonyms*** of each other. (*Example:* **contract or agreement**)

- **Related concepts:** You may want to find terms or concepts that are not exactly synonyms, but that are related to each other. Often, you will know that cases or other documents of the type you are looking for will use one or more of these words/concepts, but you're not sure which. For instance, if we're interested in cases about a landlord's tort liability for a dangerous condition on his or her property, part of our search might be:

  landlord or tenant or property owner or guest

- **Antonyms:** Frequently, you will actually want to separate ***antonyms*** by **OR**, because the kind of case you are looking for may discuss the issue either in terms of one expression or its very opposite. For instance, if we're interested in whether a particular type of government conduct is constitutional or not, we can't be certain whether the underlying opinion will speak in terms of "constitutional" or "unconstitutional" conduct, so that part of our search should say:

  constitutional or unconstitutional[4]

- **Alternative spellings or hyphenations:** A single word may have ***alternative spellings***, or both a hyphenated and unhyphenated form. Thus to be absolutely safe, you would search for:

  judgment or judgement

  or for

  anti-trust or antitrust[5]

b. AND: Use the **AND** connector (or its equivalent, **&**) to find documents in which your search words appear in the same document, ***no matter how far apart***. Thus a search for:

expectation and damages

or its equivalent,

4. In fact, the relevant case might not use either of these words, but might speak of "constitutionality" or "unconstitutionality." Therefore, the safest search would be: **constitutional! or unconstitutional!** In general, you should make extensive use of the two "universal characters," ! and *. These are discussed more extensively *infra*, p. 2-21.

5. See the treatment of hyphens *infra*, p. 2-16.

```
expectation & damages
```

will locate only those documents in which ***both*** the word "expectation" and the word "damages" appear.

The **AND** connector will operate throughout the document, even across "segment" boundaries. As we'll discuss in much more detail later,[6] each document on the LEXIS service is divided into many different "segments," or parts. In a case, for instance, segments typically include *NAME*, *DATE*, *COURT*, *OPINION*, etc. If I'm interested in cases discussing whether a defendant in a product liability suit can assert the defense of contributory negligence, and I search for:

```
contributory and product liability
```

I will get cases in which the word "contributory" occurred in, say, the majority opinion (the *OPINION* segment) and the phrase "product liability" occurred in the dissent (the *DISSENT* segment). So to avoid getting too many irrelevant documents, I will often want to use a "tighter" connector, like **W/P**, **W/S** or **W/n**, all discussed below.

c. **W/P and W/S:** The **W/P** and **W/S** connectors tell the LEXIS service to look for documents with search words that occur together in the *same paragraph* (**W/P**) or *same sentence* (**W/S**). The **W/** in the name of this connector stands for "within." These two search operators were added to the LEXIS service in 1995.

Thus to find all documents in which the phrase "antitrust" appears in the same paragraph as the word "oil," you'd enter:

```
antitrust W/P oil
```

and to have the two terms be in the same sentence you'd enter:

```
antitrust W/S oil
```

You'll want to use **W/P** or **W/S** when you're looking for a fairly tight relationship between the two search terms, but you don't want to be tied down to a particular number of words separating them (as would be the case if you used the **W/n** connector, described next). When in doubt about whether it's **W/P** or **W/S** you should use, use **W/P** since it's more inclusive and thus safer.

An advantage of **W/P** and **W/S** is that they tie in to the *thought process* of the person who wrote the document — two words might be 40 words apart physically, but if they were in the same paragraph, that would be an indication that they were part of the writer's same thought, so you as searcher might well want them to constitute a "hit." Conversely, two words might be only several words apart, but separated by a paragraph division, and you might not want them to be a hit.

You cannot combine the "proximity" connectors (**W/n** and **PRE/n**, described next) directly with **W/S** or **W/P**. If you try to do this, you'll get an error message. For exam-

6. See *infra*, p. 2-23.

ple:

retirement W/S benefit PRE/2 plan

will give you an error message.

However, you can *in*directly — by use of **AND** or **OR** — combine proximity connector search phrases with **W/S** or **W/P** search phrases:

(retirement W/20 benefit) OR (retirement W/P benefit)

or

(finance PRE/2 plan) AND (retirement W/S benefit)

Lastly, you can use the **W/S** and **W/P** connectors more than once in the same search, and can use them together. Thus:

newspaper W/S recycling W/S neighborhood

or

newspaper W/S recycling W/P neighborhood

i. NOT W/S and NOT W/P: W/S and W/P can also be paired with the word "NOT", to find documents in which there is at least one occurrence of a particular word or phrase that is not within the same sentence (or paragraph) as some other particular word or phrase. Thus

benefits NOT W/S retirement

would find all documents in which the word "benefits" occurs in at least one sentence in which the word "retirement" does not occur (whether or not there are any sentences in which "benefits" and "retirement" both appear, and regardless of whether "retirement" occurs elsewhere in the document).[7]

d. W/n: The **W/n** connector tells the LEXIS service to look for documents with search words that occur within *n* words of each other. The *n* in **W/n** can be any number between 1 and 255. The **W/** in the name of this connector stands for "within." Thus

antitrust w/10 oil

means "all documents where the word 'antitrust' occurs within 10 words of the word 'oil.' "

Here are some special rules on how **w/n** operates:

- Only non-noise words count. Thus a search on:

  freedom w/2 press

  will retrieve documents containing the phrase "freedom of the press," because both

7. You probably won't use **NOT W/S** and **NOT W/P** very often. For more about the concept of "NOT," see the discussion of **NOT W/n**, *infra*, p. 2-9, **NOT W/SEG**, p. 2-10, and **AND NOT**, p. 2-10.

"of" and "the" are noise words, so the service considers "freedom" and "press" to be adjacent to each other in such a document.

- Two words that are adjacent to each other satisfy a request of **`W/1`**, but two words that are separated by one intervening word do not. Thus a search for:

  `richard w/1 nixon`

  will find "Richard Nixon," but will not find "Richard M. Nixon."[8]

- The words linked by the **`W/n`** connector can appear in ***either order***. Thus a search for

  `freedom w/2 press`

  will retrieve not only documents containing the phrase "freedom of the press" but also a document containing the phrase "he agreed to press for freedom to compete. . . ."

- No matter how large the value of *n*, **`W/n`** will not connect words that are in ***different segments***. Thus if you search for:

  `freedom w/99 association`

  you will not find a document in which the last word of the *OPINION* segment is "freedom" and the fourth word of the *DISSENT* segment is "association" (even if *DISSENT* is the segment immediately following *OPINION*).

i. **What value to set for *n*:** The value you will set for *n* in your **`W/n`** connector will depend on the type of relationship you anticipate between the two linked search words. This is a matter of judgment, and there are no hard-and-fast rules. Here are some guidelines that LEXIS-NEXIS suggests:

To link words in the ***same phrase***, or the words in a ***person's name***, use an *n* from 3 to 5. Thus:

`john w/3 kennedy`

will find "John Fitzgerald Kennedy" as well as "John Kennedy", and:

`willful w/5 misconduct`

will find occurrences of "willful and wanton misconduct," not just "willful misconduct."

To link words in roughly the ***same sentence*** use *n*=10-15.[9] Thus if we were looking for statements concerning strict liability for defective products, we would anticipate that the phrase "strict liability" would be found in roughly the same sentence as the word "defective," but we would not be sure whether the two words would be adjacent, or in what order they would come. Therefore, we would proba-

8. Even a single letter standing by itself will constitute a "word" for purposes of the LEXIS service. See the discussion of what constitutes a word, *infra*, p. 2-13.

bly search for something like:

strict liability w/10 defective

To link words in the ***same paragraph***, or in ***nearby paragraphs***, use *n*=25-100.[10] Thus if we wanted to find cases in which the court discusses whether contributory negligence is a defense in a strict product liability case, a relevant case might be one in which the two phrases were separated by one or more sentences, and might even be one in which the two phrases were in different, but nearby, paragraphs. In this instance, an appropriate search would probably be something like:

strict liability w/50 contributory negligence

e. PRE/n: The **PRE/n** connector is exactly like **W/n**, except that the search word to the left of the connector must ***precede*** the word to the right. For example, a search for:

cable pre/2 television

will retrieve documents containing the phrase "cable television" but not ones containing the phrase "television cable."

The main applications of **PRE/n** are:

- Searching for a person by ***first and last names***. (Example: **bill pre/3 clinton**)
- Searching for ***citations*** when you know only the names of the parties, and you want to eliminate opinions in which the same parties might have been involved but listed in opposite order. For instance, the Supreme Court's celebrated abortion decision is *Planned Parenthood v. Casey*, but there are other decisions (including prior lower court proceedings in the same case) when the parties were reversed in the caption. A search for

  planned parenthood pre/10 casey

  will succeed in getting the Supreme Court decision, while excluding the lower court decision in *Casey v. Planned Parenthood.*
- Searches where you are looking for a ***phrase***, and having the words of the phrase appear in reverse order would change the meaning completely. Thus if we want cases on Workers' Compensation, a search for

  workers pre/3 compensation

---

9. Of course, if you know that you want documents where the words occur in *exactly* the same sentence, you can use the **W/S** connector, described on p. 2-5 above. However, much of the time you know that you want documents where the words occur in "approximately" the same sentence, such as one word near the end of one sentence and the other word near the beginning of the next sentence. Therefore, you'll often want to use **W/10** or **W/15**, rather than **W/S**, to err on the side of over-inclusiveness.

10. Alternatively, you can use **W/P** to find words occurring together in exactly the same paragraph; see p. 2-5 above. As with **W/S**, however, you'll often be safer using the more approximate **W/n** connector (e.g., **W/50**) than the ultra-precise **W/P**.

will work better than

```
workers w/3 compensation
```

since the latter will also turn up cases involving the phrase "compensation of workers," which is likely to have a completely different meaning.

In general, you should be very sparing of your use of **PRE/n**. You may have identified a phrase that you think will characterize the type of document that you are looking for, but it is quite easy for you to overlook that the words of that phrase may occur in the opposite order. If you're looking for cases about product liability, for instance, you may be tempted to search for

```
strict pre/3 liability
```

but this would fail to find cases in which the court says, "In this situation, the defendant's liability is strict. . . ."

The best use of **PRE/n** is as a way to find names of people, **John pre/3 Kennedy**, for instance. But even here, keep in mind that the underlying documents may recite the names in last name, first name order (in an alphabetical list, for instance).

So when in doubt, use **W/n** rather than **PRE/n**.

f. **NOT W/n:** The **NOT W/n** connector causes the service to look for documents in which the first word is found, but only if there is at least one instance of this first word that is not within *n* words of the second word.

You will not need to use **NOT W/n** very often. The classic illustration of when you might need it is when you are searching for references to the federal Racketeer Influenced and Corrupt Organizations Act, commonly referred to as "RICO." If you search simply for all documents containing the word RICO, you will find, in addition to the ones you want, every document mentioning Puerto Rico. Consequently, you should search for:

```
rico not w/2 puerto
```

This will find all documents where there is at least one occurrence of the word "RICO" that is not adjacent to an occurrence of "Puerto."[11]

Now that the LEXIS service has a new connector, **ALLCAPS**[12], you should need **NOT W/n** even less often. For instance, you could find references to the RICO statute (and eliminate references to Puerto Rico) by:

```
allcaps(rico)
```

11. As long as there is one reference that is a stand-alone "RICO" without "Puerto" next to it, the fact that elsewhere in the document, the phrase "Puerto Rico" occurs will not prevent the above search from finding the document.

12. See the treatment of **ALLCAPS** and other case-related connectors *supra*, p. 2-1.

g. **W/SEG:** The **`W/SEG`** connector is similar to the **`AND`** connector, except that the two search words must be in the ***same segment*** as each other. For instance, the search:

`bankruptcy w/seg discharge`

would not retrieve a case in which the word "bankruptcy" appeared only in the majority opinion, and the word "discharge" appeared only in the dissent, because these are treated by the LEXIS service as being different segments. For a document to be retrieved by this search, there would have to be at least one segment (no matter which one) in which both words appeared.[13]

The **`W/SEG`** connector is utilized mainly in certain heavily-segmented non-legal files such as those in the *NAARS* library.[14]

h. **NOT W/SEG:** This connector is the opposite of the **`W/SEG`** connector. It looks for documents that have at least one segment in which the first search word appears but in which the other search word does not appear. For instance, the search:

`indians not w/seg baseball`

retrieves documents with at least one segment where the word "Indians" appears but the word "baseball" does not. (As long as there was one segment in which "Indians" occurred and "baseball" did not, the document would be retrieved even though it also included other segments where both of these words appeared, or segments in which "baseball" appeared but "Indians" did not.)

i. **AND NOT:** The **`AND NOT`** connector tells the LEXIS service to find documents in which the search word that follows this connector is excluded.

`AND NOT` is the most dangerous of all connectors, because a single occurrence of a word can cause the exclusion of what would otherwise be a perfectly relevant document. For instance, suppose that you are interested in looking for cases involving liability for design defects, but you want to rule out the large percentage of design-defect cases that are about automobile design defects. You could theoretically search for:

`design defect and not (automobile or vehicle)`

But this might cause you to miss a perfectly on-point case involving a design defect in, say, a trampoline, merely because somewhere in its opinion, the court cites another case and mentions that that other case involved an automobile found to have a design defect.

C. **Combinations of connectors:** Much of the power of the LEXIS service comes from your ability to ***combine*** two or more connectors within a single search. Virtually any combination of words or phrases, no matter how complex the logical interactions among the search words, can be put into a single search if you are patient.

---

13. You can view the list of available segments in a given file by typing **`.se`** [ENTER] while in that file. See p. 2-23 for more details.

14. *NAARS* is the National Automated Accounting Research System Library. See *infra*, p. 8-14.

1. **Priority of connectors:** If you remember your junior high school math, there is an important concept called "order of operations," which describes the order in which you the mathematician are to interpret the arithmetic symbols in an expression. For instance, if you see the expression Πr^2, the "order of operations" rules tell you: do the squaring first, then do the multiplication (and if you do the multiplication first, you will get a very wrong answer). A similar "order of operations" applies to the connectors used in the LEXIS service, to tell us the order in which the computer will evaluate the connectors and the words they link.

   Here is the order of operations of LEXIS connectors:

   ```
    (1) OR
    (2) W/n  PRE/n  NOT W/n
    (3) W/S
    (4) NOT W/S
    (5) W/P
    (6) NOT W/p
    (7) W/SEG
    (8) NOT W/SEG
    (9) AND
   (10) AND NOT
   ```

   Before we see how this order works, let me give you an additional sub-rule, which will deal with class (2) above: if two or more connectors fall in class (2) (that is, you have two **W/n**'s, or one **W/n** and one **PRE/n**, etc.), first you see whether the *n*'s are the same or different. If they are different, the connector with the ***smallest number*** operates first. If the *n*'s are the same, they operate left to right.

   Let's take a moderately complicated example to see how this order of operations works:

   product or strict w/3 liability and design w/10 defect or flaw

   Here are the steps the service will take in interpreting this complex search:

   - Because **OR** has the highest priority, the system will first put "product or strict" as a logical grouping. It will then do the same with "defect or flaw."
   - Since we have two connectors with *n* in them (**W/3** and **W/10**), the service will take the one with the lower number first, and form a grouping around it. Thus we would first have a grouping between the sub-group "product or strict" and the word "liability."
   - Now, we would move to the next higher *n*, the **W/10** connector. This would create a grouping between the word "design" and the sub-group "defect or flaw."
   - The only connector left is **AND**, which of the connectors in our search has the lowest priority. Therefore, the last linking that the service would do would be to tie the group "product or strict w/3 liability" together with the group "design w/10 defect or flaw."

   You can see the final result better if I insert parentheses to indicate the groupings:

   ((product or strict) w/3 liability) and (design w/10 (defect or flaw))

So the service will first find all documents where either the word "product" or "strict" occurs within three words of the word "liability." From among this set, the service will then look for any documents where the word "design" occurs within 10 words of either the word "defect" or the word "flaw."

Thus the following (hypothetical) document would qualify:

> (on p. 49:) This suit charges the defendant, a manufacturer of swingsets, with having introduced a design defect into its Model 12b Super Jungle Girl outdoor swingset. Plaintiff's parents were among the approximately 12,000 purchasers of this set between 1985 and 1989. . .
>
> (on p. 51:) . . . American courts universally subject a manufacturer to strict liability for any products that are unreasonably dangerous and are the proximate cause of an injury to the plaintiff.

2. **Using parentheses to change the order of operations:** You sometimes might not get exactly the documents you want if you let the service use the standard order of operations. Fortunately, LEXIS gives you a way to avoid the standard order of operations: by using ***parentheses***, you can make whatever order you wish.

Suppose, for instance, that you want all cases that either mention the concept of moving for a dismissal, or that cite to Rule 12. The following search, although plausible at first blush, would cause you to miss relevant documents:

```
move or motion w/3 dismiss! or rule 12
```

The LEXIS service would look for:

```
(move w/3 dismiss!) or (move w/3 rule 12) or
 (motion w/3 dismiss!) or (motion w/3 rule 12)
```

Since we want any case mentioning "Rule 12," even if it makes no mention of "move" or "motion," this search will miss relevant cases. To get what we want, we would use parentheses:

```
(move or motion w/3 dismiss!) or rule 12
```

Now, the LEXIS service will look for two sets of cases: those in which either "move" or "motion" falls within three words of "dismiss!," and those in which Rule 12 is mentioned.

a. **Multiple parentheses:** Frequently, you will want to use multiple parentheses within a single search. For instance, if you are looking for documents containing either or both of two named individuals, you will probably want to put parentheses around each pair of names. Thus:

```
warren w/3 christopher or lloyd w/3 bentsen
```

would find you documents mentioning "Warren Lloyd," which you don't want. The following search would get you exactly what you want:

```
(warren w/3 christopher) or (lloyd w/3 bentsen)
```

By the way, I recommend using **W/n** rather than **PRE/n** in looking for the names of individuals. **PRE/n** is dangerous because there are many documents that list people last name first. A search for **(warren pre/3 christopher)** will not retrieve a document listing this person as: Christopher, Warren. Also, remember that it's a good idea to use an *n* of at least 2, preferably 3, to deal with the possibility of middle initials or middle names.

b. **Nested parentheses:** You can even use ***nested*** parentheses, i.e., one set of parentheses within another. Thus the following search reprinted from above would leave no doubts about the order of operations:

```
((product or strict) w/3 liab!) and (design w/10 (defect!
or flaw))
```

The more complex your logic in defining what kind of documents you want to see, the more you are likely to need parentheses, including nested parentheses. For an awful-looking illustration, but one that I think is an effective search, see p. 4-46, *infra*.

D. What constitutes a "word" on the LEXIS service: As I described earlier, the LEXIS service finds documents satisfying your search request by first looking in a master dictionary that contains every word in the underlying documents. What, then, is a ***"word"*** for purposes of this dictionary? This is an absolutely vital issue: if you misunderstand how the LEXIS service defines words, and you look for a particular string of characters on the assumption that it is a word when it is not, you will miss documents, and never know what you are missing.

For instance, suppose that a case on the LEXIS service cites to a particular statutory section as: §305. Suppose that you, the searcher, mistakenly assumed that the service's master dictionary would contain an entry for 305 (without the section sign). Your search for 305 would not find this document, because in fact the LEXIS service lists it in the dictionary as a single word, §305.[15]

The rules for what constitutes a "word" in the LEXIS service are fairly technical. Here they are, in perhaps more detail than you want (until you've got a problem that requires precise knowledge):

1. **The "no intervening spaces" rule:** Generally, a "word" in the LEXIS service consists of ***letters, numbers or other symbols***, with ***a space before, a space after, and no spaces in the middle***.

   For instance, each of the following would be considered a "word," and would be placed as a single entry in the LEXIS service's dictionary, assuming that when it appeared in a document it was both preceded and followed by a space:

   ```
   etc.
   401k
   McPherson
   §2105.06
   2105.06
   1041
   ```

15. I discuss how to search for section references *infra*, p. 2-16.

```
habeas
A
2.45
1:00
I.B.M.
17,34
```

2. **Symbols:** I said just above that a word is something that has "no spaces in the middle." This is true, as a general rule. But the precise reality is a little more complicated. Certain symbols are ***treated like spaces*** for purposes of determining what constitutes a word. Furthermore, some of these symbols have additional special rules associated with them. Here, then, is a pretty exhaustive (if not exhausting) discussion of special symbols on the LEXIS service, and how they influence what counts as a word:

   a. **Parentheses:** When parentheses occur in a document, they are treated ***like spaces***. Consider the three following hypothetical documents on the LEXIS service:

   Document 1 — contains: **`10 b`**
   Document 2 — contains: **`10(b)`**
   Document 3 — contains: **`10b`**

   Because an open parentheses is treated by the system like a space, Documents 1 and 2 would be indexed identically in the master dictionary of the LEXIS service, that is, as two words, the word "10" and the word "b." Therefore, to find these two documents, you would search for:

   ```
   10 b
   ```

   That is, you would search for this as a phrase.[16] What's most important to note is that Documents 1 and 2 are quite different from Document 3. **`10b`** will be indexed as a single word, "10b," in the dictionary. Therefore, our search for **`10 b`**, which retrieves Documents 1 and 2, will ***not*** retrieve Document 3.

   Consequently, if you were not sure which of these three forms the underlying document would take, your safest search would be:

   ```
   10 b or 10b
   ```

   b. **Periods:** Periods are ***treated like spaces except*** when:

   - the period is both preceded and followed by a number. Thus:

     ```
     98.6
     ```

     is one word.

   - the period is preceded by a space, and followed by a number. For instance:

     ```
     .341
     ```

16. You could, alternatively, search for: **`10(b)`**. This is because, in a search statement as well as in an underlying document, the LEXIS service interprets the "(" as being a space, so the system interprets your search for 10(b) as saying, "Find me all documents where the word '10' occurs immediately before the word 'b'."

is one word.

- the first period is preceded by one and only one alphabetic character, and is followed by any number of sets of single alphabetic characters and periods, with no intervening spaces. For instance:

  `I.B.M.`

  is one word (because the period after the "I" is preceded by one and only one alphabetic character, and that same period is followed by any number of single letters each of which is in turn followed by one period, and there are no intervening spaces anywhere between the "I" and the "." following the "M"). The dictionary for a document containing this expression will have a single entry, "I.B.M.", and you would search for it by typing **`I.B.M.`**

By contrast, if the document contains the company name written as follows:

`I. B. M.`

(with spaces after each period), this would be put into the dictionary as three separate words, the word "I", the word "B", and the word "M", so a search for **`I.B.M.`** would not find this variant.

You cannot disregard the periods in an abbreviation like "I.B.M." A search for **`I.B.M`**. will as I just noted find documents listing the name as "I.B.M.," but will not find documents listing the name as "IBM". Conversely, a search for **`IBM`** will not find documents listing the name as "I.B.M." Therefore, as with parentheses, you must be careful to specify both possible variants; the ideal search is:

`I.B.M. or IBM`

As another illustration of how periods work, consider a document that contains the following corporate name: I.G. Farben. The "I.G." is a single word (since the first period in it is preceded by one and only one alphabetic character, and is followed by one or more letters each of which is followed by a period, with no intervening spaces). The word "Farben," of course, is a separate word. Therefore, to find the document, we would search for:

`I.G. Farben`

Note that a search for:

`IG Farben`

does not succeed.

i. **Equivalents:** The LEXIS service's use of ***"equivalents"*** changes, for some commonly occurring abbreviations, the rule I stated just above that you cannot regard an abbreviation with periods as being the same as an abbreviation without periods. I discuss equivalents more extensively *infra*, p. 2-20 and in Appendix A. For now, consider an abbreviation like "U.C.C." Because the LEXIS service treats "U.C.C." and "UCC" as being equivalents, here you ***can*** search for "UCC" and get documents mentioning "U.C.C." (and, conversely, you can search for "U.C.C." and get documents mentioning "UCC"), even though you cannot do this with "I.B.M." and "IBM" (since "I.B.M." and "IBM" are not equivalents).

In general, corporate and personal names (e.g., FDR) will ***not*** have equivalents set up for them, but names of ***government departments*** and many other generic abbreviations will have equivalents (e.g., "I.R.S." and "IRS" are equivalents, as are "C.P.A." and "CPA").

c. Hyphens: A hyphen in the underlying document is treated by the LEXIS service as the equivalent of a space. Thus if the underlying document contains "pre-trial," the LEXIS service will put this in the dictionary as the word "pre" and the word "trial." Therefore, you can find this document by a search on the phrase:

```
pre trial
```

However, if the underlying document contains the word "pretrial," this will, of course, be put in the dictionary as "pretrial." Therefore, a search on "pre trial" will not find a document containing "pretrial." The safest strategy, consequently, is to use, in your search, both the two-word and the one-word variant of any word which can be hyphenated:

```
pre trial or pretrial
```

By the way, you can use a hyphen in your search with good results. The LEXIS service interprets the hyphen in your search as if you had typed a space, just as it does for underlying documents. Thus if you search for **`pre-trial`**, you will find cases containing "pre-trial," as well as cases containing "pre trial" (but you will not find cases containing "pretrial").

d. Section symbol (§) or paragraph symbol (¶): The LEXIS service gives a quite special treatment to the symbols § and ¶.

i. §: The § symbol is ***not*** treated as a space by the LEXIS service. Therefore, if the underlying document contains the word written as "§401," you will ***not*** be able to search for this document by doing a search for "401." Instead, you must search for "§401".

But how do you search for "§401," especially if you are using a garden-variety PC, which does not have a key labeled "§"? Actually, when the LEXIS service encounters a § symbol in an underlying document, it stores it as a @ symbol. Therefore, use the @ symbol to represent a § symbol. Thus to find a document containing §401, you would search for:

```
@401
```

You must also consider the possibility that the author of the underlying document either did not use a § at all, or put a space after the § and before the number. Thus a judge writing about the statutory section controlling federal diversity jurisdiction may have written:

(1) 28 U.S.C. 1332 or
(2) 28 U.S.C. § 1332 or
(3) 28 U.S.C. §1332

To be safe, you will want to search for:

```
@1332 or 1332
```

That way, the request for "@1332" will find Document 3, and the request for plain old "1332" will find Documents 1 and 2.

ii. **Paragraph symbol:** If the paragraph symbol (¶) occurs in an underlying document, the LEXIS service, when it enters the document into its system, converts the paragraph symbol to the letter "p." Therefore, you want to search on the letter "p." As with the § symbol, you will want to cover both the situation where the paragraph symbol is up against the number, and that in which the two are separated by spaces. Thus to find documents citing "¶55,978" of the CCH Labor Cases Looseleaf Reporter, you would search for:

```
cch w/3 (p55,978 or p 55,978)
```

e. **Commas:** The LEXIS service treats commas like a space, ***except when the comma is both preceded and followed by a number.*** If the comma is so preceded/followed, then it is a character that is part of the word. Thus in the previous illustration, we searched for:

```
p55,978
```

not `p55978` and not `p55 978`

(All this assumes, of course, that the underlying document writes the word as "p55,978.")

f. **Apostrophe:** The LEXIS service treats an apostrophe in two quite different ways, depending on whether the apostrophe is being used to indicate the possessive or not.

Where the apostrophe is being used in the underlying document to indicate the possessive, the LEXIS service treats the apostrophe as a space, and also ignores the letter "s" if any following the apostrophe. Thus if the underlying document refers to "the president's pardon power," this document can be retrieved by a search for:

```
president pardon power
```

(This happens as part of the service's general ability to pluralize the singular, singularize the plural, possessivize the unpossessive, and unpossessivize the possessive. See *infra*, p. 2-19.)

Where the apostrophe is ***not*** used to indicate possession, then the apostrophe is just another symbol — it is not treated as a space, and it becomes part of the word. Thus to find opinions by Justice O'Connor, we would search for:

writtenby(o'connor)

g. **Semi-colon:** A semi-colon in the middle of a word is ignored by the system. If the semi-colon occurs at the *end* of a word, as would be the case when it is used for its conventional purpose of indicating the end of a clause, then the semi-colon is not deemed to be part of the word. Thus a document saying, ". . . the president resigned; a new president was inaugurated," could be retrieved by a search on the word "resigned."[17]

h. **Colon:** The LEXIS service treats a colon in a document like a space, unless the colon is both immediately preceded and immediately followed by a number. Thus to retrieve a document stating that "the hearing resumed at 2:00 p.m.," you would search for:

2:00

i. **Question mark:** The LEXIS service treats a question mark (?) in a document as being a space.

j. **Ampersand:** The LEXIS service treats an ampersand (&) in a document as being a space.[18]

k. **Dollar sign:** The dollar sign ($) in a document is treated as a space. (For example, if the underlying document contains the word "$5,644,540.00," you can find this document by a search for either:

$5,644,540.00

or

5,644,540.00[19]

l. **The slash (/) symbol:** The slash (/) is treated as a space.

m. **The plus (+) and minus (-) symbols:** The plus sign and minus sign are treated as spaces. Therefore, if you are searching for numbers that may have these symbols in front of them, you will probably want to simply ignore the symbol and not use it as part of your search statement.

3. **Noise words:** There are certain words that are so common that the LEXIS service does not want to use up space in the dictionary by listing every occurrence of these words. These words that are too common to index are called "***noise words***." Since a noise word is not put into the dictionary, it is not searchable on the LEXIS service.

---

17. When a semi-colon appears in a *search statement* (as opposed to appearing in a document), it has a special meaning; see the discussion of the SHORT CUT feature *infra*, p. 2-48.

18. When the ampersand appears in a *search statement*, it's an equivalent to the **AND** connector. See *supra*, p. 2-4.

19. Observe that this example illustrates, in addition to the fact that the dollar sign is a space, the fact that commas are treated as real characters when they are inside of numbers, and that the same is true of periods. Thus a search for **5,644,540.00** finds a well-known case about forfeiture whose title includes a dollar amount written like that, but a search on **5644540** does not find this case.

Here are some of the common classes of noise words on the LEXIS service:

Personal Pronouns: he, she, they
Most forms of the verb "to be": be, is, was
Some conjunctions: and, as, because

In case you should ever need it, Appendix B contains the ***complete*** list of noise words for the LEXIS-NEXIS services.

Normally, your best strategy is to omit any word that you know to be a noise word from your search request. Thus if you are looking for cases mentioning "justice of the peace," and you realize that "of" and "the" are noise words, your best search is:

```
justice peace
```

Not only does the LEXIS service not index noise words, but it also does not "increment the word counter" when it encounters a noise word in the underlying document. Therefore, in an underlying document which contains the phrase "justice of the peace," the dictionary will record the word "justice" as coming immediately before the word "peace," so the above search will work exactly as you would like it to work.

If you do use noise words in a search, no real harm will occur. The service will warn you that you have used non-searchable words, but will then process your search as if you had not typed the words at all. (Consequently, you may get documents with *other* stop words in between "justice" and "peace," such as a document containing the sentence, "He is a crusader for justice and for peace.")

E. Plurals and equivalents: There are two main situations in which searching for one word on the LEXIS service will get you additional variants. These two situations involve plurals/possessives and equivalents.

1. **Plurals and possessives:** The LEXIS service automatically searches for the ***singular, plural and possessive*** forms of words that have three or more characters, and that form their plurals by adding an "s" or "es."

   Examples:

   boy = boys = boy's = boys'
   box = boxes = box's = boxes'

   Thus if we search for **boy**, we will find underlying documents containing any of the following words: boy, boys, boy's, boys'. The same is true if we search for **boys** or **boy's**.

   The LEXIS service does a similar transformation on words that form their plural by changing the final letter from "y" to "ies":

   city = city's = cities = cities'

   a. **Irregular plural endings:** For words that have ***irregular*** plurals — those that are pluralized by means other than adding "s," "es" or "y-changed-to-ies" — the LEXIS service searches for the possessive, but ***not*** for the plural. Thus if you search for "children," you will find documents containing "children's," but not documents containing the word "child" or the word "child's."

Also, LEXIS does not automatically find the plural of words ending in "us" or "is". Thus a search for "bonus" will find documents containing the word "bonus'," but not documents containing the word "bonuses."

b. Controlling for singular vs. plural: As the result of a 1993 innovation, you can now ***turn off*** this automatic transformation of singulars to plurals and plurals to singulars. Here are the new, special search commands that will do this:

SINGULAR — retrieves only the singular and singular possessive forms
PLURAL — retrieves only the plural and plural possessive forms

Thus if we want to find references to James Connor, but not references to James Connors, we would search for:

```
james pre/3 singular(connor)
```

Nesting: The **SINGULAR** and **PLURAL** connectors can be nested inside parentheses used for segment limitation[20]. For instance, if we want the word "Connor" (but not the word "Connors"), and we want to make sure that the word "Connor" is used in the *NAME* segment, we can search as follows:

```
name(singular(connor))
```

2. Equivalents: Many words have commonly-used ***alternative spellings*** or ***abbreviations***. A number of these alternatives have been programmed into the LEXIS service as "***equivalents***," so that a search for one also finds documents referring to the other. Thus if you search for "IRS," the LEXIS service will automatically find all documents containing "I.R.S.," and a search for "Cal" finds all documents containing "California."

Some of the equivalents programmed into the LEXIS service are:

Certain abbreviations of legal terms (*memo = memoranda = memorandum*)
Abbreviations for numbers under 21 (*second = 2nd, five = 5*[21])
Abbreviations for the names of institutions (*F.B.I. = FBI*)

Appendix A contains the complete list of equivalents for the LEXIS-NEXIS services.[22]

a. Additional observations: Three points are worthy of special note concerning equivalents:

- Observe that *sec = § = section*. Therefore, in your search statement, you can use the @ symbol[23] and you will find documents that use any of these three ways of expressing the concept of "section."
- The two-digit ***postal abbreviations*** for states are ***not necessarily*** equivalents of

20. The technique of segment-limiting is discussed on pp. 2-23 to 2-26 below.

21. But although 5th and fifth are equivalents, and 5 and five are equivalents, 5th and 5 are not, and five and fifth are not. In other words, ordinal numbers are equivalents with each other but not with cardinal numbers.

22. Appendix A covers only the LEXIS service. Somewhat different equivalents apply in the NEXIS service.

23. Remember that @ is the way you represent the § symbol on a PC keyboard; see *supra*, p. 2-16.

the full state name. For instance, "N.Y." and "NY" are equivalents of each other, but a search for either of these will not find documents mentioning "New York." Similarly, a search on "CA" will find documents mentioning "CCA" or "C.C.A.,"[24] but not documents mentioning "California" or "Cal." or "Calif."

- A big use of equivalents is to free you from the need to worry about periods in the abbreviations of institutional names. Thus you don't have to worry about whether the underlying document refers to "N.L.R.B." or "NLRB," because a search for one will find documents containing either variant — thus you can safely use either `N.L.R.B.` or `NLRB` in your search statement. In general, it is easier to leave out the periods if you are working with an abbreviation that appears on the equivalents list.

F. **Universal characters (! and *):** Whenever you do a search on the LEXIS service, you run the risk of specifying a particular search word, but missing documents that contain close variants of that search word. The pre-programmed equivalents that I just described are one way that the LEXIS service helps you solve this problem. A more powerful way is by the use of the two universal characters, **!** and *****. In brief, the ! is a multi-character universal symbol, and the * is a single-character symbol; each helps you capture multiple word variants from a single stem.

1. **!:** The exclamation point (!) is a substitute for ***any number*** of additional characters at the ***end*** of a ***word root***. Thus a search for:

   ```
   insur!
   ```

   will find documents using the word "insure," the word "insured," the word "insuring," and the word "insurance."

   a. **! can equal zero characters:** The exclamation symbol equals any number of characters, including ***zero***. Thus a search for:

   ```
   stock!
   ```

   will find occurrences of the word "stock," as well as occurrences of "stockholder" and "stocking."

2. ***:** The asterisk (*) substitutes for any other ***single character*** that might be in a word. How an asterisk is interpreted by the LEXIS service depends on whether it is inside the word, or at the right-hand edge of the word.

   a. **Inside a word:** When an asterisk is used ***inside*** a word, a character ***must*** appear in the space held by the asterisk. This point is especially important when you consider that multiple asterisks may be used in sequence. Thus a search for:

   ```
   bl**d
   ```

   will find five-character words like "blood," "blind" and "blond," but it will not find a four-character word like "bled," because when an asterisk is used inside a word a char-

---

24. This is apparently because "C.A." is sometimes used as an abbreviation for Court of Appeals, which LEXIS treats as an equivalent to Circuit Court of Appeals.

acter must appear in the space held by the asterisk.

Inside-the-word asterisks are useful in dealing with spelling variations, and irregular plurals. Thus:

*wom*n = woman, women*
*advis*r = advisor, adviser*

b. End-of-the-word asterisk: An asterisk can also be placed at the ***end*** of a root word. Here, too, you can use multiple asterisks in sequence. However, there is a key difference: when stacked at the end, the asterisks indicate the maximum number of characters that ***could*** (but need not) be used. For example, if you search for:

```
litiga***
```

the service will retrieve documents using the words "litigant" and "litigate" (even though each of these uses only two of the three available asterisks[25]), as well as "litigated" and "litigable." But the service will not retrieve "litigating" or "litigation," because there are not enough asterisks to account for all the characters needed to complete these words.

3. Miscellaneous: Some other rules and tips about universal characters:

- The ! may be used ***only*** at the ***end*** of the word, not in the middle. An * may be used in the middle or at the end, but ***not as the first letter*** of a word. (Thus you cannot search for "**constit!" to find occurrences of both "constitutional" and "unconstitutional.")
- Be careful before putting ! at the end of short words or at the end of word stems that have a large number of variants — you may end up with a large number of unwanted words. For instance, a search on **`tax!`**, in addition to finding you words related to taxation, will also find "taxonomy," "taxi," "taxidermy," etc.
- A good but often overlooked use of universal characters is with ***numbers***, to help you search statutes or regulations. Suppose, for instance, that you're dealing with a state administrative regulation scheme where subsections are marked off by periods: 1332.024.1. You'd now like to find all references to either 1332, 1332.024, 1332.024.1, or any similar variant. A search for:

```
1332!
```

will give you what you want.[26]

By the way, if you use ! or * with a number, you cannot do arithmetic comparisons or

25. In fact, the underlying document need not have *any* characters in the positions represented by the stacked asterisks. Thus a search for **`stock******`** will find a document containing the word "stock".

26. You might think that this would also be a good way of dealing with references that use parentheses rather than periods, e.g., 1332(a)(1). But here, the technique will not work quite as you would expect. I explain on p. 2-14 that a parenthesis acts as a space, so that an underlying document containing the expression "1332(a)(1)" will actually be indexed as three consecutive words, 1332 a 1. Therefore, your search on 1332! will find each occurrence of 1332, but so will a plain old search on 1332. So you don't get anything extra by including the ! when you're searching for statutory references that are built around parentheses.

date comparisons based on the value of the number.[27] Thus whereas you can say, **`date bef 1992`**, you cannot say, **`date bef 199*`** (though you can obtain the same result by **`date bef 1990`**).

G. Segment searching: Each document on the LEXIS service is divided into distinct "segments," or portions. Cases, for instance, are divided into segments called *NAME*, *NUMBER*, *COURT*, *CITE*, *DATE*, *OPINION*, etc. I will discuss segment searching in greater detail later on in the treatment of finding cases,[28] but for now, let's go over some basics of searching based on segments.

1. Segment-searching generally: The LEXIS service has a specific syntax for looking for a particular search word or phrase within a particular segment:

```
segment-name(search words)
```

Thus to find all documents containing the words "Exxon" in the *NAME* segment, we would do the following search:

`name(exxon)`[29]

You can put inside the parentheses not just a single-word search, but a multi-word search with several connectors, and even nested parentheses. In fact, there is no limit to the complexity of the search that you can put inside a segment identifier. For instance, if we want to find all cases in which either the phrase "Exxon Shipping" or the phrase "Exxon Transportation" occurred in the *NAME* segment, we could do the following search:

```
name(exxon pre/2 (shipping or transport!))
```

a. Get list of segments: You can easily get a list of the segments contained in any particular file. Once you have logged into a file, just press the [SEGMENTS] key (Shift-F10, or type **`.se`**), and you will see the list. Here, for instance, is a list of the segments in a typical file of cases (in this instance, the *GENFED* library, *COURTS* file):

---

27. Arithmetic comparisons are discussed *infra*, p. 2-26.

28. See *infra*, p. 4-33.

29. Actually, LEXIS lets you either use or omit a space between the segment name and the search word, so that **`name (exxon)`** would also have worked. All examples in the text omit the space.

The following names may be used as a segment name in your search request:

CITES	CLASSIFICATION	CONCUR	CONCURBY
COUNSEL	COURT	DATE	DISPOSITION
DISSENT	DISSENTBY	HEADNOTES	HISTORY
JUDGES	NAME	NOTICE	NUMBER
OPINION	OPINIONBY	OPINIONS	SYLLABUS
WRITTENBY			

The following name may be used with the arithmetic operators:
DATE

This will not tell you much about the contents of each segment. For this, you will need to use the GUIDE feature.[30] You can access GUIDE by entering **`.gu`** after you have entered a file.

b. Group segments: Some segments in the LEXIS service are ***"group"*** segments. A group segment is a segment-name that includes the contents of various ordinary segments. For instance, in most files containing cases, there are segments called *OPINIONBY* (containing the name of the judge who wrote the majority opinion), *CONCURBY* (the name of the judge who wrote the concurrence), and *DISSENTBY* (the name of the judge who wrote the dissent). If you want to see all opinions by a particular judge, and you don't care whether what she wrote was a majority, concurrence, or dissent, then you would use the group segment, *WRITTENBY*, which contains the *OPINIONBY, CONCURBY* and *DISSENTBY* segments. Thus to find all opinions by Justice Scalia, you would search for:

`writtenby(scalia)`

2. **Restricting your search by date:** One of the most useful kinds of segment-searching is searching based on ***dates***. The syntax for doing this is a little different from the standard segment-searching syntax which we reviewed above. You don't use parentheses, and you use three special connectors, **`aft`**, **`bef`** and **`is`**.

Thus to find documents whose date is later than 1989, you would search for:

`date aft 1989`

For documents whose date is earlier than July 1, 1992, you would search for:

`date bef july 1, 1991`

For documents whose date is precisely April 15, 1993:

`date is 04/15/93`

30. GUIDE is discussed further infra, p. 2-76.

To find all documents whose date is in the last half of 1992:

```
date aft june 30, 1992 and date bef 1993
```

a. **Variants in form of date:** The LEXIS service gives you extreme flexibility in the form in which you can enter the date itself. In typing the date as part of your search, you can:

- Drop the day, or the day and month (but not the year).
- Use either slashes (/) or hyphens to separate the pieces.
- Use either a four-digit year or a two-digit year.
- Use either the full name of a month, or its common abbreviation.
- For the numerical representations of the months January through September, represent the month either with a leading zero or without, i.e., 08 or 8.

Thus the LEXIS service will, like a human research assistant, behave reasonably when given any of the following forms of date:

```
09-30-92
09-30-1992
09/30/1992
09/30/92
sept 30, 1992
september 30, 1992
09-92
9/92
09/92
09/1992
sept 1992
september 1992
1992
```

i. **Month abbreviations:** Here are the acceptable abbreviations for months:

January=Jan
February=Feb=Febr
March=Mar
April=Apr
June=Jun
July=Jul
August=Aug
September=Sep=Sept
October=Oct
November=Nov
December=Dec

b. **Special symbols:** Instead of using **aft**, **bef** and **is**, you can use the arithmetic symbols > (in lieu of **aft**), < (in lieu of **bef**), and = (in lieu of **is**).

c. **Dropping of month or day:** When you drop the day, or the month and day, and use the **bef**, **aft** or **is** connectors, the system behaves the way a smart assistant would behave. Thus **date bef 1990** is interpreted to mean "date bef Jan 1, 1990," and **date is July 1992** is interpreted to mean "date aft June 30, 1992 and date bef August 1, 1992."

d. **Date restriction by file choice:** Before we leave the subject of date restrictions, keep in mind that you will often be able to do meaningful date restrictions just by your ***choice of file***. For instance, if you're interested in cases from all federal courts, but only relatively modern decisions, you can use the *NEWER* file (in the *GENFED* library), which will limit you to cases decided since 1945.

3. **Arithmetic comparisons:** The LEXIS-NEXIS services also let you do ***arithmetic comparisons*** on certain segments. The idea is similar to that behind date comparisons. You will rarely need to use arithmetic comparisons in traditional legal databases, but you will frequently want to use this in the more financially-oriented databases, such as many of those in the *NEWS* and *COMPNY* libraries.

   For instance, let's suppose that you need to identify all specialty retailers with sales of less than $200 million, who over the last five years have seen their earnings grow by at least 6%. (You might need to do this if you're practicing Mergers & Acquisitions law, or if you've left the practice of law for the theoretically greener pastures of investment banking.) You would choose the *COMPNY* library, the *DISCLO* (for "Disclosure") file[31], and you would do the following search:

```
sic-codes(5311) and net-sales < 200,000,000 and
 eps-growth > 6
```

   (The segment **sic-codes** refers to the SIC codes assigned by the federal government to represent different types of businesses, such as "Specialty Retailer" or "Printer". **net-sales** is a segment that contains the gross revenues of the business. **eps-growth** is a segment containing a number that represents the company's percentage increase in Earnings Per Share over the last 5 years.)

   When I did this search, LEXIS-NEXIS gave me one name, "Proffitt S Inc.," a specialty retailer with 1993 fiscal year sales of $128 million and a five-year earnings-per-share growth rate of 18.9%. Do not consider this to be a stock tip.

H. Online Thesaurus: When you're thinking of words to use in your search request, you can get some help from the ***Online Thesaurus*** feature that LEXIS-NEXIS added in 1995.[32] To use the

31. Many lawyers consider *DISCLOS* and other financially-oriented files on the LEXIS-NEXIS services to be among the most valuable assets on the services. They are discussed beginning on p. 8-13.

32. There's been a comparable thesaurus available for use with the FREESTYLE feature for a while; the new Online Thesaurus being discussed here works with Boolean searching.

Online Thesaurus, you must first be in a library and file. Then, type **thes** , followed by the word(s) — enclosed in parentheses — for which you want to find synonyms.

For example, to find a list of synonyms for the word "contract," you'd type:

```
thes(contract)
```

You'd then see this screen:

SYNONYM SELECTION

Synonyms for: CONTRACT
Enter synonym numbers to include in search and press ENTER (e.g. 1,2,3-4)

<=1> Exit Thesaurus

---------- Term Variations ----------

1	contracted	2	contracter	3	contracting
4	contractor				

5	accord	6	accordance	7	agreement
8	bargain	9	binding agreement	10	collective agreement
11	compact	12	concordat	13	covenant
14	embodied terms	15	entente	16	mutual agreement
17	mutual pledge	18	mutual promise	19	mutual undertaking
20	negotiated agreement	21	pact	22	pactum
23	promise	24	ratified agreement	25	set terms
26	settlement	27	stated terms	28	stipulation
29	understanding	30	written terms		
31	articles of agreement				

For further explanation, press the H key (for HELP) and then the ENTER key.

If you want to use some of the supplied synonyms in your search, you can avoid retyping them by just typing the number for each synonym. (Thus if we wanted to add "agreement," "bargain" and "pact" to our search, we'd just type **7, 8, 21** [ENTER]).

The system will then leave the synonym screen, and will create an "or'd" search built around the word you specified and the synonyms you selected. Continuing with our example, the system would return us to the main search screen with the following search filled in:

```
(contract or agreement or bargain or pact)
```

We'd then have the option of editing this search, or sending it directly to the LEXIS-NEXIS service. From here on, we'd use our regular Boolean commands.

If you don't want to select any of the synonyms (or want to type them manually), you can leave the synonym display by clicking on the **<=1>** LINK, or typing **=1**.

I. **The "Related Concepts" command:** Just as the Online Thesaurus command lets you find additional synonyms for your search terms, a command called ***"Related Concepts"*** lets you find concepts that are related to, though not necessarily synonymous with, a given search term. The Related Concepts command was added by LEXIS in 1996, and is in my opinion an important tool that you should spend some time mastering.

1. **How it works:** To use the Related Concepts command, just include the word **`rel`** before a search term, and put the search term in parentheses. Thus if you were researching "mad cow disease," and wanted to find other concepts related to it, you might search for:

   `rel(mad cow)`

   At this point, you'll see the "Related Concepts Selection" screen:

```
RELATED CONCEPTS SELECTION
TOPIC: "MAD COW"
Enter concept numbers of interest and press ENTER (e.g. 1,2,3-4)
 <=1>  Exit Related concepts
-----------------------------------------------------------------------------
  1 disease              2  mad cow disease
  3 beef                 4  British
  5 cattle               6  Britain
  7 European Union       8  farmer
  9 EU                  10  scientist
 11 infected            12  sheep
 13 meat                14  cow disease
 15 John Major          16  herd
 17 risk                18  Creutzfeldt-Jakob
 19 researcher          20  crisis
 21 protein             22  BSE
 23 consumer            24  health
 25 slaughter           26  tissue
For further explanation, press the H key (for HELP) and then the ENTER key.
```

   Now, if you want to include any of these terms in your search, type their numbers. For instance, if we wanted to carry "Creutzfeldt-Jakov" and "BSE" into our search, we'd type **`18, 22 [ENTER]`**

   Typing the numbers doesn't actually put the terms into the search; it merely carries them over into the main search screen, where you can type them in, perhaps as part of a bigger search. For instance, after we typed **`18,22 [ENTER]`**, we'd get the following screen:

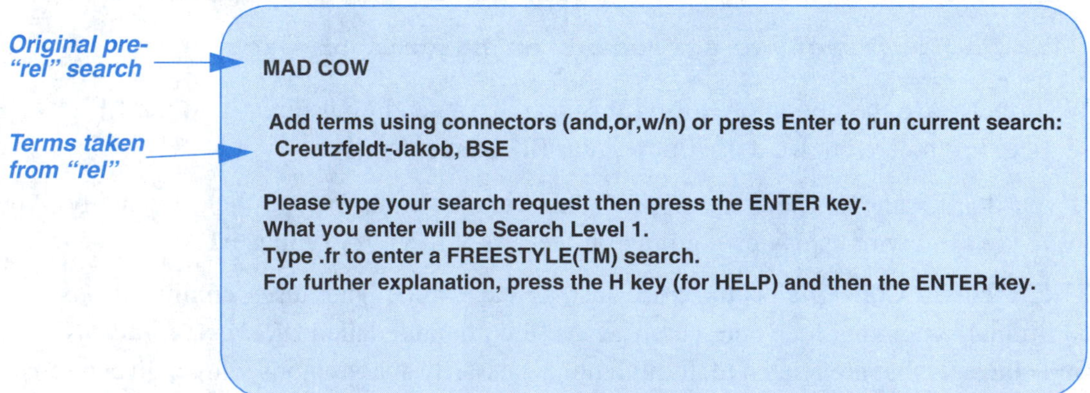

Original pre-"rel" search
MAD COW
Terms taken from "rel"
Add terms using connectors (and,or,w/n) or press Enter to run current search:
Creutzfeldt-Jakob, BSE
Please type your search request then press the ENTER key.
What you enter will be Search Level 1.
Type .fr to enter a FREESTYLE(TM) search.
For further explanation, press the H key (for HELP) and then the ENTER key.

   At this point, to use these two terms, we'd hand-type them in after "mad cow". (In other words, the only thing that typing the numbers of the terms — "18" and "22" in the above example — does, is to put those terms in your main search screen, where you can review them and manually copy them.)

2. **Relative to current file:** The Related Concepts command operates ***relative to your current file***. In other words, when you use **`rel`**, the system gives you a list of words and phrases that, judging by the current file, are frequently linked to your key word or phrase. The system does this by compiling statistical frequency tables that express how often, in the current file, particular words and phrases are found together in the same document. Thus when we did our **`rel(mad cow)`** command, the system said to us, in effect, "In the *ALLNWS* file [the file we were in when we issued the command], in documents that contain 'mad cow,' there is a tendency for the document to also contain the following words and phrases, so these are likely to be related in some way to 'mad cow.' "

3. **Uses:** I find that the Related Concepts command is especially useful when I'm looking in a current-events file, such as *ALLNWS* (in the *NEWS* library).[33] It's less useful — but still sometimes helpful — when I'm looking in a strictly law-related file like one containing cases or statutes.

    a. **Illustration:** Our above search on "mad cow" is illustrative. If I were just starting out my research on mad cow disease, I think I'd find it useful to see entries for "Creutzfeld-Jakob" and "BSE" (both of which are diseases, the former a human disease related to mad-cow disease, and the latter an acronym for bovine spongiform encephalopathy, the scientific name for mad-cow disease itself.) I might also get some help from "British," "Britain" and "John Major" (to suggest that the disease has some sort of connection with Britain) and from "European Union" and "EU" (to clue me in to a connection with the EU, which has in fact banned imports of British beef on account of mad-cow disease.) True, I could have discovered these related aspects eventually by reading the actual documents, but the Related Concepts list gives me a way to get a quick overview of "angles" from which my core concept might be viewed.

J. **Finding the most relevant documents with the ATLEAST search command:** An intriguing connector, **`ATLEAST`**, lets you limit your search to what will probably be the ***most relevant*** documents. **`ATLEAST nn (`*`search term`*`)`** finds only documents containing at least *nn* occurrences of *search term*.

For instance, let's suppose that we were interested in cases discussing a defendant's liability to a bystander who suffers emotional distress while watching an injury to a friend or relative. In the *GENFED* library, *MEGA* file, a search for:

```
emotional distress w/50 bystander
```

retrieves over 700 cases, too large a number to read. We could tighten the **`W/n`** connector, but this will not necessarily rule out the less relevant documents, merely those that happen to use the search words we want farther apart from each other. But with the **`ATLEAST`** connector, we

33. See p. 8-1 for more about this file.

can make sure we see just those documents that use each of our search phrases many times. For instance, we can take the results of the above search, and add the following Modification:[34]

`and atleast 20 (emotional distress and bystander)`

This finds us, from our 700 or so cases which use the two words within 50 words of each other, just those documents that have at least 20 occurrences of "emotional distress" and also 20 occurrences of "bystander." There turn out to be just 23 of these cases (as of mid-1995), and, as you would suspect, they are highly relevant to our issue. For instance, the fifth case of the 23 turns out to have 50 occurrences of "emotional distress" and 20 occurrences of "bystander," and is a comprehensive review of California's approach to the problem of liability to bystanders who watch others be injured.

You can use phrases, as well as the **AND** and **OR** connectors, inside the parentheses of an **ATLEAST** search. However, you cannot use **W/n**, **PRE/n**, or any other connector. Thus

`atleast 20 (emotional distress or bystander)`

will work, and so will

`atleast 10 (emotional distress and bystander)`

but

`atleast 20 (emotional w/10 distress)`

will not.

The **ATLEAST** connector is interpreted by reference to search "units." Thus **ATLEAST 20 (emotional distress)** retrieves documents containing at least 20 occurrences of the phrase "emotional distress." **ATLEAST 20 (distress and bystander)** retrieves documents where there are at least 20 occurrences of "distress" and 20 occurrences of "bystander," but these two words do not necessarily have to ever be close to each other in the document.

The **ATLEAST** connector works especially well in conjunction with the FOCUS feature. I describe what FOCUS does extensively below,[35] but the basic idea is that it helps you do a kind of mini-search against the pool of documents you have already retrieved. For instance, after we searched for "emotional distress w/50 bystander" and got 700 or so documents, we could then do the following FOCUS operation:

`focus atleast 20 (emotional distress)`

This would tell us, out of our 700 documents, how many have at least 20 occurrences of the phrase "emotional distress." Let's say the answer is that 13 documents qualify. Now, we can look at each of these 13, and see highlighting of just those places in each document where "emotional distress" occurs (without being distracted by the occurrences of "bystander.")

34. The MODIFY feature is discussed below, p. 2-37.

35. See *infra*, p. 2-41.

You can do much the same thing with the MODIFY feature.[36] The MODIFY feature adds a "clause" beginning with a connector (usually AND or OR) to your prior search request. Thus if our original search was "emotional distress w/50 bystander" and retrieved 700 documents, we could press the [MODIFY] key (Alt-F8, or type **m**), and then type:

```
and atleast 20 (emotional distress and bystander)
```

to winnow our 700 documents down to just those containing at least 20 occurrences of each of our two key phrases.

Using either the FOCUS or MODIFY feature, you can make multiple requests to travel from most relevant to less relevant documents. For instance, having retrieved our original 700 documents, we could type:

```
focus atleast 20 (emotional distress and bystander)
```

After looking at the retrieved documents (or immediately, if there were no retrieved documents), we could then type:

```
focus atleast 10 (emotional distress and bystander) and
  not atleast 20 (emotional distress and bystander)
```

to get documents falling in the more-than-10-but-less-than-20 range.

II. DISPLAYING YOUR DOCUMENTS

A. What to do after you execute the search: After you have entered your search request, the service will tell you the number of documents that satisfy your search request:

((COVENANT OR AGREEMENT) W/3 COMPETE) AND DATE AFT 1970

Your search request has found 261 CASES through Level 1.
To DISPLAY these CASES press either the KWIC, FULL, CITE or SEGMTS key.
To MODIFY your search request, press the M key (for MODFY) and then the ENTER key.

For further explanation, press the H key (for HELP) and then the ENTER key.

If you're getting more documents than you think you can reasonably read, or fewer than you think there should be, you will want to refine your search in various ways.[37] But assuming that the number of documents you have retrieved is a sensible number to review (typically between

36. See the discussion of MODIFY *infra*, p. 2-37.

37. See especially the discussion of the MODIFY feature, *infra*, p. 2-37.

5 and 50), you will want to glance through the documents on screen.

B. The display formats: There are six display formats available for the on-screen review of documents:

- KWIC format, which shows you, for each retrieved document, those portions of the document containing "hits";
- CITE format, which shows you citations of the documents found by your search;
- FULL format, which shows the full text of your document;
- VAR-KWIC format, which is the same as KWIC, but with more text surrounding each "hit";
- SEGMTS format, which lets you display, for each document, those segments which you specify;
- SuperKWIC format (available only in FREESTYLE), which shows you the portion of the document containing the most occurrences of search terms.

Now, let's take a more detailed look at each of these.

1. **The KWIC™ format:** The KWIC format is perhaps the most useful of all the display formats on the LEXIS service. KWIC stands for "**K**ey **W**ord **I**n **C**ontext," an apt description of what this format does. KWIC shows you just those portions of the document that contain one or more "hits," i.e., words that you've searched on. To get to KWIC format, just press the [KWIC] key (F5, or type **.kw**.)

   KWIC shows you a 25-word "***window***" of text around your "hits." This window consists of 25 searchable words on either side of the hit.[38] The search words themselves are highlighted.

   The big utility of the KWIC format is that ***it allows you to determine whether a document is relevant, without your having to read the whole document.*** For instance, suppose we're looking for cases discussing when a writing is necessary for a contract for the sale of goods. If we search for:

   ```
   agreement w/10 (writing or memorandum) w/10 signature and
   sale of goods
   ```

   and we retrieve documents, one of the documents looks like this when viewed in KWIC format:

38. More precisely, you see 25 searchable words on either side in the LEXIS service, and 15 searchable words on either side in all other services, such as the NEXIS and MEDIS® services.

276 Md. 247, *; 346 A.2d 231, **;
88 A.L.R.3d 406; 18 U.C.C. Rep. Serv. (Callaghan) 52

OPINION:

... [*248] [**232] appellant, and Dr. Herbert H. Hughes, the defendant-appellee, was not enforceable because the writing evidencing the contract, though signed by an agent of the appellee, was inadequately subscribed inasmuch as the agent did not have authority to execute such a memorandum on behalf of the doctor. Without determining whether the circuit court was correct in holding that this agreement cannot pass muster under the signature requirement of @ 2-201 (1), we conclude that it can be enforced under @ 2-201 (3)(b) since Dr. Hughes admitted in his testimony at trial that the contract was made. Consequently we will ...

... [*250] [**232] conclusion [**233] which appellee does not challenge on this appeal. Nonetheless, the court decided that the contract was unenforceable under @ 2-201 (1) of the UCC, which reads:

"Except as otherwise provided in this section a contract for the sale of goods for the price of $ 500 or more is not enforceable by way of action or defense unless there is some writing sufficient to indicate that a contract for sale has been made between the parties and signed by the party against whom ...

Notice that each occurrence of a search word is highlighted, and that you can see multiple "windows" into the opinion, each containing one or more hits plus the surrounding words. Thus on the above screen, we see a window into page 248 of volume 276 of the Maryland Reports, and another window into page 250 of that volume.[39]

2. **The CITE format:** The CITE format displays the citations or bibliographic references of the documents found by your search. I often find that, after I've been notified by the system of how many documents my search has found, CITE format is the best way to begin looking at those documents.

   You display the CITE format by pressing the [CITE] key (F7 on a PC keyboard, or type **`.ci`**). If you're retrieving cases, a sample first screen of cites would look something like this:

39. The hard-copy page corresponding to where you are on the screen is represented by [*248] and [*250] on the above screen. These are called Star Paging cites and are discussed further *infra*, p. 4-57.

LEVEL 1 - 21 CASES
1. A & G CONSTRUCTION CO., INC., Appellant, v. REID BROTHERS LOGGING CO., INC., Appellee, REID BROTHERS, LOGGING CO., INC., Cross-Appellant, v. A & G CONSTRUCTION CO., INC., Cross-Appellee., Nos. 2360, 2388, Supreme Court of Alaska, 547 P.2d 1207; 19 U.C.C. Rep. Serv. (Callaghan) 37, March 1, 1976
2. MIKE KRELING, Appellant, v. SAUL WALSH et al., Respondents, Civ. Nos. 15092, 15272, 15273, Court of Appeals of California, Second Appellate District, Division One, 77 Cal. App. 2d 821; 176 P.2d 965, January 29, 1947, A Petition for a Rehearing was Denied February 19, 1947, and Appellant's Petition for a Hearing by the Supreme Court was Denied March 27, 1947.
3. HOFF COMPANIES, INC., dba Hoff Building Center, an Idaho corporation, Plaintiff-Appellant, v. Robert DANNER, Defendant-Respondent, No. 18880, Court of Appeals of Idaho, 121 Idaho 39; 822 P.2d 558; 1991 Ida. App. LEXIS 240; 16 U.C.C.R. Serv. 2d(Callaghan) 974, November 27, 1991, Filed, Released for Publication January 24, 1992., As Corrected December 2, 1991. Petition for Review Denied January 24, 1992.
Each document has a number; you can display a document by typing its number

Notice that each document in the CITE display has a number to its left. You can go instantly to the text of the document by pressing its number and then [ENTER]. If you do this, the document will be displayed in KWIC format.

3. **The FULL format:** The FULL format, as you would expect, shows the complete text of the document. When you look at a document in FULL format, you can be confident that you will see all of its segments, even if these do not contain any hits. If you have just finished a search, and have not used [CITE], [KWIC] or any other display key, pressing the [FULL] key (F6, or type `.fu`) will show you the first document, and the first page of that document. If you have already been looking at a document in [KWIC], [VAR KWIC] or [SEGMTS] format, and you change to [FULL], you will see the complete text of the document starting at approximately the point you were viewing in the other format. (If you now want to go to the beginning of the document, press the [FIRST PAGE] key (Shift-F6), or type `.fp`.)

4. **The VAR-KWIC format:** The VAR-KWIC format is the same as KWIC format, except that by default, it doubles the size of the window around your search words. Thus in a LEXIS file, VAR-KWIC will show you by default 50 words on either side of each search word; in a NEXIS file, the default is 30 words on either side.

   VAR-KWIC also allows you to ***set your own window size***. That is, if *n* is the number of words shown on either side of each "hit," you can choose to set *n* to any value you want from 1-999. To do this, type the number you want for *n*, and press the [VAR KWIC] key (Shift-F5). (If you are using dot commands, type **.vk*nn***, where *nn* is the window-size, e.g., `.vk75` for a 75-word window on either side of each hit.)

5. **The SEGMTS format:** The SEGMTS format lets you view just those segments you want to see. For any segment(s) you specify, you see the whole segment(s).

   In contrast to the other display formats, pressing the [SEGMTS] key (Shift-F10, or type `.se`) does not immediately show you the document in your chosen display format.

Instead, the system displays the segments available for viewing, and prompts you to type the segments you wish. You specify multiple segments to see by separating the segment names with commas.

Actually, in most files there are "mandatory segments," which will display even if you don't request them. These mandatory segments generally serve to identify the document. In a case file, for instance, you will get the name, court, citation and date even if you don't ask for these.

If you ask for a segment, and the particular document has no information in that segment, the name of that segment does not display.

6. **The SuperKWIC format:** The SuperKWIC format is available only through the FREESTYLE feature. SuperKWIC displays the most heavily weighted block of text, i.e., the portion of the document containing the most occurrences of the various search terms. There is just one SuperKWIC block in each document, but it may be several screens long.[40]

C. **Navigating among and within documents:** You will, of course, want to move around among documents, and within a single document.

1. **Navigating among documents:** You can move to the next document by pressing the [NEXT DOC] key (F3, or type **`.nd`**). You move to the previous document by pressing [PREV DOC] (F4, or type **`.pd`**.) To go to the first document in your set of search results, use the [FIRST DOC] (Shift-F7 or type **`.fd`**.)

   You can also skip documents by using a number before the [NEXT DOC] or [PREV DOC] key. Thus to move five documents forward:

   `5`[NEXT DOC]

   (With dot commands, you do this as **`.nd5`**.)

   Remember that if you are looking at the list of documents in CITE format, you can go directly to the document you want by typing its number, shown at the left-hand part of the citation listing. When you do this, you will be in KWIC format in the selected document.

2. **Paging within a given document:** To page around in the document you are already looking at, you similarly have a choice of three function keys:

   [NEXT PAGE] (F1, or type **`.np`**)
   [PREV PAGE] (F2, or type **`.pp`**)
   [FIRST PAGE] (Shift-F6, or type **`.fp`**)

   As with moving from document to document, you can skip pages by typing a numeral first. Thus to move five pages forward, you would press:

   `5` [NEXT PAGE] (or type **`.np5`**)

40. SuperKWIC is discussed and illustrated more extensively *infra*, p. 2-61, as part of the detailed discussion of FREESTYLE.

To move six pages backward:

6 [PREV PAGE] (or type **`.pp6`**)

You can also move around within a document by use of the Star Paging feature, which lets you go to that portion of a case (or other document) that fell on a particular page of the original hard-copy case report.[41] For instance, to go the part of a case that fell on 471 U.S. 543, once you were on any part of the case, you would type:

`p*543`

D. Display order: Documents display in a particular ***order*** on the LEXIS service. For most files, documents are normally displayed in ***reverse chronological order***. That is, the most recent documents are displayed first.[42]

1. **Different courts from the same jurisdiction:** In a file of cases from a single state, but from multiple courts within that state, cases from the highest court are shown first (in the standard reverse chronological order), followed by cases from the next-highest court, and so forth. Thus in library *STATES*, file *PA*, we would see all Pennsylvania Supreme Court cases first (newest to oldest), then all Pennsylvania Superior Court cases (again, newest to oldest), followed by Commonwealth Court cases (newest to oldest), and, lastly, Philadelphia County Reporter cases.

2. **Files with multiple jurisdictions:** Some case files contain cases from multiple jurisdictions. When this happens, you will see all cases from one jurisdiction (grouped from highest court to lowest court within that jurisdiction, and newest to oldest within a given court), followed by the next jurisdiction, etc. Thus in the interests of research, I logged into the *GENFED* library, *MEGA* file (containing all federal and state cases), and asked for all cases less than one month old, in which a word starting with the initial "Z" appeared somewhere in the *NAME* segment. (Not exactly the kind of search that a firm would want to pay $300 an hour to perform.) The several hundred cases that satisfy the search request were shown to me in the following order:

    U.S. Supreme Court

    U.S. Courts of Appeals (not sorted by individual circuit, but in newest-to-oldest order, so that, say, a Fourth Circuit case decided very recently was followed by a slightly older Sixth Circuit case, followed by a slightly older Fifth Circuit case, etc.)

    U.S. District Court cases (organized the same way as Court of Appeals cases, that is, not grouped by District but sorted by date)

    U.S. Bankruptcy Court decisions

    Alabama cases (Supreme Court, followed by Court of Civil Appeals)

---

41. Star Paging is described more extensively on p. 4-57.

42. When you use the FREESTYLE feature, the default display order is "most relevant to least relevant," rather than "newest to oldest." Indeed, seeing the most relevant documents first is one of the major benefits of using FREESTYLE. See *infra*, p. 2-65 for more about display order in FREESTYLE.

Arizona cases

and so forth through to Wyoming cases

3. **The `.rank` command, for relevance-ranked order:** The display order described above is the "default" order, but you can vary that order. In particular, you can have the documents displayed in ***"relevance" order***, with most-relevant listed first. So if you're getting huge lists of documents, and you don't see any easy way to pare them down, you may want to take advantage of this "most-relevant first" sorting method.

   You do this with the **`.rank`** command.

   a. **How to use it:** Here's how to use **`.rank`**:

      ❑ First, conduct a search, just as you ordinarily would.

      ❑ Next, either before or after you've displayed your documents, type:

      `.rank [ENTER]`

      Now, your documents will be shown most-relevant to least-relevant.

   b. **How "relevance" is measured:** How does the service determine "relevance"? The method is the same one used for relevance-ranking in FREESTYLE, LEXIS' plain-English searching method.[43] Essentially, the idea is that each time a document uses one of your search terms, that document is awarded "relevance points." The document with the most points is deemed "most relevant." (However, not all search terms are weighted equally — the rarer a term is, the more points are awarded when the term occurs in a particular document.)

      i. **Most "hits" first:** So in an approximate sense, the more "hits" a document has, the higher it will be listed.

III. REFINING YOUR SEARCH

A. **The MODIFY feature:** After you do an initial search, you will probably want to refine it. Perhaps you found too many documents to read at one pass. Or, conversely, perhaps you found almost no documents that satisfied your search request. The LEXIS service is a truly interactive search system, that lets you use information from the system to constantly refine your searches. The MODIFY feature is the principal, and most cost-effective, means of refining your search.

   1. **Why you should use MODIFY:** Beginning users of the LEXIS-NEXIS services often try to cram a great deal of specificity into a single search. Then, if the search fails to come up with a reasonable number of documents, or the right type of documents, the beginner frequently starts almost from scratch, typing a new search that contains most of the original search words plus some changes.

43. See the discussion of FREESTYLE beginning on p. 2-50, *infra*.

With MODIFY, the approach is quite different. Typically, you start with a fairly broad search, which uses only a couple of fairly generic search words. After seeing how many documents this generic search produces, and browsing through some of these documents, you use MODIFY to ***add*** additional search words to your search, forming a new "level." After reviewing this newer (typically smaller) pool of documents, you may use MODIFY again to produce still another level.

Here are some of the advantages of using the MODIFY feature to refine your search a little bit at a time, rather than using a series of completely new searches by means of the [NEW SEARCH] key:

- First and foremost, ***economics***. Most LEXIS subscribers choose to be charged principally on a per-search basis.[44] Every time you use the [NEW SEARCH] key, you are billed for a new search. If you modify an existing search, you incur ***no additional search charges***, even if you do this through, say, five levels.
- When you use [NEW SEARCH], you effectively wipe out the results of your prior search. For instance, you cannot display the results of the prior search. When you use MODIFY, by contrast, you always have access to the pre-modified version of the search, and its results (by using the [DIFF LEVEL] key as described below).
- You save typing, because you only need to add new search words, not re-type words you used in the prior version of the search.

2. **How MODIFY works:** Let's take a look, then, at how you can use MODIFY to refine your search.

Let's assume that your research problem is a federal civil procedure one: your hypothetical client is a small chemical manufacturer that has been the subject of several federal diversity product liability suits brought by individual plaintiffs, but you would like to explore the possibility of instead having the suits consolidated into a single FRCP 23(b)(1) class action, so that all present and future suits of this type can be disposed of at once.

Let's assume that you begin by choosing a large library and file (*GENFED/COURTS*), and you begin by doing a fairly broad, exploratory search:

```
23 b 1 w/50 class action
```

This search produces way too many cases (over 700), and lowers your efficiency because you'll spend a lot of time digging through them. Now, instead of retyping your prior search and adding new words to it, you use MODIFY at no cost. To do this, you type the letter **m** and press [ENTER]. (Alternatively, you can use the [MODIFY] key, but most people simply type **m**. Notice that this is not a "dot" command — you type **m** rather than **.m**.) Then, you type your "new" search words.

Because you are modifying your existing search request, rather than starting a new search request, you must link the modification with the original request. You do this by starting your modification with a ***connector***. Typically, this will be **AND** or **OR** — if you are nar-

44. See the discussion of LEXIS pricing, *supra*, p. 1-20.

rowing things down, you will use **AND**, and if you are expanding the pool of documents you will use **OR**. Since most people start with a fairly broad search and narrow things down, most MODIFY requests begin with **AND**.

After you have typed the new words (and before you execute the modification by pressing [ENTER]), your screen will look something like this:

Be sure to start your MODIFY request with a connector, usually AND or OR

```
and limited fund

Your search request is:
 23  B  1 W/50  CLASS  ACTION

Number of CASES found with your search request through:
 LEVEL  1...   714

Please enter the modification to your search request (Level 2).
REMEMBER to start your modification with a CONNECTOR.

For further explanation, press the H key (for HELP) and then the ENTER key.
```

In this instance, adding a modification of **and limited fund** to our original search seems to produce good results: the number of cases goes down from over 600 to less than 75. This modified search produces exactly the same results as we would have gotten had we done everything in a single search: **(23 b 1 w/50 class action) and limited fund**. (The advantage, of course, is that we got to see that the initial search was too broad, and to refine it, without incurring any extra search charges.)

As long as you have begun with a connector, you can use any combination of words, phrases or connectors for the rest of the modification. Thus a perfectly plausible modification might be:

and class action w/3 (limited fund or fixed fund) and punitive damages.

a. **Multiple levels:** A MODIFY request produces a new ***"level"*** — the original search is called "level 1" and the second set of search words is called "level 2" (so that after four modifications, you would have five levels). You can create up to 255 levels, though you will seldom need more than four or five. After each modification, you create an additional one the same way, by typing **m**, then adding a new search word or words preceded by a connector.

b. **Limitation:** Observe that MODIFY is not quite the equivalent of being able to do a free-ranging edit of your research — you can only ***add new words***, not change anything that's already there. And, you may not be able to produce exactly the sort of logical relationships you want, due to the way priority of connectors works. For instance, suppose that your first search was:

```
punitive and class action and 23 b 1
```

Now, you realize that as long as a case contains "class action" and "23 b 1," it will be appropriate if it uses ***either*** the word "punitive" or the word "exemplary." There is no way to use MODIFY to add exemplary as an alternative to punitive — if you simply type **`m`** and then the words **`or exemplary`**, the service will interpret your modified search as if it read:

`punitive and class action and (23 b 1 or exemplary)`[45]

You can combat this problem to some extent by putting a word that you are very likely to want to edit as the last word in your initial search. For instance, if our original search had been:

```
class action w/50 23 b 1 and punitive
```

we could have added a modification of "or exemplary" and had things work out as we intended.

Additionally, you can make MODIFY more usable by being sure to use parentheses around each logical grouping in your initial search(es). For instance, suppose that our initial search was:

```
23 b 1 w/50 class action
```

Now, we would like to add to this all documents using the phrase "mass tort" (whether or not these documents mention 23(b)(1) or class action). There is no way we can do this by modification, because if we add a modification of "or mass tort," the service will interpret our search as being:

```
23 b 1 w/50 (class action or mass tort)
```

(because by the order of connectors, an **OR** connector always binds more tightly than a **`W/n`** connector). On the other hand, if the original search had been:

```
(23 b 1 w/50 class action)
```

we could now add a modification of **`or mass tort`** and have things work out the way we would like — the modified search will be read as:

`(23 b 1 w/50 class action) or mass tort`[46]

3. **Viewing different levels:** After you have used MODIFY one or more times, you may wish to go back to the pool of documents retrieved by an earlier level. You can do this by

---

45. This is because there are no parentheses in the search as modified, and by the order of connectors an **OR** binds more tightly than an **AND**.

46. Shapiro, *LEXIS: The Complete User's Guide*, pp. 69-70, notices this problem and suggests this solution.

using the [DIFF LEVEL] key (Shift-F8, or type **.dl**). This key stands for "Different Level," as you might guess.

Thus if you had a search with three levels, and you wished to view the documents retrieved by the second level (i.e., the documents retrieved as a result of the first modification), you would type "2," then press the [DIFF LEVEL] key. (As a dot command, you would do this by entering **.dl2**.)

a. **Printing different level:** You can also print all documents found at any level of your research. To do this, you must first be at that level (using [DIFF LEVEL] if you are not already at that level), then press the [PRINT ALL] key.[47]

4. **Changing a previous modification:** You may modify a previous modification. You do this by typing the number of the level you wish to change, then **m**.

   For instance, suppose you had the following search:

   Level 1 (original search): **23 b 1 w/50 class action**

   Level 2 (first modification): **and limited fund**

   Level 3 (second modification): **and punitive damages**

   Now, you realize that when you did the first modification, you should have looked for documents containing either "limited fund" or "fixed fund." You can do this by typing **2m** [ENTER], then the words: **and limited fund or fixed fund**.

   Modifying a prior level has the effect of ***wiping out*** any ***subsequent*** levels. For instance, if we modified the second level as I've just described, the third level, adding the words "and punitive damages," would be wiped out as if you had never created that level.

5. **Ending with [NEW SEARCH] or other changes:** You can only modify the "current" search. Therefore, if you press the [NEW SEARCH] key, you lose the ability to modify any searches done before you pressed that key. The same holds true if you do a change of library or change of file.

B. The FOCUS™ feature: A second means of refining your search is the FOCUS feature. FOCUS is a very powerful feature that lets you quickly locate — and highlight — key words in your retrieved documents, even if these key words are different from the ones that you searched on. Thus you can zero in on words that were not part of your search request at all, and, conversely, you can eliminate from the highlighting process words that *were* part of your search request. You can think of FOCUS as being a kind of second search-and-display software package, that operates on a group of documents that you've already retrieved with the regular LEXIS software.

1. **Adding new words:** First, let's look at how the FOCUS feature can help you add ***new search words*** to run against the pool of documents you have already retrieved. One reason you might want to do this is to divide a large pool of documents into several sub-piles. For instance, let's suppose that you've got a summer job working for a plaintiffs' product lia-

47. Printing is described in further detail *infra*, p. 2-82.

bility lawyer, who has decided that she wants to build up a practice of suing vehicle manufacturers. She would like you to get a picture of which manufacturers have been sued a lot recently, and would like you to pay special attention to truck manufacturers. You might go about this by getting a large pile of cases representing all vehicle-related product liability suits, and then dividing this into piles. To do this, you would first do a conventional search such as the following:

```
(product or strict) w/3 liability and vehicle and
 (car or truck) and date aft 1995
```

This search (when done on *GENFED/MEGA*) gives 358 cases. Now, you could use the FOCUS feature to show you just those cases involving, say, GM trucks, which you've heard have been attracting a lot of litigation recently. To do this, you would type, on the command line, the word **`focus`** (or just **`.fo`**) followed by your new search that would concentrate on GM trucks:

Type your FOCUS request on the command line, to narrow the effect of the main search

focus gm or g.m. or g.m.c. or general motors or chevrolet w/3 truck

(PRODUCT OR STRICT) W/3 LIABILITY AND VEHICLE AND (CAR OR TRUCK) AND DATE AFT 1995

Your search request has found 358 CASES through Level 1.

To DISPLAY these CASES press either the KWIC, FULL, CITE or SEGMTS key.
To MODIFY your search request, press the M key (for MODFY) and then the ENTER key.

For further explanation, press the H key (for HELP) and then the ENTER key.

The system will now respond that 13 of the 358 cases satisfy the search request you made using the FOCUS feature. You can then use any of the conventional display formats to display these 13 cases. Typically, we would want to use the KWIC format now, to home in on just the place where GM trucks are mentioned. Here is what one of the 13 cases looks like when viewed in the KWIC format:

Only terms found in the document from using the FOCUS feature are highlighted in the KWIC format; thus "strict" is not highlighted even though it was part of the original search statement

> **1997 U.S. Dist. LEXIS 4068, *2**
>
> **FOCUS**
>
> **pickup truck in a westerly direction on U.S. Highway 74 in Columbus County, North Carolina when he collided with a 1977 Chevrolet pickup truck that had been operated in an easterly direction by Henry Lambert. Mr. Hilburn died shortly thereafter as a result of the injuries, which the Plaintiffs attribute to the accident.**
>
> **------------------Footnotes------------------**
>
> **n3 The Plaintiffs' seek damages under the following theories: (1) negligence in the design of the fuel tank system on the 1977 Chevrolet pickup truck; (2) breach of an implied warranty; (3) willful and intentional misconduct; (4) strict product liability; and (5) fraudulent concealment.**
>
> **-----------------End Footnotes-----------------**
>
> **The Plaintiffs, as well as their decedent, were all North Carolina residents at the time of the accident. ...**
>
> **... [*3] arising out of any alleged defect or any failure in relation to a product shall be brought more than six years after the date of initial purchase for use or consumption.**

In addition to the fact that we have been able to narrow our 358 cases down to just the 13 that involve GM trucks, we also get good control of ***highlighting*** and the operation of KWIC format — the *only* blocks of material we will see using the KWIC format on the results of a FOCUS search are those that contain search words from the FOCUS feature request, not those containing search words from our overall request. Thus in the above screen, we see blocks referring to "GM trucks," not those referring to our original search words like "product liability" or "car." It's as if we've created our own mini-file of vehicle product-liability suits (358 cases in this file), and are then able to perform whatever searches we want on this mini-file.

2. **Removing search words:** Because the words used in your FOCUS request need not bear any special relationship to the words used in your original request, you can use the FOCUS feature to ***eliminate*** search words as well as add them. The principal reason you may want to do this is to get better control of highlighting and the KWIC format, so that you can look just at the key portion of each document.

   For example, let's suppose that you are interested in cases involving limits on contributions to so-called "401k" employee benefit plans. To make sure that you had all the relevant cases, you might use a search with a fair number of search words, such as:

   ```
   401k or 401 k and tax! and employ! and limit w/3 contrib!
   ```

   You put commonly-occurring words (such as tax! and employ!) into the above search mostly to make sure that you were not getting cases dealing with some other kind of section 401k. Once you've found the right cases, you don't especially want to see "tax" or "employee" as key words that are highlighted, and you don't want the KWIC format to display every paragraph of the case that mentions these words. Rather, you want the KWIC format to display only those paragraphs mentioning "401k" or "contribution limits," and you want only the "401" and "contribution limits" to be highlighted. You can accomplish all of this by:

```
FOCUS 401k or 401k and limit w/3 contrib!
```

3. **Allowable searches using the FOCUS feature:** The same rules for search syntax apply in FOCUS format as in "regular" searching. Thus the same connectors (**`AND`**, **`OR`**, **`W/n`**, etc.) and the same order of operations (e.g., "the **`W/n`** connector binds more tightly than the **`AND`** connector") apply. Similarly, all of the display formats (e.g., **`KWIC`**, **`CITE`** and **`FULL`**) are available to you following a FOCUS request. Once you are in FOCUS, you remain in FOCUS until you leave it; therefore, to enter a "new" focus search, simply type the search itself, without the need to type the word FOCUS.

4. **Leaving FOCUS:** You may leave the FOCUS feature at any time. To do this, press the [EXIT FOCUS] key (Ctrl-F8, or type **`.ef`**.)

5. **Choosing between MODIFY and the FOCUS feature:** When should you use the FOCUS feature, and when should you use MODIFY? Often, either will do. For instance, to winnow down the documents already retrieved by requiring that they also contain a new search word (let's assume the new word is "punitive"), you can use MODIFY followed by **`AND punitive`**, or you can use **`FOCUS punitive`**. But for some objectives, only one of the two tools will work. Here are a couple of pointers:

   Use MODIFY if you want to:

   - expand your search to include ***new documents*** (since the FOCUS feature can only work with the documents you retrieved in your prior, "regular," search).

   Use the FOCUS feature if you want to:

   - ***control highlighting*** so as to highlight words that are different from the words of your basic search (since MODIFY highlights each search word used in either the original or the modified request); or
   - do ***multiple new requests*** off of a single original request, where some of the new requests might need to be totally independent of their predecessors (since with MODIFY, a second modification must build on the first modification).

C. **Segment-limited searching:** When you are thinking of ways to refine your search, MODIFY and the FOCUS feature, as I've just noted, will be your main tools. But another good tool for refinement is the use of segment-limited searching. For instance, if you find too many cases on a certain subject, you might want to narrow things down by using a date limitation (e.g., **`date aft 1990`**). Similarly, choosing a more specific library or file will often help you narrow things down (e.g., look at a file containing just federal cases, rather than a library containing both federal and state cases).

D. **Using the ATLEAST command:** The **`ATLEAST`** command can be useful in refining your search, since it permits you to narrow things down to the very most relevant documents. Recall

Search tip: If you ever get confused about what level you are on, and/or what searches made up your various levels, you can get a good recap of your search by pressing the letter **`r`** (for "Request"), followed by [ENTER]. This will give you a recap of your current search session. For instance, if after doing three levels you pressed "r," you would get a screen like this:

```
AND PUNITIVE DAMAGES


    DATE:  May 5, 1997
  CLIENT:  LEXIS MANUAL
 LIBRARY:  GENFED
    FILE:  COURTS

Your search request is:
 23  B  1 W/50  CLASS  ACTION
 AND  MANDATORY
 AND  PUNITIVE  DAMAGES

Number of CASES found with your search request through:
  LEVEL  1...  714LEVEL  2...  189LEVEL  3...  63

Your search request has found 63 CASES through Level 3.
To DISPLAY these CASES press either the KWIC, FULL, CITE or SEGMTS key.
To MODIFY your search request, press the M key (for MODFY) and then the
ENTER key.
```

A good thing about **`r`** is that it does not interfere with anything you were doing. For instance, after pressing **`r`** in the above screen, I could then have done an additional modification. Another good thing about **`r`** is that after using it, you can press the [PRINT-SCREEN] key to have a record of your search strategy.

that a search for **`ATLEAST nn (`*`search-term`*`)`** retrieves just those documents containing at least *nn* occurrences of *search-term*. Thus a search for:

```
atleast 20 (emotional distress and bystander)
```

would retrieve just those documents in which there are at least 20 occurrences of the phrase "emotional distress" and also at least 20 occurrences of the word "bystander." For a more complete discussion of the **`ATLEAST`** command, see *supra*, p. 2-29.

IV. GETTING A DOCUMENT WHEN YOU KNOW ITS CITATION

A. Overview: Frequently, you will know a document's citation, and you will want to look at the document itself. LEXIS-NEXIS has a number of tools to let you do this. The two main ones are the LEXSEE® feature (to find cases and other stand-alone documents such as administrative rulings) and the LEXSTAT® feature (to find parts of statutes).[48] We'll be looking in greater detail at these tools, plus others, later. For now, let me give you an overview that is organized by the type of document that you want to retrieve. Where multiple methods are available, I have chosen the one that I think is the best for that type of document.

1. **Cases:** To view a case when you know its cite, use the LEXSEE feature. You type **`lexsee`** (or **`lxsee`** or **`lxe`**) followed by the citation; you can use either an official or unofficial citation. Some examples:

   `lexsee 480 us 102` (for a Supreme Court case)

   `lxsee 812 f.2d 911` (for a U.S. Court of Appeals case)

   `lxe 123 f.supp. 484` (for a U.S. District Court case)

   `lexsee 351 a.2d 349` (for a state-court case cited by its national reporter system cite)

   `lxe 69 n.j. 123` (for a state-court case cited by its official cite)

   In general, don't worry too much about periods or spaces in your cite — the LEXSEE feature is very forgiving.

2. **Statutes:** To see a particular section of a statute, use the LEXSTAT feature.

   a. **Federal statutes:** For federal statutes, you type **`lexstat`** followed by a cite in the form of XX US CODE YYY, where XX is the title number in the U.S. Code, and YYY is the section number. Thus:

      `lexstat 28 us code 1332` (to find 28 U.S.C. §1332)

      > **Search tip:** You can use the LEXSTAT and LEXSEE features regardless of what library and/or file you are logged into. In fact, as long as you've passed the client ID screen, you don't have to be in any library or file at all to use the LEXSTAT or LEXSEE features. This "file independence" is a key reason why you want to use these two tools as much as possible.

   b. **State statutes:** To find most state statutory provisions, you use the LEXSTAT feature plus the two-digit postal abbreviation for the state, followed by the word "code" and then the section. Thus:

      `lexstat or code 273.705` (to find §273.705 of the Oregon Revised Statutes)

      Some states' statutes include a particular topic in their cite. In those states, insert the topic between the postal abbreviation and the word "code":

      `lexstat ca civ proc code 1281` (to find §1281 of the California Civil Procedure Code)

      Appendix C identifies the states that require inclusion of a code topic, and gives you a

48. For a detailed discussion of the LEXSEE feature, see p. 4-30; for the LEXSTAT feature, see p. 5-12.

list of the abbreviations for the code topics in these states.

3. **Regulations and administrative rulings:** For administrative regulations and rulings, you will use either the LEXSEE or LEXSTAT feature, depending on the type of document.

   Use the LEXSEE feature for documents that are basically adjudications, such as administrative rulings; use the LEXSTAT feature for documents that are basically statutory, such as regulations.

   a. **Federal:** Here is how to get the text of some types of federal administrative documents:

      To find a section in the Code of Federal Regulations:

      `lexstat 23 cfr 750.110` (to retrieve 23 C.F.R. §750.110)

      To find a document in the Federal Register:

      `lexsee 50 fr 51242` (to find Federal Register cite 50 F.R. 51242)

      To find federal tax materials:

      `lexsee rev rul 88-2` (to retrieve Revenue Ruling 88-2)

      `lexsee rev proc 88-6` (to retrieve Revenue Procedure 88-6)

      `lexsee plr 8753003` (to retrieve Private Letter Ruling 8753003)

      To find administrative decisions by federal agencies, where these are available on the LEXIS service:

      `lexsee 50 ferc p61, 095` (to retrieve a decision of the Federal Energy Commission)

      `lexsee 1990 sec no-act lexis 268` (to retrieve an SEC no-action letter)

   b. **State administrative codes:** Some states' administrative codes are now available on LEXIS. To get them, you use the LEXSTAT feature:

      `lexstat 25 ca admin 4` (to retrieve Title 25, Section 4, of the California Code of Regulations)

4. **U.S. Constitution:** The U.S. Constitution is part of the United States Code Service on the LEXIS service. Therefore, use the LEXSTAT feature to find constitutional provisions, as if they were statutory provisions:

   `lexstat uscs const amend 4` (to display the text of the Fourth Amendment)

5. **Law reviews:** To see a law review article[49], use the LEXSEE feature:

49. For a list of law reviews available on LEXIS, together with the LEXSEE abbreviations for the reviews' names, see Appendix D.

lexsee 68 cornell 1 rev 1 (finds the article beginning on page 1 of vol. 68 of the Cornell Law Review)

lexsee 61 ncl rev 1 (finds article at p. 1 of vol. 61 of North Carolina Law Review)

6. **ALR articles:** For ALR articles, use the LEXSEE feature:

lexsee 55 alrfed 583

V. THE SHORT CUT FEATURE

A. What SHORT CUT is: The SHORT CUT feature lets you bypass the menu screens by using semicolons. If you can anticipate the next two or more steps you will want to take, SHORT CUT gives you a way to take these multiple steps in a single typed line.

SHORT CUT lets you stack the commands together on a single line, using semicolons instead of the normal [TRANSMIT] key as a command-separator. Instead of function keys, in SHORT CUT you use the dot commands.

Suppose, for instance, that on behalf of client XYZ Corp., we want to search the *GENFED* library and the *MEGA* file, perform the search "distress w/3 bystand!," and look at the retrieved documents in CITE format. Beginning at the client I.D. screen, we can do all of this with a single typed line of instructions:

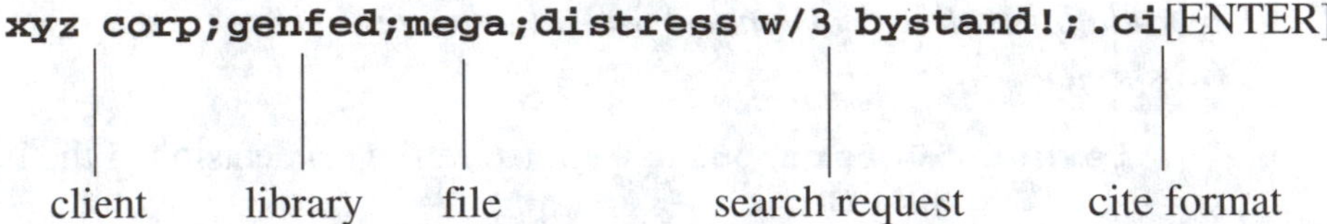

Observe that each command is separated by a semicolon, and that we do not need to put a space between the semicolon and the next command. When you use a SHORT CUT, the semicolon is the equivalent of pressing the [ENTER] key.

For your ease of reference, here is a list of common commands, and the dot commands that you would use in SHORT CUT to perform these functions:

Boolean = **.bool**	More Like This = **.more**
Change File = **.cf**	Next Document (skip ahead *n* docs) = **.nd***n*
Change Library = **.cl**	Next Page (skip ahead *n* pages) = **.np***n*
CITE display format = **.ci**	New Search = **.ns**
Client (enter new value for) = **c**	Previous Document (go back *n* docs) = **.pd***n*
Commands On = **.con**	Previous Page (go back *n* pages) = **.pp***n*
Commands Of = **.cof**	Print All = **.pa**
Different Level = **.dl**	Print displayed Screen = **.sp**
Eclipse Search, Save = **.sav**	Print Document = **.pr**
Eclipse Search, Recall = **.rec**	PRINT MANAGER (Access) = **.pm**
Exit Service = **.es**	Save Search in LOG = **.keep**
First Document = **.fd**	Saved Search (Access) = **.log**
First Page = **.fp**	SEGMTS display format = **.se**
FOCUS (enter this feature) = **.fo**	Sign Off = **.so**
FOCUS (exit this feature) = **.ef**	SuperKWIC = **.sk**
FREESTYLE = **.fr**	VAR-KWIC display format = **.vk**
FULL display = **.fu**	VAR-KWIC display format with window of *nn* words = **.vk***nn*
KWIC display format = **.kw**	
MODIFY = **m**	

One of the most common ways of using SHORT CUT is as an easy way to repeat a search in a different library. Let's suppose, for instance, that we had already run our search "emotional distress w/10 bystander" in the *GENFED* library, *MEGA* file. Now, we want to change to the *STATES* library, *COURTS* file, and run the search again; also, we want to go into KWIC format once we have rerun the search. Here's the command we would type:

```
.cl;states;courts;;.kw
```

The ";;" represents the [ENTER] key, and directs the service to *re-execute the previous search*. The ";;" must be at the end of the command stack (except that it can be followed by a display format, such as ".kw" in the above example).

Another thing I frequently use SHORT CUT for is to simplify the printing of those documents that, after inspection, I think are worth saving in hard copy. (I don't want to use [PRINT ALL] if I can avoid it, since this keeps every document retrieved by my current search request. Instead, I want a simple way of looking at a case and then saying "print just this case.") When I see a case I want to have printed, I type the following command:[50]

```
.pr;.fu;y;.nd
```

The ".pr" says "print the document I am now looking at"; the ".fu" says "do the print-out in FULL display format" (I might have used ".ci," ".kw," ".vk100," etc.); the "y" confirms my print request; the ".nd" tells the system to go on to the next document.

50. The command shown in the main text works if you're printing to an attached printer or to your computer's hard disk. If you are set up to print to a Stand Alone Printer (see *infra*, p. 2-91), you would use the following, slightly different, SHORT CUT command: **.pr;1;y;.nd**

I also frequently use a very modest form of SHORT CUT to save me just one or two key strokes. For instance, let's suppose that having looked at some documents from my previous search, I am ready to enter a new search, for "emotional distress w/10 liability." Instead of pressing [NEW SEARCH], waiting for the screen to display, and then typing my search, I can do both at once:

`.ns; emotional distress w/10 liability` [ENTER]

In fact, you'll find that the greatest use of SHORT CUT is not to stack four or five commands together, but two or three easy ones — a change of library and file, the issuance of a new search, or the specifications for a print request.

VI. PLAIN-ENGLISH SEARCHING WITH FREESTYLE™

A. Introduction to FREESTYLE: Probably the biggest software innovation from LEXIS-NEXIS in years is the FREESTYLE™ feature. The FREESTYLE feature, introduced in 1993, lets you enter searches in ***plain English***, instead of having to worry about carefully structuring your search with connectors such as **AND** and **OR**. But the FREESTYLE feature is much more than merely a means of doing plain English searching on the LEXIS-NEXIS services — it gives you, for the first time, the ability to see the most relevant documents first, a "profile" for each document showing which search terms occur in it, and a lot more.

1. **When to use:** Here are some of the situations in which you should consider using the FREESTYLE feature:

   - You want to give the service some words and phrases in a plain-English-like manner without worrying about **AND**, **OR**, **W/**__, parentheses, and the like.
   - You're dealing with a broad legal issue or concept, which can be expressed in many different ways (e.g., enforceability of non-competition agreements), rather than with a highly specific topic (e.g., proper names, or tightly-defined phrases like "res ipsa loquitur").
   - There is a large number of cases that will be somewhat relevant to your problem, and you'd like to see your documents in ***most-relevant-first*** order, rather than in the usual highest-court-first order.
   - You'd like to see a ***profile*** of each document, showing which of your search terms occurred in the document. (A key aspect of the FREESTYLE feature is that unless you specify otherwise, your search words are not "mandatory," i.e., a document could be selected even though one or more of your search words are not present in it).[51]

2. **"Associative retrieval":** The FREESTYLE feature uses a modern search technique called ***"associative retrieval"*** to find documents for you. To understand how associative

51. Although not all of your search terms must be present in the document for it to be retrieved, the document must have at least one search term in it before the FREESTYLE feature will retrieve it.

retrieval works, and how it's different from ordinary "Boolean"[52] searching, we need to first look at some of the underlying assumptions used by the Boolean approach.

A key unstated assumption of the Boolean approach is that the ***number of occurrences*** of a search word in the underlying document does not matter — the universe of underlying documents is divided into those that contain the word at least once, and those that don't contain it at all. Thus if our search consists solely of the word "car," we get those documents that contain the word "car" at least once, and the service makes absolutely no distinction between a document containing the word once and a document containing the word 100 or 1,000 times.[53] It's up to the user to examine each of the retrieved documents, and to select the ones that the user believes to be most relevant — the service gives no assistance in determining relevance.

A service using associative research, by contrast, ***does*** keep careful track of ***how many times*** a given word occurs in the document. Even more important, an associative research service attempts to use frequency and other information to help ascertain which are the ***most relevant*** documents for your research problem. In its most primitive form, the service takes two or more search words (without your describing any logical relation between them), and tries to find those documents that make the most intense use of the words you're looking for.

A concrete example may make the distinction between Boolean and associative-retrieval techniques clearer. Suppose that your client was injured in an accident that occurred while she was riding a motorcycle, and you are contemplating bringing a product liability suit against the cycle's manufacturer. Let's put aside for the moment the problem of finding cases that are product liability cases (rather than, say, contracts cases), and let's just focus on finding cases involving the right type of product. Let's furthermore assume that the most highly relevant cases would be ones about motorcycles, but we think we need to look at cases involving automobiles (since there are a lot of these), and even cases involving "vehicles" (since: (a) a case about a motorcycle might speak about "vehicles"; and (b) lots of things are neither motorcycles nor automobiles, but are vehicles, such as trucks, jeeps, etc., and we may be interested in these).

If we are doing a Boolean search, we'll probably need to do a search like:

```
motorcycle or automobile or vehicle
```

This search will, of course, retrieve any case in which any of those three words appears. From the resulting (probably large) pile of documents, there is no way for the service to

52. "Boolean" searching refers to searching built on the **AND**, **OR**, **W/n** and **NOT** search connectors. Every search technique we have looked at so far — and, in fact, all LEXIS-NEXIS searching until the advent of FREESTYLE — has been based on the Boolean approach.

53. Of course, the ATLEAST operator represents a slight deviation from this general rule. See *supra*, p. 2-29. Even with ATLEAST, however, once a document satisfies the ATLEAST operator, it is treated the same as any other document satisfying that ATLEAST command — the system makes no attempt to decide which document has "more" occurrences of the word or phrase we're interested in, or to decide which document is more relevant. As we'll see in a minute, associative research does do these things, and indeed relies heavily on them.

tell us which are the most relevant documents, so we'll have to examine them all. If the service could give us those cases with the highest number of "hits" first, this would be some assistance; but even this would not really suffice, since a document mentioning the very common word "automobile" multiple times may actually be less relevant than a document mentioning the less common "motorcycle" a few times.

Now, let's look at how an associative retrieval service would tackle the same problem. We would feed the service our three search terms — we would probably not use the **AND** or **OR** connectors, just the three terms:

motorcycle automobile vehicle

The service will first find all cases using any of these words (just as the Boolean system would). But now, the associative retrieval service does a ***statistical analysis*** of the underlying documents. One factor the service takes into account is ***how many times*** each of the search words occurs in each of the documents — the higher number of hits, the higher the estimated ***relevance*** of the document.

But the next enhancement to the statistical analysis is perhaps the most useful and ingenious. The more ***uncommon*** the search word is in the whole file, the ***higher the weight*** the service attributes to it in ranking the retrieved documents. Let's suppose, for instance, that in the particular file we're looking at, "motorcycle" occurs 100 times, "automobile" occurs 1,000 times and "vehicle" occurs 1,000 times. The service would give each occurrence of "motorcycle" a 10 times higher "weighting" or point value, than it would each occurrence of "automobile" or "vehicle." The service thus reasons, "A document that contains a rare word that the searcher is interested in is more valuable than a document that contains a common word that the searcher is interested in." In terms of our example, a document containing two occurrences of "motorcycle" would be deemed more relevant than one containing 10 occurrences of "automobile" and 5 of "vehicle."

You can probably sense why an associative-retrieval feature is most valuable where the topic is the most vague, or at least the least-capable of being reduced to a few words or phrases that must occur in the underlying document. If we're interested in cases where one of the parties is Exxon Corp., the straight-forward, old-fashioned Boolean approach gives us everything we need quickly and easily. But if we want cases involving the enforceability of non-compete agreements — keeping in mind that this concept might be expressed as "agreement not to compete," "non-compete contract," "restrictive covenant," etc., and keeping in mind that the most relevant cases are likely to have these phrases repeated multiple times — associative research becomes a very good tool to get us the most relevant documents first.

3. **Where you can use:** You can use the FREESTYLE feature in virtually every LEXIS-NEXIS library and file. The only exceptions are the citation services (SHEPARD'S and Auto-Cite), and the *QUOTE* and *DESOS* libraries (which are not available under your Educational Subscription anyway).

B. Formulating a search with FREESTYLE: Let's take a look, then, at how to search with the FREESTYLE feature.

1. **Changing into FREESTYLE:** The FREESTYLE feature is in a sense a "mode" that you're in — you leave the normal Boolean "mode," and go into FREESTYLE "mode." To do this, you simply enter the dot command `.fr`. Assuming that you've previously selected a library and file[54] you'll see the following screen:

```
Enter your FREESTYLE(TM) Search Description.
 Enter phrases in quotation marks.
 Example:  What are the requirements for a "day care center" license?

 Type .bool to exit FREESTYLE and run a Boolean search.

For further explanation, press the H key (for HELP) and then the ENTER key.
```

If at any point you want to return to ordinary Boolean searching, type `.bool`.

For the remainder of our discussion of the FREESTYLE feature, we'll assume that we're in the *GENFED* library, *MEGA* file.

2. **Do search in plain English:** Now, enter your search in plain English. "Speak" to the computer in a sentence that is more or less how you would describe your research problem to another human being. For instance, if we wanted to find cases concerning a biological mother's right to revoke her consent to the child's adoption after the adoption has become final, we could ask the service the following question:

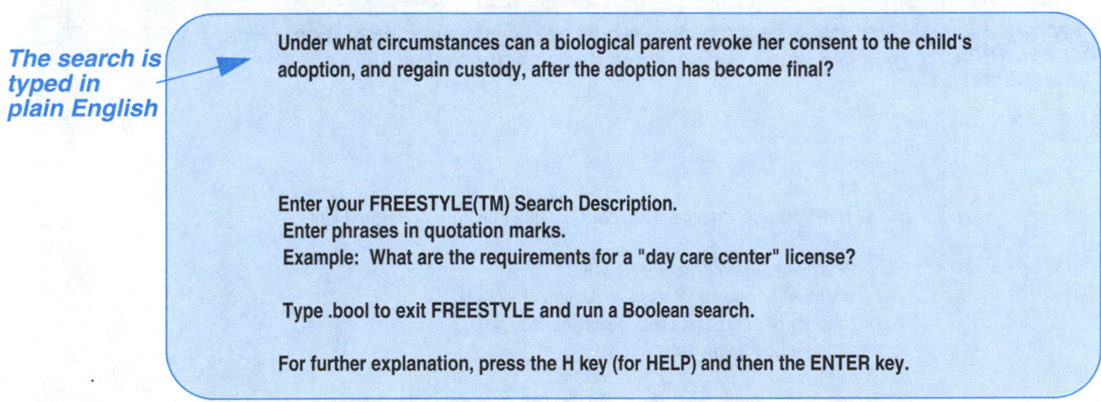
The search is typed in plain English

```
Under what circumstances can a biological parent revoke her consent to the child's
adoption, and regain custody, after the adoption has become final?

Enter your FREESTYLE(TM) Search Description.
 Enter phrases in quotation marks.
 Example:  What are the requirements for a "day care center" license?

 Type .bool to exit FREESTYLE and run a Boolean search.

For further explanation, press the H key (for HELP) and then the ENTER key.
```

After we've keyed in this search, we press the [ENTER] key, just as with a Boolean

---

54. You can use the `.fr` command to enter the FREESTYLE feature even if you have not already selected a library and file. However, you will not notice any difference in your interactions with the service until you do select a library and file and are about to enter a search.

search. Instead of immediately resolving the search, however, the service gives us a second display, in which we can do certain refinements:

FREESTYLE(TM) SEARCH OPTIONS

Press ENTER to start search.
To use a Search Option, enter an equal sign followed by the number.

Search Description:
UNDER WHAT CIRCUMSTANCES CAN A "BIOLOGICAL PARENT" REVOKE HER CONSENT TO THE CHILD'S ADOPTION AND "REGAIN CUSTODY" AFTER THE ADOPTION HAS BECOME FINAL ?

Press ENTER to start search.
<=1> Edit Search Description
<=2> Enter/edit Mandatory Terms
<=3> Enter/edit Restrictions (e.g., date)
<=4> Synonyms and Related Concepts
<=5> Change number of documents Current setting: 25

For further explanation, press the H Key (for Help) and then the ENTER key.

We'll talk about each of these five options below. For now, let's assume that we ask the service to perform the search we've already typed in, with no further refinement. We do this by pressing [ENTER] again. The service responds as follows:

Your FREESTYLE search has retrieved the top 25 documents based on statistical ranking. Search terms are listed in order of importance. Terms after the * occurred too frequently to enhance your search.

The search is reconstituted by the system

"BIOLOGICAL PARENT" "REGAIN CUSTODY" REVOKE ADOPTION ADOPTION CHILD'S CONSENT FINAL * BECOME AFTER A CAN CIRCUMSTANCES UNDER

Press ENTER to view documents in KWIC or use Full, Cite or Segmnt keys.

<=1> Browse documents in SuperKWIC (.SK)
<=2> Location of search terms in documents (.where)
<=3> Number of documents with search terms (.why)
<=4> Change document order (.sort)

For further explanation, press the H key (for HELP) and then the ENTER key.

Looking closely at the search as the service has "reconstituted" it, we see that LEXIS has performed a search based on the words it has determined to be the essential words and phrases of the search, "biological parent," "regain custody," "revoke," "adoption," "child," "consent" and "final." It has not assumed any particular logical or proximity relation among these terms (except for the phrases, shown with quotes around them). The service has listed the terms in what it believes to be "most important to least important" order. It has disregarded "become," "after," "a," "can," "circumstances," and "under" as terms that occur too frequently to be of use.[55]

Later, we'll take a detailed look at how we could check out the success of our search by looking at some background statistics associated with the results. For now, let's just assume that this first search comes up with promising results, but that we want to do better. Therefore, let's now look at some of the ways we can ***refine*** the search.

a. **Edit the search:** First, we can edit the basic search. To do this, we type **`m`** to modify the search, and then **`=1`** to "Edit Search Description." [56] We can then use the arrow keys, the delete key, and other conventional editing techniques to change the basic plain English search. For now, let's not do this.

b. **Use synonyms:** We can use ***synonyms*** in the plain English search. To do this, we put the synonym(s) in ***parentheses*** to the right of the term for which it is a synonym. In doing this, the two terms do not have to be perfectly synonymous — we're simply telling the service that the two terms are roughly equivalent. Thus if we wanted to express the idea that the cases we're looking for might involve either a "parent" or a "mother" or "father," we could reformulate our search as follows:

```
under what circumstances can a biological parent
 (mother father) revoke her consent . . .
```
[57]

i. **Thesaurus:** The FREESTYLE feature comes with an online ***thesaurus*** to help you select appropriate synonyms. After you have entered a Search Description, you can select "Synonyms and Related Concepts" from the list of options at the bottom. (It's option 4 on the screen shown in the middle of p. 2-54 above.) You'll see a screen like the one on the top of the next page, from which you choose the item for which you'd like to see thesaurus entries. Thus on the example from the next page, you could type **`8`** to see synonyms for the word **`adoption`**.

Once you've selected a term for which you'd like to see thesaurus entries, the online thesaurus works basically the same way as it does with Boolean searching, except that it's limited to legal terms.[58]

55. Some but not all of these words are words that happen to be "noise words" on the LEXIS service. (See *supra*, p. 2-18 for a description of noise words.) Even a word that is not a noise word, and is thus in the master dictionary, will be disregarded during a FREESTYLE search if the word occurs so frequently that the LEXIS software makes the judgment that documents containing these words are no more relevant than documents not containing them.

56. "Search Description" is how the FREESTYLE feature's prompts and help screens refer to the plain English part of our search. The Search Description is contrasted with "Mandatory Terms," "Restrictions," and other aspects of the search, all of which we will be discussing below.

57. I have added ellipses (. . .) here to indicate that the whole search is not reproduced.

58. See *supra*, p. 2-26 for a description of how the online thesaurus works with Boolean searching.

```
TERM SELECTION
Enter numbers for related concepts or synonyms. Example: 1,2,3,6-10
  <=1> Return to Search Options

 1 Related concepts for your search description

Search Terms found in thesaurus
-----------------------------
 2 UNDER
 3 CIRCUMSTANCES
 4 CAN
 5 REVOKE
 6 CONSENT
 7 CHILD'S
 8 ADOPTION
 9 AFTER
10 BECOME
11 FINAL
```

ii. Related Concepts: A nifty new feature is the "Related Concepts" feature. You can have the LEXIS-NEXIS service suggest whole concepts — typically, multi-word phrases — that are related to the concepts embodied in your Search Description. To access the Related Concepts feature, type **`<=4>`** ("Synonyms and Related Concepts" from the screen on p. 2-54 *supra*, the same choice that we used to get to the Thesaurus list). From the resulting screen (the one shown above), type **`1`** for "Related Concepts for your Search Description."

You'll then see a listing like the following, showing you words and phrases that the service believes are "related to" the concepts in your Search Description:

```
RELATED CONCEPTS SELECTION
Related concepts for your search
Enter concept numbers to include in search and press ENTER (e.g. 1,2,3-4)
 <=1> Return to Search Options   <=2> Return to Term Selection
--------------------------------------------------------------------------
 1 natural parent                   2 custody
 3 children                         4 natural mother
 5 adoptive parent                  6 best interest
 7 best interests of the child      8 final decree
 9 parental right                  10 adopt
11 custody of the child            12 decree
13 minor                           14 natural father
15 parental                        16 adoption decree
17 minor child                     18 surrender
19 abandonment                     20 executed
21 fraud                           22 habeas corpus
23 justifiable cause               24 probate
25 visitation                      26 withdrawn
```

As you can see, you can enter the number of a phrase, and it will be automatically included as part of your FREESTYLE search. (For more about Related Concepts, see p. 2-27, which discusses the feature in connection with Boolean searching.)

c. **Phrases:** You can also use ***phrases*** in a FREESTYLE search. If you do this, the service will only count a document as being possibly relevant if the entire phrase, not just one or more of the component words, occurs in the document. To do this, we put the phrase in ***quotation marks***. Thus if we wanted to give weight to documents containing the phrase "biological parent" (and did not want to attach any importance to the fact that a document contains just the word "biological" or the word "parent" in isolation), we would rewrite our search as follows:

```
under what circumstances can a "biological parent" revoke
 her consent . . .
```

FREESTYLE automatically recognizes some commonly-used phrases on its own ('biological mother," for instance). You can tell that FREESTYLE has recognized a phrase because it puts the phrase in quotes when it "echoes back" your search to you after you press [ENTER]. If you know that you want a particular phrase to be treated as a phrase, put the quotes in manually — it can't hurt. Conversely, if FREESTYLE supplies quotes when you don't want them, you can use "Edit Search Description" (**=1**) to remove the quotes manually.

We can combine phrases and synonyms. Thus if we wanted documents containing either "biological parent" or "biological mother," and wanted to make sure that "regain custody" was a phrase, we could search for:

```
under what circumstances can a "biological parent"
("biological mother") revoke her consent to the
child's adoption, and "regain custody" after the
adoption has become final
```

d. **No Boolean operators or wild cards:** Because the FREESTYLE feature has been trained to recognize plain English, there are some types of search logic that you cannot use in a FREESTYLE command:

i. **No Boolean:** Thus you cannot use the ***Boolean*** search connectors, **AND**, **OR**, **NOT**, **W/S**, **W/P**, **W/n** and **PRE/n**. (You can use the words "or," "and" and "not," but they will not have the logical meaning that they would have in regular Boolean LEXIS searching. Instead, they will be treated as noise words or words occurring too frequently to have relevance, and will basically be disregarded.)

For **AND** and **OR**, there is an alternative way through the FREESTYLE feature to accomplish the same result. For the concept behind **AND** (that the document must contain the word or phrase on either side of the **AND**), you can accomplish the same result by using the Mandatory feature, described below. For **OR**, you can accomplish basically the same idea by using synonyms.[59]

There is no way through the FREESTYLE feature to simulate the effect of **NOT**, **W/S**, **W/P**, **W/n**, and **PRE/n**.[60]

59. For instance, you can say **parent (mother father)**, a use of synonyms that means, in effect, **parent or mother or father**.

ii. No wild cards: Similarly, you cannot use the universal characters "!" and "*" in a FREESTYLE search. If you want several variants, you should do this by use of synonyms. Thus in our above search, if we thought that a case might say either "revoke," "revoking" or "revocation," we should rewrite the search so that it reads something like:

```
under what circumstances can a biological parent revoke
(revoking revocation) her consent . . .
```

e. Mandatories: As I mentioned earlier, an ordinary FREESTYLE Search Description does not ***require*** that any particular search term occur in a retrieved document — for instance, if you specify four words to look for, a document might be retrieved as one of the most relevant ones even though it contained just two of the four search words. But the ***"Mandatory Terms"*** feature lets you say that one or more words or phrases ***must*** be in the document for it to be retrieved.

"Enter/Edit Mandatory Terms" is one of the choices on the main search screen. See the screen on p. 2-54 as an example. If you have already done a search and you want to change it to include a Mandatory Term, type **m** (for MODIFY). At this point, Enter/Edit Mandatory Terms should be choice 2, which you can select by typing **=2** or double-clicking on the **<=2>** symbol.

Now, we would enter the Mandatory Terms. As with the ordinary Search Description, we can enter phrases by using quotation marks, and we can enter synonyms by using parentheses. (If synonyms are used in an Mandatory Term statement, then the underlying document must contain one, but not necessarily all, of the synonyms.) Thus in our adoption problem, let's suppose that we decided that "consent," "final" and "adoption" should be Mandatory Terms. We would type these Mandatory Terms into the top part of the screen, as shown here:

```
consent adoption final

Search Description:
UNDER WHAT CIRCUMSTANCES CAN A "BIOLOGICAL PARENT" REVOKE HER CONSENT TO
THE CHILD'S ADOPTION, AND REGAIN CUSTODY, AFTER THE ADOPTION HAS BECOME FINAL

Enter Mandatory Terms that must appear in documents and press ENTER.
Enclose phrases in quotation marks and synonyms in parentheses.

Type .bool to exit FREESTYLE and run a Boolean search.

For further explanation, press the H key (for HELP) and then the ENTER key.
```

---

60. However, once you have a search set retrieved by means of a FREESTYLE search, you can then use the FOCUS feature to further narrow the search. The FOCUS feature works in the traditional Boolean way, so that you can use **NOT**, **W/__**, **PRE/__**, etc., in your FOCUS search. The interaction of the FOCUS and FREESTYLE features is discussed further *infra*, p. 2-65.

Your Mandatory Terms will usually be ones that are also part of your Search Description. But the service does not require this — you can have a word be Mandatory even though you don't want it to be part of your Search Description. You might want to do this when you want to insist that all documents contain a particular word, but you don't want the number of occurrences of that word to play a role in the FREESTYLE feature's relevance ranking.[61]

A nifty feature, the **`.where`** command, lets you see where your search terms are used in the retrieved documents. We'll be covering **`.where`** in more detail below.[62] For now, let's just look at the screen we get after using **`.where`** following the running of our adoption search with the newly-added Mandatory Terms:

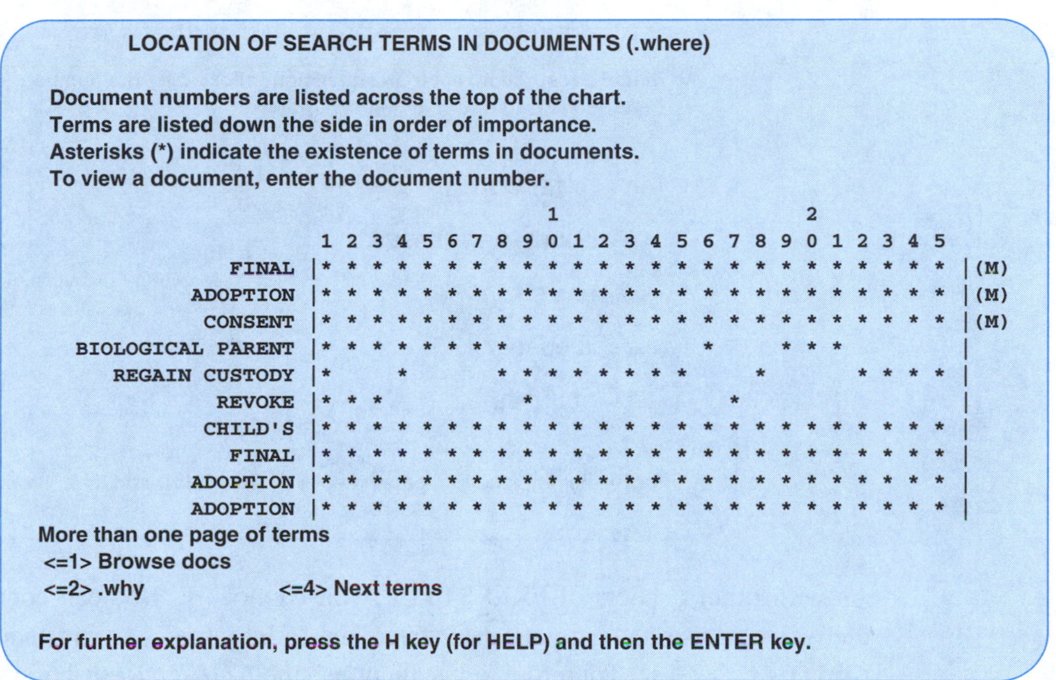

LOCATION OF SEARCH TERMS IN DOCUMENTS (.where)

Document numbers are listed across the top of the chart.
Terms are listed down the side in order of importance.
Asterisks (*) indicate the existence of terms in documents.
To view a document, enter the document number.

```
                                     1                   2
                   1 2 3 4 5 6 7 8 9 0 1 2 3 4 5 6 7 8 9 0 1 2 3 4 5
            FINAL |* * * * * * * * * * * * * * * * * * * * * * * * * |(M)
         ADOPTION |* * * * * * * * * * * * * * * * * * * * * * * * * |(M)
          CONSENT |* * * * * * * * * * * * * * * * * * * * * * * * * |(M)
BIOLOGICAL PARENT |* * * * * * * *               *     * * *         |
   REGAIN CUSTODY |*     *       * * * * * * * *     *       * * * * |
           REVOKE |* * *           *             *                   |
          CHILD'S |* * * * * * * * * * * * * * * * * * * * * * * * * |
            FINAL |* * * * * * * * * * * * * * * * * * * * * * * * * |
         ADOPTION |* * * * * * * * * * * * * * * * * * * * * * * * * |
         ADOPTION |* * * * * * * * * * * * * * * * * * * * * * * * * |
```

More than one page of terms
<=1> Browse docs
<=2> .why **<=4> Next terms**

For further explanation, press the H key (for HELP) and then the ENTER key.

What's interesting for our present purposes is that we can see at a glance that "final," "adoption" and "consent" occur in each of the 25 retrieved documents, as indeed they should. Observe that Mandatory Terms are shown by "(M)" at the right of this display.

By the way, my quick review of the first few documents retrieved by adding the Mandatory Terms indicates that the order is shuffled somewhat, and that the average relevance of these top documents is indeed somewhat increased.

f. **Restrictions:** You can also add certain ***"Restrictions"*** to your FREESTYLE search. Restrictions correspond roughly to ***segment-limited searching*** in the Boolean world.[63]

61. Only words occurring in the Search Description are weighted for determining each document's relevance.

62. See *infra*, p. 2-62.

However, only some types of Segment-limitation can be used in the FREESTYLE feature, and the types depend on which file you are in. To use Restrictions, type **`m`** (for Modify), then select "Enter/Edit Restrictions" from the list of choices (choice 3 on the screen on p. 2-54 above).

In an ordinary case-law file, there are five types of Restrictions you can enter: ***DATE***, ***COURT***, ***NAME***, ***JUDGES*** and ***COUNSEL***. *DATE* allows you to use AFT, BEF and IS,[64] and the others allow you to look only for an exact match. Thus if we want to limit ourselves to cases decided after June of 1989, we would double-click on **`[=1]`**, then type **`aft 6/89`**. To find only cases decided by a New Jersey court, we would click on **`[=2]`**, then type **`New Jersey`**. After making these two sample changes, our screen would look like this:

To use a restriction, enter an equal sign followed by the number.
Press ENTER to return to Search Options.

<=1> DATE: AFT 6/89

<=2> COURT: NEW JERSEY

<=3> NAME:

<=4> JUDGES:

<=5> COUNSEL:

For further explanation, press the H key (for HELP) and then the ENTER key.

As with other aspects of FREESTYLE, you cannot use Boolean connectors (except that you can use **`AND`** in your date statement, to let you say, for instance, **`aft 6/89 and bef 1/93`**). Therefore, you cannot use the *COURT* Restriction to find all cases occurring in either New Jersey or New York.

If you want to remove a Restriction that you have previously set, you cannot do this simply by erasing the Restriction term. Instead, you need to select the Restriction you want to delete, then type **`=0`** (or double-click) to delete that Restriction.

g. Number of documents: By default, the FREESTYLE feature retrieves only the *25* documents that it considers to be most relevant. But you can manually set this number to anything you want from 1 to 1,000. To do this, you type **`m`**, then select **`<=5>`**, "Change Number of Documents." (See the screen on p. 2-54.) Whatever new number you select will apply to all of your searches until the end of the day (2 a.m. Eastern time).

63. See *supra*, p. 2-23.

64. See *supra*, p. 2-24.

C. Viewing the search results: Once you have executed your FREESTYLE search, you will of course want to view the search results. Viewing is very similar to viewing in the ordinary Boolean mode — you have a choice among the KWIC, FULL, CITE, VAR-KWIC and SEGMTS display formats. Let's concentrate here on some of the ways in which viewing the results of FREESTYLE searches is different from the viewing of Boolean results.

1. **SuperKWIC™:** You have a sixth display format available, the ***SuperKWIC*** format. This format is available ***only*** through the FREESTYLE feature. The SuperKWIC format displays the ***most heavily weighted*** block of text, i.e., the portion of the document that is most likely to match your search request. There is just one SuperKWIC block in each document, but it may be several screens long. Here, for instance, is what the first substantive screen of the SuperKWIC format looks like for one of the documents retrieved by our adoption-custody search as it stood on p. 2-54:

903 F.2d 212, *; 1990 U.S. App. LEXIS 7870, **

May 15, 1990, Filed

SUBSEQUENT HISTORY: As Corrected.

OPINION:

... [*216] [**14] brought on behalf of herself and as a class action on behalf of all persons similarly situated, is described by Davis in her brief on this appeal as follows:

This action seeks injunctive relief and a declaratory judgment that the Pennsylvania Adoption Act is unconstitutional because it mandates the use of a vague, misleading and contradictory ' consent' form pursuant to which natural parents give up their children for adoption through private intermediaries. Among other things, the consent form deceptively characterizes their rights when they consent to an adoption, and misleads them as to the consequences attendant upon their timely and legal revocation of such consent. The action also seeks to have declared unconstitutional (a) the failure of [**15] Pennsylvania law to provide for prompt and expeditious due process to natural parents after they timely revoke their consent to adoption, and (b) those procedures of Pennsylvania law which impermissibly distinguish between two classes of natural parents who timely revoke their consent to adoption --

The advantage of SuperKWIC is that you can look at a single screenful and have your best chance at determining whether the document is a relevant one.

The easiest way to use the SuperKWIC format is to type **`.sk`**. Alternatively, at the listing of features available after you have finished the search (see the screen on p. 2-54 for an illustration), SuperKWIC is the first item, so you can type **`=1`** or double-click with your mouse on **<=1>**.

You can shift between SuperKWIC and any of the other display formats just by pressing the key, or typing the dot command, for that other format. Thus to go from the SuperKWIC to KWIC format, just type **.kw** or press the KWIC key (F5).

2. **Seeing how the service chose:** In ordinary Boolean searching on the LEXIS service, the service does not select one document "over" another — all documents satisfying the search request are retrieved, and are not ranked in order of their expected relevance. But the process of document selection with the FREESTYLE feature is different in two respects: first, the service assigns different weights to different search terms, based on their rarity, with no term required to be in the underlying document;[65] second, documents are ranked in order of their relevance. Therefore, it will be important to the searcher to be able to tell what weight the service assigned to the various search terms and, perhaps, how much more relevant the service thinks one document is than another. The FREESTYLE feature gives you two excellent tools with which to do this, the **WHERE** screen and the **WHY** screen.

   a. **The where screen:** The **where** screen tells you which documents contain each of your search terms. On the screen that appears after you have told the service to do your search, **.where** is option **<=2>**. (See the screen on p. 2-54.) To use the feature, you can either type **=2** (or with a mouse click on **<=2>**), or type **.where** as you would type any other dot command. For our adoption search as it stood on p. 2-54, **.where** takes two screens to display all data, which I've combined into a single screen:

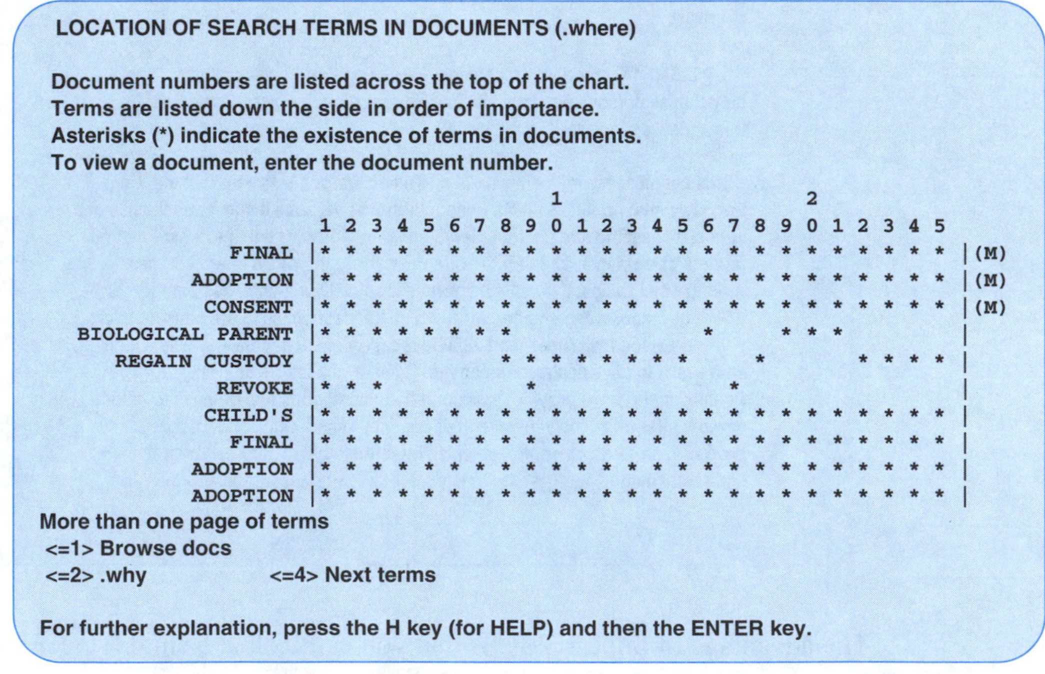

LOCATION OF SEARCH TERMS IN DOCUMENTS (.where)

Document numbers are listed across the top of the chart.
Terms are listed down the side in order of importance.
Asterisks (*) indicate the existence of terms in documents.
To view a document, enter the document number.

```
                                     1                   2
                   1 2 3 4 5 6 7 8 9 0 1 2 3 4 5 6 7 8 9 0 1 2 3 4 5
            FINAL |* * * * * * * * * * * * * * * * * * * * * * * * * |(M)
         ADOPTION |* * * * * * * * * * * * * * * * * * * * * * * * * |(M)
          CONSENT |* * * * * * * * * * * * * * * * * * * * * * * * * |(M)
BIOLOGICAL PARENT |* * * * * * * *               *     * * *         |
   REGAIN CUSTODY |*     *       * * * * * * * *     *       * * * * |
           REVOKE |* * *           *               *                 |
          CHILD'S |* * * * * * * * * * * * * * * * * * * * * * * * * |
            FINAL |* * * * * * * * * * * * * * * * * * * * * * * * * |
         ADOPTION |* * * * * * * * * * * * * * * * * * * * * * * * * |
         ADOPTION |* * * * * * * * * * * * * * * * * * * * * * * * * |
```

More than one page of terms
<=1> Browse docs
<=2> .why **<=4> Next terms**

For further explanation, press the H key (for HELP) and then the ENTER key.

Mandatory Terms are listed first, and are indicated by "(M)" on the right. As we would

65. Except for Mandatory Terms, of course.

expect, “final,” “adoption” and “consent” are all present in all of the 25 retrieved documents.

After the first three listings on the above screen, we come to the non-Mandatory terms.[66] These non-Mandatories are listing in descending order of how important the system considered them to be in deciding which documents were “best.”

We can see that the ***number of times*** that a term appears in a document must count. Otherwise, document number 22, which contains every single term (both Mandatory and non-Mandatory) at least once would be ranked higher than, say, document 2, which does not contain “revoke.”

I find that a good use of **`.where`** is to let you check that the service understood your search request as you intended it. Thus it permits us to see that the service understood that we wanted to treat “final,” “adoption” and “consent” as Mandatory Terms. Similarly, we can see that there are fewer stars in the higher-numbered (less “good”) documents, indicating that these have fewer of our search terms in them, on average.

The **`.where`** command (like the **`.why`** command, described below) can be used *at any time* — for instance, when you’re viewing cases. Just type **`.where`** (or **`.why`**) on the command line.

b. The `why` screen: The **`why`** screen gives you statistical information on a per-search-term rather than per-document basis. As with **`.where`**, there are two ways to access **`.why`**. First, you can select it from the list of choices that you get once you have completed the search; it’s the third choice, which you access by typing **`=3`** or clicking with your mouse on **`<=3>`**. Alternatively, you can just type **`.why`**.

For our custody search, here’s what the **`.why`** display looks like:[67]

66. Actually, as you’ll notice, our three Mandatory Terms are also repeated in the non-mandatory grouping, since we use those terms in the Search Description portion of our search. The information presented for these three terms is the same, so we’ll ignore it.

67. Again, I’ve actually combined two screens into one.

NUMBER OF DOCUMENTS WITH SEARCH TERMS (.why)

	Documents Retrieved	Documents Matched	Term Importance (0-100)
FINAL	25	5835	(M) Mandatory
ADOPTION	25	5835	(M) Mandatory
CONSENT	25	5835	(M) Mandatory
BIOLOGICAL PARENT	12	17	31
REGAIN CUSTODY	15	27	28
REVOKE	5	336	14
CHILD'S	25	884	9
FINAL	25	5835	1
ADOPTION	25	5835	1
ADOPTION	25	5835	1
Total retrieved:	25		

More than one page of terms
<=1> Browse docs
<=2> .where <=4> Next terms
For further explanation, press the H key (for HELP) and then the ENTER key.

The most interesting column on this display is the right-most column, "Term Importance." Possible values are 0-100. The rarer a term is in the underlying file, the higher the point value it is given. The service does not assign ***any*** points merely by virtue of the fact that a term is "mandatory."[68] Ignoring the Mandatory listings at the top, we see that the highest-weighted term is "biological mother," with a value of 23, and that the terms "final," "adoption," and "consent" have the minimum Term Importance of 1. Thus a document that used "biological mother" once (for 23 points) would be deemed more relevant than one that used "consent to final adoption" five times.

The middle column, "documents matched," also contains some useful information. The numbers here represent the number of documents that contain the term in question, *and* also satisfy all Mandatory Terms. Thus in *GENFED/MEGA* (the library and file where I performed this search), there are many more than 271 documents containing the phrase "regain custody." But there are only 271 documents that contain "regain custody" *plus* "adoption," "final," and "consent."

It can also be instructive to compare the values in the "documents matched" column with those in the left-hand "documents retrieved" column. Less than 1% (more precisely, 25 in 14775) of the documents containing "adoption" made the final cut. By contrast, over 10% (17 out of 168) of the documents containing "biological mother" made the cut, illustrating the much higher importance that the service gave to this term.

68. Thus if you list a term as a Mandatory Term, but do ***not*** use that term as part of your Search Description (the plain-English part of the FREESTYLE search), then all documents the service selects will of course have that Mandatory Term, but the number of occurrences of that term will not play any role in the service's decision about which the most relevant documents are.

All of this might suggest ways we can improve our search. For instance, I suspect that "revoke" is getting too much weight, and "adoption" is not getting enough. There is no way to increase the weight to be given to "adoption." But if we can diminish the weight given to "revoke," we can effectively increase the relative weight given to "adoption." One way to do this is by making certain that "revoke" is used *only as part of a phrase*. Thus if we reformulate the search to use "revoke consent" as a phrase, we will eliminate the significance of the isolated word "revoke," and thus effectively upgrade the importance of "adoption," "consent," etc. Keeping the Mandatory Terms the same as before ("final," "consent," and "adoption,") and revising just the Search Description part of the search to read as follows:

```
CAN A "BIOLOGICAL PARENT" ("BIOLOGICAL MOTHER") "REVOKE
 CONSENT" ("REVOKE HER CONSENT", "REVOKE HIS CONSENT",
 "REVOKE THEIR CONSENT") TO AN ADOPTION, AND "REGAIN
 CUSTODY", AFTER THE ADOPTION HAS BECOME FINAL
```

we get the following weighting of search terms:

	Documents Retrieved	Documents Matched	Term Importance 0-100)
BIOLOGICAL MOTHER	9	168	23
REVOKE THEIR CO...	24	216	22
REVOKE HIS CONSENT	24	216	22
REVOKE HER CONSENT	24	216	22
REVOKE CONSENT	24	216	22
REGAIN CUSTODY	12	271	20
BIOLOGICAL PARENT	16	294	20
FINAL	25	14775	1
ADOPTION	25	14775	1
Total Retrieved:	25		

We see that "revoke their consent," "revoke his consent" and "revoke her consent" actually get a *much higher* Term Importance (22 points) than the original stand-alone "revoke" (13 points). The difference is that a document gains no relevance by simply having a stand-alone "revoke." My subjective impression is that, looking at the retrieved documents, they are indeed, on average, more relevant to our adoption problem than the ones I got the first time around (though there is a significant overlap between the two piles of documents).

3. **Sort order:** The default sort order you get when using the FREESTYLE feature is, of course, most-relevant to least-relevant. But you can change the default order to the standard order used in Boolean searching (highest court followed by next-highest court, and within a given level of court, most-recent to oldest) by typing **`.sort`**.

4. **FOCUS:** The FOCUS feature works the same way when you are using the FREESTYLE feature as it does in the ordinary Boolean mode. However, because FOCUS lets you use ***proximity*** and ***Boolean*** operators, it is an especially valuable addition to FREESTYLE, which does not otherwise support these features.

   Suppose, for instance, that we had the 25 most relevant documents satisfying our revised search on custody. We would now like to see just those documents, and just those places in the documents, where the phrase "revoke his consent" or "revoke her consent" occurs in close proximity to "adoption" (thus eliminating those cases where what is being revoked is consent to something other than an adoption). We could do the following FOCUS request:

```
focus revoke w/10 consent w/10 adoption
```

This FOCUS request happens to be satisfied by 21 of our 25 cases, helping us at least a little bit to narrow things down further, and certainly helping us to go right to that portion of each document containing these words in close proximity.

Similarly, you can use the FOCUS feature to regain the use of universal characters. Thus:

```
focus revo! w/10 consent w/10 adopt!
```

will give us some additional variants.

Remember that FOCUS cannot enlarge our pool of documents beyond those already retrieved by our basic FREESTYLE search. What it can do, for us, however, is to winnow down the retrieved documents somewhat further, and bring us to particular parts of those documents. You might want to try setting the number of documents to be retrieved by the FREESTYLE feature to a number higher than the standard 25,[69] and then using FOCUS to narrow that bigger pool down somewhat. Also, keep in mind that the ***order*** in which you see your documents after using the FOCUS feature will still be in most-relevant-first order, which is probably what you want.[70]

Because FOCUS is a separate feature or "service," you are not really "in" FREESTYLE anymore once you have given a FOCUS request. Therefore, special FREESTYLE features like **.where**, **.why** and SuperKWIC will not work here. To leave FOCUS and return to FREESTYLE, type **.ef** ("Exit FOCUS").

5. **The "More Like This" Command:** Once you've found a document that's especially "on point," you can ask for "more documents like this one." You do this by typing the **.more** command; the system then constructs a FREESTYLE search based on the unique characteristics of your specimen case.[71]

6. **Displayed commands in FREESTYLE:** While you are displaying documents in FREESTYLE, you can cause a list of ***dot commands*** to appear at the bottom of the display screen, for easy reference. To do this, enter **.con** (for "commands on"). To turn the commands off, enter **.coff**.

D. Printing: Printing of documents occurs the same way when you're using the FREESTYLE feature as in ordinary Boolean searching. Thus you can use the [PRINT DOC] key (Shift-F3, or type **.pd**) and the [PRINT ALL] (Shift-F4, or type **.pa**) just as in Boolean searching. By the way, you can select SuperKWIC as your format for printing, by typing **.sk** as the format to use.

---

69. See *supra*, p. 2-60 for how to do this.

70. Remember that you can shift the order to a chronological-within-particular-court order, as discussed *supra*, p. 2-65.

71. **.more** is discussed extensively beginning *infra*, p. 2-67.

E. **Returning to Boolean:** At any time, you can leave the FREESTYLE feature and return to Boolean mode just by typing **`.bool`**. If you have already done one or more searches through FREESTYLE and you then return to Boolean mode, your shift will be treated as being the equivalent of a NEW SEARCH command, so you will not be able to see the documents that made up your most recent FREESTYLE solution set after you shift to Boolean.

VII. FINDING "MORE OF THE SAME" WITH .more

A. **Finding "more of the same":** Suppose you've found a very "on point" document, and you wish you could find others that are a lot like it. The **`.more`** feature, introduced by LEXIS-NEXIS in 1995, lets you do this automatically.

B. **How .more works:** The basic idea behind **`.more`** is that you find a "specimen" document, and then ask the system to find other documents that resemble it. The LEXIS service does this by automatically formulating a FREESTYLE search that combines the search terms you originally used when you found the specimen document, plus those additional search terms that seem (to the LEXIS software) to best exemplify or characterize the specimen document.

C. **An illustration:** Here's a practical example of the steps you'd take in using **`.more`**

1. **Find a specimen document:** First, we find a specimen document. We can do this using either Boolean or FREESTYLE searching. Let's suppose, for instance, that we want to find documents on the same topic we explored in the FREESTYLE section above, i.e., the right of a biological parent to revoke her consent to the child's adoption, and regain custody, after the adoption. Using either a Boolean search, or a FREESTYLE search like the one on p. 2-54, we get a set of documents. We browse through them, until we find the "best" single document. Let's assume that we decide the best one is *In the Matter of Andersen*, 99 Idaho 805, 589 P.2d 957 (1979).[72]

2. **Type .more:** Next, we type **`.more`** [ENTER]. The service responds by taking the search we used to find the specimen document, and editing it (in FREESTYLE mode) to add those characteristics that seem to set our specimen case apart from other cases.[73] Using *In the Matter of Andersen* as our specimen case, we get the following FREESTYLE search when we type **`.more`** :

---

72. As it happened, the one I decided was "best" was also the one that FREESTYLE made its "top pick," but this would not necessarily be the case.

73. Essentially, the service looks for words that appear frequently in our specimen case.

New search terms added by .more begin here

FREESTYLE(TM) SEARCH OPTIONS

Press ENTER to start MORE search or .em to return to original document.
Search terms were added to the end of your Search Description.

Search Description:
UNDER WHAT CIRCUMSTANCES CAN A "BIOLOGICAL PARENT" REVOKE HER CONSENT TO THE CHILD'S ADOPTION, AND "REGAIN CUSTODY" AFTER THE ADOPTION HAS BECOME FINAL, TERMINATION, CUSTODY, "PARENTAL RIGHTS", TERMINATED, MOOT, VISITATION, INTERMEDIARY, PARENTAL, REVOKE, "TERMINATION PROCEEDING", TERMINATING, MOOTNESS, "71 L. Ed. 2d 599", "455 U.S. 745", "102 S. Ct. 1388", "103 S. Ct. 1660"

Various ways to edit the way the .more search will be carried out

Press ENTER to start search.
<=1> Edit Search Description
<=2> Enter/edit Mandatory Terms
<=3> Enter/edit Restrictions (e.g., date)
<=4> Synonyms and Related Concepts
<=5> Change number of documents Current setting: 25
For further explanation, press the H key (for HELP) and then the ENTER key.

a. **Terms added by `.more`:** Because we used a FREESTYLE search to find our specimen document, **`.more`** began by reproducing that FREESTYLE search verbatim. It then added its own recommended search terms on to the end of the search we wrote. In the above screen, the terms added by LEXIS begin after the word "final". (If we had found the specimen document by using a Boolean rather than FREESTYLE search, LEXIS would transform our Boolean into a FREESTYLE search, then add its own recommended terms to that "synthetic" FREESTYLE search.)[74] Here are some things to note about how **`.more`** adds its own terms to the searcher's FREESTYLE search:

74. For instance, I entered the following Boolean search: **`"biological parent" w/10 "revoke consent" and adoption and "regain custody"`**. When I selected one of the retrieved cases as my specimen case, then typed **`.more`**, the service converted my Boolean search into the following "synthetic" FREESTYLE search: **`"BIOLOGICAL PARENT" W/10 "REVOKE CONSENT" ADOPTION "REGAIN CUSTODY", REVOCATION, 115-B, EXTRAJUDICIAL, "ADOPTION PROCEEDING", ADOPTIVE, REVOKE, BIOLOGICAL, COMMENCEMENT, 30-DAY, IRREVOCABLE, CUSTODY, ADVISE, COMMENCED, "63 N.Y.2d 927", "99 A.D.2d 35"`**. (The search term "W/10" in the synthetic FREESTYLE search isn't very helpful, since you can't use the W/n or PRE/n operators in a FREESTYLE search. In fact, the system treated "W/10" like any other word to be found in the documents; however, since the system didn't make "W/10" — or any other word or phrase — mandatory, no harm was done. None of the resulting 25 documents contained "W/10". However, to be safe I could, and should, have edited out the "W/10" from the FREESTYLE Search Description before continuing with the **`.more`** command.)

i. **Citation to specimen case:** If your specimen document is a case[75], the system will always add the citation(s) — in this case, "88 Idaho 485" and "401 P.2d 541" — to the list. This will usually have the effect of giving substantial weight to cases that cite the specimen case. (Of course, you can remove the citations by use of the "Edit Search Description" function before you continue, if you *don't* want this effect to occur.)

ii. **Phrases:** The system will add not only individual words but also ***phrases***. For instance, in the above screen, you can see that the system added the phrases "natural mother" and "adoption decree." Apparently the system is able to tell that certain combinations of words are commonly used as phrases, and determines that other cases using the same phrases as the specimen case are especially likely to be "like" the specimen case.

iii. **Statutes and rules:** The system will often identify a ***statutory or rule citation*** as a term that should be added. For instance, in footnote 72 on p. 2-68, you'll see that because the specimen case frequently used the phrase "115-B" (a statutory section), the system added "115-B" to the list of search terms. As with the case citation, this type of statutory addition may have the effect of making the resulting search narrower — less general and certainly less "multi-jurisdictional" — than you'd like, so you may want to edit it out.

iv. **No mandatories or synonyms:** The system apparently does not make any terms that it adds ***"mandatory."***[76] Nor does it seem to select ***synonyms*** for any terms that occur in the specimen document. (But you may add Mandatory terms or Synonyms using the editing features of FREESTYLE after the system has generated its FREESTYLE query from your specimen document.)

3. **Edit the FREESTYLE search:** After the system has given us its machine-generated FREESTYLE search, we may well want to edit that search. That is, there's a good chance that even before we run the search, we'll see that it's not optimal. For instance, it may have picked up specialized jargon from our specimen case that has very little to do with the issue we're researching.

   By way of example, look at the footnote on p. 2-68. Notice that the machine-generated FREESTYLE search included "115-B" (a statutory reference) and "30-day" (a reference to a particular period in which to do something under the law of the state applicable to the specimen case (New York, as it happened).) If we were most interested in New York cases, we might leave these references in. But if we were interested in getting a broad cross-section of cases from around the country dealing with our adoption-revocation issue, we'd probably want to remove these state-specific references.

   To do this, we'd select **`=1`** ("Edit Search Description") from the screen showing us the FREESTYLE search generated by the system. (The screen on p. 2-68 is an example.)

---

75. **`.more`** can be used with specimen documents that are not cases, such as newspaper articles, ALR reports, etc. See *infra*, p. 2-72.

76. See *supra*, p. 2-58 for a discussion of Mandatory terms in FREESTYLE.

Then, we'd simply erase any terms we didn't want. Similarly, we could add any terms we wanted.

We could also make certain terms Mandatory, or enter Restrictions (e.g., date), or select synonyms from the Thesaurus. In fact, any type of editing that we could do in a "regular" FREESTYLE search, we can do with a search generated by **`.more`**.

4. **Run the search:** Next, we'd run the search generated by **`.more`** . From here on, using **`.more`** is just like using any other FREESTYLE search. Thus:

- We see the top 25 documents, with "most relevant" first. (The "most relevant" — and thus first-listed — document will almost always be the specimen document itself. If it isn't, something's probably gone wrong, so you should use **`.why`** and **`.where`** to investigate further.)
- We can use **`.why`** to see what weighting the system has given to each word or phrase in the search, and to see how many of the retrieved documents contained that word or phrases.
- We can use **`.where`** to see which particular documents contain which search terms.

5. **Leaving `.more`: `.more`** is in a sense a "mode," something you're "in." Therefore, once you've finished with your **`.more`** work, and you want to return to the place where you first invoked **`.more`**, you do so by typing **`.em`** [ENTER].

D. What things `.more` finds: So what's the net benefit of **`.more`**? Does it find you stuff you probably wouldn't have otherwise found? It seems to me that the answer is "yes," subject to a few qualifications.

1. **Illustration:** First, a brief example of **`.more`**'s ability to find new things. In the adoption/custody problem that we used as the basis for our tour of **`.more`**, **`.more`** generated a list of 24 cases (not counting the "specimen" case, which **`.more`** will always retrieve.) Of these 24 cases, 14 were not part of the 25 "top" cases that the original FREESTYLE search found.[77]

2. **Finds associated terms:** The main utility of **`.more`** is its ability to generate additional search terms that "go together" with the ones you've already thought of. These will often be obvious once the system points them out to you, but they can nonetheless be easy to overlook. For instance, in the adoption/custody problem, compare the list (produced by **`.why`**) of search terms from my original FREESTYLE search with the list from the **`.more`** search:

---

77. I didn't ask the original FREESTYLE search to go beyond its "top 25," so it's possible that some of the "new" 14 cases found by **`.more`** were ones that would have ranked, say, 26-50 under the original FREESTYLE search.

Terms Used by original (Human-Authored) FREESTYLE Search

	NUMBER OF DOCUMENTS WITH SEARCH TERMS (.why)		
	Documents Retrieved	Documents Matched	Term Importance (0-100)
BIOLOGICAL MOTHER	17	168	23
REGAIN CUSTODY	12	271	20
BIOLOGICAL PARENT	25	294	20
REVOKE	19	1022	13
CHILD'S	25	4897	5
FINAL	25	14775	1
ADOPTION	25	14775	1
CONSENT	25	14775	1
Total Retrieved:	25		

Terms Used by `.more` (machine-generated) Search

	NUMBER OF DOCUMENTS WITH SEARCH TERMS (.why)		
	Documents Retrieved	Documents Matched	Term Importance (0-100)
401 P.2d 541	2	11	62
88 Idaho 485	2	11	62
BIOLOGICAL MOTHER	8	718	38
ADOPTION DECREE	18	1135	35
BIOLOGICAL PARENT	16	1189	35
REGAIN CUSTODY	15	1789	33
ADOPTIVE	25	7286	25
NATURAL MOTHER	24	8087	24
IRREVOCABLE	17	21844	18
BABY	24	24546	18
REVOKE	23	47439	14
EMOTIONAL	22	70518	12
REVOCATION	19	66757	12
MAGISTRATE	2	100127	10
HABEAS CORPUS	11	127332	9
ADOPTION	25	133323	9
CUSTODY	25	253843	6
DECREE	20	365656	4
Total Retrieved:	25		

You can see that among the search terms added by **`.more`** are these quite obviously relevant ones: "adoptive," "natural mother," "irrevocable," "baby," and "revocation." None of these is startling — all might be expected to be found in the type of case we're looking for. Nonetheless, for what it's worth, I did not have the acumen to include them in my original FREESTYLE search, and the system has deduced from close inspection of the specimen case that these terms might be helpful. **`.more`** is especially useful in pointing out *variants* of a search word that you've chosen; for instance, I used "revoke," but **`.more`** pointed out "irrevocable" and "revocation" as variants.

Additionally, **`.more`** can sometimes give you additional terms that you wouldn't think were relevant, but that turn out to be. For instance, **`.more`** added the phrase "habeas corpus," which I thought was irrelevant. But it turns out that in some states, if a natural parent wants to get her baby back from the adoptive parents, she does so by instituting a habeas corpus proceeding. So **`.more`** can sometimes truly expand your knowledge of what words and phrases will be relevant to your search.

The downside is that `.more` also often adds some terms that are found in the specimen case and that are *not* especially likely to be found in the type of case we're looking for. In our adoption problem, for instance, `.more` added "emotional" and "magistrate," neither of which is very helpful. One reason this occurs is because `.more` has no way to know *which aspects* of the specimen case are the ones you're interested in. In any event, you can easily overcome this problem by simply removing the irrelevant terms before pressing [ENTER] to perform the actual `.more` search.

3. **What cases it finds:** Apart from suggesting new search terms, does `.more` find useful new cases? Again, I'd say the answer is basically "yes." Of the 24 cases retrieved by `.more` in our adoption problem,[78] 14 turn out to be ones that were *not* found by my FREESTYLE search. When I went through these 14, they seemed to be pretty relevant; at least as relevant, in fact, as the cases found by my original FREESTYLE search.

   By the way, the "new" cases (that is, those not previously found by FREESTYLE) tend to cluster in the bottom, lower-ranked, area of the pile found by `.more`. Thus of the top 10 cases found by `.more`, 8 were ones previously retrieved by my FREESTYLE search. But of the next 14, 12 were new ones that FREESTYLE hadn't previously found.

   Also, keep in mind that because `.more` uses the cite to your specimen case as a search term, cases citing your specimen case will gain an "advantage." If your specimen case is a true landmark case (e.g., a Supreme Court case that makes — not merely restates — the law in a particular domain), this will probably be what you want. But if your specimen is merely illustrative rather than authoritative (e.g., it's from a small state, and you want cases from all over the country), you may find the heavy weight given to the cite to be undesirable. In that case, you should remove the cite by editing the `.more` search before you run it.

E. Other aspects of `.more`: Here are some other things about `.more` that you might want to know:

1. **Coverage:** You can use `.more` to search in most libraries and files in the LEXIS-NEXIS services, including federal and state case law, state and federal statutes, ALR articles, law reviews, the full text of bills, news and business articles, etc. You cannot use `.more` with LEXSEE or LEXSTAT documents, with Auto-Cite or SHEPARD'S Citations Service, or with financial materials.

   a. **Changing files or libraries:** In fact, once you've done a `.more` search on one library/file, you can change library and/or file, and apply the same `.more` search to the new library/file. This will happen automatically: if you are in `.more` "mode," and you press the [Change Library] or [Change File] key, the same `.more` search will reappear on your screen.

---

78. I say "24" because I don't count the specimen case, which of course is virtually always retrieved by the `.more` search.

2. **Mandatory terms:** If you begin with a FREESTYLE search and use a mandatory term, the term will be carried over to your **`.more`** search, but it will not be mandatory. (Of course, you can then make it mandatory by editing it.[79])

3. **Restrictions:** Similarly, restrictions that you use in your original FREESTYLE search will not automatically be carried over to **`.more`**. Thus if you restricted your FREESTYLE search to a certain date range, or a certain court, these restrictions won't automatically become part of your **`.more`** search. Again, however, as with Mandatory terms, you can wait for the system to generate the **`.more`** search and then add these restrictions manually using the editing functions.[80]

VIII. SOME SPECIAL FEATURES

Introductory note: The LEXIS service has a number of special features, tools that let you accomplish particular research tasks easily. We've encountered a couple of these special features already, such as the LEXSEE and LEXSTAT features. I think it is useful to have, in a single place, a brief description of all of these special features for reference. Our detailed treatment of each feature occurs elsewhere — the brief treatment here is intended so that you can browse through the list to see if there is a feature that accomplishes the particular thing you want to do.

A. The LEXSEE feature, to see a case or other single document: The LEXSEE feature, as we've seen, lets you find the full text of a ***case*** or case-like document. You type the word LEXSEE followed by the citation. The LEXSEE feature lets you find the document you're looking for without choosing a library or file, and without losing your "place," i.e., your current search results or the document you were viewing.

The LEXSEE feature can be used to find the full text not just of a case, but also a law review article, ALR annotation, administrative law document (e.g., the *Federal Register*), IRS document, or other stand-alone document. Essentially, you use LEXSEE to find any document except something that is essentially statutory.[81]

A couple of examples:

To find a case: **`lexsee 132 ariz 337`**

To find a law review article: **`lexsee 70 cal l rev 1201`**

To leave the LEXSEE feature and return to "regular" LEXIS, type **`res`** (for "resume").

B. The LEXSTAT feature, to retrieve a statutory section: The LEXSTAT feature lets you retrieve the full text of a section of a ***statute*** by its citation. As with the LEXSEE feature, you can find the document you are looking for without having to choose a specific library and file,

79. To do this, you'd go to the main **`.more`** screen as shown on p. 2-68, then type **`=2`** .

80. On the main **`.more`** screen as shown on p. 2-68, you'd type **`=3`** .

81. The details of how to use LEXSEE are covered *supra*, p. 2-46 and *infra*, p. 4-30.

and without losing your place in the search you are already doing. You just type **lexstat** followed by the citation.[82]

Some examples:

To find a federal statutory provision: **lexstat 28 uscs 1332**

To find a state code provision: **lexstat oh code 1701.95**

To find the provision from a specially-named state statute:
lexstat ca pub util code 2874

To leave the LEXSTAT feature and return to "regular" LEXIS, type **res** (for "resume") on the command line.

C. The LEXCITE® feature, to find all documents referring to a given citation: The LEXCITE feature finds all documents containing references to a particular citation. Its primary use is to find all documents referring to a particular case by that case's citation; but it can also find references to other types of documents, such as law review articles, agency decisions, and ALR annotations.[83]

Unlike the LEXSEE and LEXSTAT features, to use the LEXCITE feature you have to be in the particular library and file that you would like to search. For instance, to find all cases that cite *Webster v. Reproductive Health Services*, 492 U.S. 490, you would select an appropriately large library and file (e.g., *GENFED/MEGA*), and then type:

lexcite (492 us 490)

The service will then find every case anywhere in the *MEGA* file that cites *Webster*. You can get immediately to the cite by using the KWIC display format. An extra benefit is that you can supply any of the parallel citations to your cited case, and the LEXCITE feature will find all cases citing that case by any of the parallel citations. For instance, you could supply the S.Ct. or L.Ed. cite for *Webster*, and find cases citing *Webster* that use only the U.S. cite for that case.

1. **No need to specify "LEXCITE":** You don't even have to tell LEXIS explicitly that you want to use LEXCITE. Instead, just supply the citation itself as part of your search request, and the service will recognize that you want to do a LEXCITE search.

D. Star Paging, to track hard-copy interior-page cites: The Star Paging feature lets you identify which particular page of the hard-copy reporter any given page of your on-screen opinion falls on. For instance, suppose that you are looking at the Supreme Court's decision in *Harper & Row v. Nation Enterprises*, 471 U.S. 539. You find a particular passage which you would like to quote, and you would like to be able to indicate in your writing what actual page of the U.S. Reports (or the S.Ct. or L.Ed. Reports) that quotation falls on. By looking for the Star Paging reference inserted before the particular passage, you can identify the page of U.S. Reports on which that quote actually fell. You might see something like this:

In justifying the pardon, Ford goes out of his way to assure the reader that "com-

82. LEXSTAT is discussed further *supra*, p. 2-46 and *infra*, p. 5-12.

83. LEXCITE is discussed in more detail *infra*, p. 9-17.

> passion for Nixon as an individual [*573] hadn't prompted my decision at all." n. 9 Rather, he did it because he had to "get the monkey off my back one way or the other." n. 10

This would tell you that the quotation in the Court's opinion beginning with the words "hadn't prompted my decision. . . ." fell on p. 573 of 471 U.S.[84]

E. The FOCUS feature, to spotlight key words: The FOCUS feature lets you quickly spotlight important words in your retrieved documents, even if these words were not part of your original search request. Conversely, it lets you suppress the highlighting of words that *were* part of your search request.[85]

For instance, after doing a conventional search on "product liability w/30 vehicle," you could choose to look only at those documents containing the phrase "GM truck," and to have only that phrase highlighted for you. To do this, you would type:

`focus gm truck` [ENTER]

This instruction would cause the service to further restrict your pool of documents to those containing the phrase "GM truck"; you could then see just those portions of each opinion containing that phrase by using the KWIC key (though you could also use the FULL, CITE, or other display keys, just as you can in ordinary document-displaying).

F. The `.more` command, to find more cases like the one you're viewing: Once you've found a document which you consider to be a "model" or "specimen" document, you can use the `.more` command to find more documents similar to that specimen document. `.more` will analyze the content of the specimen document, extract the most relevant words, and construct a FREESTYLE search statement using those words. To use `.more`, just be looking at your specimen document, then type `.more`.

The `.more` command works in most libraries and files, and works whether you've done either a FREESTYLE or a Boolean search to find the specimen document in the first place.[86]

G. The LINK™ feature, to see cases cited by the case you are looking at: If you are looking at a case, and you see a citation in it to another case, you can immediately see the cited case by using the LINK feature[87]. The LINK feature is a form of hypertext. Anytime a case or law review on the LEXIS service cites a case that is itself present on the LEXIS service, the citing case contains a symbol like `[=1]`; by clicking on this symbol with your mouse, you can see the cited case. (If you don't have a mouse, you can simply type `=1` [ENTER].)

For instance, let's suppose that in looking at a case, we see the following on our screen:

> . . . failure in either requirement is fatal. [=2] Exterminating Co. v. Griffin, 258 N.C. 179, 128 S.E.2d 130; [=3] Ashville Associates v. Miller, 255 N.C. 400, 121 S.E.2d 593. . .

---

84. For a more extensive discussion of Star Paging, see *infra*, p. 4-57.

85. FOCUS is discussed more extensively *supra*, p. 2-41.

86. `.more` is discussed extensively supra, p. 2-67.

87. For a fuller discussion of LINK, see *supra*, p. 1-12 and *infra*, p. 4-54.

To see the *Exterminating Co.* case, we would click on the `[=2]` symbol that occurs just before the citation to *Exterminating Co.* (or type **=2**).

H. The GUIDE feature, to get information about the system: Two related features — the GUIDE (**.gu**) command and the GUIDE library — help you find information about the LEXIS-NEXIS services by using the services themselves.

1. The GUIDE (.gu) Command: First, let's look at the GUIDE (**.gu**) command. The **.gu** command lets you get, instantly, a description of any library or file from virtually any point in your research. After you get the description, you can easily get back to where you were when you used **.gu**.

a. When you're in the library or file for which you want a description: If you're already in the library for which you want a description, just type **.gu**, and you'll immediately see a description of that library. Here, for instance, is the description you get if you're in the *GENFED* library:

General Federal Library (GENFED)

A comprehensive collection of federal legal materials of a general nature. Case law from all federal courts is available. Legislative materials include the United States Code Service, United States Public Laws, pending federal legislation, legislative histories, and the Congressional Record. Regulatory materials include the Code of Federal Regulations and the Federal Register. Administrative decisions, court rules, circuit summaries, sentencing guidelines, and legal publications are also available.

(To get a library description, you need to have signed in to the library in question, and to have not yet signed in to any file.)

Once you've signed in to a *file*, you can use the same technique to get a description of that particular file.

The descriptions of files are perhaps even more useful than those of libraries, because they tell you what kinds of documents are in the file, how far back the coverage goes, and other stuff that's pretty hard to find out otherwise. This is especially true for non-case files, like those containing publications or public records. To take a random example, the description for *DCPROP*, a file that contains property records for the District of Columbia, contains the following description:

DCPROP - DISTRICT OF COLUMBIA TAX ASSESSOR RECORDS

TO SEARCH DCPROP: Press the NEW SEARCH key or type .ns and press ENTER.

CONTENT: Data for this file is obtained primarily from the records of the tax assessor's office. Additional data sources may be used, such as the treasurer's office and county clerk's office when appropriate. This file is usually updated annually and includes:
- owner's name
- mailing address and/or property address
- parcel number
- assessed value

By the way, the initial screen you get when you type **.gu** will contain various LINK markers at the top, followed by an overview of the file. You can use these LINK markers to go right to the portion of the document you want.[88] Here's an example of the LINK markers you'd get at the top of your first screen:

<=1> Return **<=2> File Overview** **<=3> Libraries/Files**
<=4> Content Summary **<=5> Segment Description** **<=6> Sample Document**
<=7> Browse FULL document **<=8> Help Information**

b. **When you're not in the library or file:** If you're *not* already in the library or file for which you want a description, you can simply add that library or file name after the **.gu**.[89]

Suppose, for instance, that you were in *GENFED/MEGA*, and you decided you wanted a description of the *CONN* library. You'd just type:

```
.gu conn
```

and the first thing you'd get would be a description of the CONN library.

Each GUIDE "description" is a separate document, describing either a library or a file. When you type **.gu** followed by the name of a library or file, the system actually does a key-word search for the name you give it, against the "title" segment in each description. Since the name you specify may occur as a word in the title of a number of different GUIDE documents, you can (and often will) get many documents.

For instance, when you type **.gu conn**, what you get is 38 "descriptions" (documents), of which the first is a description of the *CONN* Library. Each of the remaining documents describes a different file such that the single-line "title" of the description for that file contains "CONN". Thus for **.gu conn**, if you press the [CITE] key, you'd see (as a first screenful):

LEVEL 1 - 38 DESCRIPTIONS

1. **Connecticut Library (CONN)**
2. **Connecticut Law Tribune, CLT**
3. **Connecticut Law Reviews, CTLRV**
4. **Employment and Labor Law Newsletters, EMPLAW**
5. **Environmental Law Newsletters, ENVRN**
6. **Insurance Law Newsletters, INSUR**
7. **Video Monitoring Services of America (formerly Radio TV Reports), VMS**
8. **Business Dateline Database, BUSDTL**
9. **CT - General Statutes of Connecticut and ALS, CTCODE**
10. **CT Supreme Court Cases, CONN**
11. **CT - General Statutes of Connecticut, CTCD**

You can then see any of these descriptions by pressing its number.

c. **Finding phrases, including publication names:** Remember that, as I just described, **.gu** followed by a word or phrase does a search for that word or phrase in the titles of all the descriptions. Because of this fact, you can use **.gu** to find out quickly whether a particular type of document, or a particular publication, is present on the system. Thus if you wanted to know whether the LEXIS service contains documents from the Secretary of State's office from various states, you could type:

```
.gu secretary of state
```

88. See *supra*, p. 2-75 for more about the LINK feature.

89. This technique works better for finding files than libraries, for technical reasons not worth going into.

You'd get 50 descriptions back, demonstrating that the answer to your question is "yes". In [CITE] mode, the first screenful of search results to this search looks like this:

LEVEL 1 - 50 DESCRIPTIONS
1. IL Secretary of State Corporation Filings, ILINC
2. WI Secretary of State Corporation and Ltd Partnership Filings, WISOS
3. IN Secretary of State Corporation and Ltd Partnership Filings, INSOS
4. CA Secretary of State Limited Partnership Filings, CALTP
5. CA Secretary of State Corporation and Ltd Partnership Filings, CASOS
6. DE Secretary of State Corporation and Ltd Partnership Filings, DESOS
7. GA Secretary of State Corporation Filings, GAINC
8. GA Secretary of State Limited Partnership Filings, GALTP
9. MO Secretary of State Corporation and Ltd Partnership Filings, MOSOS
10. CA Secretary of State Corporation Filings, CAINC
11. MA Secretary of State Corporation and Ltd Partnership Filings, MASOS

Similarly, to find out whether any files contain the text of *Newsweek* magazine, you'd simply type **`.gu newsweek`**.

d. Checking the segment-layout of a file, and seeing a sample document: You can also use **`.gu`** to learn about the "architecture" of a file, and to see a sample document.

When I say "architecture," I mean the way the file is organized into distinct segments. You'll remember from our discussion of segment-limited searching[90] that it's often useful to be able to limit your search to words or phrases that occur within a particular segment. You can use **`.gu`** to find out what segments a particular file contains, and what type of data is in each of those segments.

For instance, suppose we wanted to search for all *New York Times* articles by a certain author, and we weren't sure what segment an article's author is contained in. First, we'd enter **`.gu new york times`**, and from the listed documents we'd select the main description of the *Times*. Then, using the LINK markers at the top of our first screen,[91] we'd select the marker for "Segment Description" (typically, **`=5`**). We'd then get a nice listing of each segment, with information about what's in it and an illustration of how to search on it:

SEGMENT DESCRIPTIONS

BODY	**Text of the document.** **BODY (Irene Impellizzeri w/4 Italian)**
BYLINE	**Person (s) identified as the author/reporter.** **BYLINE(JOSEPH BERGER)** **Subject and location in which this information is being presented**
CATEGORY	**CATEGORY: Politics and Government (U.S.)**
CORRECTION	**The text of a published correction.** **CORRECTION (Correction Appended)**

Similarly, we can see a sample document — a combination of segment names and actual live data — for each file. To do this, select the LINK called "Sample Document" (typically, **`=6`**).

90. See *supra*, p. 2-23.

91. The markers reproduced on p. 2-77 *supra* are an example.

e. **Leaving `.gu`:** Once you've done whatever you want in **`.gu`**, you can leave it, and return to wherever you were when you invoked it, by typing **`=1`**, the LINK marker for the "return" option.

f. **Using the GUIDE library and file:** **`.gu`** is a sort of "mode" or "feature" — you go into it to get a description, then you return to whatever you were doing. The functionality of GUIDE is also available as a standalone Library/File, which you can search and use like any other library/file. In fact, even broader functionality is available this way than through **`.gu`** — **`.gu`** in effect limits you to searching for words or phrases occurring in the title segment of each description, whereas the GUIDE library/file lets you search for any word or phrase in a truly full-text way, wherever it occurs in any description document.

The most important thing you can do in the GUIDE library/file is to get help on any software feature, or other aspect of how the LEXIS-NEXIS services work. For instance, suppose we know that there's a LEXIS feature called the "Print Manager," about which we'd like some information. Here's how we'd go about finding that info.

First, we do a Change Library to *GUIDE*, and a Change File to *GUIDE*. We might do this all in one step using SHORT CUT:[92]

`.cl;guide;guide`

We then get the following screen, which makes extensive use of LINK markers:

```
LEVEL 1 - 1 OF 9379 DESCRIPTIONS
                 GUIDE - Main Menu
      Copyright 1997, LEXIS-NEXIS, a div. of Reed Elsevier Inc.
Click on a number or enter an equal sign followed by the number.

<=1>  Product Guide Descriptions for Publications or Files
<=2>  Directory of Online Services (1997 Edition)
<=3>  Search Tips (How to's)
<=4>  LEXIS-NEXIS Press Releases
<=5>  Newsletters Produced By LEXIS-NEXIS
<=6>  Terms and Conditions
<=7>  Whom to Contact
<=8>  Auto-Cite (R) Guide
<=9>  SHEPARD'S (R) Citations Guide
<=10> Training schedules
<=11> Standard segments and exclusions

<=12> Exit <=13> Sign off <=14> Help
```

You can use these LINK markers to go right to the portion of the file that you think would be most useful. For instance, if you knew that what you were looking for would be in the various newsletters produced by LEXIS-NEXIS, you'd select **=4**.

Usually, however, I find it easier to search the entire GUIDE file, without using the

92. See supra, p. 2-48 for a description of how SHORT CUT works.

markers. To do this, you simply type **.ns** followed by your search term. Thus to find out about Print Manager, we'd type (after we got the above screen):

```
.ns; print manager
```

Here is the first screenful of what we get (viewed in [CITE] mode); I show it merely to give you an idea of the various types of documents that contain information describing how the service operates:

LEVEL 1 - 15 DESCRIPTIONS
1. LEXIS-NEXIS COMMANDS AT A GLANCE, April, 1997, 1997, Issue 1
2. Directory of Online Services; Quick Reference, February, 1997, 1997 Edition, Pg. 491, LEXIS-NEXIS Commands At A Glance
3. June, 1996 , Commands, Summarized
4. June, 1996 , GO DOCS
5. June, 1996 , PRINT MANAGER
6. LEXIS-NEXIS Insight, December, 1994, Issue 6, 1994, Pg. 1, In This Issue
7. LEXIS-NEXIS Insight, December, 1994, Issue 6, 1994, Pg. 5, Tips for Using Print Manager, Lorna Hoilette, NEXIS Customer Service
8. December, 1994, Printing/Downloading
9. December, 1994, TOP 25 Non-Technical Questions & Answers
10. INFORMATION PROFESSIONAL UPDATE, September, 1994, Issue 5, 1994, Pg. 94:59, Search Strategies New Proximity Connectors, Print Features

Most of these are newsletters and marketing or customer-service documents. Together, they give you a surprisingly large amount of information about how to use any given LEXIS-NEXIS feature.

I. The ECLIPSE™ feature (Electronic Clipping Service): The ECLIPSE feature automatically updates a saved search request at daily (business days only), weekly or monthly intervals. These updates can then be printed at your school's printer or saved for storing on your own PC's disk or printing on your own printer.

To use the ECLIPSE feature, press the [SELECT SERV] key (Shift-F1, or type **.ss**), then press the [SAVE ECLIPSE] key (Alt-F3, or type **sav**), and follow the online instructions.

J. The SHEPARD'S® and Auto-Cite® citator services: The LEXIS service contains two specialized citator services, SHEPARD'S Citations and Auto-Cite.

1. **SHEPARD'S:** For virtually every case on the LEXIS service, you can find every other case (or, for that matter, law review article) that has cited the case in question. To SHEPARDIZE® a case you are viewing in the LEXIS service, type **shep** [ENTER]. To SHEPARDIZE a case you are not viewing, type **shep** followed by the case citation, such as:

   ```
   shep 410 us 113
   ```

   (which will find all federal or state cases, law review articles and ALR articles discussing *Roe v. Wade*, 410 U.S. 113.)

   To leave SHEPARD'S, type **res** (for "resume").

2. **Auto-Cite:** Auto-Cite serves somewhat the same citation function as SHEPARD'S. Auto-Cite gives you: (1) the procedural history of your opinion (both the pre-opinion history of the case and the post-opinion history, if any); (2) the full case name; and (3) a very reliable set of parallel citations. Auto-Cite is also a very good guide to help you find any ALR

annotation that cites the case you are interested in. However, Auto-Cite does not purport to give every citation to a given case, as SHEPARD'S does — Auto-Cite gives you only cases referring *negatively* to your given case.

To use Auto-Cite on a case you are currently viewing, just type **ac** [ENTER]. To use it on a case that you are not viewing, type **ac** followed by the case citation, such as:

```
ac 410 us 113
```

To leave Auto-Cite, type **res** (for "resume").

K. The KEEP and LOG commands: The KEEP command lets you store the results of multiple searches online until 2:00 a.m. Eastern time. You can then use the LOG command to retrieve a stored search request at any time and access the results from it, at no additional search charges.

To use KEEP to store the results of a search, just type **.keep** . When you use the KEEP command, a record of your searches will be stored automatically in a file called the LOG file, and you will be returned to the main menu screen.

To display the LOG later on, type **.log**. You'll see something like this:

```
<=1> KEPT SEARCH: DEMO       STATES; OHIO
PUNITIVE W/20 STRICT! OR PRODUCT W/5 LIAB!
  (LEVEL 1-15 CASES)
<=2> KEPT SEARCH: DEMO2      GENFED; US
OPINIONBY(REHNQUIST) (LEVEL 1-429 CASES)
  AND DATE AFT 8/31/87 (LEVEL 2-77 CASES)
```

The LOG lists the following information:

- client/project ID
- library and file names
- each search request made for that library and file
- any modifications adding levels to a search request
- the number of documents found by your search request (per level)

Not only does LOG let you see this summary information, but it lets you *get back to where you were in the session*. To do this, you click on the LINK marker next to each "kept search" in the LOG file (or type **=** plus the number of the marker, e.g., **=2**). Thus if we had used LOG to get the above screen, and we wanted to put our screen back in the position it was in just after we'd done the search "punitive w/20 strict! or product w/5 liab!", we'd click on the <=1> LINK marker on our screen (or we'd type **=1** [ENTER] if we didn't have a mouse). The service would now change us to the *STATES* library, *OHIO* file (where the search was originally run), re-run the search, and show us the resulting documents just as if we were doing all this from scratch. You can now read or print these documents. And best of all, *there are no new search* *charges.*

L. The FREESTYLE Search Conversion feature: Suppose you're doing a Boolean search, and the system tells you that it will find more than 1,000 documents (or that it hasn't found any documents). At this point, you can automatically convert your search to a FREESTYLE search. To do this, just type `.fr` [ENTER] after the system gives you the "more than 1,000 documents" or "no documents" message. In the case of a "more than 1,000 documents" message, the FREESTYLE search will retrieve (by default) the 25 most relevant documents. In the case of a "no documents" message, the FREESTYLE search will similarly get the 25 "most relevant" documents — but it will do this by treating all terms as non-mandatory, so that even the "most relevant" document will be one that is missing at least one of your search terms.

M. Miscellaneous features: Here is a brief description of some additional features, which are not as major as the ones just summarized, but nonetheless useful:

1. **The REQUEST command:** If you get confused about what your current search is (especially where you have created multiple levels), you can get a recap of your search by entering `r` (without any period in front of it) followed by [ENTER].

2. **The PAGES command:** If you are looking at a document, you can discover the number of pages in that document by typing the letter `p` (for pages), then [ENTER]. The service will tell you the number of pages based on the format you are viewing (so that if you are in KWIC format, you will see the number of screensful that contain hits).

3. **The HELP command:** To get HELP text that is appropriate for the library, file or service (such as Auto-Cite, SHEPARD'S, LEXSEE, etc.) you are in, you can type the letter `h` (for help) at any time.

4. **The TIME command:** To learn the time you have spent on line in your current search session, type the letter `t` followed by [ENTER].

IX. PRINTING

A. Several types of printing: There are three essentially distinct options for printing documents in LEXIS: PRINT DOC, PRINT ALL and SCREEN PRINT. PRINT DOC prints just the document you are currently looking at; PRINT ALL prints all the documents retrieved by your current search level; SCREEN PRINT prints the contents of your current screen. Each of these three types of printing has various options associated with it.

B. About printers: Before we look at these individual print options, you should have some idea of the types of printers that may exist in a law school or office that uses LEXIS.

1. **Stand Alone Printer or laser printer:** First is the Stand Alone Printer (SAP). A SAP is a dedicated printer that is connected directly to the LEXIS service by means of a phone line. Because a SAP is not attached to your computer, you can be printing one document to the SAP while you are searching or viewing other documents on your computer, thus giving you a kind of time sharing.

a. **Dual Column Print:** Most law schools have at least one SAP that is a laser printer capable of supporting a nice feature, Dual Column Print. We'll be talking about this feature more later.[93] For now, just know that, as the name implies, Dual Column Print lets you print cases or other documents in two columns, with footnotes separated and indented, in a way that makes your printout look a lot like cases reported in books.

b. **Access to your law school's SAP:** If you are accessing LEXIS from a PC at your school, you can rely on LEXIS to keep track of the SAP(s) for your school, so that if you print to the SAP, the printout will occur on an appropriate printer at the school. If you are accessing the LEXIS service from your home, the LEXIS service will know which law school you go to, and will thus "map" your ID to the appropriate SAP at the school. This will give you the ability to initiate a print request at home, in such a way that the printout will go to your school's SAP, so that you can pick it up in the morning. (You'll find this especially valuable if you want to use the Dual Column Print option, since that requires special-purpose equipment that you will not have at home.)

2. **Attached Printer:** If your PC has a printer attached to it, this printer is known as an "Attached Printer." When you want to print to an Attached Printer, the printing generally takes place after you have otherwise terminated your search session. That is, the various print requests that you "queue up" during the course of your session are held until the very end, because of the trouble PCs have with letting you do two things at once (in this case, searching and printing).

3. **Print in Dayton and mail:** Some LEXIS subscribers are set up so that one of their printing options is to have a document printed on high-speed printers at LEXIS-NEXIS headquarters in Dayton, and mailed to the subscriber by first-class mail the next business day. You do not have this option if you are using a law school ID, or if you are working from home on a personal ID given to you in conjunction with your law-student status. I will not refer to this option further.

4. **Storing to disk:** You can cause any document to be stored "to disk" rather than printed on the Attached Printer on your PC.[94] Storing to disk lets you view the information at your leisure. It also lets you manipulate the information (e.g., by moving a quote from a case into a word-processing document.)

C. **The print options in detail:** Let's now take a detailed look at each of the three main types of printing, PRINT DOC, PRINT ALL and SCREEN PRINT:

1. **PRINT DOC:** PRINT DOC causes the system to print out the document you are looking at, and no others. You may also use this command to print out *certain pages* of a document. Use the [PRINT DOC] key (Shift-F3, or type `.pr`.)

a. **Choice of printer:** After you press [PRINT DOC], the system may ask you to select a printer. Whether it does this will depend on how your LEXIS ID number is set up. If

93. See *infra*, p. 2-91.

94. See *infra*, p. 2-93 for details.

your ID is associated with a Stand Alone Printer (SAP) at your school, the system will ask you to choose from these two options:

- Print on the printer attached to your PC (or to the disk or diskette on your PC); or
- Print to the LEXIS-NEXIS printer assigned to your personal identification number.

If your ID is not associated with a SAP, you won't be asked to select a printer — the system will simply assume that your printout is to be routed to the printer attached to your computer (or your computer's hard disk), since that's the only possibility.

b. Listing of Options: After you've indicated your choice of printer, you'll be given a number of options:

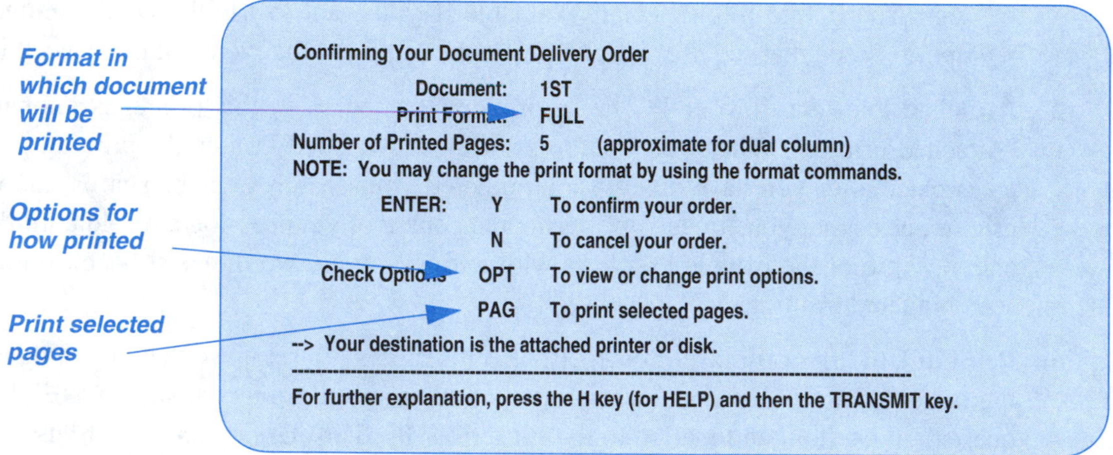

Format in which document will be printed
Options for how printed
Print selected pages
Confirming Your Document Delivery Order
Document: 1ST
Print Format: FULL
Number of Printed Pages: 5 (approximate for dual column)
NOTE: You may change the print format by using the format commands.
ENTER: Y To confirm your order.
N To cancel your order.
Check Options OPT To view or change print options.
PAG To print selected pages.
--> Your destination is the attached printer or disk.
For further explanation, press the H key (for HELP) and then the TRANSMIT key.

i. Choice of display format: The first important thing to notice about this screen is that it gives you the option of choosing ***which display format*** you would like to see your document printed in. By default, the system chooses FULL. But as you can see from the above screen, you are given the chance to press the key representing one of the other formats (KWIC, VAR KWIC, CITE or SEGMT) instead. You can also use the dot commands (**.kw**, **.vk**, **.ci** and **.se**).

ii. "OPT" to specify how the document will look: Another thing to note about this screen is that you can choose "OPT" to change your print options. If you do, you'll get the chance to tweak various aspects about how your printout will appear on the page, such as how search terms will be printed, and whether you want a cover and/ or end page.[95] Of the choices you get when you select "OPT," I find it especially useful to set either (or both) of #1 and #2 to "YES," so that in the resulting printout my search terms will be bold and/or underlined, for easy spotting.[96]

Another useful feature is "Dual Column Print." Dual Column Print works with any

95. These options are discussed more fully on p. 2-91 *infra*, as part of the discussion of "Dual Column Print."

printer that is PCL3 or PCL5 compatible.[97]

iii. **The "PAG" option to print selected pages:** A last important selection on the above screen is the "PAG" option. This option lets you specify that you only want to print ***certain pages*** from the document. An important and valuable aspect of "PAG" is that it lets you specify original ***"physical"*** page numbers, rather than "screen numbers." For instance, if you're printing *Thing v. La Chusa*, 48 Cal.3d 644, "PAG" lets you specify that you only want to print, say, pages 648-650; your printout will then contain exactly, and only, what was printed on pages 648-650 of vol. 48 of the original hard-copy Cal.3d reports.[98]

The PAG option is only available if the selected document has star pagination. (For instance, cases have it, but statutes don't).

c. **Confirmation:** Once you've used "OPT" and "PAG" to set your print options the way you want them, press ENTER to return to the prior screen (the one printed on p. 2-84 above). At this point, you can type "Y" to confirm your order or "N" to cancel it.

d. **Timing of printing:** Printing will normally not occur until you have signed off from your research session. But you can make it occur right away, if you wish:

- If you requested that printing be done on your attached printer (or your disk), you can make it happen right away by using the Print Now command. After you've confirmed your Print Doc or Print All request, type `.pn`. You'll then see a screen titled "Start Document Delivery." Enter `Y` to confirm that you want to print the document(s) right away. The document(s) will print to your attached printer or disk, whichever you specify in the dialog box that pops up next.

- If you requested that printing be done on the LEXIS-NEXIS Stand Alone Printer (SAP), you can make it happen right away by typing `.gd` (for "GO DOCS") after you issue the Print Doc or Print All request.

e. **Detailed routing instructions:** After you sign off, you will be given some follow-up questions concerning exactly how the document is to be routed. For instance, if you are sending to your Attached Printer or hard disk, the service will ask you which of these you want. Further details are given below on p. 2-91.

2. **PRINT ALL:** Use the PRINT ALL function when you want to print all (or at least several) documents from the current search level. Whereas PRINT DOC prints only the document you are currently viewing, PRINT ALL prints all or a selection of the documents at

96. With these set to "Yes," the search terms will be bold and underlined if you send the print-out directly to the printer. However, if you save the print-out to disk and then call it up into a word processor, the bolding and italics will be lost.

97. Examples of printers that support Dual Column Print are the HP DeskJet 300, 400, 500, 600 and 800 series (all of which support PCL3), the HP LaserJet 4, 5 and 6 families (PCL5) and the HP DeskJet 1200 and 1600 series (PCL5). For more about Dual Column Print, see p. 2-83 *supra*.

98. I tell you more about using "PAG" to print parts of cases, *infra*, p. 4-61.

your current search level (not necessarily including the document, if any, that you are viewing).

If you will be looking at, and perhaps printing, a significant number of documents from a given search level, PRINT ALL is probably a more attractive way of getting printouts than PRINT DOC. You could, of course, examine each document, and then while looking at a given document that you want, pressing [PRINT DOC]. But since each PRINT DOC request requires you to answer several questions, you may find it more efficient to keep a hard-copy list of the number of each document that you want to print. Then, before leaving the search level of which those documents are a part, you can do a single omnibus PRINT ALL command (using the SEL option to select individual documents, as described below).

To use PRINT ALL, press the [PRINT ALL] key (Shift-F4, or type `.pa`.)

a. **Display format:** As with PRINT DOC, you may choose a display format by pressing the appropriate format key: FULL (`.fu`), KWIC (`.kw`), CITE (`.ci`), VAR KWIC (`.vk`) or SEGMENTS (`.se`). If you choose VAR KWIC, you can widen the standard 50-word window around each hit to a number of your choosing. Thus `.vk75` would give you a 75-word window around each hit.

b. **Document delivery option:** Again as with PRINT DOC, you will next have a choice about how the document is to be delivered. Typically, you will be able to choose between the Stand Alone Printer at your school and the printer or disk drive attached to your PC.

c. **Print options:** Once you have selected a delivery option, you will see the following screen of options:

```
Confirming Your Document Delivery Order

Number of CASES:   12
   Print format:   KWIC

  TRANSMIT:         Y     To confirm your order.

                    MANY  To confirm this order and request that more than one
                          CASE may be printed on a page.

                    N     To cancel your order.

                    SEL   To print selected documents.

Check Options       OPT   To view or change print options.

--> Your destination is the attached printer or disk.
---------------------------------------------------------------------
For further explanation, press the H key (for HELP) and then the ENTER key.
```

By default, PRINT ALL will cause each document to start on a new page. But by selecting MANY from the above screen, the service will not start a new page for each document.

One of the most useful options is SEL, which lets you print selected documents. If you choose SEL, you have the chance to identify the documents you want in various ways:

- A single document (Example: **5**)
- Multiple document number separated by commas (Example: **1, 4, 7**)
- A range of document numbers separated by a hyphen (Example: **1-6**)
- A combination of the above, using both hyphens and commas (Example: **1, 4-8**)

Another useful option is OPT, which lets you set various aspects of how the documents print (e.g., whether and how search terms are highlighted). OPT functions the same way it does if you've chosen PRINT DOC.[99]

d. **Confirmation:** Once you've done anything you want to do with MANY, SEL and/or OPT, you should now (from the screen reproduced above) confirm your order by typing **y**.

e. **Timing of printing:** As with PRINT DOC, the timing of printing under PRINT ALL will depend on which printer you use. If you requested printing to the attached printer or hard disk, this will only occur when you have signed off from your research session. If you requested that printing be done on the Stand Alone Printer (SAP), the printing will happen within moments after you type "Y" to confirm the print order.

3. **PRINT SCREEN:** PRINT SCREEN, as the name implies, lets you print the contents of your current screen. The mechanism by which this works, and the choices available to you, are quite different than for PRINT DOC and PRINT ALL.

To begin with, how PRINT SCREEN works is essentially determined by which computer and operating system you are using. Let's consider the environments one at a time.

MS-DOS: Under MS-DOS, when you press the [PRINT SCREEN] key, the MS-DOS operating system, not the LEXIS-NEXIS Research Software, takes over and does the work. Under MS-DOS, pressing [PRINT SCREEN] causes a copy of whatever is on your screen to be sent directly to your local printer. Usually, your PC has been set up in such a way that the contents is sent to the parallel printer port, which is the port to which most printers on PCs are connected.

By the way, when I tell you to press the [PRINT SCREEN] key, I mean that you should press the key that the computer manufacturer has labelled as being "PRINT SCREEN." (There is no key on the LEXIS-NEXIS software template called "PRINT SCREEN.") Also, on some PCs, you will need to press Shift-[PRINT SCREEN], rather than regular [PRINT SCREEN], to cause the screen's contents to print.

An additional complication is that generally, your PC will not send a page-eject com-

99. How OPT works in PRINT DOC is summarized *supra*, p. 2-84, and discussed more fully *infra*, p. 2-91, as part of the treatment of Dual Column Print.

mand after it sends the contents of the screen. Therefore, the screen contents may sit in your printer without being told to print out. If you suspect that this may be happening, you can do either of two things: (1) you can press [PRINT SCREEN] again, in the hopes that this second copy of the screen contents will be enough to finish off the page and cause the page to be ejected; or (2) you can put your printer into the offline position (usually by pressing the On-line button on the printer), and then telling the printer to do a form feed (usually by pressing a button called "Form Feed").

MS-Windows: Under MS-Windows, there are two different senses in which you can print the contents of your current screen.

If you want to print just the raw contents of the screen in ASCII form (without seeing the menu listings at the top, or the buttons at the bottom, or any of the graphical organization of your screen), you can do this by clicking on the [PRINT SCREEN] button near the lower left of your screen.[100] You will get an unadorned printout of just the main screen contents.

Alternatively, if you want to capture the full graphical representation of the screen (with the menu items above, and the buttons below), you can do this by pressing the [PRINT SCREEN] key. A graphical representation of your screen will be placed into the Windows Clipboard. Then, to print the Clipboard contents, you will have to put those contents into a word processor. Typically, you will do this by starting your word processor, then clicking on "Edit", followed by "Paste". This technique works quite nicely with Microsoft Word for Windows, which when you paste the Clipboard contents into a document causes the printout to be neatly scaled to about five inches in width. After you have put the Clipboard contents into your document, you can print it as you would print any other word processing document, and/or save it as a document.[101]

By the way, if at any point you want to know whether you have succeeded in getting the screen contents into the Windows Clipboard, you can do this by using the Clipboard Viewer, a program usually found in the Main Program Group of Program Manager. However, there is no way to print from Clipboard Viewer.

Macintosh: On the Macintosh, to print the contents of the screen, select the menu item "Print", and then item "Screen" from within that menu. The displayed screen will then be sent immediately to the printer attached to your Macintosh.

Doing a SCREEN PRINT to the Stand Alone Printer: Regardless of whether you are using DOS, Windows or the Mac, you can cause an ASCII representation of the contents of your screen to be printed to the Stand Alone Printer. To do this, simply type `.sp` followed by [ENTER], and the screen contents will be sent to the Stand

100. This assumes you're using version 2.5 (or higher) of LEXIS-NEXIS Research Software for Windows. For lower versions, press the Ctrl key and at the same time press the accent-grave (') key (the one located above the Tab key, that looks like an open-single-quote symbol.)

101. There is no way that I know of to get a graphical representation of your screen in a single step from the LEXIS-NEXIS Research Software for Windows to your printer.

Alone Printer with your ID after you sign off.

4. **Session Record:** If you want to print or store a sequence of operations (which may include searches, the results of searches, and documents displayed in various formats), the best tool is Session Record. While Session Record is turned on, ***every*** screenful that you see gets placed into a ***file***, from which you can later print it out. You can easily turn Session Record on and off, to capture just what you want. Session Record lets you delay printing until you are off line, and lets you conduct word-searches in the recorded file. (You would then use your word processor to do offline printing and/or word-searching.)

   Session Record is not actually the best way to get a machine readable copy of cases, because you must scroll your way through every screenful of the case in order to get it into a file if this is the method you are using. (PRINT DOC or PRINT ALL, used with the option for storing to your hard disk, are better ways to do this.) The real benefit of Session Record is to capture each ***search request*** you make, so that you've got a ***record*** of what you've done. To keep a record of a search, do the search, then type the letter "r" (for "request"); you will then get a recap showing, for the current search, the client, library, file, complete search request, and level information.[102] Now, turn Session Record on so that this request is saved to a file. Turn it off, and examine the cases. If you do this for each search, you will have a record showing the details of each search request during the session. That way, if there ever arises a question about whether you looked for a certain type of document[103] you've got a record of everything you did. The safest practice of all is to print this stored session out after the session is over, and stick it in the case file.[104]

   In general, a screenful will not be recorded until you've pressed NEXT PAGE (or otherwise put new contents on the screen), so be sure not to turn Session Record off until you've gone past the screenful you're trying to record.

   The precise operation of Session Record varies depending on which operating system, and thus which Research Software, you are using.

   MS-DOS: To turn Session Record on under MS-DOS, press the [SESS REC] key (Alt-F2); there is no comparable dot command. You will then be prompted to type the name of the file in which your research should be saved. By default, you will see whatever entry you set up in the LEXIS-NEXIS Utilities Menu for the Research Software for MS-DOS.[105]

   If you have screen contents that you want to record, you must go to a new screenful (e.g., by pressing NEXT PAGE) in order for the first screenful to be recorded.

   You can toggle Session Record on or off at any time. That is, pressing the [SESS REC] key at a time when Session Record was off will turn it on, and pressing the key while

102. See p. 2-45 *supra* for an illustration of what you get when you type "r."

103. Imagine a client accusing you or your law firm of malpractice, for not having found a particular precedent!

104. Alternatively, you can keep a record of searches by using the `.keep` feature, then `.log`, and printing the results. See p. 2-81.

Session Record is on will turn it off. When you turn it on, it captures your present screen, as well as all future screens until you turn it off again. If you turn it on for the second time in a session, the system will ask you whether you want to Replace or Append to the existing contents of that file; normally, you will want to Append, so as to add onto, rather than overwriting, the prior contents from earlier in the session.

When you turn Session Record on, you will see the letters "RC" at the lower right part of your screen, to indicate that Record is on. If you turn Session Record off, the "RC" disappears.

MS-Windows: Using Session Record under Windows is similar to using it under MS-DOS, but some of the details are different.

- To use Session Record, you must first open a "recording file". To do this, from the File Menu, select New. Then, click the radio button called "Recording," and enter the name of the file into which you want your recordings to be placed. (Just enter the file name; the file will be placed in the same directory as your LEXIS-NEXIS software.)
- Then, toggle the Session Record option on and off as needed. To do this, go to the File Menu, and click on the option called "Recording On/Off." When this option is set to "On," you will see a checkmark in the left margin, and you will also see the letters RC on the status line at the bottom right part of your screen.
- As with the MS-DOS version of Session Record, once you turn Recording on, every screenful will be placed into the designated file, until you toggle recording off again.

Macintosh: Session Record on the Macintosh is similar to the Windows version.

- To get ready to Record for the first time in a session, determine the data you want to capture, then select "Session Record" from the File Menu.
- Two options appear under Session Record: 1. "Start Session Record" and 2. "Resume Session Record." Click on "Start Session Record."
- When prompted, enter a file name and a directory. Every screenful will be placed in the file until you turn off Session Recording. Data is immediately stored to the file at no charge.
- To end Session Record, select "Session Record" from the File Menu. Select "Stop Session Record." (*Note:* The "Start Session Record" option changes to "Stop Session Record" when a recording session is active). If you want to end Session

105. If you want to change your default setting for the name of the file in which your search is to be stored, start up your LEXIS-NEXIS Research Software, then select from the Main Menu item 2, "LEXIS-NEXIS Utilities Menu." From this menu, select item 2, "Set Up Research Software." You will then see the "Setup Main Menu" menu; select the line called "User Options." You will then see an entry called "Session Recording"; put the new name for the file into which you want your research stored by default. If you simply put a file name, a file with this name will be placed within the same directory that you have your Research Software (probably C:\LEXIS). However, you may specify a full path name, in order to put to the research in any directory you want.

Recording and resume at a later time with an existing file, select "Session Record" from the File Menu, then select the "Resume Session Record" option. Activating this option allows you to begin picking up data from where you left off in a previous session, and saves the new data to the existing file.

D. Routing the printout to its destination: You will need to give the service some instructions about exactly where and how to deliver your printout. The pointers that follow assume that you have chosen either PRINT DOC or PRINT ALL. (For SCREEN PRINT, see above.)

1. **Printing to the Stand Alone Printer:** If you want to print to the Stand Alone Printer associated with your ID, you must so indicate at the time you first issue your [PRINT DOC] or [PRINT ALL] request

   a. **Dual Column and other special printing:** If you are printing to a printer that supports the PCL3 or PCL5 printer control languages (whether it's your attached printer or an SAP), you will be able to take advantage of Dual Column Print and other formatted printing.[106] Once you've indicated that you want to do a PRINT DOC or a PRINT ALL, and you've selected the final destination for your printout (i.e., attached printer/ download to disk, or Stand Alone Printer), you'll see the following screen:

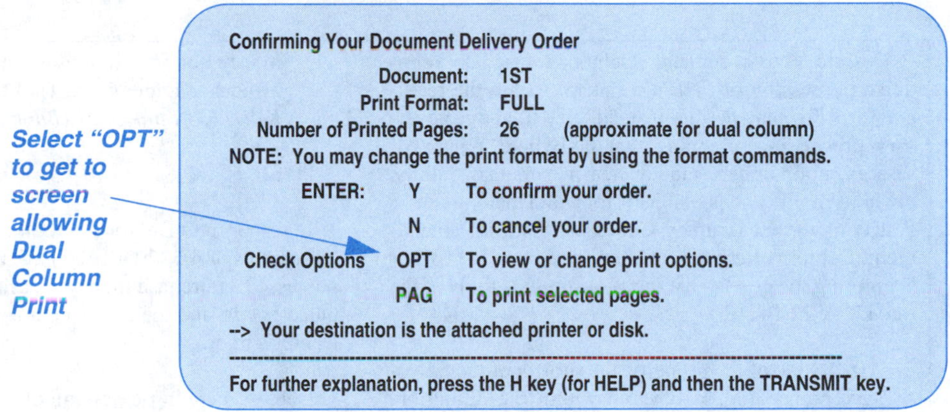

Type **OPT** and then [ENTER]. You'll get the following set of options:

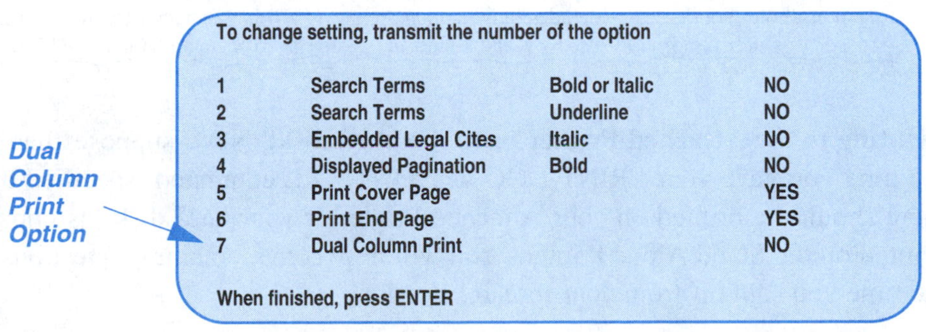

106. Examples of printers that support PCL3 or 5, and thus support Dual Column Print, are the HP DeskJet 300, 400, 500, 600 and 800 series (PCL3), the HP LaserJet 4, 5 and 6 families (PCL5) and the HP DeskJet 1200 and 1600 series (PCL5). Some non-HP printers support these protocols as well.

As you can see, you are given a considerable amount of flexibility in how you want the resulting printout to look. Thus you can choose to:

- have search words printed in bold (by setting #1 to "yes")
- underline search words (by setting #2 to "yes")
- italicize case names and cites when the document is printed in FULL format (set #3 to "yes")
- set the Star Paging entries (e.g., [*235]) to print in bold (set #4 to "yes")
- print a cover page (set #5 to "yes")
- print an ending page (set #6 to "yes,")
- most significantly, select Dual Column Print (set #7 to "yes").

The following printout, with search words in bold and underlined, with embedded legal cites in italic, and with Dual Column Print turned on, gives you a sense of what you can do with the dual column print option:

Despite FNB's demand, Debtors refused to relinquish **possession** of FNB's collateral within the requisite forty-five day period. Instead, they filed this adversary proceeding, claiming that FNB held a nonpossessory, nonpurchase-money lien in personal, family, or household goods subject to avoidance under § 522(f) of the Bankruptcy Code. n1 By trial amendment, Debtors offered as an alternative basis **[***3]** for exempting the goods, that they constituted "tools of the trade." § 522(f)(2)(b).

n1 None of the property, the subject of the adversary proceeding, is covered within the definition, household furnishings or goods. This Court adopts the definition set out in *In re Courtney, 89 Bankr. 15 (Bankr. W.D. Tex. 1988)* quoting *In re Bandy, 62 Bankr. 437, 439 (Bankr. E.D. Cal. 1986):*

'household goods . . . includes any personal property which is normally used by and found in

money lien in that item is not, avoidance under § 522(f) of the *Kelly, 133 Bankr. 811 (Bankr.*

[5]**

In response to Debtor's complaint quirements of § 522(f)(2)(B) have no possessed a purchase money security puted goods, and the goods do not qu Debtor's trade.

Debtors were in **possession** of the from the time of filing their bankrupt trial.

Factual Background

FNB has financed Debtors' farmin the 1970's. On an annual **[*838]** basis,

2. **Printing to the Attached Printer or to the hard disk:** Now, suppose that you have, at the time you gave your PRINT DOC or PRINT ALL command, specified that the document should be printed on your Attached Printer or your hard disk (as opposed to being printed on the Stand Alone Printer.) You will have some remaining questions to answer at the time you sign off from your research session.

   a. **Choosing to start delivery:** First, you'll be asked to choose whether to "Start document delivery" (choice "Y"); "Defer document delivery until you sign on again" (choice "N"), or "Route document delivery to the LEXIS-NEXIS printer assigned to your personal identification number" (choice "R"). Normally, you'll type **Y** to indicate that you want the document(s) printed right away on your attached printer or disk.

b. Selecting "File" or "Printer": Next, you'll be asked whether you want to send the document(s) to a File, the Printer, or both. Under Windows, here's what the dialog box looks like:

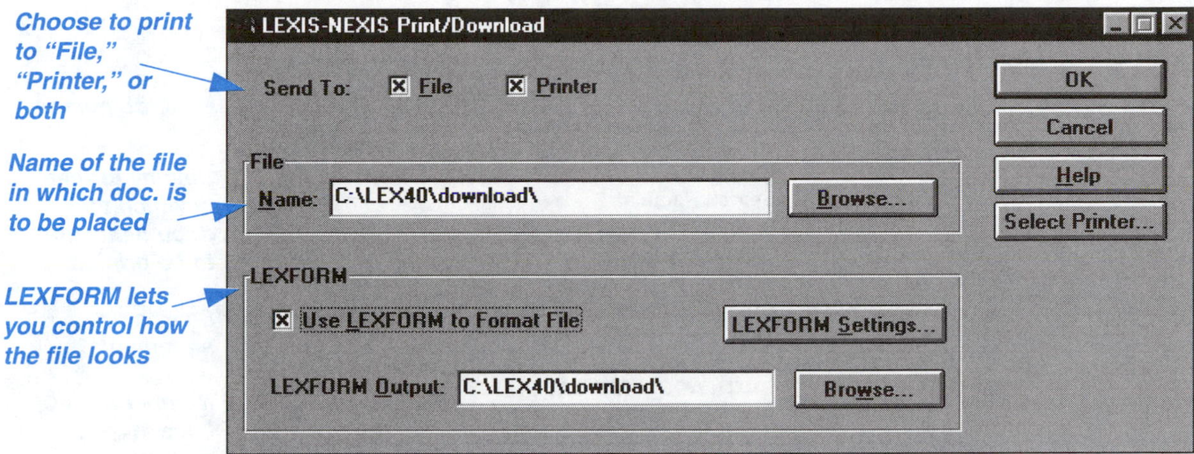

If you choose the printer: If you choose to send the document(s) to the printer, the service does not ask any further questions — it simply prints the document on your attached printer. (You can click on the "Select Printer" button to change from the Default Printer to whatever specific printer you want.)

If you store to disk: If you select "File" (whether or not you also select "Printer"), you'll have the opportunity to: (1) specify the name of the file into which the document(s) will be put; and (2) say whether you want to use LEXFORM to format the file. (We cover LEXFORM in greater detail on p. 2-95 below.)

The system will by default put your document(s) in a file in a sub-directory called "DOWNLOAD" under the directory where you've put your LEXIS-NEXIS Research Software. In an MS-Windows system, this will by default be a directory called C:\LEX40\download, as in the above screen-print. It's up to you to name the file.

Note: These document-delivery options behave the same way whether you have done a PRINT DOC or PRINT ALL command. In fact, you may have done both in a single session, in which case you will only be asked the document-delivery questions once, and a single printout or disk file containing the results of your PRINT ALL and PRINT DOC commands will be created. Also, if in a previous search session, you have told the service that you want to defer printing, the deferred print request will also be printed at this time — thus you might be getting documents you saved from a prior session done on the same day, as well as ones from the current session.

E. Controlling print-outs with Print Manager: You can get better control over how printing occurs by using "Print Manager" commands. Print Manager allows you to display your outstanding print requests, and to cancel an individual request.

To use the Print Manager, type **.gd** (for "Go Documents") and [ENTER], then type **.pm** [ENTER]. You'll get a listing of all your outstanding print requests, whether they were PRINT DOC or PRINT ALL commands (and whether they're for printing on an attached printer/disk, or on a Stand Alone printer).

For instance, after I made individual PRINT DOC requests from each of three searches, I got the following report by typing **.pm** :

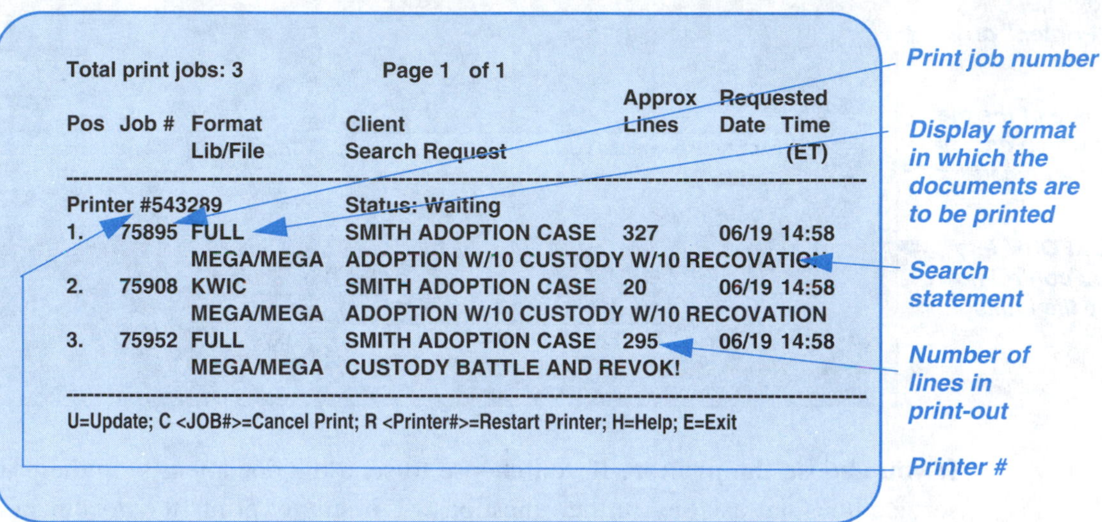

The main utility of the Print Manager is to let you ***cancel*** an individual print request. Thus if I changed my mind and didn't want to print out the documents represented by the third line in the above screen (the documents associated with the search "custody battle and revolt"), I could do this by typing, on the above screen, "c" and a space, followed by the job number:

```
c 75952
```

If you are printing to a SAP, you can use Print Manager to restart the printer if something has gone wrong (e.g., you took the printer offline to change paper). To do this, you use the "r" command, followed by the SAP's #. Thus to restart the printer referred to in the above screen, you'd type:

```
r 543289
```

If you're using PRINT ALL, you don't need to do anything special when you issue the command in order to be able to use the Print Manager later. But if you're issuing a PRINT DOC command, then you'll need to specify "Go Docs" in order to have your PRINT DOC command show up on a line of its own when you later use the Print Manager. To do this, when the system asks you to confirm after you give the PRINT DOC command, instead of just typing "Y", add the Go Docs command. You can do this by stringing the confirmation and the Go Docs command together at the confirmation screen:

```
y;.gd
```

F. **Manipulate your hard-disk print file:** If you have chosen to have your documents "downloaded" (i.e., "printed" to the hard disk rather than to paper), you may want to manipulate that disk file before printing it out. For instance, you may want to strip out the page numbers generated by LEXIS-NEXIS, or control word wrapping.

1. **LEXFORM™ (DOS & Windows):** If you are using either the MS-DOS or Windows versions of the LEXIS-NEXIS Research Software, a good tool for manipulating your downloaded file is the LEXFORM program. LEXFORM, which is called a "Downloaded File Formatter," lets you perform various format transformations (e.g., removal of header information) on your downloaded file. Here is what Windows version of the LEXFORM screen looks like that lets you select the formatting options you wish:

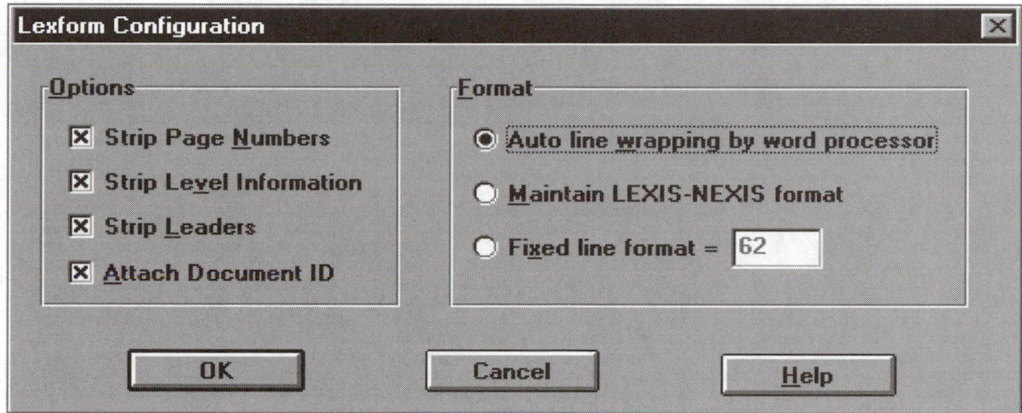

I usually run LEXFORM with the options shown as selected in the above screen-print. In particular, I find it very helpful to use the option, "Automatic line wrapping by word processor." When the LEXIS service stores a research file to your hard disk, it puts a carriage return at the end of every individual line, so that the file shows the same line breaks as you originally saw on your LEXIS screen while you were on line. But if you are printing in a smaller font, or want to use the stored information as part of some word processed document (e.g., a moot court brief), being restricted to the same line endings as are used in the LEXIS service will be very confining. Choosing the "automatic line wrapping by word processor" option lets you strip out the carriage returns from the end of each line, leaving only those carriage returns that are on the end of a paragraph. Then, when you import the document into a word processor, it is the word processor (including whatever settings you have made for line length and point size) that will determine where the lines break. I generally find that to print out a document that I have had the LEXIS service store to my hard disk, my best bet is to run the LEXFORM program, then to call the document up into a word processor. That way, the word processor can control line length, point size, and the printing of page numbers.

2. **Macintosh:** If you are working on the Macintosh, the LEXFORM program is not available at all. Here, if you want to strip out carriage returns so that your word processor can make its own line endings, you will need to use the search-and-replace feature of your word processor to do this stripping. Because you don't want to strip out the "real" paragraph symbols (the ones that are at the end of true paragraphs, as opposed to being at the

end of individual lines), you should first search for every instance in which there are two paragraph symbols in a row (representing a "true" paragraph break), and substitute some arbitrary symbol(s), perhaps something like [], a sequence that would never occur in a real document. Then, look for each occurrence of a single paragraph symbol (these will be at the end of conventional lines, rather than paragraphs), and change those to spaces. Lastly, search for the symbol you used for true paragraphs ([] in our example), and convert these back to paragraph symbols.

Chapter 3

Using Secondary Legal Authorities

Introductory note: Traditionally, law students have been taught that they should begin a research problem by looking directly at primary authorities, mainly cases and statutes. But most practicing lawyers don't do it that way, and don't believe that that's the best way. Instead, most practitioners begin their research into a problem by looking at ***secondary*** authorities, that is, narratives or commentaries about the law. I agree with this more practical view, which is why this chapter comes before the chapters on Finding Cases and on Finding Statutes.

Many excellent secondary authorities are present on the LEXIS service, and this chapter focuses on some of these. I concentrate on three main categories of secondary authority here: (1) ALR annotations, AmJur and its state-specific versions, Restatements and other similar large-scale narratives; (2) legal periodicals, including law reviews; and (3) briefs from U.S. Supreme Court cases.

I. ALR ANNOTATIONS, ENCYCLOPEDIAS, RESTATEMENTS AND OTHER NARRATIVES

A. ALR annotations: The single most useful secondary legal authority available on the LEXIS service might be the American Law Reports, commonly known as ALR. ALR is published by Lawyers Cooperative Publishing, and consists essentially of a series of "annotations." Each annotation is somewhat like a law review article, and is addressed to a single topic, often a quite narrow one. All together, ALR contains over 14,000 annotations,[1] most of which are periodically updated by the Lawyers Cooperative Publishing staff.

In general, if there is an ALR annotation that is on point to the problem you are trying to solve, you are likely to find it much more exhaustive and useful than, say, the relevant entry from a legal encyclopedia (e.g., *AmJur*). Not every narrow topic is covered, but those that are covered, are covered thoroughly.

To give you some sense of the scope of a typical ALR annotation, consider the problem of a person who has witnessed a horrible injury or death of another person close-hand, leading to emotional distress on the part of the witness. Here are some of the ALR annotations that, by their title, seem as though they may have bearing on this problem:

Relationship between victim and plaintiff witness as affecting right to recover damages in

1. Carrick, *LEXIS: A Legal Research Manual*, p. 84-85.

negligence for shock or mental anguish at witnessing victim's injury or death. 94 ALR3d 486

Recovery for mental or emotional distress resulting from injury to, or death of, member of plaintiff's family arising from physician's or hospital's wrongful conduct. 77 ALR3d 447

Right to recover damages in negligence for fear or injury to another, or shock or mental anguish at witnessing such injury. 29 ALR3d 1337

Bystander recovery for emotional distress at witnessing another's injury under strict products liability or breach of warranty. 31 ALR4th 162

So from this list you can already see that the ALR editors slice and dice a topic pretty narrowly, not just focusing on a quite specific legal issue, but often doing so within a quite specific factual context (e.g., emotional distress of witnesses in a doctor-patient setting).

1. **Case-finding tool:** An ALR annotation is primarily a ***case finding*** tool. Most courts do not regard ALR annotations as themselves constituting legal authority, so you would not typically cite an ALR annotation in, say, a brief. Instead, you use an ALR annotation to give you an overview of the law of a particular area (including an introduction to the various sub-issues arising in that area), and to lead you to cases.

2. **Structure of ALR on the LEXIS service:**

   a. **Coverage:** In hard copy, ALR has been published in the form of six series of volumes, beginning with ALR1st (first published in 1919) through ALR5th, plus ALR Federal. All of these except ALR1st are available in full text on the LEXIS service. Here are the names of the various series, together with the dates on which the original volumes in the series were published:[2]

      ALR2d: 1948-1965
      ALR3d: 1965-1980
      ALR4th: 1980-current
      ALR5th: 1992-current
      ALR Federal: 1969-current

   From 1969, all coverage of federal topics in ALR has been in the ALR Federal series, so that since that date, ALR3d, ALR4th and ALR5th are restricted to state-law topics.

   b. **ALR libraries and files:** ALR is available from a number of different libraries on the LEXIS service: *ALR*, *2NDARY*, *ENVIRN*, *GENFED*, *LAWREV*, *MEGA*, *CRIME* and *STATES*. In each of these libraries, there is a file called *ALR* that consists solely of ALR annotations.[3]

   To find an ALR annotation on point, you'll want to do a search either for words and

2. The ending date shown in this table for each series is the last date on which a new volume of annotations was published. Once published, an annotation is generally continually and indefinitely updated by the Lawyers Cooperative staff, unless it is superseded by a later newly-published annotation. For instance, even though ALR2d no longer had new volumes added to it after 1965, many annotations in that series are still being updated. As I describe later in the text, ALR annotation updates on the LEXIS service are placed right into the annotation itself, so that you do not have to look in a separate place for them.

phrases as they appear in the entire text of the annotation, or for words and phrases as they appear in the annotation's *TITLE* segment. Details on how to do this are given on p. 3-7.

c. **Structure of an annotation:** Each annotation is its own document in the *ALR* file. Each annotation has various segments:

Name of Segment	Description
PUBLICATION	Name of publication (e.g., "ALR Federal") and copyright information
TITLE	Title of annotation
BYLINE	Name of author of annotation
CITE	Citation of annotation (e.g., 93 ALRFed 706)
TCSL-REFS	List of Total Client-Service Library References, i.e., references to other Lawyers Cooperative publications, such as AmJur
CONTENTS	Table of Contents for the annotation
JUR-TABLE	Table of courts and jurisdictions, showing for each jurisdiction what sections of the annotation contain cases from that jurisdiction
TABLE-OF-CASES	Table of cases cited in the annotation, including their citations
INDEX	Subject-Matter Index for the annotation
TEXT	Text of the article

I think it may be helpful for you to get a sense of the physical look of a typical annotation. Here are a few representative portions. First, the first screen, which includes the title and the cross-references to other Lawyers Cooperative publications:

3. There are a number of other files that contain both case law and ALR annotations. For instance, in the *GENFED* library, the *OMNI* file includes federal case law plus ALR annotations, and in the *STATES* library, the *OMNI* file (a different file from the file called *OMNI* in *GENFED*) contains state case law plus ALR annotations. Therefore, a search in, say, *GENFED/OMNI* will probably give you an answer set containing both ALR annotations and case law.

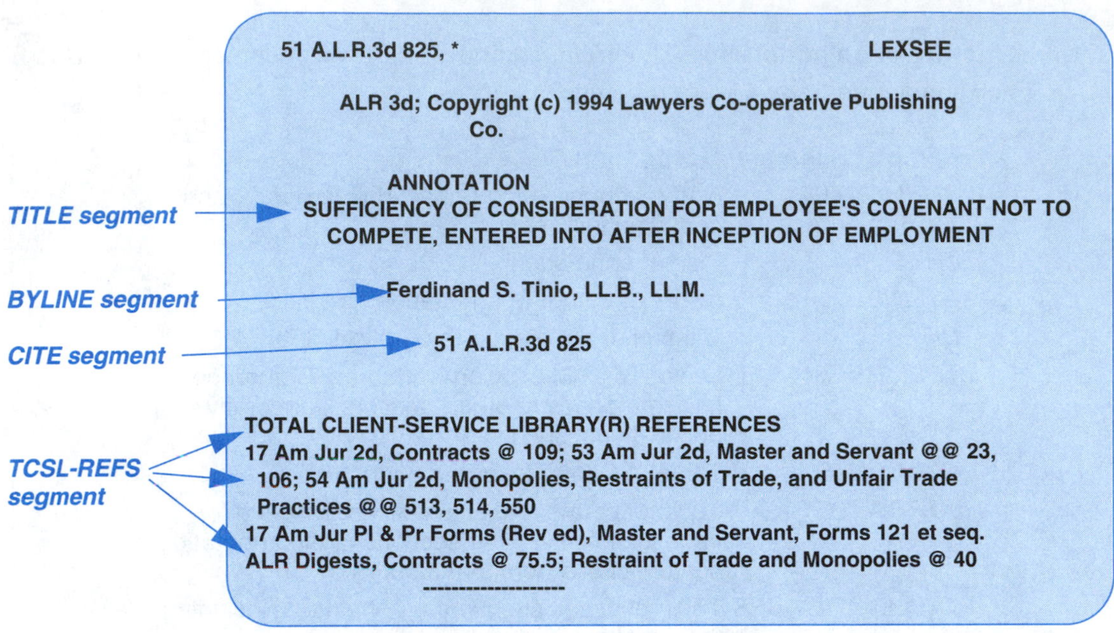

51 A.L.R.3d 825, *
LEXSEE
ALR 3d; Copyright (c) 1994 Lawyers Co-operative Publishing Co.
ANNOTATION
SUFFICIENCY OF CONSIDERATION FOR EMPLOYEE'S COVENANT NOT TO COMPETE, ENTERED INTO AFTER INCEPTION OF EMPLOYMENT
Ferdinand S. Tinio, LL.B., LL.M.
51 A.L.R.3d 825
TOTAL CLIENT-SERVICE LIBRARY(R) REFERENCES
17 Am Jur 2d, Contracts @ 109; 53 Am Jur 2d, Master and Servant @@ 23, 106; 54 Am Jur 2d, Monopolies, Restraints of Trade, and Unfair Trade Practices @@ 513, 514, 550
17 Am Jur Pl & Pr Forms (Rev ed), Master and Servant, Forms 121 et seq.
ALR Digests, Contracts @ 75.5; Restraint of Trade and Monopolies @ 40
TITLE segment
BYLINE segment
CITE segment
TCSL-REFS segment

Next, we have the Table of Contents, which is divided into sections and sub-sections:

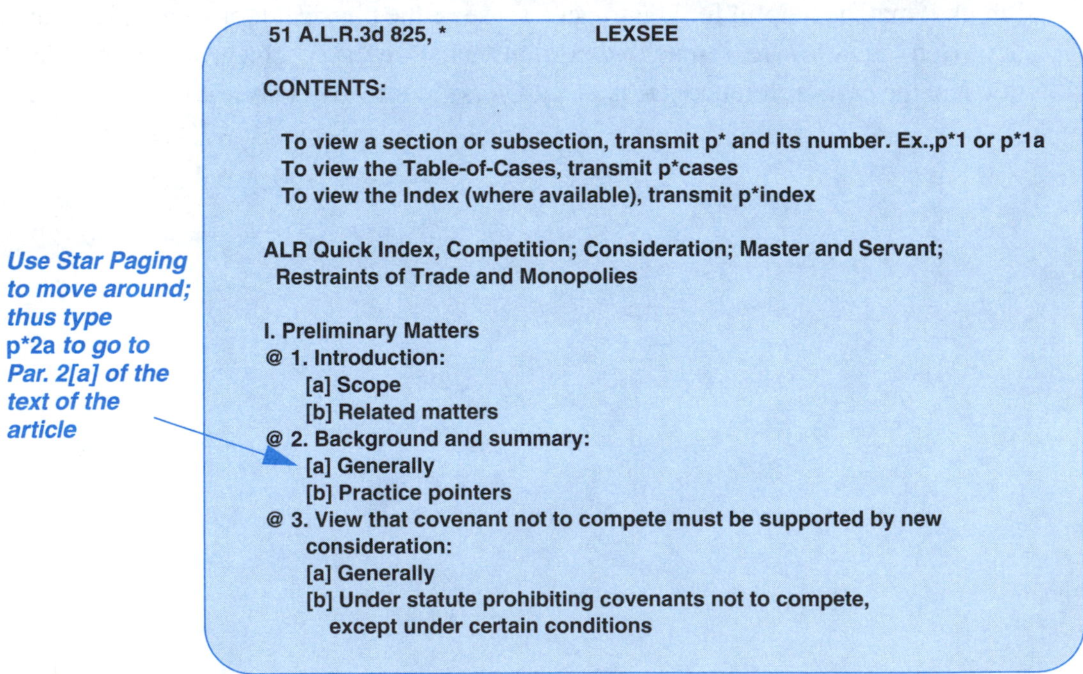

51 A.L.R.3d 825, *
LEXSEE
CONTENTS:
To view a section or subsection, transmit p* and its number. Ex.,p*1 or p*1a
To view the Table-of-Cases, transmit p*cases
To view the Index (where available), transmit p*index
ALR Quick Index, Competition; Consideration; Master and Servant; Restraints of Trade and Monopolies
I. Preliminary Matters
@ 1. Introduction:
[a] Scope
[b] Related matters
@ 2. Background and summary:
[a] Generally
[b] Practice pointers
@ 3. View that covenant not to compete must be supported by new consideration:
[a] Generally
[b] Under statute prohibiting covenants not to compete, except under certain conditions
Use Star Paging to move around; thus type p*2a to go to Par. 2[a] of the text of the article

As you can see from the prompt at the top of the screen, you can use Star Paging[4] to get to any portion of the article you wish. For instance, to go immediately to paragraph 3[a], you would simply type **`p*3a`** [ENTER].

4. See *supra*, p. 2-74, and *infra*, p. 4-57 for more about Star Paging.

Here, slightly edited by me, is a representative screen from the Text segment of an annotation:

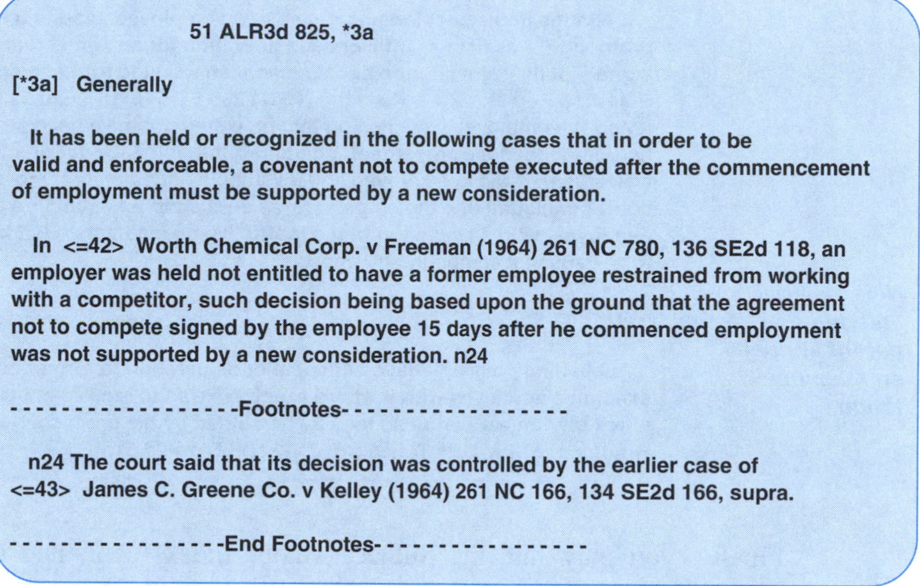

51 ALR3d 825, *3a

[*3a] Generally

It has been held or recognized in the following cases that in order to be valid and enforceable, a covenant not to compete executed after the commencement of employment must be supported by a new consideration.

In <=42> Worth Chemical Corp. v Freeman (1964) 261 NC 780, 136 SE2d 118, an employer was held not entitled to have a former employee restrained from working with a competitor, such decision being based upon the ground that the agreement not to compete signed by the employee 15 days after he commenced employment was not supported by a new consideration. n24

------------------Footnotes------------------

n24 The court said that its decision was controlled by the earlier case of <=43> James C. Greene Co. v Kelley (1964) 261 NC 166, 134 SE2d 166, supra.

----------------End Footnotes----------------

The bulk of an annotation consists of case-by-case summaries of the cases on a single point. Because the annotation author knows that he is writing about a particular legal issue (in the above screen, sufficiency of consideration for an employee's covenant not to compete, where the covenant is entered into after the employment has already begun), you often see a sharpness of focus in the case briefs that is not present in the typical West case digest system, where every legal issue in every case must be digested.

A key helpful feature in the LEXIS service's version of ALR annotations is that the ***supplementation*** is completely ***integrated*** into the annotation. This means that even though the original annotation may have been written some years ago, any newly-decided case that is on point will be incorporated into the annotation, in a constant updating process. Generally, the supplementary material is inserted at the end of a section or sub-section, and is always indicated by the message "—SUPP—." Thus (slightly edited from the original):

51 ALR3d 825, *7

A change in the position and duties of an employee, resulting in his promotion, was held a sufficient consideration for an agreement not to compete signed many years after he had commenced working for the employer, in <=142> Standard Register Co. v Kerrigan (1961) 238 SC 54, 119 SE2d 533, where the court noted the employee's admission that he would not have been kept on the job if he had not signed the agreement, pointing out that the execution of the contract was a benefit to the employee and a valuable consideration moving to him. The court concluded that the employer was entitled to an injunction against the employee, who, in violation of the restrictive covenant, had left his employment to engage in a competing business.

New material inserted as part of annual supplementation

--SUPP--

Publishing company gave sufficient consideration to former newspaper executive employed with it where executive was to receive annual installments of stock for 10-year period so long as he abided by his promise. <=143> Bradford v New York Times Co. (CA2 NY) 501 F2d 51.

Finally, you may find the Subject Matter Index (contained in the segment called *INDEX*) useful; this is an index to the particular annotation:

51 ALR3d 825, *index

FOCUS

[*index]

INDEX

Advertising expense, @ 3[b]
Annuity contract, @ 8
Automobile expenses as basis, @@ 3[a], 5
Cleaning and dyeing business, routeman for, @ 4[a]
Clothing dealer, deliveryman and bill collector for, @ 4[a]
Collective bargaining agreement, benefits under, @ 3[a]
Collector, @ 4
Commissions, consideration by agreement to pay, @ 4[b]
Conflict of laws, @ 3[a]
Continued employment, @ 4
Corporation, partnership formed into, @ 6
Credit reporting service, @ 4[b]
Deliveryman, @ 4
Frauds, statute of, @ 3[a]
Gasoline expenses, reimbursement of, @ 5
Illusory consideration, @@ 2[a], 5

3. **Searching in ALR:**

a. **Text searching:** You can, of course, search directly on the text of ALR annotations. Since these annotations are in effect articles about cases, you search the ALR text in much the same way that you would search the text of actual cases. Thus if we were interested in annotations dealing with the issue of whether a bystander who witnesses a trauma to another person may recover for emotional distress, we might search in the *ALR* library/*ALR* file, for:

```
emotional distress w/10 bystander w/10 liab!
```

b. **Search on title segment:** I have found that searches on the raw text of ALR annotations often find more annotations than I can really use, some of which are quite irrelevant. (For instance, the above search involving emotional distress found 21 annotations, some of which were obviously irrelevant judging by their titles, like "Measure and elements of damages for pollution of well or spring.") Therefore, I generally find that my best bet is to do my searching based on the *TITLE* segment. ALR annotations tend to have very descriptive and precise titles, so you can usually get considerable precision with a *TITLE*-based search, without missing relevant documents. In general, I find that when I search based on title, I need to loosen up my search restrictions a bit, by using more synonyms, and by using **AND** and **OR** rather than **W/n**. Thus for our emotional distress/bystander problem, the following search (in the *ALR* library, *ALR* file) produces five annotations:

```
title(bystander or witness and emotional distress
 or injury)
```

Two of these annotations seem right on point: *Bystander recovery for emotional distress at witnessing another's injury under strict products liability or breach of warranty*, 31 ALR 4th 162, and *Relationship between victim and plaintiff-witness as affecting right to recover damages in negligence for shock or mental anguish at witnessing victim's injury or death*, 94 ALR 3d 486.

4. **Navigating among and within annotations:** Navigating among annotations, and within a given annotation, is similar to navigation in other kinds of files. One extra feature is that, as I mentioned above, Star Paging has a special way of working in the *ALR* file: you can get to any section or sub-section simply by typing **p*** followed by the section number. Thus you can view the Table of Contents (near the beginning of the document), identify section 2[b] as something you would like to see, and go immediately to it by typing **p*2b** followed by [ENTER].

5. **Tie-in with Auto-Cite and SHEPARD's:** There is another way you can discover an on-point ALR annotation. SHEPARD'S and Auto-Cite, two citator services on the LEXIS service, pick up ALR annotations that cite a given case. So if you are using either of these tools to find later cases that cite a leading case you've located, these services will tell you about any ALR annotations that cite that leading case.

6. **Lawyers' Edition:** Reed Elsevier now publishes Lawyers' Edition, a version of the United States Supreme Court Reports. In addition to the actual text of Supreme Court cases, Lawyers' Edition frequently contains annotations on the Supreme Court's view of a particular topic. These Lawyers' Edition annotations are good overviews of how the Supreme Court thinks about a certain subject. For instance, the Supreme Court's views on abortion are well-summarized (and well-updated) in an annotation called *Supreme Court's views as to validity, under federal Constitution, of abortion laws*, 111 L.Ed.2d 879.

   These Lawyer's Edition annotations are present in the *ALR* file. You can recognize a Lawyers' Edition annotation, and distinguish it from an ALR annotation, because the *PUBLI-*

CATION segment lists the publication as being L.Ed.2d rather than ALR. The segment structure of a Lawyers' Edition annotation, and the way you search it, are the same as for an ALR annotation.

B. AmJur: Another very important resource for national-scope research is the ***AmJur 2d*** legal encyclopedia, published by Lawyers Cooperative. *AmJur 2d* is a summary of federal and state law, both substantive and procedural.

AmJur consists of about 400 "Articles." An Article covers a fairly wide swath of territory. To give one example, *AmJur 2d*'s Articles beginning with the letter "L" are as follows:

LABOR AND LABOR RELATIONS
LANDLORD AND TENANT
LARCENY
LAUNDRIES, DYERS, AND DRYCLEANERS
LEASES OF PERSONAL PROPERTY
LETTERS OF CREDIT
LEVEES AND FLOOD CONTROL
LEWDNESS, INDECENCY, AND OBSCENITY
LIBEL AND SLANDER
LICENSES AND PERMITS
LIENS
LIFE TENANTS AND REMAINDERMEN
LIMITATION OF ACTIONS
LIS PENDENS
LOBBYING
LOGS AND TIMBER
LOST AND DESTROYED INSTRUMENTS

There are two main ways in which AmJur differs from ALR:

- An *AmJur* article covers a much bigger topic than an ALR annotation, on average. Thus there are only about 400 articles in all of *AmJur*, compared with literally thousands of ALR annotations. For instance, whereas there is a single article called "Landlord and Tenant" in *AmJur*, there are over 150 ALR annotations with the word "landlord" or the word "tenant" in the title, including such specific titles as "Landlord-Tenant Security Deposit Legislation."

- An ALR annotation tends to be more or less a string of case briefs, one paragraph per case. An AmJur article, by contrast, reads much more like a traditional legal treatise. That is, it is a narrative stating general principles of law, with the case-by-case discussion limited to the footnotes (and with much less information on the particular facts and holdings about each case than you would find in an ALR annotation). In general, I think that *AmJur* is better at explaining to you the state of "the law" in an area, whereas the ALR annotations are better at finding you particular cases on point.

1. **Where to find it:** *AmJur 2d* is in the *2NDARY* Library, *AMJUR* File.

2. **Two ways to search:** You have a choice of two quite different ways in which to search the *AMJUR* file: by browsing through the Table of Contents, or by doing a full-text search. You will be given the choice between these two methods when you first log into the file. To do a full-text search, you press the [NEW SEARCH] key (F8 or type `.ns`). To browse the Table of Contents, you type **=5** [Enter].

   a. **Searching by Table of Contents:** When you search by Table of Contents (i.e., you type **=5** when you first log into the *AMJUR* file), the first thing you are shown is a list of the titles of the Articles, beginning with the "A"s:

```
LEVEL 1 - 1 OF 1 DOCUMENT
          TABLE OF CONTENTS--American Jurisprudence 2d
      Copyright (c) 1996 by Lawyers Cooperative Publishing Company
<=1>  Previous Step    <=2>  Secondary Sources Menu    <=3>  Help
<=4>  Search all sections of American Jurisprudence 2d
<=5>  View list of all American Jurisprudence 2d titles

<=6>  ABANDONED, LOST, AND UNCLAIMED PROPERTY
<=7>  ABATEMENT, SURVIVAL, AND REVIVAL
<=8>  ABDUCTION AND KIDNAPPING
<=9>  ABORTION AND BIRTH CONTROL
<=10>  ABSENTEES
<=11>  ABSTRACTS OF TITLE
<=12>  ABUSE OF PROCESS
<=13>  ACCESSION AND CONFUSION
<=14>  ACCORD AND SATISFACTION
<=15>  ACCOUNTANTS
<=16>  ACCOUNTS AND ACCOUNTING
<=17>  ACKNOWLEDGMENTS
<=18>  ACTIONS
<=19>  ACT OF GOD
```

   Typically, you would page through the screensful of Articles titles until you found a title that was of interest to you. At that point, you would view the Table of Contents for that Article by typing **=** plus the number of the document you wish to retrieve. Thus as shown in the above screen, to view the Table of Contents for the Article "Abandoned, Lost and Unclaimed Property," we would type **=6** .

   Here is what the first full page of the Table of Contents looks like for the Article in *AmJur 2d* called "Automobiles and Highway Traffic":

<=13> IX. FINANCIAL RESPONSIBILITY OR SECURITY REQUIREMENTS
<=14> X. EQUIPMENT, WEIGHT, AND SIZE OF VEHICLES
<=15> XI. TRAFFIC REGULATIONS AND OFFENSES
<=16> XII. LARCENY AND ALLIED OFFENSES; STOLEN VEHICLES
<=17> XIII .TAMPERING WITH MOTOR VEHICLES; MALICIOUS MISCHIEF
<=18> XIV. PROSECUTIONS
<=19> XV. AUTOMOBILE DEALERS FRANCHISE ACTS
<=20> XVI. IN GENERAL
<=21> XVII. GENERAL DUTY OF CARE IN OPERATION OF VEHICLE
<=22> XVIII. EFFECT OF NEGLIGENCE OF INJURED PARTY; ASSUMPTION OF RISK
<=23> XIX. VIOLATION OF STATUTE, ORDINANCE, OR REGULATION AS NEGLIGENCE
<=24> XX. PROXIMATE CAUSE; LAST CLEAR CHANCE
<=25> XXI. INJURIES TO PARTICULAR PERSONS
<=26> XXII. PERSONS LIABLE; LIABILITY FOR ACT OF ANOTHER
<=27> XXIII. IMPUTED NEGLIGENCE
<=28> XXIV. PARTICULAR CIRCUMSTANCES AND PLACE OF INJURY
<=29> XXV. PRACTICE AND PROCEDURE IN ACTIONS FOR INJURIES
<=30> XXVI. MEASURE AND ELEMENTS OF DAMAGES TO MOTOR VEHICLES

To get to a more detailed Table of Contents for any individual Roman numeral sub-title, we would again type = plus the number of the document we want to retrieve. Thus to view the sub-title "Traffic Regulations and Offenses," we would, following the above screen, type **=15**

The first full screen of the detailed Table of Contents for this sub-title looks like this:

AUTOMOBILES AND HIGHWAY TRAFFIC
XI. TRAFFIC REGULATIONS AND OFFENSES

<=6> A. In General
<=7> B. Exclusion or Restriction of Traffic on Certain Highways or Streets
<=8> C. Speed
<=9> D. Traffic Signs, Lights, and Signals; Safety Zones
<=10> E. Right of Way
<=11> F. Turning
<=12> G. Portion of Highway to Be Used; Following, Approaching, and Passing Other Vehicles
<=13> H. Slowing Down or Stopping; Backing
<=14> I. Parking; Standing
<=15> J. Rights and Duties of Pedestrians
<=16> K. Stopping, Identification, and Aid by Motorist After Accident
<=17> L. Drunken Driving and Similar Conduct
<=18> M. Reckless Driving
<=19> N. Driving in Careless Manner or in Manner Endangering Public
<=20> O. Speed Contests and Races
<=21> P. Homicide
<=22> Q. Assault and Battery

Now, we can actually view the text of the individual section, by typing = plus the number of the document as shown on the screen with an equal sign next to it. Thus to see the text of section D ("Traffic Signs, Lights and Signals; Safety Zones") of the "Automobiles and Highway Traffic" title of *AmJur*, we would type: **=9**

We would then get another, more detailed, table of contents:

TABLE OF CONTENTS--American Jurisprudence 2d
Copyright (c) 1996 by Lawyers Cooperative Publishing
<=1> HELP <=2> WORD SEARCH
<=3> DISPLAY CONTENTS IN OUTLINE FORM, SUITABLE FOR PRINTING
Return to the table of contents for:

<=4> American Jurisprudence 2d
<=5> AUTOMOBILES AND HIGHWAY TRAFFIC
<=6> XI. TRAFFIC REGULATIONS AND OFFENSES
Following retrieval of desired document, return to this table of contents by entering ".ES" or using the "EXIT SERVICE" icon
AUTOMOBILES AND HIGHWAY TRAFFIC
XI. TRAFFIC REGULATIONS AND OFFENSES
D. Traffic Signs, Lights, and Signals; Safety Zones
<=7> @ 232 Generally
<=8> @ 233 Traffic lights or signals
<=9> @ 234 Stop signs
<=10> @ 235 Safety zones

If we picked a section, we'd (finally!) get to the text of the section. Thus **=234** (for "Stop Signs") would give us text beginning as follows:

<=1> View American Jurisprudence 2d Table of Contents
American Jurisprudence, Second Edition
Copyright 1996 by The Lawyers Cooperative Publishing Company
AUTOMOBILES AND HIGHWAY TRAFFIC
XI. TRAFFIC REGULATIONS AND OFFENSES
D. Traffic Signs, Lights, and Signals; Safety Zones
7A Am Jur 2d AUTOMOBILES AND HIGHWAY TRAFFIC @ 234

@ 234. Stop signs

"Stop" signs are generally erected for the purpose of notifying motorists that they are approaching highway or street intersections, n1 and a statute or ordinance requiring motorists to stop in accordance with the mandate of such signs except when directed to proceed by a police officer or traffic control signal constitutes a valid exercise of the police power. n2

It is axiomatic that a motorist is normally under the duty of stopping in obedience to a stop sign protecting an intersection he is about to enter, n3 which means a full or complete stop, n4 and not just slowing down. n5 The fact that when a motorist reaches a stop sign there are, in his judgment or to his knowledge, no other motorists sufficiently close to the intersection to constitute a hazard does not affect or qualify the former's imperative duty to bring his vehicle to a full stop. n6 The actual stopping at a stop sign must consume more than a mere moment of time, n7 although it is not necessary that

You can page through the individual sections by using the [NEXT PAGE] command (F1, or type **.np**) and the [PREV PAGE] command (F2, or type **.pp**). To skip multiple pages, you can put a numeral after the [NEXT PAGE] or [PREV PAGE] command (e.g., enter `.np10` to jump 10 pages).

You can also "browse" through prior or succeeding sections, even though these may not be part of your answer set. To do this, you will first need to type "b," to indicate that you want to browse. Thus to go from section 234 (shown in the above screen) to the next section, 235, you would type:

b [ENTER]

This will put you in BROWSE mode. In BROWSE mode, the [NEXT DOC] (F3, or type **.nd**) and [PREV DOC] (F4, or type **.pd**) keys have the effect of moving you to the next or previous section, respectively.[5]

b. Searching by full text: You can also search the *AMJUR* file by ***full-text*** methods. Thus to find all places in *AmJur 2d* speaking about seat belts, you might search (in the *2NDARY* library, *AMJUR* file) for:

```
seat belt or seatbelt or safety belt
```

There are two segments that you are likely to find especially useful in full-text searching these files: *TITLE* and *SECTION-TITLE*. *TITLE* represents the approximately 400 major encyclopedia-like articles (e.g., "Automobiles and Highway Traffic," or "Torts" or "Unemployment Compensation.") *SECTION-TITLE* represents a "section," the smallest, most specific, unit within an article. For instance, there are over 1,100 sections to *AMJUR*'s treatment of the article "Automobiles and Highway Traffic," with names like "Bicycles and tricycles" (in the division "Governmental Regulation and Control, In General"), or "Requirements as to Bills of Sale" (in the division "Title and Ownership; Transfers and Encumbrances").[6]

If we were interested in cases involving seat belts, but only in the context of liability for an automobile accident, we might do a search limited to the *TITLE* segment as follows:

```
title(automobile or torts) and seat belt or seatbelt
 or safety belt
```

Similarly, if we wanted to see only those sections where seat belts were sufficiently central that they appeared in the title of the section, we could search for:

```
section-title(seat belt or seatbelt or safety belt)
```

To navigate within a section, or from section to section, use the same techniques (including typing "b" for BROWSE) as I described in the discussion of searching by Table of Contents.

5. BROWSE mode was actually developed to let you navigate among statutory sections. For more information about BROWSE, see *infra*, p. 5-21.

6. For the names of some other sections within this "Traffic Regulations" subdivision, see the screen reproduced on p. 3-10.

C. State-law jurisprudence products: If you are doing research that centers on the law of Florida, New York, Ohio or Texas, a series of state-law encyclopedias published by Lawyers Cooperative can help you. These are the familiar "Jurisprudence" encyclopedias, *Florida Jurisprudence, New York Jurisprudence, Ohio Jurisprudence* and *Texas Jurisprudence*. Each is a multi-volume encyclopedia covering the substantive and procedural law of the state in question. These are in essence single-state versions of *AmJur.*

The layout of these single-state *Jurisprudence* products is similar to that of *AmJur*, so refer to my discussion of *AmJur* supra.

1. **Where to find these:** The best place to find these encyclopedias is in the *STATES* or *2NDARY* libraries, where they are in files named *FLJUR, NYJUR, OHJUR* and *TXJUR*.

2. **Witkin California Treatises:** For California law, there is a set of treatises that are somewhat similar to the *Jurisprudence* products. These are four treatises by B.E. Witkin: *Summary of California Law* (file *WITSUM*); *California Criminal Law* (file *WITCRM*); *California Evidence* (file *WITEVD*); and *California Procedure* (file *WITPRO*). All can be found in the *STATES, CAL* or *BEGIN* libraries. The group file *WITKIN* combines all four. I have found these volumes to be unusually well written and useful, perhaps reflecting the fact that they are collectively the life's work of a single principal author.

   You use essentially the same search techniques (including Table of Contents browsing) as for *AmJur* and the state-law *Jurisprudence* files.

D. Restatements: The American Law Institute's *Restatements of the Law* represent the only semi-official "black letter" rendition of common law principles. As such, they make a very valuable addition to the arsenal of secondary authorities available on the LEXIS service. Also, I believe that being able to do a full-text search on both the black-letter statements of law and the comments accompanying those statements, makes the online version of the Restatements even more valuable than the hard-copy version.

1. **Titles:** All 11 of the Restatements currently in print are represented on the LEXIS service: *Agency, Conflict of Laws, Contracts, Foreign Relations, Judgments, Property, Restitution, Security, Torts, Trusts* and *Unfair Competition*. In each case, the most current version of the Restatement (usually Restatement Second) is available.

   a. **All in one file:** All of the Restatements are in a single file, *RESTAT*, in the *2NDARY* research library (which also contains other secondary materials, including *ALR,* AmJur, law reviews, etc.) After you log into the *RESTAT* file, you will see a list of the 11 Restatements. You select the one you want by typing its link (e.g., **=9** to search on the *Restatement of Torts*).[7]

2. **Searching the Restatements:** There are three different ways to search on a given Restatement: (1) browse the Table of Contents; (2) do a full-text search on the black letter rules and comments to them; and (3) do a full-text search on the Annotated Case Citations to the Restatement's rules.

7. See *supra*, p. 1-12 for a discussion of the LINK feature on the LEXIS service.

a. Table of Contents: You can browse through a given Restatement's Table of Contents, which lists the section number and section title of each of the several hundred sections making up a Restatement. To get to the Table of Contents, you log into the particular Restatement, then type **=1** . You'll then get a short list of "Divisions"; in the case of Torts 2d, for instance, there are four, with names like "Division 1 — Intentional Harms." You select the division you want by entering its link number. At that point, you'll see a section-by-section listing.

Here, for instance, is what the Table of Contents portions for Rest.2d Torts look like, beginning with §402A (the famous section on strict product liability):

To search a section, Enter = and the number for that section: e.g.=3

<=442> Section 402A - Special liability of seller of product for physical harm to user or consumer
<=443> Section 402B - Misrepresentation by seller of chattels to consumer

Topic 6 - INDEPENDENT CONTRACTORS
<=444> Section 403 - Chattel known to be dangerous
<=445> Section 404 - Negligence in making, rebuilding, or repairing chattel

Topic 7 - DONORS, LENDERS, AND LESSORS OF CHATTELS
<=446> Section 405 - Donors and lenders of chattels known to be dangerous
<=447> Section 406 - Manufacturer giving or lending negligently made chattel
<=448> Section 407 - Lessors of chattels known to be dangerous
<=449> Section 408 - Lease of chattel for immediate use

Chapter 15 - LIABILITY OF AN EMPLOYER OF AN INDEPENDENT CONTRACTOR

To go from the Table of Contents to a particular section, you simply double-click on the LINK marker next to the section, or type **=** plus the LINK number of the document to be retrieved. Thus to see the full text of §402A based on the above listing, we would type **=442**, or double-click on the **<=442>** symbol with our mouse. We would then see the full text of 402A, the first screen of which looks like this:

To be able to browse preceding or succeeding code sections, enter B. The first page of the document you are currently viewing will be displayed in FULL.

LEVEL 1 - 3 OF 6 DOCUMENTS

<=1> To search Annotated Case Citations to this Rule
<=2> To view the Table of Contents for Torts, Second, Enter =2

RESTATEMENT OF THE LAW, SECOND, TORTS
Copyright 1965, American Law Institute

RULES AND PRINCIPLES

Division Two - Negligence
Chapter 14 - Liability of Persons Supplying Chattels For the Use of Others
Topic 5 - Strict Liability

@ 402A SPECIAL LIABILITY OF SELLER OF PRODUCT FOR PHYSICAL HARM TO USER OR CONSUMER

(1) One who sells any product in a defective condition unreasonably dangerous to the user or consumer or to his property is subject to liability for physical harm thereby caused to the ultimate user or consumer, or to his

From here, we can browse through the section with [NEXT PAGE] (F1 or type **.np**) and [PREV PAGE] (F2 or type **.pp**). To browse among sections, we would type the letter "b" followed by [NEXT DOC] (F3 or **.nd**) or [PREV DOC] (F4 or type **.pd**).[8]

b. Full-text search on Rules: Alternatively, you can do a full-text search on the actual black letter Rules of the Restatement, as well as on the full text of the Comments and Reporters Notes for the Rules. To do this, you first log into the particular Restatement you want by typing its link number (e.g., **=9** for Torts). You then type **=2** to select "Rules, Comments and Notes."

You then enter your full-text search, the same as with any other file. Thus to find all places in the Rules, Comments or Reporters Notes of the *Restatement Second of Torts* where there is a discussion of a seller's liability for selling a product that causes physical harm, we might search for:

seller and product and physical harm and liab!

This search retrieves a surprisingly-high 10 documents, representing 10 sections, including the famous §402A. (Each individual section of a Restatement is a "document" for purposes of the LEXIS service.)

If you just want to find words that occur in the name of the section, do a search limited to the *CITE* segment; thus:

cite(seller and product and physical harm)

8. The techniques for browsing among sections are discussed in more detail *infra*, p. 5-21 to 5-22.

c. **Annotated case citations:** A very helpful feature of the Restatements online is the inclusion of ***Annotated Case Citations***. Each Annotated Case Citation (ACC) is a "digest" of a case that cites a particular Restatement provision. Here is what an ACC looks like for a case that cites Rest.2d §402A:

> Case Citations to the First Restatement
>
> @ 402A SPECIAL LIABILITY OF SELLER OF PRODUCT FOR PHYSICAL HARM TO USER OR CONSUMER
>
> CASE: Sumnicht v. Toyota Motor Sales, U.S.A., Inc., (1984)
>
> CITATION: <=3> 121 Wis.2d 338, 360 N.W.2d 2, 7-8, 15, 16.
>
> COURT: Supreme Court of Wisconsin
>
> TREATMENT: Quoted in footnote in support, cited in treatise quoted in discussion, comments (g), (h), and (i) quoted in support.
>
> SUMMARY: The plaintiff automobile passenger brought a products liability action against the seller and the distributor of the foreign-made automobile. The plaintiff brought the action on a theory of "second collision," alleging that a defective seat system caused his injuries. In affirming the lower court, this court held that there was evidence sufficient to support a finding that the seat system was unreasonably dangerous and was a substantial factor in causing the passenger's injuries.
>
> To LEXSEE to the full text of this case, Enter = and the highlighted number

The best way to find ACCs on a particular point is to do a search that combines the number of the rule, and any text, date or other limitation that will pin things down.

Thus suppose we wanted all ACCs that: (1) cite to Rest.2d Torts §402A; (2) mention the word "tractor" in the summary; and (3) were decided after 1990. Here's what we'd do:

- At the main Torts screen, we'd enter =3 ("Annotated Case Citations").
- At the resulting search screen, we'd enter the following search:

```
rule(402A) and tractor and date aft 1990
```

This search (as of mid-1997) finds 8 documents, i.e., 8 case annotations that meet our three requirements.

II. LEGAL PERIODICALS, ESPECIALLY LAW REVIEWS

A. **Law reviews:** The LEXIS-NEXIS services have a good collection of law reviews online. By "law review," LEXIS-NEXIS and I are referring mainly to student-run general-interest legal periodicals put out at individual law schools, such as the *Harvard Law Review*, the *Yale Law Journal*, etc. But the *LAWREV* library also includes some single-topic periodicals (e.g., *The Journal of Real Estate Taxation*), including some that are published by commercial publishers.

Law reviews are generally to be found in the *LAWREV* and *2NDARY* libraries. Also, law reviews published in a particular state are grouped in a file called *XXLRV* within the library for that state. Thus in the *NY* library, there is a filed called *NYLRV*, consisting of 36 law reviews, all published in New York state.

There are also some files that group law reviews by ***topic***. Thus all law reviews on LEXIS that specialize in tax are placed together in file *TAXLR* (in library *LAWREV*). You can see all the special-topic groupings for law reviews by looking at the first page of file listings when you log in to the *LAWREV* library.

Each law review has its own file (e.g., the *Minnesota Law Review* is contained in file *MINNLR*). Thus you can get an up to date sense of what law reviews are available by looking online at the list of files in the *LAWREV* library, starting with page 4 of the listings.

Additionally, most of the law reviews in the LAWREV library are grouped together in a combined file, *ALLREV.* Although some journal publishers have elected to have their journals kept out of *ALLREV*, you can count on finding virtually all of the law-school reviews in the *ALLREV* combined file. Therefore, when you want to do a general search for law reviews on point, the *LAWREV* library, *ALLREV* file, is definitely the thing to use.

A complete list of all titles contained in the *LAWREV* library as of April 1997 is reproduced in Appendix D. There are over 360 individual journals represented in *LAWREV*, of which most are conventional general-interest law-school law reviews.

1. **Time and scope of coverage:** Many of the law reviews that are available on the LEXIS service are covered since 1982. However, those added most recently are only available as to issues published since the review was added. When a law review is available, typically virtually all text from the issue (not just articles, but also book reviews, notes, symposia, etc.) are present in full text.

2. **Segment layout:** Here are most of the segments found in a law review "document" (typically an article):

Name of Segment	Description
PUBLICATION	Name of the publication
DATE	Date of issue
CITE	Citation to the article (e.g., "56 Tenn. L. Rev. 595")
LENGTH	Length of article (in words); this segment is arithmetically searchable
TITLE	Title of document, including a word indicating what type of document it is (e.g., "Note: Economic and critical analyses of the law of covenants not to compete")
NAME	Name of author(s)
BIO	Footnote describing the credentials of the author(s)
TEXT	Full text of the article, including footnotes
AUTHOR	*NAME* segment plus acknowledgments and biographical information about the author

3. **Searching:** Searching for law review articles is not very different from other types of searching on the LEXIS service. Here are some law-review-specific pointers:

- ***TITLE* segment:** As with ALR annotations, you may well find it easier to home in on what you want by restricting your search to words found in the title, rather than words appearing in the narrative. Thus looking for:

  ```
  title(defamation and first amendment)
  ```

  will of course find fewer, and probably more tightly focused, articles than a generic text search on

  ```
  defamation w/10 first amendment
  ```

- ***LENGTH* segment:** The *LENGTH* segment reports the number of words in the document. This segment is numerically searchable. Thus to limit yourself to documents of more than, say, 5,000 words (that is, a pretty meaty article), you could in addition to your other search words ask for:

  ```
  length > 5000
  ```

- **Using LEXSEE:** If you know the citation for the article you want to see, you can get to the article quickly with the LEXSEE feature. Just type LEXSEE followed by the citation to the article; for instance:

  ```
  lexsee 57 s cal l rev 531
  ```

  will retrieve the article appearing at this citation. (Most of the time, your common sense will stand you in good stead in trying to guess how the name of the journal should be abbreviated on the LEXIS service. To make certain, you can consult Appendix D, which lists not only each law review available on the LEXIS service but also the LEXSEE format for accessing that law review.)

- **Star Paging:** Star Paging is supported in law reviews. This lets you get to a particular hard-copy page in an article instantly, and conversely lets you determine what hard-copy page a particular sentence fell on. Thus if you were displaying (in FULL format) 57 S. Cal. L. Rev. 531, and wanted to go directly to the material on page 547 (perhaps because you knew, from the way another source cited this article, that the article discussed a certain topic on page 547), you would enter:

  ```
  p*547
  ```

  If you were looking at a screenful and saw [*547] in front of material you wanted to cite, you would know that that material was to be cited as 57 S. Cal. L. Rev. 531, 547. By the way, to use the Star Paging feature, you must be looking at the document in FULL format.

B. Other legal periodicals: Apart from law-school law reviews, there are other sorts of periodicals available on the LEXIS service, many of them in the *LAWREV* library. Some random examples include *The American Bankruptcy Law Journal* (file *AMBLJ*), *The American Journal of Law and Medicine* (*LAWMED*), *Environmental Law* (*ENVLAW*), *The Journal of*

Accountancy (*JNLACC*), *The Journal of International Law and Business* (*INTBUS*), and *The Transportation Law Journal* (*TRANLJ*); all of the ones I have just listed are present in the *LAWREV* library.

1. ABA publications: In addition, the LEXIS service contains a number of specialized law reviews published by the American Bar Association, including the following:[9]

Publication Name	File Name on LEXIS	Libraries in which Pub. can be found
Antitrust Law Journal	*ATRUST*	*ABA, TRADE*
Banking Journal	*ABABJ*	*BANKNG, MARKET, NEWS* and *UCC*
The Business Lawyer	*BUSLAW*	*ABA, BANKNG, CORP, FEDSEC, GENFED, LAWREV, LEGNEW, NEWS, REALTY, TRADE*, and *UCC*
International Lawyer	*INTLAW*	*ABA, ADMRTY, GEN-FED, INTLAW, ITRADE*
ABA Journal	*ABAJNL*	*ABA, ETHICS* and *MSTORT*
Law Practice Management	*LGECON*	*ABA, GENFED, LEG-NEW and NEWS*
Patent, Trademark & Copyright Law	*PTCLAW*	*ABA, COPYRT, LAWREV, PATENT, TRDMRK*
The Tax Lawyer	*TAXLAW*	*ABA, ESTATE, FED-TAX, LAWREV* and *STTAX*
Tort & Insurance Law Journal	*INSLJ*	*ABA, ADMRTY, IN-SURE, LAWREV, MSTORT* and *PRLIAB*

C. Legal newspapers: The LEXIS-NEXIS services also contain what can be called "legal newspapers." These are periodicals put out in a newspaper-like format that contain information about both substantive legal developments and coverage of the business of lawyering. On a national level, these publications include *American Lawyer*, *Legal Times* and *The National Law Journal*. A number of more localized legal newspapers are also present (e.g., *The New York Law Journal, Illinois Legal Times, Massachusetts Lawyers Weekly, The Connecticut Law Tribune*, etc.). The best place to find all of these legal newspapers, whether national or local, is in the *LEGNEW* library.

While in the *LEGNEW* library, don't overlook *U.S. Law Week*, which gives a very good coverage of both Supreme Court developments and lower federal court and state court developments. *U.S. Law Week* is one of the main tools I use in updating the *Emanuel Law Outlines*. It is available as file *USLW*.

9. Additional ABA law review publications are being added as this is written (mid-1997).

LEXIS-NEXIS also now contains a number of bar journals, put out by state bar associations. For instance, the bar journals of Florida, Louisiana, Michigan, Rhode Island and Utah are present, all in the *LAWREV* library. The bar journals often give good treatment of the practicalities of lawyering in a particular state.

D. Indexes to periodicals: Apart from the full text of many law reviews and other legal periodicals, the LEXIS service also contains two comprehensive ***indexes*** to these and other legal periodicals. The two are the *Index to Legal Periodicals* and the *Legal Resource Index*. You must keep in mind that both of these are ***bibliographic*** resources — they tell you such things as the author and title of a periodical article, but they do ***not*** contain the full text of the article.

Given that you have the full text of so many legal periodicals already available to you on the LEXIS service, why would you ever want to use a mere index? There are two reasons:

- each of these indexes covers a far greater number of periodicals than are available in full text on the LEXIS service, so each may lead you to an article that you can then obtain in hard-copy form; and
- both indexes have editors who classify each article, and the classification scheme can help you find articles that you might not be able to find so easily from key-word searches, even if you had the article's full text.

1. **The Index to Legal Periodicals (ILP):** The *Index to Legal Periodicals* is published by H.W. Wilson. If you were to ask a lawyer or law librarian, "How do I locate law review articles on a certain subject?" this is the answer that the vast majority would give. The index is available in the *LEXREF* and *LAWREV* libraries, as file *ILP*.

   a. **Coverage:** *ILP* tracks about 500 law reviews, bar association publications, and other legal periodicals, from the U.S. and other English speaking countries. The LEXIS service's coverage starts from 1979.

   b. **Availability:** Unfortunately, *ILP* is not available under your Education Subscription, because of publisher's restrictions. You will have to use this file at a law firm or other subscriber with a Commercial Subscription to the LEXIS service.[10]

2. **The Legal Resource Index (LRI):** The *Legal Resource Index*, like the *Index to Legal Periodicals*, gives you a bibliographic record for each article in a large number of law-related periodicals.

   a. **Advantages over ILP:** I prefer *LRI* over *ILP*, for two main reasons:

      - *LRI* covers a substantially broader base of publications, about 700 periodicals versus 500 for *ILP*. In particular, *LRI* picks up the major legal newspapers (e.g., the *National Law Journal*, *Legal Times* and the *New York Law Journal*) which *ILP* does not, and it also picks up law-related articles from general-circulation newspapers and magazines (e.g., *The New York Times*, *Wall Street Journal*). Thus when I wanted to find articles on employment-related covenants not to compete, I performed the following search in both indexes:

10. Some law school libraries also have access to *ILP*, so check with yours.

```
compete and covenant
```

LRI gave me 92 articles, compared with 46 for *ILP*.

- *LRI*'s "descriptors" (i.e., its descriptive words and phrases) in its *TERM* segment are more specific, and therefore in my opinion more useful, than the entries in *ILP*'s *DESCRIPTORS* segment. Thus whereas articles on non-competes tend to be classified by *ILP* under the phrase "employment contracts," they tend to be classified by *LRI* under the much more specific phrase "non-competition agreements." Therefore, you can home in on a subject much better, without having to worry about anticipating each word that may appear in the *TITLE* segment of the article (which is the only other textual thing you can search on in either index).

b. Availability: *LRI*, like *ILP*, is not available as part of your standard Educational Subscription. However, if your school subscribes to Legal Trac (and many do), you will be able to access it.

c. Where to find it; coverage dates: *LRI* is contained in the file *LGLIND*, available in either the *LEXREF* or *LAWREV* libraries. Coverage begins in 1977.

d. Segment layout: Here are the most important segments in the *Legal Resource Index* (*LGLIND*) file:

Name of Segment	Description
AUTH	Author of document
TITLE	Title of document
REFR	Name and citation of publication
DATE	Date of publication
TERM	Descriptors assigned by LRI editors (e.g., "Non-competition agreements")

e. Search tips:

- **General search:** Because the records are so small, you can safely do a general, rather than segment-limited search. If you're interested in non-competition agreements, the following search would be perfectly reasonable:

```
(covenant or agreement) and (competition or
  compete)
```

- ***TITLE* search**: If you have a pretty good idea of a word or phrase that would be contained in the title, a search limited to the article's title (contained in the *TITLE* segment) will often work well, for example:

```
title(covenant and compet!)
```

- ***AUTH* search:** If you know the author, use the *AUTH* segment, perhaps combined with a subject-matter-related search word:

```
auth(shadowen) and title(covenant and compete)
```

- **Descriptors:** Use the *TERM* segment, which contains descriptors assigned by the

LRI editors. The categories are quite specific. You may want to find some articles by doing a search on *TITLE*, or a non-segment-limited search, then examine the descriptors assigned by the editors to those articles. Now, you can go back and do a search on those descriptors, to find other articles that the editors have concluded are on the same subject.

For instance, when I searched for

```
compete and covenant
```

I found 92 documents. When I examined some of these, I found that the *LRI* editors assigned a descriptor called "non-competition agreement." When I searched for

```
term(non-competition agreement)
```

I got 361 references. Most of these were on point, and, obviously, many were ones that I would not easily have found through the words contained in the title (e.g., "Validity of In-term Restrictive Covenants is Still in Doubt").

III. BRIEFS FROM U.S. SUPREME COURT CASES

A. Briefs from the Supreme Court: As of the 1993/94 term, the LEXIS service offers ***merit briefs*** for cases granting certiorari and special masters. No joint appendices are collected; only appendices to specific briefs. Prior to the 1993/94 term, all briefs for cases granted cert, joint appendices and special masters are available on the LEXIS service.

1. Why use: Here are several reasons why you might want to look at Supreme Court briefs:

- To see what arguments can be made on a particular issue, so you can adapt these arguments to an issue you face;
- To find authorities (cases, statutes, secondary sources) on a particular issue;
- To see how a professionally-done brief is organized, and what style it uses.

2. Where to find: The Supreme Court briefs are found in the *GENFED* library, in the *BRIEFS* file.

a. Time delay: A brief generally appears online six to eight weeks from the date the case is argued. This means, of course, that you can generally review the briefs even before the case has been decided by the Court.

B. Segment layout: Here are the segments that you are most likely to find useful in the *BRIEFS* file:

Name of Segment	Description
NAME	Names of the parties. Contains the full names of the parties, not just the last names as in a citation. (Example: "Juan Francisco Venegas, Petitioner, v. Michael R. Mitchell, Respondent")
NUMBER	Supreme Court Docket Number (e.g., "No. 88-1725")

Name of Segment	Description
TERM	Term of the Supreme Court (e.g., "October Term, 1989")
DATE	Date the Brief was filed with the Court.
TYPE	Type of brief, and for which party it is submitted. (e.g., "Brief for the Respondent" or "Brief of the State of New York as Amicus Curiae")
COUNSEL	Names of the lawyer(s) and firm(s) submitting the brief
AUTHORITY-CITED	Cases, statutes, court rules and other authorities cited in the brief, as listed in the Table of Authorities
STATS-INVOLVED	Statutes involved in the case, if not listed in the *AUTHORITY-CITED* segment
QUESTIONS	Questions presented by the case
STATEMENT	Statement of the case
SUMMARY	Summary of the Argument made in the brief
TEXT	Text of the brief
CONCLUSION	Conclusion of the brief

C. Some search tips: Here are some tips for finding Supreme Court briefs in the *GENFED* library, *BRIEFS* file:

- If you know the approximate names of the parties in a particular case you're interested in, use the techniques for finding decisions by case name.[11] Don't try to hit the exact name as listed on the brief, which will include first names, status of the parties (e.g., "Respondent"), and other distractions. Don't use "v." as in a caption. Use the *NAME* segment. Thus search for:

  ```
  name(planned parenthood and casey)
  ```

  not

  ```
  name(planned parenthood of southeastern pennsylvania
    v. casey)
  ```

- If you're searching by issue, use the same techniques you would use to find cases if you knew the issue.[12] If you get too many documents when you search without a segment limitation, use the *QUESTIONS* and *STATEMENT* segments, so you'll only get those briefs where the words you're looking for are very central to the case.

- If you know that there are a few leading cases in the area you're interested in, and you want to find briefs from other cases on the same subject, use the *AUTHORITY-CITED* segment as a kind of citator.[13] For instance, if you knew that *Planned Parenthood v. Casey* was an important recent abortion case, and you wanted to see briefs in subsequent abortion cases

11. These are discussed *infra*, p. 4-34.

12. These are discussed *infra*, p. 4-41.

13. Citators, which are used to find other cases citing a leading case you've already found, are discussed *infra*, p. 9-1.

that may have come before the Court, you could search (in library *GENFED*, file *BRIEFS*) for:

```
authority-cited(planned parenthood w/20 casey)
```

- If there is a statute that's central to your problem, look for references to the statute in both the *AUTHORITY-CITED* and *STATS-INVOLVED* segments, since there's no way to be sure which of these segments will contain the reference in any particular brief. Thus to find references to the Civil Rights Attorney's Fee Awards Act of 1976, 42 U.S.C. 1988:

```
authority-cited(28 pre/3 1254) or stats-involved(28 pre/3
1254) and date aft 1993
```

Chapter 4

Finding Cases

Introductory note: In this chapter, we're going to take a close look at how you can use the LEXIS service to find relevant cases. Before we start, let me tell you one thing that you will probably find surprising: in your post-law school life as a "real lawyer,'' cases will frequently not be the most important form of raw materials you'll use. In most legal problems, statutes and the regulations promulgated under them are probably more important than cases.

Therefore, although we're taking a close look at cases before we look at statutes or regulations, keep in mind that usually, you will be going at things in the opposite way: first, you'll try to find out whether there is a statute or regulation on point. If there is, you'll usually begin to get at cases by looking for ones that are decided "under'' the relevant statutory provision. But even in this scenario, the case-finding techniques I discuss in this chapter will be useful for getting additional cases.

I. THE CASE-REPORTING SYSTEM GENERALLY

A. Published vs. unpublished cases: Before we get into a detailed discussion of how to use the LEXIS service for case-finding, let's get a brief overview of American case law from a general rather than LEXIS specific perspective. The first distinction you should make is between ***"published''*** and ***"unpublished''*** opinions.[1] An opinion is deemed "published'' when it is broadly disseminated, in either an official or unofficial reporter (a distinction that I'll get to in a minute). A synonym for "published," by the way, is "reported." Contrary to what you might think, many opinions are never published at all — they exist solely as a typewritten document, copies of which are held by the judge and by the clerk of the court, but which are not disseminated much further.

1. Federal opinions: In the *federal* system, the likelihood that a particular opinion will be published depends on the level from which it originates. All Supreme Court decisions are, of course, widely published (by the "official'' U.S. government reporter and by several "unofficial'' commercial publishers). About half of U.S. Court of Appeals decisions are

1. When I say "opinion'' in this chapter, I mean a judge's attempt to set forth the facts of a controversy, and to rule on a point of law relating to those facts. Most litigated controversies never result in an "opinion'' at all — this is true even of cases that are tried to a jury and result in a verdict. Therefore, if you should read in a newspaper account that a particular matter was tried and resulted in a verdict, do not be surprised if you cannot locate a judicial opinion from the case — putting aside the "published'' vs. "unpublished'' distinction which I am about to discuss in the text, there may simply not be an opinion of any sort.

published today.[2] At the federal District Court level, only a very small percentage — estimated at about 15% — are ever published.[3] (But as we'll see, a significant number of otherwise-unpublished District Court opinions are present on LEXIS.)

2. **State opinions:** As with the federal system, not all ***state*** opinions are reported. In general, nearly all decisions of the ***highest court*** of each state (usually, but not always, called the "Supreme Court" of that state) are published. Most states provide for publication of decisions of their ***intermediate appeals*** courts, where these exist. In only a very few states — New York is the most notable example — are any state ***trial court*** opinions published, and even in these, only a small minority are.

3. **Stages of publication:** When an opinion is "published," it actually goes through several stages of publication.

   a. **Slip opinions:** First, it is published as a ***"slip opinion,"*** that is, a stand-alone pamphlet containing just the opinion(s) in one case. Slip opinions are usually not very widely disseminated.

   b. **Advance sheets:** The first widely-disseminated form that a published opinion takes is when it appears in the ***"advance sheets."*** Advance sheets usually take the form of a paper-bound pamphlet, containing all of the published opinions decided during, say, a two-week period by a particular court or group of courts. Most states that publish their own "official" reports (see below), and all of the West Reporters, publish advance sheets.

   c. **Bound volume:** Finally, the published opinion is included in a ***bound*** volume. The bound volume usually collects the opinions from several advance sheets, and has more elaborate finding aids, like subject indices and case tables, than do the advance sheets.

   d. **Electronic form:** Fairly early in the cycle — usually during the slip opinion stage — most opinions are also ***electronically published*** on the LEXIS service. Some courts transmit "machine-readable" copies of the cases to the LEXIS service; for other courts, the service has the material keyed from the hard-copy opinion.

B. "Official" vs. "unofficial" reports: It is also important to distinguish between ***"official"*** and ***"unofficial"*** reports. An "official" report is one published by (or at least under the auspices of) the court system from which the opinion originated. An "unofficial" report is one published by a private, commercial publisher.

1. **Federal system:**

   a. **Supreme Court:** The decisions of the U.S. Supreme Court are published both officially and unofficially. The official reporter is the *U.S. Reports* (abbreviated in citations as *U.S.*), put out by employees of the federal government. There are several unofficial Supreme Court reporters, most notably the *Supreme Court Reporter* (published by West Publishing Co., and abbreviated as *S.Ct.* in citations) and the *United*

2. Cohen, Berring & Olson, *How to Find the Law*, p. 43.

3. Carrick, *LEXIS: A Legal Research Manual*, p. 39

States Supreme Court Reports, Lawyers' Edition (published by Lawyers Cooperative, and cited as *L.Ed.*).

b. **U.S. Courts of Appeals:** Surprisingly, there is ***no*** official reporter for ***U.S. Court of Appeals*** decisions. That is, although each Court of Appeals publishes some or all of its opinions in single-case "slip opinion" form, the U.S. government does not collect or publish Court of Appeals opinions in either advance sheet or bound-volume form![4] The main hard-copy source for published U.S. Court of Appeals decisions is the West Publishing Company, which as you probably know publishes these decisions in the Federal Reporter (the modern version of which is cited as *F.2d*).

c. **Federal District Court opinions:** Similarly, there is no official reporter for federal District Court opinions. The sole systematic hard-copy publisher of these cases is again West Publishing, which publishes them as the Federal Supplement (cited as *F.Supp.*).

2. **State decisions:** Traditionally, every state published officially at least the opinions of its own highest court. Today, most states continue to publish officially their highest-court opinions, but some states have discontinued their official reporters.

a. **Highest-court opinions:** Highest-court opinions from every state are included in the West National Reporter System. As we'll see in detail later, these opinions are also included on the LEXIS service.

b. **Lower-level state decisions:** Even of those states still publishing official reports, not all publish intermediate-level appellate decisions in these official reports. All state intermediate-level appellate courts are, however, included within the National Reporter System, though, as I noted above, some decisions from these mid-level courts are not published at all. (Again, as we'll see shortly, virtually all published mid-level decisions are also available on the LEXIS service.) Few state trial-level decisions are published in either the official or unofficial reports.

C. **Preview of what cases are on LEXIS-NEXIS:** Let's now take a brief look at what cases are present on the LEXIS service.[5] We'll be examining this subject much more closely below (see p. 4-15), but for now, let's get a brief overview.

1. **Federal cases:** In the federal system, the LEXIS service's coverage is as broad as, I think, any sane researcher could want: essentially all published opinions of the Supreme Court, the Courts of Appeal and the District Courts are present, back to 1789.

2. **State decisions:** The LEXIS service's state coverage is not quite as encyclopedic, but still very extensive. The decisions of each state's highest court are included, with every state covered from at least 1965 (and with 36 states covered from 1944 or earlier). The most

---

4. When I describe this fact to even experienced litigators, they are often somewhat amazed. None of them, of course, has *seen* an officially-published collection of federal Court of Appeals decisions, but they are usually incredulous that the mighty federal government has never seen fit to handle this prototypically-governmental function.

5. This information is current as of May, 1997. By the time you read this, more may have been added.

populous states tend to have the longest coverage (e.g., New York from 1884, California from 1883, and Texas from 1886). In addition, state intermediate-level appellate opinions are covered from all states that officially publish such opinions, and from some states that do not publish them; however, the starting date for intermediate-level courts is usually somewhat later (e.g., California Court of Appeal decisions begin in 1944).

3. **Reported vs. unreported:** For the time periods covered, virtually every case that is reported in either an official or unofficial hard-copy reporter is picked up in the LEXIS service. Additionally, a significant number of unpublished cases are covered.[6]

II. COMPARING TRADITIONAL AND COMPUTER-ASSISTED RESEARCH METHODS

A. Review of traditional methods: Let's now compare traditional and computer-assisted methods for finding cases. I realize that we haven't yet focused in any detail on how one can find cases using a computer-assisted system like the LEXIS service. But even before we get to the details of case-finding with the LEXIS service, I'd like you to have some idea of the high-level differences between traditional and CALR methods.

1. **Use of digests:** The traditional method of case-finding makes heavy use of digests.[7] Most commonly, you'll be using the digest/key number system utilized by West Publishing. Let's review briefly how you would use the West digest system to find cases dealing with a particular issue.[8]

   a. **Select proper digest:** First, you'll need to select the proper digest volume(s). For multi-jurisdiction research, the odds are that you will need to consult anywhere from two to dozens of different digest volumes.

   b. **Select key numbers:** Next, you would select one or more key numbers whose entries you would read. You would probably do this by looking in the Descriptive-Word Index for the digest and also by browsing the topical outline at the start of one or more major headings (e.g., "Contracts" or "Automobiles") in the main portion of the digest.

   c. **Read digest entries:** Once you have found one or more key numbers (e.g., Automobiles #246(28)), you would start to read the individual digest entries. Depending on how densely populated the particular key numbers you're searching are, you may have to scan hundreds of digests to find the few that are relevant to your precise issue.

6. See p. 4-15 *infra*.

7. I am assuming that you have already used secondary materials to get the "lay of the land" — I recommend that you start your research this way whether you will be using traditional methods, CALR, or both. To cite a few examples, you should use *ALR Reports*, legal encyclopedias like *AmJur*, single-subject treatises, looseleafs, and other narrative materials. These are described much more fully in the previous chapter; see *supra*, p. 3-1.

8. My overview here is not intended to teach you how to do digest-style research. I assume that you already know how to do this, and I'm just reviewing the main features of digest-searching so that we can compare these with CALR.

d. Read some cases: After you have found a few cases that, judging by their digests, are apparently relevant, you would probably want to read those cases, to see whether you are on the right track. You might then check to see whether there are other key numbers represented in those cases, which would lead you to other digest topics to research. Also, you might want to look at a few cases cited by the cases you are now reading, and check what key numbers those cited cases have been classified under.

e. Check other key numbers: If in the prior step you discover additional key numbers that seem to have relevant cases associated with them, you would then go back to the digest to look at these new key numbers, and repeat the read-digests/read-cases steps outlined above.

f. Other materials: Of course, at several points during this process, you would probably bring in additional tools. For instance, if you found a case that was major and very much on point, you would be likely to "SHEPARDIZE"[9] it to discover cases citing this key case; you would then read these additional cases, see if that turned up any new key numbers, etc. You might also have discovered a statute that was relevant, in which case you would SHEPARDIZE the statute to find other cases discussing that statute; you would also read the annotated statutes[10] to discover cases involving that statutory section. (For the rest of our discussion of case-finding, let's simplify matters by assuming that there are no relevant statutes.)

B. Preview of CALR: Let's now take a very general overview of how we would go about finding relevant cases using the LEXIS service. Again, for simplicity's sake we'll assume that no statute is on point, and that our prior secondary-source research has given us only a general lay of the land, and not the names of any cases. At the most general level, here's how we would go about case-finding:

a. Try representative words, or do a FREESTYLE search: First, we would make an initial attempt to put together a search based on words and phrases that we think would be present in relevant cases. For instance, if we were interested in tort cases allowing a bystander to recover for emotional distress at seeing a car run over a friend in the street, we might search for:

```
bystander and emotional distress and (friend
or relative)
```

Alternatively, you might do a FREESTYLE search here (e.g., **`May a bystander recover damages for emotional distress at seeing an accident happen to a friend?`**)

b. Read cases online: Next, we would take at least a quick online look at some of the retrieved cases, to see whether our first search produced the right sort of case, and

---

9. SHEPARD'S Citations are a powerful system for finding all cases that cite the case you are interested in. See p. 9-2 for an extensive discussion of SHEPARD'S, including the online version of SHEPARD'S available on the LEXIS service.

10. See *infra*, p. 5-19.

whether it produced too many or too few. To do this, we would probably use the KWIC format.

c. **Refine search:** Based on this initial review of cases, we would probably refine our search. We might do this either by expanding the net (making the search more forgiving, to find more cases), or we might narrow the search, to get rid of unwanted cases. We might go through this refine cycle of ''refine search and scan the retrieved cases'' several times.

d. **Use of other materials:** If our prior secondary-source research gave us the names of cases, we might look at these cases online, to see what kind of search words appear in those cases, again helping us refine our search further. Similarly, we might SHEPARDIZE any especially important case we found (we would probably do this SHEPARDIZING online[11]), and read the cases produced by SHEPARD'S to see whether these give us any additional words to search upon.

C. **Weaknesses of the traditional method and how CALR helps:** Let's now take a look at some of the weaknesses of this traditional digest-oriented research method. In doing so, I don't mean to pick on West Publishing. But I think that the system has real weaknesses, and that these weaknesses have become accentuated as our law has become more complex and specialized and as the number of reported cases has grown exponentially; I also think that the LEXIS service does a lot to overcome these weaknesses. Here are the six biggest weaknesses I see: (1) the ''missing case'' problem; (2) the ''needle in a haystack'' problem; (3) the "you can't do that at all'' problem; (4) the ''out of state'' problem; (5) the "I relied on the headnote, your Honor" trap; and (6) the "But your Honor, that case was only decided this week" humiliation.

1. **The ''missing case'' problem:** The first — and I suppose in many ways the scariest — problem with relying on the West digest system is the ***''missing case''*** problem. By this, I do not mean that a reported case is not present at all in the digest volume — I mean that it is ***misfiled***, so that you, the searcher, won't find it. There are two main scenarios by which this can come about, the ''unexpected category'' scenario and the "change of category'' scenario.

a. **Unexpected category:** The ***"unexpected category''*** scenario is the most dangerous of all. Here, the West editor has placed the case in a key number where you would simply ***never expect to find it***, so that you never check that category.

Consider, if you will, the strange case of *People v. Martinez,*[12] a case which disappeared into the ether for nine years until it was rematerialized by a judge with a computer terminal.[13] In *Martinez*, the Appellate Division (a New York intermediate appeals court) held that bail jumping is a single, non-continuous offense (rather than

---

11. See p. 9-3 for a description of how to SHEPARDIZE any case you see cited in a document that you're viewing on LEXIS.

12. 400 N.Y.S.2d 96 (1st Dept. 1977).

13. If I sound like Rod Serling with this introduction, it's because there is something *Twilight Zone*-like about this story.

an offense that is deemed to be repeated every day that the bail jumper remains at liberty). Usually the "single offense vs. continuous offense" distinction is relevant for *statute of limitations*[14] purposes. But the issue in *Martinez* was the date of the offense for purposes of a "habitual offender" statute (by which an offender's past crimes, committed within the last *n* years, could lead to a harsher penalty for the present crime). The West editors created only one headnote for this part of the case, and put it into the "Successive Offenses and Habitual Criminals" key number within the topic Criminal Law. West did not put any headnotes into the "Bail" key numbers or into the "Criminal Law — Limitation of Prosecutions" key numbers, where West typically places criminal cases concerning the statute of limitations.

The statute of limitations on bail jumping is five years in New York. For nine years after *Martinez* was decided, district attorneys in the two counties within the First Department (whose appellate court had decided *Martinez*) brought many bail-jumping prosecutions where the prosecution began more than five years after the offender first jumped bail — the prosecutors argued that bail jumping was a continuous offense, so that the statute of limitations would not even start to run until the offender ended his bail-jump and reappeared in court. Neither defense lawyers nor judges (nor, apparently, the prosecutors themselves) ever seems to have realized that the relevant appeals court had already decided this issue adversely to the prosecution, in *Martinez*. Finally, a trial court judge using CALR discovered the "missing" case, in *People v. Barnes*, 499 N.Y.S.2d 343 (Sup.Ct.N.Y.Co. 1986). The judge explained the above facts, then asked,

> How can a case which is clearly controlling on a particular issue properly serve as a precedent when it is virtually unknown and undiscoverable? This dilemma evokes the age-old query — is there a sound if a tree falls in the forest but nobody hears it? Apparently, the district attorneys of New York and Bronx Counties have not yet "heard" the holding in the *Martinez* case. . . .

The judge noted that in contrast to traditional research methods, "the *Martinez* case can be retrieved by the use of a computer . . . by entering variations of the phrase 'continuous offense bail jumping'."

The *Martinez/Barnes* example may seem to be bizarre and unusual. But it points up a more fundamental problem with headnotes, however well done. The headnote/digesting process will only work if the editor is able to identify not only every issue which the court thinks it's talking about, but every issue as to which ***later researchers*** may want to examine the opinion. It's hard to fault the particular editor who digested the *Martinez* case — it would have taken considerable insight for the editor to have noticed that the continuous nature of bail jumping would be relevant not only to the issue "What crimes count for purposes of the 'habitual offender' statute?" but also to the issue, "When does the statute of limitations start to run on bail jumping?," an issue not remotely relevant in *Martinez* itself.

14. A statute of limitations, as you may know, establishes the time limit within which a particular type of action, such as a criminal prosecution, must be brought.

As Bob Berring, a law professor who is the librarian at the University of California-Berkeley Law School, explains, the headnote system works only to the extent that the headnote editor is able to *anticipate the thoughts* of the person who will be doing research, perhaps several decades later; West and its editors are trying to create a "Universe of All Thinkable Thoughts." As our law grows in complexity, and as the sheer number of reported cases burgeons,[15] this mission becomes less and less possible.

By contrast, CALR clearly does not suffer from this weakness. If new legal issues arise over the years, or if a searcher wants to look for judicial language that may be incidental to the precise issue in the reported case, the searcher simply has to formulate an electronic search request that captures the right key words. As the judge in *Barnes* suggested, a searcher could readily have found *Martinez* from a search such as **`bail jumping and continuous offense,`** and it would not matter what issue the judge in *Martinez* (or the headnote editor digesting *Martinez*) thought was the important issue or context.

b. The "changing categories" problem: Contributing to the "missing case" problem is the "change of category" sub-problem. As the law develops over the space of decades, even the ***names of categories*** that we lawyers use to think about legal problems changes too. A lawyer searching several decades worth of cases has to ask herself not only, "How would a West editor today classify this case?" but also "How would a West editor in 1985 or '75 or '65 have classified this case?"

Consider, for instance, cases raising issues relating to a child's out-of-wedlock status. Until about 1976, cases on this subject were grouped under the major topic "Bastards." From 1976 to 1980, the somewhat-less-judgmental phrase "Illegitimate Children" was used. Finally, in 1981, West shifted to the absolutely-politically-correct phrase "Children Out-of-wedlock."[16] So a researcher in 1995 would have to ***know*** (or discover) that these swaps had taken place, so she could check all three as she went back in time. This is certainly a discoverable fact (looking in the Descriptive Word Index for each digest volume, under the phrases "Illegitimate Children" and "Legitimation," would have picked up the phrases actually used by West in each instance), but the procedure is certainly cumbersome at best, and a trap for the unwary at worst.

2. The "needle-in-a-haystack" problem: The next major problem is the ***"needle-in-a-haystack"*** difficulty. In essence, this problem arises when a searcher is looking under a "correct" key number (that is, a key number into which the relevant cases have in fact been placed by the West editors), but there are ***so many cases*** in those categories that it's very hard to pick out the ones you are interested in. Sometimes, you may simply be burdened by having to read hundreds of digest entries, but at least you'll be able to tell from a given case's digest entries whether it's one you want or not; other times, you may not even

15. West estimates that about 60,000 new cases appear in its National Reporter System each year.

16. I can see from this that I will have to become more up-to-date in my *Constitutional Law* outline, where I classify the subject as "Illegitimacy." Like West editors, I too am a child of my time — I wrote the first edition of *Constitutional Law* in the early 1980's, and seem to have used the phrase that was in vogue then.

be able to tell whether the case is a "good" one without reading the case itself. Either way, you may have to do a tremendous amount of work.

The West editors have tried to minimize this problem, by slicing the key numbers into ever-narrower sub-numbers. For instance, suppose your research problem involves damage to your client's car when he stored it at a private parking garage. The car was stolen from under the nose of the attendant and later recovered in battered condition; assume further that the parking stub contained fine print disclaiming all liability for theft of a stored car. You have reason to believe that courts often distinguish between public and private garages in assessing tort liability.

For this problem, the West key number system would give you a fairly narrow slice of cases: the major topic "Automobiles" has a key number, #372, which contains cases involving "Storage of vehicles; parking facilities — injury to or loss of vehicle or contents." In fact, underneath that, we have key number #372(2) covering "Limitation of liability" for such cases. But this is as far as the classification scheme goes — every case in the National Reporter System involving the relatively broad issue of whether a disclaimer on a parking stub limits the garage owner's liability for any kind of damage to the stored vehicle will be collected within this one category. The searcher has to read one or more headnotes for every such case in order to pick out the ones involving theft (as opposed to some other sort of damage), in order to pick out the ones involving a private vs. public garage if that appears to make a difference, or in order pick out any other further-narrowing fact or issue.

a. Decennial Digest: The problem is at its worst when you the searcher have decided that, for one reason or another, you need to look at cases from all over the nation. (For instance, this may be because the case is one of first impression in your own state, or because you are doing, say, a moot court project involving the hypothetical state of "Columbia" which has no precedents of its own.) You will need to use a combination of Decennial Digests and General Digests. As you may be aware, there are now two complete multi-volume sets for each Decennial Digest beginning in 1976 (Part 1 and Part 2, each covering five years), and about 12 non-cumulative volumes of the General Digest for each year after the most recent Decennial Digest. You would have to look in each of these volumes in order to complete just the digest portion of your research project.

Example: Suppose you, a researcher working in 1995, need to research our little "theft of car from parking garage, with disclaimer on the parking ticket" problem. Suppose further that you decide that you need to look at 30 years' worth of cases from all American courts. Here is a list of volumes that you would need to consult:

1992-95 — General Digest (48 volumes)

1986-91 — Tenth Decennial Digest, Part 1 (1 vol.)

1982-86 — Ninth Decennial Digest, Part 2 (1 vol.)

1976-81 — Ninth Decennial Digest, Part 1 (1 vol.)

1966-76 — Eight Decennial Digest (1 vol.)

1956-66 — Seventh Decennial Digest (1 vol.)

Total: 53 volumes

In each volume of the General Digest, there is a chart showing, for each key number, which heretofore-published General Digest volumes contain one or more cases from that key number; thus the searcher may be able to eliminate some volumes. But in a broadly-populated key number, most of the General Digest volumes will have one or more cases. I conducted a search of Automobiles 372 back to 1956, and was required to read 170 headnotes from 12 different volumes. Only 47 of these seemed to involve thefts from garages, and less than half of these gave any indication that they involved private as opposed to municipal garages.

b. **Search for un-indexed key words:** A different aspect of the "needle-in-a-haystack" problem is that your research problem may turn completely on ***words or phrases that simply have never been the subject of a West headnote classification scheme.***

Consider, for instance, product liability problems where the precise identity of a particular product, or narrow product group, is what identifies a useful case from a not-so-useful one — thus we are interested in Ford trucks built from 1985-1990, or Toro lawnmowers, or a small-but-generic category like trampolines. West does not — and probably couldn't even if it wanted to — classify cases according to the precise type of product involved. Therefore, if your problem is, say, whether the manufacturer of a trampoline is liable to a child injured on it where the maker did not post a prominent warning label, you would probably have to read through the headnotes on hundreds, maybe thousands, of "failure to warn" cases to find just those involving trampolines.

c. **"Intersection" or "multi-category" cases:** Finally, the "needle-in-a-haystack" problem can arise where what is of interest to you is the ***intersection*** between two or more categories. For instance, suppose that you want to find cases involving discrimination against black female employees. West has a very nice series of key numbers for racial discrimination: "Civil Rights — Discrimination by reason of race, color or national origin." It also has a nice set of categories for sex discrimination: "Civil Rights — Sex discrimination." But nowhere does it have a category for "Combined Sex and Race Discrimination" or anything like it. You would need to read each headnote in each of the two categories to discover whether the case in fact involved a black woman employee, a mind-numbing task.[17]

By contrast, a CALR system would take care of the problem easily: you would just search (perhaps in library *GENFED*, file *NEWER*) for something like:

discriminat! and (black w/1 (female or wom!) w/15 (employ! or work!)) [18]

17. This example is suggested by Delgado and Stefancic, *Why Do We Tell the Same Stories?: Law Reform, Critical Librarianship, and the Triple Helix Dilemma*, 42 Stan. L. Rev. 207, 219 (1989).

3. **"You can't do that at all":** What I call the "you can't do that at all" problem is the legal-research equivalent of "you can't get there from here." Sometimes you need to search on things that simply ***aren't picked up in the headnotes at all.***

   a. **Name of judge:** Most dramatically, you sometimes need to find all cases decided by a ***particular judge***.[19] There is simply no way to tell from a headnote what judge wrote the opinion. On the LEXIS service, by contrast, it's easy: a Boolean search for

   `writtenby (brown)`

   will retrieve all opinions (majority, concurrence or dissent) issued by any judge named "Brown." (You might have multiple judge Browns, so you would probably combine this search with a search by particular court.)

   Alternatively, if you want to find all cases in which a particular judge cast a vote (even if that judge merely joined someone else's opinion rather than writing her own opinion), you can do this with the **`judges`** segment; thus

   `judges (brown)`

   finds all cases in which a judge named "brown" cast a vote.

   b. **Name of counsel:** Similarly, you may want to find cases in which a particular ***lawyer*** or law firm represented one of the parties.[20] Here, too, no amount of headnote-reading will get you what you want. A search on the LEXIS service will, instantly. To find all discrimination cases in which the firm of Jones, Smith and Brown represented one of the parties, just do the following Boolean search (perhaps in library *GENFED*, file *NEWER*):

   `discrimination and counsel (jones and smith and brown)`

   (The counsel listings on the LEXIS service typically include both the name of the individual lawyer and the name of his/her firm.)

   c. **Names of parties:** You might want to search for all cases, or cases of a particular type, in which a ***litigant*** named X was one of the parties.[21] Here, too, much of what you want to do simply cannot be done with headnotes. True, the headnote entry seems to give you the "name" of the case, and thus, the names of the parties. But where there are multiple plaintiffs or multiple defendants, only the first of each is listed in the headnote, and the one you want may not necessarily be the first one. Furthermore, you may have to wade through hundreds of cases in a particular key number to find the one whose party-name is the one you are looking for.

   As with judges and counsel, looking for the name of a particular party is simple on the

18. Alternatively, you could use a FREESTYLE search, such as **`What conduct constitutes discrimination against black female employees?`**

19. See *infra*, p. 4-35, for some reasons why you might want to do this.

20. See *infra*, p. 4-38 for reasons why.

21. See *infra*, p. 4-34 for reasons why.

LEXIS service. Thus to find all cases involving Exxon Shipping Corp., you would simply do a Boolean search for:

```
name (exxon shipping)
```

d. By particular court(s): Finally, you might want to search for all cases decided by a ***particular court*** or courts. Again, this is easy on the LEXIS service. You can usually accomplish it by selecting the right library and file combination; for instance, to restrict yourself to appellate cases decided by the federal Sixth Circuit, you would choose library *GENFED*, file *6CIR*. If there were no library/file combination that was exactly what you wanted, you could limit the search by name of court; thus to find only cases deciding by federal district judges located in the Northern District of Ohio, you could do a Boolean search in library *GENFED*, file *6DIST*[22], for:

```
court(Ohio and Northern)
```

4. The ''out-of-state case'' problem: The next problem, the ''out-of-state cases'' problem, is not so much a problem with headnotes as it is a problem with the way reporters are structured, and the way law libraries (especially libraries at, say, public interest agencies or smaller law firms) are maintained. Let's suppose that your problem is a state-law one, and that you have decided that you need cases from nearby states, and also from nearby federal courts interpreting the law of those nearby states. You have two related problems:

(1) the ''fit'' between the jurisdictions you're interested in, and the setup of the digests serving those states, may not be very good. Consequently, you're likely to have to look in a lot of different places. For instance, let's suppose that you're in New York, and you need cases from Connecticut and New Jersey, as well as federal cases from New York, Connecticut and New Jersey. You will need to look at the Atlantic Digest (to cover Connecticut and New Jersey), the New York Digest (for New York), and the Federal Practice Digest (for federal cases from those states). On the LEXIS service, it would be easy to search for just the courts you need: you would go into the *MEGA* library, and select both the *2MEGA* file (which would you give you U.S. Supreme Court cases, federal case law from the Second Circuit, including the District Courts in the Second Circuit, and state case law from Connecticut, New York and Vermont, the three states making up the Second Circuit), and the *3MEGA* file (which would do the same for the Third Circuit, including state cases from New Jersey, which is one of the states in the Third Circuit).

(2) Your library, if it is something less than a law-school or large-law-firm one, may not have all of the reporters you need for this kind of multi-jurisdiction research. Many smaller libraries, for instance, have the federal reporters and the reporters of the state where the library is located, but not others. On the LEXIS

22. The *6DIST* file is limited to cases decided by the federal district courts located in the 6th Circuit. See Appendix F-2 for more information about files within the *GENFED* library.

service, of course, virtually ***all*** reported cases are always accessible to you from your terminal, no matter where you are.

5. **The "I relied on the headnote, Your Honor" trap:** The next problem is not a necessary difficulty with doing traditional research, but traditional researchers are likely to suffer from the problem. What you are supposed to do, of course, is to read the headnotes, pick each possibly relevant case, and then *read the case itself.* But many a busy lawyer sooner or later falls into the trap of *relying on the headnote*, and assuming that the case says what the headnote says it says. The results can be embarrassing to the lawyer and worse for the client.

The cases are filled with judicial scorn for headnotes, and for lawyers who rely on them.[23] My award for "Most Vitriolic Judicial Language on the Subject of Unjustified Reliance on Headnotes'' goes to Judge Kocoras, of the federal district court for the Northern District of Illinois, who referred to:

> . . . Yet another instance of bungling by [the plaintiff's] lawyers. Sloppily relying on a headnote (which has been misprinted), without bothering to read the actual text of the opinion, they misstated the holding of a case to this court. Rather than supporting them as they say it does, this case actually goes directly against their position.[24]

Many other opinions similarly stress that the headnote, even when written by the ***official reporter*** for the court, let alone by an unofficial West editor, is not the law, and that a lawyer who relies on the headnote is a foolish one.[25]

---

23. For my next book, I plan to follow in the spirit of books like "Men Who Won't Commit, and Women Who Love Them,'' by publishing "Headnote Editors Who Err, and Lawyers Who Rely on Them.''

24. *Buchanin v. Blase*, No. 83 C2932, Slip Op. (N.D.Ill. July 30, 1984).

25. Here are some more examples: *Bisso v. Inland Waterways Corp.*, 349 U.S. 85 (1955), Mr. Justice Frankfurter dissenting ("[These cases] are to be assessed, of course, according to time-honored rules for reading cases — that cases hold only what they decide, not what slipshod or ignorant headnote writers state them to decide; that decisions are one thing, gratuitous remarks another.''); *U.S. v. Detroit Timber & Lumber Company*, 200 U.S. 321 (1906) ("The headnote is not the work of the court, nor does it state its decision. . . . It is simply the work of the reporter, gives his understanding of the decision, and is prepared for the convenience of the profession in the examination of the reports. . . . [T]he headnote [at issue here] is a misinterpretation of the scope of the decision.''); *In re Hessler*, 549 A.2d 700 (D.C.App. 1988) ("The summary of the case and the relevant headnote in the Atlantic Reporter are misleading. . . .''); *Forbes v. The National Rating Bureau, Inc.*, 223 So.2d 764 (D.C.App.Fla. 1969) ("The first two headnotes preceding [the] opinion [in Brill v. Jewett] purport to say what the writer of Florida Jurisprudence says the case stands for, but the case does not hold what the reader of Florida Jurisprudence is led to think. . . . We cannot repeat too often that headnotes are not holdings. We recognize that lawyers are busy people, but careful case analysis is required and frequently reveals the headnote to be a misleading guide to the holding of the court in a particular case.''); *Hardiman v. State*, 436 A.2d 923 (Ct.Spec.App.Md. 1981) ("The lead headnote in McCoy seems to espouse that upon which the State relies. We remind the State, however, that it is the holding of Court, not the opinion of a headnoter, that provides us the authority we must follow.''); *Rooney v. McEachern*, 321 A.2d 270 (N.J.Super. 1974) ("Although the decision in Batistich is clear enough, the headnote in the report is misleading. . . . This points up the danger to a lawyer in relying on a headnote.'').

By the way, the method by which I found these cases about the dangers of headnotes is itself a nifty illustration of the kind of search one can do on the LEXIS service. I found most of these cases simply by doing a Boolean search (in library *GENFED*, file *MEGA*) for:

```
headnote w/10 (rely! or misleading or misled or
misprinted)
```

To the extent that you're doing your primary case finding on the LEXIS service, you obviously won't have the headnote-reliance problem: you'll be reading material in the case itself, not in the headnotes, so there will be nothing unofficial to rely on.

6. **The "But Your Honor, that case was only decided last week'' humiliation:** About the most embarrassing thing that can happen to a lawyer — or at least a litigator — is to rely publicly on what turns out to be ***out-of-date law***. When I was a law student, in the mid-1970s, this usually took the form of relying on a case which, if SHEPARDIZED, would be seen to have been reversed on appeal, or overruled by a later case. Today, the bigger risk is that one's key case has been reversed or overruled by a decision that is too new to have even been picked up by SHEPARD'S hard-copy service, but which is very much present on the LEXIS service.

As we'll be discussing at greater length below,[26] the time gap between when an opinion is released by the judge and when it appears on the LEXIS service is remarkably brief, a mere hour for U.S. Supreme Court decisions and, perhaps more remarkably, less than 48 hours for many lower federal court decisions and state Supreme Court decisions. By contrast, it is likely to be several weeks after release before cases show up in advance sheets or in the printed version of SHEPARD'S.

A friend of mine recently told me a story showing how humiliating it can be to cite out-of-date law. While giving a speech at a Continuing Legal Education seminar in a field where he was acknowledged to be an expert, he extensively discussed a particular federal district court decision. But soon after he finished, a federal judge in the audience said, "Don't you know that decision was overruled last week by the Seventh Circuit? All you had to do was check recent Seventh Circuit cases yesterday on LEXIS, the way I did, and you wouldn't have made a mistake like that."

The moral seems to be, if you're not as up-to-date as the most up-to-date electronic service could get you, you're a walking target for a malpractice suit.

D. Integrating traditional research and CALR: Does all of this mean that I think you should drop traditional hard-copy methods and use CALR exclusively? Not at all. I think that traditional print sources can add a lot to your research. But I do think that the backbone of your approach to case-finding should be CALR, not print. Here's how I would go about integrating the two for case-finding:

1. **Start with secondary sources:** Start with secondary sources, like legal encyclopedias, law reviews and treatises. Many of these can be found online (like ALR, Restatements and

26. See *infra*, p. 4-17.

the *ALLREV* law reviews file, all on the LEXIS service). Use these secondary sources to: (1) get an overview of the subject, including identification of what are likely to be central phrases that would appear in suitable cases; and (2) get the names/cites of some leading cases.

2. **Search for more cases:** Go online to the LEXIS service. Use the central phrases you found in step 1, as well as the leading cases you found in step 1, to get more cases. The way you'll use the central phrases, of course, is by simply searching for all cases containing those phrases (as I'll show you in more detail below). The way you'll use the leading cases is by searching for other cases that cite or are cited in those key cases (using tools like SHEPARD'S, Auto-Cite, LEXCITE, and LINK).[27]

3. **Read your cases:** Now, read the cases you've found so far. You can do this either online or in hard-copy. Inspect these cases to: (1) make sure you're on the right track, i.e., that you've analyzed the problem in a basically-correct way and are finding relevant cases; and (2) locate additional central words and phrases, by seeing the language that these cases use in discussing the issue.

4. **Go online again:** Go back online, and: (1) search on the new words or phrases to get additional cases; and (2) use the new cases to lead you to additional cases by using SHEPARD'S and other citator tools.

III. WHAT CASES ARE ON LEXIS-NEXIS

A. **What courts are covered, and from when:** The case law databases on the LEXIS service give you, in my opinion, practically every reported case (and many unreported cases) likely to have a bearing on the vast majority of legal problems. The precise coverage of federal and state law on the LEXIS service is shown in Appendix E-1 and E-2. Here's a brief summary:

- Virtually all reported federal cases (Supreme Court, Court of Appeals and District Court) since 1789.
- Virtually all reported cases from the highest court of each state, since 1969 (and in most instances much earlier). All reported cases from intermediate state courts, most of them since the early 1980s or earlier.
- Many unreported cases from both the federal and state systems, often going back thirty years or more.

1. **Reported cases:** For the periods of coverage shown in Appendix E-1 and E-2, the LEXIS service has virtually every reported case (whether the case was reported in the official reporter, the unofficial West reporter or both).

2. **Unreported cases:** Additionally, the LEXIS service contains a substantial number of ***unreported*** cases, that is, cases that do not appear in any Official Reporter for the jurisdic-

27. See *infra*, p. 4-49 and p. 4-54, where I discuss using one case to find other related cases.

tion nor in the West National Reporter System. The prevalence of such unreported opinions varies sharply from jurisdiction to jurisdiction:

a. **Federal:** From the federal system, there are essentially no unreported U.S. Supreme Court opinions at all. But at least half of all U.S. Court of Appeals cases are unreported, and the LEXIS service includes many of these. The federal District Court story is even more dramatic: recall[28] that West's F.Supp. reporter, the only general federal District Court case reporter, picks up only about 15% of all substantive federal District Court opinions. The LEXIS service picks up a substantially higher number. For instance, LEXIS contains 20,736 federal District Court decisions decided in 1992, the last complete year available at the writing of this edition. Of these, 5,704 appeared in F.Supp. The remaining 15,032 — nearly three-quarters of the total — are cases which were never picked up at all in F.Supp.

b. **State court decisions:** A somewhat similar pattern occurs on the state-court front. There are practically no unreported cases available on the LEXIS service from each state's highest court, since all of those cases appear in the state's official reports (if there are official reports),[29] or in the West National Reporter System. The picture changes somewhat at the intermediate-appellate level, however. In many states, the printed reporters and LEXIS are comparable in their coverage of intermediate-appellate decisions; for instance, California and New York both publish officially all of the intermediate-level decisions (from the Court of Appeal in California and the Appellate Division in New York) that those states consider important, and LEXIS coverage from these courts is essentially the same as the print coverage. But in other states, the rule is quite different. For instance, in Texas for 1992, there were over 1200 Court of Appeals cases that were unpublished but appear on the LEXIS service, and in Tennessee for 1992, there were nearly 800 Court of Appeals cases that were never published but appear on the LEXIS service.

> **Safety Tip:** You must always be careful before citing an unreported case as precedent. Many jurisdictions, by court rule, treat unpublished decisions as being without precedential value, and forbid litigants from citing to these cases even if they appear on the LEXIS service. See, e.g., Rule 90(i) of the Texas Rules of Appellate Procedure. Other courts allow citation to unreported cases, but only if a copy of the case is served on the other side. (LEXIS tells you when the case you are looking at is not freely citable under local court rules.) Of course, even where you are not permitted to cite to an unreported case, reading the case may lead you to other cases or authorities of value to you.

B. **No editorial judgment by LEXIS-NEXIS:** In the print world, judges, publishers and reporters frequently exercise judgment in determining what should be published. In the West

28. See *supra*, p. 4-2.

29. See *supra*, p. 4-3.

National Reporter System, for instance, while every U.S. Supreme Court decision is reproduced, federal judges make decisions about which of their Court of Appeals and District Court opinions to forward to West for publication, and West editors then exercise considerable judgment in deciding which of these decisions to reproduce. Similarly, in states having an official reporter system, the official in charge of the reporter (who is himself typically called the "State Reporter," leading to considerable confusion) typically exercises considerable judgment in deciding what to print. In New York, for instance, the official known as the Reporter for the State of New York chooses only a minority of the available cases from the mid-level appellate courts in New York, and an even smaller percentage of trial-court cases, to appear in the official Appellate Division and Miscellaneous Reports, respectively.

But the procedure is quite different at the LEXIS service. Essentially, LEXIS-NEXIS puts up in full text *every opinion* that it receives from federal and state courts around the country. Most of the time, it is up to the individual judge whether to send a copy of the case to the LEXIS service. In some jurisdictions, the LEXIS service receives its cases from a central state source (e.g., the Official Reporter), who makes some decisions about which cases should be forwarded to the LEXIS service. The important thing to remember is that LEXIS-NEXIS exercises no editorial discretion — any case it receives, it puts online without scrutinizing the case for usefulness.

C. **Currentness:** How up-to-date is the LEXIS service? The answer depends on the jurisdiction. There are two sources of delay: (1) the time between when the case is released by the judge, and when the LEXIS service is able to get a hard copy or electronic copy of that case; and (2) the gap between when the LEXIS service gets a copy of the case, and when it puts the case up. Typically, the former accounts for most of the total delay between release and online availability. The following chart gives some general guidelines.

Court	Delay
U.S. Supreme Court	1 hour
U.S. Courts of Appeals	24 hours for published opinions; 5-10 days for unpublished ones
U.S. District Courts	24-72 hours
State Supreme Courts	24-96 hours

Note: Actual currentness varies sharply from jurisdiction to jurisdiction. Among federal District Courts, for instance, decisions from those located in the Second Circuit typically come on within one week, whereas those located in the Eighth Circuit take more than two weeks. Similarly, among state Supreme Courts, those of the New York Court of Appeals appear within several days, whereas those of Illinois take several weeks. These discrepancies seem to relate more to the release practices of the various courts than they do to the LEXIS service's diligence.

D. Segments for case law: The table below shows how case law typically appears on the LEXIS service. To the left of the table, printed in bold, are the names of the segments (e.g., the *NAME* segment, which contains the names of all parties). In the boxed area is shown the text of a typical case, as you would see it on your LEXIS screen. (The lines separating the segments have been added to make the chart clearer.)

State Case Law
Sample Document-Segment Description

NAME	Morris et al. v. Savoy Morris v. Savoy
NUMBER	No. 89-1807
COURT	Supreme Court of Ohio
CITE	61 Ohio St. 3d 684; 576 N.E.2d 765; 1991 Ohio LEXIS 2117
DATE	February 20, 1991, Submitted August 27, 1991, Decided
HISTORY	SUBSEQUENT HISTORY: [***1] As Amended. PRIOR HISTORY: On Order from the United States District Court, Northern District of Ohio, Eastern Division, Certifying Questions of State Law, No. C88-3649-A.
DISPOSITION	DISPOSITION: Judgment accordingly.
HEADNOTES (written by court)	HEADNOTES: Malpractice -- Physicians -- R.C. 2307.43, which sets a cap on general damages that may be awarded for medical malpractice, is unconstitutional.
COUNSEL	COUNSEL: Jeffries, Kube & Monteleone Co., L.P.A., J. Michael Monteleone and Richard A. Vadnal, for petitioners. Jacobson, Maynard, Tuschman & Kalur Co., L.P.A., Robert C. Maynard, Jerome S. Kalur, Thomas H. Terry III and Robert C. Seibel, for respondent. [PORTION OF TEXT DELETED TO SHORTEN SAMPLE DOCUMENT]
JUDGES	JUDGES: Wright, J. Moyer, C.J., and H. Brown, J., concur. H. Brown, J., concurs separately. Holmes, J., concurs in part and dissents in part. Sweeney and Resnick, JJ., concur in part and dissent in part. Douglas, J., not participating.
OPINIONBY	OPINIONBY: WRIGHT

Sample continued on next page

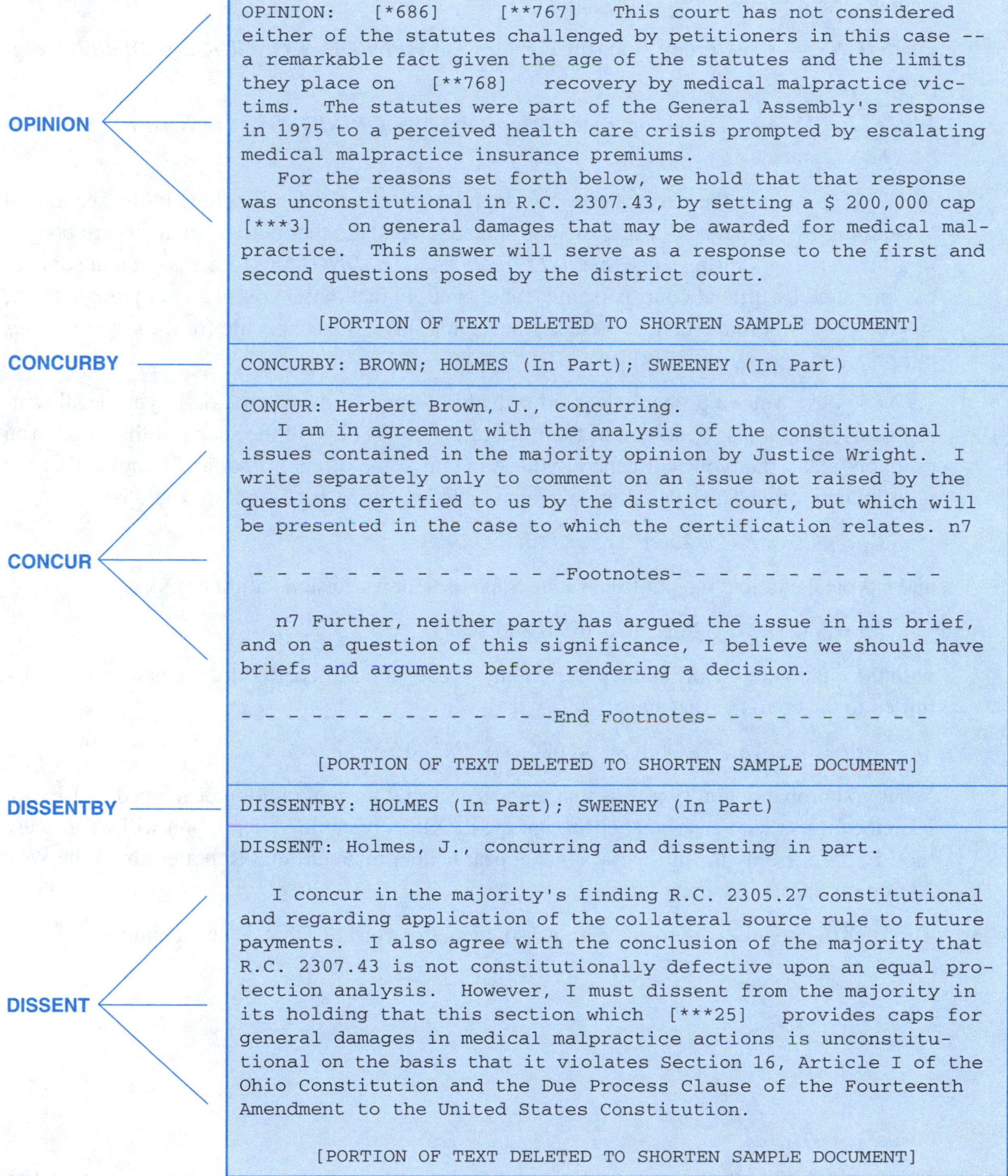
OPINION: [*686] [**767] This court has not considered either of the statutes challenged by petitioners in this case -- a remarkable fact given the age of the statutes and the limits they place on [**768] recovery by medical malpractice victims. The statutes were part of the General Assembly's response in 1975 to a perceived health care crisis prompted by escalating medical malpractice insurance premiums.

For the reasons set forth below, we hold that that response was unconstitutional in R.C. 2307.43, by setting a $ 200,000 cap [***3] on general damages that may be awarded for medical malpractice. This answer will serve as a response to the first and second questions posed by the district court.

[PORTION OF TEXT DELETED TO SHORTEN SAMPLE DOCUMENT]

CONCURBY: BROWN; HOLMES (In Part); SWEENEY (In Part)

CONCUR: Herbert Brown, J., concurring.

I am in agreement with the analysis of the constitutional issues contained in the majority opinion by Justice Wright. I write separately only to comment on an issue not raised by the questions certified to us by the district court, but which will be presented in the case to which the certification relates. n7

- - - - - - - - - - - - - - -Footnotes- - - - - - - - - - - - -

n7 Further, neither party has argued the issue in his brief, and on a question of this significance, I believe we should have briefs and arguments before rendering a decision.

- - - - - - - - - - - - - - - -End Footnotes- - - - - - - - - - - -

[PORTION OF TEXT DELETED TO SHORTEN SAMPLE DOCUMENT]

DISSENTBY: HOLMES (In Part); SWEENEY (In Part)

DISSENT: Holmes, J., concurring and dissenting in part.

I concur in the majority's finding R.C. 2305.27 constitutional and regarding application of the collateral source rule to future payments. I also agree with the conclusion of the majority that R.C. 2307.43 is not constitutionally defective upon an equal protection analysis. However, I must dissent from the majority in its holding that this section which [***25] provides caps for general damages in medical malpractice actions is unconstitutional on the basis that it violates Section 16, Article I of the Ohio Constitution and the Due Process Clause of the Fourteenth Amendment to the United States Constitution.

[PORTION OF TEXT DELETED TO SHORTEN SAMPLE DOCUMENT]

Additionally, the following segments may appear in some cases:

NOTICE — This segment contains any notices published by the court concerning the finality of the decision or the limitation on the use of the decision as precedent.

SYLLABUS — This segment contains a summary of the facts and history of a case and the points of law in the decision (found in cases from U.S. Supreme Court, and cases from the state courts of Illinois, Kansas, Oklahoma and West Virginia)

OPINIONS — This group segment contains the *OPINION*, *CONCUR* and *DISSENT* segments.

WRITTENBY — This group segment contains the *OPINIONBY, CONCURBY* and *DISSENTBY* segments.

We'll be discussing the various case-law segments in greater detail below, in the section on "searching by segment."[30] For now, you should understand that not all segments are present in all case files — for instance, the *SYLLABUS* and *HEADNOTES* segments contain summaries prepared by official court personnel, and some (in fact most) courts do not prepare these, so you would not find either of these segments in a single-state case file from a state that does not prepare them.

E. LEXIS cites: You've probably learned something about forms of citation in your legal writing course, and a real treatment of the rules of citation is beyond the scope of this book. You probably recall that you will generally have to cite to the official reporter (if any) and/or the unofficial reporter. Thus a citation to a reported federal appeals court case would be:

Chromiak v. Field, 406 F.2d 502 (9th Cir. 1969)

and a typical citation to a published state Supreme Court decision would be:

Morris v. Savoy, 576 N.E.2d 765 (Ohio 1991)

with the citation to the official reporter, if any, added, at least where the document will be submitted to the courts of that state:

Morris v. Savoy, 61 Ohio St. 3d 684, 576 N.E.2d 765 (1991)

What you probably don't know is that there is a special form of citation developed by LEXIS-NEXIS, for use with cases that appear on the LEXIS service. In general, you will want to use the LEXIS cite only for those cases that appear neither in an Official Reporter nor in the West National Reporter System.[31]

The LEXIS cite takes the form: year, jurisdiction, the word "LEXIS," and a number:

---

30. See p. 4-33, *infra*.

31. In fact, *The Blue Book*, that 343-page compendium of citation wisdom prepared by the Columbia, Harvard, Penn and Yale Law Reviews, sets out even stricter rules for when cites to LEXIS, and its competitor WestLaw, should be used. According to *The Blue Book*, Rule 10.3.1(b), "If a case is not available in an official or preferred unofficial [i.e., West] reporter, cite to another unofficial reporter, to a service, to a widely used computer database [such as LEXIS], to a slip opinion, or to a newspaper, ***in that order of preference***." (emphasis added.) So basically, CALR sources come near the bottom of the totem pole.

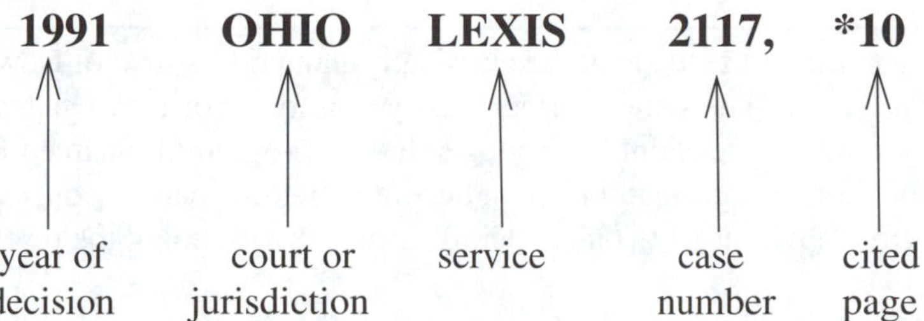

You will not find LEXIS citations for cases decided earlier than 1987, since it was only in that year that the LEXIS service began its own citation system.

You can also cite to an individual "page" when you use a LEXIS cite. One difference from ordinary hard-copy cites is that the number that follows the word "LEXIS" is a case number, not a page number, and the page numbers for each case start at 1. LEXIS page breaks occur roughly every 1200 characters and do not correspond to the amount of text that fits on the screen. The citation shown in the above diagram cites to page 10 of the case.

F. Court-Assigned cites: A few court systems (e.g., the federal 6th Circuit, and the New York and Louisiana state courts) have implemented their own official ***electronic citation systems***. When a court system adopts an official electronic citation system, searchers can use a single citation to find the case on any CALR system, and can do so even before the case has been published in hard-copy form.[32] Some courts are furnishing not only a cite representing the "starting point" (in essence, the first page) of the case, but also "interior cites," so that a person can cite to any particular portion of a case.[33]

IV. FINDING CASES ON LEXIS-NEXIS

A. Sample problem: Let's now look at the nuts and bolts of how you look for cases on the LEXIS service. To give us a framework, I've made up a little research problem. (I did not work backward in developing this problem. That is, what I did not do was to locate some juicy case, and then set up the facts to see whether you could find the case. Instead, I invented the factual setting out of whole cloth, with no idea what kinds of precedents either hard-copy or CALR research would find. In that sense, at least, this should be a pretty good "real world" problem.)

32. Because of these benefits, the Automation and Technology Committee for the U.S. Judicial Conference has proposed a Standard Electronic Citation System, by which a single "electronic cite" could be used to retrieve and refer to any federal case on both LEXIS and Westlaw. See 56 Fed. Reg. 38457. As of May, 1997, the proposal had not been adopted. This was due in part to opposition by West Publishing Co., whose own propriety citation system stood to become less valuable if the Standard system were adopted.

33. That is, some courts are adopting their own equivalent to "Star Paging." See *supra*, p. 2-74, and *infra*, p. 4-57. The ABA has, similarly, recommended a "vendor-neutral" and "medium-neutral" citation system under which cases would be numbered sequentially as they are published, and each paragraph within a case would be numbered. See *Legal Times*, April 14, 1997, p. 6.

Sample Research Problem

You are a summer associate at the classically-named law firm of Dewey, Cheatham & Howe. The senior partner calls you into her office to give you the following problem. The client is a young software programmer named Harry Hacker, who (for reasons that will soon become obvious) can pay only a small retainer — that's why lowly you are being entrusted with doing the research on this tricky case.

Harry began work on January 2, 1995 for a software development company, Billable Hours Systems (BHS), which specializes in software packages that run on personal computers and that help a law firm handle its time-keeping and billing. In the interviews leading to Harry's being hired, the owner of BHS, Bill Daily, never mentioned that Harry would be expected to sign a non-compete agreement. Induced by the high salary and good working conditions he had been led to believe he would have at BHS, Harry resigned from his prior programming job, and accepted BHS's offer of at-will employment. Harry's prior employer was disturbed at Harry's leaving, and told him as he left, "You'd better hope the new job works out, because even if you come crawling back here I won't take you back."

After Harry had been on the BHS job for six months, Bill Daily handed him a one-page agreement, and said, "Sign this, all of our programmers have to sign it." The document turned out to be a non-competition agreement, under which Harry promised BHS that if Harry were to leave BHS' employ for any reason (even being fired without cause), Harry would not, for one year after his date of departure, write any software for use in a legal time and record keeping system, where Harry could reasonably expect that the resulting system would be sold anywhere in the United States. There were no other restrictions placed upon Harry in the document. The document also stated that in the event that Harry violated the provisions of the agreement, BHS could obtain equitable relief against him. Bill did not otherwise offer any change in the relationship in return for Harry's signing the non-compete, and Harry did not ask for any modification in the business deal. Harry reluctantly signed the document.

Harry's work for DBS involved highly-trained, but by no means unique, programming skills. When Harry did the work, it was Harry, not Bill or any other DBS employee, who figured out all technical issues, including how to program the system and how to debug the resulting software. Bill did, however, supply the "specs" which described, from the user's point of view, how this particular time and billing system should operate.

The job went along swimmingly for about 18 more months. Then, one day Harry met Dave Dobetter, the owner of a small software company that desired to bring out a better legal time and billing system. Lured by a promise of a bigger salary, Harry agreed to quit BHS and join Dobetter's company, Dobetter Systems, Inc. (DBS). Harry completely forgot that he had ever signed the non-compete with BHS, gave two weeks notice to BHS, and then turned up on DBS's payroll.

> As soon as Bill Daily found out that Harry was working for DBS, and was working on a new, competitive, legal time and billing system, Daily brought suit against Harry, Dobetter and DBS, seeking to enjoin Harry from continuing to work on the system. Harry is not convinced that DBS will adequately litigate the case (especially since DBS is annoyed at Harry for not mentioning the non-compete in the first place), so Harry has come to Dewey, Cheatham & Howe for advice.
>
> The senior partner wants you to analyze the case and its underlying issues, and find relevant precedent. All parties are located in the mythical state of Columbia, which has no relevant precedents, and no relevant statutes.

B. Approach to sample problem: Before we get into the nitty-gritty of how you can use the LEXIS service to research this problem, let me sketch out how I think you should plan on proceeding:

1. **Identify the main subject:** First, identify the main subject you're dealing with. Here, within the discipline of Contracts, we're dealing with "non-compete agreements" or "covenants not to compete".

2. **Secondary sources:** Next, go to the secondary sources. In this instance, I would (and in fact did) look at: (1) hornbooks such as Farnsworth on Contracts; (2) the Second Restatement of Contracts; (3) encyclopedias like *ALR* and *AmJur 2d*; (4) law reviews and (5) perhaps even (gasp) a law-school outline, such as the *Emanuel Law Outline* in Contracts. Of these, categories (2), (3) and (4) are available online on the LEXIS service.

   a. **Developing Boolean search terms:** My experiences in doing this first-tier research show how using secondary materials can help you come up with words and phrases that will aid you in later steps. I decided to start with a Boolean (rather than FREESTYLE) search because I wanted to limit myself to the *TITLE* segment, and there's no way to do that in FREESTYLE.

   I began my search with ALR articles, and looked (in library *2NDARY*, file *ALR*) for the two phrases that I was quite confident would produce the kind of annotation I was looking for:

   ```
   title(non-compete or non-competition)
   ```

   To my amazement, I got no documents at all. Since I didn't believe that there were no annotations on point, I broadened my search (still in *2NDARY/ALR*) to:

   ```
   title(compet!)
   ```

   This produced a lot of irrelevant citations (e.g., annotations about antitrust restraints on competition), but it also produced some relevant articles, thus showing me what I had been doing wrong — in formal legal writing, the concept of "non-compete" is much more likely to show up as "covenant against competition" or "covenant not to compete" or "agreement not to compete." Revising my search in this manner, I got some good annotations like *Enforceability of Covenant against Competition in Accountant's Employment Contract* and *Sufficiency of Consideration for Employee's*

Covenant not to Compete, Entered into after Inception of Employment. These in turn gave me both an overview of the law, as well as some good cases. Similarly, the broadened search, when applied to law reviews (library *LAWREV*, file *ALLREV*), gave me good articles like *Economic and Critical Analyses of the Law of Covenants Not to Compete* and *Involuntary Nonservitude: The Current Judicial Enforcement of Employee Covenants Not to Compete — A Proposal for Reform*. These law review articles were mostly sophisticated jurisprudential or economic analyses, but each of them had a three or four page section in which current law was summarized, with plenty of citations.

b. **FREESTYLE alternative:** Alternatively, I could explore the secondary sources with a FREESTYLE search. For instance, again in *ALR/ALR*, I could have typed:

```
Is an employee "covenant not to compete" enforceable?
```

Note my use of quotes in the FREESTYLE search, to set off something that I want to use as a phrase.

3. **List the issues and rough-out searches:** Now that you've had an overview of the law of non-competes from secondary sources, it's time to make a list of issues (and possible defenses) that are relevant. Apart from sharpening your thinking generally, this will help you decide which types of cases, out of the tens of thousands decided nationally concerning non-competes over the last 30 years, will help you the most. Here's what my list of issues would look like at this point, for our sample problem:

Issue 1: Where the employee has already been on the job for some time before he signs the non-compete, does the employer have to give separate or new consideration for the non-compete, or is it sufficient that the employer merely continues the at-will employment? (This issue was suggested to me by seeing the ALR annotation entitled *Sufficiency of Consideration for Employee's Covenant not to Compete, Entered into after Inception of Employment*.) This issue suggests Boolean searches[34] such as (in library *MEGA*, file *NEWER*):

```
(covenant not to compete) and (additional consideration or
new consideration or separate consideration)
```

Issue 2: Where an employer commissions software, and the employer furnishes user specifications to the employee (but the employee solves all technical problems without employer assistance), has the employer given the employee access to a trade secret? (I learned from my reading of the Farnsworth hornbook and the Emanuel *Contracts* outline that non-competes on employees tend to be enforced only where the employee is using confidential information/trade secrets, or is using the employer's customer lists.

34. For these issues, Boolean searches seem to work a little better than FREESTYLE searches. For instance, in the above sample search for Issue 1, there's no easy way to capture in FREESTYLE the concept of "additional consideration or new consideration or separate consideration."

Since there are no customer lists here, I realized that DBS could only win by showing Harry had access to, and was now using, trade secrets.) This issue suggested a Boolean search like (still in *MEGA/NEWER*):

```
(covenant not to compete) and trade secrets
```

Issue 3: Is a restraint on a certain type of activity that applies to the entire United States unreasonably broad? (From my secondary sources, I learned that even where the employee has had access to, and is using, trade secrets or customer lists belonging to the employer, the restraint will not be enforced unless it is reasonable in scope, both in terms of type of activity, geographical area, and duration.) This issue suggested a Boolean search like (in *MEGA/NEWER*):

```
(covenant not to compete) and unreasonable and scope and
  (time or duration)
```

4. **First pass of online case research:** Now, you should be ready to look for cases. You know that your "own'' jurisdiction (in this instance, the mythical state of Columbia) has no precedents, so you need to look at law from all around the nation. Therefore, a search in the *MEGA* library, *NEWER* file (giving us all federal and state cases decided since 1945), would be a good place to start. If we wanted to use Boolean searching,

```
covenant not to compete
```

would be a good first search. If we wanted to use FREESTYLE,

```
when is a "covenant not to compete" enforceable?
```

would be a good first search.

For each good case, use SHEPARD'S[35] and Auto-Cite[36] to find later cases that reverse, overrule, distinguish or rely on your principal case.

5. **Read the cases:** After you've found 5-10 good cases, read them to: (1) make sure you're on the right track; and (2) identify additional words and phrases to use in additional research. You can do this reading either online or offline (perhaps via a copy that you retrieve from the LEXIS service and store onto your hard disk, then print on your computer's printer).[37]

6. **Use `.more` to find more cases:** Select the most-relevant or most-representative single case of those you read in Step 5 as a "specimen" case. Then, go back online and use the `.more` ("More Like This") feature to find additional ones that resemble it.[38]

   a. **How to use `.more`:** A very brief recap of how to use `.more`: when you're looking at the specimen case, just type `.more`. You'll be given the 25 cases that are "most like"

35. See *infra*, p. 9-2.

36. See *infra*, p. 9-12.

37. See *supra*, pp. 2-82 to 2-95 for details about how to store-to-disk and print.

38. See supra, p. 2-67 for a detailed description of how to use `.more`.

your specimen case. When you're finished browsing through these, type `.em` (for "EXIT MORE") to return to "regular" (either Boolean or FREESTYLE) searching.

7. **Use new words and phrases:** Also, use the new words or phrases you found in step 5 to look for cases citing, or cited by, the new cases you found in step 5.

C. Case libraries and files on LEXIS-NEXIS:

Before we can search for cases, we've got to select an appropriate library and file.

There are literally hundreds of different case files on the LEXIS service, grouped in dozens of libraries. Here, I can give you only a brief introduction to some of the more commonly-used ones, and to the general layout of case law on the service. (For more precise information, you should obtain a copy of the *LEXIS-NEXIS Directory of Online Services*, published annually and available from your LEXIS representative.[39])

When you first log in to the services, you will see a list of all libraries, which takes two screensful. Here they are:

LIBRARIES -- PAGE 1 of 2
Please ENTER the NAME (only one) of the library you want to search.
- For more information about a library, ENTER its page (PG) number.
- To see a list of additional libraries, press the NEXT PAGE key.

NAME	PG	NAME	PG	NAME	PG	NAME	PG	NAME	PG	NAME	PG	NAME	PG	NAME	PG
General Legal						Public Records				Helps		Financial		Nexis	
MEGA	1	2NDARY	2	LAWREV	3	ALLREC	4	INSOLV	5	EASY	6	COMPNY	7	NEWS	22
GENFED	1	ALR	2	MARHUB	3	ASSETS	4	LEXDOC	5	GUIDE	6	INVEST	7	REGNWS	22
STATES	1	BNA	2	LEXREF	3	DOCKET	4	LIENS	5	PRACT	6	NAARS	7	TOPNWS	22
CODES	1	ABA	2	HOTTOP	3	FINDER	4	VERDCT	5	TERMS	6	QUOTE	7	LEGNEW	22
CITES	1	CAREER	2			INCORP	4			CATLOG	6	D&B	7	CMPGN	22
LEGIS	1	CLE	2							CUSTOM	6	BLMBRG	7	WORLD	22

Area of Law														Medical	
ACCTG	8	CORP	9	ETHICS	10	HEALTH	11	LEXPAT	12	PUBHW	13	TORTS	14	GENMED	15
ADMRTY	8	CRIME	9	FAMILY	10	IMMIG	11	M&A	12	REALTY	13	TRADE	14	EMBASE	15
ADR	8	EMPLOY	9	FEDCOM	10	INSURE	11	MILTRY	12	STSEC	13	TRANS	14	MEDLNE	15
BANKNG	8	ENERGY	9	FEDSEC	10	INTLAW	11	PATENT	12	STTAX	13	TRDMRK	14		
BKRTCY	8	ENVIRN	9	FEDTAX	10	ITRADE	11	PENBEN	12	TAXANA	13	UCC	14		
COPYRT	8	ESTATE	9			LABOR	11	PUBCON	12	TAXRIA	13				

Enter .NP for Individual States, International Law and more News information

First Page of LEXIS-NEXIS Library Listings

39. This Directory is also available online as a document in the *GUIDE* library, *GUIDE* file (see *infra*, p. 2-76) and as a Folio "infobase" which you receive as part of the LEXIS-NEXIS Office for Legal Education (see *infra*, p. 12-8).

LIBRARIES -- PAGE 2 of 2
Please ENTER the NAME (only one) of the library you want to search.
- For more information about a library, ENTER its page (PG) number.
- To see a list of additional libraries, press the PREV PAGE key.

NAME	PG	NAME	PG	NAME	PG	NAME	PG	NAME	PG	NAME	PG	NAME	PG	NAME	PG
---Individual States---								---Int'l Law---				---News---			
ALA	16	IND	16	NEB	17	RI	17	AUST	19	NILAW	20	APOLIT	23	EXEC	24
ALAS	16	IOWA	16	NEV	17	SC	17	CANADA	19	NZ	20	BUSFIN	23	GEODEM	24
ARIZ	16	KAN	16	NH	17	SD	17	COMCAS	19	PHLIPP	20	BUSREF	23	MARKET	24
ARK	16	KY	16	NJ	17	TENN	17	ENGGEN	19	SAFRCA	20	CMPCOM	23	MKTRES	24
CAL	16	LA	16	NM	17	TEX	17	EURCOM	19	SCOT	20	ENTERT	23	PEOPLE	24
COLO	16	MAINE	16	NY	17	UTAH	18	HKCHNA	19	SING	20			SPORTS	24
CONN	16	MD	16	NC	17	VT	18	IRELND	19	UK	20	---Int'l News---			
DEL	16	MASS	17	ND	17	VA	18	MALAY	19	UKCURR	20	ASIAPC	25	MDEAFR	25
DC	16	MICH	17	OHIO	17	VI	18	MEXICO	19	UKJRNL	20	DUTCH	25	NSAMER	25
FLA	16	MINN	17	OKLA	17	WASH	18			UKTAX	20	EUROPE	25	TXTLNE	25
GA	16	MISS	17	ORE	17	WVA	18	---French Language---				GERMAN	25		
HAW	16	MO	17	PA	17	WISC	18	INTNAT	21	PRIVE	21				
IDA	16	MONT	17	PR	17	WYO	18	LOIREG	21	PUBLIC	21				
ILL	16							PRESSE	21	REVUES	21			PROFIL	18

Second Page of LEXIS-NEXIS Library Listings

If you're interested in cases, the main libraries that will be of interest to you on the first screen above are *GENFED*, *MEGA* and *STATES*. (Most of the other libraries listed on the first screen are single-subject libraries that contain case law but also contain statutes, regulations, law reviews, etc.; for instance, the *ADMRTY* library contains federal and state case law, federal statutes, federal regulations, and secondary materials, all on the subject of admiralty.)

From the second screen reproduced above, you will mainly be interested in the individual state libraries (e.g., the *ALA* library for Alabama, *ALAS* for Alaska, etc.).

Now let's get an overview of what's in some of these libraries. Assuming that you know you want to search libraries and files consisting solely of case law, and ones that are not limited to single subjects, you will want to use the *MEGA*, *GENFED* and *STATES* libraries.

1. **The *MEGA*™ library:** The *MEGA* library is called by LEXIS-NEXIS the "Federal/State Case Law Combined Library,'' and is the most complete case law library on the service. The most obvious use you might make of the *MEGA* library is where you want to retrieve both state and federal case law from a single search (though you may also use it when you want to limit your research to the state and federal courts of a particular region). Appendix F-1 contains a brief explanation of some of the files contained in the *MEGA* library.

   Of the files in the *MEGA* library, the largest by far is the *MEGA* file; LEXIS-NEXIS describes the *MEGA* file as "a ***one-stop search of all available federal and state case law***.'' So at least when you are living in the wonderful cost-free world of the law student LEXIS user, and you don't care what jurisdiction cases come from, the *MEGA* file is your obvious first choice.[40]

In the *MEGA* library, each state has a file that contains all the federal district cases from that state; this file bears the name *XXDIST*, where *XX* is the state's two-letter postal abbreviation (e.g., *CADIST* for California). Also, each state has an *XXALL* file that contains all state and federal caselaw that originated from the geographic boundaries of that particular state. Additionally, you can use "custom file selection" to ***combine*** several files in the *MEGA* library to do a single search; for instance, if you wanted to search in state-court cases from Kansas, Nebraska and Missouri, as well as cases from the U.S. Supreme Court, you would specify your file as being:

KSDIST, NEDIST, MODIST, US[41]

2. **The *GENFED* library:** If you know that your research will be centered around federal case law, you should begin with the *GENFED* library. Here are the first two screens' worth of files in the *GENFED* library:

Please ENTER, separated by commas, the NAMES of the files you want to search. You may select as many files as you want, including files that do not appear below, but you must enter them all at one time. To see a description of a file, ENTER its page (PG) number.

FILES - PAGE 1 of 10 (NEXT PAGE for additional files)

NAME	PG	DESCRIP	NAME	PG	DESCRIP	NAME	PG	DESCRIP
-----COURTS GROUP FILES--			---------SUPREME COURT---------			-------------RULES--------------		
MEGA	11	Fed & State Cts	US	1	US Supreme Court	RULES	24	Federal Rules
OMNI	1	Fed Cases & ALR	USPLUS	12	US,BRIEFS,PRE-VU	----ADMINISTRATIVE-----		
COURTS	1	Fed Cases	BRIEFS	12	Argued from 9/79	ALLREG	16	FEDREG & CFR
CURRNT	1	Cases w/in 2yrs	USTRAN	12	Sup.Ct Transcripts	FEDREG	16	Fed. Register
NEWER	3	Cases from 1944	USLIST	12	Sup.Ct Summaries	CFR	16	Code of Fed.Reg
SUPCIR	1	US,USAPP & CAFC	USLW	12	US Law Week	COMGEN	14	Comp.Gen.Decs.
FED	8	CAFC,CCPA,CIT.	---------LEGISLATIVE---------			-----SECONDARY SOURCES----		
--------U.S. COURT FILES------			RECORD	19	CongRec frm 1985	SSMEGA	33	All Secondary
US	1	US Supreme Ct	BILLS	27	All Bills Files	ALR	33	ALR &L.Ed.Annos
USAPP	1	Cts of Appeal	PUBLAW	15	US Public Laws	RESTAT	33	Restatements
DIST	1	District Courts	USCODE	15	USCS & PUBLAW	EXTRA	11	In the News...
CLAIMS	2	Ct. Fed. Claims				PUBS	38	Legal Pubs

To search by Circuits press NEXT PAGE. NOTE: Only court files can be combined.

First Page of Files in *GENFED* Library

40. In the real world where you pay for LEXIS usage, the standard charge for a search in the *MEGA* file is $105.

41. Custom file selection is discussed further, *infra*, p. 4-38.

Please ENTER, separated by commas, the NAMES of the files you want to search.
You may select as many files as you want, including files that do not appear
below, but you must transmit them all at one time. To see a description of a
file, ENTER its page (PG) number.
FILES - PAGE 2 of 10 (NEXT PAGE or PREV PAGE for additional files)

NAME	PG	NAME	PG	NAME	PG	NAME	PG	NAME	PG	NAME	PG
-----------C I R & D I S T---------				------------C I R C U I T-----------				----------D I S T R I C T---------			
1ST	5	8TH	6	1CIR	9	8CIR	9	1DIST	10	10DIST	10
2ND	5	9TH	7	2CIR	9	9CIR	9	2DIST	10	11DIST	10
3RD	5	10TH	7	3CIR	9	10CIR	9	3DIST	10	DCDIST	10
4TH	5	11TH	8	4CIR	9	11CIR	9	4DIST	10	CIT	2
5TH	6	CADC	8	5CIR	9	DCCIR	9	5DIST	10	CVA	2
6TH	6	FED	8	6CIR	9	CAFC	9	6DIST	10	TC	2
7TH	6			7CIR	9	CCPA	2	7DIST	10	BANKR	2
		MILTRY	2					8DIST	10	CUSTCT	2
								9DIST	10	COMCT	2

-----------------------------CASES BY CIRCUIT AFTER 1911-------------------------------

Press NEXT PAGE for Cong. Record. Note: Only court files can be combined.

Second Page of Files in *GENFED* Library

Appendix F-2 gives a description of some of the more important files in the *GENFED* library.

3. **The *STATES* library:** Another very important library is the *STATES* library. As its name implies, it concentrates on matters of state law, mostly state case law. Here are the main case-law files located in the *STATES* library:

Please ENTER, separated by commas, the NAMES of the files you want to search.
You may select as many files as you want, including files that do not appear
below, but you must enter them all at one time. To see a description of a
file, ENTER its page (PG) number.
FILES - PAGE 1 of 12 (NEXT PAGE for additional files)

NAME	PG	DESCRIP	NAME	PG	NAME	PG	NAME	PG	NAME	PG
--------------GROUP COURT FILES--------------			-----------------------------STATE CASE LAW-------------------------							
MEGA	61	Federal & State Courts	ALCTS	1	ILCTS	16	MTCTS	30	RICTS	46
OMNI	51	State Courts & ALR	AKCTS	2	INCTS	17	NECTS	31	SCCTS	47
COURTS	61	State Courts	AZCTS	3	IACTS	18	NVCTS	32	SDCTS	48
HIGHCT	61	State Cts of Last Resort	ARCTS	4	KSCTS	19	NHCTS	33	TNCTS	49
-------------------GROUP FILES-------------------			CACTS	5	KYCTS	20	NJCTS	34	TXCTS	50
ALLCDE	61	All State Codes	COCTS	7	LACTS	21	NMCTS	35	UTCTS	52
ALLAG	61	Attorney General Ops.	CTCTS	8	MECTS	22	NYCTS	36	VTCTS	53
STTRCK	51	State Bill Tracking	DECTS	10	MDCTS	23	NCCTS	38	VACTS	54
-------------SECONDARY SOURCES------------			DCCTS	11	MACTS	24	NDCTS	39	VICTS	55
SSMEGA	64	Comb Secondary Sources	FLCTS	12	MICTS	26	OHCTS	40	WACTS	56
ALR	64	ALR & L.Ed. Annos	GACTS	13	MNCTS	27	OKCTS	41	WVCTS	57
RESTAT	64	ALI Restatements of Law	HICTS	14	MSCTS	28	ORCTS	42	WICTS	58
EXTRA	63	In the News . . .	IDCTS	15	MOCTS	29	PACTS	43	WYCTS	59

First Page of Files in *STATES* Library

If you know you need state court decisions, and don't want anything else, use the *COURTS* file within the *STATES* library. If you want just the highest court of each state, use the *HIGHCT* file. Observe that the *MEGA* file, which combines federal and state case law, exists within the *STATES* library just as it does within the *GENFED* library. For the whole set of reported case law (regardless of court) from a particular state, you have two choices: (1) you can use the *STATES* library, and the *XXCTS* state case law file (e.g., *ALCTS* for Alabama), as shown in the above screen; or (2) you can use the individual state library for the state in question, and the *XXCASE* file in that library (e.g., for Alabama cases, the *ALA* library and the *ALCASE* file).

4. **How to do some common things:** Here is a list of the more common things you might want to do, together with my suggestion for the library and file in which you can do them:

If You Want to Find...	Use this Library/File Combination:
All American case law on the LEXIS service	*MEGA/MEGA*
All federal case law	*GENFED/COURTS*
All federal case law from the Supreme Court and the Courts of Appeal	*GENFED/SUPCIR*
Federal case law from the last couple of years	*GENFED/CURRNT*
All federal case law of the modern (post-1944) era	*GENFED/NEWER*
Case law from a particular U.S. Court of Appeal	*GENFED/1CIR*, *GENFED/2CIR,* etc.
All federal cases from a particular Circuit, including cases by the Court of Appeals and the District Courts in that Circuit	*GENFED/1ST, GENFED/2ND, etc.*
All cases from any American state court	*STATES/COURTS*
All cases from a particular state	[The appropriate Individual State Legal Library] / *XXCASE*. (Example: For Alabama cases, use the *ALA* library, *ALCASE* file.)
Cases from the court of last resort of all states	*STATES/HIGHCT*
All state cases from those states located in a particular federal Circuit	*STATES/1ST, STATES/2ND,* etc. (Example: For state cases from Conn., N.Y. and Vermont, which are the states located in the federal Second Circuit, use *STATES/2ND*)

D. **Searching if you know the citation for a case:** Let's now begin our look into the actual nuts and bolts of finding cases on the LEXIS service. First, let's assume that you know some form of ***citation*** for a particular case, and you want to see the text of the case.

1. **Using the LEXSEE feature:** The easiest way to call the case up on your screen when you know one of its citations is by the use of the LEXSEE feature.

The LEXSEE feature permits you to specify a citation, and instantly see the case. Why is this better than doing a conventional LEXIS search for the cite you are interested in? There are several reasons:

- You can use the LEXSEE feature at any time after the client identification screen, even before you have selected a library and file (or if you are in a library or file different from the one you think the cited case would be found in). This lets you save yourself the bother of figuring out what library/file your case would be in.
- LEXSEE is a hypertext-like feature, in the sense that you don't "lose your place" when you use it. For example, suppose you are reading a law review article on-screen when you see that the article cites a case that you would like to read. You can use the LEXSEE feature to show you the cited case.[42] When you've done reading and/or printing the cited case, you can "resume" your regular research by typing **`res`** (or pressing the [RESUME] key (Ctrl-F5)); you will be put back in the same law review article, at the same place, you were in when you started the LEXSEE search.
- LEXSEE is astonishingly fast, typically taking less than five seconds to show you the first page of the case.
- LEXSEE is very "forgiving," in that it accepts a number of variations on the form of citation (e.g., 45 Cal App 3d 605, 45 Calapp3d 605 and 45 Cal.App.3d 605 would all be acceptable ways to enter the cite).
- The LEXSEE feature knows that you are looking for the case whose *own citation* is the one you have entered, and that you are not looking for other documents that contain in their body the citation you are looking for. (You could accomplish the same result by doing an ordinary LEXIS search limited to the Cite segment, but LEXSEE is a little more straightforward when you are trying to find the cited case itself.)

Let's now take a look at how you use the LEXSEE feature in practice. To add a quasi-realistic flavor to our exercise, let's take a case which we think is relevant to our non-compete problem, *James C. Green Co. v. Kelley*, 261 N.C. 166, 134 S.E.2d 166 (1964), which we found from reading an annotation in ALR. Here's how we would use LEXSEE to find this case:

- First, remember that you can use the LEXSEE feature no matter where you are on the LEXIS service. So it doesn't matter what library or file you are in (and you don't in fact have to be in any file at all, as long as you've already gotten past the log-in and client ID screens.)
- Type **`lexsee`** followed by the citation. You can use either an official or unofficial (e.g., West) citation. Thus for the *Green* case, you would type either:

  `lexsee 261 nc 166`

  or

42. You can also use LINK, which lets you type just a few characters (e.g., "=12") to see the cited case. See the discussion of LINK *infra*, p. 4-54.

```
lexsee 134 se2d 166
```

- You will almost immediately see the full text of the cited case, beginning with the first page. You can use any of the navigating keys to move around in the case. Thus you can use the [NEXT PAGE] key (or type **.np**), [PREV PAGE] (or type **.pp**), and [FIRST PAGE] (or type **.fp**). You can arrange to print the case with [PRINT DOC] (or type **.pd**).
- When you have done whatever you want to do with the case, you can leave LEXSEE (which is in a sense a ''mode'' that you go into and out of), and "resume" your regular research, by typing **res** (or pressing the [RESUME] key (ctrl-F5)).

I find that the biggest trick in using the LEXSEE feature successfully is to get the citation into the right form. This is not too hard to do, because the LEXSEE feature is very forgiving of stylistic variations in citation. Essentially, the rules on cites go like this:

- You must have a space between the volume number and the start of the reporter-name and you must have another space between the reporter-name and the page number:

  ```
  134 se2d 166
  ```

- You may put spaces in the middle of the words of the reporter-name, but you don't have to.
- You may put periods at the end of the words of the reporter-name, but again, you don't have to.

Thus whereas *The Bluebook* insists that the correct form for the reporter that contains federal Court of Appeals decisions is written:

```
F.2d
```

with a period after F, no period after d, and no space between the period and the ''2,'' any of the following LEXSEE citations will work:

```
435 F.2d 995
435 F2d 995
435 F. 2d. 995
435 F.2d. 995
435 F 2d 995
```

Also, case doesn't matter — **703 f.2D 1261** would work just as well as the more conventional **703 F.2d 1261**.

Appendix G contains a list of valid LEXSEE Citation Formats for case reporters and other sources.

Apart from using the LEXSEE feature to retrieve documents based upon their official or unofficial cites, you can also use LEXSEE if you know the LEXIS cite. (Remember that the LEXIS service has been assigning its own citations to case law and other materials since 1987.) Thus if you happened to have the LEXIS cite for *Morris v. Savoy* and didn't have the Ohio state or Northeastern cite, you could do the following search:

```
lexsee 1991 Ohio lexis 2117
```

By the way, you can use the LEXSEE feature not just to find cases, but most other documents on the LEXIS service that have some sort of "cite" associated with them. Law reviews and the regulatory decisions of administrative agencies are examples. (But you can't use LEXSEE to retrieve documents from the NEXIS or Public Records services.)

a. **CITES Assistant:** Instead of using "raw" LEXSEE — the method I've been discussing — you might want to use CITES Assistant, which is essentially a "prompted" version of the LEXSEE feature. Just enter `.ca` to invoke the CITES Assistant feature, and follow the online instructions when you're prompted to enter information. CITES Assistant is helpful if you're having trouble retrieving a document through LEXSEE, or if you don't recall how to use LEXSEE.[43]

E. **Segment searching:** In your arsenal of LEXIS weapons, one of the most valuable is the ability to use ***segment searching*** fluently. Nowhere is this more true than in searching for cases. Frequently, you will want to search for cases based on the names of the parties, cases decided by a particular judge, cases from a particular court, cases where a particular attorney represented one of the parties, cases decided within a certain range of dates, etc. In all of these instances, the only reliable way to get what you want is to limit your search by segment.

1. **Getting a list of the segments for a database:** Before we look at each of these situations in detail, let's examine how you can get a ***list*** of available segments for a particular database, in case you never knew or have forgotten what segments are in the database. As you would expect, the segmentation of documents varies from one file to another. When you are in a particular file, you can see a list of segments for that file by being at the new-search screen and then pressing the [SEGMTS] key (shift-F10, or type `.se`). For library *MEGA*, file *MEGA*, you get the following display:

```
The following names may be used as a segment name in your search request:

CITES          CLASSIFICATION   CONCUR       CONCURBY
COUNSEL        COURT            DATE         DISPOSITION
DISSENT        DISSENTBY        HEADNOTES    HISTORY
JUDGES         NAME             NOTICE       NUMBER
OPINION        OPINIONBY        OPINIONS     SYLLABUS
WRITTENBY

The following name may be used with the arithmetic operators:
DATE
```

As you can see, you learn the names of the segments, but you don't learn anything about what's in each segment beyond what you can glean from the name itself.

To learn more precisely what is in each segment in the current file, your best bet is to use the GUIDE feature. Type `.gu`, then select "Segment Description" (usually `=5`). You'll get a detailed explanation of the contents of each segment. You can also see a sample document (usually accessed by `=6`), broken down into its individual segments.[44]

43. CITES Assistant is discussed further, p. 9-20 *infra*.

2. **Searching on parties' names:** It will often be the case that you don't know the citation for a case, but merely know the ***names of the parties***. Examples of why you might want to do this include: (i) you want to know whether your present adversary has had cases like this, how your adversary has handled these issues in the past, whether the adversary might be collaterally stopped from taking a particular position now, etc.; (ii) you suspect that your present adversary may be a "vexatious litigant" who has brought many similar nuisance suits in the past, in which case you can use the fact of these past suits to impeach the litigant's credibility; or (iii) you represent a would-be plaintiff in a products liability context, and you don't know who made the particular instance of the product in question (e.g., a birth control pill), so you want to get the names of all companies that have been defendants in the past in suits of the type you are planning to bring. I recognize that in all of these scenarios, reported cases may represent only a small portion of total relevant suits, but reported cases still furnish a good place to start.

For any of these names-of-the-parties problems, you will want to do a segment-limited search based on the *NAME* segment.

You would think that the best way to do this would be to use the name of the case as it is commonly referred to (e.g., "*Roe v. Wade*," "*Marbury v. Madison*," "*Brown v. Board of Education*"). However, this method will rarely work to find the case bearing that name. The reason is that the *NAME* segment on the LEXIS service generally includes the full names of the parties, and their status as litigants. When you type the simplified version of the names, you will not get a hit. For instance, consider the Supreme Court's 1993 pronouncement on abortion, commonly known as "*Planned Parenthood v. Casey.*" If you do the following search:

```
name(planned parenthood v. casey)
```

you would get only a case whose name included those four words in exactly that sequence, with no intervening words or abbreviations; such a case doesn't in fact exist, so you'd get nothing. The case you want is represented on the LEXIS service with the following information in the *NAME* field:

Planned Parenthood of Southeastern Pennsylvania, et al., Petitioner 91-744 v. Robert P. Casey, et al. . . .

Therefore, what you really want to do in searching based on the names of the parties is to skip the "v.," and use only the ***one or two words for each party*** best identifying that party. Thus for *Planned Parenthood v. Casey*, here is the search I would recommend (perhaps in *GENFED/NEWER*):

```
name(planned parenthood and casey)
```

Observe that this search specifies that the word "Planned" must be next to the word "Parenthood," but that there is no specified proximity relationship between the phrase "Planned Parenthood" and the word "Casey." This might be over-inclusive (for instance,

44. For more about GUIDE see *supra*, p. 2-76.

if there were a lower court case called "*Casey v. Planned Parenthood*," it would find this case as well.)

You generally want to leave out common abbreviations like "Co.," "Corp.," "Inc." and "Comm."

You will want to use only two words in total if this gives you a fair crack at identifying the case; this will be so, for instance, if one of the two words is relatively uncommon. Thus for the case of *Pacific Mutual Life Insurance Co. v. Haslip*, a search on:

name(pacific and haslip)

in *GENFED/NEWER* will do the trick nicely, because although there may be a lot of cases with the word "Pacific" contained in the name field, there will be very few with "Pacific" found together with "Haslip." (In fact, the word "Haslip" is so rare that a search limited to U.S. Supreme Court cases — which I describe how to do below — containing the word "Haslip" in the *NAME* field would probably narrow things down enough all by itself.)

Where you have no uncommon words in the case name, you will probably want to put two or more words together as a phrase, or use the **w/** connector. Our search on **name(planned parenthood and casey)** above is one example. Another would be, to find *Pacific States Telephone & Telegraph Co. v. Oregon*:

name(pacific w/5 telephone and oregon)[45]

(If we didn't use proximity, and tried to search on this case based on two identifying words, we would probably come up with too many cases: **name(pacific and oregon)**, for instance, would almost surely be very over-inclusive.)

Another use of the *NAME* segment is to find all cases in which a particular person or entity has appeared as a litigant. If we wanted to find all cases where Toyota Motors, or its affiliates, had appeared as parties, for instance, we would search for:

name(toyota)

By the way, after you do a search on parties' names and the system tells you that you have one or more cases satisfying your search, it's often useful to use the [CITE] key (or type **.ci**) to see a brief listing of the names and cites of the cases retrieved, to quickly see which ones are relevant.[46]

3. **Search for judge:** You may wish to find all cases containing opinions written by a ***particular judge***. Some of the reasons why you might want to do this are: (i) you are going to appear before that judge, so you want to know how he/she thinks about a particular issue; (ii) you're looking for a judicial clerkship, and when you go to your interview with judge X, you want to be able to discuss some of his more interesting recent cases with him; or (iii) you're already on a judicial clerkship with judge Y, and before you draft an opinion,

45. Remember that the order of connectors is such that **w/__** "binds more tightly" than **and**, so **pacific w/5 telephone and oregon** is interpreted as **(pacific w/5 telephone) and oregon**.

46. See p. 2-32 above for a fuller discussion of CITE and other LEXIS-NEXIS display formats.

you'd like to be sure that you don't conflict with anything she has previously said in other opinions.

There are four segments in the LEXIS service's case law files that contain the names of judges: *OPINIONBY, CONCURBY, DISSENTBY* and *WRITTENBY.*

The *OPINIONBY* segment contains the name of the judge who wrote the majority opinion in the case. The *CONCURBY* segment contains the name of each judge who concurred in the court's result. The *DISSENTBY* segment contains the name of each judge who wrote a dissenting opinion. The *WRITTENBY* segment is a group segment, containing the *OPINIONBY, CONCURBY* and *DISSENTBY* segments. If you want to see all opinions by a particular judge, and you don't care whether the opinions are as author of the majority opinion, concurring or dissenting, then you would search on the *WRITTENBY* group segment.

All four of these "opinion authorship'' segments contain the judge's last name only.

Where the judge you are interested in has a very unusual last name, that last name alone will probably identify the opinions that you want. For instance, to find all opinions by Antonin Scalia (without worrying about whether the opinion was written before or after he was appointed to the Supreme Court), you could search in *GENFED/NEWER* for:

```
writtenby(scalia)
```

Where the last name is more common one, you will probably want to combine the judge's name with the court on which he or she sits. The *COURT* segment is discussed immediately below, but for now you can assume that it gives you a way to more or less identify the court you want. Thus suppose we wanted to find all cases that contain dissents by Thurgood Marshall. A search for **dissentby(marshall)** would produce dissents written by *any* judge named Marshall, regardless of what court; since the name is a common one, we would be left with many opinions by judges whose last name was Marshall but whose first name was not Thurgood. Since we don't have access to the first names, we would use the *COURT* segment to limit ourselves to the U.S. Supreme Court:

```
court(united states and supreme) and dissentby(marshall)
```

(Even this would not eliminate cases by that other great "Marshall'' on the Supreme Court, John. To do this, we would probably add a date limitation as well: **date aft 1950**, say.)

4. **Searching for opinions from a particular court:** You can use the *COURT* segment to limit your search to cases from a ***particular court***. As with the names of parties,[47] you will generally want to pick just a couple of key words, rather than trying to reproduce the entire phrase by which the court is identified in the file. Thus to retrieve cases decided by the "Court of Appeal of California, Second Appellate District, Division 2,'' the following search, done in *STATES/COURTS*, would work if you got it exactly right:

```
court(court of appeal of california second appellate
 district division 2)
```

47. See *supra*, p. 4-34.

but it would be cumbersome and prone to error. The following search (still in *STATES/COURTS*) would work just as well, require less typing, and be less susceptible to mis-typing:

```
court(appeal and california and second and division 2)
```

The ability to search by court is actually not as important as you might think, because you will frequently have the ability to choose a library and file that contain exactly the court, and only the court, you want. For instance, to limit yourself to cases from the Oklahoma Court of Criminal Appeals, you could select a large file (e.g., in the *STATES* library, the *MEGA*, *OMNI* or *COURTS* files), then search on:

```
court(oklahoma and criminal appeals)
```

But you could do this more neatly simply by selecting the *OKLA* library, and the *CRMAPP* file, which consists solely of Oklahoma Court of Criminal Appeals cases.

Nonetheless, there will be times when you cannot narrow your search to exactly the right court(s) by careful file selection, and will have to use the *COURT* segment. Here are two illustrations of when and how you might do this:

You need to find cases from:	You would search in/for
Federal District Courts for the Northern District of Illinois	*GENFED/DIST*, **court(northern and illinois)**
First or Second Department of the Appellate Division of New York State	*STATES/COURTS*, **court(new york and appellate division and first or second)**

The LEXIS service's concept of "equivalents" makes court-limited searching easier.[48] For instance, if you are interested in limiting your search to cases decided by the Eighth Circuit Court of Appeals, either of the following searches, when done in the *GENFED* library and the *USAPP* file, will do the trick:

```
court(eighth)
```

or

```
court(8th)
```

An important use of court-limited searching is where you want cases from more than one jurisdiction or region, and no database is limited to just the ones that you want. For instance, if you wanted to find federal cases from the northeastern area known as the "tristate" area (New York, New Jersey and Connecticut), you could not accomplish this by even the most careful file selection, but you could easily do it by:

48. For a list of all LEXIS equivalents, see Appendix A.

Library: **GENFED**
File: **OMNI**
Enter: **court(2nd or 3rd or new york or new jersey or connecticut)**

By the way, you ***cannot*** use the two-letter abbreviations for states when doing court-limited searches: you must use **court(connecticut)**, not **court(ct)**.

Another trick to consider is that you may be able to avoid the need for court-limited searching by ***combining*** files. For example, in both the *GENFED* and *STATES* libraries, the vast majority of files can be combined to make a "custom file selection."[49] For instance, suppose that we were researching a community property problem, and wanted to search just case law from the eight states that follow community property principles for the distribution of marital property. We could select the *STATES* library; then, in specifying our file, we could type the following entry:

AZCTS, CACTS, IDCTS, LACTS, NVCTS, NMCTS, TXCTS, WACTS

This would give us all the case law available on LEXIS from those states (not just case law from the highest court of each state), and would not require us to include a court-segment limitation on each search we do in the session.

However, don't assume that every file can be combined with every other file within a library; the on-screen file listings within a particular library will tell you which files cannot be combined with others for custom file selection; often, custom file selection will not be allowed because the two or more files you want to combine do not have the same segment layout.

5. **Searching for a particular attorney:** You will sometimes want to search for all cases in which a particular ***attorney*** or law firm appeared. Reasons you might want to do this include: (i) you will be interviewing with the firm and would like to know what sort of matters they have handled; (ii) you're going to be opposing lawyer Jones in a matter, and you'd like to get some sense of her track record and advocacy skills; or (iii) you're an in-house counsel at a corporation, and someone has suggested that your corporation retain the firm of Jones and Smith on a particular matter, and you'd like to get a sense of their expertise.

The segment you will use for this purpose is called the *COUNSEL* segment. Most of the time, the *COUNSEL* segment contains the full name of individuals who appeared, as well as the name of any firm that has appeared, including the firm of which the named individual is a partner or associate. You can count on the individual's name being rendered as: first name last name. Therefore, when searching for an individual, you should search using **pre/3**:

name(alan pre/3 dershowitz)

The use of **pre/3** lets you avoid having to worry about middle names (even the rare case

49. See *supra*, p. 1-29.

where someone has two middle names or two middle initials), yet will usually not be over-inclusive. Also, you may want to consider the possibility of using universal characters in the name. For instance, if I didn't know that Alan Dershowitz's name was spelled "Alan,"[50] I might want to search (perhaps in *MEGA/NEWER*) for:

```
counsel(al! pre/3 dershowitz)
```

The *COUNSEL* information is surprisingly comprehensive; here, for instance, is what the *COUNSEL* listings look like from the appellate case that was at the center of the movie *Reversal of Fortune*:

LEVEL 1 - 1 OF 1 CASE

State v. Claus von Bulow.

No. 82-462-C.A.

Supreme Court of Rhode Island

475 A.2d 995; 47 A.L.R.4th 455

April 27, 1984;

SUBSEQUENT HISTORY: Petition for Reargument Denied May 24, 1984

COUNSEL: Dennis J. Roberts II, Attorney General; Stephen R. Famiglietti, Assistant Attorney General; Sharon O'Keefe, Special Assistant Attorney General; Susan E. McGuirl, Deputy Attorney General, For Plaintiff

Alan M. Dershowitz, Cambridge, MA; John A. MacFadyen, III (Vetter & White), Providence; Susan Estrich/Jeanne Baker/David Fine/Joann Crispi, of counsel; Mark D. Fabiani/Stephanie Cleverdon, on brief, For Defendant

JUDGES: Murray, J. wrote the opinion. Bevilacqua, C.J., Kelleher, Weisberger,

Nonetheless, remember that a search on the *COUNSEL* field will usually turn up just reported decisions, and in the state courts, those reported decisions will generally be limited to appellate decisions.

6. **Searching by date:** Searching by the ***date*** of a decision is one of the most useful forms of segment-limitation. I have already covered the basics of date searching,[51] and I will not repeat these here. But let's take a quick look at how date searching can be used when looking for case law in particular.

If you look at the actual text of a case, you are likely to find that the date "area" contains more than one date: thus you may find a date on which the case was "argued" or "submitted" to the court, a date on which the case was "decided," and a date on which the case

50. Of course, reading sports-page coverage of Mike Tyson, or business-section coverage of Leona Helmsley, is more than enough to remind me that the spelling is "Alan." Some lawyers you search for, however, may be slightly less famous.

51. See *supra*, p. 2-24.

was "filed." The date of decision is the only one you can be certain will be present in the file. Also, the dates other than decision (date argued, date submitted, date filed) may or may not be searchable, but the date of decision is always searchable.

Only dates found in the *DATE* segment are searchable. Thus if you know that the case you are interested in mentions, in its *text*, "May 25, 1990," you may not use the **`date is`** or **`date aft`** search syntax to find that date buried in the text. Instead, you have to do an ordinary textual search, and you must write out this date-string in pretty much the way it is to be found in the case itself; thus you would search for:

```
may 25, 1990
```

not, say,

```
5/25/90
```

A date must always be ***combined*** with some other type of search operation. Thus you may not simply look for:

```
date aft december 31, 1992
```

But even an additional search criterion based on the name of the court will be enough added search information to make the request legal; thus the following search would work:

```
date aft 12/31/92 and court(kansas)
```

Observe that you can use date searching to create your own online "advance sheets" for a particular court (perhaps combined with a particular issue). Thus to see all cases decided by the Michigan Supreme Court in the last month (viewed as of the date I am writing this), I would search (perhaps in *STATES/COURTS*) for:

```
court(michigan and supreme) and date aft april 15, 1993
```

7. **Searching on a docket number:** There is one last segment which you may find occasionally useful in case law searches: the ***docket number***. The docket number is assigned by the court when the case is first filed; a typical docket number consists of a two-digit year prefix, a hyphen, and then a multi-digit number representing the case's relative position within that court's cases file that year:

no. 89-1807

for instance. The docket number is included in the LEXIS segment called *NUMBER.*

Letters rather than numbers are sometimes used in the first part of the docket number, and an abbreviation for the court or type of matter may be stuck in the middle of two numbers, such as "92 CIV. 7703." Therefore, the safest way to search for a docket number is by using the **AND** connector:

```
number(92 AND 7703)
```

By the way, if there is a hyphen, you can simply type the hyphen as if it were just another letter; thus the following search would be effective:

```
court(ohio and supreme) and number(89-1807)
```

F. **Searching by topic or issue:** So far, we've assumed that you have information pointing you to a particular case or cases. Now, let's assume that you know merely what topic or issue you want to find cases about. I'll assume that you've already done enough research (typically by use of secondary sources) so that you've crystallized your topic or issue fairly tightly; what we're now going to examine is how you turn this crystallized issue into one or more LEXIS searches, and how you use the results of one search to help you determine what the next search should be.

1. **Formulate the issue:** For starters, you will need a crisp statement of the issue. I recommend that you write out, in long-hand, without too many abbreviations or ellipses, a statement of the issue as you now see it. For instance, consider our sample non-compete problem on p. 4-22; let's assume the issue we want to research is the one arising out of the fact that our client Harry Hacker had already entered his new job, and worked there for six months, before he was essentially forced to choose between signing the non-compete and losing his job. Our issue statement might look something like this:

   When an employee, long after his employment has begun, signs a covenant not to compete, does the lack of new or separate consideration for the signing constitute a defense to the covenant's enforcement?

   Notice that I have carefully written the issue in fairly formal terms, similar to those in which a judge might couch the issue in his decision. For instance, I have used the phrase "covenant not to compete'' rather than the more informal "non-compete.'' The reason I have done this is to suggest to myself as accurately as possible what phrases or words are likely to pop up in decisions of the sort I am looking for.

2. **Formulate a rough search:** Next, you should formulate a rough version of your first search. In this step, don't worry too much about being precise, or about eliminating superfluous language — you'll have a chance to do this later.

   a. **Boolean:** If you're using Boolean searching, the rough search might look like this:

   ```
   covenant not to compete and employment and long after and
   (new or additional) w/5 consideration and defense and
   enforce!
   ```

   b. **FREESTYLE:** If you're using FREESTYLE searching, the rough search might be a variant of your hand-written search referred to in 1. above, perhaps something like:

   ```
   When an employee signs a "covenant not to compete" after
   the commencement of his employment, does the lack of "new
   consideration" or "separate consideration" constitute a
   defense to enforcement of the non-competition agreement?
   ```

3. **Edit the rough search:** Now, you should edit the rough search.

   a. **Boolean:** If you're using Boolean searching, this editing step will mean that you'll remove words or phrases that won't narrow down your pool of retrieved documents very much, or by contrast, will narrow it down too much. You will also want to remove noise words[52] from the search. Editing our rough search, we would have the following:

covenant w/3 ~~not to~~ compete and employment ~~and long after~~ and (new or additional) w/5 consideration ~~and defense and enforce!~~

I removed "not to" because these are likely to be noise words; I removed "long after" because the concept of a long passage of time between two events can be expressed in too many different ways ("long after," "sometime later," "two years later," "one year after," etc.), and I decided that it was probably easier to abandon the concept of passage of time entirely. I decided that "defense" and "enforce!" didn't narrow the results down very much, because in almost every n on-compete litigation, defenses are raised, and the enforceability of the clause is at issue. I also decided that some words or phrases needed to be added; for instance, the case might refer to an "agreement not to compete" rather than a "covenant not to compete." Similarly, a case might speak of "separate consideration" rather than "new consideration" or "additional" consideration. Therefore, my fully edited search, ready to be used online, might be:

((covenant or agreement) w/3 compet!) and ((new or additional or separate) w/3 consideration)[53]

We're now ready to run the search online. We'll run this search on the *MEGA* library, *MEGA* file, since we want federal and state cases from throughout the U.S. When we do so, here's what we get:[54]

((COVENANT OR AGREEMENT) W/3 COMPET!) AND (NEW OR ADDITIONAL OR SEPARATE) W/3 CONSIDERATION

Your search request has found 599 CASES through Level 1.
To DISPLAY these CASES press either the KWIC, FULL, CITE or SEGMTS key.
To MODIFY your search request, press the M key (for MODFY) and then the ENTER key.
For further explanation, press the H key (for HELP) and then the ENTER key.

52. See *supra*, p. 2-18.

53. Observe that I use parentheses liberally. If I had really mastered the priority of connectors, as described *supra*, p. 2-11, I might be able to construct this search without using parentheses. But I always worry that if I don't use parentheses, I won't know whether a search like: **covenant or agreement w/3 compet!** will be interpreted as **(covenant or agreement) w/3 compet!** or by contrast, as **covenant or (agreement w/3 compet!)**. (The latter is in fact how the search would be interpreted.) It just seems easier to me to use parentheses, though this is by no means the "official LEXIS-NEXIS position."

Obviously, we'd prefer not to have to read through 599 cases, so we'd better find some way to narrow the search. There are two things we can do immediately: (1) we can limit our search to cases arising in an employment context (as opposed to a sale-of-business context); and (2) we can confine ourselves to, say, the last 20 or 25 years of cases, at least until we have a better idea of what sorts of key phrases we're looking for.

b. **FREESTYLE:** If you're using FREESTYLE searching, the "edit" step will typically involve specifying Mandatory Terms and Restrictions, and perhaps adding some synonyms. Thus we might make "compete," and "consideration" Mandatory Terms. Similarly, we might add some synonyms to the main FREESTYLE search, which we do in parentheses; for instance,

> **When an employee (worker) signs a "covenant not to compete" (non-compete) after the commencement (beginning) of his employment (job), does the lack of consideration ("new consideration" "separate consideration" "fresh consideration) constitute a defense to enforcement (enforceability) of the non-competition agreement?**

4. **Narrowing things down:** Next, we'll want to narrow things down.

a. **Use the Modify key to narrow things down (Boolean):** If we're using Boolean searching, we'll now use the MODIFY feature[55] to narrow our search further. In general, you will find that the MODIFY feature is extremely useful as you go through the process of narrowing down (or occasionally, widening) your search. To modify, you type the letter **m** and then press [ENTER]. (Alternatively, you can use the [MODIFY] key, but most people simply type **m**. Notice that this is not a "dot" command — you type **m** not **.m**) . After we enter the **m** command, we get a screen like this:

```
Your search request is:
(COVENANT OR AGREEMENT) W/3 COMPET! W/15 (NEW OR ADDITIONAL OR
SEPARATE) W/3 CONSIDERATION

Number of CASES found with your search request through:
  LEVEL  1...   599

Please transmit the modification to your search request (Level 2).
REMEMBER to start your modification with a CONNECTOR.

For further explanation, press the H key (for HELP) and then the
ENTER key.
```

As you see, the service reproduces your current search, and asks you to type your

54. Throughout this whole mock search session, I have invented each search first, written it into the manuscript, and only then have I run it online. I tell you this not to impress you with my honesty, but to show you how the real-life process of online searching has many a pitfall, and the good researcher is not the one who never stumbles on the pothole, it's the one who can climb out again.

55. The MODIFY feature is discussed *supra*, p. 2-37.

modification. You only type the ''new'' portion of the search, and you must begin that with a connector (usually **`and`** but occasionally **`or`**). In this instance, we want to add our two new concepts (limiting the search to the employment context, and to cases from the last two or three decades), so we would type on the command line:

`and employ! and date aft 1970`

This narrows things down to 361 documents, still too many, but a good start.

b. FREESTYLE: If we're using FREESTYLE, we can't use Modify in quite the same way. But we can accomplish much the same thing. After browsing through the "top 25" documents retrieved by our original FREESTYLE search, we'd type **`m1`** (FREESTYLE's "modify" command), then **`=1`** in order to be able to edit our search. Also, we'd go back to the Mandatory Terms section (perhaps to make "employment" mandatory), and back to the Restrictions section (perhaps to limit ourselves to cases after 1970).

5. View some retrieved cases: Probably it's time to look at a few of these documents, to discover whether there are some good ways to narrow the population further — at this point, we're not interested in analyzing what seem to be the ''good'' cases, we're more interested in analyzing the ''bad'' cases to figure how to get rid of them.[56]

A quick navigation through the first few retrieved cases, using the CITE, FULL and KWIC[57] formats shows us one major problem immediately: we are picking up anti-trust cases, in which the court says something like, ''This agreement had an anti-competitive effect.'' A quick way to fix this is by removing **`compet!`** from our search and substituting **`compete`**, since the kinds of case we want will almost always use the word **`compete`** and will not rely on the word **`competitive`** .

To make this change in our search request, we'll ***"back modify"*** search level one. To do this, we type **`m1`** , which signifies that we want to change something in our level-one search. Then, we'll position our cursor on the "!" of "compet!", and replace it with an "e". Then, we'll put the cursor all the way to the right-most part of the search (since the system reads only what's to the left of the cursor.)[58]

At the same time, it's probably also wise to tie the ''non-compete'' portion of the opinions more tightly together with the ''new or additional or separate consideration'' portion — otherwise, we may get (and in fact seem to be getting) cases that only briefly speak about a non-compete issue (perhaps an issue from another case being cited by the court), and then discuss consideration as part of a completely separate legal issue. So we want to use a prox-

56. For the remainder of this section, we'll assume, in the interests of simplicity, that we're using only Boolean searching. If we were using FREESTYLE, one thing we might do differently is to use SuperKWIC as our "mode" of display, by typing **`.sk`**. See *supra*, p. 2-61 for more about SuperKWIC.

57. The use of these and other document-display keys in navigating through case law is discussed further *infra*, p. 4-55.

58. Back-modifying a search doesn't save any money; it costs the same as a fresh search. But it does save you from having to re-key the entire search request.

imity connector (**w/**) to link these two parts of the search. Our restated search would look something like this:

```
((covenant or agreement) w/3 compete) w/15 ((new or
additional or separate) w/3 consideration) and employ!
and date aft 1970
```

This search request, when run in library *MEGA*, file *MEGA*, retrieves 95 cases. This is a small enough number that we can hope to look at each individual case to see whether it's on point.

Now, we seem to be getting mostly the right sort of case. Here are interesting parts of two of the first few cases retrieved by this search:

1991 U.S. App. LEXIS 21736, *11
FOCUS

consideration in order to be enforced. <=15> Collier Cobb & Associates, Inc. v. Leak, 61 N.C. App. 249, 252, 300 S.E.2d 583, 585, review denied, <=16> 308 N.C. 543, 304 S.E.2d 236 (1983). In addition, "when the relationship of employer and employee is already established without a restrictive covenant, any agreement thereafter not to compete must be in the nature of a new contract based upon a new consideration." <=17> James C. Greene Company v. Kelley, 261 N.C. 166, 168, 134 S.E.2d 166, 167 (1964); <=18> Kadis v. Britt, 224 N.C. 154, 163, 29 S.E.2d 543, 549 (1944). In contrast, under Florida law, the courts have held that covenants not to compete are founded on adequate consideration despite the fact that the employee worked for the employer before [*12] signing the covenant. See <=19> Criss v. Davis, Presser & La Faye, P.A., 494 So.2d 525, 526 (Fla. Dist. Ct. App. 1986), review denied, <=20> 501 So.2d 1281 (Fla. 1986); <=21> Tasty Box Lunch Co. v. Kennedy, 121 So.2d 52 (Fla. Dist. Ct. App. 1960).

The district court found that Florida's requirement of consideration and North Carolina's requirement differed significantly. In the abstract, this is

This material shows us we're on the right track

791 F. Supp. 1280, *1286; 1991 U.S. Dist. LEXIS 20126, **17
FOCUS

covenant not to compete, after successfully obtaining the rider which allowed them to opt out of the covenant if they resigned their positions before November 19, 1989. The defendants were [*1287] told they would not be paid unless they signed this agreement.

4) In addition to the non- ...

... [*1287] [**18] rights it may then have in relation to such misconduct.

. . .

Although the Ohio Supreme Court has not ruled on the issue, it appears to be settled law in Ohio that a promise of continued employment, standing alone, does not provide consideration for a promise not to compete. E.g., <=23> Prinz Office Equipment Co. v. Pesko, 1990 Ohio App. LEXIS 367 (1990); <=24> Cohen & Co. v. Messina, 24 Ohio App. 3d 22, 25, 492 N.E.2d ...

Again, we're on the right track

6. **Storing-to-disk cases or screens:** These cases, and others that are part of the 95 cases we retrieved with the most recent search, seem to be enough on point that they're worth capturing in hard copy. We might want to store-to-disk the entire text of some of these cases, if they seem very much on point; to do so, we would probably use the [PRINT DOC] key.[59] Or, we might just find one or two screensful of interest; for instance, we might see a statement of law that looks interesting, even though the case itself is not too much on point. If so, we might use [PRINT SCREEN] to capture just that screenful.[60]

7. **Pick up new words and phrases:** One very important thing we would like to do now is to pick up ***additional words and phrases*** that can be the basis for additional searches, or for modifications to our existing search. For instance, recall that we did not really capture the concept of a non-compete signed after the employee had already been on the job for some time. Looking at our first few cases, which discuss this issue, we see some good phrases that help encapsulate this concept:

    employment relationship was already established

    continued at-will employment

    outset of employment

    mid-employment

    We might, for instance, take the search that we last used above, and modify it with the following line:[61]

    ```
    and (employment w/10 (already established) or continued
    or outset or mid)
    ```

    So our search now looks like this[62]:

    ```
    ((covenant or agreement) w/3 compete) w/15 ((new or
    additional or separate) w/3 consideration))
    and date aft 1970 and (employment w/10
    already established or continued or outset or mid)
    ```

    When we make this modification, and again run the search against *MEGA* library, *MEGA* file, we see that our 95 cases are now whittled down to 43, a number that can be comfortably read in one sitting. Inspection of these cases show that a very high percentage of them are just what we want: cases about workers who are already on the job when they are given a non-compete document and told that they must sign it in order to keep their jobs, but are

59. See the fuller discussion of PRINT DOC *supra*, p. 2-83.

60. See the full treatment of PRINT SCREEN *supra*, p. 2-87.

61. Again, for simplicity we'll assume that we're using only Boolean searching. If we were using FREESTYLE, we'd edit the search in the way described on p. 2-52, but the general strategy would be the same.

62. Don't worry about whether you can enter such a long search into LEXIS. You can type multiple lines' worth of a search; just keep typing on the command line, and your search will "wrap" from one line to the next. The wrapping may occur in the middle of a word, but don't worry about this either. LEXIS-NEXIS recommends that you try to keep your searches to no more than three lines (though you'll note that I didn't do this in the final version of the search above).

given no other consideration for signing it. Our search (though it looks kind of unwieldy) is now so on point that we might go further back in time, by relaxing our **`date aft 1970`** limitation.

This relatively-successful search illustrates two things: (1) to really capture the "good" cases and eliminate the "bad" ones, you will often have to come up with a much more sophisticated, and lengthy, search than you ever thought at the outset that you would need; and (2) you'd better learn to use parentheses for such complex searches, or you'll never be able to figure out how the system is interpreting your search.

8. **Use the FOCUS feature (Boolean and FREESTYLE):** The FOCUS feature can be extremely useful, especially when you are taking an online look at cases or other documents that you have retrieved through a complex, multi-word search. You'll recall[63] that the FOCUS feature lets you take the results of a search request, and then choose which words you want to highlight. Remember that to use FOCUS, you do your search, get your list of documents, and then type **`.fo`** or press the [FOCUS] key. You then use basically standard LEXIS search syntax to indicate which words you would like to see highlighted.

You can, and should, use FOCUS whether you got your search results by Boolean searching or by FREESTYLE. FOCUS works exactly the same way whichever of these two search methods you're using.

In the case of our non-compete problem, our search statement is so complicated, and uses so many common words, that trying to zero in on the key portion of each opinion is very difficult — for instance, we can be sidetracked by a blizzard of highlighted occurrences of words like "employment" or "employee" or "agreement." The words that will really help us identify whether a particular retrieved case is on point will tend to be the words "compete" and "consideration." So we can type **`.fo`**, and then the words:

```
compete or consideration
```

Since these words were already used in our search statement, the system not surprisingly tells us that all 43 of our prior retrieved documents satisfy the FOCUS request. (But if we had used words in our FOCUS statement that were *not* part of our original search request, as FOCUS lets us do, then probably not all of the 43 originally-retrieved documents would satisfy the FOCUS request.) Now, when we look through each document in FOCUS format (which behaves similarly to KWIC format), the only highlighting we will see will be of the words "compete" and "consideration," and the only chunks of text we will see are those chunks that happen to contain either of these words.

63. See the discussion of FOCUS *supra*, p. 2-41.

1987 U.S. Dist. LEXIS 6929, *8

FOCUS

Nor would granting Defendants leave to amend their answer unfairly prejudice Plaintiffs. Even if Plaintiff did not initially know of Defendants' lack of consideration argument, Plaintiff obviously knew of the defense by the time it addressed the equitable claims in its post-trial brief, as Plaintiff specifically referred to the issue. Plaintiff cannot now complain of prejudice, as it chose to refrain from addressing the defense by arguing that it had been waived. Thus, Defendants may amend their answer to assert lack of

Defendants' lack of consideration claim is based on the fact that Mr. Halmi did not sign the agreement until fifteen years after his initial employment. The confidentiality agreement at issue is akin to the situation where a covenant not to compete is signed in mid-employment. See <=8> Henry Hope X-Ray Products, Inc. v. Marron Carrel, Inc., 674 F.2d 1336, 1342 (9th Cir. 1982) (Court relied upon cases involving covenants not to compete to determine viability of anti-competition agreement). Several courts have held that a restrictive covenant will fail absent new consideration if it is not signed at the outset of employment. Hollingsworth [*9] <=9> Solderless Terminal Co. v. Turley,

Only "compete" and "consider-ation," not other search words, are highlighted after we run FOCUS

Notice that in the above example, the word "employment," and the phrases "mid-employment" and "outset of employment," are not highlighted, even though they were part of the search request. Notice also how much easier it will be to see whether the case is really on point.

9. **Use universal characters freely:** When you are doing research for cases, you should use ***universal characters*** freely. Recall that the two universal characters in the LEXIS service are the `*` (to represent a single missing character) and the `!` (to represent any number of additional characters at the end of a word root).[64] So, for instance, in our above search session, we used **`employ!`** — the concept of an employment relationship might be expressed by the word "employment," or by the fact that the defendant was an "employee"; use of the exclamation point universal character saves us from having to figure out which is being used by the underlying case.

10. **Using the ATLEAST command (Boolean):** If you're using Boolean searching, make extensive use of the **`ATLEAST`** command.[65] This will help you limit your search to those documents which, because they have the highest number of occurrences of your search words, are the most likely to be relevant. The best use of **`ATLEAST`** is in conjunction with the FOCUS and MODIFY features. For instance, after we found our 43 documents as a result of our refined search on p. 4-46 above, we could look at the very most relevant ones by adding the following refinement:

64. See the more extensive discussion of universal characters *supra*, p. 2-21.

65. In FREESTYLE, you can't use ATLEAST. However, because the way FREESTYLE works is to give you the "most relevant" documents first, and because relevance is determined by how many times the various search terms occur, you're getting much the same "find me the most occurrences" functionality automatically through FREESTYLE as you get "manually" by using ATLEAST in a Boolean search.

```
focus atleast 10 (compete and consideration)
```

which would show us just those documents, from the original 43, in which both the word "compete" and the word "consideration" occur at least 10 times — these are likely to be the most relevant documents of the 43.

G. **Finding other cases related to your principal case:** Now, let's suppose that you have identified one or more cases as "key" or "principal" cases for your problem. You'll want to use this key case to do three things: (1) find cases that cite your key case; (2) find additional cases that are "like" your key case; and (3) look at the cases cited by your key case.

1. **How to find cases citing your principal case:** How do you find cases citing your principal case? The LEXIS service lets you do this in two quite distinct ways: (1) using the LEXIS service's own LEXCITE® feature; and (2) using two third-party "citator" tools, SHEPARD'S and Auto-Cite.

   a. **LEXCITE:** The LEXCITE feature lets you find all cases (as well as other types of documents) that contain a given citation. That is, you tell LEXCITE the citation for your principal case, and it will find every other case that, in its body, cites your principal case. You can then browse through these other cases using the familiar display formats (KWIC, FULL, etc.).

   Because the LEXCITE feature is essentially just another search connector, you can combine LEXCITE with other connectors. Thus to find cases citing *Roe v. Wade*, 410 U.S. 113, but only if the citing case was decided after 1992 and mentions "viability", we could do the following search:

   ```
   lexcite (410 us 113) and date aft 1992 and viability
   ```

   An especially valuable attribute of the LEXCITE feature is that it will find not only cases citing your principal case by whichever citation you give to LEXCITE, but also those cases that cite your principal case by ***any parallel citation*** (even if the citation you give to LEXCITE does not appear anywhere in the citing case). For example, let's suppose that my principal case is a U.S. Supreme Court case decided six months ago, for which I have only the U.S. Law Week cite: 59 U.S.L.W. 4251. I type:

   ```
   lexcite (59 uslw 4251)
   ```

   The service gives me back every case in my current library/file citing the case of *Feist Publications, Inc. v. Rural Telephone Service Co.* (the case published at 59 U.S.L.W. 4251), even if the citing cases use the U.S., S.Ct. or L.Ed.2d forms of citation and not the U.S.L.W. form.

   In fact, the LEXCITE feature is smart enough to be able to handle virtually ***any*** citation under which a case is published anywhere; thus you can give LEXCITE a special-purpose looseleaf citation, and it will usually work. Two examples:

   `lexcite (44 e.p.d. P37,400)` (retrieves the appropriate case from the CCH Employment Practices Decisions looseleaf reporter).

   `lexcite (fed.sec.l.rep. P960,633)` (retrieves the appropriate case from the CCH Federal Securities Law Reporter looseleaf).

By and large, the abbreviations recognized by the LEXCITE feature are the same as those recognized by the LEXSEE feature; therefore, you can use Appendix G (LEXSEE Citation Formats) as a guide as to how to enter your LEXCITE request. (LEXCITE can find not only references to cases, but also references to other legal documents, including law review articles, agency decisions and *Federal Register* documents.)

By the way, a new feature called ***"Automatic Citation Recognition"*** now makes it even easier to use LEXCITE. You don't actually have to use the word "LEXCITE" in your search — whenever you enter a citation as part of your cite, the LEXIS service automatically recognizes it as a citation, and converts it to a LEXCITE search. Thus for the first search given in this section, on p. 4-49, we could simply have entered:

```
410 us 113 and date aft 1992 and viability
```

The service will interpret this exactly as if our search had contained the words **`lexcite(410 us 113)`**.

Observe that LEXCITE will find you even ***unreported*** cases citing your principal case, provided that the unreported case is present on the LEXIS service, and is present in the file that you are logged into at the time you issue the LEXCITE request. Thus the many thousands of otherwise unreported federal district court cases, for instance, are available to you as they would not be with other citator methods (e.g., SHEPARD'S, whether the hard-copy or the online version.)

Since you often will not know what jurisdiction the cases citing your principal case will be from, you will cast the widest net if you use the biggest file, which will always be *MEGA* (found in either the *MEGA* library or the *GENFED* library).

b. The third-party citators (SHEPARD'S and Auto-Cite): Of the methods of finding cases that cite your principal case, LEXCITE casts the widest net — it will retrieve more cases (as well as other types of documents) containing the requested citation than any other method I know of. But the LEXCITE feature is also the least critical method: it tells you nothing about ***how*** the case was cited, and you must do a lot of work on your own to figure out which of the citing cases is relevant to the point you were researching. By contrast, two third-party citators available on the LEXIS service, SHEPARD'S and Auto-Cite, give you some critical analysis of the citing cases, but their net is somewhat less wide. We discuss these two citators in much greater detail later in this book.[66] So for now we will only touch on their features.

i. SHEPARD'S: SHEPARD'S is the more comprehensive of the two third-party citators. Essentially, it will show you every reported case, law review article and ALR annotation that cites the case you give it. It is more analytical than LEXCITE in that for some cases, it tells you *how* your principal case was cited, by giving you words, chosen by the SHEPARD'S editors, to describe the cited case's treatment

66. See *infra*, p. 9-2 for SHEPARD'S and *infra*, p. 9-12 for Auto-Cite.

within the citing case (e.g., "criticized," "distinguished," "explained," "followed," "overruled," etc.). Additionally, SHEPARD'S is extremely good at showing the ***history*** of your principal case, both its history before the opinion you are starting from and its history after your opinion (especially critical if you want to be sure that your case was not reversed on appeal).

You can access the online version of SHEPARD'S from pretty much anywhere within the LEXIS service. At the command line, you type **shep** or **sh** followed by the citation of the case you want to SHEPARDIZE. Assume, for instance, that you were in the *MEGA* library, *MEGA* file, and had just discovered the principal case (at least for purposes of our non-compete problem) of *James C. Greene & Co. v. Kelley*, 261 N.C. 166 (1964). From the command line, you would type:

shep 261 nc 166

The service will then give you a choice of what types of citing references you'd like to see:

```
33 Citing References
James C. Greene Co. v. Kelley, 261 N.C. 166, 134 S.E.2d 166 (1964)
SHEPARD'S Signal: Caution - Possible negative treatment
------------------------------------------------------------------------
<=1> or <ENTER> Show All Citing References and Parallel Cites

<=2> Show References with Negative Analyses
Available Analyses: Distinguished

<=3> Show References with Positive Analyses
Available Analyses: Followed

<=4> Show References with ANY Analysis

<=5> Restrict References by Jurisdiction, Analyses, Headnote, or Date

<=6> Exit SHEPARD'S Citations

<=7> Help
```

If you want the fullest treatment — all citing references (whether the analysis of our case is positive or negative), plus all parallel cites — you would type **=1**. If you did so, here is the first screen of references you'd get:

Double-clicking on this LINK will take you to the citing case

Shows how the citing case handled the cited case (e.g., "Distinguished" or "Followed")

```
Copr. 1997 Shepard's
                33 Citing References
Citations to: James C. Greene Co. v. Kelley, 261 N.C. 166, 134 S.E.2d 166
(1964)
SHEPARD'S Signal: Caution - Possible negative treatment
Restricted:  No Restrictions
Double-click on a number or enter an equal sign followed by the number.
<=1> Restrictions  <=2> Show Negative Refs  <=3> Exit SHEPARD'S  <=4> Help
---------------------------------------------------------------------------
North Carolina
 Triangle Leasing Company Inc. v. McMahon, 327 N.C. 224
  <=10> p.228, Headnote: 2
 Whittaker General Medical Corp. v. Daniel, 324 N.C. 523
  <=11> p.527, Headnote: 3
 Engineering Associates Inc. v. Pankow, 268 N.C. 137
  <=12> p.139, Headnote: 2
 James C. Greene Co. v. Arnold, 266 N.C. 85
  <=13> Distinguished p.88, Headnote: 2
 Leonard v. Baker's Shoe Store Inc., 261 N.C. 781
  <=14> Followed p.781, Headnote: 2
 Milner Airco Inc. of Charlotte North Carolina v. Morris, 111 N.C. App. 866
  <=15> p.869
```

You can decide to display only "Negative References" (by typing **=2** at the above screen); in that case, you'll see just those citing cases that have handled the cited case by distinguishing it, criticizing it, questioning it, or, most drastically, overruling it.

Alternatively, you can choose to see only "Positive Analyses" (choice **=5** from the original menu). Most notably, this will give you any cases that have "Followed" your cited case.

Additionally, there are various customization options. We discuss SHEPARD'S in greater detail beginning on p. 9-2 below.

After you've viewed and/or printed whatever you want in SHEPARD'S, you can return to the exact place you left off in the LEXIS service by typing **=3** [ENTER] (which brings you to the "Resume Options" screen), followed by **=2** .

ii. Auto-Cite: Auto-Cite does not purport to give you every case or other authority citing your principal case. But when a citation to your case has been written up by the people who prepare Auto-Cite (the editors at Lawyer's Cooperative Publishing), they frequently tell you a little more than SHEPARD'S does about the way in which your principal case is discussed in the citing case. Also, Auto-Cite skips those cases that merely include your principal case as a string cite, and focuses on those citing cases that discuss, negatively, the merits of your principal case.

As with SHEPARD'S, you can be essentially anywhere in the system at the time you issue a SHEPARD'S request. To issue an Auto-Cite request for *International Shoe Co. v. Washington*, 326 U.S. 310 (1945), we would type, from the command line (without worrying about what library or file we were in):

```
ac 326 us 310
```

Auto-Cite responds with the following as the first of a number of screens:

Auto-Cite (R) Citation Service, (c) 1993 Lawyers Cooperative Publishing

326 US 310: Screen 1 of 15

CITATION YOU ENTERED:

International Shoe Co. v. Washington*1, 326 U.S. 310, 90 L. Ed. 95, 66 S. Ct. 154, 161 A.L.R. 1057 (1945)

SUBSEQUENT TREATMENT HISTORY:

(among conflicting authorities noted in United States v. Ten Thousand Dollars ($10,000.00) in United States Currency, 860 F.2d 1511, 1988 U.S. App. LEXIS 14846 (9th Cir. Cal. 1988)

(disagreed with by United States v. One Lot of $25,721.00 in Currency, 938 F.2d 1417, 1991 U.S. App. LEXIS 15245, 20 Fed. R. Serv. 3d (Callaghan) 1152 (1st Cir. Mass. 1991)))

Alternate presentation formats are available.
For further explanation, press the H key (for HELP) and then the ENTER key.
To return to LEXIS, press the EXIT SERV key.

Observe that Auto-Cite seems to be giving us some real editorial analysis, describing the way in which the citing cases have discussed *International Shoe*.

As with SHEPARD'S, when you've finished using Auto-Cite, you can return to the exact place you were in in the LEXIS service by typing `res` (for "resume").

2. **Finding more cases like your central case (`.more`):** Now, let's move to the second task we'd like to perform with our central case: finding additional cases that resemble it. Here, we use the powerful new "`.more`" feature.[67]

To do this, all we need to do is to be looking at the central case. Then, we type `.more` . The system will now generate a new FREESTYLE search (whether we've been using Boolean or FREESTYLE searching up to this point), which will include elements from our most recent "hand-made" search, plus elements that the computer has determined characterize the specimen case. We then can (but need not) edit this "machine-generated" search before running it.

Keep in mind that when your central document is a case,[68] `.more` will always make the cite of that case one of the search terms. If you've already followed step 1 above — that is, you've used specialized tools like LEXCITE and SHEPARD's to find cases citing your

67. See supra, p. 2-67 for a more detailed discussion of `.more`.

68. `.more` can also be used with central documents that are not cases, such as newspaper articles or public record documents.

central case — you probably won't want **`.more`** to include the cite, because you'll be traversing old ground.[69]

3. **How to find cases cited by your central case:** Finally, let's use the LEXIS service to immediately lay our hands on cases that are ***cited*** by our central case. Here, we have two approaches: the LINK™ and LEXSEE features.

   a. **When you're looking at the central case, use LINK:** If you are already looking at the central case, the LINK feature is by far the best way to get to any case cited in the central case. You'll recall[70] that LINK is a form of hypertext, introduced by LEXIS-NEXIS in 1993. You use LINK by clicking on those **`<=1>`** symbols that are scattered throughout cases.

   Let's suppose we're looking at a screenful of our central case, *James C. Greene & Co. v. Kelley*:

261 N.C. 166, *168; 134 S.E.2d 166, **167 LEXSEE

of law, made out a complete defense.

The courts generally have held that restrictive covenants not to engage in competitive employment are in partial restraint of trade, and hence to be enforceable they must be (1) in writing, (2) supported by a valid consideration, and (3) reasonable as to terms, time, and territory. Failure in either requirement is fatal. <=2> Exterminating Co. v. Griffin, 258 N.C. 179, 128 S.E. 2d 139; <=3> Asheville Associates v. Miller, 255 N.C. 400, 121 S.E. 2d 593; <=4> Welcome Wagon v. Pender, 255 N.C. 244, 120 S.E. 2d 739; <=5> Paper Co. v. McAllister, 253 N.C. 529, 117 S.E. 2d 431; <=6> Thompson v. Turner, 245 N.C. 478, 96 S.E. 2d 263; <=7> Ice Cream Co. v. Ice Cream Co., 238 N.C. 317, 77 S.E. 2d 910; <=8> Sonotone Corp. v. Baldwin, 227 N.C. 387, 42 S.E. 2d 352; <=9> Kadis v. Britt, 224 N.C. 154 29 S.E. 2d 543, 152 A.L.R. 405.

Links to cited cases

It is generally agreed that mutual promises of employer and employee furnish valuable considerations each to the other for the contract. However, when the relationship of employer and employee is already established without a restrictive covenant, any agreement thereafter not to compete must be in the nature of a new contract based upon a new consideration. <=10> Kadis v. Britt, supra. Therefore, the employer could not call for a covenant not to compete without compensating for it.

Help Quit Auto-Cite Shepards LEXSEE LEXSTAT FOCUS

   We'd like to look at *Welcome Wagon v. Pender*, 255 N.C. 244. If you're using the Windows version of the LEXIS Research Software, you can simply double click on the **`<=4>`** symbol on the screen, and the service will show you the first page of the *Welcome Wagon* case. (If you're using the MS-DOS or Mac versions, you just type **`=4`** .)

69. You can instruct **`.more`** to drop the cite from the FREESTYLE search that **`.more`** generates, by using **`.more`**'s edit feature. See supra, p. 2-69.

70. See *supra*, p. 1-12 for an introduction to the LINK feature.

We can then navigate through this case using NEXT PAGE (or **.np**), PREVIOUS PAGE (or **.pp**), etc.; we can print it, and do various other document-level tasks. One of the best features of LINK is that it "saves your place'': we can get back to where we were (looking at *James C. Greene v. Kelley*) by entering **res** (for "RESUME"), or **.es** (for "EXIT SERVICE).[71]

By the way, if you don't want to display the LINK markers at all times, you can toggle them off and on by typing **.linkoff** and **.linkon** .

b. **LEXSEE:** If you are not looking at the central case, but have one or more citations for which you would like to see the case, you'll want to use the LEXSEE feature. I've discussed this feature extensively at other places in this book,[72] so I won't repeat the discussion here. Suffice it to say that no matter what library or database you are in, you can instantly see the full text of any case by typing **lexsee** followed by the citation. Thus to find the *Welcome Wagon* case even if we weren't looking at a citation to that case, we would just type:

```
lexsee 255 nc 244
```

To leave the LEXSEE feature, and get back to where you were at the time you used it, you can press the [EXIT SERV] key or type **.es** .

V. DISPLAYING CASES AND PRINTING THEM

A. **Displaying cases:** Once you've done a search that has produced a manageably-small number of cases, you'll of course want to look at those cases. Recall that there are five main display formats on LEXIS: CITE, KWIC, FULL, VAR KWIC and SEGMENTS.[73] In addition, if you've done a FREESTYLE search, you can use the SuperKWIC display format.

1. **Some tips on displaying:** Let's look at how you can best use these formats in looking through cases. Here are some tips from my practical experience:

a. **Start with CITE:** Start by using CITE (the [CITE] key or **.ci**). The CITE display will give you the names of the parties, the court and the date, and you will be able to see multiple cites at once:

---

71. This assumes that we got *James C. Greene v. Kelley* by means of an ordinary LEXIS search. If we got it through the LEXSEE feature, and we then used LINK to go to a different case, entering **res** or **.es** will not return us to *Greene*, but will instead put us back to wherever in the LEXIS service we were when we used LEXSEE.

72. See, e.g., p. 4-30 *supra*.

73. See the full discussion of each of these formats *supra*, p. 2-32 *et seq*.

LEVEL 1 - 493 CASES

1. FEDERAL TRADE COMMISSION v. SUPERIOR COURT TRIAL LAWYERS ASSOCIATION ET AL.,
No. 88-1198, SUPREME COURT OF THE UNITED STATES, 493 U.S. 411; 110 S. Ct. 768; 1990 U.S. LEXIS 638; 107 L. Ed. 2d 851; 58 U.S.L.W. 3468; 58 U.S.L.W. 4145; 1990-1 Trade Cas. (CCH) P68,895, October 30, 1989, Argued, January 22, 1990, * Decided * Together with No. 88-1393, Superior Court Trial Lawyers Association et al. v. Federal Trade Commission, also on certiorari to the same court.

2. COPPERWELD CORP. ET AL. v. INDEPENDENCE TUBE CORP., No. 82-1260, SUPREME COURT OF THE UNITED STATES, 467 U.S. 752; 104 S. Ct. 2731; 1984 U.S. LEXIS 115; 81 L. Ed. 2d 628; 52 U.S.L.W. 4821; 1984-2 Trade Cas. (CCH) P66,065, December 5, 1983, Argued, June 19, 1984, Decided

3. UNITED STATES v. GRINNELL CORP. ET AL., No. 73, SUPREME COURT OF THE UNITED STATES, 384 U.S. 563; 86 S. Ct. 1698; 1966 U.S. LEXIS 2988; 16 L. Ed. 2d 778; 1966 Trade Cas. (CCH) P71,459; 1966 Trade Cas. (CCH) P71,789, March 28-29, 1966, Argued, June 13, 1966, Decided * * Together with No. 74, Grinnell Corp. v. United States, No. 75, American District Telegraph Co. v. United States, No. 76, Holmes Electric Protective Co. v. United States and No. 77, Automatic Fire Alarm Co. of Delaware v. United States, also on appeal from the same court.

4. FEDERAL TRADE COMMISSION v. CEMENT INSTITUTE ET AL., No. 23, SUPREME COURT OF THE UNITED STATES, 333 U.S. 683; 68 S. Ct. 793; 1948 U.S. LEXIS 2709; 92 L.Ed.

You would be surprised how often you can tell that a case is probably irrelevant just by looking at its display as this appears in CITE. In the above screen, for instance (which was retrieved by my first search for cases on the topic of non-competes), I immediately suspected that any case involving the Federal Trade Commission probably was not relevant, so I didn't need to read further in the first or fourth case on the above screen.

b. Go from CITE to KWIC: Starting from the CITE display, I usually find it best to take the next look at a case in KWIC (Key Word In Context) format. LEXIS makes this especially easy to do from the CITE display: you just type the number of the case, followed by [ENTER]. Thus if I were looking at the above screen, and wanted to see the second case (the *Copperweld* case), I would merely type:

2 [ENTER]

The case is then immediately shown in KWIC format. Recall that KWIC shows you some summary information (for a case, it shows you the names of the parties, the docket number, the court, the citations, the date and the disposition), and then shows you 25 words on either side of any "hit."[74] If you're looking at a case, this gives you a pretty good sense of context. Thus for our favorite case of *James C. Greene v. Kelley*, if we searched for

74. For all LEXIS-NEXIS databases, KWIC shows you 25 words on either side. But for the MEDIS®, NEXIS, LEXIS® Financial Information™ and NAARS Services, KWIC shows you 15 words on either side.

`already established w/15 compete`

the first screen of the KWIC display for this case would look as follows:

```
LEVEL 2 - 2 OF 2 CASES

JAMES C. GREENE COMPANY, a North Carolina Corporation v.
L. E. KELLEY, JR.

No. 461

Supreme Court of North Carolina

261 N.C. 166; 134 S.E.2d 166

January 17, 1964, Filed

DISPOSITION: Affirmed.

OPINION:

... [*168] [**167] N.C. 154 29 S.E. 2d 543, 152 A.L.R. 405.

It is generally agreed that mutual promises of employer and employee furnish
valuable considerations each to the other for the contract. However, when the
relationship of employer and employee is already established without a
restrictive covenant, any agreement thereafter not to compete must be in the
```

Search words are shown highlighted

c. **Look at good cases in FULL:** Once you have a case displayed in KWIC that merits closer review, then, of course, you probably want to look at it in FULL format. The nice thing about the interaction between KWIC and FULL is that if you're in KWIC looking at the particular chunk of material that interests you, and you press FULL, the display starts off at the same place you were in in KWIC.

   I rarely find much use, at least in case-viewing, for the VAR KWIC and SEGMENTS formats.

2. **Moving around within a document:** You will also, of course, need to move around within a given document. For the most part, it will be obvious how to do this. You can use the [NEXT PAGE] (type **`.np`**), [PREV PAGE] (**`.pp`**) and [FIRST PAGE] (**`.fp`**) keys. When you are in KWIC format, the [NEXT PAGE] key brings you to the next screenful that contains a hit, which may be many pages of underlying information away from where you were when you pressed the key.

   a. **Star Paging:** One important aid in moving around within a case is the ***Star Paging*** feature. Star Paging permits you to move directly to a particular page number of the case; "page number'' is interpreted by reference to the pagination that occurred in the original hard-copy reporter.

   Let's suppose that you have consulted a source that cites to: *Harper & Row v. Nation Enterprises*, 105 S.Ct. 2218, 2237. You would like to be able to find not only this case on the LEXIS service, but that *particular page* (2237). If you're thinking like a computer programmer (God help you if you are), you'll realize that there is no necessary correspondence between screensful and hard-copy pages, so there would ordinarily be no way to find exactly those words which appeared on page 2237 of 105 S.Ct. But the LEXIS service has inserted into all case law ''Star Paging'' for all major reporters.

Here's how we would go about seeing 105 S.Ct. 2237. First, we would get the appropriate case up on the screen, probably by doing a LEXSEE search for the basic citation, 471 U.S. 539 or 105 S.Ct. 2218. The first screenful of the case looks like this:

LEVEL 1 - 1 OF 1 CASE

HARPER & ROW, PUBLISHERS, INC., ET AL. v. NATION ENTERPRISES ET AL.

No. 83-1632

SUPREME COURT OF THE UNITED STATES

471 U.S. 539; 105 S. Ct. 2218; 1985 U.S. LEXIS 17; 85 L. Ed. 2d 588; 53 U.S.L.W. 4562; 225 U.S.P.Q. (BNA) 1073; 11 Media L. Rep. 1969

U.S., S.Ct. and LEXIS cites, listed in that order

November 6, 1984, Argued
May 20, 1985, Decided

PRIOR HISTORY: [***1]

CERTIORARI TO THE UNITED STATES COURT OF APPEALS FOR THE SECOND CIRCUIT.

DISPOSITION: <=1> 723 F.2d 195, reversed and remanded.

Help Quit Auto-Cite Shepards LEXSEE LEXSTAT FOCUS

Looking at the citations at the beginning of the case, we see that the U.S. cite is given first, the S.Ct. cite is given second and the LEXIS cite is given third. The order of the citation types determines the number of stars we use in Star Paging. Thus since the U.S. cite is listed first, we would get to any page by typing **p****nnn***, where nnn is the page number in the U.S. cite we're looking for. We get to any page of the S.Ct. cite by typing **p******nnn***, and to any page number of the LEXIS cite by typing **p***nnn**. Thus to find page 2237 of S.Ct., we would type on the command line:

```
p**2237
```

The service will immediately move us to the correct page, and will in fact put the beginning of that hard-copy page on the top of our screen:

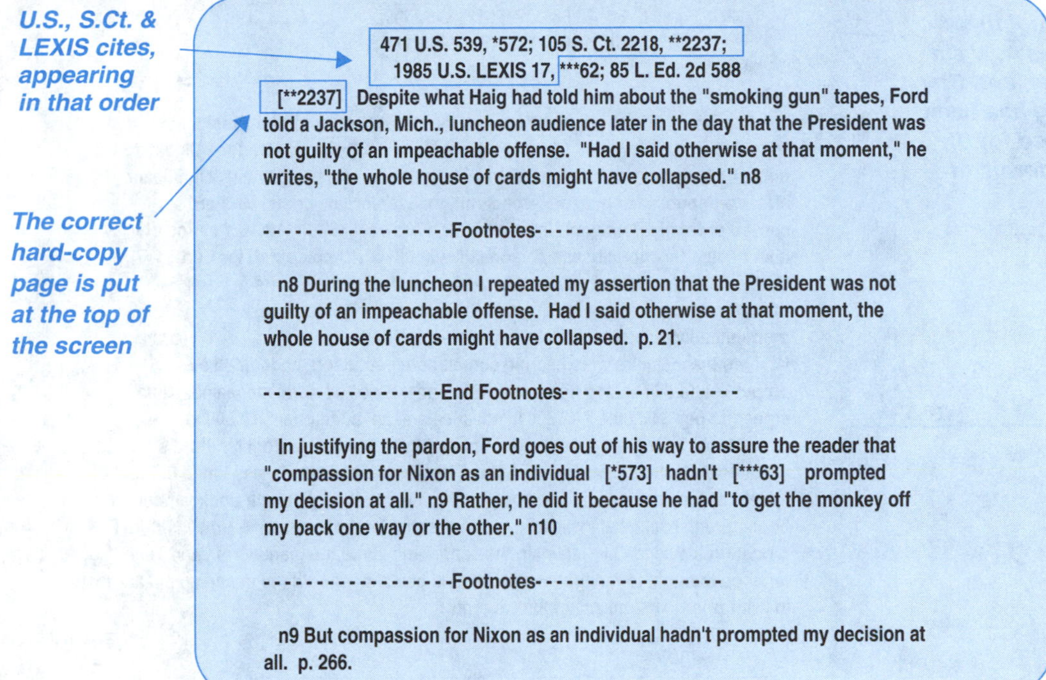
U.S., S.Ct. & LEXIS cites, appearing in that order
The correct hard-copy page is put at the top of the screen
471 U.S. 539, *572; 105 S. Ct. 2218, **2237;
1985 U.S. LEXIS 17, ***62; 85 L. Ed. 2d 588
[**2237] Despite what Haig had told him about the "smoking gun" tapes, Ford told a Jackson, Mich., luncheon audience later in the day that the President was not guilty of an impeachable offense. "Had I said otherwise at that moment," he writes, "the whole house of cards might have collapsed." n8
------------------Footnotes------------------
n8 During the luncheon I repeated my assertion that the President was not guilty of an impeachable offense. Had I said otherwise at that moment, the whole house of cards might have collapsed. p. 21.
-----------------End Footnotes-----------------
In justifying the pardon, Ford goes out of his way to assure the reader that "compassion for Nixon as an individual [*573] hadn't [***63] prompted my decision at all." n9 Rather, he did it because he had "to get the monkey off my back one way or the other." n10
------------------Footnotes------------------
n9 But compassion for Nixon as an individual hadn't prompted my decision at all. p. 266.

Observe that at the start of each screenful after the first one, a citation header at the top of the screen shows you what page you're on for each of the reporters, and how many stars the LEXIS service has assigned to that reporter. Thus on the above screenful, we see that we are now on page 572 of 471 U.S. (which LEXIS has given one star to), page 2237 of 105 S.Ct. (two stars), and page 62 of 1985 U.S. LEXIS 17 (three stars).

By the way, you can sometimes get Star Pagination even for reporters that are not shown at the top of the screen as having any stars. You do this by typing the word **`star`** followed by the abbreviation for the reporter for which you would like to see Star Pagination. Thus if you are dealing with Supreme Court cases, you can always see the Star Paging for Lawyers Edition (L.Ed. and L.Ed.2d) by typing:

```
star led [TRANSMIT]
```

After we issue this command while looking at the *Harper & Row v. Nation* case, here's what we get:

Star Paging for L.Ed. is now single star, and Star Paging has been dropped for the other forms of cites.

85 L. Ed. 2d 588, *595; 471 U.S. 539; L.Ed.2D
105 S. Ct. 2218; 1985 U.S. LEXIS 17

[*596] I

In February 1977, shortly after leaving the White House, former President Gerald R. Ford contracted with petitioners Harper & Row and Reader's Digest, to publish his as yet unwritten memoirs. The memoirs were to contain "significant hitherto unpublished material" concerning the Watergate crisis, Mr. Ford's pardon of former President Nixon and "Mr. Ford's reflections on this period of history, and the morality and personalities involved." App. to Pet. for Cert. C-14 -- C-15. In addition to the right to publish the Ford memoirs in book form, the agreement gave petitioners the exclusive right to license prepublication excerpts, known in the trade as "first serial rights." Two years later, as the memoirs were nearing completion, petitioners negotiated a prepublication licensing agreement with Time, a weekly news magazine. Time agreed to pay $ 25,000, $ 12,500 in advance and an additional $ 12,500 at publication, in exchange for the right to excerpt 7,500 words from Mr. Ford's account of the Nixon pardon. The issue featuring the excerpts was timed to appear approximately one week before shipment of the full length book version to bookstores. Exclusivity was an important consideration; Harper & Row instituted procedures designed to maintain the confidentiality of the manuscript, and Time retained the right to renegotiate the second payment should the material appear in print prior to its release of the excerpts.

Notice that not only do we now have Star Paging for L.Ed., but that Star Paging is "single star," and the stars for all the other forms of citation have been dropped both from the headers and from the underlying text, so we won't get distracted.

Apart from using Star Paging to guide you to the page number you already know you want to see, Star Paging is useful in making sure you give correct cites. Let's suppose you want to quote, or cite to, the words "despite what Hague had told him. . . ." Since you can determine on what page these words fell in both major Supreme Court reporters, you can cite to that particular page number without looking at either hard-copy reporter. (You can see this from the Star Paging on the screen on p. 4-59 above — it's 471 U.S. 539, 572; 105 S.Ct. 2218, 2237).

3. **Using [DIFF LEVEL] to shift levels:** If your current search has more than one level, you might want to view documents that you obtained at a previous level. You can do this by pressing the number of the preceding level, and then pressing the [DIFF LEVEL] key (or transmit **`.dl`** and the number of the level) to get the documents found at that level. Thus if you had used the MODIFY feature twice on the current search (so that you had three levels), and you wanted to go back to look at documents that were present in the first level but not in either of the later two, you would type:

```
1[DIFF LEVEL]
```

(Or, you could type the following dot command: **`.dl1`**).

You will now be shifted to this level, and your regular display keys (CITE, KWIC, etc.) will show you documents from the first level.

4. **Using the SuperKWIC display format:** If you did your searching in FREESTYLE, you should make extensive use of the SuperKWIC display format. This format displays the most heavily weighted block of text, i.e., the portion of the document containing the most occurrences of significant search terms. There is just one SuperKWIC block in each document, but it may be several screens long.[75]

You can put yourself in SuperKWIC by just typing **`.sk`** , or by selecting **`=1`** from the screen that comes up after you finished your FREESTYLE search. (Once in Super-KWIC, if you want a different display format, you can just press the key, or type the dot command, for that other display format.)

B. Printing cases: Printing cases is not very different from printing other sorts of documents. However, here are some special tips about printing cases:

1. **Printing parts of cases:** Often, only a small part of a case (even as little as one paragraph) will be relevant to you. Cases can often be unexpectedly long, and printing the whole case can drown you in a large stack, tie up your school's printer and waste paper. To avoid this, there are two different approaches you can take:

   a. **Use [SCREEN-PRINT]:** The first approach is to use [SCREEN-PRINT]. To do this: (1) first, get yourself to the first screenful of the case, and press [SCREEN PRINT] so that you've got a record of the full name and citation of the case; (2) then advance to the page whose text is of interest to you (perhaps by using KWIC), and do a screen print of that page as well. (You'll want to be sure you have Star Paging for the screenful you are looking at, in case you need to give a Star Paging cite; this may require you to print the screens before and after the one you're interested in.)

   b. **Use the PAG option in [PRINT-DOC]:** The second approach is to use [PRINT-DOC], and to use the "PAG" option within [PRINT-DOC]. To do this, press [PRINT-DOC] while you're looking at the case you want to print, then select "PAG" from the confirmation screen.[76] When you list the page number(s) you want, list the page numbers *as they appear in the original printed report*. For instance, if you're printing pages from 48 Cal.2d 644, and you wanted the "third" and "fourth" pages of that case, you'd specify **`646-647`** (not 3-4) as the pages for PAG to print.

   Because the PAG option uses the page numbers as they appeared in the original printed volume, you'll need to use the Star Paging notations in the case to know what page numbers to specify. These will generally be of the form: [*646] , placed as the first "word" in a paragraph.[77] The PAG option works only on the "primary" Star Paging cites in a case, i.e., the cites indicated by a single star, rather than by two or more stars.[78]

2. **[PRINT-ALL]:** If you are going to use the [PRINT ALL] key, consider using a display format other than [FULL]. For instance, frequently just getting a list of the cites for each

75. For more about SuperKWIC, see *supra*, p. 2-61.

76. The "PAG" option to [PRINT-DOC] is discussed in more detail *supra*, p. 2-85.

77. See *supra*, p. 2-74 for more about Star Paging.

case in your search set will suffice; more often, printing out each case in KWIC format will work very nicely, since you will have the first screenful (containing the citation), as well as those chunks containing hits, without material that you don't need.

3. **Printing to Disk:** If you're working from home, you should consider "printing" the results of your [PRINT ALL] or [PRINT DOCUMENT] request to ***disk*** rather than directly to paper. Some benefits of this approach are: (1) you'll be online for a shorter time, since printing to disk happens much faster than printing to paper, even if you've got a laser printer; (2) if you're printing from your stored disk file and something goes wrong with the printer, you will have an opportunity to fix the problem and reprint, without having to retransmit from Dayton; and (3) you'll now have a stored, machine readable version of your materials, which you can incorporate in your writing (e.g., to quote one or more paragraphs of a case without having to retype it), and which you can search on (e.g., by using the word search feature of any word processor).

4. **Dual-Column Print:** If you've got access to a printer that supports the PCL3 or PCL5 printer-control language (e.g., an HP LaserJet), you may want to take advantage of ***dual-column print***.[79] This format is especially nice for cases, since it mimics a printed reporter, and takes much less paper.

5. **Customize the look of your cases:** Similarly, you'll probably want to customize the look of your printed cases, by bolding or italicizing search terms, italicizing citations, printing cover or end pages, etc. These options are described further *supra*, p. 2-91.

---

78. You can reverse this, however. For instance, for a California case, by default the "primary" Star Paging is to Cal. 3d, and the "secondary" (indicated by two asterisks) is to P.2d. You can enter the following command: `star p2d`. This will temporarily transform P.2d into the primary Star Paging for that case. (See p. 4-59 *supra* for more about this.) Then, you can list P.2d page numbers for purposes of the PAG option.

79. See *supra*, p. 2-91.

Chapter 5

Statutory Law

Introductory Note: Statutes are the bedrock of modern American law. It is hard to find a legal problem in which no federal or state statute is on point. For most legal problems, before you start to look for cases, you will want to see whether there is a statute on point; only after reading any applicable statutes should you start to look for cases. In fact, when you do read cases, the first cases you will read will frequently be those construing a particular statutory provision that you have already located.

The LEXIS-NEXIS services are as useful in finding out whether there is a statute on point as in locating appropriate cases. You can search the full text of all federal and state statutes, plus the tables of contents to statutes. And for many jurisdictions, you can search and view digests of cases construing a particular statutory provision, by using online "annotated statutes" such as United States Code Service.

I. FINDING CONSTITUTIONS

A. Researching the U.S. Constitution: The best way to search for the text of, or information about, the U.S. Constitution, is by using a special file devoted solely to the Constitution. This is the file *USCNST*, in the *GENFED* library.

1. **Segment layout:** The most important segments in the *USCNST* file are as follows:

Name of Segment	Description
CITE	Name of Article or Amendment, plus section (e.g., "USCS Const. Amend. 14, @ 1")
SECTION	Number of section, and text of section name (e.g., "Section 1. Citizens of the United States.")
TEXT	Full text of the individual clause, or if no clause exists, the full text of the entire section
HISTORY	Details on how and when the clause or section was enacted
NOTES	Extensive annotations regarding the clause, including ALR references, law review references, and case digests

2. **What is a document:** A document in the *USCNST* file consists of an individual clause (e.g., Article I, Section 3, Clause 7, concerning judgment in cases of impeachment). If the section is not divided into clauses, then a document consists of the entire section (e.g., Amendment 14, Section 1).

3. **Searching the U.S. Constitution:** Here are some tips on how to do searches about the U.S. Constitution in the *USCNST* file:

   a. **Finding a particular clause or section:** Often, you will know the number of an amendment or clause. The best way to retrieve that amendment or clause is by using the *CITE* segment.

      Thus to retrieve Article I, Section 3, Clause 7 (relating to judgment in cases of impeachment), you would search (in *GENFED/USCNST*) for:

      ```
      cite(art I @ 3 pre/5 cl 7)
      ```

      Note several special things about this search:

      - You search for "art," not "article" (since the underlying document uses "art," and "art" and "article" are not equivalents on the LEXIS service).
      - For the article number, you must use the Roman Numeral (I, not 1).
      - To indicate the section, you use the @ symbol[1] and you put a space between the @ and the number of the section.
      - You use "cl," not "clause."

      Similarly, to find Section 1 of the Fourteenth Amendment, you would search (again in *GENFED/USCNST*) for:

      ```
      cite(amend 14 @ 1)
      ```

      Here, note that we search for "amend," not "amendment," and that the amendment portion of the cite is expressed as "amend 14," not "14th amend."

   b. **Full text search:** Sometimes, you will know a combination of words or phrases that appear in the Constitution itself, and you will want to get the full text of the section in question. Here, you will simply do a key word search on the *TEXT* segment. For instance, if you know that somewhere in the Constitution there is a reference to freedom of speech and of the press, you might search (again in *GENFED/USCNST*) for:

      ```
      text(freedom w/10 (speech or press))
      ```

      This search will, of course, retrieve the entire text of the First Amendment, since that amendment is not broken down into sections or clauses.

   c. **Searching annotations:** One of the most useful aspects of the *USCNST* file on the LEXIS service is the wealth of ***annotations*** about each clause or section. These are prepared by the editors of Lawyers Cooperative, as part of the U.S. Code Service.

      The annotations are contained in the *NOTES* segment. This segment contains extensive citations to ALR articles and law review articles, but its greatest value will probably be for its digests of literally thousands of cases construing the Constitution. In searching for annotations, keep in mind that a "document" consists not of a single case

1. See *supra*, p. 2-16.

digest, but rather, the entire set of digests for a section or clause of the constitution. Therefore, you will want to make extensive use of the **W/n** connector, rather than the **AND** connector, to narrow your search appropriately.

Suppose, for instance, that you want to see digests of cases discussing whether it is a violation of the defendant's due process rights for the police or prosecutors to hypnotize a witness. You might search (still in *GENFED/USCNST*) for:

```
notes(hypnosis w/20 due process)
```

This search finds us a single document (whose *TEXT* segment consists of the text of the Fourteenth Amendment, Section 5),[2] and each individual annotation is basically a paragraph. Looking at this document in KWIC format (F5, or type **.kw**), we see the following:

> **USCS Const. Amend. 14, @ 5 (1993)**
>
> **NOTES:**
>
> **... detailed description of victim's prehypnotic memory, where officer's only training was a 4-day seminar on the subject, and where testimony was uncorroborated. Little v Armontrout (1987, CA8 Mo) 819 F2d 1425.**
>
> **Defendant's** due process **rights were violated when state trial court refused to appoint expert in** hypnosis **for him to counter rape victim's post-hypnotic identification since** hypnosis **expert might have explained how victim might have been influenced, without realizing it, by improper suggestion. Little v Armontrout (1987, CA8 Mo) 835 F2d 1240.**
>
> **Defendant's** due process **rights to fair trial were not violated by use of hypnotically refreshed testimony where witness' knowledge independent of hypnosis sessions defeats inference that** hypnosis **was unduly suggestive or that hypnotically enhanced detail of witness' trial testimony were product of impermissible suggestions or techniques by hypnotist and where opportunity for effective cross-examination of witness was available. Bundy v Dugger (1988, ...**
>
> **... only in suggestive settings causing substantial likelihood of either misidentification or identification induced by impermissible suggestions. Williams v Armontrout (1989, CA8 Mo) 877 F2d 1376.**
>
> **Rape defendant's** due process **rights were not violated by pretrial** hypnosis **of victim where her prehypnosis statement to police officers was similar to her posthypnosis testimony and her testimony was corroborated by**

We can now use the LEXSEE feature to read any of these cases without losing our place in the *USCNST* file.

i. **Location of annotations:** Sometimes, the segment containing annotations for a particular clause (the *NOTES* segment) is part of the document containing the clause itself, as you would expect, even though that clause is not the last clause of the section. For instance, annotations concerning Article I, Section 6, Clause 1 occur at the end of the document consisting of Clause 1, as you would expect. But at other times — especially in the coverage of amendments — the *NOTES* segment comes only at the end of the *whole amendment*, not at the end of each clause or

2. All the annotations for the 14th Amendment are placed in the document whose *TEXT* segment contains just §5, as is further explained *infra*, p. 5-4.

section. Thus all notes concerning the Thirteenth Amendment come at the end of the document containing Section 2 (the last section) of that amendment, even notes pertaining to Section 1 (which is in its own document). The same is true for the Fourteenth Amendment — all notes (and thus annotations) for the Fourteenth Amendment come as part of the document covering Section 5 of that amendment.

ii. **Table of Contents to annotations:** You may also find it useful to look at what is essentially a ***Table of Contents*** to the annotations, found in each document that contains annotations. This Table of Contents comes just before the annotations themselves start, and after the citations to ALR articles and law review articles. The Table of Contents is surprisingly detailed (over 500 entries just for the Fourteenth Amendment), and the digests themselves are grouped according to Table of Contents numbers. Here, for instance, is a small part of the Table of Contents entries concerning the Due Process Clause:

USCS Const. Amend. 14 @ 5 (1995)

71. Generally
72. What constitutes "property"
73. What constitutes "deprivation" or "taking" of property

2. Particular Means of Deprivation
74. Limitations on acquisition, ownership, or disposition of property
75. -Provisions pertaining to aliens
75.5. Regulation of employment
76. Regulation of decedents' estates and inheritance
77. Regulation of marital property interests
78. Regulation of education and schools
78.5. Regulation of insurance
79. Regulation of refuse disposal
80. Laws affecting riparian and other water-related interests
81. Statutory repeal or modification
82. Abatement of nuisance

If we were interested in cases involving regulation of education as violations of the Due Process Clause, we could, having seen Table of Contents entry 78 on the above screen, now enter the following request:

```
focus 78 w/10 (education w/4 school)
```

If we now press [ENTER], using the [NEXT PAGE] key (F1, or type **`.np`**) will quickly bring us to the annotations classified under "78. Regulation of education and schools."[3]

3. Actually, for technical reasons I won't bore you with, after you've done your FOCUS request, you will probably want to do something like **`75`**[VAR-KWIC] (Shift-F5, or type **`.vk75`**). Then, when you press [NEXT PAGE], you'll get to the start of the annotations under "#78." At this point, change to FULL format (F6, or type **`.fu`**). Now, you'll be able to read all the annotations under #78, involving the regulation of education.

B. State constitutions: The constitutions of each of the 50 states are also available on the LEXIS service. There are two ways to get at these. First, you can choose the Individual State Library, and then choose the file called *XXCNST* (where XX is the postal abbreviation for the state) in that library. (For instance, the California Library is named *CAL*, and there is a file *CACNST* in that library.) Alternatively, a state's constitution is included as part of a group file containing the Code for that state; thus you can choose the general *CODES* library, and then a file whose name is *XXCODE* (example: library *CODES*, file *CACODE*, for the California Code).[4]

Both of these sources — the *XXCNST* file in the Individual State Library, and the *XXCODE* file in the *CODES* library — have identical segment layouts. This segment layout is essentially the same as it is for the U.S. Constitution (discussed above), except that in addition to the segments present in the U.S. Constitution file, the state constitutional files have a segment called *STATUS*, which tells you the date through which the document is current (e.g., "This section is current through the 1992 Supplement (1991 Session)").

1. **Tips for searching:** Techniques for searching the state constitution files are essentially the same as for searching the U.S. Constitution. As in the U.S. Constitution, each state constitution document consists of a single section of the constitution. If you know the citation to a section and want to see the section, your best technique is to use the *CITE* segment:

```
cite(const art I and @ 3)
```

(If you are in the file *XXCNST* in the individual-state library, all documents would be part of the constitution, so the reference to "const" in the above search would not be necessary; but if you are using the *XXCODE* file in the *CODES* library, the reference to "const" would be necessary to distinguish constitutional documents from statutory ones.)

By the way, you can check ***all*** state constitutions with a single search, if you wish. In library *CODES*, select the file called *ALLCDE* (which is a group file consisting of all state code files); then, in addition to your key word search, make sure to specify that the *HEADING* segment contains the word "constitution." Thus to find all state constitutional provisions that seem to be dealing with school or pupil assignments (to find those constitutions that deal with problems of busing), you might search for:

```
heading(constitution) and text((school or pupil)
 w/10 assign!)
```

II. FINDING FEDERAL STATUTES

A. Federal statutes generally: Before we talk about how to do federal statutory research on the LEXIS service, it's worth looking briefly at federal statutes from a general perspective, rather than one specific to LEXIS.

4. For our extensive discussion of state codes, see *infra*, p. 5-27.

1. **Public Laws, published as slip laws:** When Congress first enacts a statute, it is published as a ***slip law***, a separately-published pamphlet containing the text only of that statute. When published as a slip law, the statute is cited by its Public Law number, such as P.L. 101-336 (which happens to be the Americans with Disabilities Act of 1990). The number before the hyphen represents the number of the Congress which enacted the law; thus the Congress that enacted the ADA was the 101st Congress. The number following the hyphen is the chronological number of the law in that session of Congress; thus the ADA was the 336th statute passed by the 101st Congress.

2. **Session Laws (Statutes at Large):** The next form in which the statute is published is as part of a ***"Session Laws"*** or ***"Statutes at Large"*** volume. After Congress completes each annual session, all laws it enacted are published in a Session Law publication called the United States Statutes at Large. Statutes at Large are cited in the form "*Volume-#* Stat. *Act-#*"; thus the statute that first enacted the Americans with Disabilities Act is cited as 104 Stat. 330.

   The U.S. Government Printing Office has been running behind in publishing the Statutes at Large — currently there is a delay of about three or four years between the end of each annual session of Congress and the appearance of the bound Statutes at Large volumes.[5] Two private publishers put out a commercial version of the Statutes at Large: *United States Code Congressional and Administrative News* (published by West Publishing Co.), and the Advance pamphlets to the *United States Code Service* (published by Lawyers Cooperative Publishing).

   a. **Similarity to slip laws:** The form in which a statute occurs in the Statutes at Large is very similar to that in which it appears in the slip laws. In the Statutes at Large volume, each Act is printed on a stand-alone basis, without reference to any pre-existing federal statutes that the new Statute may have amended, and without reference to any subsequent statutes that may have amended the Statute you are looking at.

3. **Codified statutes:** Because of the difficulties in doing research in chronological publications like slip laws and Statutes at Large (especially the problems of checking for prior or subsequent statutes, referred to in the prior paragraph), most federal statutory research is done on the "***codified***" version of the federal law, the United States Code. The U.S. Code divides all of federal statutory law into 50 distinct subject matters, called "Titles," such as "Commerce and Trade," "Copyrights," "Food and Drugs," "Internal Revenue Code," "Judiciary and Judicial Procedure," "Postal Service," etc. All Statutes at Large having to do with a particular subject are grouped in the appropriate Title. Within a Title, the material is divided into Chapters, and then into Sections; Sections are numbered continuously within each Title.

   a. **Section numbering:** When a statute is codified, i.e., brought from its original Statutes at Large version and placed into the appropriate portions of the U.S. Code, the ***section numbering*** of the statute generally does *not* remain intact. For instance, in the Americans with Disabilities Act, the Statutes at Large version places the general ban

5. *How to Find the Law*, p. 150.

on private-employer discrimination into section 102 of the Act. In the U.S. Code version, this anti-discrimination language is placed in section 12112 (more precisely, as 42 U.S.C. §12112).

b. Amendments: When a statute is codified, repealed sections are removed, and any sections that have later been ***amended*** are merged together with the amending language to form a new and accurate composite version.

This means that a given provision in the U.S. Code may derive from two or more Statutes at Large — this is exactly what happens when one statute amends a previously-enacted statute. For instance, when the ADA was originally enacted in 1990, its anti-discrimination section had no provision dealing with the foreign operations of U.S. Corporations. But if you look today at 42 U.S.C. §12112 (which for the most part is identical with section 102 of 104 Stat. 327, the original version of the ADA), you will find a lengthy provision, §12112(c), called "Covered Entities in Foreign Countries" — this was placed into 42 U.S.C. §12112 by a later Statute at Large, 105 Stat. 1071, or P.L. 102-166, which was part of the Civil Rights Act of 1991. This example illustrates why the most reliable body of statutory material to look at is always the U.S. Code, not the Statutes at Large or the Public Laws — the U.S. Code represents your best chance of finding all related materials in a single place. Of course, you still risk missing relevant information while looking at an apparently-relevant U.S. Code version (there may be some relevant provision somewhere else in the Code), but your odds of seeing the whole picture in front of you are much better.

c. Form of citation: The U.S. Code is always cited in the form "*Title-#* U.S.C. *Section-#*." Thus the Americans with Disabilities Act, in its U.S. Code formulation, is cited as 42 U.S.C. §12101 et seq.

d. Utility of Statutes at Large: If the U.S. Code has the material organized nicely by subject matter, with all amendments plugged into the appropriate position, why would one ever want to go back to the Statutes at Large or the Public Laws? There are two reasons:

- First, the process of codification is ***not instantaneous***. Even if you are looking at the U.S. Code online (e.g., in the LEXIS service's version, the United States Code Service), there can be a gap of a few months between the time a public law is enacted, and the time when the U.S. Code is harmonized to show the new statute.[6]
- Second, ***legislative history*** is organized according to the particular public law, not the U.S. Code section. To return to our example of the Americans with Disabilities Act, if we wanted to find the legislative history of those portions dealing with discrimination abroad by U.S. corporations, we would need to discover which public law added those sections (this turns out to be P.L. 103-25, not P.L. 101-336, which enacted the basic ADA provisions), and then read the Congressional Committee Reports for that Public Law.

6. See the further discussion of this issue *infra*, p. 5-22.

B. Overview of federal statutes on the LEXIS-NEXIS services: Federal statutes on the LEXIS-NEXIS services parallel the hard-copy publications described above. Each individual act is collected in a file of Public Laws, and the codified version of federal statutes is collected in the U.S. Code Service.

1. **Public Laws:** Federal Public Laws are collected in the file *PUBLAW*, which can be accessed from a number of libraries, including *GENFED* and *CODES*. (Henceforth, I will assume that all federal statutory materials are accessed from the *CODES* library, which is the single most comprehensive library of state and federal statutory materials on the LEXIS service.)

   a. **Nature of *PUBLAW* file:** The *PUBLAW* file contains the full text of each Public Law (essentially, each statute) enacted by Congress, beginning with the 100th Congress, Second Session (which began in February 1988).[7] Each statute in the *PUBLAW* file constitutes a separate document. A statute is usually available online within 10 working days after it became law.

   b. **Segment layout:** The segment layout for the *PUBLAW* file is simple:

Segment Name	Description
HEADING	Contains the number of the Public Law (e.g., "Public Law 101-336"), the number of the Congress that enacted it (e.g., "101st Congress"), and the number of the House or Senate Bill which corresponds most closely to the enacted law (e.g., "S. 933").
CITE	The citation to the Public Law, with the P.L., House or Senate, and Statutes at Large citations included (e.g., "101 P.L. 336; 1990 S. 933; 104 Stat. 327").
SYNOPSIS	A one-sentence description of the nature or purpose of the statute (for instance, in the case of the Americans with Disabilities Act of 1990, "An Act to establish a clear and comprehensive prohibition of discrimination on the basis of disability").
DATE	Date of enactment of the statute.
TEXT	Full text of the statute.

   c. **Using LEXSEE to retrieve:** We'll be discussing in greater detail below how you should search in the *PUBLAW* file. For now, just know that if you have the Public Law citations, you can quickly retrieve the law by using the LEXSEE feature. Thus to retrieve the Americans with Disabilities Act of 1990, P.L. 101-336, you would type the following command:

   lexsee 101 pl 336 [ENTER]

7. The text of Public Laws enacted prior to the 100th Congress, Second Session, are not available on the LEXIS service.

2. **The U.S. Code:** Because the official printed version of the U.S. Code (put out by the Government Printing Office) runs so far behind the actual statutes, the LEXIS service uses one of the two main commercial, annotated, versions of the U.S. Code: the ***United States Code Service*** (USCS). In addition to being far more up-to-date than the government-printed U.S. Code, the USCS contains extensive ***annotations*** to the Code of Federal Regulations and to court decisions construing each statutory provision (which the U.S. Code does not).

   a. **Where to find it:** The best place to find the full text of the USCS is in the *USCODE* file, which is contained in the *GENFED* and *CODES* libraries. Actually, *USCODE* is a group file; it groups together individual files containing the entire U.S. Code, Constitution, Public Laws, and various other things (e.g., references to the Code of Federal Regulations.) Unless you are confident that you want to work only with a single Title, you should use the group file *USCODE* so as to be sure not to miss any statutory provision because you are incorrect about what Title to look in.

      i. **Using LEXSTAT:** We'll be talking about how to search the USCS in detail below. For now, if you know the Title and section number you want, you can use the LEXSTAT feature. Thus if you happen to know that the Americans with Disabilities Act was codified beginning at 42 U.S.C. §12101, you could quickly get access to this section by:

      ```
      lexstat 42 uscs 12101
      ```

      You could then view neighboring sections by pressing "b" (for "Browse"), followed by the [Next Doc] and [Prev Doc] keys.

   b. **Segment layout:** Because of the importance of being able to search federal statutes accurately, I reproduce here a sample USCS provision, together with labels showing you which segment each piece of material is in:

United States Code Service
Sample Document-Segment Description

```
                         UNITED STATES CODE SERVICE
              Copyright (c) 1993, Lawyers Cooperative Publishing
```

STATUS

```
         ***THIS SECTION IS CURRENT THROUGH THE 102ND CONGRESS,
                               2ND SESSION
```

HEADING

```
               TITLE 42. THE PUBLIC HEALTH AND WELFARE
 CHAPTER 126. EQUAL OPPORTUNITY FOR INDIVIDUALS WITH DISABILITIES
```

CITE

```
                        42 USCS @ 12101 (1993)
```

SECTION

```
               @ 12101. Congressional findings and purposes
```

TEXT

```
(a) Findings.  The Congress finds that--

   (1) some 43,000,000 Americans have one or more physical or
mental disabilities, and this number is increasing as the popula-
tion as a whole is growing older;

   (2) historically, society has tended to isolate and segregate
individuals with disabilities, and, despite some improvements,
such forms of discrimination against individuals with disabili-
ties continue to be a serious and pervasive social problem;

   (3) discrimination against individuals with disabilities per-
sists in such critical areas as employment, housing, public
accommodations, education, transportation, communication, recre-
ation, institutionalization, health services, voting, and access
to public services;

       [PORTION OF TEXT DELETED TO SHORTEN SAMPLE DOCUMENT]
```

HISTORY

```
HISTORY: (July 26, 1990, P.L. 101-336, @ 2, 104 Stat. 328.)

REFERENCES IN TEXT:
   "This Act", referred to in this section, is Act July 26, 1990,
P.L.  101-336, 104 Stat. 327, popularly referred to as the Ameri-
cans with Disabilities Act of 1990, which appears generally as 42
USCS @@ 12101 et seq. For full classification, consult USCS
Tables volumes.

SHORT TITLES:
   July 26, 1990, P.L. 101-336, @ 1(a), 104 Stat. 327, provides:
"This Act may be cited as the 'Americans with Disabilities Act of
1990'.".  For full classification of this Act, consult USCS
Tables volumes.
       [PORTION OF TEXT DELETED TO SHORTEN SAMPLE DOCUMENT]
```

Sample continues on next page

NOTES
(material shown plus Cross References and Ancillary Law)

```
NOTES:

CODE OF FEDERAL REGULATIONS
49 CFR Parts 27, 37.

RESEARCH GUIDE

AMERICANS WITH DISABILITIES:
   1 Am Disab, Programs, Services and Accommodations @@ 1:5, 2:1,
2, 3:1, 4, 11--13, 52, 182, 302, 4:1--5, 45, 56,67.

LAW REVIEW ARTICLES:
   Stein, A new 'bill of rights' for millions: the Americans with
Disabilities Law 1 (Winter 1991).
   Geslewitz, Understanding the 1991 Civil Rights Act. 38 Prac
Law 57 (March 1992).
   Ebert; Perkins, Jr., New era of employment litigation: over-
view of Americans With Disabilities Act. 34 Res Gestae 318 (Janu-
ary 1991). Trial 56, December 1990.
       [PORTION OF TEXT DELETED TO SHORTEN SAMPLE DOCUMENT]
```

CASENOTES

```
               INTERPRETIVE NOTES AND DECISIONS
   Action filed against state division of vocational rehabilita-
tion for violating Americans with Disabilities Act (42 USCS @
12101 et seq.) is not frivolous, where the plaintiff contends
that division discriminated against him by requiring him to be
examined by psychiatrist or psychologist in violation of his
religious beliefs, because prohibition against discrimination
includes medical examinations and inquiries pursuant to 42 USCS @
12112(d) and what constitutes discrimination in employment prac-
tices may arguably constitute discrimination by entities provid-
ing employment services.  Kent v Director, Missouri Dept. of
Elementary & Secondary Educ., etc. (1992, ED Mo) 792 F Supp 59,
59 CCH EPD para. 41743.
       [PORTION OF TEXT DELETED TO SHORTEN SAMPLE DOCUMENT]
```

c. **Extra materials:** In addition to the text of the statutory section, there are a number of other elements added to USCS by its editors:[8]

- The effective date of the section (in the *HISTORY* segment, following the label "EFFECTIVE DATE OF SECTION:");
- Details about any amendment to a section, and the date on which the amendment was added (in the *HISTORY* segment, following the label "AMENDMENTS:");
- References to those provisions in the *Code of Federal Regulations* containing regulations implementing the statute (in the *NOTES* segment, following the label "CODE OF FEDERAL REGULATIONS");

8. You won't be able to find all of these in the sample USCS document reprinted above.

- Cross-references, i.e., other places in the USCS to which the current section refers (in the *HISTORY* segment, following the label "REFERENCES IN TEXT:");
- *AmJur* and *Lawyers' Edition* references related to the section;
- Law review articles related to the section (in the *NOTES* segment, following the label "LAW REVIEW ARTICLES"); and
- Individual case digests of cases construing the section (in the *CASENOTES* segment, following the label "INTERPRETIVE NOTES AND DECISIONS").

d. **Table of contents:** There is a USCS Table of Contents, contained in the file *USTOC* (available in the *CODES* and *GENFED* libraries). This can be searched in a hypertext-like way, and is a good way to get a feeling for how a Title or Chapter of the U.S. Code is organized. We'll examine below how to use this Table of Contents.

C. **Finding federal statutes on the LEXIS-NEXIS services:** Let's look now at using the LEXIS service to find federal statutes.

1. **If you know the cite:** If there is specific statutory provision you're interested in, and you know its citation, it's easy to retrieve and display the section on the LEXIS service.

a. **If you know the Public Law cite:** First, let's suppose you know the Public Law cite. In this situation, you want to use LEXSEE, since a Public Law is similar to a case — that is, it is a single document that is not really connected to any other documents. Thus if we happen to know that the statute which first enacted the Americans with Disabilities Act was P.L. 101-336, we would simply type:

```
lexsee 101 pl 336
```

Remember that you can use the LEXSEE feature regardless of what library or file you are logged into, and indeed, you can use it even if you are not logged into any library or file (as long as you have gotten past the client ID screen).[9]

Since LEXSEE is a "service," you return to ordinary searching by pressing the [EXIT SERV] key (Shift-F2, or type **.es**).

b. **If you know the U.S.C. cite:** If the citation you have is to the U.S. Code, then you use the LEXSTAT feature. Thus if we knew that the main provision barring discrimination against the handicapped in the private sector was 42 U.S.C. §2112, we could retrieve that section immediately by:

```
lexstat 42 uscs 12112
```

Actually, we don't have to use **uscs** in our cite; **usc** and **usca** will also work.

As with LEXSEE, you can use the LEXSTAT feature regardless of what library or file you are in, so long as you are past the client identification screen. You return to ordinary searching by pressing the [EXIT SERV] key (Shift-F2, or type **.es**.)

You can use the [NEXT PAGE] and [PREV PAGE] keys (type **.np** and **.pp**) to move

9. For more about LEXSEE, see *supra*, p. 4-30.

around in the section. If you want to be able to see adjacent sections, type the letter **b**, which will put you in "BROWSE" mode, at which point you can use the [PREV DOC] (**.pd**) and [NEXT DOC] (**.nd**) keys.[10]

You can also use the CITES ASSISTANT feature[11] if you have trouble remembering how to structure a LEXSTAT search. Just type **.ca** at any point in your research, then select **=3** to retrieve a statute.

2. **If you know the popular name:** Frequently, you will not know either the Public Law or U.S. Code cite, but will know the ***"popular name"*** of the statute. For statutes enacted within the last few decades, the statute itself lists the popular name by which the statute can be referred to. To go from the popular name to the U.S. Code section(s), we would use the Table of Acts by Popular Names, which is part of the U.S. Code Service on the LEXIS service. Let's assume that we want to find the sections in the U.S. Code that contain the material first enacted as the Americans with Disabilities Act of 1990.

   First, we would go into library *CODES*, and choose file *USNAME*. (This is listed on the second page of files within the CODES library.) The *USNAME* file, because it is essentially a table, has a bit different structure from most files on the LEXIS service. There are 26 documents in the *USNAME* file, each of which covers all popular names beginning with a particular letter.

   If you know the precise popular name that you are interested in, then you should use the *USNAME* file as if it were a dictionary or encyclopedia, and turn to the appropriate "page." To do this, you use the Star Paging feature built into this file. First, you specify the letter your popular name starts with.[12] Then, you supply up to three letters (representing the first three letters in the popular name) when you give your Star Paging request. Thus for the ADA, we would specify starting-letter "A", and we'd then type:

   p*ame

   to find all popular names that begin with the letters AME. Here's what we get (after we scroll through about three prior screensful of Acts whose popular names begin with AME):

10. Browsing within a statute is discussed more fully *infra*, p. 5-21.

11. This feature is discussed more extensively *infra*, p. 9-20.

12. That is, you give the service a letter, and you thereby choose a "document" that contains all popular names beginning with that letter. As you would expect, *USNAME* consists of 26 documents.

```
USCS Pop. Name A 1995, *AME

  June 26, 1953, ch 152, 67 Stat. 81, 36 USCS @@ 97, 98.
  April 12, 1974, P.L. 93-267, 88 Stat. 85, 36 USCS @ 97.

AMERICANS WITH DISABILITIES ACT OF 1990
  July 26, 1990, P.L. 101-336, 42 USCS 12101 note.
  Nov. 21, 1991, P.L. 102-166, 42 USCS @@ 12111, 12112, 12209.
  Jan. 23, 1995, P.L.  104-1, 42 USCS @ 12209.

[*AMN]   Enter p* and up to three letters to jump elsewhere.
     To view a P.L. after 100-242 use LEXSEE  -- e.g.  lexsee 102 pl 166
     To view a USCS section use LXSTAT        -- e.g.  lxstat 42 uscs 5101

AMNESTY ACTS (REMOVAL OF DISABILITIES UNDER
FOURTEENTH AMENDMENT)
  May 22, 1872, ch 193, 17 Stat. 142.
  June 6, 1898, ch 389, 30 Stat. 432.

AMNESTY PROCLAMATIONS
  Dec. 8, 1863, No 11, 13 Stat. 737.
  May 29, 1865, No 37, 13 Stat. 758.
  Dec. 25, 1868, No 15, 15 Stat. 711.
```

Looking at this entry, we learn two things:

- 42 U.S.C. 12101 et seq. seems to be where the Act has been codified; and
- Three different Public Laws (enacted in 1990, 1991 and 1995) seem to deal with the material. Since the ADA is "The Americans with Disabilities Act *of 1990*," apparently the 1990 P.L. sets forth the main statutory provisions of the ADA, and the 1991 and 1995 Public Laws must have amended the ADA, probably in this sections codified as 42 U.S.C. §§ 12111, 12112 and 12209.

Now that we know that the material we want is in or around 42 USCS 12101, we can use LEXSTAT to call that section up.

The second way of using the *USNAME* file is by using the FOCUS feature. If we didn't know the exact popular name of the Act we were interested in, but knew that it had the word "disabilities" in it, we could (starting from the main screen we see after logging into *USNAME*, a screen that tells us there are 26 documents, one for each letter of the alphabet) type the following FOCUS request:

```
focus disabilities
```

The system responds that 13 of the 26 total documents satisfy this search request. Pressing CITE will show us a list of these documents, but the list is not very informative, since it simply shows us the letter covered by that document (e.g., the first document reads "USCS Pop. Name A 1992," the second one "USCS Pop. Name C 1992," etc. But by using KWIC to go through these documents, we quickly discover an entry for the abbreviation ADA, which tells us to "See Americans with Disabilities Act." Paging down a little further, we find the actual entry for "Americans with Disabilities Act of 1990," which as we saw before tells us what we want to know, namely what U.S. Code sections are affected by this Act.

a. **Finding a particular statutory section:** Suppose you're interested in not only a popular name, but also a particular section number within the popular name (e.g., "Section 102 of the Americans with Disabilities Act"). Using the *USNAME* file in the way described above won't really do the job, because you'll end up with either a possibly-long list of U.S.C. sections, or just the starting U.S.C. section, and you want to know where *your particular section* is codified. But you may be able to home in on just the section you want by doing a search in a case-law file, such as *GENFED/COURTS*.

   That is, you can hope that some judge has cited the act by its section number within its popular name, and then also given you its U.S.C. cite. So for Section 102 of the ADA, we could search in *GENFED/COURTS* for something like:

   ```
   102 w/10 ((americans w/3 disabil!) or (ada))
   ```

   When I did this search, I got 61 cases. The seventh of these contained the sentence (which I got to immediately using KWIC format): "In cases where a discriminatory practice involves the provision of a reasonable accommodation pursuant to section 102(b)(5) of the Americans with Disabilities Act of 1990 (42 U.S.C.A. @ 12112(b)(5)), or regulations ..." So I knew that section 102 of the Act had been codified at 42 U.S.C.A. 12112.

3. **If you know some words or phrases likely to be found:** Now, let's assume that you do not know either the cite or the popular name (or even any words likely to be found in the popular name), but that you do know words or phrases likely to be found in the statute itself.[13] In this situation, you may want to do a full text search of the U.S. Code itself.[14]

   Searching the full text of the U.S. Code is similar to searching the full text of cases — you simply try to find a word, phrase or combination of words and phrases that is likely to be present in the thing you are looking for.

   One problem with looking for words and phrases in the overall body of federal statutory law is that you are likely to retrieve a large number of documents. (A document, in the U.S. Code file, consists of a single statutory section with its associated history and annotations.) Suppose, for instance, that you didn't know the name of any Act dealing with disabilities, but you had the feeling that the right statutory provisions would mention the words "Americans," "disabilities," and perhaps "employment." Here are some possible search requests and the number of documents they retrieve from the U.S. Code (library *CODES*, file *USCODE*):

   `americans and disabilities` (retrieves 1,176 documents)

---

13. I'm assuming that you know that there is a particular statute on point, and have some idea of what it contains. I discuss below the somewhat different problem where you merely have an issue, and don't know whether there are any, or how many, statutes on point.

14. You may also want to do a search of the Table of Contents of the U.S. Code. I discuss how to do this in the treatment of searching on an issue, *infra*, p. 5-16.

americans w/10 disabilities (617 documents)

disability w/10 employment (354 documents)

On the other hand, it is certainly possible in most instances to string together enough words or phrases that you will home in on what you want. For instance, if we add the word "discrimination" to our search (even while dropping "Americans"), here's what we get:

disability w/10 employment w/10 discrimination (retrieves 36 documents)

Of these 36 documents, five indeed turn out to be sections that are part of 42 U.S.C. 12101 et seq. and deal with employment. The CITE display for these documents shows that they are all part of the Chapter titled "Equal Opportunity for Individuals with Disabilities, Employment" (or are part of the general definitions before the "Employment" Chapter begins), so we have indeed discovered "the right stuff."

When you are doing word or phrase searching in the U.S. Code, don't forget that a "document" in that file is defined in a very narrow way, to represent only a ***single section*** plus the notes and annotations to that section. This severely restricts the use of the **AND** and **OR** connectors: if 42 U.S.C. 12101 uses the term "employment" (but not the term "discrimination") and 42 U.S.C. 12102 uses the term "discrimination" (but not the term "employment"), a search for "employment and discrimination" will not retrieve either of these sections. For this reason, when you don't have a pretty good idea of the name of the statute you are interested in, your safest bet is to use the techniques described below for issue-searching, which include extensive use of the index and table of contents to the U.S. Code.

4. **Searching when you know only an issue or facts:** Now, let's tackle the toughest aspect of federal statutory research: you have an issue or facts, but you have no direct knowledge that there is even a federal statute on point, let alone what the identity of that statute might be.

Let's consider the following research problem:

Federal Statutory Research Problem

> You are still a summer associate at Dewey Cheatham and Howe. A client of the firm, Bill Payer, tells you the following sad story. Bill was a salaried worker of modest means. About four years ago, Bill got into a dispute with his landlord, Larry Lessor — Bill went on a rent strike on the grounds that Larry was not supplying adequate heat, and Larry brought an action to evict Bill for nonpayment. When the action came to trial, Larry got a verdict of $1,500 (representing three months of unpaid rent), but Bill got a verdict of $1,300 on his counterclaim (representing the damages to him from six months of inadequate heat). The judge entered a judgment against Bill for the $200 difference, which Bill promptly paid. Bill has since moved to a different apartment. Bill now wants to buy a house, and has applied for a mortgage. Two banks have rejected

Federal Statutory Research Problem

his application, on the grounds that a credit report shows that he had a judgment recorded against him by Larry Lessor for $200 for unpaid rent. The credit report was issued by Credit Reports Inc. (CRI), with whom Bill has spoken. Bill has told CRI the facts about the dispute (including the fact that he recovered nearly as much on his counterclaim as Lessor was claiming), but the people at CRI have told Bill that since the $200 judgment was in fact entered against him, there is nothing they can do about the fact that this item appears in the credit report.

Your boss would like you to figure out whether there is anything useful that the firm can do for Bill.

Before we begin, keep in mind that the entire body of federal statutory materials is very large, statutes are often written in a roundabout way with a lot of jargon rather than commonplace words, and it is therefore cumbersome to rely on word or phrase searching in the statutory materials directly. Therefore, I recommend that you use the Table of Contents of the U.S. Code as the first line of attack on this sort of issue-problem, and search the statutes themselves only after you have taken this other step. Let's take a look at how to do this in the context of our credit report problem:

a. Using the Table of Contents to the U.S. Code Service: The ***Table of Contents*** to the U.S. Code Service is found in the *CODES* library, *USTOC* file. When you first sign into this file, you see a list of all 50 Titles to the U.S. Code. Because you frequently won't know which Title (if any) the material you want is in, you're best off going right to a key word search of the Table of Contents file. To do this, double-click on the **<=2>** symbol at the top of the first screen when you log into the file (or type **=2**). You will then be prompted to enter your search. Enter a typical key word search, such as:

```
credit w/10 report
```

You will look at the retrieved documents in CITE format (F7, or type **.ci**); each document is a Table of Contents entry for a particular Title, and a particular Chapter within a Title. Here is what one of the screens of the CITE display retrieved by the above search looks like:

```
LEVEL 1 - 15 DOCUMENTS
(c) 1994 Lawyers Cooperative Publishing *** THIS DOCUMENT IS CURRENT
THROUGH P.L. 103-262, APPROVED 5/31/94 ***

6. TITLE 15. COMMERCE AND TRADE CHAPTER 41. CONSUMER CREDIT
PROTECTION CONSUMER CREDIT COST DISCLOSURE CREDIT BILLING,
TABLE OF CONTENTS--UNITED STATES CODE SERVICE Copyright (c) 1994 Lawyers
Cooperative Publishing *** THIS DOCUMENT IS CURRENT THROUGH P.L. 103-262,
APPROVED 5/31/94 ***

7. TITLE 16. CONSERVATION CHAPTER 36. FOREST AND RANGELAND RENEWABLE
RESOURCES PLANNING WOOD RESIDUE UTILIZATION, TABLE OF CONTENTS--
UNITED STATES CODE SERVICE Copyright (c) 1994 Lawyers Cooperative Publishing
*** THIS DOCUMENT IS CURRENT THROUGH P.L. 103-262, APPROVED 5/31/94 ***

8. TITLE 18. CRIMES AND CRIMINAL PROCEDURE PART I. CRIMES CHAPTER 47.
FRAUD AND FALSE STATEMENTS, TABLE OF CONTENTS--UNITED STATES CODE
SERVICE Copyright (c) 1994 Lawyers Cooperative Publishing *** THIS DOCUMENT
IS CURRENT THROUGH P.L. 103-262, APPROVED 5/31/94 ***
```

Document 6 on the above screen looks like it may be relevant to our problem; if we type **6** [ENTER], we see the following screen:

```
LEVEL 1 - 6 OF 15 DOCUMENTS

TABLE OF CONTENTS--UNITED STATES CODE SERVICE
Copyright (c) 1994 Lawyers Cooperative Publishing
*** THIS DOCUMENT IS CURRENT THROUGH P.L. 103-262, APPROVED 5/31/94 ***

<=1>  HELP     <=2>  WORD SEARCH
<=3>  DISPLAY CONTENTS IN OUTLINE FORM, SUITABLE FOR PRINTING

Return to the table of contents for:
<=4>  UNITED STATES CODE SERVICE
<=5>  TITLE 15
<=6>  CHAPTER 41
<=7>  CONSUMER CREDIT COST DISCLOSURE

          TITLE 15. COMMERCE AND TRADE
       CHAPTER 41. CONSUMER CREDIT PROTECTION
         CONSUMER CREDIT COST DISCLOSURE
                CREDIT BILLING
<=8>  Preceding @ 1666.
<=9>  @ 1666      Correction of billing errors
<=10> @ 1666a     Regulation of credit reports
```

At the bottom of the above screen, we see the first three lines of detailed Table of Contents entries for that portion of Title 15, Chapter 41, dealing with "Consumer Credit Cost Disclosure" and "Credit Billing" — as you can see, 15 U.S.C. §1666a appears to be called "Regulation of Credit Reports," and may be of interest to us. Now, we can use the LINK feature to see the section itself. That is, if we click on **`<=10>`**, we can look at this section, which turns out to be somewhat relevant.

b. Full-text search on statutes: Now, let's suppose you're ready to do a full text search on the statutes themselves. For this, you will use file *USCODE*, located in the *CODES* library. Remember that a "document" consists of a single Code section, plus associated notes and annotations.

Because there is so much federal statutory material, and because it is so hard to predict what words or phrases will appear in the individual section you want, be prepared to get a veritable blizzard of search results. For instance, when I search on "credit w/10 report," I get 234 documents (sections) satisfying the request. Many of these are, of course, completely irrelevant (e.g., a provision governing the Congressional Budget Process, speaking of "reports on legislation providing new budget authority, new spending authority, or new credit authority. . . ."). The sheer number of documents retrieved shows why you want to use the Table of Contents to the U.S. Code Service before tackling the U.S. Code itself.

One way to cut down on the number of unwanted documents retrieved is to limit your search to the segment *UNANNO*. This is a group segment that includes just the *HEADING, CITE, SECTION, TEXT* and *HISTORY* segments — it does not include the *NOTES* segment (which contains cross-references to other materials, including law reviews) or the *CASENOTES* segment (which includes annotations to cases construing the statutory provision). For instance, the search "credit w/10 report," when restricted to the *UNANNO* group segment, retrieves only 159 documents, rather than the original 234.

Another useful segment is the *SECTION* segment, which contains the "Name" of the individual statutory section. A search limited to the *SECTION* segment is especially useful where a full-text search is finding an overwhelming number of documents. For instance, a search (in *CODES/USCODE*) on:

```
section(credit reports)
```

finds only three sections, one of which is 15 U.S.C. §1666a, which is a relevant (though by no means the sole relevant) section. By the way, the *SECTION* segment also contains the number of the section, but not the Title the section is in; thus for the section that would be cited as 15 U.S.C. §1666a, the *SECTION* segment does not contain "15," but does contain "@ 1666a."

c. Read case annotations: When you do find a statutory provision that is on point, you will want to read the ***case annotations*** associated with that section. Probably the easiest way to get to the case annotations is to use the SEGMENTS format: once you're looking at a statutory section (perhaps in FULL or KWIC format), enter:

```
.se;casenotes
```

This command will cause the LEXIS service to take you directly to the *CASENOTES* segment for the section; the segment will show up on your screen under the title "Interpretive Notes and Decisions." Here is what the first page of case annotations looks like for 15 U.S.C. §1681i,[15] which turns out to be the most relevant section for our credit bureau problem:

```
15 USCS @ 1681i (1994)        LEXSTAT

INTERPRETIVE NOTES AND DECISIONS
1. Generally
2. Informing consumers of their right to correct files
3. Noting consumer's dispute
4. Deletion of inaccurate or unverifiable information

1. Generally
  While negligence may be inferred from defendant's lack of cross-referencing
in its filing system, where there was no evidence of damage to plaintiff as
result of defendant's failure to delete inaccuracy in report, there was no
willful violation of 15 USCS @ 1681i(a) where corrected information obtained in
subsequent investigation had been provided. Hauser v Equifax, Inc. (1979, CA8
Neb) 602 F2d 811.
  There was evidence from which jury could find negligent violation of 15 USCS
@ 1681i where, upon defendant credit reporting agency's receipt of notice of
dispute over account from debtor's attorney, agency called creditor to reverify
report and consulted man they knew to have had disagreements with debtor in past
```

If there are many annotations for a particular statutory provision, you may want to use the full text search capabilities of the service to narrow in on the relevant ones. In our problem, for instance, we know we are interested in credit reports, so once we had identified the right section, we might search (in *CODES/USCODE*) for:

```
cite(15 w/3 1681(i)) and casenotes(credit w/3 report)
```

By the way, reading the cases associated with the statutory provision can often give you a lot of insight into how the section is used, as well as furnishing formal precedent. For instance, returning to Bill's problem with Credit Reports Inc., based solely on our reading of 15 U.S.C. §1681i itself we might not think that Bill would necessarily have the right to recover in damages from Credit Reports Inc. if CRI fails to heed our request to include Bill's statement of his side of the dispute. But paging through the annotations to 15 U.S.C. §1681i, we come upon the following one:

15. That is, if you do a LEXSTAT for **15 uscs 1681i**, then enter **.se;casenotes**, this screen (slightly edited) is what you get.

15 USCS @ 1681i (1993)　　　　LEXSTAT

There was evidence from which jury could find negligent violation of 15 USCS @ 1681i where, upon defendant credit reporting agency's receipt of notice of dispute over account from debtor's attorney, agency called creditor to reverify report and consulted man they knew to have had disagreements with debtor in past since, in view of individual's involvement with debtor, contacting only him was insufficient to reverify entry as agency was required to do under @ 1681i(a), and if there was no other authority to verify account, agency should have deleted information altogether as is required by @ 1681i(a). Pinner v Schmidt (1986, CA5 La) 805 F2d 1258.

Good case on point for our research problem →

Consumer states actionable claim against credit reporting company under 15 USCS @ 1681i(a), where consumer notified company of full circumstances surrounding $ 414 state-court judgment against him--that he had been awarded $ 608 on his counterclaim and was therefore net winner in litigation against landlord--yet company inexplicably had not effected deletion from credit report nor recorded information provided by consumer, because @ 1681i(a) provides remedy for unreasonably incomplete reports. Grant v TRW, Inc. (1992, DC Md) 789 F Supp 690.

Under 15 USCS @ 1681i agency bears at least some burden of evaluation of information received upon reinvestigation, and knowledge of dispute between consumer and creditor may affect agency's ability to rely upon information received from creditor upon reinvestigation; agency violated @ 1681i deletion requirement where agency, which had included in report entries indicating that

This case — which, like ours, involves a dispute with a landlord in which both sides recover against the other — suggests that there is an implied federal right of action for damages against a credit bureau that does not comply with the requirements of §1681i.

The case annotations in the U.S. Code Service do not purport to be complete — that is, the editors choose only what they consider to be the most important cases construing a statute, not all cases (or even all reported cases) construing a statute. Therefore, once you have located a statutory provision on point, you will want to use other techniques to make sure that you have read all or most of the cases construing that statute. I discuss these methods in Chapter 9 on Citators; for instance, you will want to do an ordinary search, in the appropriate case files, to find cases citing the statutory section.

5. **Using the BROWSE feature:** Recall that in the *USCODE* file, each statutory provision is its own document. Yet you will often want to look not only at the statutory section containing the key words you have been searching, but adjacent sections. The LEXIS service provides a special way to do this. Once you have retrieved a given section (whether by searching for its key words or by using the LEXSTAT[16] feature), you can then go into BROWSE. To go into BROWSE, type the letter **`b`**, followed by [ENTER]. Now, each time you press the [NEXT DOC] and [PREV DOC] keys (**`.nd`** and **`.pd`** respectively), these keys will not have their usual meaning of "go to the next [or previous] document containing a hit"; instead, they will be interpreted to mean "go to the next [or previous] section adjacent to the one we are currently on, even if it does not contain a hit." Thus if you were looking at 15 U.S.C. §1681i, you could advance to the next section, §1681j ("Charges for

16. See pp. 5-12 to 5-12 for how to use LEXSTAT to retrieve a *USCODE* section.

Disclosures") by pressing [NEXT DOC], then to §1681k by pressing [NEXT DOC] again, etc.

You can type a number before [NEXT DOC] or [PREV DOC] to move that number of sections forward or backward. Similarly, you can type a number before [NEXT PAGE] and [PREV PAGE], which will cause you to move that number of pages forward or backward within the section you are already on.

Once you have typed the letter "b" to go into BROWSE mode, you are automatically put in FULL format. You cannot use KWIC or VAR-KWIC, because the whole idea of browsing is to let you see adjacent statutory sections that do not necessarily have any hits. Highlighting is also turned off while you are in BROWSE mode. You can use SEGMENTS format (Shift-F10, or type **`.se`**) and CITE format (F7 or type **`.ci`**). To leave BROWSE mode, you simply type the letter "b" again, and you will be returned to whatever section you were looking at when you first typed "b." If you are confused about whether you are in BROWSE mode, you will see the symbol "=B=" at the upper right-hand portion of your screen when you are in this special mode.

D. Making sure your research is up-to-date: The U.S. Code Service is quite up-to-date, but you cannot rely on it to contain the full text of a statute enacted in the very recent past. In general, statutes seem to get into the USCS about 2-3 months after they are first enacted — thus when I look at a statutory provision in the USCS on August 21, 1995, I see a notation that the section is "current through P.L. 104-12, approved 5/18/95."[17]

Therefore, to reduce the chance that you may miss a relevant statute that has very recently been enacted, you should be sure to check the Public Laws file (filename *PUBLAW*, in the *CODES* library).[18] The full text of each Public Law generally is entered into the *PUBLAW* file within 10 working days of enactment, so the *PUBLAW* file will typically be about six weeks more up-to-date than the *USCODE* file.

If you want to be extra diligent in making sure that nothing has happened recently, you can go to the current-Congress ***Bill Tracking*** file. This file, named *BLTRCK* (in the *CODES* library) tracks the status of every bill pending in the current Congress. It contains a one-sentence synopsis of the purpose of each bill. If the bill has become law, *BLTRCK* will tell you so by including the words "became Public Law" (followed by the actual P.L. citation) in the segment called *STATUS*. For instance, to check whether any bill introduced in the current Congress included the word "health" in its synopsis, and became law, we could search in *CODES/BLTRCK* for:

```
synopsis(health) and status(became public)
```

The *BLTRCK* file is updated by Noon (EST) on the day following any House or Senate activity.

---

17. A legend showing the currentness of each section is placed on the screen near the top of the display of that section. See the screen at the top of p. 5-18 for an illustration. In general, on any given day, all sections of the USCS bear the same "current through. . . ." designation.

18. The operation of this file is discussed further *supra*, p. 5-8.

E. Tracking pending legislation: You may need to track ***pending*** legislation. For instance, you may be working for a law firm that does lobbying for a particular group or on a particular issue. Within the *CODES* library, there are three files that can help you do this kind of tracking. We will consider each, but only briefly.

The *BLTEXT* file includes the full text of ***every bill introduced*** in the current Congress (in the *TEXT* segment), together with segments like *CITE, SYNOPSIS, DATE* and *SPONSOR*. If your client was a local phone company who was hoping that Congress would deregulate the long-distance phone industry, you could report to your client about every bill now pending that would do that, by searching in the *BLTEXT* file for something like:

```
telecom! w/5 (regulat! or deregulat!)
```

Because so many bills are introduced in Congress (over 40,000 in the 102nd Congress, which was in session from 1991-92), you will tend to be deluged with information if you use *BLTEXT* as your principal place to search. A better first place to look is in the *BLTRCK* file, which is a Bill Tracking file that shows you the status of each bill pending in the current Congress. This file will show you, among other things, the number of co-sponsors (in the *TOTAL-COSPONSORS* segment), and the actions that have been taken with reference to the bill (in the *ACTIONS* segment). Since there is also a *SYNOPSIS* segment, you can do some Subject Matter searching, as well as impose some other limitations that will theoretically restrict you to bills that have some reasonable chance of passage. In our phone deregulation example, for instance, we could search in *CODES/BLTRCK* for:

```
synopsis(telecomm! or telephone) and total-cosponsors
> 5
```

to limit ourselves to bills that have more than a few cosponsors (on the theory that such bills are more likely to pass than those sponsored by only a few individuals).

Lastly, there is actually a file on the LEXIS service that purports to tell you the odds that any given bill will pass. This is the *BLCAST* file. Since it does not include any *SYNOPSIS* segment, you will probably need to locate bills you are interested in through a textual search on the *BLTEXT* or *BLTRCK* files, then do a search on the particular bill number in *BLCAST*. (*BLCAST* does, however, include the full text of the Title of the bill, in the *TITLE* segment, so you can do some limited textual searching there.) For instance, with our phone problem, suppose we discover that a Senate bill (S652) would deregulate the entire telecommunications industry. By searching *CODES/BLCAST* for:

```
bill-number(s 652)
```

we discover that the bill has already passed the Senate Commerce Committee, and that the publishers of the *BLCAST* file (Information for Public Affairs, Inc.) believe that there is a 79% chance that the bill will pass the relevant House Committee and a 71% chance that it will get all the way to become law.

F. Legislative history: You can do some of your federal ***legislative history*** research on the LEXIS service. Legislative history is the story of how a bill came to be law. When you research the legislative history of a federal statute, you examine documents such as the debates on the floor of the Congress concerning the bill, the reports by the House and Senate committees that had responsibility for the bill, hearings conducted by those committees, and other legislative documents.

1. **Legislative history on the LEXIS service:** This is not the place for an extended discussion of how to do legislative history on federal statutes. I will instead give you brief guidance on the types of legislative history research you can do on the LEXIS service, with an occasional note about how you can do something in hard-copy that you cannot do on the service.

   a. **Committee Reports:** The single best source of legislative history is the ***Reports*** by the House and Senate committees that had responsibility for the bill, and the Report by the conference committee that reconciled differences between the House and Senate versions of the bill. A Committee Report on a bill will usually take you through each section of the (not-yet-enacted) statute, and give you insight into what the committee thought the section did, and how it should be interpreted.

   The LEXIS service now contains the full text of nearly all Committee Reports (and even Sub-Committee Reports) released by the House and Senate since January, 1990. These are in library *LEGIS*, file *CMTRPT*.

   If you know the popular name of the bill on which you want a report, you may want to use the *TITLE* segment in *CMTRPT*. Thus:

```
title(americans w/3 disabil!)
```

   finds all Reports from 1990 or later on the Americans with Disabilities Act.

   For Reports issued prior to 1990, the LEXIS service's coverage is limited to five main subject areas; these are as follows:

Subject Matter	Principal Statutes Covered	Library/File
Bankruptcy	Bankruptcy Reform Act of 1978	LEGIS/BKRLH
Banking (mainly S&L Bailout)	FIRREA	LEGIS/FIRREA
Environmental	Clean Air Act, CERCLA, NEPA, Superfund	LEGIS/ENVLH
Estate Taxation	Estate tax portions of Internal Revenue Code	LEGIS/ESTLH
Securities	Securities Act of 1933; Securities Exchange Act of 1934 (plus recent amendments)	FEDSEC/LEGIS
Tax	Internal Revenue Code (all versions since 1954)	LEGIS/TAXLH

   i. **Hard-copy Committee Reports:** If you need a Committee Report for a subject area that is not covered in the files described above, the best source is the *U.S. Code Congressional and Administrative News*, which includes one or more Committee Reports for most major statutes.

b. *Congressional Record:* The other major source of legislative history consists of the floor debates in Congress about the bill, before it is passed. The hard-copy source for everything said on the floor of Congress, as you probably know, is the *Congressional Record*, published by the U.S. government. Fortunately, the full text of every *Congressional Record* published since 1985 is available online on the LEXIS service.

To search the *Congressional Record* successfully online, you should first determine which session of Congress debated the bill in question — this will, of course, generally be the session that passed the bill. The year the bill was passed will usually tell you what you need to know, in conjunction with the following little chart:

Number of Congress	Dates in Session
105th	1997-98
104th	1995-96
103rd	1993-94
102nd	1991-92
101st	1989-90
100th	1987-88
99th	1985-86

(Alternatively, the session-matched-to-dates information is contained in the *LEGIS* library, *RECORD* file.)

Next, you want to log in to the appropriate file. All Congressional Record files are located in the *LEGIS* library. The full text of the Congressional Record (both houses) for a given session is in a file bearing the name of that session: *104TH*, *103RD*, *102ND*, *101ST*, *100TH* and *99TH*. (There are sub-files, containing the debates from just a single house, but usually you won't need to bother with these.)

At the time debate occurs on a bill, the bill is not yet law. Therefore, you can't search for the statute by its Public Law number, let alone by its U.S. Code cite (unless a bill under debate amends some previously-enacted law that the speaker mentions by its U.S. Code cite). Therefore, you will need to know the bill number by which the bill was known in Congress (e.g., H.R. 223 or S. 133). Probably the easiest way to discover this information is to locate the statute or the Public Law on the LEXIS service, using the *CODES* library, *PUBLAW* file;[19] at the start of the text of a Public Law in this file you will see the number of the House or Senate bill, preceded by the year in which the bill was introduced (e.g., for the Americans with Disabilities Act of 1990, you will see the cite "1990 S. 933," at the start of the text for P.L. 101-336).

Let's suppose that we need to know more about the drug-use portions of the Americans with Disabilities Act (which, in brief, say that an employer can discriminate on the basis of present drug use, but not on the basis of past drug use if that drug use is not continuing). After choosing the right Congressional Record file on the LEXIS service (in this case, *101ST* in the *LEGIS* library), we might search for:

19. See *supra*, pp. 5-8 to 5-9, for details about how to do this.

```
text(s 933 and drug w/5 use)
```

The *TEXT* segment of a Congressional Record file contains the actual text of the words spoken on the floor, which is what we want. (Limiting ourselves to the TEXT segment has an additional advantage: if we try to search for "s 933" without restricting to a single segment, LEXIS thinks "s" means we are trying to sort the retrieved documents. By putting the "s" inside a segment, in the search word **`text(s 933)`**, there is no ambiguity.)

Don't count too much on the persuasiveness of *Congressional Record* debates when you are trying to establish legislative history. Members of Congress are notorious for making statements on the floor just to get them into the *Congressional Record* so as to influence the legislative history, in a way favorable to the member's own views, even if these views are not shared by most of the other members of Congress voting on the bill. For this reason, Committee Reports (especially the majority report on a bill) are vastly more persuasive as to what Congress intended.

By the way, you can also find speeches by a given member of Congress, by using the *SPEAKER* segment. Thus to find documents in which Senator Bob Dole has spoken about the balanced budget, you could search (perhaps in *LEGIS/104TH*) for:

```
speaker(dole) and budget w/3 balanc!
```

c. **Summaries of legislative histories (*CISLH*):** A good source for researching legislative histories is the Congressional Information Service Legislative Histories file, *CISLH*, in the *CODES* library. This file contains, for statutes enacted after 1969, a citation to every House and Senate committee report on the bill, a reference to the pages of the Congressional Record where the bill was debated, and a citation to the printed volume of each set of hearings conducted on the bill. While the *CISLH* file does not contain the full text of any of these materials, you can order the full text of any of them from CIS (located in Bethesda, MD) using citation numbers listed in the *CISLH* file. Also, the *CISLH* file contains LINK markers identifying those documents that the LEXIS service has online in other files; thus you can click on the LINK marker for a document and see that document immediately, if it exists in full text anywhere on LEXIS.

i. **Searching by Public Law number:** To find the *CISLH* listings relating to a statute, you'll usually want to use the LH (legislative history) segment, coupled with the statute's Public Law number. Thus:

```
lh(101-336)
```

will find all *CISLH* listings that relate to Public Law 101-336.

ii. **Use at start:** You may well want to search *CISLH* at the *start* of your legislative-history research, so you'll have a list of primary documents (committee reports, etc.) that you should then look at.

III. FINDING STATE STATUTES

A. The hard-copy side: The process by which state statutes are published parallels the federal side. A statute is first published in slip-law form, and is usually referred to as a Chapter or Act. At the end of the legislative year, all the laws passed by the legislature are published in a form called Session Laws. Periodically, the newly-enacted laws are put into a subject-by-subject codification, typically called the [state-name] State Code.

1. **Official vs. unofficial:** As in the federal context, state statutory materials have both an official and unofficial incarnation. Most practitioners use a commercially-published version of their state's code, which contains annotations after each section (with references to a section's history, cases construing it, administrative regulations, etc.). Every state has at least one commercially-published annotated code, and some states have two. A subscription to an annotated code usually includes advance sheets containing the full text of each bill, published shortly after the bill's enactment. These advance sheets are similar to Session Laws, except that they are much more timely than the state's own officially-published Session Laws. In most states, the commercially-published advance sheets containing each law as it is passed are collectively called an "Advance Legislative Service." The two biggest publishers of annotated codes and accompanying Advance Legislative Services are the Michie Company, a sister unit of LEXIS-NEXIS (with about two dozen states) and West (with about 20 states).

B. State statutes on the LEXIS-NEXIS services: State statutes are present on the LEXIS-NEXIS services in much the same way that federal statutes are.

1. **Codes:** The statutes of all 50 states (plus D.C., Puerto Rico and the U.S. Virgin Islands), are available in codified form on the LEXIS service. Most, but not all, of the codes are annotated.

2. **Where to find:** All state codes are available in both the *CODES* library and the *STATES* library; in either case, the name of the file containing a single state's code is *XXCODE*, where *XX* is the state's postal abbreviation. Thus the Mississippi Statutes Annotated are found in *MSCODE*. (In addition, a state's code can be found in the library for that individual state, under the name *CODE*; thus in the library *COLO*, the Colorado library, there is a file called *CODE*, which contains the Colorado Revised Statutes.)

   a. **Archive versions:** The files described above contain, as you would expect, the current version of a state's code. In addition, for all states the LEXIS service keeps online the code as it stood at various ***earlier points in time***, usually one, two and three years earlier. This is useful for the many legal problems that require you to know what a state's statutory law was at an earlier moment, when it may have been different from what it is now (e.g., a criminal prosecution for a crime whose definition has been changed in the interim).[20]

---

20. You can find the archived version of any state's code in the *CODES* library, in a file named *XXARCH* (where *XX* is the postal abbreviation of the state). Within this *XXARCH* file, you can specify which of the earlier versions you want to search (e.g., the code as it stood in 1991, in 1992, etc.)

b. **Search of all state codes simultaneously:** Occasionally, you might want to search the codes of all states simultaneously; this can be useful, for instance, to find those states that have dealt with a particular problem. To do this from within the *CODES* library, select the *ALLCDE* file, which is a group file consisting of all of the Individual State Code files.

c. **Segment layout:** Here is the segment layout for files containing state codes:

Name of Segment	Description
STATUS	Contains the date through which this version of the code is current (e.g., "This section is current through the 1992 Supplement (1992 regular session)"). Also contains citations to recently enacted legislation (slip laws) that have affected the code section.
HEADING	Contains number and name of Title, number and name of Chapter, and possibly of sub-chapter (e.g., "Title 3.1. Agriculture, Horticulture and Food. Chapter 9. Produce Markets. Article 1. Produce Market Authorities")
CITE	Contains citation to the section (e.g., "Va. Code Ann. Section 3.1-48 (1992)")
SECTION	Section number, plus name of section (e.g., "@ 3.1-48 Market Authorities Authorized to be Established")
TEXT	Full text of statutory section
HISTORY	Usually contains year of previous versions of the Code containing the section, and the number of the section within those previous codes (e.g., "Code 1950 @ 3-79.2; 1975 c.135")
NOTES	References to secondary sources such as ALR or law review articles, as well as digests of cases interpreting the statutory section.
CASENOTES	Contains digests of cases that interpret the statutory section. This segment is a sub-set of the *NOTES* segment.
UNANNO	This is a group segment that consists of the *HEADING, CITE, SECTION, TEXT* and *HISTORY* segments (i.e., everything but the *NOTES* and *CASENOTES* segments)

3. **Public Laws:** Public Laws or Session Laws — that is, the uncodified form of a statute, as enacted by the state legislature — are widely available on the LEXIS service. Since a commercial hard-copy publisher generally publishes these Session Laws as part of its Advance Legislative Service advance sheets (see *supra*), the LEXIS service includes the letters "ALS" in the names of these files. The easiest way to get at a particular state's Session Laws is by using the *CODES* library, and a file named *XXALS*, where *XX* is the state's

postal abbreviation; thus New York Session Laws are in library *CODES*, file *NYALS*. (The same file is located in the individual state libraries; thus Wisconsin's Session Laws can be found in a file called *WIALS* in the *WISC* library.)

C. **Researching state statutes:** Since researching state statutes on the LEXIS service is so similar to researching federal statutes, I touch only on the highlights here. In general, any search tactic I discussed in the federal statutory context can be emulated in the state context.

1. **If you know the code cite:** If you have a cite to a state's codified version of its statutes, you can use the LEXSTAT feature to see that statutory section. Thus to see California Business and Professional Code §1627.7, you would type:

   `lexstat cal bus prof 1627.7`[21]

   Remember that you can use the LEXSTAT feature regardless of what library and file you are signed into (and, indeed, even if you are not signed into any library or file). Once you have used the LEXSTAT feature, to return to ordinary searching, enter **`res`** (for RESUME).

   In general, the abbreviation you use with the LEXSTAT feature is the two-digit postal code, followed by the word "code," followed by the section. Thus to see section 30-2806 of the Nebraska Revised Statutes, you would type:

   `lexstat ne code 30-2806`

   Some state codes have a subject matter in their name; in this instance, you will need to type the abbreviation for the subject matter. Thus:

   `lexstat ny gen mun 370`

   `lexstat ca pub util code 2874`

   See Appendix H for a list of statutes available on the LEXIS service, together with the LEXSTAT format for those statutes.

   a. **If you have a Session Law cite:** If you do not have a cite to the codified version of the statute, but do have a cite to its Session Law (or some other cite identifying it by reference to the uncodified law passed by the legislature), use the LEXSEE feature. Thus if you know a certain statute was passed by the Alabama legislature in 1991 as Public Act 159, you could retrieve it by:

      `lexsee 1991 al pub act 159`

2. **If you have an issue:** If you need to find all statutes on a particular issue, handle this task generally the way you would handle it for a federal statute.

   a. **Table of Contents:** Make use of the ***Table of Contents***, which exists for each state statute. This table is organized in a hierarchical way, and you can navigate from one

21. The Help screens within LEXSTAT will give you details about the proper abbreviations for use in a LEXSTAT request.

level to the next by use of the LINK feature, just as you can with the U.S. Code's counterpart, *USTOC*.[22]

Alternatively, you can do a text search on a state statutory Table of Contents file. Thus if we wanted to find any California statutes involving the rights of a natural father when the birth mother proposes to give the child up for adoption, we might choose the *CATOC* file in the *CODES* library, select **=2** (to perform a word search), and do a search of:

`adoption w/10 father`

The Table of Contents usually contains the full title of each individual section; the titles are often quite detailed (e.g., Cal. Civ. Code §7017 is entitled "Rights of Parent upon Other Parent's Relinquishment or Consent to Adoption of Child; Petition to Terminate Parental Rights of Father"), so a key word search on the Table of Contents file will often get you what you want.

Each state's statutory Table of Contents file can be found in the *CODES* library, in a file named *XXTOC*, where *XX* is the state's postal abbreviation followed by the letters "TOC" (thus California's is in file *CATOC*).

b. Full text of statutes: Alternatively, you can of course search the full text of a state's statutes. As in the federal case, this can be cumbersome due to the awkward wording of most statutes. To narrow your search, you may find it useful to use the *SECTION* segment, which contains not only the section number but the name of the section. This can be a substitute for doing a key word search in the Table of Contents file; thus we could do our adoption search by choosing library *CODES*, file *CACODE*, and searching for:

`section(adoption and father)`

If you are searching in an annotated statute file, and are being deluged by hits that occur in the annotations rather than in the statutory text, you may want to search the *UNANNO* group segment, which includes everything except the *NOTES* segment (which is the segment containing the annotations and cross-references).

3. Navigating within a statute: Once you have retrieved a statutory section and are looking at it, you may want to read adjacent sections even though these may not contain hits. To do this, type the letter **`b`**. This will put you into BROWSE mode. When you are in BROWSE mode, [NEXT DOC] (the F3 key, or type **`.nd`**) and [PREV DOC] (F4 or type **`.pd`**) will move you to the next and previous sections, respectively. While in BROWSE mode, you will not see highlighting.[23]

D. Updating your research: You will want to make sure that your state statutory research is up-to-date. In general, the Session Laws are more up-to-date than the codified version of a state

---

22. See *supra*, p. 5-18 for an explanation of how to use the LINK feature within the United States Code Service Table of Contents file, *USTOC*.

23. For more information about BROWSE mode, see *supra*, p. 5-21.

statute. Therefore, after you have done your primary research into the state's code, you should log in to the Advanced Legislative Service file,[24] so you can check the full text of statutes passed in the current session. Most ALS files are updated within a week or so of passage of a new law, in contrast to several months or more for the codified version of a state's statutes.[25]

E. **Tracking pending legislation:** You can also use the LEXIS service to track ***pending*** legislation. There are two types of files in which you can do this kind of research: bill text files and bill tracking files.

1. **Bill text files:** For all states, you can get the full text of every bill pending in the legislature. These files bear the name *XXTEXT*, where *XX* is the two digit postal abbreviation for the state (e.g., *MATEXT* for Massachusetts full-text bills). All of these files are in the *CODES* library.

2. **Bill tracking:** For all states, you can do bill tracking. There is a file named *XXTRCK*, where *XX* is the state postal abbreviation (e.g., *KYTRCK* for Kentucky bill tracking), located in the *CODES* library. For each bill pending in the current session of the legislature, there is a document in the *XXTRCK* file giving you, among other things, a one or two sentence synopsis of what the bill would do (in the *SYNOPSIS* segment), status information (e.g., "to Senate Committee on Appropriations"; "Passed Senate," etc.); and words and phrases summarizing the categories affected (e.g., "Law and Justice"; "Administrative Agencies," "Lobbying and Political Practices") in the *SUBJECT* segment.

F. **Legislative history:** Doing legislative history research on state statutes is extremely difficult even with the world's largest hard-copy library at your fingertips. In contrast to the federal system, there is usually just not very much legislative history available on most state statutes; for instance, the type of extensive committee reports that accompany federal legislation usually do not exist in the state statutory world. In any event, there is practically no useful legislative history you can do on the LEXIS service, except in the few instances where the annotations following a section of the state code (remember that the annotations are usually found in the *NOTES* segment of a *CODE* file), or a case construing a statutory provision, give you some legislative history. No other online service contains any appreciable volume of state legislative history materials either.

---

24. See *supra*, p. 5-28 for details.

25. For more about ALS files and the Session Laws they contain, see *supra*, pp. 5-27 and 5-28.

Chapter 6

Administrative Law

Introductory Note: Your law school education has acculturated you (or soon will) to the belief that most law is made by courts, and, to a lesser extent, legislatures. But if you look at how "the law" influences most businesses and individuals, you will find that it is probably ***government agencies*** that have the most profound effect on daily life. Some random examples:

- Who gets to own and run a television station, cable TV system or mobile phone system, and what services they can offer and at what price (the Federal Communications Commission);
- How stock in public companies gets issued, and traded after issue (the federal Securities and Exchange Commission);
- How gas, electric, water and telephone companies offer and price their services (state Public Utility Commissions);
- How the environment is protected (the federal Environmental Protection Agency, plus state environmental agencies);
- How we compute and pay our taxes (the Internal Revenue Service and state Tax Commissions); and
- How crime is prosecuted and punished (the federal Department of Justice, plus state and local law enforcement agencies).

Each of these agencies creates several different types of "law." They promulgate "regulations," which are general pronouncements, similar to statutes in their tone. They also issue "rulings" and "administrative decisions," both of which are dependent on the facts of individual situations and are thus more like case law. Regulations, rulings and administrative decisions together make up what is commonly referred to as "administrative law."

You can use the LEXIS service for the majority of your federal administrative law research, and for some of your state administrative law research.

I. FEDERAL ADMINISTRATIVE LAW

A. Federal administrative law generally: Federal agencies divide administrative law materials into statute-like rules and regulations on the one hand, and case-like administrative rulings and decisions on the other hand. Nearly all commonly-used hard-copy federal administrative materials are published by the U.S. Government itself, not by commercial publishers as in the world of case law and statutes.

1. **Regulations and rules:** When Congress decides to regulate a certain subject area, in addition to the statutory provisions imposing the broad-scale regulations, Congress typically creates a federal administrative agency to implement the statute. This agency is empowered to promulgate ***regulations***, which are detailed rules implementing the statute and filling in gaps left by the statute. For instance, Congress has decided to regulate the sale and trading of securities, and has by statute forbidden the use of any manipulative or deceptive device in connection with the purchase or sale of any security (in §10(b) of the Securities Exchange Act of 1934). But Congress has left it to the Securities and Exchange Commission to enact a detailed regulation putting meat on the bones of this general statutory provision (which the SEC has done in the form of SEC Rule 10b-5, which is much more specific).

   The two most important hard-copy embodiments of federal regulatory law are the ***Federal Register*** and the ***Code of Federal Regulations***. These are in a sense analogous to Session Laws and codified statutes, respectively[1] — a regulation is first enacted and published in a stand-alone form in the *Federal Register*, and then is "codified," i.e., put together with other regulations on the same subject, in the *Code of Federal Regulations*.

   a. **The *Federal Register*:** The *Federal Register* is published by the federal government following each business day. The *Federal Register* is the basic chronological source for everything that happens in the administrative branch of government — not only every administrative regulation, but also lots of other administrative and executive business (e.g., Executive Orders, Presidential proclamations, notices of hearings, issuances of licenses, etc.) is published in the *Federal Register*.

      A regulation first sees the light of day by being published in "proposed" form in the *Federal Register*. Then, after a period in which the public can comment on the regulation, the regulation is published in "final" form in the *Register* (often with changes since the proposed version, so that a comparison between proposed and final form can be useful in figuring out the agency's intent).

   b. **The *Code of Federal Regulations*:** Final rules and regulations are codified in the *Code of Federal Regulations* (C.F.R.). The C.F.R. divides all administrative law into 50 subject titles; each title is divided into parts, which are sub-divided into sections. After the first five titles (which describe the organization of the federal government), the remaining titles each cover a single subject (e.g., Banks and Banking, Food and Drugs, Internal Revenue, Labor, Postal Service, Transportation, etc.).

      The C.F.R. now takes up about 150 volumes, which are published by the government in soft cover. Each individual volume is published once a year, and there is no hard-copy supplementation. Because publishing the C.F.R. is such a huge task, the govern-

1. See *supra*, p. 5-6.

ment prints it in four groups as of four different dates:

Titles	Current As of	Publication Date
1-16	January 1	Shortly after January 1
17-27	April 1	Shortly after April 1
28-41	July 1	Shortly after July 1
42-50	October 1	Shortly after October 1

So the C.F.R. in its official print form is basically four sets of "snapshots" of "current" regulatory law. But although each is nearly current as of the moment of publication, it can be more than a year out of date by the end of its annual cycle.[2]

2. **Administrative decisions and rulings:** An administrative agency generally also has the responsibility of applying its regulations to specific fact patterns. These case-like decisions by agency personnel are sometimes called ***"administrative decisions"*** and sometimes called ***"rulings."*** (Rulings tend to be non-binding on the agency in later similar fact situations, whereas administrative decisions have more force of precedent.) For instance, the National Labor Relations Board, as part of its job of administering the nation's labor laws, conducts administrative trials to determine, say, whether a particular company management has committed an Unfair Labor Practice; the case is tried to an Administrative Law Judge, and culminates in an administrative decision that in format and content is similar to a judicial opinion. There are more administrative decisional materials than can be covered in this book; some of the more important are treated below in our specific discussion of decisions and rulings on LEXIS.

B. Federal administrative law on the LEXIS-NEXIS services:

1. **Federal regulations on LEXIS-NEXIS:** The full and up-to-date contents of both the *Federal Register* and the *Code of Federal Regulations* are available on the LEXIS service, so you can research federal regulations thoroughly on the system.

   a. **The *Federal Register:*** If you want the full text of the *Federal Register*, it is available in file *FEDREG*, located in both the *CODES* and the *GENFED* libraries. Additionally, many of the special-purpose libraries contain just those documents from the Federal Register pertaining to that topic; examples of such special-interest libraries include Bankruptcy (*BKRTCY* library), Copyright (*COPYRT*), Federal Securities Law (*FEDSEC*), Labor (*LABOR*), and Patent (*PATENT*).[3] In each of these special-purpose libraries, the *Federal Register* materials are in a file called *FEDREG*.

   The full text of each day's *Federal Register* comes online by 5:00 PM (EST) of the day

2. As you'll see below, p. 6-4, the LEXIS version of the C.F.R. is, by contrast, much more up-to-date than the G.P.O.'s print version.

3. Many of the special purpose libraries are discussed in greater detail beginning *infra*, p. 7-1.

the text is released by the Government Printing Office.

i. Segment layout: The most important segments in the *FEDREG* file are as follows:

Name of Segment	Description
AGENCY	Name of agency (e.g., "Department of the Treasury")
SUB-AGENCY	Name of sub-agency within the agency (e.g., "United States Customs Service," which is a branch of the Dept. of the Treasury)
CFR	Cite to that part of Code of Federal Regulations which is being affected, cited by Title, Part and name of section (e.g., "47 C.F.R. Part 76 Cable TV Act of 1992 — Cable rate regulations")
NUMBER	Any number assigned by the agency to its proceeding (e.g., "FCC 93-304")
DATE	Date of the Federal Register issue in which the document appears (which can be searched by **BEF**, **AFT** and **IS**)
ACTION	Status of the rule or regulation, i.e., proposed, final, interim (e.g., "Interim Rule with request for comments")
SUMMARY	Two or three sentence summary of what the rule or regulation does
DATES	Effective date of the regulation; date by which comments are due; other dates (e.g., "This Interim Rule becomes effective February 14, 1991. Comments due April 15, 1991")
CONTACT	Person to contact for more information, or to whom comments should be sent; generally contains telephone number and/or address
TEXT	Full text of regulation or other document
HEADING	This is a group segment, which combines the *AGENCY, SUB-AGENCY, CFR, NUMBER* and *ACTION* segments

b. The *Code of Federal Regulations:* The entire current text of the *Code of Federal Regulations* is available as file *CFR*, located in both the *CODES* and *GENFED* library. In addition, individual C.F.R. Titles are located in the special-subject libraries to which they pertain (e.g., Title 49, dealing with Transportation, is available in the *TRANS* library). If you don't know which Title you are interested in, your best bet is the *CFR* file in the *CODES* or *GENFED* library.

As noted above,[4] in the G.P.O's hard-copy version of the C.F.R., each Title is updated once a year, and the update date varies from Title to Title; the print version of a given Title can thus be as much as 15 months out-of-date. However, the LEXIS version of the C.F.R. is actually much more up-to-date, as the result of new procedures adopted by LEXIS-NEXIS in 1994-95. Each week, Michie (a sister unit of LEXIS-NEXIS)

4. See *supra*, pp. 6-2 to 6-3.

takes all the changes that have appeared in the Federal Register, and ***"integrates"*** those changes into the appropriate places in the LEXIS version of the C.F.R. Therefore, when you search the C.F.R. on the LEXIS-NEXIS service, you're seeing the regulatory scheme in a form that is rarely more than two weeks behind the Federal Register.[5]

i. Segment layout: Here is the segment layout for the *CFR* file:

Name of Segment	Description
TITLE	Title number and title name (e.g., "Title 47 — Telecommunication; revised as of October 1, 1991")
CHAPTER	Chapter number and name; subchapter letter and name (e.g., "Chapter I — Federal Communications Commission. Subchapter C — Broadcast Radio Services")
PART	Part number and name; subpart letter and name (e.g., "Part 76 — Cable Television Service. Subpart A — General")
HEADING	A group segment, consisting of the TITLE, CHAPTER and PART segments
SECTION	Section number and name (e.g., "@ 76.5 Definitions")
NOTES	Editorial information, including effective date and description of structural changes
CITE	Citation to C.F.R. (e.g., "47 C.F.R. 76.5")
TEXT	Full text of C.F.R. section
HISTORY	Citations to and dates of the *Federal Register* pages where the CFR section was first published and later amended (e.g., "37 F.R. 3278, Feb. 12, 1972")
AUTHORITY	Citation to statute authorizing the regulation (e.g., "47 U.S.C. 152, 153, 154, 301, 303")

c. Finding a document by its C.F.R. or F.R. cite: You will frequently want to find a regulation in the *Federal Register* or the C.F.R. by its cite. Here's how to do it:

i. Federal Register: The best way to retrieve a document from the *Federal Register* when you have its cite is to use the LEXSEE feature.[6] Thus:

```
lexsee 56 fr 16048
```

Federal Register documents are generally cited by reference to the first page of the document. Thus the document retrieved by the above LEXSEE request is a multi-page document that started on page 16048 of volume 56 of the *Federal Register*. (A new volume of the Federal Register is published each year, so the volume number

5. Because of this possibility of an up-to-two-weeks gap, you'll still want to check the Federal Register for the last two weeks to make sure nothing really recent affected the regulations you're interested in.

6. LEXSEE is used with "non-codified" materials, and LEXSTAT is used with "codified" ones. The distinction is discussed on p. 5-6 above. Since the *Federal Register* is non-codified, LEXSEE is used.

increases by one each year.)

By the way, the LEXIS service contains the complete *Federal Register* back to July, 1980.

ii. C.F.R.: To retrieve a regulation by its C.F.R. cite, use the LEXSTAT[7] feature. Thus:

```
lexstat 37 cfr 1.628
```

will retrieve section number 1.628 from Title 37 (Patents, Trademarks and Copyrights) of the C.F.R.

You can only use LEXSTAT to retrieve a *particular section* of the C.F.R., not to retrieve an entire Part.[8]

By the way, just as you can use the BROWSE feature to browse through adjacent sections when looking at a statutory code,[9] so you can use the BROWSE function to do this with the C.F.R. Thus if we were looking at 37 C.F.R. 1.628, we could type the letter **b**, and then use the [PREV DOC] (F4, or type **.pd**) and [NEXT DOC] (F3 or type **.nd**) to view 37 C.F.R. 1.627 and 37 C.F.R. 1.629 respectively.

As you would expect, a LEXSTAT search on the C.F.R. cite will always retrieve the latest published version of that C.F.R. cite, so you won't have to worry about inadvertently getting a now-obsolete version (though prior versions of the C.F.R. back to 1981 are also available online, as I describe below). However, keep in mind that the online version of C.F.R. itself can be a couple of weeks out of date, so to be absolutely sure of currentness you always need to update your research by checking the *Federal Register.*[10]

d. Finding regulations when you know the cite of the federal statute: Frequently, you will have identified a federal statute, and will need to find any regulations implementing that statute. There are several ways to do this; they are not mutually exclusive, and you should consider doing all of them to leave no stone unturned:

- First, look at the statutory section in the U.S. Code Service; the *NOTES* segment of the USCS contains cross-references to the Code of Federal Regulations. The easiest way to do this is to do a LEXSTAT search on the USCS citation, and then enter:

```
se; notes
```

This will put you right into the *NOTES* segment. Then you can examine the material that follows the status line in *NOTES* called "CODE OF FEDERAL REGULA-

---

7. See the prior footnote. The C.F.R. is codified.

8. Each "Part" in the C.F.R. groups together multiple sections dealing with a single issue. To find an entire Part, your best bet is to do a regular LEXIS search on the *TITLE* segment together with the *PART* segment: **TITLE(47) AND PART(76)**. This will find all sections within the specified Part, and you can examine them one at a time.

9. See *supra*, p. 5-21.

10. I describe in detail how to do this *infra*, p. 6-8.

TIONS:"

Thus if we knew that we were dealing with 12 U.S.C. 1818 (governing a bank's termination as an insured depository institution), we would do:

```
lexstat 12 usc 1818
```

This would show us section 1818; **.se; notes** would put us into the *NOTES* segment, where we would find, under the status line "CODE OF FEDERAL REGULATIONS:" the line "Federal Deposit Insurance Corporation, termination of insured status, 12 CFR Part 307."

Occasionally, this technique will produce a reference to a particular CFR section, in which case you can retrieve the section by using the LEXSTAT feature. But the vast majority of the time, the references you will get from the U.S. Code Service will not be references to a particular CFR section, but instead, to a particular Part, as in the above example. You will not be able to use LEXSTAT when all you know is the title and the part.[11] Instead, you will have to do a segment-limited search. Thus if, as in the above example, the U.S.C. reference was to 12 CFR Part 307, you would then log in to the *CODES* library, *CFR* file, and do the following search:

```
title(12) and part(307)
```

- Second, you can (and should) now use the opposite tack: search the *CFR* or *FEDREG* file for any references to the U.S.C. cite that you have. Thus to find any entries in *CFR* that mention 42 U.S.C. 12101 (the first section of the Americans with Disabilities Act), you would do a conventional search for a statutory section, perhaps:

```
42 pre/20 12101
```

Don't try to look for phrases; use **PRE/n** instead. A reference in the body of a regulation will often list a number of sections, e.g., "47 U.S.C. 225, 283, 318 and 611." A search for **47 usc 611** will not find a document with such a reference, but **47 pre/20 611** will.

The technique described just above will find every regulation in the C.F.R. mentioning a particular statute, even if the reference is a fleeting one that has nothing to do with the core of the regulation. If you get overwhelmed with documents when you do this kind of broad search, you can narrow it by limiting yourself to regulations whose *AUTHORITY* segment lists the statute you are interested in. Thus:

```
authority(42 pre/20 12101)
```

produces fewer regulation sections (and ones more directly relevant to our statute, the Americans with Disabilities Act) than does a non-segment-limited search on the same U.S. Code section. (This technique works for the C.F.R., but does not work the *Federal Register*, which has no segment analogous to *AUTHORITY.*)

11. See p. 6-6 above.

e. Searching when you know an issue or fact pattern: When you have an issue or a fact pattern, but no form of cite, you can do key word searching just as you would with a case or statute. Thus if you wanted regulations having to do with wheelchair-access in office buildings, you might look in the *CFR* and *FEDREG* files (both of them in the *CODES* library) for:

```
(wheelchair w/5 access!) and (office w/5 building)
```

There is no very useful index to either the *Federal Register* or the C.F.R. available online, so a full text search on the materials themselves is pretty much what you have to do if you do not have a cite to either the governing statute or to the *Federal Register*/C.F.R. document itself.

If you know what administrative agency would promulgate the regulations you're interested in, then you can use a segment limitation. In the *CFR* file, the segment called *CHAPTER* contains the name of the agency; in the *FEDREG* file, there is a separate segment called *AGENCY.* Thus if we know that we want cable television rate regulations promulgated by the Federal Communications Commission, we could search in the *CODES* library, *CFR* file for:

```
chapter(communications commission) and (CATV or cable)
 and rate
```

and in the *CODES* library, *FEDREG* file for:

```
agency(communications) and (cable or CATV) and rate
```

f. Updating your research: Normally, you will do your most intensive regulation research in the *CFR* file, since you know that that file had the entire current body of regulations contained within it on the date it was published (which, if you will recall, is once per year). The *FEDREG* file, by contrast, contains all the regulations enacted since 1980, and if you search the whole thing, you will come up with many since-repealed or since-amended regulations, which will just confuse you. Therefore, you will usually only want to use *FEDREG* to ***update*** your C.F.R. research. To do this, take the following steps:

- Do your C.F.R. research. For each regulation you find, check the line at the top the document, which will tell you the date as of which that C.F.R. Title is current (e.g., "This section is current through the 6/19/95 issue of the Federal Register.") When you write down the cite to each of these C.F.R. sections, write down not only the particular section, but the Part of which that section is a portion (since the *Federal Register*, which we will be looking at in the second step, generally cites to the Part rather than to the section). Thus for the Americans with Disabilities Act, we would write down citations such as "49 C.F.R. Part 27" (not just "49 C.F.R. 27.1").
- Now, change to the *FEDREG* file. Do a search that is limited to the *CFR* segment and limited by date. Thus for our Americans with Disabilities problem, if we knew that the C.F.R. was current as of 6/12/95, and the C.F.R. materials we found were in Title 49, Part 27, we would search in *CODES/FEDREG* for:

```
cfr(49 and 27) and date aft 6/12/95
```

From the documents retrieved in this way, you will want to home in on those that affect just the particular section(s) you're interested in, since a Part often includes many sections, and the sections affected by the particular *Federal Register* document you are looking at may not be the ones you are interested in at all. The best way to do this homing in is to use the FOCUS feature[12] together with the particular section number. Thus after doing the above search for Title 49, Part 27, if we were particularly interested in section 27.3, we would do the following request:

```
focus 27.3
```

This will let us, using the [KWIC] key, get right to any reference to "27.3" within any document affecting 49 C.F.R. Part 27. (You don't want to use the entire C.F.R. cite in your FOCUS request, because the full cite may never occur in the underlying document. References to existing C.F.R. materials usually read like this: "Section 890.205 is revised to read as follows. . . ." — in such a reference, there is generally no place where the C.F.R. Title and the section are in close proximity to each other.)

g. **Going back in time in the C.F.R. and the F.R.:** Occasionally you will need to ascertain not what the state of regulation is today, but what it was at *some earlier date*. You can do this in both the C.F.R. and the *Federal Register*, as long as you are dealing with a date in the 1980s or later.

   i. **Federal Register:** The *Federal Register* is like a newspaper — one daily "issue" is never really superseded by later issues. Therefore, the LEXIS service keeps online all issues of the *Federal Register* since July 1980. Consequently, you can check whether a certain event happened within a certain time frame by using a **DATE BEF** and **DATE AFT** limitation:

```
catv or cable and rate and date aft 1982 and
 date bef 1986
```

   Of course, this won't by itself tell you every regulation that was ***in force*** during that period, only those regulations that were in some way ***changed*** (so that a regulation enacted in 1979, and still in force in 1984, would not show up by this technique).

   ii. **C.F.R.:** The LEXIS service also keeps online every annual version of the C.F.R. since 1981. These are all stored in the *GENFED* library, in a series of files named *CFRNN*, where *NN* is the last two digits of the year (e.g., file *CFR87*, for the 1987 Code of Federal Regulations).

12. See *supra*, p. 2-41.

2. **Court rules:** If you will be litigating in federal court, you will need to master a variety of ***court rules***. Many of the relevant ones can be found on the LEXIS service. Here is a summary of some of the more important ones; all are found in the *GENFED* library:

Name of File	Description
FRAP	Federal Rules of Appellate Procedure
BKRULE	Federal Rules of Bankruptcy Procedure, and official bankruptcy forms
FRCP	Federal Rules of Civil Procedure
FRCRP	Federal Rules of Criminal Procedure
FRE	Federal Rules of Evidence
SUPRUL	U.S. Supreme Court Rules
1CRUL . . . through *11CRUL*	Federal Courts of Appeal, First Circuit Rules . . . through Eleventh Circuit Rules
DCRUL	D.C. Circuit Rules
FCRUL	Federal Circuit Rules

a. **Segment layout:** The segment layout for most of these files is as follows:

Name of Segment	Description
HEADING	Description of type of rule (e.g., "Federal Rules of Civil Procedure, V. Depositions and Discovery")
CITE	Citation to the individual rule (e.g., "USCS Fed. Rules Civ. Proc. R. 34 (1992)")
SECTION	Number of rule, and name of rule (e.g., "Rule 34. Production of Documents and Things and Entry Upon Land for Inspection and Other Purposes")
TEXT	Full text of rule
HISTORY	History of amendments, and references to Advisory Committee Notes and other related rules and legislation

3. **Decisions and rulings:** Many federal agency ***decisions*** and ***rulings*** are available on the LEXIS service. A full treatment of these is beyond the scope of this book. Many of the decisions and rulings are parts of special-purpose libraries, which are summarized in the next chapter.[13] Here are a few random files to give you some idea of the kinds of decisions and rulings available on the system:

a. **Tax:** Relating to tax, and found in the *FEDTAX* library:

File Name	Description
PLR	Private Letter Rulings
GCM	General Counsel Memoranda
AOD	Actions on Decisions

13. See *infra*, p. 7-1.

b. **Justice:** Relating to the U.S. Department of Justice, and found in the *GENFED* library:

File Name	Description
USAG	Opinions of the U.S. Attorney General

c. **Environmental:** Relating to environmental law, and found in the *ENVIRN* special-purpose library:

File Name	Description
CONDEC	EPA Consent Decrees
CAA	Clean Air Act Decisions
INTDEC	Department of the Interior, Interior Decisions

d. **Labor and employment law:** Relating to labor and employment, and found in the *LABOR* special-purpose library:

File Name	Description
NLRB	National Labor Relations Board decisions
EEOC	Equal Employment Opportunity Commission decisions
OSAHRC	Occupational Safety and Health Review Commission decisions
ERISA	ERISA letter opinions

e. **Banking:** Relating to banking law, and found in the *BANKNG* special-purpose library:

File Name	Description
THRIFT	Office of Thrift Supervision General Counsel opinions, Federal Home Loan Bank Board General Counsel opinions
FDIC	FDIC Interpretive Letters and Enforcement Decisions
COMGEN	Comptroller General decisions

f. **Securities law:** Relevant to securities law and found in the *FEDSEC* library:

File Name	Description
NOACT	SEC No-Action Letters
SECREL	SEC Releases, Administrative Decisions and Administrative Proceedings Rulings
CFTC	Commodities Futures Trading Commission orders and decisions

4. **Presidential documents:** Many documents relating to the presidency are contained in the *PRESDC* file, in the *GENFED* library. These documents include Executive Orders, Proclamations, presidential messages to Congress, speeches, press conferences and the like.

The *GENFED* library also contains various State Department documents (including the Department of State Dispatch, formerly known as the Department of State Bulletin) in the *DSTATE* file.

II. STATE ADMINISTRATIVE LAW

A. Introduction: State administrative law coverage on the LEXIS service is growing rapidly.

B. State administrative codes: Most states have an ***administrative code***, that is, an arrangement of their administrative regulations by subject matter; a state administrative code is analogous to the *Code of Federal Regulations*.[14] At this point, the complete administrative codes of 32 states are available on the LEXIS service. All of these codes are found in the *CODES* and *STATES* libraries, in a file named *XXADMN*, where *XX* is the two-letter postal abbreviation for the state (e.g., *FLADMN*, for the Florida Administrative Code). A typical segment layout for a state administrative code file is as follows:

Name of Segment	Description
CITE	Citation to a particular administrative code section (e.g., "OAC 123:1-7-15" for an Ohio Administrative Code section)
RULE	Rule number and name (e.g., "123:1-7-15 State Managerial and Supervisory Classifications")
TEXT	Full text of code section
EFF-DATE	Effective date of section
HISTORY	History of code section
NOTES	Annotations, including cross-references, statutory references and case digests

1. **State registers:** Some states also have a ***register***, a daily or weekly publication showing changes to the state's administrative regulations. (These are analogous to the Federal Register.) At this writing, the registers of three states — Pennsylvania, Texas and New Mexico — are available on LEXIS-NEXIS. These are found in files named *XXREG* (where *XX* is the state's postal abbreviation) in the *CODES* library, as well as in a file of the same name in the individual state library (e.g., *TEXREG* in the *TEX* library.)

C. State Attorney General decisions: For all 50 states, the LEXIS service contains state ***Attorney General opinions***. These are generally opinions giving advice about the legality of a proposed statute or other governmental conduct. All Attorney General files are located in the *STATES* library, and have the name *XXAG*, where *XX* is the two-digit postal abbreviation for the state (e.g., *ARAG* for Arkansas Attorney General opinions). These files are also available as a file called *AG* in each individual state library (e.g., file *AG* in the *OHIO* library.)

D. Other state agency decisions: State agencies, like federal ones, sometimes publish their decisions, but this is much less common than in the federal arena. Here are some of the state administrative decisions available on the LEXIS service:

---

14. The C.F.R. is discussed *supra*, p. 6-2.

1. **Public Utility Commissions:** For 17 states, the LEXIS service contains the state's ***Public Utility Commission*** files. These states are California, Connecticut, Delaware, Florida, Illinois, Indiana, Louisiana, Maryland, Michigan, Minnesota, Missouri, New York, Ohio, Pennsylvania, Texas, Washington and Wisconsin. All of these files are in the *STATES* library (as well as the *UTILTY* library), and have the name *XXPUC*, where *XX* is the two-digit postal abbreviation (e.g., *DEPUC*, for Delaware Public Service Commission files).

   In addition, LEXIS contains the full text of a commercial publication, Public Utilities Reports (Fourth), which includes selected full-text decisions from the Public Utility Commissions of all 50 states plus the federal system. These are in library *UTILTY*, file *ALLPUR* (all 50 states and federal, combined), and files *XXPUR* (one for each state, with *XX* the state's postal abbreviation).

2. **Environmental agencies:** For 10 states, the LEXIS service contains state ***environmental agency*** decisions. The states are California, Florida, Georgia, Illinois, Louisiana, Michigan, New Jersey, New York, Ohio and Pennsylvania. The files are in the *STATES* and *ENVIRN* libraries, and have the name *XXENV*, where *XX* is the two-digit postal abbreviation (e.g., *LAEVN*, for Louisiana Department of Environmental Quality).[15]

3. **Tax:** For all 50 states, various state ***tax-related*** administrative documents are available (often including rules, regulations, rulings, Private Letter Rulings, and other material whose categories varies from state to state). These can all be found in the *STATES* library, in a file named *XXTAX*, where the *XX* is the two-letter postal abbreviation (e.g., *MOTAX*, for Missouri Tax Commission decisions, orders and other materials).

4. **Security agencies:** For about 29 states, the LEXIS service contains states' ***securities*** regulatory materials (including orders, decisions, releases and No-action Letters). These can be found in the *STATES* library, in a file named *XXSEC*, where *XX* is the two-digit postal abbreviation (e.g., *FLSEC*, for Florida Division of Securities materials).

E. State court rules: The LEXIS service now carries ***court rules*** for all 50 states, plus the District of Columbia and Puerto Rico. The file name for each state's rules is *XXRULE*, where *XX* is the postal abbreviation for the state. These files can be found in the *STATES* library, or in the individual state libraries. The segments include *HEADING, CITE, RULE, TEXT, HISTORY* and *NOTES*.

15. In addition, state environmental *regulations* for all 50 states are available in the *ENVIRN* library. The files are named *XXEVRG*, where *XX* is the state's postal abbreviation (e.g., *ILEVRG* for Illinois Environmental Regulations.)

Chapter 7

Specialized Legal Research

Introductory Note: This chapter contains an overview of a number of subject areas, and LEXIS tools for searching in those areas. In over 40 areas of law, the LEXIS service has grouped different types of materials, such as cases, statutes, regulations, secondary sources, etc. into a single-subject library (e.g., the *FEDTAX* library for federal tax, and the *INTLAW* library for international law). I have chosen six areas to highlight:

Federal Tax
Securities and Corporate
Labor and Employment
Intellectual Property
Environmental
Foreign and International

After these highlights, I list various other specialized libraries.

I. FEDERAL TAX RESEARCH

A. Introduction: Federal tax research is a large and arcane specialty — few lawyers who do not consider themselves "tax lawyers" are even minimally competent at it. I personally do not fall into either the category of "tax lawyer" or the category of "non-tax-lawyer who is minimally competent in tax research." Therefore, for both space and competency reasons, my treatment of doing tax research on the LEXIS service will be enough to give you a sense of the lay of the land, but not enough to come close to making *you* competent.

B. Overview of tax research generally: Let me begin by listing some of the types of materials that a researcher might look at in trying to solve a federal[1] tax problem:

- The ***Internal Revenue Code***, which is essentially a set of federal statutes. (In any version of the U.S. Code, the I.R.C. appears as Title 26.)
- Regulations interpreting the Internal Revenue Code. These are called ***"Treasury Regulations,"*** and are written by the Treasury Department.

1. LEXIS also has a wealth of materials relating to *state* tax law and administration. Many of these are in the *STATES* library, in files named *XXTAX*, where *XX* is the state's postal abbreviation. State tax materials are beyond the scope of this discussion.

- IRS releases, which fall into several sub-categories, of which the most important are:
  - *Revenue Rulings*, which apply the law to particular fact situations presented by taxpayers, but which are deemed by the IRS to be of somewhat general interest.
  - *Revenue Procedures*, which are published statements about the practices and procedures of the IRS.
  - *Private Letter Rulings*, which like Revenue Rulings apply the law to specific fact patterns presented by taxpayers, but which in contrast to Revenue Rulings have precedential value only to the taxpayer to whom the letter is addressed. (Other taxpayers search PLRs for indications of IRS policy.)
  - *Technical Advice Memoranda*, which are similar to Private Letter Rulings, but which are written by the IRS in response to an IRS agent's request.
  - *General Counsel Memoranda* (legal memos by the IRS' Office of Chief Counsel advising IRS personnel on legal issues) and *Actions on Decisions* (memos prepared by IRS lawyers in the Tax Litigation Division).
  - The *Internal Revenue Manual*, which describes the IRS' internal operating policies and procedures.
- Federal tax ***case law***, which can come from any district or federal appeals court, but can also come from a special-purpose court, the United States Tax Court.
- ***Legislative history***, mainly reports and lengthy explanations of tax legislation from the House Ways and Means Committee, the Senate Finance Committee and the Joint Committee on Taxation.
- Secondary ***looseleafs*** and other narratives about tax law, published by commercial publishers such as RIA and BNA.
- ***Daily tax news***, such as *Tax Notes Today* and *BNA Daily Tax Report*.
- ***Tax periodicals***, such as *The Journal of Taxation* and the *Tax Law Review*.
- ***International*** tax news and tax treaties, as published by commercial publishers like Tax Analysts and the International Bureau of Fiscal Documentation.

C. **Strategy for tax research:** The order in which you use these sources while researching a problem is likely to depend both on your personal style and your degree of expertise in tax law. If you are a beginner, you will probably find it best to begin with secondary materials and periodicals to get an overview, then follow those leads into the Code, regulations and other primary documents. True tax professionals, by contrast, usually know — or very quickly discover — which IRC section(s) is at issue, and immediately look at that section, and regulations and releases about it, going to secondary materials only later. In the treatment that follows, I proceed from official to unofficial sources, even though that is probably not the order in which you will do your research if you are a beginner.

D. **The Internal Revenue Code and regulations under it:** For the Internal Revenue Code and the regulations under it, as for most aspects of federal tax law, what you need will generally be found in the *FEDTAX* library, a special-purpose library consisting solely of tax-related (both state and federal) materials.

1. **The Code:** There are two files each of which contains the full text of the Internal Revenue Code: *USCS* and *CODE*. The *USCS* file consists of Title 26 from the United States Code Service, published by Lawyers Cooperative Service.[2] The *CODE* file is a different version of Title 26, prepared by RIA, a tax publisher. Of the two, *USCS* has two features that you are likely to find advantageous which *CODE* does not:

   - Since *USCS* is part of the complete United States Code Service version of the U.S. Code, its segment layout is the same as that of the complete *USCS* file,[3] and you are likely to be familiar with it from research you have done into the non-tax parts of the United States Code;

   - *USCS* has extensive annotations, including cross-references to the appropriate Treasury Regulations, citations to law review articles on point, and, most importantly, digests of thousands of cases on point. (The annotations are contained in the *NOTES* segment.)

   You can do a key word search in either the *USCS* or *CODE* file (both in the *FEDTAX* library), as you would expect to be able to do, for instance:

   ```
   entertainment expense w/30 deduct!
   ```

   If you happen to know the number of an IRC section, you can use the LEXSTAT feature:

   ```
   lexstat 26 uscs 274
   ```

   (to get the *USCS* version) or:

   ```
   lexstat irc 274
   ```

   (for the *CODE* version).

2. **Treasury Regulations:** Once you find a section of the IRC that is on point, you will almost always want to look at the regulations enacted by the Treasury Department interpreting that section. These are called ***Treasury Regulations***. They are numbered in a scheme that parallels the IRC. Thus a regulation construing IRC §274 would have a number like 1.274-2. (The number in front of the decimal point indicates the type of regulation. "1" indicates Income Tax, "20" indicates Estate Tax, "25" stands for Gift Tax, "301" stands for Procedure and Administration, and "601" stands for IRS Procedural Rules. The number after the decimal point and before the hyphen is the IRC section; the numbers and letters after the hyphen indicate the hierarchy of rules interpreting that particular IRC section.)

   Final Treasury Regulations are contained in the *FEDTAX* library, *REGS* file. Proposed Treasury Regulations (which, as their name indicates, have not yet taken effect), are in the *FEDTAX* library, *P-REGS* file.

---

2. See *supra*, p. 5-9 for the discussion of the USCS.

3. This segment layout is summarized *supra*, p. 5-10.

If you know an IRC section and want to see the final Treasury Regulations for that section (but don't know the exact cite to the regulation itself), you can do a key-word search that takes into account the structured way in which regulations are numbered. Thus for regulations construing IRC 274, you would search for (in the *FEDTAX* library, *REGS* file):

```
26 cfr 1.274!
```

This will find regulations 1.274-1, 1.274-2, 1.274-3, and anything else interpreting §274. (This technique should work for proposed regulations, in the *P-REGS* file, as well.)

E. IRS Releases:

1. **Revenue Rulings:** Revenue Rulings are found in the *CB* file in the *FEDTAX* library. The reason the file is called *CB* is that Revenue Rulings are published in the IRS' ***Cumulative Bulletin***, a publication detailing the IRS' internal procedures.

   More precisely, a Revenue Ruling is first published in the weekly Internal Revenue Bulletin; the IRB is then cumulated twice a year, in the Cumulative Bulletin. A Revenue Ruling therefore has several different citations — initially, it might be cited as "Rev. Rul. 93-21, 1993-13 I.R.B. 11" (the first cite means the 21st Revenue Ruling issued in 1993; the second cite means the 13th issue of the Internal Revenue Bulletin published in 1993, p. 11). Once a particular issue of the IRB has been replaced by a Cumulative Bulletin, a CB cite is added as another parallel cite: "1993-2 C.B. 212," for instance.

   Therefore, if you know any of the three forms of cite for a Revenue Ruling, you can use LEXSEE to get the document:

   ```
   lexsee rev rul 93-70
   ```

   or

   ```
   lexsee 1993-33 irb 17
   ```

   or

   ```
   lexsee 1993-2 cb 294
   ```

   The text of a Revenue Ruling mentions the IRC sections, and the Treasury Regulations, to which the Revenue Ruling relates. Therefore, you can do searches in the *CB* file for Revenue Rulings having to do with a particular section or Treasury Regulation. For instance, to find all Revenue Rulings having to do with IRC §274 or Regulation 1.274(d), you can search (in *FEDTAX/CB*) for:

   ```
   document(rev rul) and (274 or 1.274 d)
   ```

   A useful segment is the *HILITE* segment, which contains a synopsis of the ruling — you may want to do a search limited to the *HILITE* segment, to retrieve fewer, more relevant, documents.

2. **Revenue Procedures:** Revenue Procedures are treated almost identically to Revenue Rulings. Therefore, you find them in the *CB* file, and they have the same three forms of citing (e.g., "Rev. Proc. 93-21, 1993-13 I.R.B. 11, 1993-2 C.B. 679").

Techniques for searching Revenue Procedures, and for using the LEXSEE feature to retrieve by cite, are the same as for Revenue Rulings.

3. **Private Letter Rulings:** IRS Private Letter Rulings are found in the *PLR* file in the *FEDTAX* library. The cite for a PLR is essentially a file number, like "9237003" (the first two digits are the year of issuance, the next two digits are the week of issuance, and the last three digits are the number within that week).

   PLRs contain references to the IRC sections to which they relate. Thus to find all PLRs relating to IRC §274, you would search (in *FEDTAX/PLR*) for:

   `heading(section 274)`[4]

   Also, the verbal title of each IRC section is also included in the file. Since the verbal title for §274 is "Disallowance of Certain Entertainment Expense," instead of searching for PLRs relating to §274, you could search for PLRs in which the words "disallowance," "entertainment" and "expense" occur in the *HEADING* segment.

4. **Technical Advice Memoranda:** Technical Advice Memoranda are also included in the *PLR* file. (In fact, TAMs are identical to PLRs except that they originate in response to an agent's request or an audit, rather than in response to a taxpayer's request.) The citation form and the segment layout are the same as for PLRs.

5. **General Counsel Memoranda:** General Counsel Memoranda are contained in their own file, named *GCM*. Cross-references to Code sections are done in the same way as for PLRs.

6. **Actions on Decisions:** Actions on Decisions are contained in their own file, named *AOD*.

7. **Internal Revenue Manual:** If you have an issue relating to the IRS own internal procedures, you will find the various sub-manuals included in the Internal Revenue Manual very helpful. All of these are contained in the file called *MANUAL*. To search the Manual for Code sections, use the TEXT segment. Thus to find all portions of the Internal Revenue Manual having to do with IRC §274, you could search (in *FEDTAX/MANUAL*) for:

   ```
   text((irc or i.r.c. or code or section or 26) pre/5 (274
   or @274))
   ```

F. **Legislative history:** The legislative history of tax laws is well covered on the LEXIS service. The file *LEGIS* (in the *FEDTAX* library) contains the full text of Committee Reports from the House Ways and Means Committee, the Senate Finance Committee, and the House-Senate Conference Committee, for all the tax bills since 1954. Joint Committee on Taxation "Blue Books" and prints are also available in this file.[5]

---

4. You may notice that in the retrieved documents, the IRC section number is sometimes preceded by a leading zero (e.g., "Section 0274"). Don't worry about this in your search statement — your search on the number without the leading zero (e.g., **`section 274`**) will find the documents that have the leading zero.

5. For general information about legislative history for federal statutes, see *supra*, p. 5-23.

G. Tax case law: A full range of tax case law is present on the LEXIS service. The best single source is the *CASES* file in the *FEDTAX* library; this combines tax cases from the Supreme Court, Courts of Appeal, District Courts, and, most importantly, the Tax Court. The Tax Court cases consist of both full Tax Court opinions as well as Memorandum Decisions. An additional feature of this library is Commissioner's Acquiescence and Non-Acquiescence Tables for Tax Court opinions — these tell you, for each Tax Court case which the IRS lost, whether the IRS agrees to accept the ruling and reasoning in future similar fact situations.

H. Third-party collections: There are a number of extensive overviews of the law of federal taxation available on the LEXIS service. Some of these are ones that began their existence as looseleaf services, published by commercial publishers. Here, I can only scratch the surface of what is available on LEXIS. Four of the most useful third-party sources are RIA's *Federal Tax Coordinator 2d*, RIA's *U.S. Tax Reporter*, BNA's *Tax Management Portfolios*, and Tax Analysts' *Tax Notes* Magazine.

1. **RIA's Federal Tax Coordinator:** RIA's *Federal Tax Coordinator 2d* (file *RIAFTC*, in library *FEDTAX*) is a thorough narrative on the entire Internal Revenue Code. One big advantage of it is that it is organized into chapters on the basis of subject matter, rather than using the IRC section-number organization employed by most other tax publishers. Much of the information is simply written, and the service has a transactional bent — if you have such and such a tax problem, here are the methods (including documents) by which you solve it. Thus if I look in *FEDTAX/RIAFTC* for

   `(meal w/10 entertain!) w/20 expens!`

   one of the 18 documents retrieved is entitled "Deduction for Entertainment Expenses and Club Dues," which has a sub-section called "Meal and Entertainment Deduction Limit." This tells me, in language understandable to an ordinary person (as opposed to a tax professional) that "The amount allowable as a deduction for any expense for food or beverages may not exceed 50% of the amount otherwise allowable as a deduction." The editors then give me a nice little illustration: "A business meal costs $ 200. Tax and tip come to $10 and $30, respectively. The amount deductible is $ 120 (i.e., 50% of $ 240)." This kind of clear and practical writing about tax is a lot rarer than you might think.

   The *RIAFTC* file robustly supports Star Paging. At the beginning of each major section ("Deduction for Entertainment Expenses and Club Dues" in the above example), you are given a Table of Contents of sub-sections; you can get to any sub-section by typing **`p*`** followed by the sub-section's four-digit number (e.g., **`p*2135`** to get to the "Meal and Entertainment Deduction Limit" discussed above).

2. **RIA's U.S. Tax Reporter:** RIA's *U.S. Tax Reporter* (file *FED*, in library *FEDTAX*) is the online version of RIA's full-scale multi-volume federal tax looseleaf service. It contains the full text of the Code and Regulations, the full text of relevant Committee Reports, plus extensive editorial analysis by RIA's editors. A segment called *IRC* gives you an easy way to find all references in the service to a particular Code section (e.g., **`irc(274)`**).

3. **BNA Tax Management Portfolios:** One of the favorite secondary sources of serious tax professionals is the *Tax Management Portfolio* series published by BNA. These are

divided into the Federal Income Tax Series (file *TMUS* in libraries *FEDTAX* and *BNA*), the Estates, Gifts & Trusts Series (in file *TMEGT* in libraries *FEDTAX*, *BNA,* and *ESTATE*), and the Foreign Income Series (in file *TMFOR* in libraries *FEDTAX* and *BNA*).

A *Tax Management Portfolio* is a document whose hard-copy runs about 50-200 pages, devoted to a fairly narrow segment of tax law. The entire Portfolio series consists of several hundred of these documents. If you can find a Portfolio that is more or less on point for your issue, you are likely to learn just about everything there is to know about the law and practice in this area. Each Portfolio is prepared by an expert practitioner specializing in the particular subject.

To give you a sense of the specificity of a Portfolio, the discussion of limits on deductions for meals and entertainment is found in a Portfolio entitled "Entertainment, Meals, Gifts and Lodging — Deduction and Record Keeping Requirements." This Portfolio runs nearly 1,000 screensful on the LEXIS service, and has 1,438 footnotes. The Portfolios are kept up to date quite regularly — the one on Entertainment, Meals, etc. was last updated two months before the day I searched on it.

You can usefully search any Portfolios by key word, section, or both.

Another helpful publication, especially if you are trying to follow recent developments, is the BNA *Daily Tax Report*, which as the name suggests is published each business day. This is available in file *BNADTR* (in libraries *FEDTAX* and *BNA*.)

4. **Tax Analysts:** If you want to be certain that your research is up-to-date as to all legislative, judicial and IRS developments, a good source is two files published by Tax Analysts: *TXNMAG* (containing the weekly *Tax Notes* magazine) and *TNT* (containing a daily publication, *Tax Notes Today*); both are in the *FEDTAX* library.

   TNT is especially encyclopedic. It includes, in addition to materials available from lots of other sources, information that is not widely available, such as: details about federal tax legislation being proposed by individual members of Congress; the text of selected Committee Hearings; comments submitted by the public about proposed regulations; details of *pending* Tax Court cases — in short, just about everything that moves on the face of the tax earth. One illustration: a search in *TNT* in May, 1997 for[6]

```
entertainment w/3 expense w/10 meal and date aft 1992
```

   found 529 different documents.

I. **Tax periodicals:** Some other tax-related periodicals available on the LEXIS service (all in the *FEDTAX* library) are:

Name of Publication	File
Journal of Accountancy	JNLACC
Tax Advisor	TAXADV
Estate Planners Alert (RIA)	ESTATE

6. *TNT* is an "automatic display file": when you first log in to it, you see the text of that day's issue. Therefore, you have to enter **.ns** before you can actually do the archive search that I'm illustrating.

Name of Publication	File
Employee Benefits / Executive Compensation Alert (RIA)	BENEF
Weekly Alert (RIA)	WEEKLY
Pension and Benefits Daily (BNA)	BNAPEN
Estate Planning	ESTPLN
Journal of International Taxation	JITAX
Journal of Partnership Taxation	JPTAX
Journal of Real Estate Taxation	JRETAX
Journal of Taxation	JTAX
Taxation for Accountants	TAXACC
Taxation for Lawyers	TXLAW
Pension Reporter (RIA)	PENSN
Tax Notes Weekly Magazine	TXNMAG
Tax Notes International Mag.	TNIMAG
State Tax Notes Magazine	STNMAG
Letter Ruling Review	LTRMAG
Exempt Organization Tax Rev.	EOTMAG
Insurance Tax Review	ITRMAG
Tax Practice and Controversies Magazine	TPCMAG
Tax Management Weekly (BNA)	TMWEEK
Tax Management Compensation Planning Journal	TMCPJ
Tax Management Estate Gift & Trust Journal	TMEGTJ
Tax Management Real Estate Journal	TMREJ
Tax Management Memorandum	TMMEMO
NYU Tax Law Review	NYUTAX
Univ. of Virginia Tax Review	UVATAX
American Journal of Tax Policy	AMJPT

II. SECURITIES AND CORPORATE RESEARCH

A. **Federal Securities Law:** The LEXIS service has grouped a number of materials related to federal securities law in the *FEDSEC* library.

1. **Securities statutes, rules and regulations:** Securities law centers around the Securities Act of 1933 and the Securities Exchange Act of 1934. These Acts are administered, of course, by the Securities and Exchange Commission.

a. **Statutes:** Federal statutes governing securities regulation — Titles 7, 12 15, 18 and 31 of the U.S. Code — are grouped in the file *USCS* in the *FEDSEC* library. The main Title governing securities regulation is Title 15.

You can search these using the same techniques as you would for searching the entire

United States Code.[7] If you want to search the U.S. Code, Federal Register and C.F.R. provisions on securities simultaneously, you can do so by using the *CODREG* file.

b. Rules and regulations: Rules and regulations enacted by the SEC, like other agency rules, are published in the Federal Register, and then codified in the CFR. The *FEDREG* file in the *FEDSEC* library contains just those *Federal Register* portions relating to the SEC and the Commodity Futures Trading Commission. Similarly, the *CFR* file in the *FEDSEC* library contains just those portions of the Code of Federal Regulations relating to securities regulation (Title 12 and Title 17). You can search the relevant *Federal Register* and CFR provisions together by using the *ALLREG* file.

The SEC's interpretations of its regulations, together with data on the SEC's proposed and final approvals of new and changed rules, are included in the *SECREL* file in the *FEDSEC* library. You can also search the CFR text and the SEC releases together by using the *RULREL* file.

You may wish to find an SEC Rule which you know by its common rule number (e.g., SEC Rule 10b-5, which prohibits fraud in connection with the purchase or sale of any security). The easiest way to do this on the LEXIS service is in the *CFR* file (since an SEC rule is a regulation and is thus included in the *Code of Federal Regulation*). However, the naming and numbering conventions in *CFR* do not match the SEC's own rule numbers, at least not quite exactly. SEC Rules are generally found in 17 CFR 240; the Rule number is indicated by the data to the right of the decimal point following the 240. Thus the SEC's Rule 10b-5 is published in the CFR as 17 CFR 240.10b-5. You can use the *LEXSTAT* feature to find SEC Rules in the CFR. Thus you could find the full text of Rule 10b-5 by:

```
lxt 17 cfr 240.10b-5
```

Actually, not all SEC rules are in Part 240 of the CFR — just those on the Securities Exchange Act of 1934, which tend to be among the most important. The following table will tell you, for each of the statutes administered by the SEC, the CFR Part number containing the rules and regulations on that statute:

Part 230 — Securities Act of 1933
Part 240 — Securities Exchange Act of 1934
Part 250 — Public Utility Holding Company Act of 1935
Part 260 — Trust Indenture Act of 1939
Part 270 — Investment Company Act of 1940
Part 275 — Investment Advisers Act of 1940
Part 300 — Rules of the Securities Investor Protection Corp.

c. Other SEC materials: The SEC releases other types of information to the public. The two most important sources of SEC documents are:

i. Releases: First, the SEC issues many "releases" on various topics. These can be found, in their entirety, in the *SECREL* file in the *FEDSEC* library. Significant

7. See *supra*, p. 5-12 for details.

releases are also published in the *Federal Register*, so you will find some overlap between the contents of *SECREL* and the contents of *FEDREG*.

ii. No-action Letters: Second, the SEC frequently issues No-action Letters. These are somewhat similar to IRS Private Letter Rulings,[8] in that a private party, such as a would-be issuer of stock or a security exchange, sets out a factual pattern and asks the SEC to say whether the applicant's proposed action would be lawful. Past published No-action Letters are frequently relied on by securities lawyers as an indication to what conduct is likely to be allowed by the Commission. No-action letters from 1971 forward (as well as "interpretative" and "exemption" letters) can be found in the *NOACT* file.

d. Cases: If you want to find cases construing the federal securities laws, your best source is the *COURTS* file in the *FEDSEC* library, which includes securities cases from all federal courts.[9]

2. Filings with the SEC: Every publicly-traded company is required to file various reports with the SEC. Some of the most important are the form 10-K (an annual report filed with the Commission), the 10-Q (a report filed quarterly with the Commission) and the Annual Report to Shareholders. Nearly all of these SEC reports, if filed in 1987 or later, can be found in the *FEDSEC* library.

The following table shows you some of the types of SEC filings available in the *FEDSEC* library, together with a brief description and the name of the file:

Type of Filing	Description	File Name
10-K	Annual Report to the SEC	*10-K*
10-Q	Quarterly Report to the SEC	*10-Q*
Annual Report	Annual Report to Shareholders	*ARS*
Proxy Statement	Document sent annually to shareholders, in connection with election of Board of Directors	*PROXY*
8-K	Report of unscheduled material event or corporate change (e.g., change in control, acquisition or disposition of assets, bankruptcy, etc.)	*8-K*
20-F	Annual Report to the SEC filed by foreign issuers whose shares trade on U.S. stock exchanges	*20-F*
Prospectus	Document issued in connection with sale of securities; describes the securities and the issuer	*PROSP*
Registration Statement	Mainly, documents filed with the SEC to register securities before they are offered to the public	*REG*

Group Files:

8. See *supra*, p. 7-5.

9. If you want to find a *state*'s interpretation of an issue of federal securities law, use the *MEGA* file (in the *FEDSEC* library), which contains both federal and state case law.

Type of Filing	Description	File Name
	SEC filings received by the Electronic Data Gathering Analysis and Retrieval (EDGAR) System, including 10-Ks, 10-Qs, Proxies, 8-Ks, Registrations, Prospectuses, and Williams Act filings	*EDGARP*
	All available SEC full-text filings (i.e., all of the above types of filings)	*FILING*
	All available SEC filings, both full-text and abstract (i.e., all of the above, plus various acquisition, shareholder and other abstracted info.)	*SEC*

A useful segment in searching most of these files is the *COMPANY* segment; thus you can find all SEC filings filed by American Express since 1991 by the following search in the *FEDSEC* library, *FILING* file:

```
company(american express) and date aft 1991
```

You might be interested to know that the SEC now requires that companies filing reports with the SEC do so ***electronically***. This is done via the SEC's so-called ***"EDGAR"*** (Electronic Data Gathering Analysis and Retrieval) system. Nearly all the filings you retrieve in the *FEDSEC* library are ones that were electronically filed in the first place, if the filing took place after mid-1996.

You don't have to worry about whether the document you're looking for was filed under EDGAR or not — EDGAR and non-EDGAR documents are generally mixed together in the files listed in the above chart, and both types of documents are searched pretty much the same way.[10]

An important benefit of the EDGAR system is timeliness — EDGAR-filed documents are now generally online within 2-10 days of the time they're accepted by the SEC.[11]

A last good resource for filings is the *ACCESS* file. This file lets you specify a company name (or the company's ticker symbol), and then see a one-line listing for each SEC filing since 1967 by that company. If the filing is online on the LEXIS service as an EDGAR document, an asterisk so indicates, and you can see the filing itself by clicking on the reference to it.[12]

3. **National Association of Securities Dealers:** The *FEDSEC* library also contains several files dealing with the *National Association of Securities Dealers* (NASD), which is the trade association for dealers in over-the-counter (OTC) stocks. NASD also operates NASDAQ, the second largest stock market in the U.S. These NASD-specific files include

10. There are some extra segments, and other special features, available in EDGAR-filed documents. For instance, EDGAR-filed documents on the LEXIS service have a Table of Contents that lets you move directly to the portion of the document that you want to see. If you want to limit yourself to EDGAR-filed documents, you can do this by using the *EDGARP* (for "EDGAR-Plus") group file.

11. Another benefit is completeness. Unlike most paper-filed filings in *FEDSEC*, EDGAR-filed documents include the full text of exhibits, including exhibits incorporated by reference.

12. You can also order a hard-copy of any document (whether available online or not) from Disclosure, Inc., the publisher of the *ACCESS* file, by using the document number that *ACCESS* gives you.

MANUAL (the official manual of NASD rules and regulations), *DISCIP* (records of NASD disciplinary actions against member firms and individual brokers),[13] and *NOTICE* (rules changes, summaries of disciplinary actions, and other general information about NASD).

4. **Third-party analysis:** The LEXIS service contains a number of commercially-published services and journals relating to securities law. The one that you are most likely to find useful for a broad range of securities problems is BNA's *Securities Regulation and Law Report*, which exists mainly as a print looseleaf service that is widely subscribed to by securities lawyers, but which also exists as an online file (file *SECREG* in the *FEDSEC* library). This Report contains summaries of virtually every court case relating to securities law, as well as a wide variety of SEC and statutory actions relating to the field. You can usefully search in *SECREG* by either key words (e.g., "manipulative device"), statutory reference (e.g., "15 USC 78j"), or SEC Rule number (e.g., "Rule 10b-5").

5. **Commodities:** The *FEDSEC* library also includes LEXIS' offerings relating to the regulation of ***Commodities***. Thus statutes governing commodities are encompassed within the *USCS* file; the rules and regulations of the Commodity Futures Trading Commission (CFTC) are included in the *CFR* and *FEDREG* files; cases about commodities, and various CFTC letters, decisions and no-action letters, are placed in the *CFTC* file.

B. State securities laws: Apart from the federal securities regulatory scheme, each state has its own system of regulating securities. The LEXIS service contains a State Securities Library, *STSEC*.

The *STSEC* library consists of state case law concerning securities law, mainly the securities laws of the state where the court sits. To find cases for the nation as a whole, use the *CASES* file in *STSEC*. To find cases from a particular state, use the individual file devoted to that state within the *STSEC* library. To get the state abbreviation, you will need to look at the file listings for the *STSEC* library. (*Example:* Massachusetts securities cases are found in the file *MASS*.)

The *STSEC* library also contains ***administrative*** materials from 31 states. These are orders, no-action letters, releases, and the like, issued by each state's agency or commission regulating securities. For a single state, use the state-specific file within *STSEC* (e.g., the *ILL* file for no-action letters and orders of the Illinois Securities Department). The administrative materials of all 31 states are grouped together in the *ADMIN* file.

C. State corporate law: If you are researching state corporate law, as opposed to securities law, use the Corporate Law Library, *CORP*. In this library, the LEXIS service has gathered all state cases having to do with corporate law.

To search on an issue of corporate law from a national perspective, without regard to the level of the court, use the *OMNI* file.

To research matters of corporate law from not only all state courts but also from the federal courts construing Delaware corporation law, use the *MEGA* file.

To limit yourself to cases construing Delaware corporate law (including both Delaware state courts and federal courts construing Delaware corporate law), use the *DECORP* file.

---

13. You can use *DISCIP* to find out whether a particular broker has been found guilty of wrongdoing.

To research the corporate law of a particular state, select the appropriate state file from the *CORP* library (e.g., *IND* for Indiana corporate law cases); in order to know the appropriate abbreviation for each state, you will have to use the list of files when you first log in to the *CORP* library.

D. State corporation information: Rarely in law school, but quite often in the practice of law, you will have occasion to find out information about a corporation as listed in the records of a state's Secretary of State. For instance, you may want to know who is listed as the Chairman of the Board, what the listed address is, whether the corporation's status is active or inactive, what the date of the corporation or state of incorporation are, etc. (Or, you may want to know whether a name for a new corporation is available, something that can be determined only by seeing whether the proposed name, or one very similar to it, is already in use.)

You can do much, but by no means all, of this in the *CORP* library. Corporate filing information from the Secretary of State's records from about 17 states have been entered into the LEXIS service. Information about limited partnerships have also been entered, for some of these states. The following table shows you approximately what is available to you under your Educational Subscription:

State	Corporation Records	Limited Partnership Records
California	X	X
Colorado	X	X
Connecticut	X	
Delaware[a]		
Georgia	X	X
Illinois	X	
Indiana	X	X
Maryland	X	X
Massachusetts	X	X
Michigan	X	X
Missouri	X	X
Nevada	X	X
New York	X	X
Ohio	X	X
Pennsylvania	X	X
Texas	X	X
Wisconsin	X	X

a. See discussion of Delaware below

These records typically show not only filings in a state that is the corporation's home state (that is, its state of incorporation), but also filings in a state if an out-of-state corporation has filed to do business there. (For instance, IBM has filed as a "foreign corporation" in all 50 states.)

If you don't know what state a particular corporation has filed in, the best file to use on the LEXIS service is the *ALLSOS* file, which combines the records from all of the states listed above. When in *ALLSOS*, you will typically want to use the *NAME* segment, which contains the name of the corporation. Thus to find all filings by IBM in any of the above states, you would search in library *CORP*, file *ALLSOS*[14] for:

```
name(international business machines)
```

Observe that Delaware is not included in the list of states whose records are present on the LEXIS service. The LEXIS service does not have Delaware corporation filings; however, it provides a gateway to the Delaware Secretary of State's own computer system, from which these records may be searched. To do this, you would change to the *DESOS* file. However, you do not have access to *DESOS* if you are using your Educational Subscription, due to the licensing agreement between the Delaware Secretary of State and LEXIS-NEXIS.

If you know the particular state whose filings you are interested in, you can usually look at the records of just that state (for both corporation and limited partnership information) by selecting file *XXSOS*, where *XX* is the two-digit postal abbreviation for the state (e.g., *CASOS* for California corporation and limited partnership filings). For a few states, there is no *XXSOS* file, so you should try a file named *XXINC* (where *XX* is the two-digit postal abbreviation), which will contain just the corporation (not limited partnership) filings for that state.

III. LABOR AND EMPLOYMENT LAW

A. Introduction: Both the federal government and the states extensively regulate the employment relationship. To research an issue involving labor law or employment law on the LEXIS service, you will first have to decide whether you are mainly interested in federal law or state law, because these are treated in two completely separate libraries, *LABOR* (for most federal materials) and *EMPLOY* (for all state materials, and a few federal materials).

B. Federal labor law: Federal labor law is treated mainly in the *LABOR* library, which the LEXIS service refers to as the Federal Labor Library.[15] Like other special-interest libraries on the LEXIS service, this one contains a variety of statutes, regulations, cases, administrative agency materials, and third-party commentary. This library covers not only traditional labor law (i.e., the regulation of unions and collective bargaining), but also the federal law of employment discrimination, and occupational health and safety. For any labor law problem, also do a quick check in the *EMPLOY* library — which contains mostly state-law materials — before you conclude your research, because state employment law issues will often overlap with federal issues.[16]

1. **Statutes:** Federal statutes governing any of these labor-related areas can be found in the *USCS* file in the *LABOR* library.[17]

---

14. After logging in to this file, you must enter `.ns` before doing a search.

15. As its name suggests, the Federal Labor Library (*LABOR*) contains mostly federal materials. But it also has some state labor-law materials (e.g., the *MEGA* file in *LABOR* contains both federal and state materials, and the state *XXPER* files contain selected states' Public Employee Reporters.)

16. State employment law is discussed briefly *infra*, p. 7-16.

2. **Regulations:** Labor-related items from the *Federal Register* are collected in the *FEDREG* file. Those portions of the *Code of Federal Regulations* having to do with labor are collected in the *CFR* file.[18]

3. **Cases:** Federal cases relating to labor law are grouped in the *COURTS* file. Federal and state cases are grouped together in the *MEGA* file.

4. **Administrative agency materials and third-party sources:** The special value of the *LABOR* library lies in its collection of administrative agency materials and secondary commentaries put out by commercial publishers. Going agency by agency, here are some highlights:

   a. **Collective bargaining and union law (National Labor Relations Board):** Unions and collective bargaining are governed by the National Labor Relations Board. NLRB decisions are collected in the *NLRB* file. Some of the Board's General Counsel Advice Memoranda ("Go" and "No Go" letters) are collected in the file *NLRBGC*.[19] These two files are also combined in a group file called *BOARD*.

      i. **BNA reporters:** The LEXIS service also contains online versions of several popular looseleaf reporters relating to unions and collective bargaining, published by BNA. These include the Daily Labor Report (file *DLABRT*), the Labor Relations Reference Manual (file *LRRM*), and Labor Relations Reporter Analysis/News (file *LRRNEW*).

   b. **Employment discrimination (EEOC):** Laws on employment discrimination are administered by the Equal Employment Opportunity Commission (EEOC). LEXIS has several files containing material authored by the EEOC:

      - EEOC decisions in private-sector disputes are collected in the *EEOC* file.
      - EEOC decisions in public-sector disputes are collected in the *EEOPUB* file.
      - The EEOC Compliance Manual is in the *EEOMAN* file.

      i. **BNA materials:** Again, BNA publishes useful looseleafs on EEOC law, with online versions present on the LEXIS service. *Examples: The BNA Labor Relations Reporter Individual Employment Rights Newsletter* (file *IERNEW*) and *BNA Labor Relations Reporter Individual Employment Rights Cases* (file *LRRIER*).

   c. **Occupational health and safety (OSHA):** On-the-job safety is governed by the Occupational Safety and Health Review Commission, part of the Department of Labor. Decisions of the Commission are collected in file *OSAHRC*. In addition, OSHA Inspection Reports may also be found in the file *OSHAIR*.

---

17. You search this file the same way you search any other file consisting of United States Code sections; see *supra*, p. 5-12 for details.

18. You search these two files the way you would search the larger all-inclusive versions of these files. See *supra*, p. 6-4 (*CFR*), and *supra*, p. 6-3 (*FEDREG*) for more details.

19. Other types of General Counsel Memoranda are found in the *DLABRT* file.

i. **BNA materials:** There are several BNA publications available on OSHA-related subjects: *Occupational Safety & Health Reporter* (file *OSHR*), and *Occupational Safety & Health Daily* (file *BNAOHD*).

d. **Americans with Disabilities Act:** The Americans with Disabilities Act (ADA), since it affects not only employers but also government agencies, builders of office buildings and lots of others, is administered by multiple agencies, mostly the EEOC.

The LEXIS service has grouped together all of its ADA-related materials into a group file called *ADAALL*. There are also individual files related to particular aspects of the ADA (e.g., House and Senate Reports in *ADACOM*, *Federal Register* materials in *ADAFR*, federal case law in *ADAFCL*, BNA's *ADA Cases* in *BNAADA*, and agency decisions in *ADAAGY*).

C. **Pensions and benefits:** If you are researching a subject related to pensions and benefits, you are better off in the special-purpose *PENBEN* library than in the *LABOR* library (though *LABOR* does have some pension-related materials). As with other special-purpose libraries, *PENBEN* has a file of cases (*COURTS*), a file of statutory provisions (*USCS*), a file of regulations (*CFR*) and a file of *Federal Register* documents (*FEDREG*).

Most of the materials in the *PENBEN* library are related to the corporate planning and tax aspects of pensions, rather than to the worker's-rights aspects.

Materials from two government agencies are available: Opinion Letters from the Pension Benefit Guarantee Corporation (in file *PBGC*), and Department of Labor Letter Opinions regarding ERISA (in the *ERISA* file).

Once again, BNA is widely present, with publications such as the *BNA Pension Reporter* (file *PENSN*), and *Pensions and Benefits Daily* (file *BNAPEN*). Also, see the *RIA Employees Benefit Alert* (file *BENEF*), and the magazine *Pensions & Investments* (file *PENSM*).

D. **Social Security law:** If you have a problem relating to Social Security, you have two places to go on the LEXIS service: the *EMPLOY* library[20] and the *PUBHW* library. Here are some of the files in these libraries related to Social Security:

- Federal case law, in the *COURTS* file (in both the *EMPLOY* and *PUBHW* libraries).
- Social Security Rulings, in the *SSRULE* file (both libraries).
- The *Social Security Bulletin*, in the *ASAPII* file in both the *EMPLOY* and *PUBHW* libraries.

E. **State employment law:** The LEXIS service's materials on state employment law are found mainly in the *EMPLOY* library; in fact, the LEXIS service calls this the State Employment Law Library, even though it contains some federal materials as well as state materials.

1. **Statutes:** The entire code for each state (including but not limited to employment-related titles) have been pulled into a file called *ALLCDE*.[21]

20. Other aspects of the *EMPLOY* library are discussed below, in the context of state employment law.

21. Search this file the way you would search files of state statutes in the *CODES* library; see *supra*, p. 5-29 for details.

2. **Cases:** Cases from all states on employment law are grouped in the file *OMNI*. If you just want to see cases from the highest court of states, use the *HIGHCT* file. For cases from a particular state, select the file dedicated to that state (e.g., *FLA* for Florida employment cases).

3. **Public Employees:** For problems involving the rights of public employees under state law, the LEXIS service has a special file containing decisions from nine states (California, Florida, Illinois, Indiana, Michigan, New Jersey, Ohio and Pennsylvania). This is the *ALL-PER* file. (Alternatively, you can find the public employee decisions for a single one of these states in file *XXPER*, where *XX* is the two-digit abbreviation for the state, e.g., *INPER* for Indiana public employee decisions.)

4. **Worker's Compensation:** Worker's Compensation decisions for 12 states are now available on the LEXIS service. These states are California, Colorado, Florida, Illinois, Michigan, Missouri, New Jersey, New York, Ohio, Oregon, Pennsylvania and Washington. These files are all named *XXWORK* (where *XX* is the 2-letter state-name abbreviation; thus *CAWORK* for California). The files can be found in the *EMPLOY* library, as well as in the library of each individual state.

   a. **Newsletters:** Additionally, there are a number of newsletters wholly or partly devoted to worker's comp issues (e.g., LRP Publications' *Florida Worker's Compensation Law Bulletin* and *Illinois Worker's Compensation law Bulletin*). These can be found grouped in the *EMPLAW* file in the *EMPLOY* library.

IV. INTELLECTUAL PROPERTY LAW

A. **Introduction:** In the broad area of intellectual property law, the LEXIS service has special-purpose libraries for patent law (the *PATENT* library), for trademark law (library *TRDMRK*) and for copyright law (library *COPYRT*).

B. **Patents:** The *PATENT* library on the LEXIS service is the most fully developed of the three intellectual property libraries. The *PATENT* library features not only law, but also the full text of patents themselves, as well as many patent-related publications.

1. **Statutes:** Those portions of the U.S. Code relating to patents (Title 35 of the U.S.C.) are in file *USCS* in the *PATENT* library.

2. **Regulations:** Codified regulations governing patents are in file *CFR*. *Federal Register* documents relating to patent issues are in file *FEDREG*. (The contents of both the *CFR* and *FEDREG* files are combined in the *ALLREG* file.)

3. **Cases:** Patent-related case law from the entire federal court system is grouped into file *FEDCTS*. (In addition, court decisions are grouped together with administrative decisions, in the *CASES* file.)

4. **Administrative materials:** Two main bodies of administrative agency materials relating to patents are also available:

a. **Board of Patent Appeals and Interferences:** Decisions by the Board of Patent Appeals and Interferences (as well as decisions of its two predecessors, the Board of Patent Interferences and the Patent and Trademark Office's Board of Appeals), are found in the file *PATAPP*.

b. **Patent awards:** The LEXIS service includes the ***full text of patents*** issued since the mid-1970s. More precisely, the LEXIS service contains, in the *PATENT* library, the following files:

Name of File	Description
ALL	Combined *UTIL*, *DESIGN*, *PLANT*, *REEXAM*, *REISS* & *SIR* files
UTIL	Utility patents from Dec. 1974 (plus selected utility patents from 1971-1974)
DESIGN	Design patents from Dec. 1976
PLANT	Plant patents from Dec. 1976
REEXAM	Reexamination certificates
REISS	Reissue patents
SIR	Defensive publications
ASSIGN	Assignee and class
ABSTCL	Abstracts & claims

(There are also various chronological patent files, each covering all patents issued during a particular period of time. Thus there are files named *PATXX*, where *XX* is a number from 75 to 95; for instance, *PAT82* contains only patents issued in 1982. There are also files named *71-79*, *80-89* and *90-CUR*, covering patents issued in 1971-79, 1980-89 and 1990 to the present, respectively.)

There are over 40 possible segments in a utility patent, so listing and describing them all is impractical. Here are a few of the segments you may find useful for searching:

Name of Segment	Description
PATNO	Patent number, with commas in it (Example: "4,566,112")
DATE	Date patent was issued by the Patent and Trademark Office
TITLE	Brief one-sentence title (e.g., "User interface with multiple workspaces for sharing display system objects")
INVENTOR	List of inventor(s), by last name, first name, city and state (e.g., "Card, Stewart K., Los Altos Hills, California")
ASSIGNEE	Person or entity to whom the patent has been assigned (e.g., "Xerox Corporation, Stamford, Connecticut (02)")
FILED	Date on which patent application was filed
ABST	Abstract, usually about 2-6 sentences in length

Name of Segment	**Description**
CLAIMS	Text of all claims in the patent
US-CL	U.S. Claim numbers, corresponding to the PTO's Manual of Classification (e.g., "364#918," for class 364 — Electrical Computers and Data Processing Systems, sub-class 918 — Commerce/Business)
REF-CITED	References cited, i.e., other U.S. and foreign patents cited in the application, by number (e.g., "4,132,896" for a U.S. patent; "2035769" for a U.K. patent)
DRWDESC	Brief description of the drawings
DETDESC	Detailed description of the invention

Because you have the full text for patents, you can find some relevant patents by doing a key word search. You will be safest doing this without any segment limitation — the bulk of the patent application, including the portions called "Background of the Invention" and "Brief Summary of the Invention," are not in any segment, so you must use a non-segment-limited search to find these portions.

Thus if you represent a software developer who would like to know what patents relate to a windowing system used on a computer, your preferred search would be a fairly general one (in library *PATENT*, file *ALL*) like:

```
software w/30 windowing
```

The Patent and Trademark Office maintains a system of classification, which can help you find relevant patents. To do this, first select the *INDEX* file (still in the *PATENT* library), which is the Index to the Manual of Classification. Then do a key word search on this file, to discover which classification numbers may be relevant. For instance, you might search for **`computer w/25 systems`** to discover what classification numbers include these words. This search will then give you some classification numbers (e.g., "364#400"). Now, you can change to the *CLMNL* file (still in the *PATENT* library), which is the Manual of Classification itself. If you now search for something like

```
class 364
```

you will get a document containing the entire sub-classification scheme for class 364 (a class identified as "Electrical Computers and Data Processing Systems"). Assuming that you are interested in 364#918, you could, while looking at the class 364 document, request

```
focus 918
```

This will show you not only that 364#918 is "Commerce/Business," but will also show you the sub-sub-classifications (e.g., 364#918*10, for "Accounting/Billing" within "Commerce/Business").

Now, you can use the sub-classification to find the patents that have been issued under that classification. Returning to the patent file (let's assume that you are looking for a utility patent, so you choose the *UTIL* file in the *PATENT* library), you would search for:

```
us-cl(364#918)
```

to find all patents issued under class 364 (Electrical Computers and Data Processing Systems), sub-class 918 (Accounting/Billing). Now, you can browse through these patents or, preferably, use the FOCUS or MODIFY features to narrow the grouping further. (You cannot, unfortunately, search on the lowest-level of classification, the sub-sub-classes; thus if you tried to search for **us-cl(364#918*20)**, you will not get any hits.)

If you are able to locate a patent that seems relevant, and you wish to find any other, later, patent applications that cite that patent, you can do so by using the *REF-CITED* field; thus to find all patents citing Patent 4,132,896, you would search (in library *PATENT*, file *ALL*) for:

```
ref-cited(4,132,896)
```

> **Caution:** Patent searching is an art form, so if you are a generalist (e.g., a business lawyer), you should normally leave the final patent searching on which your client will rely to a specialist. Also, remember that only patents issued since the mid-1970s are even on the LEXIS service.

c. **Patent imaging:** A really neat, and major, enhancement to the LEXIS service's patent coverage is patent ***imaging***. Most patents are accompanied by drawings representing the invention. You can download these drawings right into your computer, for any patent issued since 1975. And you can do this with pretty standard computer equipment.[22]

If you're technically-minded, you'll realize that drawings aren't "text" — they have to be transmitted as much bulkier "bit-mapped" images. So instead of about 1,000-2,000 bytes per page of text, the image page is about 15,000 bytes (after extensive compression). But on a 28,800 baud modem, a page of drawing takes only about 7-10 seconds to transmit.

To get the drawings associated with a patent, first retrieve the full text of the patent by one of the methods described above, using the *LEXPAT* library and the *ALL* file. Then, double-click on the **=1** LINK at the top of the screen. You'll then see the first drawing for that patent, in a separate window.

At the top of the next page is what one of the drawings for the main patent for the automobile airbag — a most valuable patent indeed! — looks like. (If you want to find it online, a search in library *LEXPAT*, file *ALL*, for **patno is 5,364,124** will do the trick).

22. Patent imaging requires Microsoft Windows, plus a modem running at at least 9600 baud, and a VGA or higher monitor.

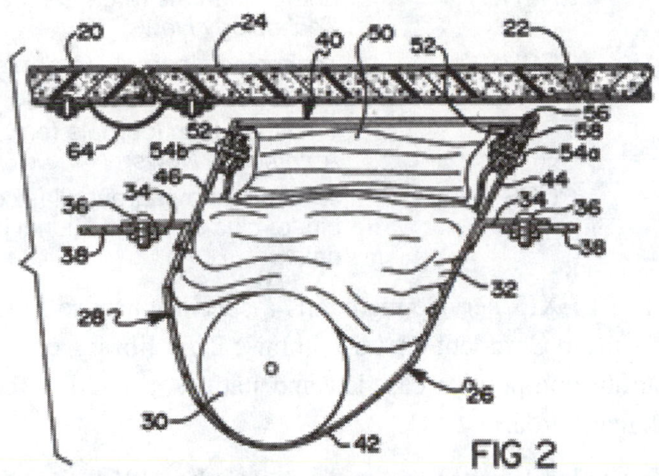

Patent drawing of Auto Airbag,
Pat. No. 5,364,124

Patent imaging on the LEXIS service may well be a harbinger of other types of online document imaging (e.g., the actual page of a newspaper, with photos and charts). Already, LEXIS has added Trademark imaging; see p. 7-22 below.

5. **Periodicals:** There are a number of patent law periodicals available in the *PATENT* library, including

File	Name of Journal
AIPLA	American Intellectual Property Law Assoc. Quarterly Journal
HRVTEC	Harvard Univ. Journal of Law & Technology
LAWTEC	Journal of Law and Technology
PTCLAW	ABA Patent, Trademark and Copyright Committee Reports and Summary of Proceedings
BNAPTD	BNA Patent, Trademark and Copyright Law Daily
PTCJNL	BNA Patent, Trademark and Copyright Journal

Additionally, some non-legal journals, covering areas of technology that often involve patents, have been placed in the *PATENT* library. The list of all the journal names is not feasible to print here. Here, however, are the names of the group files covered:

File Name	Description
COMM	Communication journals
CMPTRS	Computer journals (e.g., *PC Magazine*)
ELTRNC	Electronics journals (e.g., *Electronic News*)

File Name	Description
ENERGY	Energy journals (e.g., *Genetic Technology News*)
TECHNY	Technology journals (e.g., *Technology Review*)
TRANS	Transportation journals (e.g., *Automotive News*)
PUBS	All of the above group files combined, plus some additional journals

C. Trademarks: The LEXIS service maintains a special-purpose library called *TRDMRK*, the Trademark and Unfair Competition Law library. This library covers both federal and state trademark and unfair competition case law and statutes, as well as federal administrative decisions in the trademark area.

1. **Statutes:** For federal trademark statutes, use the *USCS* file. For state statutes, use the *ALLCDE* file.

2. **Federal regulations:** For federal regulations, use the *CFR* file (for the portions of the *Code of Federal Regulations* relating to trademarks and unfair competition), and the *FEDREG* file (for *Federal Register* documents relating to trademark, unfair competition and trade secrets). To search both the *CFR* and *FEDREG* files together, use the *ALLREG* file.

3. **Cases:** For federal case law on trademark and unfair competition law, use the *FEDCTS* file. For state case law on trademarks, unfair competition, and trade secrets, use the *STCTS* file.

4. **Trademark filings:** The LEXIS service now has a quite complete set of federal and state trademark filings. These are in library *TRDMRK*; the most complete file is *ALLTM* (all federal and state trademarks).

   Since a trademark filing can be "for" either words, a design, or both, your searching can also be for either/both:

   - To find trademarks that use ***words*** similar to the words of a proposed mark, use the *WORDS* segment. Thus a search on:

     ```
     words(intelli!)
     ```

     will find all trademarks on words that begin with the letters "intelli".

   - To find trademarks that use a ***design*** similar to the design of a proposed mark, search for words describing the design element. Do this using the *DESIGN* segment. Thus:

     ```
     design(moon)
     ```

     will find any designs that have been classified as being in the shape of a moon.

   - If you want to find all marks that *either* use the word(s), or are in the shape described by that word(s), use the *TRADEMARK* segment. Thus:

     ```
     trademark(apple!)
     ```

will find any trademarks that either contain the letters "apple" or have been classified as looking like an apple.

a. Other segment-limited searching: You can do a number of other types of segment-limited searching on the trademark filings in *TRDMRK/ALLTM*. Two examples:

- To see all trademarks within a particular ***class*** of goods or services, do an initial search on words or design elements, then use the FOCUS feature together with the *CLASS* segment. Thus:

  ```
  design(apple);focus class(clothing)
  ```

  will find all designs in the shape of an apple, but only if the trademark has been placed by the Patent & Trademark Office (PTO) into the class "clothing."

- To see all trademarks owned by, or assigned to, a particular person or company, use the *OWNERS* and *ASSIGNMENTS* segments. Thus:

  ```
  owners(pepsico) or assignments(pepsico)
  ```

  will find all trademarks ever owned by, or assigned to, Pepsico corp. (You might want to search on the *WORDS*, *DESIGN*, or *TRADEMARK* segments first, to narrow down the types of marks, and then search for owners or assignee by using the FOCUS feature.)

b. Imaging, for design marks: When the trademark is for a design (as opposed to word), the LEXIS service now can give you the ***image*** of that design, a really cool feature that rivals the service's treatment of patents.

When a trademark includes a design, you'll see a LINK marker at near the top of each screenful displaying the text information for that trademark; you'll also see the words "Get Trademark Design" near that LINK marker. Just double-click on the link marker to see the design. Since it's a "bit-map," it takes a little while (perhaps 7-10 seconds on a 28.8 modem) to download.

To mix in a little advertising into our technical discussion, here's what the "judge" logo registered by us (Emanuel Publishing Corp.) looks like, when retrieved from the *ALLTM* file:

5. **Periodicals:** Here are the trademark periodicals available:

File Name	Description
AIPLA	American Intellectual Property Law Association Quarterly Journal
BNAPTD	BNA Patent, Trademark and Copyright Law Daily
PTCJNL	BNA Patent, Trademark and Copyright Journal
PTCLAW	ABA Patent, Trademark and Copyright Committee Report and Summary of Proceedings
TMR	U.S. Trademark Association Journal, The Trademark Reporter

D. **Copyright law:** The LEXIS service contains a special-purpose Copyright Law library, *COPYRT.*

1. **Statutes:** Federal copyright statutes are in the *USCS* file.

2. **Regulations:** Federal copyright regulations are in the *CFR* file (for regulations codified in the Code of Federal Regulations) and in the *FEDREG* file (for Federal Register documents). To search both the *CFR* and *FEDREG* files together, use the *ALLREG* file.

3. **Cases:** Federal copyright-related case law is in the *FEDCTS* file.

4. **Periodicals:** Periodicals available in the *COPYRT* library are the same as the first four listed above for the Trademark (*TRDMRK*) library.

V. ENVIRONMENTAL LAW

A. **Introduction:** The LEXIS service' coverage of federal and state environmental law is vast. We can only touch the surface here. In general, the LEXIS service's coverage includes not only the legal aspects of environmental regulation (statutes, regulations, cases, and administrative agency decisions) but also much site-specific information (e.g., the location of Superfund sites and parties potentially responsible for cleaning them up).

B. **The *ENVIRN* library:** The library devoted to environmental law is *ENVIRN*, which contains both state and federal environmental law materials. Everything mentioned below is in the *ENVIRN* library unless otherwise noted.

1. **Statutes:**

a. **Federal statutes:** Federal statutes relating to the environment are collected in file *USCS.*

i. **Legislative history:** Legislative histories for the principal environmental statutes (Clean Air Act Amendments of 1977, CERCLA, NEPA, and Superfund) are collected in the *ENVLH* file.

b. State statutes: The entire text of all states' statutes (including but not limited to those governing the environment) are grouped in the *ALLCDE* file.

2. **Regulations:**

a. Federal regulations: Federal environmental regulations are placed in the *CFR* file (for the *Code of Federal Regulations*), and the *FEDREG* file (for *Federal Register* documents).

b. State regulation: The ENFLEX® collection of state regulations on environmental matters, health and safety, and transportation of hazardous materials, for all 50 states, is contained in the *ENVIRN* library. The files are named *XXEVRG*, where *XX* is the state's postal abbreviation. (*ENVIRN* also has environmental regulations for a number of foreign countries, such as *UKENV* for Britain and *EUENV* for the European Community.)

3. **Case law:**

a. Federal case law: Environment-related case law from the federal system is collected in file *COURTS* (in the *ENVIRN* library).

b. State case law: State environment-related case law from certain states — California, Florida, Georgia, Illinois, Louisiana, Michigan, New Jersey, New York, Ohio and Pennsylvania — is grouped in the *STCTS* file (in the *ENVIRN* library). Additionally, each of these states has a file in that library, called *XXCTS* (where *XX* is the 2-letter state abbreviation, such as *CACTS* for California.)

4. **Administrative agency decisions:**

a. Federal: The LEXIS service has a full complement of federal agency decisions regarding the environment, in the *ENVIRN* library. Unless otherwise noted, all decisions are from the EPA:

File Name	Description
AHERA	Asbestos Hazard Emergency Response Act Decisions
CAA	Clean Air Act Decisions
CWA	Clean Water Act Decisions
CERCLA	Comprehensive Environmental Response, Compensation & Liability Act Decisions
CONDEC	EPA Consent Decrees
EPCRA	Emergency Planning & Community Right-to-Know Act Decisions
EPAAPP	EPA Appeals Board Decisions
EPAGCO	EPA General Counsel Opinions
FIFRA	Federal Insecticide, Fungicide & Rodenticide Decisions
IBIA	Interior Board of Indian Appeals Decisions

File Name	Description
IBLA	Interior Board of Land Appeals Decisions
INTDEC	Department of the Interior — Interior Decisions
MPRSA	Marine Protection, Resources & Sanctuaries Act Decisions
MWTA	Medical Waste Tracking Act Decisions
NPDES	National Pollutant Discharge Elimination Decisions
PSD	Prevention of Significant Deterioration Decisions
PWS	Public Water Supply Decisions
RCRA	Resource Conservation & Recovery Act Decisions
SARA	Superfund Amendments & Reauthorization Act Decisions
SDWA	Safe Drinking Water Act Decisions
TSCA	Toxic Substances Control Act Decisions
UIC	Underground Injection Control Decisions
NOAA	National Oceanic Atmospheric Administration Decisions
OSAHRC	Occupational Safety and Health Review Commission Decisions
AGENCY	All of the above combined

b. State agency decisions: Environmental agency decisions from 10 states are also available in the *ENVIRN* library:

File Name	Description
CAENV	California Water Resources Control Board Decisions
FLENV	Florida Environmental and Land Use Decisions
GAENV	Georgia Board of Natural Resources Decisions
ILENV	Illinois Pollution Control Board Decisions
LAENV	Louisiana Department of Environmental Quality Decisions
MIENV	Michigan Department of Natural Resources Decisions
NJENV	New Jersey Department of Environmental Protection Decisions
NYENV	New York Department of Environmental Conservation Decisions

File Name	Description
OHENV	Ohio Environmental Board of Review Decisions
PAENV	Pennsylvania Environmental Hearing Board Decisions
ALLENV	Group file, containing all of the above

5. **Site-specific information:** The *ENVIRN* library contains very detailed facility site records that give you information about environmental hazards, risks, assessments, and actions at hundreds of thousands of properties throughout the United States. Here are some of the files containing site-specific information:

File Name	Description
AIRS	Aerometric Information Reporting System
CERCLS	Comprehensive Environmental Response Compensation and Liability Site Information System
EPADKT	EPA Civil Enforcement Docket
ERNS	Emergency Response Notification System
FINDS	EPA Facility Index System
FTTS	FIFRA and TSCA Tracking System
LUST	Leaking Underground Storage Tanks
NPDESF	National Pollutant Discharge Facilities
NPLDSC	National Priorities Site Description
NPLIST	National Priorities List
OSHAIR	OSHA Inspection Reports
PRP	Potentially Responsible Parties/ Superfund Enforcement Tracking System
RCRIS	Resource Conservation and Recovery Information System
RODS	EPA Superfund Records of Decision
SITE	All sites appearing in one of the above- or below-listed databases
SPL	State Priorities List
SWS	Solid Waste Sites
TRIS	Toxic Release Inventory System
USTAST	Underground/Aboveground Storage Tanks

I am not an environmental lawyer, so I have no idea what most of the above files are. But just by browsing through a couple of them, I have been able to discover a couple of ways in which an ordinary lawyer might be able to use some of this data:

- Suppose your client is about to buy a piece of real estate. For all sorts of reasons (including liability under state law imposed on a property owner), it would be unwise for your client to buy a property that has toxic waste buried on it. You can use the *CERCLS* file (*ENVIRN* library) to determine whether the federal government has identified the site as having toxic waste on it. You can use the *FACILITY-ADDRESS* segment of this file to do the inquiry:

```
facility-address(echo ave! and new rochelle and 10801)
```

since street address, city name and state and zip are all included in this segment.[23] This information is probably not specific enough to let you know that there is or is not a toxic waste problem, but at least it may put you on notice that a problem may exist.

- Your client is about to purchase a dry cleaner. You know that dry cleaners use toxic solvents, and are required to file reports with the EPA detailing their volume and how they dispose of the materials. You can check to see whether the seller has complied with the filing requirements, by using the *RCRIS* (Resource Conservation and Recovery Information System) file (*ENVIRN* library), and using the *FACILITY-NAME*, *FACILITY-STREET* and *FACILITY-STATE* segments:

```
facility-name(colonial cleaners) and facility-street
  (north ave!) and facility-zip(10801)
```

6. **Secondary publications:** The *ENVIRN* library contains a number of secondary publications analyzing environmental law. Some of them are:

File Name	Publication Name
BNACRD	BNA Chemical Regulation Daily
BNAIED	BNA International Environmental Daily
CHEMRG	BNA Chemical Regulation Reporter
ENVREP	BNA Environment Reporter
INTENV	BNA International Environment Reporter
TOXICS	BNA Toxics Law Reporter
BNANED	BNA National Environment Daily
BNASED	BNA State Environment Daily
BNAED	BNA Daily Environment Report
BNATLD	BNA Toxics Law Daily
ENVAFF	Boston College Environmental Affairs Law Review
ENVLAW	Environmental Law (law review)
NEWS	ELR News and Analysis

23. Alternatively, you might do the same search, but without the *FACILITY-ADDRESS* segment-limitation. This may give you hits you don't want (e.g., hits where the address belongs to the office-building headquarters of a company that owns a toxic-site that's located elsewhere), but it reduces the risk of overlooking something.

File Name	Publication Name
ADMIN	ELR Administrative Materials
LIT	ELR Litigation Materials

7. **Industry publications:** The LEXIS service has gathered a number of trade journals from various industries (e.g., coal mining, petroleum refining, paper making) into several files. The most comprehensive of these is the *ALLNWS* group file, containing environment-related articles from about 70 trade journals, general-circulation newspapers and general-interest magazines.

VI. FOREIGN AND INTERNATIONAL LAW

A. Introduction: The LEXIS service contains an ever-increasing wealth of materials on both foreign law (that is, the law of countries other than the U.S.) and international law (the law governing the relations among nations). For instance, more than 60 new country-law files were added to the LEXIS service during 1996.

B. Law of foreign countries:

1. **Martindale Digest:** An excellent place to begin your research into the laws of foreign countries is in Martindale-Hubbell's International Law Digest. This digest of laws describes the major points of each covered country's laws, legal systems and governments. Over 60 countries are covered; the European Community and the individual Canadian provinces are also covered. This digest (which is in English) can be found in the *MARHUB* or *INTLAW* libraries, *INTDIG* file.

   Now, let's turn to specific areas of the world:

2. **Commonwealth and Irish law:** The countries of the British Commonwealth, as well as the Republic of Ireland, are especially well-represented on the LEXIS-NEXIS services.

   a. **U.K law:** Laws of the United Kingdom are covered in the *ENGGEN, UK, UKJNL* and *UKCURR* libraries. Some of the materials are:

   - Reported caselaw from 1938 and unreported caselaw from 1980, including the House of Lords, Court of Appeal (Civil Division), Privy Council, and others, in the *CASES* file
   - Statutes (Public General Acts of England and Wales) from 1267, in the *STAT* file.
   - Statutory instruments (Regulations, Rules and Orders), in the *SI* file. (You should typically search statutes and statutory instruments together, in the *STATIS* group file.)
   - Parliamentary bill status, and other current awareness topics, in the *UKCURR* library. (Bills in progress are in the *BILLS* file.)
   - Double taxation instruments, in the *DTAX* file.
   - UK law journals, in the *ALLJNL* file.

i. **Northern Ireland:** Cases from Northern Ireland (reported ones from 1945 and unreported ones from 1984) are in the *NILAW* library, *CASES* file.

ii. **Scotland:** Hard-to-find Scottish cases (reported ones from 1947 and unreported ones from 1982) are in the *SCOT* library, *CASES* file.

b. **Canadian law:** Canadian law is covered in the *CANADA* library.

Reported caselaw from across Canada can be found in these files: *DLR* (Dominion Law Reports), *CCRIM* (Canadian Criminal Cases), *CPR* (Canadian Patent Reporter) and LAC (Labour Arbitration Cases).

Summaries of recent unreported cases from across Canada can be found in the *CANSUM* file.

c. **Australian law:** Australian law is covered in the *AUST* library. Some of the files containing cases are *AUSMAX* (all Australian cases), *HIGHCT* (High Court), *FEDDEC* (Federal Court), *FAMDEC* (Family Court), *IRTDEC* (Immigration Review and Refugee Tribunals), *AATDEC* (Administrative Appeals Tribunal), *ACTDEC* (Australian Capital Territory Supreme Court), *SASDEC* (South Australian Supreme Court), *TASDEC* (Tasmania Supreme Court), *NSCDEC* (Northern Territory Supreme Court), and *NSWUNR* (New South Wales unreported).

Australian federal legislation can be found in these files: *CONACT* (Constitution and Acts of Parliament); *CURACT* (Current Amended Acts); *NUMREG* (new numbered rules and regulations); and *CURREG* (Current Amended Rules and Regulations).

Australian law journal indices are in the *AGIS* and *ALLI* files. The full text of 16 journals can be found in the group file *AUJNLS*.

d. **New Zealand:** Reported cases from 1958 are in the *NZ* library, *NZCAS* file.

e. **Malaysia and Brunei:** Malayan, Singapore and Brunei caselaw reported in the *Malayan Law Journal* from 1955 is in the *MALAY* library, *MALLJ* file.

f. **Singapore:** Singapore cases reported in the *Singapore Law Journal* from 1965 are in the *SING* library, the *SINGLR* file.

g. **Hong Kong:** Hong Kong cases reported in *Hong Kong Cases* from 1947 are in the *HKCHNA* library, *HKCAS* file.

h. **South Africa:** South African cases reported in *Butterworths Constitutional Law Reports* from July 1994 are in the *SAFRAC* library, *SACLR* file.

i. **Republic of Ireland:** Irish reported cases from 1950 and unreported cases from July 1985 can be found in the *IRELND* and *IRLAW* libraries, *CASES* file.

j. **Commonwealth Cases Group Files:** All UK, Irish and Commonwealth cases can be searched at once in the *COMCAS* library, *ALL* or *ALL1* group files.

3. **France:** The other major body of foreign case law available on the LEXIS service is French law, including (all in French):

- French private caselaw (library *PRIVE*, file *CASS*);

- French public and administrative caselaw (library *PUBLIC*, file *BIBLIO*);
- The Constitution of France, plus current laws and decrees (library *LOIREG*, file *JO*);
- Various French Codes (library *LOIREG*, file *CODES*);
- The official bulletins of the French ministries (library *LOIREG*, file *BO*); and
- Various legal periodicals (library *REVUES*).

4. **Mexico:** There is a new collection of federal and state laws from Mexico (presently in Spanish). This collection, in the *MEXICO* library, includes:
   - Mexican Constitution and federal laws, in the *MXCNST* and *MXFED* files.
   - Laws of the Federal District of Mexico, in the *MXDIST* file.
   - Jurisprudence from the Supreme Court of Mexico, in the *MXJUR* file.
   - Laws of the states of Mexico, in the *MEXICO* file.
   - Laws by topic, in the *MXAMB*, *MXCOM*, *MXELEC* and *MXFISC* files.
5. **Russia and China Laws:** Economic laws from the Russian Federation and the Peoples Republic of China can be searched in the *INTLAW* library, *RFLAW* and *CHINAL* files.

C. International law, including treaties:

1. **Treaties:** Some of the materials on international Treaties and Agreements are:
   - Basic Documents of International Law (*BDIEL* file);
   - Treaties in force to which the U.S. is a party, from 1783 (*USTRTY* file);
   - GATT, NAFTA and NAFTA Panel Decisions (*GATT*, *NAFTA* and *NAFDEC* files, respectively)
   - Various U.S. Department of State materials (*DSTATE* file);
   - Various international legal materials, including treaties, analysis, ICJ decisions, etc., collected by the American Society of International Law (*ASIL* file);
   - International Tax Treaties and news (*IBFD* file).
2. **European Community materials:** The LEXIS service also contains material relating specifically to the law of the European Community, including (all files in the INTLAW library unless otherwise noted):
   - European Communities law (CELEX database) (in English in the *ECLAW* file, and in French in the *EURCOM* library, *JOCE* file). Abstracts of Series L & C notices can also be found in the *EURCOM* library, *SPICER* file.
   - European Court of Justice cases (in English in the *ECCASE* file, and in French in the *INTNAT* library, *CJCE* file).
   - EC Treaties and Agreements (*ECTY* and *ASIL* files); and
   - European Commission decisions applying fair competition rules (*COMDEC* file).

- Latest news from the EC/EU (*ECNEWS* file).

3. **Human Rights Materials:** Decisions from the European Court of Human Rights are available (in English in the *ECCASE* file, and in French in the *INTNAT* library, *CEDH* file). Human rights reports prepared by the U.S. Department of State can be searched in the *DSTATE* file.

D. U.S. law: Finally, the *INTLAW* library includes various American materials relating to international matters. These include:

- International law as applied by U.S. courts (*CASES* and *COURTS* files);
- *Restatement of the Law Third, Foreign Relations* (*FORREL* file);
- Federal statutes (*USCS* file); and
- Federal regulations (*CFR* file for the *Code of Federal Regulations*, and *FEDREG* file for *Federal Register* documents).

VII. OTHER SPECIALIZED LIBRARIES

A. Introduction: There are other specialized law libraries on the LEXIS service, which I do not have space here to cover but which I can list:

Name of Library	Description
BANKNG	Federal Banking library
BKRTCY	Federal Bankruptcy library
FEDCOM	Federal Communications library
ENERGY	Federal Energy library
ESTATE	Federal Estate, Gift and Trust library
ETHICS	Ethics library (principally state law on legal ethics plus ABA publications on the subject)
FAMILY	Family Law library (state and federal materials)
FEDSEN	Federal Sentencing library
HEALTH	Health Law library
IMMIG	Immigration library
INSRLW	Insurance Law library
TRADE	International Trade library
MSTORT	Mass Torts library
MEDMAL	Medical Malpractice library
M&A	Mergers and Acquisitions library
MILTRY	Military Justice library
PRLIAB	Products Liability library
PUBCON	Federal Public Contracts library
PUBHW	Public Health and Welfare library (principally Social Security law)

Name of Library	Description
REALTY	Real Estate library (federal and state)
UTILTY	Public Utilities Law library
TRADE	Federal Trade Regulation library
TRANS	Federal Transportation library
UCC	Uniform Commercial Code library

Chapter 8

NEXIS® and Other Law-related Information

Introduction: So far, all of the materials we've talked about have been law-specific ones, ones whose primary users are lawyers. But there is another major category of materials on the services, consisting of materials designed for a non-lawyer audience, but which are nonetheless very relevant to lawyers. Most of these are placed in what LEXIS-NEXIS calls the "NEXIS service."[1] On the NEXIS service, you can find the full text of hundreds of newspapers, magazines, wire services, newsletters, stock reports, medical journals, public records, etc.

LEXIS-NEXIS originally created the NEXIS service (some years after it first came out with the LEXIS service's case law libraries) with the intent of selling to the world at large the same sorts of full-text searching as it had sold so successfully to lawyers in the form of the LEXIS service. But in actuality, almost half of the usage of the NEXIS service today is by lawyers. The reason is that there are a tremendous number of occasions during which a lawyer needs to know information that can be found in non-legal-specific publications, like general-interest newspapers or industry-specific trade journals. Consequently, my focus in this chapter is on how to use the NEXIS service in law-related ways; that is also why I have titled this chapter "NEXIS and Other Law-Related Information."

I. THE *NEWS* LIBRARY

A. Introduction to the *NEWS* library: Within the 25 or so libraries that LEXIS-NEXIS has grouped under the phrase "the NEXIS service," the largest by far is the library named *NEWS*. The NEXIS service refers to this library as being the "General News and Business" library. It comprises more than 2300 full-text[2] publications: U.S. and foreign newspapers, magazines, trade journals, newsletters, wire services and broadcast transcripts. In the 1997 *LEXIS-NEXIS Directory of Online Services* hard-copy publication, the small-print listing of publications in the *NEWS* library, double-column with one line per publication, takes 32 pages!

1. Within the NEXIS service, there is a large library called the *NEWS* library. But there are other libraries within the NEXIS service, such as the *CMPCOM* library (for materials on computers and communications), the *MARKET* library (materials on marketing), the *PEOPLE* library (materials concentrating on biographical or people-related news), etc. In the discussion that follows, assume that the materials being talked about can be found in the *NEWS* library unless otherwise noted.

2. Material in abstracted form is available from an additional 1,000 sources.

B. Coverage of *NEWS*: Let's take a closer look at the types of publications available within the *NEWS* library. Unless I note otherwise, all of these publications are available in ***full text***.[3]

1. **Newspapers:** The *NEWS* library contains nearly 1,000 full-text and selected-full-text ***newspapers***. Many of these are single-city newspapers of general circulation (e.g., *The Chicago Tribune*). But others are special-topic newspapers (e.g., *Investor's Business Daily, The Philadelphia Business Journal*, and *The Sporting News*, to take a few examples at random).

   a. **Major newspapers:** Most of the largest-circulation general newspapers in America are included in the *NEWS* library (*PAPERS* file). Here are some of them:

      Atlanta Journal and Constitution (from Jan. 1991)
      Boston Globe (from Sept. 1988)
      Chicago Tribune (from Jan. 1985)
      Christian Science Monitor (from Jan. 1980)
      Cincinnati Enquirer (from Nov. 1990)
      Cleveland Plain Dealer (from Nov. 1992)
      Dallas Morning News (from Oct. 1992)
      Detroit News (from Jan. 1990)
      Denver Post (from Aug. 1988)
      Houston Chronicle (from Sept. 1991)
      International Herald Tribune (from July 1991)
      Los Angeles Times (from Jan. 1985)
      Minneapolis Star Tribune (from Sept. 1991)
      Newsday (from Jan. 1988)
      New York Times (from June 1980)
      Orlando Sentinel Tribune (from Jan. 1990)
      Pittsburgh Post Gazette (from July 1990)
      Rocky Mountain News (from Dec. 1993)
      Sacramento Bee (from Nov. 1988)
      St. Louis Post Dispatch (from Jan. 1989)
      Seattle Times (from Jan. 1990)
      San Francisco Chronicle (from Oct. 1989)
      South China Morning Post (from July 1992)
      Times of London and *Sunday Times* (from Jan. 1990)
      USA Today (from Jan. 1989)
      Washington Post (from Jan. 1977)

   b. ***The New York Times:*** Of these, *The New York Times* is worthy of a special note. *The Times* is usually considered to be the unofficial "newspaper of record" of America. It is an enormous newspaper, one that gives detailed treatment not just of general news items, but of events in the worlds of law, business and finance, culture, fashion, education, sports, and most other major fields of human endeavor. Couple this with the fact that the full text of *The Times* is available on the NEXIS service from June, 1980, and you have a single source (in file *NYT* in the *NEWS* library) that can give you information about an exceptional range of topics. One author has referred to *The Times* as "the crown jewel of NEXIS offerings."[4]

---

3. Actually, what is reproduced is the full text of every *news* item, but not necessarily the text of other types of items. For example, *NEWS* files omit classified advertisements, the text of cartoons, mast-head and subscription information, and the like.

4. Shapiro, *LEXIS: The Complete User's Guide*, p. 252.

c. **Special-purpose newspapers:** Some of the more important ***special-purpose*** newspapers are:

Advertising Age (from Jan. 1986)
American Banker (from Jan. 1979)
Automotive News (from Jan. 1988)
Electronic News (from Jan. 1983)
The Financial Times (from Jan. 1982)
Investors Business Daily (from Jan. 1990)
Pensions and Investments Age (from Jan. 1987)
The Sporting News (from Jan. 1989)

Additionally, a large number of local business newspapers and journals are present (e.g., *Arkansas Business*, *Austin Business Journal*, *Baltimore Business Journal*, to cite only the first few).

Note: You can search all of these newspapers — indeed all newspapers present in the *NEWS* library — by using the *PAPERS* group file. Or, you can search just the files of a particular newspaper, since each paper has its own file (e.g., *NYT* for *The New York Times*). Group file selection is discussed further *infra*, p. 8-4.

2. **Magazines:** There are over 150 magazines and journals in the *NEWS* library.

a. **Major magazines:** To cite only a few of the most famous of these magazines:

Billboard
Business Week
BYTE
Consumer Reports
Forbes
Fortune
Harvard Business Review
Inc.
Life
Money
The Nation
The New Republic
Newsweek
PC Magazine
People
Playboy
Popular Science
Psychology Today
Saturday Evening Post
Sports Illustrated
Time
U.S. News & World Report

You can search all of the *NEWS* library's magazine files at once by using the *MAGS* group file.

3. **Wire services:** So far, nearly all of the sources we have examined in this book would be available to you in hard-copy form from either a well-equipped law library or a well-equipped general library. But now we come to an extraordinary resource that is not really available, so far as I know, in any other way apart from the LEXIS-NEXIS services: the collection of back files from ***wire services***.

The principal job of a wire service is to supply its newspaper, TV and radio station clients with news information that the client can re-publish. Historically, wire service stories have been considered of ephemeral importance — the newspaper may reproduce the story, but if it does not do so, the wire service's own files have been considered to be of little importance. Yet the total word-count of news stories prepared by the wire services each day is probably greater than the word-count of stories run in the 100 largest American daily newspapers. Wire services are especially useful if you want to find a story that was of too localized interest to be picked up in one of the major-city newspapers. There are over 140 wire services present in full text on the NEXIS service, too many to list here. Most of the files go back only for several years, but some go back as far as the mid 1970's. More than half of them are foreign-based, making the wire service files especially good sources of foreign news stories. Here is a sampling of the wire services available:

Agence France Presse (from May 1991) (file *AFP*)
The Associated Press (world, national, business and sports wires, from Jan. 1977) (file *AP*)[a]
The PR News Wire (from Jan. 1980) (file *PRNEWS*)
Reuters:
- *Reuter Business Report* (from May 1987) (file *REUBUS*)
- *Reuter Financial Service* (from Jan. 1987) (file *REUFIN*)
- *Reuter North America News* (from April 1979) (file *REUNA*)
- *Reuter World Service* (from Oct. 1982) (file *REUWLD*)

Gannett News Service (from Jan. 1989) (file *GNS*)
States News Service (from Aug. 1984) (file *SNS*)
TASS (the *Telegraph Agency of the Soviet Union*) (from Jan. 1987) (file *TASS*)
United Press International:
- *UPI World, National, Business and Sports* wires (from Sept. 1980) (file *UPI*)
- *UPI State and Regional* wires (for Nov. 1980 to one year ago, use *UPSTAT*; for the most recent 12 months, use *UPSTCU*)

a. The AP wires are not available on your Educational Subscription.

To give you some idea of the huge volume of material available, in the *REUNA* (*Reuter* North American news wire service) file alone, there are 87,577 stories from 1996!

4. **Newsletters:** The *NEWS* library also includes hundreds of industry newsletters, grouped in the file *NWLTRS*; many of these are also available each in its own file. Some random examples: *East European Energy Report*; *Money Laundering Alert*; *Bank Automation News*; *Food Chemical News*; *Asbestos Abatement Report*; *European Cosmetic Markets*.

5. **Transcripts:** Another unusual category consists of ***transcripts*** of TV and radio news broadcasts. Examples include: transcripts from ABC News broadcasts, CNN, *The News-Hour with Jim Lehrer*, and National Public Radio. These are all available in the group file *SCRIPT*. Frequently, law-related stories — especially ones dealing with recent Supreme Court decisions — are broadcast on these programs, so I find these transcripts are often useful as a form of legal research.

6. **Abstract files:** The vast majority of files in the *NEWS* library are full-text, that is, full articles reproduced with the consent of the publisher. For about 1,500 sources, however, the NEXIS service merely supplies abstracts (for which no copyright permission is needed). Examples of abstracted publications include *The Wall Street Journal*, *The Philadelphia Inquirer* and *The Miami Herald* (all in file *INFOBK*). There are also some special-purpose abstract collections available, such as Banking Information Source Select (file *BISSEL*), which abstracts publications about financial services companies, and the Insurance Information Institute's Abstracts (file *IIABS*), abstracting thousands of insurance-related articles. All abstract files are also available in a group file, *ALLABS*.

C. **Group files:** Most publications covered in full text in the *NEWS* library are available each in its own single-publication file (e.g., file *NYT* for *The New York Times*). But normally, you will not want to limit yourself to a single publication when you do research in the NEXIS service. Therefore, you will usually want to use one or more group files.

If you're in a group file and would like to know what individual publications it contains, you can do this with the **.gu** command. While in the file, just type **.gu** [ENTER], and you'll see the GUIDE write-up on the group file; you can then scroll through a list of each publication in the group.[5]

Here is an overview of some of the available groupings within the *NEWS* library:

1. **By date:** All full text *NEWS* library files are available in two files that are organized by ***date***:
   - The *CURNWS* file contains all "current" stories, that is, those two years old or newer.
   - The *ARCNWS* file contains all stories too old to be included in the *CURNWS* file. This means all stories that are more than two years old.
2. **By source:** *NEWS* library files are also available in a series of group files that are organized by ***source***. That is, you can choose to search just magazines, just newspapers, etc. The most important source groupings are as follows:[6]
   - The *MAGS* group file covers more than 200 national, regional and local magazines available on the NEXIS service.
   - The *MAJPAP* file covers all "major newspapers" on the NEXIS service. These are the 60+ newspapers that LEXIS-NEXIS has determined to be the most important ones. For example, the *Boston Globe, Chicago Tribune, Christian Science Monitor, Houston Chronicle, Los Angeles Times, Newsday, New York Times, Seattle Times, San Francisco Chronicle, Minneapolis Star Tribune, USA Today* and *Washington Post* are among the papers included in *MAJPAP.*
   - The *PAPERS* group file includes all newspapers available in the *NEWS* library. At this writing, this includes more than 220 international, national, regional and local papers.
   - The *NWLTRS* file contains all newsletters available on the NEXIS service, of which there are more than 1,278 at this writing.
   - The *SCRIPT* file contains transcripts of broadcast programs.
   - The *WIRES* file contains stories from the more than 140 worldwide wire services covered by the NEXIS service.
3. **By subject:** The *NEWS* library's stories have also been sliced up by subject.
   - The *BUS* file contains stories from newspapers, magazines, wire services and TV news transcripts covering business-related topics. A given publication either is included in the *BUS* file (in which case every story in it is included, even those that are not busi-

5. For more about the GUIDE feature, see p. 2-76.

6. Since the NEXIS service seldom puts full text and abstract articles together in the same group file, unless otherwise noted all of the group files discussed below contain only full-text stories.

ness-related) or is not (in which case no story is included, even if it is business related). Thus business stories from the *New York Times* are not included in this group file. The file consists mainly of local business newspapers (e.g., *Denver Business*) and industry trade journals and newsletters (e.g., *Industrial Distribution*).

- The *FIN* group file includes the full text of all publications that primarily cover financial markets and investing. (*Examples: American Banker*; *The Bond Buyer*; *Financial World*; *Investors Business Daily*; *Securities Week*.)
- The *NON-US* group file includes publications and wire services that primarily cover foreign affairs. (Examples: *Agence France Presse* wire service; *The Economist*; *The International Herald Tribune*; *The Toronto Star*.)
- The *LGLNEW* file includes publications that primarily cover legal news. (Examples: *American Lawyer*; *Connecticut Law Tribune*; *Legal Times*; *National Law Journal*; *New York Law Journal*; *U.S. Law Week*.)
- The *PERSON* group file includes publications and wire services focusing on biographical information and general news of individuals. (*Examples: People* magazine; the *NYTBIO* file, which culls selected biographical stories from *The New York Times*.)
- The *TRDTEC* group file, which includes publications covering a trade, science or technology. (*Examples: AutoWeek*; *Communications Daily*; *InfoWorld*; *Nuclear News*.)

4. **By region:** The *NEWS* library takes its general-interest publications, and those specializing in business, and carves them up into regional groupings. In general, a publication will appear in only one of the regions, even if it covers news from around the nation. (For instance, the *New York Times* (*NYT*) file appears only in the Northeast Region file.) The names of these group files are: *NEAST* (Northeast region); *SEAST* (Southeast region); *WEST* (West region); *MWEST* (Midwest region).
5. **Abstracted:** All files consisting of abstracts rather than full-text stories are placed into a grouping of their own, the *ALLABS* group file. In addition, abstracts of current stories (those two years old or newer) are in a smaller file called *CURABS*, and all stories too old for *CURABS* are placed in *ARCABS*.

D. **Things you might do on the NEXIS service:** Why should you, the law student, care about the NEXIS service? After all, you're interested in "the law," not in general news stories, industry developments, or matters of technology. The short answer is that the law reflects human activity, and the average lawyer has a surprisingly large need for information that is not of the sort found in cases, statutes and regulations. Here are a few somewhat randomly-selected ways in which a lawyer or law student might use the NEXIS service:

1. **Making a client dossier:** Suppose your firm has been retained by a new client, XYZ Corp. You can use the NEXIS service to find out lots of information about XYZ, its executives, its competitors, its industry, etc. This will in turn help you: (1) get up to speed on XYZ's business and legal problems more quickly, without tying up XYZ's executives in lawyer briefings; and (2) impress XYZ's executives (including its all-important general counsel) with your uncannily deep and current knowledge.

2. **Client development:** Suppose that you specialize in representing a particular industry, pharmaceuticals, let's say. You can use the NEXIS service to keep up with what's going on in the pharmaceuticals industry, so you'll know where opportunities for generating legal business may reside. For instance, if you read that ABC Corp. files 20 New Drug Applications each year with the FDA, you can write to ABC's general counsel and offer your expertise in the law of New Drug Applications.

3. **Expert witnesses:** Suppose you are a plaintiff's tort lawyer — specializing in product liability suits against automobile manufacturers, let's say. You have a case involving a 1987 Scorpion manufactured by Thunder Motors, and you think your client was burned because the fuel tanks improperly ruptured in the collision. You can use the NEXIS service to search for newspaper and wire-service accounts of other suits involving the Scorpion (or other cars with fuel tank problems), so as to share insights or documents with other plaintiff's lawyers, or to find an automotive design engineer who will serve as your expert witness in testifying that the fuel tank was defective.

4. **Due diligence:** You are a mergers and acquisitions lawyer. Your client is about to acquire 123 Chemicals, Inc., a chemical manufacturer. You can use the NEXIS service as part of the due diligence process, to find out whether your client would be buying a pig in a poke. For instance, you can review 123's EPA filings,[7] find the states where it has qualified to do business,[8] or see whether there have been suits brought against it.[9]

5. **Litigation fact checking:** You can check facts that are relevant in a litigation you are handling. For instance, if your client was injured when a motorist went through a stop sign at a particular intersection, and you are suing the city because you think the stop sign should have been replaced by a traffic light, you may be able to check local newspapers and wire service reports to identify other accidents that have taken place at the same intersection (indicating that the city had notice of the need for a traffic light there).

6. **Job searching:** You are a law student who is about to be interviewed for a job with Dewey, Cheatham & Howe. You can use the NEXIS service to search for all mentions of the firm in press accounts, which are likely to reveal firm activities that you would not find out about merely by consulting reported decisions (e.g., pro bono activities by the firm, charitable activities by partners, press conferences in which a lawyer from the firm made statements on behalf of a client, etc.). This information can help you: (1) learn whether the firm is right for you; and (2) impress the interviewer with your awesomely detailed knowledge.

7. **Personal development:** The final category is not truly law-related. It refers to ways of using the NEXIS service to make your non-work life more pleasant or stimulating. Some examples:

    - You're going to be in New York next week on business. You have a fondness for Indian

7. See *supra*, p. 7-27.

8. See *supra*, p. 7-13.

9. See *infra*, p. 8-17.

food. You can search *The New York Times* for recent reviews of Indian restaurants.

- You plan to take a vacation in southern Italy soon. You can find travel columns in newspapers and magazines to give you an idea of which towns to visit, and which tour operators to consider.
- The wood floors in your house look dull and unpolished. You can search newspapers and magazines for info on what polish to use, and where to buy or rent a floor polishing machine.
- You need to buy a new car, and need a four-door sedan with front wheel drive and a large amount of rear-seat leg room. You can search for reviews in newspapers and magazines (e.g., *Consumer Reports*) to narrow down your choice. Also, if you want to use a car-buying service to save you the need to haggle with your local dealer, you can locate a good service.
- Your friend or relative has an unusual medical condition. You can search for newspaper articles mentioning the names of well-regarded specialists in your area, and find out in general terms what the state-of-the-art techniques are for treating the condition. (For more specialized medical info, you can use the *MEDIS*® service, described *infra*, p. 8-14.)

In short, a large portion of what the average human being is interested in sooner or later gets reflected in the pages of the hundreds of newspapers, magazines, wire services, etc., available on the NEXIS service. On literally dozens of occasions during the past couple of years, I have been able to come up with highly specialized information for my family and friends, who think of me as some sort of information wizard. Frankly, I'm amazed that the NEXIS service is not more widely used by non-lawyers, though of course the service's pricing structure has something to do with this. At least while you're still in law school, enjoy the free access!

E. Searching on the NEXIS service: Let's now look at some details of how you can profitably search the *NEWS* library.

1. **Generally:** In general, the *NEWS* library is no different from any other library on the LEXIS-NEXIS services. You sign into the library the same way, you use the same search connectors and search syntax, and you display and print documents in the same way.
2. **Segments:** Here is the segment layout of a typical file in the *NEWS* library:

Name of Segment	Description
PUBLICATION	The name of the publication (e.g., "The New York Times")
DATE	Date of the issue in which the article appeared; this is arithmetically searchable (e.g., **`date aft 1991`**)

Name of Segment	Description
SECTION	Name of the section of the publication in which the article appears. These vary sharply from one publication to another (e.g., for *The New York Times*, section entries include "Foreign Desk," "Metropolitan Desk," "Science Desk," and various Sunday-issue only desks like "Book Review Desk" or "Travel Desk." For *The Washington Post*, sections include "Book World," "Editorial," "Metro" and "Style.") You can generally get a list of sections for a publication by going into GUIDE (type **.gu** while in the publication), then looking at the section-name listings at the end of GUIDE's discussion of that publication's segment names.)
LENGTH	Length of the article in words. This segment is arithmetically searchable and sortable (e.g., length > 100; sort by longest to shortest)[a]
HEADLINE	Headline of the article
BYLINE	Name of the author of the article
DATELINE	City in which the events in the article occurred, or from which the story was filed
LEAD	Approximately the first 50 words of the story
BODY	The full text of the story, not including the special segments like *HEADLINE* and *BYLINE*
GRAPHIC	The type of graphic accompanying the document (e.g., "cartoon," "chart," "diagram," "graph," "map," "photo," "table," etc.) This segment also includes the text of any caption.
TYPE	A term categorizing the story (e.g., "analysis," "biography," "national news," "interview," "letter," "obituary," "review," "editorial," etc.) (Not all publications have this segment.)
HLEAD	A group segment combining the *HEADLINE* and *LEAD* segments of the document.

a. For more information about sorting by article length, see *infra*, p. 8-10.

3. **How to do some common things:** Let's take a look at how to use the NEXIS service to do some common types of searches. Because the techniques you would use will often depend upon the precise vocabulary used by the publication itself (e.g., the names of the sections), my examples assume that you are primarily interested in researching *The New York Times* — you will have to adapt these examples for other publications.

- **Locating a review of a book, movie, restaurant, etc.:** To call up reviews of a book, movie, restaurant, play, etc., use the *TYPE* segment and the name of the item:

```
type(review) and body w/3 evidence and madonna
```

(Sure enough, this search produces, in the *NYT* file, two reviews of the movie *Body of Evidence*, starring Madonna. One review says that "As a suspense film . . . it is possibly one of the worst ever made." The other calls it "a sluggish courtroom melodrama relieved only by unintentional laughter." Unfortunately, my wife has already rented this film from Blockbuster, so I will have to see it tonight or leave the bedroom.)

- **Finding front page stories:** To find major stories, you will often want to restrict yourself to those appearing on page one. You will usually want to do this using the *SECTION* segment, such as:

```
date aft 6/1/93 and section(page 1) and somalia
```

However, you must be careful to take into account the varying ways that newspapers record their page numbers. Many papers, for instance, use a section letter in addition to the number, and this gets carried over onto the NEXIS service. Thus whereas the *SECTION* segment for *The New York Times* would typically read something like "section 1; page 1," for *The Washington Post* the entry in the *SECTION* segment would read something like "first section; page A1." So for *The Washington Post*, you would want to search for **section(a1)**.

- **Using the *HEADLINE* segment:** You can home in more rapidly on suitable articles by making good use of the *HEADLINE* segment, since you are less likely to find irrelevant stories that way. Thus if you are interested in recent stories about welfare reform, a search in *The New York Times* file for:

```
headline(welfare and reform) and date aft 1992
```

produces only 45 stories, but they are quite relevant; by contrast, the search:

```
welfare w/20 reform and date aft 1992
```

produces over 1,000 stories, many of them of little relevance (e.g., ones listing welfare reform along with various other electoral issues).

- **Sorting:** The NEXIS service's files, in contrast to most LEXIS files, have segments on which you can ***sort*** your search results. To discover, for a particular file that you have logged into, which segments are sortable, type the letter **s** followed by [ENTER].

For most NEXIS service files, the segments you can sort on include *DATE, SECTION,* and *LENGTH.*

You can sort on more than one segment, in which case the documents will be sorted first on the segment you list first, then on the second, etc. Thus if, after typing **s** , you type:

```
section, date
```

the service will first sort by the contents of the *SECTION* segment, and then by *DATE* within a given section.

The normal sequence in which documents are sorted is ascending. In the case of an alphabetic field, "ascending" means from A to Z. In the case of a numeric segment, it means smallest to largest; in the case of a date, it means earliest to latest. Thus to reverse the usual sort order that you get if you don't specify a sort at all (which is sorted by date, newest first), you would simply type:

```
date
```

after you specified that you wanted to sort by typing the letter **s**. You can reverse the normal sorting sequence by putting the characters **-d** immediately following the name of the segment. Thus to sort by *LENGTH*, largest to smallest, you would type:

```
length-d
```

By the way, sorting on length is probably the most useful sorting you can do in the NEXIS service's files, since it lets you concentrate on the largest (or the smallest) articles first.

F. **The *REGNWS* Library:** Another "news-like" library that you may want to use is the *REGNWS,* or "Regional News," Library. *REGNWS* consists mainly of more than 100 full-text American daily newspapers. It includes some very large newspapers with meaningful circulations outside their state of publication (e.g., the *New York Times*), but doesn't include newspapers with a truly national focus (e.g., *USA Today*). *REGNWS* also includes the UPI State & Regional wire service, plus certain transcripts of radio and TV programs. As near as I can tell, practically everything in the *REGNWS* library is also contained in the much-larger *NEWS* library.

1. **Cost:** There's not much of a cost advantage in using *REGNWS* instead of the big *NEWS* library. For instance, a search on the *ALLNWS* file (old and new stories) in *REGNWS* costs the same $60 as a search on *ALLNWS* in the *NEWS* library.

2. **State-by-state coverage:** Why, then, would anyone ever use *REGNWS*? The main reason is ***state-by-state selectivity***: *REGNWS* lets you specify a state (or custom combination of states), and then gives you just stories from publications in that state. This can help you avoid being drowned in detail.

   For example, let's suppose you're looking for stories on a particular event that you know took place in Florida. Because of the localness of the story you either believe that almost all coverage came from Florida news sources, or you're only interested in Florida news sources even if out-of-state sources may have covered the story. Within the *REGNWS* library, you'd select the *FLNWS* file, and be given only sources that are published within Florida.[10]

10. If what you want is a full region of the U.S., rather than one or a few states, you'll probably be better off in the appropriate regional file in the *NEWS* library (e.g., the *NEAST* group file). See p. 8-6 above.

II. OTHER LAW-RELATED LEXIS-NEXIS SERVICES

A. Introduction: So far in this chapter, we have considered only files within the *NEWS* library. But the law-related (as opposed to specifically legal) materials on the LEXIS service go beyond this one library. There are other libraries within what LEXIS-NEXIS calls its "NEXIS service"; there are also other "services" apart from the LEXIS and NEXIS services. I consider each of these in turn.

B. Other NEXIS libraries: Within "the NEXIS service"[11] there are other libraries apart from the *NEWS* library. These are likely to be somewhat peripheral to your needs, so I merely list some of them here:

Library Name	Description
CMPGN	The Campaign Library (dedicated solely to the news surrounding political campaigns and current-office holders)
CMPCOM	The Computers and Communications Library (concentrates on the news and technology surrounding the computer, telecommunications and electronics industries).
ENTERT	The Entertainment Library (focuses on facts pertaining to the entertainment industry, i.e., movies, TV and music)
EXEC	The Executive Branch Library (news coverage of the Executive Branch and federal government agencies)
LEGNEW	The Legal News Library (general news about the U.S. legal industry and legal profession; includes publications like *American Lawyer, Legal Times, National Law Journal, Texas Lawyer,* etc.)
MARKET	The Marketing Library (covers advertising, marketing, market research, public relations, product announcements, and other marketing-related items)
PEOPLE	The People Library (concentrates on biographical or people-related news, issues and events)

11. There's really no functional significance to LEXIS-NEXIS' distinction between libraries that are in "the NEXIS service" and other libraries, such as those that LEXIS-NEXIS puts in "the LEXIS service," the MEDIS service, etc. You don't log into a particular "service"; you log into the LEXIS-NEXIS services as a whole, and then into a library within a service. So services are merely a LEXIS-NEXIS classification scheme for grouping libraries.

Library Name	Description
SPORTS	The Sports Library (contains the full text of *Sports Illustrated* and *The Sporting News*, as well as the Sports section of many major newspapers and newswires)
LEXPAT®	The U.S. Patent and Trademark Office Library (full text of U.S. patents since at least 1976, plus various other filed information about patents; material in the *LEXPAT* library is also available in the *PATENT* library)

C. The LEXIS® Financial Information™ Service: The LEXIS Financial Information service contains three libraries designed mainly for use by investors. However, lawyers practicing in the corporate area will sometimes find useful information here. For instance, a mergers and acquisitions specialist might want to retrieve quickly the SEC reports filed by a target corporation. Similarly, a lawyer specializing in bringing shareholders' derivative litigation might want to use these materials to search for securities-related wrongdoing by potential corporate defendants. The libraries contained in the LEXIS Financial Information service are as follows:

1. **The *COMPNY* library:** The *COMPNY* library consists of:
   - Reports by investment banks and brokerage houses about whole industries, and about individual companies. (These are mainly available in the *INVTXT* file.)[12]
   - Filings by corporations and individuals with the SEC, including 10-K, 10-Q, 8-K, Annual Report to Shareholders, Proxy Statement, Tender Offer, Acquisition, Outstanding Corporate Event, Insider Trading, Registration Statement, and other filings. (The most inclusive files containing SEC filings are the *FILING* and *SEC* files. Another important file of company financial information is *DISCLO* ("Disclosure").)
   - Profiles of U.S. public and private companies, plus foreign companies (especially the *BDS*, *SPCO*, and *ICC* files.)
   - Company and Economic News, especially from wire services. (The most inclusive file is *ALLNWS*.)
   - Corporate profiles for both public and private companies (e.g., Standard & Poor's Register, in the *SPCORP* file).
   - Mergers and acquisition news stories (in the file *M&ANWS*).
2. **The *INVEST* library:** The Analysts Research (*INVEST*) library consists solely of company and industry research reports. This library is not included on your Educational Subscription.

12. Only a few of the many hundreds of reports on individual companies or entire industries are available on your Educational Subscription, so you will need to use a Commercial Subscription to get at most of these.

3. **The *NAARS* library:** The National Automated Accounting Research System (NAARS) library is provided by the American Institute of Certified Public Accountants. It has two main components:

   - Accounting and audit literature, such as accounting rules promulgated by the Financial Accounting Standards Board. (The accounting literature is mainly in the *LIT* file.)
   - The full-text financial statement of annual reports for many publicly traded companies from 1984-1994. Because the purpose of this file is to help accountants properly prepare financial statements and the footnotes to them, this file does not contain the Letter to Shareholders or other important components of the Annual Report to Shareholders; therefore, for finding out about a company's business, you are better off using the *FILING* and *SEC* files in the *COMPNY* library.

D. The MEDIS® Service: The MEDIS service contains medical information. It is comprised of three libraries, *GENMED*, *MEDLNE* and *EMBASE*.

1. ***GENMED*:** The General Medical (*GENMED*) library consists mainly of the full text of various medical journals and newsletters. Some of the publications covered are "updated" (that is, coverage continues through the latest edition of the journal), whereas others are "archived" (that is, the MEDIS service's coverage stopped with some past issue). The full-text updated journals available to you on your Educational Subscription are:

File Name	Description
CURJNL	Combined updated journals
JNCI	*Journal of the National Cancer Institute*
LANCET	*The Lancet*
PED	*Pediatrics*
PHR	*Public Health Reports*
SGO	*Journal of Amer. Coll. of Surgeons (formerly Surgery, Gynecology & Obstetrics)*

2. ***MEDLNE*:** The *MEDLNE* library contains ***bibliographic*** (rather than full text) information from over 3,500 worldwide medical journals dating back to 1966. *MEDLNE* is a public domain database that is prepared by the National Library of Medicine. You can best think of *MEDLNE* as a super-index to medical literature; each "document" in it, rather than being the full text of an article, consists of bibliographic information, often including a several-sentence abstract of the article (prepared by the article's author and published at the beginning of the article itself). Normally, you will use *MEDLNE* to find references to articles that may be of interest, and you will then get the full text of the article itself from a medical library or from the publisher.

3. ***EMBASE*:** Another bibliographic medical library is EMBASE (library *EMBASE*, file *EMBASE*). Like *MEDLNE*, it includes abstracts of articles from thousands of medical journals from around the world. The *EMBASE* file has its own set of descriptors and codes, so you might want to use it even if you've already used *MEDLNE*, because *EMBASE* may have classified an article differently from *MEDLNE*.

E. The LEXIS® Country Information™ Service: The LEXIS Country Information service gives you economic and general information about a region, or a single country, at a time.

1. **The regions:** For this service, LEXIS-NEXIS has divided the world into four regions (plus a "group region"), each of which is represented as a library. These regions are:

Library Name	Description
ASIAPC	Asia/Pacific Rim region (includes all of Asia plus Australia and New Zealand)
EUROPE	Europe (including the countries formerly included in the U.S.S.R.)
MDEAFR	Mideast/Africa
NSAMER	North/South America (principally covers Latin and South America, but also contains American and Canadian information relevant to international trade)
WORLD	Combines *ASIAPC, EUROPE, MDEAFR* and *NSAMER* files

2. **Files:** Within each regional library, the material is organized in various formats. Some of the more interesting "slices" in each library are:

- The file *ALLNWS* (available in each regional library), which contains all news stories in the library;
- The file *BUSANL* (available in each regional library), which includes all "business analysis" for the region; and
- Individual-country files, one for each country in the region. (*Examples:* In the *ASIAPC* library, there is a separate file for each of the 21 countries in the region, including files named *CAMBOD, HKONG, NKOREA*, etc.)

F. The LEXIS® Public Records Online Service: The LEXIS Public Records Online service consists of eight libraries: (1) the *ASSETS* library (property records); (2) the *DOCKET* library (court index and docket information); (3) the *FINDER* library (person and business locator; not available under the educational subscription); (4) the *INCORP®* library (state corporation, limited partnership and DBA filings); (5) the *INSOLV* library (bankruptcy filings); (6) the *LIENS* library (UCC filings, plus certain other lien and judgment filings); (7) the *VERDCT* library (information about verdicts and settlements in civil cases); and (8) the *ALLREC* library (a compilation of all of the above public information.)

1. **Property records (the *ASSETS* library):** The *ASSETS* library gives you detailed information about the ownership of individual parcels of real property throughout much of the U.S. The information is collected from county tax assessors' and recorders' offices in 41 states and the District of Columbia. The *ASSETS* library allows you to discover asset ownership, owner's mailing address, assessed tax valuation, recent property sales and deed transfers, and other aspects of real property ownership. At present, some or all of the counties in the following states are available online: AK, AL, AZ, CA, CO, CT, DE, FL, GA, HI, IL, IN, IA, KS, KY, LA, MD, MA, MI, MN, MS, MO, MT, NV, NJ, NM, NY, NC,

OH, OK, OR, PA, RI, SC, TN, TX, UT, VA, WA, WV and WI (plus DC and the Virgin Islands).[13]

At the lowest level, the property records are organized by county (e.g., file *NYPBRO* for Bronx County, New York). The county records for any given state are all grouped together in at least one, and often two or three, statewide files. More precisely, for each state (of the 41 covered) there is a file named *XXPROP* (where *XX* is the two-digit postal abbreviation, such as *NJPROP* for New Jersey), representing the Tax Assessor's records. In addition, for 27 states (AZ, CA, CO, CT, FL, GA, HI, IL, KY, MD, MA, MI, MN, MO, NV, NJ, NY, OH, OR, PA, RI, TN, TX, UT, VA, WA and WI, and the District of Columbia) there is a file called *XXSALE* (e.g., *NJSALE*), which contains the Deed Transfer records. In a state which has both *XXPROP* and *XXSALE* files, these are combined together in an *XXOWN* (e.g., *NJOWN*) file.

Since a *XXPROP* file exists for all 41 of the states covered by the *ASSETS* library, in any of these states you can find out whether a person owns property by doing a search[14] on the person's first and last name, such as:

```
smith w/5 fred!
```

Because of the possibility of people with the same name, you may want to add additional information to your search. You can do this by selecting the file for a single county, or perhaps using a zip code or city name in conjunction with the *ADDRESS* segment, e.g.:

```
smith w/3 fred! and address(san diego)
```

However, you should be aware that not all records contain all pieces of information; for instance, some don't have the zip code.

In those 27 states where Deed Transfer records are available, you will be able to find out when the property was acquired, and how much the buyer paid for it.

Keep in mind that of the 41 states covered in some form or another in the *ASSETS* library, only for seven states (AZ, CA, FL, HI, MD, MT and TN)[15] is full ***state-wide*** tax-assessor information available; for the balance, only records from selected counties are present. Also, when a state has records for only selected counties, these records generally don't have deed-transfer information, just current-owner information.

There are few if any legitimate uses to which you are likely to be able to put the *ASSETS* library in your work as a law student. However, in your work as a summer associate, lawyer in a private firm, prosecutor, etc., there may be many uses. Three that immediately occur are:

- You have obtained a judgment for your client against John Doe, and you would like to

13. You can also research FAA aircraft registration records (file *AIRCFT*), as well as boat registrations from the U.S. Coast Guard (file *USBOAT*) and from Florida (file *FLBOAT*).

14. In order to do a search in this file, you'll first have to enter **.ns** after you log in.

15. The District of Columbia and the Virgin Islands also fall into this group.

locate and file liens against any property he owns so that your client can collect on the judgment.

- You are considering whether to sue John Doe for a client, and would like to know whether he has assets that are sufficient to make it worthwhile to pursue him (since a judgment against a person with no assets is worth nothing). If you do not know which state a person is likely to own property in, and you do not want to take the time to go through all 42 state-wide files, you can use the *ALLOWN* file, which groups all 42 state files together. However, the *ALLOWN* file is not accessible through your Educational Subscription.
- You are a prosecutor who is prosecuting, or is about to prosecute, John Doe, and you would like to lay the groundwork for seizing his assets pursuant to federal or state forfeiture statutes.

2. **Court dockets (the *DOCKET* library):** For 13 states (CA, CT, DE, FL, IL, ME, MA, NJ, NY, OH, PA, RI, and TX) you can search court docket information, in the *DOCKET* library. You can learn such things as the names of the parties, filing date, court, and docket or case number. These filings are generally in a file called *XXCIVL*, where *XX* is the state's postal abbreviation.

   The main utility of the *DOCKET* library is to allow you to discover whether a particular person has been involved in litigation in the past. If you find that there has been litigation, you can then obtain the actual pleadings and other case information from the court where the proceeding took place.[16]

   The *XXCIVL* file for a particular state generally covers only civil cases, and only state-court ones. Also, the entire state is not necessarily covered. For instance, for California, what is available in file *CACIVL* is the Civil Case Index for Superior Court for 10 counties (mainly the highest-population ones).

   For a few states, criminal court dockets are also available (e.g., *CACRIM*, covering the Superior Court criminal dockets for L.A. and Orange Counties). And for some states the federal civil docket is included (e.g., file *USCACD*, covering federal cases filed in the Central District of California, or file *USNYSD*, covering the Southern District of New York.)

   Lastly, bankruptcy filings are available for 44 states and D.C., in the *ALLBKT* file.

3. **Corporation information (the *INCORP* library):** Information about corporations incorporated in, or registered to do business in, 44 states and D.C., is available in the *INCORP* library. Limited-partnership information for 35 states is also included. This information is also included in several other libraries (e.g., the *CORP* library), and is discussed elsewhere.[17] DBA ("Doing Business As...") filings for 47 states and D.C. are available in the *ALLDBA* file.

---

16. You can actually use the LEXDOC® feature to order copies of the pleadings while you are still online looking at a particular docket entry for a case. However, LEXDOC is not available as part of your Educational Subscription.

17. See *supra*, p. 7-13.

4. **Liens (the *LIENS* library):** The Liens Library (*LIENS*) gives information about several different types of filings: UCC filings, state-court judgments, and federal and state tax liens.

   a. **UCC filings:** Security interests in personal property, filed under Article 9 of the Uniform Commercial Code, are available online for all 50 states and the District of Columbia. There is a file for each state (named *XXUCC*, where *XX* is the two-digit state abbreviation); also, information from all states is combined in the *ALLUCC* file.

   b. **State-court judgments and liens:** State-court judgments and liens are present from 38 states (AZ, AR, CA, CO, CT, DE, FL, HI, ID, IL, IN, IA, KS, KY, LA, ME, MA, MN, MO, NE, NV, NH, NJ, NM, NY, ND, OH, OK, OR, PA, RI, SD, TX, UT, VT, WA, WI, and WY). These are in files named *XXJGT*, where *XX* is the state's postal abbreviation. In general, all courts of a state are covered. All of these are grouped in the *ALLJGT* file.

   c. **Federal and state tax liens:** Tax liens filed by federal and state tax authorities are available from six states (CA, DE, IL, NJ, NY and PA) in files named *XXTXLN*, where *XX* is the state's postal abbreviation.

5. **Verdicts and settlements (the *VERDCT* library):** Jury verdicts in civil cases, and pre-trial settlements, usually do not become widely available. For example, if you look only at reported cases (which basically means appellate cases), you will glimpse only a small portion of jury verdicts, and almost no settlements. Yet the practitioner often has a great need for this information, to answer questions like, "What's the likely recovery for a young man's loss of a leg in New York?" or, "Who is good at bringing highway-design negligence cases against municipalities in Southern California?" or, "What expert structural engineer can I get to analyze whether and why the brakes failed in my client's car, leading to a crash?"

   The Verdicts library (*VERDCT*) is designed to answer this sort of question. The library consists of about 15 files. Most of them are single-state verdict and trial reporters. Four are national reporters, the files *ATLA*, *SHEPJV*, *NLJVER* and *JVR*. You can search all the verdict files at one time in the *ALLVER* file.

   Of the four national reporters, *JVR* is far and away the most comprehensive, both in terms of number of verdicts and settlements covered, and detail furnished on each one. *JVR* is put out by Jury Verdict Research, Inc., the leading hard-copy publisher of verdict and settlement information. Because of its excellent coverage, I will concentrate on the *JVR* file here.

   Here are some of the segments covered in the *JVR* file:

Segment Name	Description
NAME	A group segment containing the case name, medical experts and technical experts.
NUMBER	Docket number of case (e.g., "Case No. H-26059")
DATE	A group segment containing various dates (e.g., verdict date, incident date), usually a month and year

Segment Name	Description
TOPIC	Principal topic of case (e.g., "Products Liability — Clothing")
RESULT	Who won the case (e.g., "Plaintiff Verdict" or "Defense Verdict"). If plaintiff won, the amount won, with commas (e.g., "$ 1,300,00"). In the case of a plaintiff verdict, the verdict is broken down by type (e.g., "Compensatory: $ 40,000; Punitive damages: $ 35,000"). If a settlement, the word "Settlement" is used together with the amount.
INJURY	Nature of injury (e.g., "Lumbar vertebra fracture"; "wrongful termination"; "death"; "subdural hematoma")
STATE	Name of state, expressed in both words and two-digit postal abbreviation
COUNTY	Name of county where case was tried or settled
COURT	Name of court where case was filed (e.g., "district," "supreme")
COUNSEL	Names of plaintiff's and defendant's counsel; usually includes firm name, individual lawyer's name, city and state of the lawyer (e.g., "Maloney, Gallup, et al. by Joseph V. McCarthy, Buffalo, NY")
SUMMARY	A several sentence summary of the facts, including a description of the damages, the legal and factual arguments made by both sides, and the outcome of the suit (e.g., "A male suffered a closed head injury and a soft-tissue injury to the back when his vehicle collided with a vehicle operated by the male defendant and owned by the co-defendant company at an intersection. The plaintiff contended that the defendant was negligent for failing to yield the right of way. The plaintiff was found 100% negligent.")
EXPERTS	Names and cities of experts for each side, together with their specialty (e.g., "Plaintiff experts: Ruple, Charles, Austin, TX — Accident Reconstructionist. Defendant experts: Bodner, Seymour, Edison, NJ — Engineer.")

Here are some illustrations of the kinds of things you could do with the *JVR* file, and how to do them:

- You are a practicing lawyer, but not a tort specialist. A woman you know wants you to represent her daughter in a suit against the manufacturer of her daughter's pajamas, which burst into flame from a spark. You would like to refer the case to a lawyer specializing in this type of case. You should search for descriptive words likely to appear in the document, and limit the search to the appropriate state:

  ```
  burn! and pajamas and state(ny)
  ```

  You would then review the various cases, and interview the person shown as the plaintiff's attorney in the cases that seem to have been successfully resolved for the plaintiff either by settlement or verdict.

  If you wished, you could limit your search to verdicts or settlements above a certain size, in addition to the other criteria, by using the *RESULT* segment. Thus:

  ```
  result > 1,000,000 and burn! and pajamas
  ```

- You would like to find out how much a certain type of injury is "worth." Obviously, this will depend not just on the medical description of the injury, but on the monetary damages it causes (so that a 30-year-old construction worker who loses an arm will presumably have greater damages than a 72-year-old retired homemaker who suffers the same loss). Nonetheless, you will often find it useful to read accounts of cases involving the particular type of injury at issue in your case. For this, you can use the *INJURY* segment:

```
injury(finger w/3 amputation)
```

- You need to find an expert witness, preferably one who has successfully represented your side of the controversy. Typically, you will want to use a key word summarizing the type of expert you need, plus, perhaps, locational information and verdict information. For instance, if you need a urologist to give expert testimony for the plaintiff in a surgical malpractice case in which your client was rendered impotent, and you don't want to have to bring the expert in from too far away to attend trial in Massachusetts, you might search for:

```
malpractice and impoten! and
 experts(urolo! and ma or ct or ri)
```

  Unfortunately, there is no good way to ask the service for just those documents in which there is some data (as opposed to emptiness) in the *EXPERTS* segment. However, as you can see from the above search, you can require that the service give you only documents containing a particular state in the *EXPERTS* field, so that you can use this to find those documents that may involve a urologist from a particular state.

  There is, however, an easy way to find just those cases in which the urologist testified on behalf of the plaintiff rather than for the defendant. In addition to the single segment, *EXPERTS*, which contains both the names of the plaintiff's experts and the defendant's experts, there are the segments *P-DOCTORS* (names of medical expert witnesses for plaintiff) and *D-DOCTORS* (same, but for defendant).[18]

  Forensic Services Directory: By the way, another good source for leads to expert witnesses is the Forensic Services Directory (filename *EXPERT*, in library *LEXREF*), which contains information on about 5,000 experts with technical scientific or medical knowledge in more than 6,500 subject areas.[19]

- You are suing a doctor, and would like to know whether he has ever been sued in cases that have either gone to trial or been settled. You can do a full-text search on the name of the doctor, together with location information, to get likely candidates. However, the names of the parties are preserved only in the *NAME* segment, and generally only the last name appears; therefore, you will have to order the pleadings themselves from the court, if available, to know whether you have the right party.

18. Non-medical experts are listed in the *P-EXPERTS* and *D-EXPERTS* segments.

19. The *EXPERT* file is not included in your Educational Subscription, but would be available under your employer's general Commercial Subscription.

- You know that the other side will be presenting testimony by a particular expert. You can use the *EXPERTS* segment to find out whether that expert has ever testified before. This segment contains both first and last name, so your search can be quite precise. Once you get the names of cases where this person testified, you can: (1) possibly get a transcript of the testimony, so as to impeach him if he takes a different position now, or to learn what kind of witness he is; and (2) talk to the lawyer who cross-examined the expert, to get some ideas.

Chapter 9

Citators

I. OVERVIEW

A. Citators in general: During the course of any research project, you will develop one or more principal cases, statutory provisions, or other critical documents. You will then need to find later cases or other legal writings that cite your principal document. (For now, let's assume your principal document is a case.) There are several reasons why you might want to do this, of which the two most important typically are:

- You want to find additional authority, and finding cases or law review articles that cite your principal case is a good way to find relevant authority; or
- You need to be sure that your principal case still represents "good law," that is, that it has not been reversed by a higher court, overruled by a later decision, superseded by a statute, or otherwise invalidated; finding all later references to your principal case is a good way to make sure this invalidation has not occurred.

Tools that help you find citations to your principal case are called "citators." The LEXIS service effectively has three citators within it:

- SHEPARD'S®
- Auto-Cite®
- The LEXCITE® feature

We will consider each of these in turn.

B. When should you use each one: You'll get a better sense of the differences among these three tools as we go through our detailed discussion. But here, I can give you a broad sense of when you would use each one, and how they differ:

1. **SHEPARD'S:** The main utility of SHEPARD'S is to show you a large, almost completely inclusive, list of references to your principal case. One of its key benefits is that for every reference that cites your principal case, SHEPARD'S editors have done an editorial analysis. That is, they have evaluated the impact of the citing case on your principal case to determine if it is being overruled, criticized, distinguished or just mentioned. Neither of the other two services does this in a way that is both as inclusive and as precise.

   In general, if you are only going to use one of the three citators, and you want to be able to home in on relevant authority quickly, SHEPARD'S is probably your best bet.

2. **Auto-Cite:** Auto-Cite is a "citation verification service." It provides substantially different material than a true "citator." Auto-Cite gives you the caption and cite of your case in Bluebook sequence. It notes parallel references. It provides the complete appellate history of your case. It also gives you an "answer set" of cases, consisting of two types of cases: (1) certain subsequent cases that may weaken your case's precedential value; and (2) certain earlier cases upon which your case has had a negative impact. In addition, Auto-Cite will refer you to annotations in ALR that explain or discuss any case in the Auto-Cite answer set.

3. **The LEXCITE feature:** The LEXCITE feature is basically a streamlined way of using the broad LEXIS service as a citator. You pick a particular library and file, and then you feed LEXIS the cite you're interested in. The service then returns with all documents whose text includes that citation.

   The key advantages of LEXCITE are that its results are very complete, very current, and completely "in context." (I discuss these advantages in more detail on p. 9-17 below.)

II. SHEPARD'S CITATIONS

A. **What SHEPARD'S is and does:** SHEPARD'S Citations, as you probably know, has for more than a century consisted of hard-copy books showing, for every case, every later case that has cited that first case. The LEXIS version of SHEPARD'S fulfills this same function, but in a quite different, and highly automated, way.

B. **1500 reporters:** SHEPARD'S on the LEXIS service covers more than 1500 different hard-copy reporters, practically the entire universe of reporters.

1. **Law reviews:** In addition to cases that cite your principal case, SHEPARD'S also tracks ***law review articles*** that cite your case. See p. 9-6.

2. **Statutes:** You can also now SHEPARDIZE ***statutory provisions***. Thus you can find all cases mentioning a particular section of a federal or state statute. See p. 9-9.

3. **Code of Federal Regulations and federal rules:** You can SHEPARDIZE for mentions of the ***CFR*** and ***federal rules*** in cases. See p. 9-10.

C. **Currentness:** New citing references and analyses are ***updated every day*** upon receipt from SHEPARD'S.

D. **Coding of analyses:** In my opinion, the most useful feature of SHEPARD'S online is that you can use the editors' "bright-line" editorial analysis of how the citing case has treated the cited case. That is, the editors decide whether Case B has "overruled" Case A, "distinguished" it, "questioned" it, etc. SHEPARD'S use of these predefined analysis terms gives you great control over "what kind" of references you want to see: you can choose to see only "negative treatments," only cases following your case, only cases overruling your case, etc.

1. **Comparison:** By contrast, LEXCITE makes you do your own editorial analysis of the citing case — there's no automated way to see, say, just those cases that treat your case negatively.

E. **How to use SHEPARD'S on the LEXIS service:** Let's now look in detail at how to use the online version of SHEPARD'S to find cites to cases. We'll be SHEPARDIZING™ *Kelley v. R.G. Industries*, 497 A.2d 1143, 304 Md. 124 (1985), a torts case allowing the victim of an armed robbery to recover in strict liability against the manufacturer of the cheap "Saturday Night Special" handgun used in the robbery.

1. **Getting started:** There are two different techniques by which you can get "into" SHEPARD'S. With either of these techniques, you can with a single step both enter SHEPARD'S and furnish the identity of the case you want to SHEPARDIZE.

   a. **While viewing the case:** If you are currently viewing the case that you want to SHEPARDIZE, giving the command to SHEPARDIZE the case is trivial. Simply type:

      `shep` [ENTER]

      and the initial SHEPARD'S screen for the case will be displayed for you almost instantly. (To return to the case itself, use the LINK marker for "Exit SHEPARD'S," usually **`=3`**)

   b. **While doing anything else:** If you are not viewing the case you want to SHEPARDIZE, you can still SHEPARDIZE the case you want in a single step. No matter where you are on the service or what you are doing, to SHEPARDIZE 497 A.2d 1143, you would simply type:

      `shep 497 a2d 1143` [ENTER]

      As you would expect, you indicate the citation in the usual format:

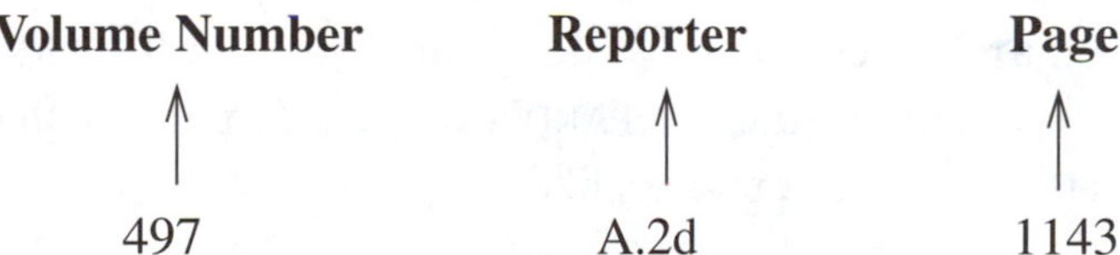

      There must be a space between the volume number and the reporter, and another space between the reporter and the page number. "Page number" refers to the page upon which the case ***begins***, not some interior page in the opinion. (If you supply an interior page, however, SHEPARD'S will detect that this is an interior page, and will "fallback" to the correct SHEPARD'S listing for the initial page of the case that contains that interior page.)

      i. **Abbreviations:** You use basically the standard abbreviations for the reporters. SHEPARD'S is fairly forgiving about the form of abbreviations — for example, it will accept a reporter name with or without interior spaces, with or without interior periods, and in capital letters or lower case, so that any of the following will work:

```
307 n w 2d 12
307 n.w.2d 12
307 N.W.2d 12
307 N. W. 2d 12
```

I usually find it most convenient to not include either periods or spaces, and to use lower case, so that I would type:

> **`307 nw2d 12`** [ENTER]

The abbreviations themselves are pretty much the standard ones you would expect. Thus for the main federal and regional reporters, you can use:

`us`	**`ne2d`**
`f2d`	**`nw2d`**
`fsupp`	**`p2d`**
`a2d`	**`so2d`**
`calrep` (Cal. Reporter)	**`se2d`**
`nysupp` (New York Supp.)	**`sw2d`**

For the state reporters, the abbreviation by which the reporter would be cited in Blue Book form will generally be fine; thus:

`ariz` (Arizona Reports)
`cal` (California Supreme Court Reports)
`calapp3d` (California Appellate Reports Third Series)
`ga` (Georgia Reports)
`mo` (Missouri Supreme Court Reports)
`ny2d` (New York Court of Appeals Reports, Second Series)
`tex` (Texas Supreme Court Reports)
`texcivapp` (Texas Civil Appeals Reports)

2. **The initial screen and its elements:** After your request to SHEPARDIZE a particular cite, you receive the first page of the SHEPARD'S display screen for that case. For 497 A.2d 1143, here's what the first screen looks like:

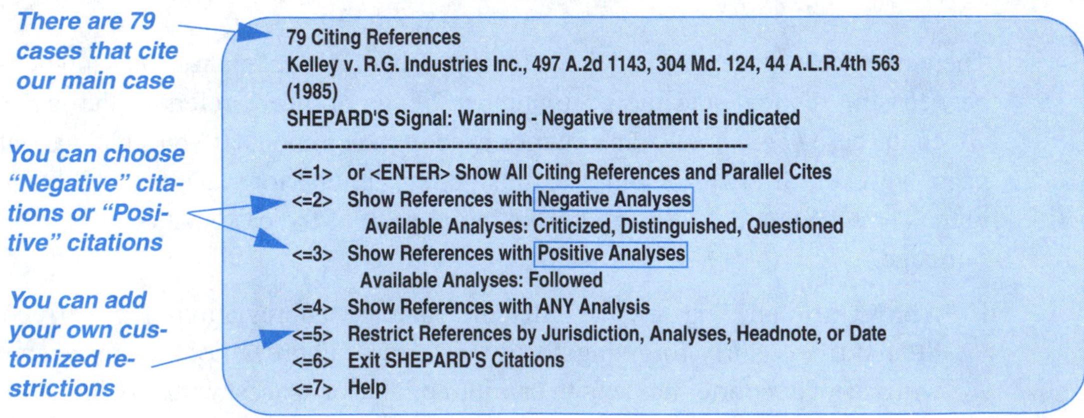

There are 79 cases that cite our main case
You can choose "Negative" citations or "Positive" citations
You can add your own customized restrictions
79 Citing References
Kelley v. R.G. Industries Inc., 497 A.2d 1143, 304 Md. 124, 44 A.L.R.4th 563 (1985)
SHEPARD'S Signal: Warning - Negative treatment is indicated
<=1> or <ENTER> Show All Citing References and Parallel Cites
<=2> Show References with Negative Analyses
Available Analyses: Criticized, Distinguished, Questioned
<=3> Show References with Positive Analyses
Available Analyses: Followed
<=4> Show References with ANY Analysis
<=5> Restrict References by Jurisdiction, Analyses, Headnote, or Date
<=6> Exit SHEPARD'S Citations
<=7> Help

Some comments about this screen:

- Notice that the first line tells you how many "citing references" (cases and law review articles) cite your main case.

- If the number of citing references is not too large, you may want to ***display them all***. To do this, select the =1 LINK marker, by double-clicking on that marker or by typing **=1**.
- If you know that you're interested only in whether your main case is ***still good law***, you may want to limit yourself to references with ***"Negative Analyses."*** (If none of these overrules or otherwise casts real doubt on the continued validity of your case, you're home free.) To do this, choose **=2** . (Notice that the "Available Analyses" portion of the **=2** entry tells you exactly which negative analyses are represented somewhere among the retrieved documents — in this case the "Criticized," "Distinguished" and "Questioned" analyses are present somewhere.)
- Conversely, you may be looking just for ***support*** for your position. In that case, you may want to see only those cases that view your case ***"Positively."*** To do this, choose **=3** . (The entry for **=3** shows you which positive analyses are represented among the documents.)
- Your greatest flexibility comes with use of LINK marker **=5**, "Restrict References by Jurisdiction, Analyses, Headnote, or Date." I talk further about this option on p. 9-6.

Here is what the master list of citations for *Kelley* look like, if we choose **=1** so as to display all citing references (regardless of whether they're positive or negative):

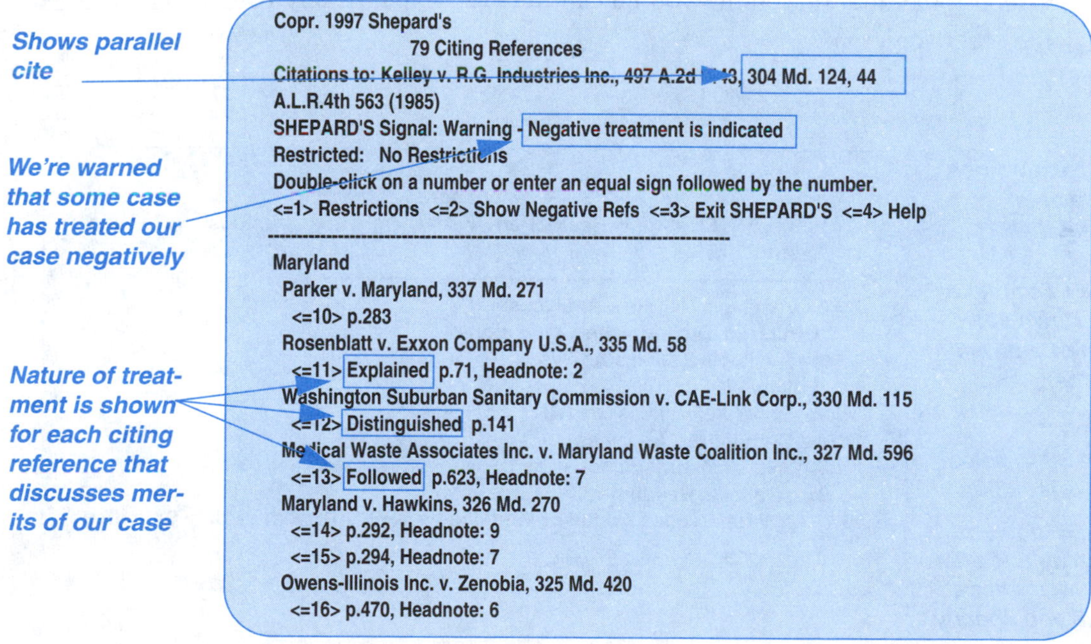
Copr. 1997 Shepard's
79 Citing References
Citations to: Kelley v. R.G. Industries Inc., 497 A.2d 1143, 304 Md. 124, 44 A.L.R.4th 563 (1985)
SHEPARD'S Signal: Warning - Negative treatment is indicated
Restricted: No Restrictions
Double-click on a number or enter an equal sign followed by the number.
<=1> Restrictions <=2> Show Negative Refs <=3> Exit SHEPARD'S <=4> Help

Maryland
Parker v. Maryland, 337 Md. 271
<=10> p.283
Rosenblatt v. Exxon Company U.S.A., 335 Md. 58
<=11> Explained p.71, Headnote: 2
Washington Suburban Sanitary Commission v. CAE-Link Corp., 330 Md. 115
<=12> Distinguished p.141
Medical Waste Associates Inc. v. Maryland Waste Coalition Inc., 327 Md. 596
<=13> Followed p.623, Headnote: 7
Maryland v. Hawkins, 326 Md. 270
<=14> p.292, Headnote: 9
<=15> p.294, Headnote: 7
Owens-Illinois Inc. v. Zenobia, 325 Md. 420
<=16> p.470, Headnote: 6

Notice that we can change what type of references we'd like to see at this point, either by selecting **=2** to see Negative ones, or by selecting **=1** to impose our own customized set of restrictions (as I discuss below).

3. Order of references: The master list of references has a particular order:

- *History References.* To begin with, SHEPARD'S gives you "History References," which are the citations for the cit*ed* case itself, including earlier and later stages of that same case.
- *Cases*. The citing cases begin with whatever the jurisdiction was of the case whose cite you gave to SHEPARD'S. In this instance, 497 A.2d 1143 is a Maryland case, so Maryland citations as reported in the Maryland Reporter are first; next come Maryland cases as reported in the Atlantic Reporter. Federal citations are then arranged by court level (U.S., L.E., L.E.2d, S.C., F., F.2d, F.3d, F.Supp. and F.R.D.). Then citations from states other than Maryland are arranged alphabetically by state name.
- *ALR annotations*
- *Law review articles*
- *Legal treatises*
- *Periodicals and newsletters*

Within each of the above subgroupings, the newest citation appears first and the oldest last (except "History References," which are chronological.)

4. Customizing your restrictions: Perhaps the most powerful aspect of SHEPARD'S on LEXIS is the ability to customize precisely the restrictions you want to impose on the citing references. To get to the "Restrictions" screen, select **=1** from the above cite-display screen, or =5 from the initial options screen shown on p. 9-4. Here's what the resulting screen looks like (assuming you haven't already imposed any restrictions through use of the other screens):

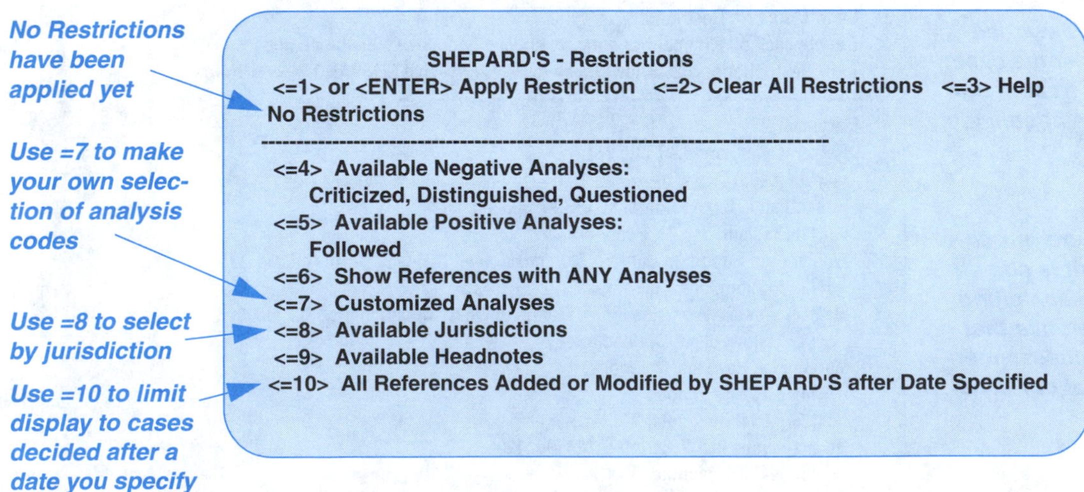

Here are the main things you can do from this screen:

- You can make your own ***selection of analysis codes*** for which you want to see cases. Thus you can choose to see, say, just cases that have "criticized" or "distinguished" your case. To do this select **=7** ("Customized Analyses"). You'll then see a screen that lets you choose from among the applicable analyses:[1]

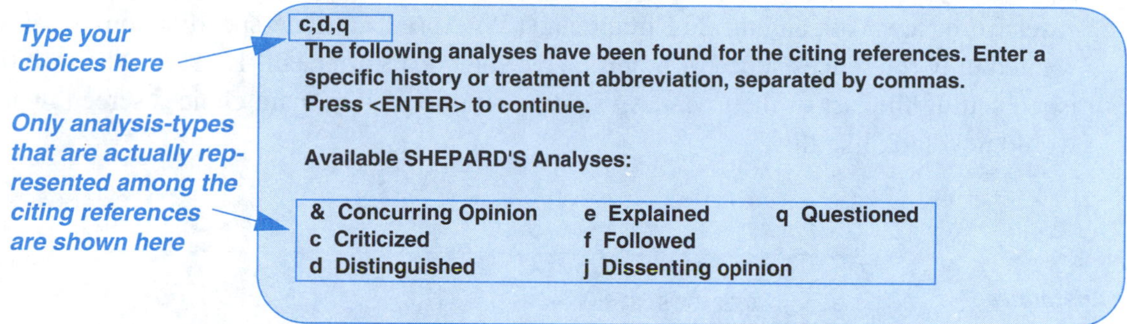

- You can choose to see only citing cases from ***particular jurisdictions***. To do this, select =8 ("Available Jurisdictions.") Here's the display you'll see:

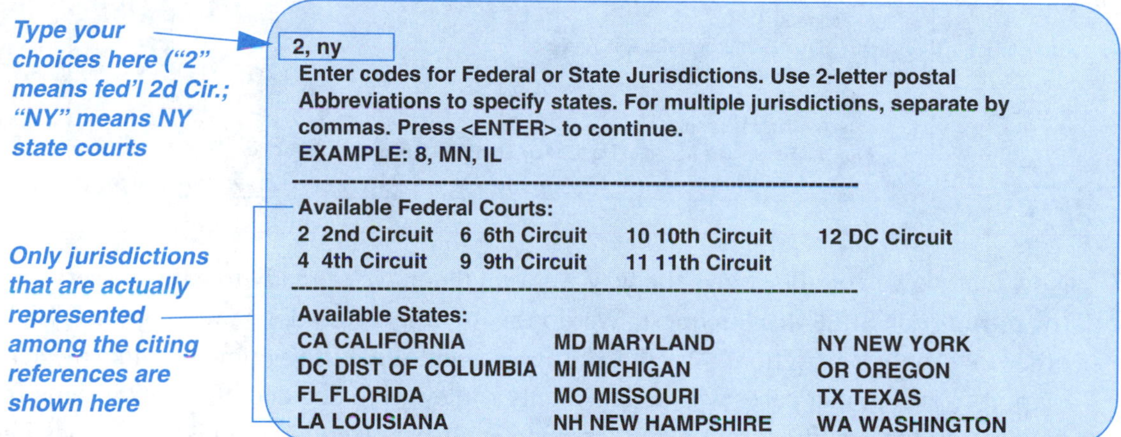

Type your choices here ("2" means fed'l 2d Cir.; "NY" means NY state courts
Only jurisdictions that are actually represented among the citing references are shown here
2, ny
Enter codes for Federal or State Jurisdictions. Use 2-letter postal Abbreviations to specify states. For multiple jurisdictions, separate by commas. Press <ENTER> to continue.
EXAMPLE: 8, MN, IL
Available Federal Courts:
2 2nd Circuit
4 4th Circuit
6 6th Circuit
9 9th Circuit
10 10th Circuit
11 11th Circuit
12 DC Circuit
Available States:
CA CALIFORNIA
DC DIST OF COLUMBIA
FL FLORIDA
LA LOUISIANA
MD MARYLAND
MI MICHIGAN
MO MISSOURI
NH NEW HAMPSHIRE
NY NEW YORK
OR OREGON
TX TEXAS
WA WASHINGTON

- You can restrict yourself to citing references that refer to a ***particular syllabus/headnote*** in the cited case. For instance, if we determined from our reading of the *Kelley* case that the relevant headnote for our purposes was [6], we could specify that we only want to see citations that refer to that aspect of *Kelley* summarized by headnote [6]. To do this, select **=9** ("Available Headnotes"), then type the number(s) of the headnote(s) for which you want to see all cites.

- You can restrict yourself to citing references added or modified by SHEPARD'S ***after a particular date***. To do this, select **=8** ("All References Added or Modified by SHEPARD'S after Date Specified.")

1. The system shows you only those analyses that actually apply, i.e., those that at least one citing reference falls into. So if no citing case, say, criticizes your main case, you won't see a listing of "c" — criticized, on the Customized Analyses screen.

As you use each of these options, you're brought back to the same screen shown on p. 9-6, but with your newly-established settings reflected near the top of the screen. Thus suppose we did the following things: (1) we used **=7** ("Customized Analyses") to say that we wanted only cases that use analysis-codes "c" ("Criticized"), "d" ("Distinguished") and "q" ("Questioned"); (2) we used **=8** ("Available Jurisdictions") to say we wanted only cases from New York and the 2d Circuit; and (3) we used **=8** (date-specification) to say we wanted only references added or modified by SHEPARD'S after Jan. 1, 1995. When we finished setting the last of these values, we'd be returned to the main choices screen, which would now look like this:

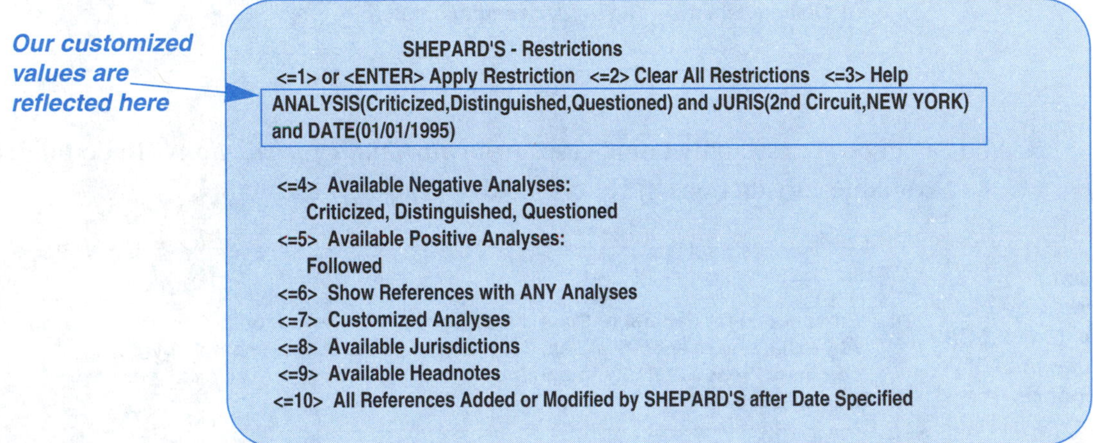

Now that we've got all settings the way we want them, we're ready to have the service run (or re-run) our SHEPARD'S request. We do this by selecting **=1** or pressing [ENTER], in order to "Apply Restriction." We'll then see a screenful of citing references like the screen on p. 9-5, except that cases will be listed only if they were decided after 1995, came from the federal 2d Circuit or from New York state, and criticized, distinguished or questioned *Kelley*.

5. **Viewing the citing references:** When you're looking at the list of citing references, if you want to see one of the listed cases, double-click on its LINK marker. (Thus on the screen p. 9-5, if you wanted to see *Rosenblatt v. Exxon*, you'd double-click on the **=11** marker.)

   You'll then be shown the citing reference in context, i.e., with the citation displayed, together with the surrounding text:

The citation is shown in context

Additional short-cites are also shown

```
335 Md. 58, *71; 642 A.2d 180;                    Md.
                1994 Md. LEXIS 74; 38 ERC (BNA) 1908
OPINION:
  ... [*71]   stated that because the defendant had no right of ownership or
control of the site, its liability was limited to negligence, and could not be
enlarged, under the circumstances, to a liability without fault.  <=17>  Id. at
213-14.
  We similarly limited the doctrine in <=18> Kelley v. R.G. Industries,
Inc., 304 Md. 124, 497 A.2d 1143 (1985), holding that it was not applicable to
hold the manufacturer or marketer of a handgun liable to a person injured by the
handgun during the course of a crime. We said:

"The thrust of the doctrine is that the activity be abnormally dangerous in
relation to the ...
  ... [*71]   in the use of a handgun in the commission of a  crime, on the
[*72]   other hand, bear no relation to any occupation or ownership of land.
Therefore, the abnormally dangerous activity doctrine does not apply to the
manufacture or marketing of handguns." <=19> 304 Md. at 133 (citations
omitted).

Thus, we have applied the doctrine only to claims by an occupier of land
```

Actually, the system puts you in KWIC mode in the citing case. You can then browse around in that case, using the various modes (e.g., FULL or VAR-KWIC). If you want to go back to the list of citing references in Shepards, type:

`res shep` [ENTER]

(which stands for "Resume SHEPARD'S").

F. **Shepardizing statutes:** You can also Shepardize a ***statute***. SHEPARD'S now covers ***all federal and state statutes.***

You follow essentially the same process as for a case: just type **`shep`** followed by the citation to the statute. Thus to find references to the main section of the Americans with Disabilities Act, you would enter:

`shep 42 uscs 12112` [ENTER]

The displays are pretty much the same as they are for cases. One difference is that the first screen you get divides the citing references based on whether they cite to just your statutory section alone, or as part of a range of sections, and upon whether they cite to a sub-section within your section. Thus the above request on 42 uscs 12112 produces the following initial screen:

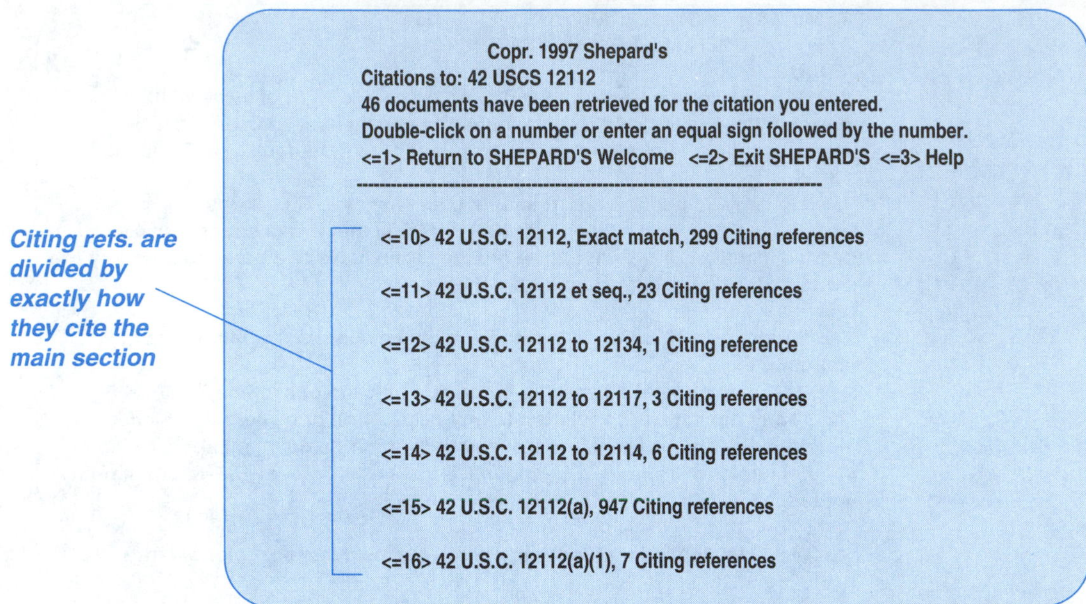

Copr. 1997 Shepard's
Citations to: 42 USCS 12112
46 documents have been retrieved for the citation you entered.
Double-click on a number or enter an equal sign followed by the number.
<=1> Return to SHEPARD'S Welcome <=2> Exit SHEPARD'S <=3> Help
<=10> 42 U.S.C. 12112, Exact match, 299 Citing references
<=11> 42 U.S.C. 12112 et seq., 23 Citing references
<=12> 42 U.S.C. 12112 to 12134, 1 Citing reference
<=13> 42 U.S.C. 12112 to 12117, 3 Citing references
<=14> 42 U.S.C. 12112 to 12114, 6 Citing references
<=15> 42 U.S.C. 12112(a), 947 Citing references
<=16> 42 U.S.C. 12112(a)(1), 7 Citing references
Citing refs. are divided by exactly how they cite the main section

Another difference from Shepardizing case citations is that when you display a case that cites a statute, the service puts you at the beginning of the page containing the statutory cite, rather than at the precise place on that page where the statutory cite occurs — it's up to you to find the statutory cite on the page.

If you're looking at a citing reference and want to return to the master list of cites, type

`res shep`

just as if it had been a case cite that you were Shepardizing.

G. CFR and Federal Rules: You can also now use SHEPARD'S to find citations to ***federal rules*** (e.g., the Fed. R. of Civ. Proc.) and to the ***Code of Federal Regulations.*** Thus:

`shep frcp 26`

will find you all cases, law review articles, and annotations, citing Fed. R. Civ. Proc. 26 (including a separate listing by the sub-section of the rule, such as just those sources citing FRCP 26(a)).

H. Printing your SHEPARD'S results: You can ***print*** the master list of citing references just as you can print any other document. While looking at that list (a sample of which appears on p. 9-5), just select Print Doc (type **`.pd`** [ENTER] or double-click the Print Doc icon). The "document" that you're printing is the master list of all citing references.[2]

I. Navigating into, out of, and within SHEPARD'S: Here are some tips about how to navigate into, out of and within SHEPARD'S (some of these are a review of things already discussed):

2. If you've customized the display (e.g., by selecting just citing references that give a certain treatment to your main case), then the print-out you get from Print Doc will list just those same citing references.

- To get into SHEPARD'S when you are looking at the case you want to SHEPARDIZE, type:

  `shep`

  or press the [SHEP] key (Ctrl-F2, or type **`.sh`**).

- To get into SHEPARD'S when you are not looking at the case you want to SHEPARDIZE, type "shep" followed by the cite; thus:

  `shep 573 p2d 443`

  This will work regardless of what file or library you are in (and, in fact, you do not have to be in *any* library or file).

- To jump from the SHEPARD'S list of citing reference to a particular citing reference, double-click on the LINK marker next to that reference as shown on the display screen.

- To return to SHEPARD'S after asking to see the text of the citing reference type:

  `res shep`

- To leave the SHEPARD'S display screen to get back to whatever you were doing (e.g., the regular LEXIS service) when you first gave the command to SHEPARDIZE, type **`res`** (for "Resume").[3]

- To SHEPARDIZE a second cite while you are already looking at the SHEPARD'S display for a first cite, simply type the second cite with nothing in front of it:

  `20 cal3d 413`

1. **Maneuvering within SHEPARD'S:** Where your main SHEPARD'S display for a particular citation spans more than one screen, as will usually be the case, you can maneuver among these screens readily. You can use the [NEXT PAGE] and [PREV PAGE] keys (F1 and F2, respectively, or **`.np`** and **`.pp`**). You can move ahead multiple screensful at a time by using a number before the [NEXT PAGE] or [PREV PAGE] key; thus to move ahead nine screens, type:

   `9` and press F1 (the [NEXT PAGE] key)

   or type **`.np9`**.

2. **Printing from within SHEPARD'S:** If you want to ***print*** the list of SHEPARD'S citations, type:

   `.pd`

   (or double-click the Print-Doc icon) while looking at the list.

3. **Getting help:** To receive assistance while in the SHEPARD'S Citations Service, type **`h`** (for Help) and press [ENTER]. Within the online Help is a list of citation formats, abbreviations, and SHEPARD'S Citations Analyses Definitions.

3. After you type **`res`**, you'll need to select **`=1`** to return to the main LEXIS search screen.

III. Auto-Cite

A. What Auto-Cite is and does: Auto-Cite is an electronic citation verification service. It is maintained by LEXIS-NEXIS. Auto-Cite was devised as a way for legal editors to check the validity of cases when writing publications like ALR. Here is what Auto-Cite does:

- Auto-Cite gives you the ***name***, date of decision and jurisdiction of your case, in Bluebook form.
- Auto-Cite gives you the ***complete appellate history*** of your case. That is, it tells you about developments in the case both before and after the decision whose cite you supply.
- Auto-Cite gives you cases outside your case's appellate chain that have ***diminished the value of your case as precedent.*** (This information appears in the "Subsequent Treatment History" section of the Auto-Cite response.) Auto-Cite also gives you cases upon which your case has had a negative impact; those cases appear in the "Makes Negative Reference To" section.
- Finally, Auto-Cite gives you extensive information on ***ALR annotations*** that cite the case you entered or that cite other cases in the Auto-Cite response.

B. Coverage of Auto-Cite: Auto-Cite covers cases, as well as some non-case materials, such as Revenue Rulings and Revenue Procedures. All of the standard federal, regional and official state reporters are covered. Many specialty looseleaf reporters (e.g., the *CCH Bankruptcy Law Reporter* and the *CCH Employment Practice Service*) are also covered. You can supply Auto-Cite with a cite to any of over 460 reporters.

C. Using Auto-Cite: Let's take a look now at how to use Auto-Cite:

1. Getting started: You can get into Auto-Cite in four different ways:

a. If you are looking at a court case or IRS Ruling, and you would like to view the ***full*** Auto-Cite treatment of that document, you simply type:

`ac` [ENTER]

and you will immediately see the Auto-Cite information for that document.

b. If you are not looking at the case or other document you want to check, and want the full Auto-Cite treatment, then you type "ac" followed by the citation. Thus:

`ac 573 p2d 443` [ENTER]

(To return to whatever you were doing previously, such as regular LEXIS research, enter `res` [for "Resume"].)

c. If you are looking at a court case or IRS Ruling, and you would like to view the ***short*** Auto-Cite treatment of that document, you simply type:

`aca` [ENTER]

and you will immediately see the short-form Auto-Cite information for that document.

d. If you are not looking at the case or other document you want to check, and want the short Auto-Cite treatment, then you type "ac" followed by the citation. Thus:

aca 573 p2d 443 [ENTER]

(Again, to return to whatever you were doing previously, such as regular LEXIS research, enter **res** [for "Resume"].)

We'll talk more about the difference between the "full" and "short" forms of Auto-Cite below and on p. 9-16 *infra*.

2. **Form of citation:** Auto-Cite will basically accept the standard abbreviations for reporters, even without punctuation. Thus any of the following abbreviations would work:

us
f2d
fsupp
a2d
ariz
calrptr
revproc (for a Revenue Procedure)
revrul (for a Revenue Ruling)

As with SHEPARD'S, I find that you are best off omitting periods, and running the abbreviation together (e.g., **calapp3d**).

If you are not sure whether a reporter is covered in Auto-Cite or what abbreviation you should use, you can check the Auto-Cite section of the *GUIDE* library for a current list of reporters, coverage and abbreviations. To do this, enter the *GUIDE* library, *GUIDE* file, and then enter **=8** to receive assistance on Auto-Cite.

3. **The display (in "full" form):** The Auto-Cite display is designed to help you find information efficiently. When you enter a citation, the response you get is in an outline format. Each response may include five sections, which are, in order of appearance, Subsequent Appellate History, Subsequent Treatment History, Prior History, Citation You Entered Makes Negative Reference To, and Annotations Citing the Case(s) Indicated Above With Asterisk(s). Each Auto-Cite response includes just those sections for which there is information, so a particular response may be missing some sections.

Assuming that you asked for the "full" Auto-Cite treatment (by using "ac" rather than "aca"), here's what the first screen would typically look like:

Auto-Cite (R) Citation Service, (c) 1995 Lawyers Cooperative Publishing

410 US 113: Screen 1 of 16

CITATION YOU ENTERED:

<=1> Roe v. Wade*1, 410 U.S. 113, 35 L. Ed. 2d 147, 93 S. Ct. 705 (1973)

SUBSEQUENT APPELLATE HISTORY:

reh'g denied, <=2> Roe v. Wade, 410 U.S. 959, 35 L. Ed. 2d 694, 93 S. Ct. 1409 (1973)

SUBSEQUENT TREATMENT HISTORY:

and (criticized by <=3> Webster v. Reproductive Health Services*2, 492 U.S. 490, 106 L. Ed. 2d 410, 1989 U.S. LEXIS 3290, 109 S. Ct. 3040, 57 U.S.L.W. 5023 (1989))

Alternate presentation formats are available.
For further explanation, press the H key (for HELP) and then the ENTER key.
To return to LEXIS, press the EXIT SERV key.

Before we get into the details of this screen, notice that you have LINK markers next to each citation. To see a particular decision, double-click on the marker next to it (e.g., click on **=3** on the above screen to see *Webster*, which criticized our principal case.)

Now, let's take a look now at the individual parts of an Auto-Cite response. (Not all cases will have all parts.)

The ***Citation*** portion shows you the names of the parties, plus all parallel cites:

<=1> Roe v. Wade*1, 410 U.S. 113, 35 L. Ed. 2d 147, 93 S. Ct. 705 (1973)

This is an extremely useful aspect of an Auto-Cite response, since it lets you do an instant check of the accuracy of your citation.

Procedural developments that have occurred since your case was decided appear in the ***Subsequent Appellate History*** section of the response. For instance:

reh'g denied, <=2> Roe v. Wade, 410 U.S. 959, 35 L. Ed. 2d 694, 93 S. Ct. 1409 (1973)

The Subsequent Appellate History section provides information on any subsequent proceedings in your case, provided they have been reported either in hardcopy or on the LEXIS service. For example, if your case has been reversed or affirmed, that information will appear in this section. There are over 350 history phrases that may appear in this section.

The ***Subsequent Treatment History*** section shows you how later cases referred to your principal case. For instance:

and (criticized by <=3> Webster v. Reproductive Health Services*2, 492 U.S. 490, 106 L. Ed. 2d 410, 1989 U.S. LEXIS 3290, 109 S. Ct. 3040, 57 U.S.L.W. 5023 (1989))

and (criticized by <=4> Planned Parenthood of Southeastern Pennsylvania v. Casey*3, 120 L. Ed. 2d 674, 1992 U.S. LEXIS 4751, 112 S. Ct. 2791, 60 U.S.L.W. 4795, 92 Daily Journal D.A.R. 8982, 6 Fla. L. Weekly Fed. S 663 (U.S. 1992)

The Subsequent Treatment History is limited to later cases that refer ***negatively*** to your principal case. Treatment History cases appear after one of 14 standard phrases:

Overruled by
Overruled as stated in
Overruled in part
Overruled in part as stated in

Disapproved by
Disapproved as stated in

Not followed by
Not followed as stated in

Criticized by
Criticized as stated in
Criticized but Reluctantly
Followed as stated in

Superseded by Statute
as stated in

Among Conflicting Authorities
Noted in

The case(s) listed following any Treatment History phrase ending in "as stated in" describe the negative effect of a *third* case (*not* the citing case) on your case. For instance, if Auto-Cite shows you that your case has been "Overruled as stated in" Case X, it means that the court in Case X recognizes that your case was effectively overruled by another decision (not Case X). The overruling decision itself may not specifically mention your case; you must read Case X to determine how the precedential value of your case has been affected.

The ***Prior History*** portion of Auto-Cite shows you what happened in the case of which your opinion is part, before that opinion was handed down. Here is an example, showing what happened in *Roe v. Wade* before the Supreme Court's landmark opinion:

PRIOR HISTORY:

Roe v. Wade*4, 314 F. Supp. 1217 (N.D. Tex. 1970)

juris. postponed, <=25> Roe v. Wade, 402 U.S. 941, 29 L. Ed. 2d 108, 91 S. Ct. 1610 (1971)

mot. granted, mot. denied, <=26> Roe v. Wade, 404 U.S. 813, 30 L. Ed. 2d 43, 92 S. Ct. 38 (1971)

mot. granted, <=27> Roe v. Wade, 404 U.S. 879, 30 L. Ed. 2d 160, 92 S. Ct. 195 (1971)

mot. granted, <=28> Roe v. Wade, 404 U.S. 934, 30 L. Ed. 2d 247, 92 S. Ct. 267 (1971)

mot. denied, <=29> Roe v. Wade, 404 U.S. 981, 30 L. Ed. 2d 365, 92 S. Ct. 442 (1971)

The ***Annotations*** portion of Auto-Cite gives you ALR annotations citing the indicated case:

ANNOTATIONS CITING THE CASE(S) INDICATED ABOVE WITH ASTERISK(S):

***1 "Choice of evils," necessity, duress, or similar defense to state or local criminal charges based on acts of public protest, <=33> 3 A.L.R.5th 521, secs. 3, 5.**

Recoverability of cost of raising normal, healthy child born as result of physician's negligence or breach of contract or warranty, <=35> 89 A.L.R.4th 632, sec. 3.

Right of child to action against mother for infliction of prenatal injuries, <=36> 78 A.L.R.4th 1082, sec. 2.

Recoverability of compensatory damages for mental anguish or emotional distress for tortiously causing another's birth, <=37> 74 A.L.R.4th 798, secs. 12, 21, 24, 25.

Validity of state statutes and regulations limiting or restricting public funding for abortions sought by indigent women, <=40> 20 A.L.R.4th 1166.

The Annotation section gives you not only ALR annotations citing your principal case, but also annotations citing any subsequent case that is picked up by Auto-Cite in its Subsequent Treatment History portion. To see if a case has an ALR annotation citing it, look at the Citation or Subsequent Treatment History listing for that case to see if there is an asterisk followed by a number — if there is, ALR annotations citing that case are collected under the asterisked number in the Annotations portion. Thus in our current example (see the screen on p. 9-14 above), the Citation listing for *Roe v. Wade* has "*1" after it; the Annotations section then puts a "*1" in front of the group of ALR annotations that cite *Roe* (see this page, above). Similarly, the Subsequent Treatment History listing for *Webster v. Reproductive Health Services* (same screen on p. 9-14) has a "*2" after it, meaning that ALR annotations citing *Webster* will be collected under "*2" in the Annotations section. (The "*2" part of the sample Annotations section is not reproduced above.)

If you see an ALR annotation that you would like to read or print right away, you can use the LEXSEE feature to do this. Thus to read the "Choice of Evils…" annotation listed as the first entry in the above annotations list, we would type:

```
lexsee 3 alr5th 521.
```

4. **Using the short "aca" form:** If you don't want as much detail, you can use "aca" (short for "Auto-Cite Assistant") instead of "ac." This form gives you just one level of detail about each of the Subsequent-History cases, none of the Prior History, and none of the Annotation information. The main function of aca is to give you a brief snapshot of whether the case is still good law, by giving you one brief entry for certain (and by no means all) cases that case doubt on the validity of your current case.

   For example, whereas the complete "ac" Auto-Cite treatment for *Roe v. Wade* runs to 6 printed pages, here's the entire substantive treatment of that case with aca:

Auto-Cite (R) Citation Service, (c) 1997 Lawyers Cooperative Publishing
410 US 113: Screen 1 of 2
CITATION YOU ENTERED:

<=1> Roe v. Wade, 410 U.S. 113, 35 L. Ed. 2d 147, 93 S. Ct. 705 (1973)

SUBSEQUENT APPELLATE HISTORY:

reh'g denied, <=2> Roe v. Wade, 410 U.S. 959, 35 L. Ed. 2d 694, 93 S. Ct. 1409 (1973)

SUBSEQUENT TREATMENT HISTORY:

and (criticized by <=3> Webster v. Reproductive Health Services, 492 U.S. 490, 106 L. Ed. 2d 410, 1989 U.S. LEXIS 3290, 109 S. Ct. 3040, 57 U.S.L.W. 5023 (1989)) and (criticized by <=4> Planned Parenthood v. Casey, 505 U.S. 833, 120 L. Ed. 2d 674, 1992 U.S. LEXIS 4751, 112 S. Ct. 2791, 60 U.S.L.W. 4795, 92 Daily Journal D.A.R. 8982, 6 Fla. L. Weekly Fed. S 663 (1992))

and (not followed by <=5> Jane L. v. Bangerter, 809 F. Supp. 865, 1992 U.S. Dist. LEXIS 20167 (D. Utah 1992))

and (criticized in <=6> A Woman's Choice-East Side Women's Clinic v. Newman, 904 F. Supp. 1434, 1995 U.S. Dist. LEXIS 17086 (S.D. Ind. 1995))

To display additional Auto-Cite information for this citation, type ACO (for Auto-Cite Outline) and press the ENTER key.

You can leave aca and go to the full form by typing **aco** [ENTER] at any time. Conversely, you can leave the full form and go to the short (aca) form at any time by typing **aca** [ENTER].

5. **Auto-Citing an ALR annotation:** Just as you Auto-Cite a case, you can Auto-Cite an ALR annotation. This will tell you whether the annotation is still "good law."

6. **Printing or saving Auto-Cite histories:** There are three ways to print or save the information you're retrieved via Auto-Cite:

   - Use the [PRINT DOC] key (Shift-F3, or type **.pr**) to print the whole Auto-Cite response (if you're in "aca," you'll just get a print-out of this short form);
   - Use the [SESS REC] key (Alt-F2, or type **.sr**) to record your session onto your hard disk for later use;
   - Use your PC's [PRINT SCREEN] key to print individual screens.

IV. THE LEXCITE® FEATURE

A. **About LEXCITE:** The LEXCITE feature is actually a streamlined way of using the basic LEXIS service as a citator.

LEXCITE lets you find citations to cases, as well as citations to the U.S. Code, ALR, law reviews, the Federal Register, and Comptroller General Opinions. You cannot use the LEXCITE feature to track citations to certain other types of documents: state statutes and most administrative materials, for instance.

The best way to think of LEXCITE is probably as a different kind of search connector, one which understands a citation and is able to look up the parallel citations. Thus if you want to find all cases in a certain library/file that mention *James C. Greene Co. v. Kelley*, 261 N.C. 166, you would perform the following search on the file of your choice:

```
lexcite(261 nc 166)
```

This will find not only cases citing to *Greene* by the cite we supplied (261 N.C. 166), but also cases citing to it only by its parallel cite, 134 S.E.2d 166. In other words, the LEXCITE feature takes the citation you give it, checks a listing of parallel cites, and then performs a search on all of the parallel versions.

When you receive your results from LEXCITE, the names of the parties in the case, as well as the citation itself, are highlighted in the text of the case. You can then use the KWIC format (F5, or type **.kw**) to see the specific place in the citing case where the citation occurs.

B. Advantages: Here are what I see as the advantages of using LEXCITE:

- its results are very ***complete*** (since all documents on LEXIS, including unpublished opinions, are searched);
- its results are very ***current*** (since the moment a document goes online, cites contained in it can be picked up by LEXCITE);
- it shows you the ***context*** in which your principal case is cited;
- it automatically searches for ***parallel citation*** references (so if you search for, say, a Cal.2d cite, you'll find cites to the matching P.2d cite); and
- it lets you customize your search so that you retrieve only cases citing your case and dealing with a ***specific issue***, a function not available through Auto-Cite, and only available through SHEPARD'S by using headnote analysis.

C. Disadvantages: But LEXCITE, like the other two services, has some disadvantages as well:

- No editor has gone through to identify the editorial treatment and pigeonhole it for each citing case. Therefore, if you want to know whether any case has, say, overruled your principal case, you must read *every* case retrieved by your LEXIS citator search.
- Using the LEXIS service as a citator will typically be somewhat more expensive than using either of the other two citators.[4]

4. For instance, to find every reference to your principal case in any later federal or state case, you would typically have to do a LEXCITE search in a file like *NEWER* in the *MEGA* library (all federal and state cases since 1945); this would cost $84 in standard Transactional search charges. By contrast, an Auto-Cite or SHEPARD'S search for a single principal case would cost $3.50. (However, if you then did a LEXSEE search for each case reported by Auto-Cite or SHEPARD'S, the total cost might not be less than for a LEXIS search. Also, of course, if you are on an Educational Subscription, or some other subscription that has a low or zero marginal cost per search, searching with LEXCITE might not be more expensive than Auto-Cite or SHEPARD'S.)

- You must choose a particular library and file in which to search (whereas you don't have to do this in SHEPARD'S or Auto-Cite).

D. When to use: Here are the situations in which using the LEXCITE feature is an especially attractive alternative to using SHEPARD'S:

- Use LEXCITE to find the ***very latest cases*** citing your principal case (since a case will usually be discoverable in this manner within a week or two of its availability from the deciding court);
- Use LEXCITE if it is important to you to be able to discover ***unpublished*** cases as well as published ones (since SHEPARD'S covers only published cases, though SHEPARD'S does include a wide variety of reporters, including various looseleaf services, in its category of "reported" cases).
- Use LEXCITE when you need a printout with each citation in ***context***.[5] In SHEPARD'S, by contrast, you can't get a report showing each cite in context. (You can, while online, travel from the SHEPARD'S display screen to the cite in context on the LEXIS service and back again. But you cannot in a single step produce a printout showing each citing reference's context.)

E. Using LEXCITE: Let's look at some of the details of using LEXCITE.

1. **Choosing a library and file:** Unlike finding citing cases through SHEPARD'S and Auto-Cite, LEXCITE requires you to choose a particular library and file combination, and will find only cases present in that library/file. Thus if you were interested in all cases from federal and state courts citing to your principal case, you will need to use a large library/file (e.g., *MEGA* library, *MEGA* file). There is a special library, the *CITES* library, that is designed to be used with the LEXCITE feature; it groups for you several files that, because of their largeness or up-to-dateness, are good repositories of citing cases. The main files included in the *CITES* library are:

   MEGA (All federal and state court cases, regardless of date)
   1YEAR (All federal and state court cases decided in the last roughly 12 months)
   FED (All federal court cases, whenever decided)
   STATES (All state court cases, whenever decided)

   These four files are counterparts of ones available in other libraries, and there is no particular cost advantage in using the version found in the *CITES* library. For instance, the *MEGA* file costs the same $105 per search when you use the version of it found in the *CITES* library as when you use the identical version called *MEGA* in the *MEGA* library.

2. **Combining LEXCITE with other search words:** You can combine a LEXCITE term with other search words. Thus if you were only interested in those cases citing the *James*

5. To do this, you would press [PRINT ALL], and tell the system to use KWIC format for the printout. This is described in more detail *supra*, p. 2-85.

C. Greene case if the citing case mentioned *Greene* in close proximity to the word "competition," you could accomplish this by:

```
lexcite(261 nc 166) w/10 competition
```

3. **No need to specify "LEXCITE":** Actually, LEXCITE is now so "intelligent" that you don't even need to tell the service explicitly that you want to use LEXCITE. Instead, just supply the citation itself as part of your search request, and the service will recognize that you want to do a LEXCITE search. Thus if you want to find all cases that cite to the case appearing at 449 U.S. 383 (which happens to be *Upjohn v. U.S.*), and that use the phrase "attorney-client privilege," just search for:

```
449 us 383 and attorney-client privilege
```

The service will recognize that you've entered a citation, presume that you want to use LEXCITE, and reformulate your search this way before executing it:

```
lexcite(449 us 383) and attorney-client privilege
```

Then, just as if you had manually specified that LEXCITE was to be used, the service would find you cases citing *Upjohn*, even if the cite was to one of the alternative forms (e.g., 101 S.Ct. 677).

4. **Charges:** Because the LEXCITE feature is simply used as another search connector, search charges are the same as they would be for any other LEXIS search. (This makes LEXCITE more expensive than SHEPARD'S or Auto-Cite on a per-principal-case basis).

V. THE *CITES* LIBRARY, AND THE *CITES ASSISTANT* FEATURE — ASSISTANCE IN CITE-CHECKING

A. Introduction: If you need assistance in cite-checking, two special forms of it are available on the LEXIS service: the *CITES* library, and the CITES Assistant feature. Each gives you a step-by-step "prompted" method of selecting which cite-checking method (SHEPARD'S, Auto-Cite and LEXCITE) you wish, and then using that method.

B. The CITES library: When you log into the *CITES* library (which is a library like any other) the service will prompt you for which of the methods of cite checking you wish to use. Combining the first two screens into one, what you see is:

```
Please ENTER the NAME of the file you want to search. To see a description
of a file, type its page number and press the ENTER key.

        FILES - PAGE 1 of 2 (NEXT PAGE for additional files)
NAME    PG  DESCRIP
 ------ CITATION SERVICES --------

CA      1   Cites Assistant
AC          AUTO-CITE Citation Service
SHEP        SHEPARD's Citation Service

        FILES - PAGE 2 of 2 (PREV PAGE for additional files)
NAME    PG  DESCRIP

---- LEXCITE --------
MEGA    1   Federal & State Court Cases
1YEAR   1   MEGA FILE within 1 year
FED     1   Federal Court Cases
STATES 1    State Court Cases
    EXAMPLE
Select a file and ENTER:
lexcite(490 us 107)
To perform a LEXCITE search in other libraries, CHANGE LIBRARY (.cl) and select
the appropriate LIBRARY and FILE, e.g., .cl;ny;cases;lexcite(61 ny2d 481).
Use the LEXCITE search to quickly find the full-text of cases referencing your
citation, as well as parallel cites, and "id" and "supra" references.
```

If you want to use SHEPARD'S or Auto-Cite, you simply enter **AC** or **SHEP**. If you want to use the LEXCITE feature, enter the name of the file that contains the type of cases in which you want to look (e.g., *MEGA*, to get federal and state cases without regard to date). The service then gives you instructions to help enter your citation. There is no difference between using these services through the *CITES* library or in the traditional manner; the *CITES* library merely gives you a framework — a "prompted" method — which you may need if you're unfamiliar with the standard way of using them.

C. **CITES Assistant:** The "CITES Assistant" feature is available either through the *CITES* library (by taking the first option, "CA", shown on the above screen), or by typing **.ca** from any point in your research. When you enter CITES Assistant, you'll be presented with the following list of options:

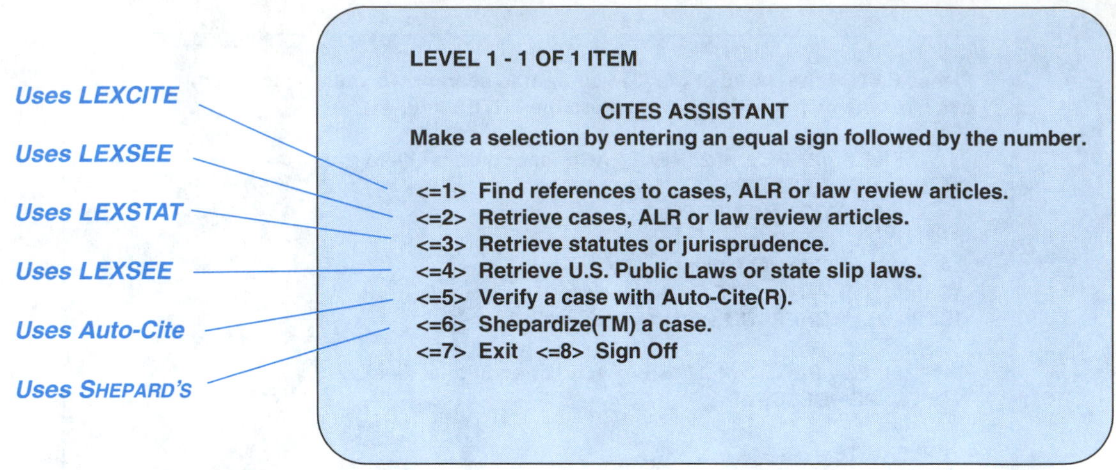

Uses LEXCITE
Uses LEXSEE
Uses LEXSTAT
Uses LEXSEE
Uses Auto-Cite
Uses SHEPARD'S
LEVEL 1 - 1 OF 1 ITEM
CITES ASSISTANT
Make a selection by entering an equal sign followed by the number.
<=1> Find references to cases, ALR or law review articles.
<=2> Retrieve cases, ALR or law review articles.
<=3> Retrieve statutes or jurisprudence.
<=4> Retrieve U.S. Public Laws or state slip laws.
<=5> Verify a case with Auto-Cite(R).
<=6> Shepardize(TM) a case.
<=7> Exit <=8> Sign Off

As you can see from my annotations to the left of the above screen, CITES Assistant gives you prompted access to LEXCITE (for references to cases), LEXSEE (to retrieve the specified case or public law) and LEXSTAT (to retrieve the specified statutory section),[6] as well as to Auto-Cite and SHEPARD'S.

Once you've selected a function from the above screen, the service will prompt you to enter a citation; it will then perform whatever function you've chosen. Like the *CITES* library, the CITES Assistant merely provides a framework for you if you're unfamiliar with how to access these functions in the standard way.

If while you're using any of the functions you accessed through CITES Assistant, you want to get back to the main CITES Assistant screen, enter **res** (for "Resume"). If you want to leave CITES Assistant completely, you must first get back to the main screen (by typing **res**), then select **=7**.

VI. FINDING CITES TO STATUTES AND OTHER NON-CASE MATERIALS

A. Finding cites to statutes: You can use the main LEXIS service in order to find references to statutes.[7]

Finding citations to statutes is tricky because of the diverse ways in which a given statute can be cited. Consider, for instance, the Americans with Disabilities Act, which is codified in Title 42 of the U.S. Code, beginning with §12101. There are many different ways in which the Act might be cited, including:

6. LEXSTAT is described in Section VII, *supra*, p. 2-73.

7. Actually, now that SHEPARD'S can be used to find cites to all federal and state statutes (see *supra*, p. 9-9), I find that it's usually a better method than the "LEXIS as citator" method described here. However, because the LEXIS-as-citator method is the only way to combine a search for statutory citations with a search for keywords in the citing reference (e.g., **42 u.s.c. @ 12101 w/10 disabilit!**), I go into considerable detail about this method here. Also, note that LEXCITE (see p. 9-19) cannot be used to find citations to statutes.

42 U.S.C. §12101
42 U.S.C. § 12101
42 U.S.C.A. § 12101
42 U.S.C.S. § 12101
42 U.S.C. §§ 12101-12213
Section 12101 of Title 42

Before we look at search options for finding statutory cites, let's review a couple of rules regarding punctuation, which I discussed in detail earlier in the book:[8]

- All section-signs on the LEXIS service are represented by use of the at-symbol (@), not the section-sign (§). Thus a document on the LEXIS service referring to the Americans with Disabilities Act would say **`42 u.s.c. @ 12101`** , not **`42 u.s.c. § 12101`**.

  Similarly, when you search for a section-sign, you should use the @ symbol,[9] so that your search would be:

  `42 u.s.c. @ 12101`

- A section-sign that bumps up against the following number is indexed by the LEXIS service as a single word. A section-sign followed by a space followed by the number is indexed as two separate words. Thus if you search for:

  `@12101`

  you will find documents containing "@12101" but not documents containing "@ 12101." Similarly, a search for "@ 12101" will not find documents that contain "@12101."

- Parentheses are treated as spaces by the LEXIS service. This is true both as to the underlying document and your search request. Therefore, to find underlying documents that contain 12101(a)(2), you can search for:

  `12101(a)(2)`

  (Transparently to you, both the underlying document and your search will be treated by the LEXIS service as containing three separate words, "12101," "a" and "2," which will be searched for as if they were a phrase.)

Now then, let's develop some strategies for looking for statutory citations:

- Search for both the variant with and the variant without a section symbol. Thus for the Americans with Disabilities Act, you would want to search for:

  `@12101 or 12101`

  (The first term will find all occurrences of "@12101," which is how §12101 will be represented on the LEXIS service, and the second term will find "@ 12101".)

---

8. See supra, p. 2-14.

9. Alternatively, you could in your search statement use **`sec`** or **`section`** instead of **`@`**. These three things are all equivalents.

- In general, it is worthwhile to include the Title number as well as the section number. Thus for a federal statute, you would be better off to search for:

  ```
  42 w/5 (@12101 or 12101)
  ```

  than to search for plain old:

  ```
  @12101 or 12101
  ```

  because the presence of the Title number restricts the number of false hits. Of course, you must be aware that there may be citations that will not use the Title number at all, but these should be rare.

- If you want a particular sub-section, don't be afraid to use that section in your search, because the rule on parentheses described above will protect you. Thus you can search for:

  ```
  42 w/5 (@12101(b)(3) or 12101(b)(2))
  ```

- Consider the possibility that the statute you are interested in may be cited by means of something other than its codified cite. For instance, it may be cited by its Session Law number (e.g., "P.L. 101-336" or "Pub. L. No. 101-336"), by its Statutes at Large number (e.g., "104 Stat. 328"), or by its name (e.g., "Americans with Disabilities Act of 1990").

  Therefore, ideally you would search on all of these things, either in successive searches or, better still, as one omnibus search to find everything. In the case of the Americans with Disabilities Act, your search might look like this:

  ```
  (americans disabilities act) or (42 w/5 @12101 or 12101)
  or 101-336 or (104 pre/5 328)
  ```

B. Administrative regulations: Pretty much the same considerations apply to the process of finding citations to regulations.

For a cite to the ***Code of Federal Regulations***, you can generally safely use "CFR" in your search statement, because you don't have to worry about there being varying ways in which the underlying document may refer to the source (just "CFR" or "C.F.R.," which can both be searched by looking for "CFR"). Also, you can be pretty confident that the title will be part of the citation. However, you need to remember that there may be a substantial gap between the title and the section number, because of the way different sections are often cited all at once (e.g., "24 CFR Parts 200, 201, 203 and 208"). Also, remember that periods in the middle of numbers do not cause word breaks, so that if a document contains "203.42," this will appear in the LEXIS service dictionary as a single word, and can be searched for that way.

Putting all this together, a good, conservative (i.e., not likely to miss things) method of looking for §203.42(a) of Title 24 of the CFR would be:

```
24 w/3 cfr w/10 (@203.42(a) or 203.42(a))
```

If you are dealing with a ***Treasury Regulation***, you can generally be safe in looking for the regulation without a section-sign attached to it (since the section-sign usually has a space after it in this sort of cite), and you can also generally put in any hyphens. Parentheses may confuse the services in this type of cite, so substitute spaces for parentheses. Thus the following search for a Treas. Reg. would do what you would expect it to do:

```
1.105-4 a 3 i
```

C. Constitutions: Searching for a cite to a particular part of a ***constitution*** can be tricky, mostly because constitutions frequently use Roman numerals as part of the numbering scheme. Also, constitutions frequently use ordinal numbers ("fifth," "second"). You get a little help with the ordinal problem from the LEXIS service, because the written-out form is made equivalent to the numeric short form for numbers 20 and under (so that "fourteenth" and "14th" are equivalent). But cardinal and ordinal numbers are not made equivalent to each other (so that "14" and "14th" are not equivalents).

You are best off using the short numerical form, but including cardinal, ordinal and Roman numeral forms, together with the word "article" or "amendment." Thus to find all references to the Fourteenth Amendment, a good search would be:

```
amendment w/5 (14 or 14th or xiv or xivth)
```

You will often want to combine some descriptive words together with the cite to the article or amendment you are interested in, such as:

```
due process w/20 amendment w/3 (5 or 5th or v or vth)
```

D. Rules: You can also use the LEXIS service to find references to a particular ***rule***, such as a Federal Rule of Civil Procedure, or a local court rule. As with other types of citations, you need to be alert to the fact that there are different ways in which a particular rule can be cited. Thus for Federal Rule of Civil Procedure 23, a good search would be:

```
23 w/5 (rule or frcp or f.r.c.p. or civil or civ)
```

(You need to specify both "FRCP" and "F.R.C.P." because these two formulations are not made into equivalents by the LEXIS service.)

If you have a citation to a sub-rule, you can type the full citation, with parentheses intact. Also, the more precise your citation, the less you need to use additional identifying words like "FRCP" or "Civil," because the less risk there is that you will be getting unwanted citations. To illustrate, if we are interested in Federal Rule of Civil Procedure 23, and we search for simply:

```
23
```

we will obviously get thousands of unwanted occurrences of the number 23 having nothing to do with the Federal Rules. On the other hand, if we are interested in Rule 23(b)(3), that is a sufficiently unusual formulation that a search for:

```
23(b)(3)
```

will work relatively well. In fact, this formulation is probably ***better*** than:

```
23(b)(3) w/5 (rule or frcp or f.r.c.p.)
```

because the underlying case may refer in one place to "Rule 23" and then refer sometime later simply to "23(b)(3)."

E. Treatises and other narrative materials: You can use the LEXIS service as a citator to find references to ***treatises*** and other secondary sources. For treatises, the last name of the author(s) and one word from the title will usually work well. Thus to find references to Wright & Miller's treatise on *Federal Practice and Procedure*, a good search would be:

```
wright w/3 miller
```

because these two words are unlikely to occur naturally near each other except when the treatise is being cited. (This search shows me, by the way, that in the *MEGA* library/*MEGA* file, the Wright & Miller treatise has been cited in more than 30,000 different cases!) To find Moore's *Federal Practice* treatise, by contrast, because Moore is a common name, a good search would be:

```
moore w/5 (practice or pract)
```

For Restatements, a combination of the word "Restatement," the word representing the subject, and the section reference will usually work well. For instance:

```
(restatement or rest) w/10 torts w/10 (@402A or 402A)
```

As with all efforts to use the LEXIS service as a citator, the critical thing is to visualize the various ways in which the document you are interested in may be cited by the many different citing authors.

Chapter 10 CheckCite™, CiteRite™, CompareRite™, and FullAuthority™

Introductory Note: In 1984, two young graduates of Harvard Law School decided to abandon the practice of law and start a company to make PC software for lawyers. Their first product, which they called CiteRite™, checked a piece of writing and told you whether each cite complied with the Harvard Blue Book and how to fix it if it didn't. Other nifty products followed. Today, all of these products are owned and marketed by LEXIS-NEXIS.

This chapter consists of an overview of this "cluster" of software products, which has four components:

- *CheckCite*™, which takes your brief or other document containing cites, automatically dials up the LEXIS service to get information, and gives you a customized report showing the accuracy and standing of all cites; (CheckCite software can also retrieve, with formatting, the full text of any case, and can verify the accuracy of quotations from caselaw);
- *CiteRite*™ *II*, which checks cites for proper Blue Book or California Citation form without markers;
- *CompareRite*™, which compares two documents (typically two successive drafts) and shows you all differences between the two; and
- *FullAuthority*™, which finds all your cites and builds a Table of Authorities automatically.

Because of the expense of disks, packaging and documentation, LEXIS-NEXIS cannot routinely give these products free to law students. However, the Legal Education segment of LEXIS-NEXIS frequently runs special programs making these products available at a discount, or occasionally even free. Contact your school's LEXIS representative for details. If you would like more information about these products, or want to consider purchasing one at an educational discount, contact the main LEXIS Customer Support Hotline, 1-800-45LEXIS.

All four of the products described in this chapter are available in Windows versions, and my discussion of these products here is about that Windows version.

I. CheckCite

A. What CheckCite can do for you: CheckCite software gives you a way to automatically dial into the LEXIS service and perform various cite-checking functions. Usually, you use Check-Cite after you have written a brief or other piece of legal writing that contains citations. Starting with this piece of writing, which is usually in the form of a word-processed file, you can have CheckCite do any or all of the following for you:

1. CheckCite software can ***retrieve the full text*** of each case cited, through use of the LEXSEE feature. (In fact, it can give the case to you with underlined case names, indented quotes and even, if you use WordPerfect, dual-column format or with footnotes placed at the bottom of the page.)

2. It can ***check the accuracy*** of your citations, by using both Auto-Cite and SHEPARD'S. In doing this, it will match what you say the name of the case is with what you say its numerical cite is, and will tell you whether Auto-Cite agrees with you. It will also report to you parallel cites, and will tell you if either Auto-Cite or SHEPARD'S believes that your case starts on a different page than you say it starts on.

3. For each citation in your document, it will ***find you all or selected later cases citing your case***, by using SHEPARD'S. It not only retrieves automatically the full SHEPARD'S report for each case, but can cause SHEPARD'S to do things that you cannot make it do when you are online yourself (like limit the retrieved SHEPARD'S references to those from a single jurisdiction, or to those that are "negative").

4. For each of your citations, it can save a KWIC-like report to disk, showing each case that cites your case, together with the ***context*** in which the citation occurs (e.g., 25 words on either side of the citation itself). The CheckCite program does this by using the LEXCITE feature. You can tell CheckCite to limit this report to cases contained in a particular LEXIS service file (e.g., the file *1YEAR*, which contains only the most recent year's worth of state and federal case law).

5. It can have the CheckCite program check ***quotations*** that occurred in your document. It will check these quotes character-for-character, and report even punctuation differences!

B. A quick tour: Let's take a quick tour through CheckCite. Our purpose is not to become proficient CheckCite users — the program is too rich for that in this limited space. Instead, I want to give you the flavor of how it works, and what you can do with it. For this tour, let's assume that you are in the early stages of your research, but you have identified several significant cases. For each of these cases, you would like to: (1) make sure you have the right cite; (2) find ALR articles and law review articles discussing your case; and (3) make sure your case has not been overruled recently. Here are the steps you would take to do all this:

1. **Prepare input file:** First, you would prepare an "input file" containing the names and numerical citations of your several important cases. Thus for our non-compete problem,[1] our input file might look something like this:

1. See supra, p. 4-21.

```
Here is some regular text, without a citation.
James C. Greene Co. v. Kelley, 134 S.E.2d 166 (N.C. 1964)
American Hot Rod Assoc. v. Carrier, 500 F.2d 1269 (4th
Cir. 1974)
```

Typically, you will use a word processor to prepare this input file, and you will notify the CheckCite program of which word processor you use. CheckCite supports nearly all major word processors, including WordPerfect (for both DOS and Windows) and Microsoft Word (for both DOS and Windows). Later, when you have a full brief or memo of law ready, the fact that CheckCite can read your word-processed file without modification — and can pick the citations out of the file without your marking them in any way — will give you a powerful way of doing a last minute cite check.

Let's assume that this file is called `NONCOMP.DOC`, and that it is a WordPerfect file.

2. **Set-up session:** Now, it's time to tell the CheckCite software what to do. After we start the program, we typically start a new "session." Then, we enter the information about the session, including the location of our input file, where to put the resulting report, etc., into the main Session screen:

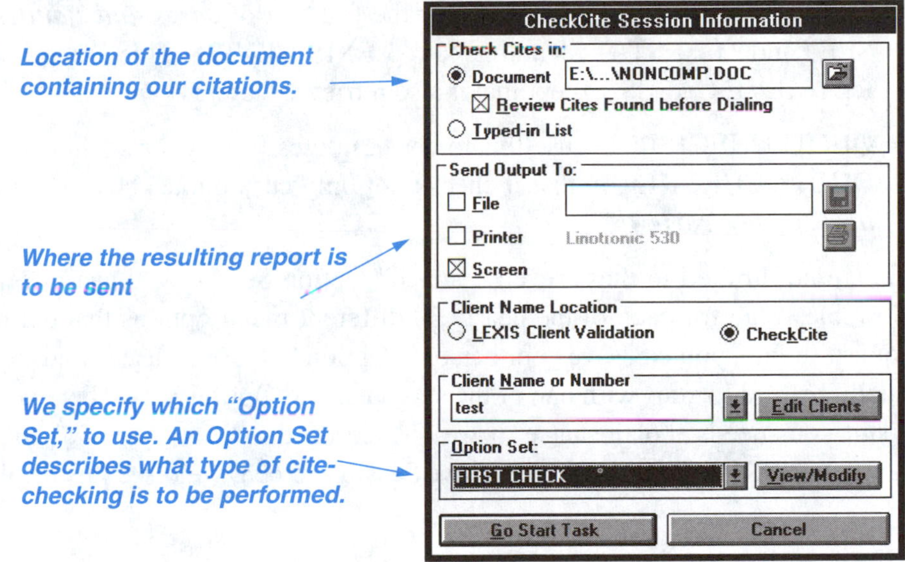

An important part of setting up the new Session is to specify which ***"Option Set"*** to use. An Option Set requests that CheckCite deliver a particular package of services. CheckCite comes with seven "canned" Option Sets. FIRST.CHECK, the one shown as selected in the above screen, is designed to be used at the beginning of your research; it checks cites using Auto-Cite (including the prior history of the case plus ALR articles citing the case); SHEPARD'S (all cases citing your case, as long as they have some treatment code); and LEXCITE (using the file *1YEAR*, which contains all federal and state cases decided in the last year). The FIRST.CHECK option set does not get you a copy of the case, or check your quotes.

The other canned option sets, described very briefly, are:

FINAL.CHECK — designed to be used ***just before you file your brief***; uses Auto-Cite (but with no prior history and no ALR articles); and SHEPARD'S (but limited to cases giving your case a negative treatment).

LATE.BREAKING — also used just before you file your brief. This checks cites using Auto-Cite (without prior history and without ALR articles) and LEXCITE (against the *1YEAR* file on LEXIS). This report includes only cites that the CheckCite software determines to have citation errors, or that have been negatively treated by a later citing case.

RETRIEVE.CASES — use this to retrieve the ***full text*** of cases. It works by using the LEXSEE feature, and will give you an enhanced output report (with underlined case names, indented quotes, and other special features; the report is in the format of whatever word processor you specify).

QUOTE.CHECKER — use the QuoteCheck™ feature to ***check case quotes*** from your document. It detects any differences between how you report the quote and how the LEXIS service version of the case reports the quote. It also reprints the paragraph containing the quote.

CASES.PLUS — use this to retrieve the full text of ***cases and statutes*** via the LEXSEE and LEXSTAT features on LEXIS-NEXIS. This report is similar to RETRIEVE.CASES, except that it also retrieves statutes.

QUOTECHECK.PL — use this to check quotes from your document. It differs from QUOTE.CHECKER in that it checks not only case quotes but also quotes from ***statutes*** and ***law reviews***.

You are not limited to these seven "canned" Option Sets — you can manually select any allowable value for each of the nearly 30 different menu options that define a CheckCite request. In fact, you can save your personal Option Sets for re-use. I find, however, that it's usually helpful to start with one of the seven canned Option Sets. Then, you can modify it to suit your needs. For instance, if we clicked on the "View/Modify" button next to the choice of "FIRST.CHECK" in the above Session screen, we'd see this display:

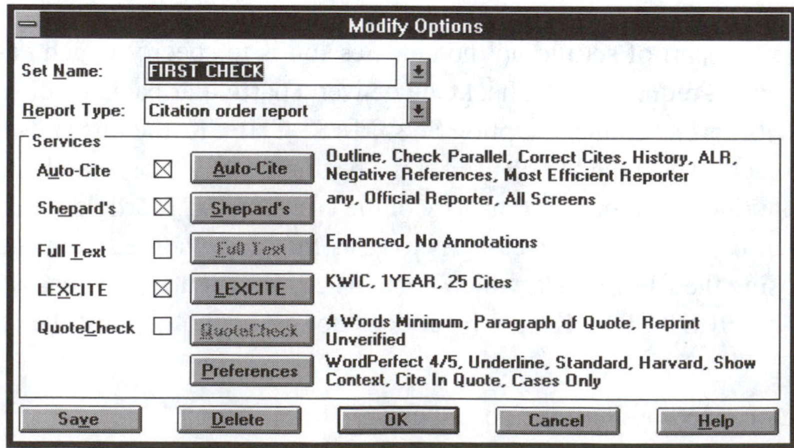

We could now redefine this to meet our needs (e.g., by re-specifying the word processor we use); then, we could either save this changed version under the original name FIRST.CHECK, or save it under a different name as a personal Option Set.

In any event, let's assume that we've specified option set FIRST.CHECK as shown in the above screen. Then, we'll click on the "OK" button, which will return us to the main Session screen (the one shown on p. 10-3). Now, we'll click on "Go Start Task," which will cause the system to begin cite-checking.

If we've checked the button called "Review Cites Before Dialing" on the main Session screen, the system will read our input document, and confirm with us each cite that it finds. Here, for instance, the system has found the *James C. Greene* cite, and gives us a chance to confirm or change that cite, or to add a new one:

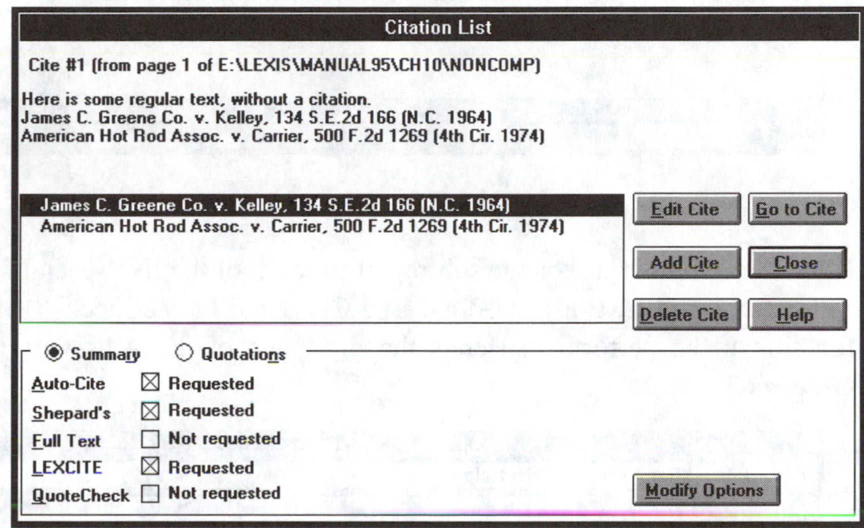

As you click on each cite in the list, the system shows you its understanding of the text of the cite, and also shows you the words surrounding that cite. Once you've confirmed that the system understands where the cites are, you close this window, and the system will then dial up the LEXIS-NEXIS services to do whatever cite-checking and/or downloading your choice of Option Set specified.

3. **Review report:** CheckCite will store to disk the items it needs for its report, then tell you that it has finished. When the report is ready, you will see the first page in your display window. (Alternatively, you could cause the report to be printed or saved to disk. The format of the report is pretty much the same regardless of whether you view it on screen or on paper.) Let's take a look at its contents.

   The first page of the report is a "summary report," which before each citation, shows you the brief results of each of the five special functions. For our *James C. Greene Co.* cite, here's what the summary report looks like:

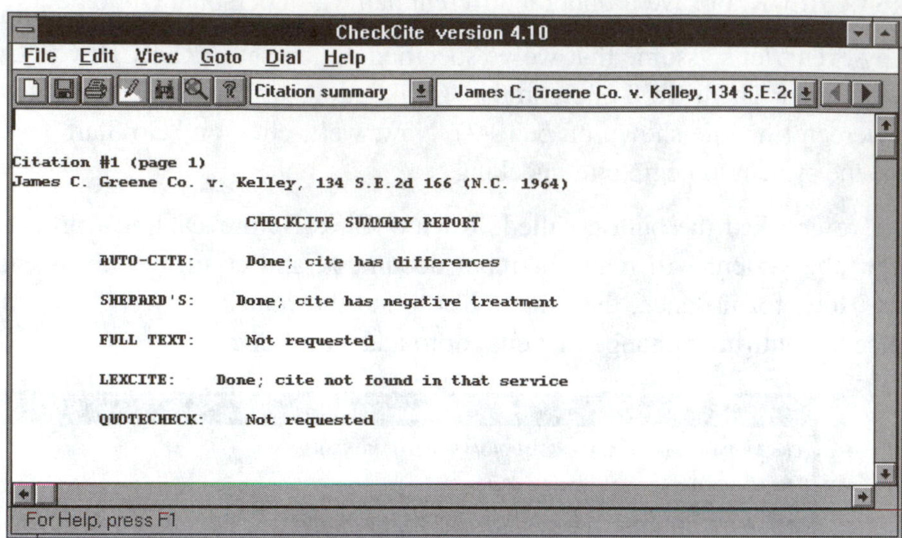

Next, there follows a separate sub-report for each of the five special functions (Auto-Cite, SHEPARD'S, full text downloading, LEXCITE and QuoteCheck™) if you asked for that function to be performed. Here's the first page of the Auto-Cite report for *James C. Greene Co.*:

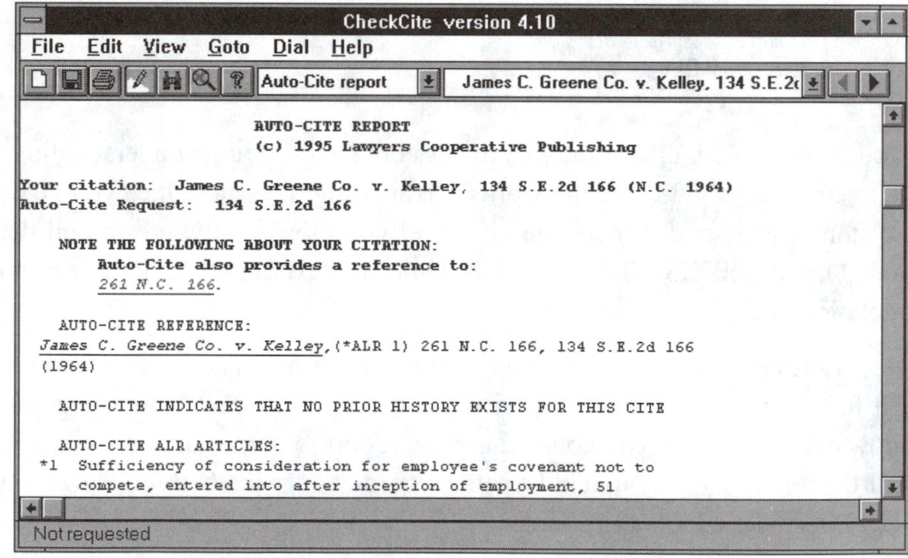

This report gives us (after repeating the cite from our document and the cite as it was requested from Auto-Cite):

- Differences between our cite and the reference from Auto-Cite (e.g., differences in the names of the parties);
- The Auto-Cite reference, consisting of the full case name and all parallel cites, plus any

subsequent history of the case and any negative references to the case in later cases;[2]

- Any prior history in the principal case, if we elected to include it; and
- Any ALR articles citing our case, if we elected to include them.

Next comes the SHEPARD'S report. Here is part of that report:

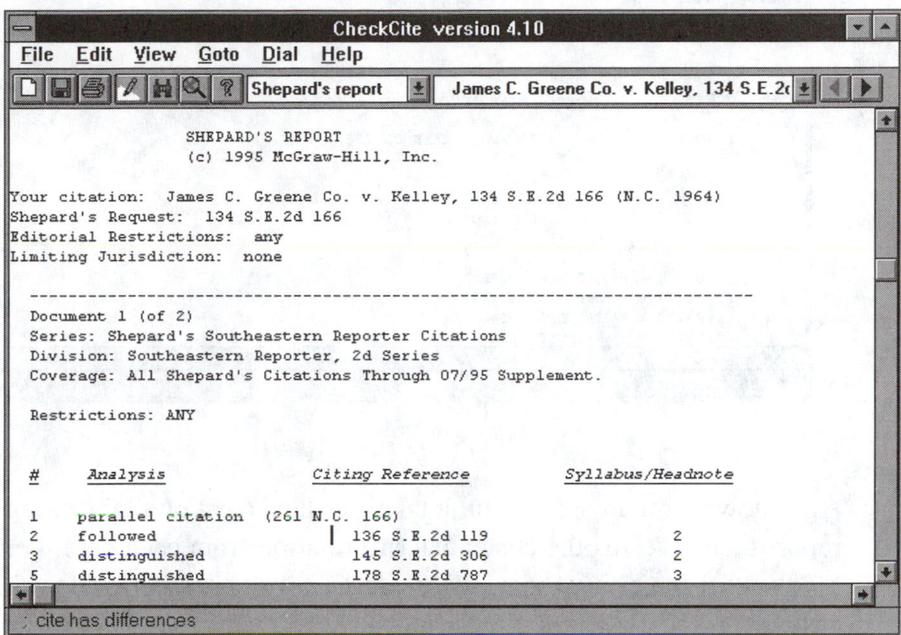

Next comes the LEXCITE report, which uses the main LEXIS service to find us any cases that cite our case. Obviously, this overlaps significantly with what is available on SHEPARD'S. The main ways in which the LEXCITE report adds value over what we have already gotten from our SHEPARD'S reports are:

- The LEXCITE report can find us cases that are on the LEXIS service but do not appear in any hard-copy reporter (unlike SHEPARD'S);
- The LEXCITE report can find cases that appeared on the LEXIS service as recently as that same day; and
- Most important of all, the LEXCITE report can show us the actual ***context*** in which our principal case is cited by the citing case, using the LEXIS service's KWIC 25-words-before-and-after-the-cite technique.

Here is the first page of the LEXCITE report for the *James C. Greene Co.* case:

2. But Auto-Cite does not purport to find every case that cites the principal case negatively; only cases negatively affecting the precedential value of the principal case are found. See *supra*, p. 9-12.

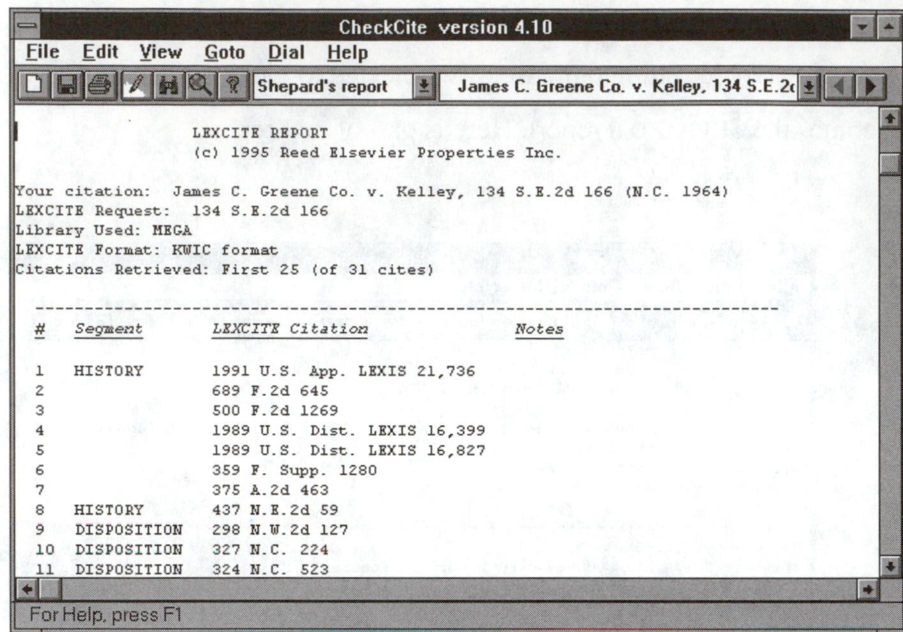

After however many screensful it takes to show a list of all the citing cases, the LEXCITE report then gives us the contextual information from each case; here is a screen showing how one of the citing cases, *Whittaker General*, cites our principal *James C. Greene Co.* case:

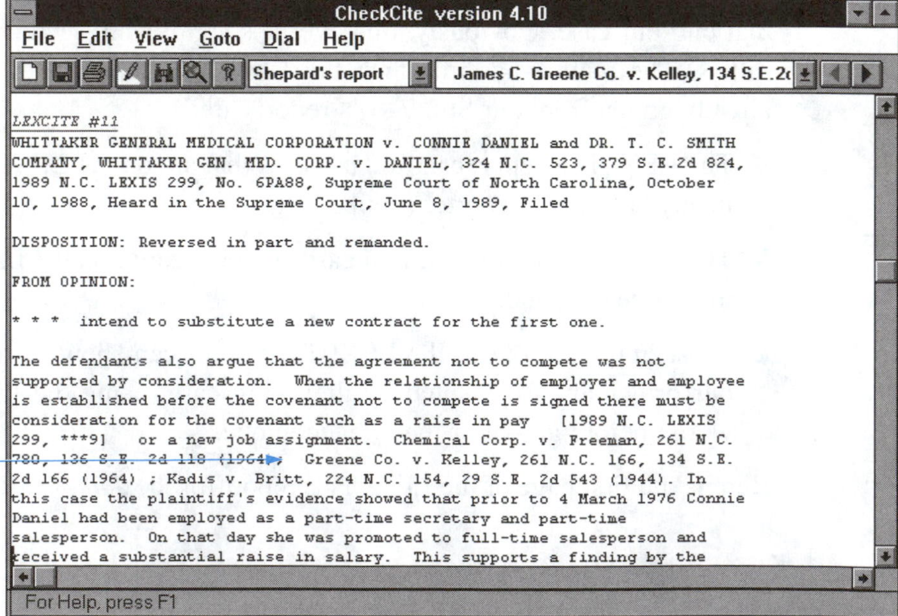

Citation to our James C. Greene case, shown in context

In my opinion, the ability to automatically prepare this kind of KWIC report can all by itself easily justify the cost of the CheckCite program — you can simply prepare a file containing a list of cites, and without any further intervention, end up with a file or stack of paper showing you the context in which each of those cases has been subsequently referred to. Add to this the ability to choose which file you want to run your LEXCITE report against (including the very valuable *1YEAR* file, so you can check for a recent overruling), and you have a very powerful tool indeed.

Since we used the FIRST.CHECK option set, these are the only sub-reports we get. If we had used different option sets, we might have also gotten the full text of the case, or a report checking our quotations; I discuss these reports below.

C. **Retrieving cases and statutes:** Another extremely valuable tool within the CheckCite toolchest is the ability to automatically pull down the ***whole text*** of one or more cases or statutory provisions. Of course, you could do this manually by use of the LEXSEE or LEXSTAT features, but having CheckCite software do it for you certainly speeds things up, especially when you have a large number of documents to store to disk. To retrieve cases, you would typically use the RETRIEVE.CASES option set. To retrieve cases plus statutes and/or law review articles, you'd use the CASES.PLUS option set.

You can have CheckCite ***"enhance"*** the full text of the document while downloading it. When you select "Enhanced Output" as an option, the CheckCite program ***underlines the case names*** and ***indents quotes***. It also prepares the file in whatever word processor format you have specified, making it especially easy to extract parts of a case to put into a piece of writing you are preparing. Perhaps most dramatically of all, if you are using WordPerfect, you can have the case retrieved for you in dual column format (without the need for any special hardware),[3] and you can print footnotes at the bottom of the page. (However, you must choose *either* dual-column printing or footnote-at-the-bottom-of-the-page printing — you can't have both in the same document.)

D. **Quote checking:** An important feature of CheckCite software is *QuoteCheck*. Here are the things that the QuoteCheck feature can do for you:

- It automatically locates the quotes in your brief or piece of writing. More precisely, it will identify as a quote text which is either: (1) preceded and followed by quotation marks ("); (2) single-spaced, and preceded by double spaced text ending in a colon; or (3) indented on each side by the same amount (for some word processors only).
- QuoteCheck then uses the LEXSEE feature to check each quote for accuracy of wording, spelling and punctuation, and gives you a report highlighting any errors in your version of the quote.
- The QuoteCheck feature verifies the cited page number for the quote — if your quote is not found on the cited page, QuoteCheck provides the corrected page number.
- If you so elect, the QuoteCheck feature will extract, from the quoted case, the paragraph

3. The main LEXIS-NEXIS service can deliver dual column format on a printout, but only for printers following the PCL3 and PCL5 printer-control languages, mainly certain HP printers. See the discussion of ordinary dual-column printing supra, p. 2-91.

containing your quote, so you can see the quote in context.

Let's see an example of the report that QuoteCheck can produce. I prepared an input file in WordPerfect format, reading as follows:

> As the court said in a leading case, "When the relationship of employer and employee is established without a restrictive covenant, any agreement thereafter not to compete must be in the nature of a new contract based upon a new consideration." James C. Greene Co. v. Kelley, 134 S.E.2d 166, 167 (N.C. 1964).

The QuoteCheck feature was smart enough not only to recognize my quote as a quote, but also to recognize from my syntax that I must have meant that the quotation was from the *James C. Greene Co.* case.[4]

Here is the relevant screenful from the report produced by the QuoteCheck feature for the above file:

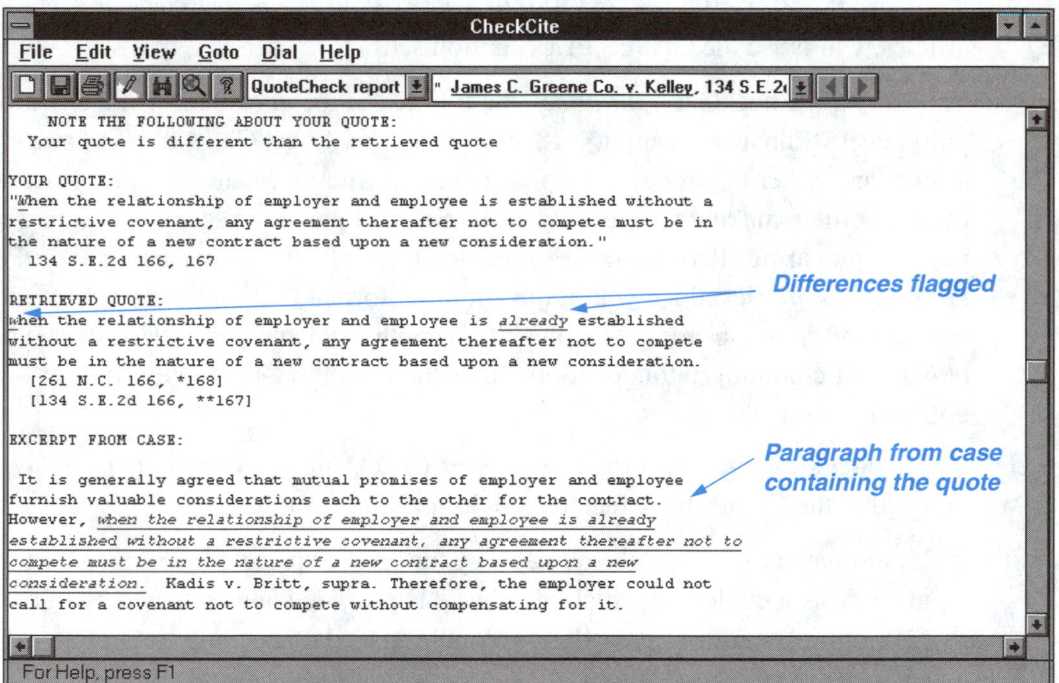

Observe that QuoteCheck has highlighted both of the differences between my quote and the retrieved quote (the punctuation on the first letter of the quote, and the fact that I dropped the word "already"). Also, the QuoteCheck feature has shown me the entire paragraph containing my quote, and confirms (in a line that's just below what you can see on the above screen-print) that it is on page 167 of 134 S.E.2d.

4. In general, QuoteCheck can "attach" a cite to a quote if the cite comes *after* the quote. Where the cite comes *before* the quote (e.g., "As the court said in *James C. Greene Co. v. Kelley*, 'When the relationship…' "), the QuoteCheck feature is sometimes — but not always — able to attach the cite and the quote to each other. However, you can manually attach a quote and a cite to each other within QuoteCheck fairly painlessly.

II. CiteRite II

A. What CiteRite II does: CiteRite II is a different kind of citation-checking software from CheckCite. You can think of CiteRite software as the "procedural" piece of the cite-checking puzzle, whereas CheckCite is the "substantive" piece. That is, whereas CheckCite software makes sure that there really is, say, a case in the reporter volume and at the page number you say there is, and that the names of the parties really are what you say they are, CiteRite checks to make sure that you have put your citation into proper ***form***.

CiteRite software can check either Blue Book or California Citation forms. It can read your word processing files, and discover the cites without your needing to mark them first. CiteRite has been laboriously programmed to understand virtually all of the rules of the Blue Book (as well as the California Citation rules), and thus can detect literally hundreds of different citation errors, including:

- Missing parallel cites.
- Incorrect reporter abbreviations (e.g., "N.Y. Supp.2d" instead of "N.Y.S.2d").
- Improper underlining.
- Improper punctuation (e.g., "W.D. Mich" instead of "W.D. Mich.").
- Improper abbreviations in case names ("In the Matter of Jones…" rather than "In re Jones…").

CiteRite II software checks citations not only to cases, but also to federal and state statutes, law review articles, books, federal legislative history, model codes, uniform codes, and services. It can handle short forms and complex string cites.

1. **Word processors supported:** Since you don't want to have to retype your citations into a different file, it's important that you be able to feed your word-processed file unchanged into CiteRite. CiteRite for Windows supports these word processors:

   AmiPro 3.0;
   WordPerfect for DOS 5.1 and higher;
   WordPerfect for Windows 5.1-6.1;
   Microsoft Word for Windows 2.0 and higher

B. A sample session: There's not enough space for me to show you the actual workings of CiteRite II software. But we can take a look at how it handles a sample text file containing cites, and what kind of report it produces when run against that file.

Here is the full text of a small sample file that I created using WordPerfect:

Plaintiff's right to relief is demonstrated by <u>In the Matter of Clark</u>, 21 N.Y. 478, 236 N.E. 2d 152, 288 N.Y. Supp. 2d 993 (1968). Defendant relies on <u>McLean v. Arkansas Bd. of Education</u>, 529 F. Supp. 1255 (W.D. Ark 1984). However, <u>McLean</u> does not stand for the proposition cited by defendant. In any event, defendant's position is clearly contradicted by the Fair Labor Standards Act, 29 U.S.C. § 200 et seq. ("FLSA").

When I ran the CiteRite program against this file, the first page of the resulting report came out as reproduced on the next page.

Sample output from the CiteRite program

```
--- Cite #1 (on page 1) ---

① In the Matter of Clark, 21 N.Y. 478, 236 N.E. 2d 152, 288 N.Y. Supp. 2d 993
(1968).

>>I<<n the Matter of Clark, 21 N.Y. 478, 236 N.E. 2d 152, 288 N.Y. Supp. ...

② Error: Use "In re" instead of "In the matter of"
See Rule 10.2.1(b)

In the Matter of Clark, 21 N.Y. 478, 236 N.E.>> <<2d 152, 288 N.Y. Supp. ...

Error: You have misspelled or mispunctuated "N.E.2d"
See Rule 6.1 and Table 1

In the Matter of Clark, 21 N.Y. 478, 236 N.E. 2d 152, 288 >>N<<.Y. Supp. ...

Error: Use "N.Y.S.2d" instead of "N.Y. Supp. 2d"
See Table 1

In the Matter of Clark, 21 N.Y. 478, 236 N.E. 2d 152, 288 >>N<<.Y. Supp. ...

③ ERROR! You cannot cite to both the N.Y. reporter and the N.Y. Supp. 2d reporter.
If these are supposed to be separate cites, place a ";" between them.
See Rule P.3 and Table 1

--- Cite #2 (on page 1) ---
McLean v. Arkansas Bd. of Education, 529 F. Supp. 1255 (W.D. Ark 1984).

McLean v. Arkansas Bd. of >>E<<ducation, 529 F. Supp. 1255 (W.D. Ark ...

④ Warning: Abbreviate this word as "Educ.", unless this cite is part of an ordi-
nary sentence.
See Table 6

McLean v. Arkansas Bd. of Education, 529 F. Supp. 1255 (W.D. Ark>> <<...

⑤ Error: You have misspelled or mispunctuated "W.D. Ark."
See Table 7

--- Cite #3 (on page 1) ---
Fair Labor Standards Act, 29 U.S.C. § 200 et seq. ("FLSA").

Fair Labor Standards Act, 29 U.S.C. § 200 >>e<<t seq. ("FLSA").

ERROR! Give all section numbers (EX: 29.101-29.199) instead of using "et seq."
See Rule 3.4(b)
```

You can get a pretty good idea of the sophistication of the product just by looking at the errors it picked up from the first two cites in this simple writing sample. But here are some features worthy of note (each number ties into the circled number which I've placed on the report):

1. The software shows you the cite as it was found in your writing, and references the page of your document that the cite was found on.

2. The program not only gives you a clear verbal description of how to correct your error, but also refers you to the appropriate rule in the Blue Book or the California Style Manual, so you can get more information. (A copy of the Blue Book is included with each copy of CiteRite.)

3. The program ranks the severity of each error. For instance, the error here is so serious that CiteRite has indicated it with the legend **ERROR!** (in contrast to **Error** for the errors it found previously).

4. Where CiteRite merely suspects an error in an ambiguous situation where CiteRite cannot be certain that there is an error, the program issues a "warning" rather than "error" message.

5. CiteRite software knows the abbreviations for nearly every reporter, state, judicial district, etc. (In fact, it knows not only the rules governing case citations, but also those governing statutes, law review articles, books, and practically any other legal authorities you might cite.)

When I was in law school, a significant part of the writing competition to make Law Review was a "substantive cite check," in which you were required to read a draft Law Review Note and comment on it both substantively and in terms of its conformance to the Blue Book. I see that the existence of CiteRite II would make the Blue-Book-conformity part of such a test meaningless today — anybody with a copy of the program could in 20 minutes do a better job than, probably, the Editor in Chief of the latest revision of the Blue Book. There are more and more things that computers do better than any human being, and I think cite-checking is now one of them.

III. FullAuthority

A. What FullAuthority does: The FullAuthority program automatically generates a Table of Authorities from your brief or other piece of legal writing. The program reads your document, and locates, alphabetizes and cross-references your citations. It also corrects some common citation errors. Once the cites have been located, the program automatically sorts each cite into the appropriate category — cases, statutes, miscellaneous, etc. Then, the system will actually prepare for you a word-processing file containing a proposed Table, with all appropriate formatting already in place, like underlining of case names, dots leading up to the page number, section titles in bold, etc.

Some of the additional features of the program are:

- It can automatically divide your cites into federal and state categories if you wish;
- It can sort statutes by either name or numerical cite;
- It lets you edit its dictionary of legal abbreviations, so that you can enable the program to recognize obscure authorities or non-standard abbreviations;

- It gives you control over the format of the Table generated by the program (e.g., single versus double line-spacing, left and right margin size; number of page references per line, indenting of second line of a citation, etc.).
- In contrast to competing products, it does ***not*** require that you ***mark*** the cites in any special way — it is smart enough to recognize them based on their native characteristics.
- It can handle up to 4,000 citations in a single brief or other document.

B. A sample session: To get a quick idea of what the FullAuthority program can do for you, let's run the program against the following snippets from a brief:

> [on page 3 of the brief:]
>
> Settlements are "highly favored in the law and upheld whenever possible because they are a means of amicably resolving doubts and prevent lawsuits." See Miller v. Republic Nat'l Life Ins. Co., 559 F.2d 426, 428-429 (5th Cir. 1977); Citizens For a Better Envt. v. Gorsuch, 718 F.2d 1117, 1126 (D.C. Cir. 1983). See also Helfand v. New American Fund, Inc., 64 F.R.D. 86 (E.D. Pa. 1974) (approving a settlement of about 5% of filed class-claims). In this case the objectors state that the settlement is "inherently unfair" and as a matter of law could never be found to be reasonable.
>
> [on page 6 of the brief:]
>
> Thus, the Clayton Act, § 4, 15 U.S.C. § 15(a), which provides for treble damages in antitrust statutes, permits prejudgment interest only for a period after service of the Complaint. See Miller, 559 F.2d at 429. See also Newberg on Class Actions 2d at 520 (1984).

We feed FullAuthority the actual word processing file containing the brief [5] (in this case, a WordPerfect document). The FullAuthority program is smart enough to be able to read the word processor's own internal page markers, so it knows what page of your brief it is reading at any moment. The program is also intelligent enough to recognize, after a case has been cited in its long form, subsequent short form references (and, if you wish, it will combine the long form and short form references into a single entry on the Table).

What you get when you run FullAuthority is a fully formatted, editable file in the native format of the same word processor you created your original document in. Here, for instance, is a printout (printed from within WordPerfect, since that's what I created my sample document in) of the Table file created when I ran the program against our little sample snippets of brief:

5. FullAuthority supports essentially the same word processing packages as CiteRite II; see the list of these supra, p. 10-11.

TABLE OF AUTHORITIES

FEDERAL CASES

①

Citizens For a Better Environment v. Gorsuch, 718 F.2d 1117 (D.C. Cir. 1983)...... 3

②

Helfand v. New American Fund, Inc., 64 F.R.D. 86 (E.D. Pa. 1974)............... 3

Miller v. Republic National Life Insurance Co., 559 F.2d 426 (5th Cir. 1977) ... 3, 6

③

FEDERAL STATUTES

④

Clayton Act, § 4, 15 U.S.C. § 15(a) 6

MISCELLANEOUS

⑤

Newberg on Class Actions 2d at 520 (1984) 6

(Actually, to be scrupulously accurate, let me confess that I made two small editing changes in the file before printing it out: I changed a section head called "UNRECOGNIZED" to "MISCELLANEOUS," and I removed the message saying that the *Newberg* cite, which is in fact a book, was not recognized by the program.)

Here are some things worthy of note about this sample report. (The numbers correspond to the circled numbers which I've placed on the report.)

1. The program expands abbreviations, if you want it to. (In this case, "Envt." was expanded to "Environment.")

2. The program is smart enough to recognize and remove explanatory second parentheticals (such as the one explaining the significance of *Helfand*).

3. The program recognizes subsequent short forms and combines them with the original long form citation. (In this case, *Miller* is cited in full form on page 3, and then in short form on page 6.)

4. The program recognizes statutes, and gives you a choice of alphabetizing them either by statute name or by number. In this case, I chose to alphabetize by statute name. The program would also have separated federal and state statutes if I had wanted it to.

5. The program recognizes books and law reviews, not just cases and statutes. It does this without requiring that any of the citations be specially marked as such in the document. (Thus in my original word processing file, I underlined the cites as I would normally do in a brief, but did not in any other way signal that something was a cite.)

IV. CompareRite

A. What CompareRite does: CompareRite is a ***"redliner"*** program. That is, it automatically ***compares two different versions of a document*** and highlights all ***changes*** between the two.

There are other redlining programs on the market, and in fact many word processors now have their own built-in redliners. But CompareRite software has been around longer than nearly all the others, and has been steadily enriched through the years. Here are some of the things that I think makes it superior:

- It can read more than 10 different word-processing formats, including Microsoft Word (DOS and Windows) and WordPerfect (DOS and Windows), and can compare a document done in one with a document done in another.
- It gives you almost complete control over how the redlined draft should look. For instance, you get several different "comparison styles," including "pinpoint" (showing changes word-by-word), "normal" (showing changes phrase-by-phrase) and "broad" (showing changes paragraph-by-paragraph). Similarly, you can decide that additions should be shown in ordinary type with brackets around them, underlined type with brackets around, bold type, etc.
- You can get a cover page, telling you which documents have been compared and how the redlined document is formatted.
- There are additional powerful features, such as the ability to compare footnotes, footnote numbers, headers and footers.

B. A sample session: Here's a glimpse at what you can get from the CompareRite program. I prepared (using WordPerfect) two different mini-documents, one of which was an edited version of the other:

First Document:

```
It is Agreed that A Company shall not assign or sublet any
part of the said parking space without the consent of B Cor-
poration in writing.  Only an automobile that is the property
of the party whose name appears on the face of this contract
can be parked in said parking space.

It is Further Agreed that in case said premises shall be
destroyed by fire or the elements, or by any other cause then
and thereupon this contract shall terminate and said A Com-
pany shall and does waive any claim for damages or compensa-
tion.
```

Second Document:

```
It is Agreed that Any Company, Inc. shall not assign or sub-
let any part of the said parking space without the consent of
Another Corporation in writing. All vehicles are to be sub-
ject to the approval of Another Corporation.  Only the vehi-
cle of the party whose name appears on the face of this
contract can be parked in said parking space.
```

I used CompareRite software's defaults for how to format our redlined document. I got the following report when I compared the two documents:

This redlined draft, generated by CompareRite - The Instant Redliner, shows the differences between -
original document : C:\COMPARE\CONTRCT3.WP
and revised document: C:\COMPARE\CONTRCT4.WP

It is Agreed that ~~<A>~~ **[Any]** Company**[, Inc.]** shall not assign or sub-let any part of the said parking space without the consent of ~~<B>~~ **[Another]** Corporation in writing. ~~<Only an automobile that is the property>~~ **[All vehicles are to be subject to the approval of Another Corporation. Only the vehicle]** of the party whose name appears on the face of this contract can be parked in said parking space.~~<~~

~~It is Further Agreed that in case said premises shall be destroyed by fire or the elements, or by any other cause then and thereupon this contract shall terminate and said A Company shall and does waive any claim for damages or compensation.>~~

As you can see, deletions are shown struck through and with angle brackets around them, and additions are shown in bold type, with regular brackets around them. (I could have used different typesetting styles to indicate these things.) At a glance, I can tell exactly how the second document differs from the first.

Chapter 11

Job Prospecting

Introduction: The LEXIS-NEXIS services can help you land a job. Whether it's a summer job or a permanent job you're looking for, and whether you're looking in the private or the government sector, you will find at least one file of prospective employers. Some of the job-search files available on the service are the Law-Firm and Corporate-Law-Department files from Martindale-Hubbell®, the LEXIS Employer Directory, Legal Support System's Employer Directory, the LEXIS Judicial Clerkship Directory, and a number of directories for government-related employment. Many of these files will permit you to automatically generate a ***mailing list*** in electronic form, which you can then word-process to create customized application letters and labels.[1]

Our discussion is basically organized by the type of job you are looking for: (1) jobs in private practice; (2) judicial clerkships; and (3) government, public interest and corporate counsel. Nearly all of the job-prospecting files have been placed in a special library, *CAREER*.

Before we begin our detailed discussion of what's on the LEXIS-NEXIS online system, however, let's first take a look at the "Career Builder" Internet website.

I. THE "CAREER BUILDER" INTERNET SITE

A. Introduction: A good online overview of LEXIS-NEXIS' career offerings is available from something called "Career Builder." Career Builder is a joint product of LEXIS-NEXIS and Martindale-Hubbell. It's available in two forms:

- as a one-diskette Folio Views infobase; and
- as an Internet web site, http://www.lexis.com/lawschool

To get the infobase version of Career Builder, contact the LEXIS-NEXIS account manager at your law school, or your LEXIS-NEXIS student representative. We'll focus here on the Internet version.

B. The Internet version of Career Builder: To visit Career Builder online on the Internet, first go to the LEXIS-NEXIS lawschool home page, http://www.lexis.com/lawschool. You'll see

1. Creation of mailing lists and customized form letters is discussed *infra*, p. 11-22.

an image simulating the entry-way to a law school, and the school's information desk. Click on the logo that says "Career Center" at the upper left.

You'll now see the following image:

"Job Board" leads you to a description of the Summer Legal Employment Guide and the LEXIS Employer Directory

"Resumé Builder" leads you to the L-N / Martindale Hubbell Student Directory

"WWW Job Search" leads you to list of "Career Related Internet Sites"

Let's talk briefly about three items of particular interest available from this screen:

- The "Job Board" area leads you to descriptions of two employment guides available on LEXIS, the *Summer Legal Employment Guide* and the *LEXIS Employer Directory.* Each of these guides is published annually. You can download each into a Folio Infobase[2] right from the website, if you follow the links that "Job Board" leads you to. Alternatively, you can search each guide online in the main LEXIS-NEXIS service. I describe the *Employer Directory* further on p. 11-13.
- The "Resumé Builder" area leads you to the Internet version of the LEXIS-NEXIS & Martindale-Hubbell Student Directory. In that directory, you can: (1) enter your resumé via the Internet, and have it available to potential employers who will view it either on the LEXIS-

2. See p. 12-8 for a description of what Folio Infobases are.

NEXIS online service or on the Internet; and (2) download sample resumés and cover letters, in a Windows word-processing format. The Student Directory feature is discussed further below.

- The "WWW Job Search" area leads you to a page called "Using the Internet to Find a Job." One of the items on this page, in turn, is a list of "Career Related Internet Sites." Some of the listings you'll find there are law-specific (e.g., www.emplawyernet.com, which is EmplawyerNet's employment information system, and www.lawjobs.com, which is the National Law Journal's Law Employment Center) and others are more generic (e.g., www.ajb.dni.us, for "America's Job Bank).

II. THE STUDENT DIRECTORY (*RESUME*)

A. The Martindale-Hubbell & LEXIS Student Directory: You can ***put your resumé online***, and have it seen by thousands of law firms, corporations and government agencies. You do this with the Martindale-Hubbell & LEXIS Student Directory.

You can enter your resumé by two different means:

- First, you can use the LEXIS-NEXIS website, http://www.lexis.com/lawschool. To use this Internet method, take these steps:
    - At www.lexis.com/lawschool, click on the "Career Center" icon.
    - Then, choose "Career Center" at the screen that shows you a law-school information center.
    - Click on the "Resumé Builder" binder.
    - Double-click on the word "resumé," towards the bottom of the screen.
- Alternatively, you can use the LEXIS-NEXIS online system. The Student Directory is in file *RESUME* in the *CAREER* library.

The rest of our discussion assumes you're using the second of these options (though there's not all that much difference between the two).

B. Key features: The Directory has many nifty features, including these:

- You make ***your own decisions*** about what information to supply, and key it in yourself. Your resumé will be online within 24 hours.
- You can supply lots of ***different types of data*** about yourself: law school name, grade point average, law school honors and extracurricular activities, practice interest, geographic preference, and work experience, to name only a few. For most items, you can decline to furnish the information if you wish.
- You can ***update*** your resumé as frequently as you wish (to reflect new activities or honors, for instance.) Updates appear online within 24 hours.
- Your resumé is ***protected*** by a personal password, which only you know, so that no one else can alter it.

- Only potential employers, ***not other students***, will be able to see your resumé, so you don't have to worry about your classmates seeing personal information (like your grade point average).
- Each piece of information (practice interest, geographic interest, etc.) is placed in its ***own segment***, for high-powered searching. Therefore, employers will be able to find you if you've got some special talent they're looking for (e.g., "Russian speaker who wants to work in the Pacific Northwest for a large firm").

C. Sample listing: Here's what a sample resumé looks like when it's been entered in the Directory:

The Martindale-Hubbell (R) & LEXIS (R) Student Directory
Jennifer A. Brown
LAST-UPDATE: 5/16/94
CURRENT ADDRESS: 1234 Main St., Dayton, Ohio, 45415
HOME PHONE: (513) 123-4567
PERMANENT ADDRESS: 123 Wabash Street, Chicago, Illinois 60610
HOME PHONE: (312) 555-1234
LAW SCHOOL: The University of Dayton School of Law, Dayton, Ohio, USA
EXPECTED GRADUATION DATE: June, 1996
LAW DEGREE SOUGHT: JD
G.P.A.: 3.2 on a scale of 4.0
CLASS RANK: Top 25%
ACADEMIC EXTRACURRICULAR ACTIVITIES: PHI ALPHA DELTA ENVIRONMENTAL LAW SOCIETY VICE PRESIDENT, RESIDENCE HALL COUNCIL
EDUCATION & PROFESSIONAL AFFILIATIONS: MEMBER, AMERICAN INST. OF CERTIFIED PUBLIC ACCOUNTANTS
PUBLISHED WORKS: AICPA JOURNAL, FEB. 1994, "HEAVY METAL ROCK MUSICIANS AND THE HOME OFFICE DEDUCTION"
RELEVANT EXPERIENCE: CLERK TO JUDGE DAVID GREEN, MONROE COUNTY (OH) COURT OF COMMON PLEAS, SUMMER 1995

GEOGRAPHIC PREFERENCE: Midwest
PRACTICE INTEREST: Large Law (> 40 attorneys), Medium Law (20-40 attorneys)
AREAS OF CONCENTRATION: Litigation, Tax
OTHER COMMENTS: FLUENT SPANISH; C.P.A
PRELAW EDUCATIONAL BACKGROUND PRELAW SCHOOL1: The Ohio State University PRELAW GRADUATION DATE: June, 1990 DEGREE ACQUIRED: BA MAJOR: Business HONORS: STUDENT GOVERNMENT PRESIDENT, PHI BETA KAPPA PRELAW EDUCATION & PROFESSIONAL AFFILIATIONS: MEMBER, BETA ALPHA PSI (Accounting Honor Society)

D. **How to enter your listing:** To enter your listing, select the *CAREER* library, *RESUME* file. Then, use the LINK markers to select the function you want to perform. For instance, the first screen you'll see offers you these choices:

Select a mode by entering an equal sign followed by the number (i.e. =1)

<=1>	**Input Your Resume'**
<=2>	**Update Your Resume'**
<=3>	**View Your Resume' (On LEXIS 24 Hrs. After Inputting Listing)**
<=4>	**Delete Your Resume'**

Of course, you'll begin by clicking <=1> (or typing **=1**). After you select each option, you'll be prompted to enter appropriate information, one segment at a time. Your completed resumé will be online for others to view within 24 hours of when you enter it.

III. JOBS IN PRIVATE PRACTICE

A. **The *LSSDIR* file:** If you are looking for a job with a private law firm, an extremely useful file is *LSSDIR*, the Legal Support System's *Employer Directory*, which is found in the *CAREER* library. *LSSDIR* contains detailed information about employers who currently forecast openings for first, second and third year law students.

1. **Coverage:** *LSSDIR* has listings, one per firm, for nearly 1,000 employers. Nearly all of these are law firms, though a smattering of corporations is also present. Most of the firms listed tend to be larger ones, of the sort who conduct annual on-campus interviews at multiple law schools.

   As you might expect from a collection of mostly large law firms, the firms are mainly from large cities.

   a. **Each office is a "document":** In the *LSSDIR* file, each individual ***office*** for a firm is treated as a separate "document." Thus for Jones, Day, Reavis & Pogue, to pick an example of a firm with a lot of offices, there are multiple documents. In general, all information contained in the document applies to that individual office only — thus the entry for Jones, Day's Irvine, California office shows five partners and no openings for 2L's, both obviously figures that are particular to that office.

b. Segments: Here is what a typical document in the *LSSDIR* file — for Jones, Day's large Cleveland office — looks like.

```
                        Private Law Firms

CITY-STATE              Ohio, Cleveland

NAME                    Jones, Day,  Reavis & Pogue

                        North Point
ADDRESS               901 Lakeside Avenue
                     Cleveland,  OH 44114
                        (216) 586-3939

                  Hiring Attorney:
HIRING-             ***********
ATTORNEY          Send Correspondence and Inquiries to:
                    Ms. Paula Nylander, Recruiting Administrator
                       (216) 586-1034

                  Other offices in Washington (estab'd 1946; 176 lawyers),
                  Dallas (1981; 136), New York (1986; 110), Chicago (1987;
OTHER-            105), Atlanta (1989; 86), Los Angeles (1973; 86), Columbus
OFFICES           (1980; 56), Pittsburgh (1989; 43), Paris (1986; 19), Irvine
                  (1991; 18), Frankfurt (1991; 15), Brussels (1989; 8), London
                  (1986; 7), Taipei (1990; 7), Geneva (1987; 3), Hong Kong
                  (1986; 3), Riyadh (1986; 3), and Tokyo (1989; 2)

                  Reasonable travel expenses are reimbursed for callback
TRAVEL            interviews;  travel expense guidelines are available on
                  request.

                  Interviews at Harvard, October 7, 1996; Chicago (1996); and
INTERVIEWS        Columbia (1996); and Michigan (1996). 1L candidates should
                  apply between December 1 and March 1.

                          1997     ---------- Employed ----------
                          Openings     1996        1995        1994

                  Lateral                            11          20
                Jud. Clerk              4(1)*         3        3(1)*
OPENINGS              3L               15(8)*      22(9)*     11(6)*
                      2L               24(7)*      17(2)*        10
                      1L                              8           9

                       * were previously summer associates
```

Sample Continued on Next Page

FIRM-COMPOSITION

Feb. 1)	Partners '96	Partners '95	SnrAssoc '96	SnrAssoc '95	Assoc. '96	Assoc. '95	Summer '96	Summer '95
Men	75	77	11	11	67	55	15	14
Women	7	8	6	4	38	32	14	11
Total	82	85	17	15	105	87	29	25
Afro-Am	1	1	0	0	2	1	3	2
Asian-Am	0	0	0	0	3	2	1	1
Hispanic	0	0	0	0	3	2	1	0
Native Am	0	0	0	0	1	1	0	0
Openly Gay								
Disabled	0	0	0	0	0	0	0	0

CURRENT-STAFF

Partners	82
Of Counsel	1
Senior Attys	17
Paralegals	66
Support	220
Total	491

PRACTICE-AREA

Practice Areas

Litigation	67
Transactional	27
Intellectual Prop.	27
Tax	24
Securities	12
Antitrust	10
Real Estate	10
Labor	8
Environmental	5
Bankruptcy	4

NEW-ASSOC

New Associates: '95: $ 70,000; '94: $ 70,000; '93: $ 70,000. (Other: Class of 1995 Associates received $4000 stipend (less taxes); Moving Expenses; Bar Review and Exam fees.) Average hours worked: 2100. Rotation is routine for: 1-2 years.

SUMMER-ASSOC

Summer Associates: '95: $ 1221/wk.; '94: $ 1221/wk.; '93: $ 1221/wk. (Other: Travel expenses.) Split summers are permitted under special circumstances (cbc weeks min.). Both joint degree and judicial clerk candidates are accepted. JudClk: '95: $ 1356/wk.; '94: $ 1356/wk.

Sample Continued on Next Page

BENEFITS	Benefits: 4 weeks vacation; cbc weeks paid paternity leave (and cbc weeks unpaid); 401(k) plan.
PART-TIME-WORK	Part-Time Work: 8 lawyers currently work part-time.
INSURANCE	Insurance: Life; Disability; Health; Dental.
PARTNERSHIP	Partnership Consideration After: 8.5 years Entering Associates Made Partners This office only Consideration After: 8.5 years '81 '82 '83 '84 '85 '86 Entering Associates 7 10 10 6 17 19 Made Partners 2 5 1 1 4 2
PRO-BONO-POLICY	Pro Bono Policy: Our lawyers have always participated in pro bono matters as their individual interests dictate. Fellowships supported: Student Funded Fellowships, National Association for Public Interest Law, National Association for Students Against Homelessness. NASAH contributor.
TEXT	A law firm stands or falls on the quality of its lawyers. The credentials and talents of Jones Day lawyers are second to none. [PORTION OF TEXT DELETED TO SHORTEN SAMPLE DOCUMENT] STRUCTURE: Jones Day is a partnership. Major Firm decisions are made by the Managing Partner after consultation with the [PORTION OF TEXT DELETED TO SHORTEN SAMPLE DOCUMENT] PRACTICE: Our practice reaches well beyond any single region and includes a wide array of major national and international concerns as well as local and regional clients. Matters often involve lawyers from several of the Firm's Offices, and on occasion lawyers from various Offices may work as a team on a major matter. [PORTION OF TEXT DELETED TO SHORTEN SAMPLE DOCUMENT]

c. **Additional segments:** There are some additional segments that you cannot notice from the above sample document. All of these relate to the number of associates or partners falling into various categories, and each segment contains, for a given document, just one number. The segments are:

Partner-related Statistics	Associate-related Statistics
MEN-PARTNER	*MEN-ASSOC*
HISPANIC-PARTNER	*HISPANIC-ASSOC*
WOMEN-PARTNER	*WOMEN-ASSOC*

Partner-related Statistics	Associate-related Statistics
NATIVE-PARTNER	*NATIVE-ASSOC*
AFRO-AM-PARTNER	*AFRO-AM-ASSOC*
GAY-PARTNER	*GAY-ASSOC*
ASIAN-AM-PARTNER	*ASIAN-AM-ASSOC*
DISABLED-PARTNER	*DISABLED-ASSOC*

The 16 segments listed above are all (and are the only) arithmetically-searchable segments. Use of these arithmetically-searchable segments is discussed further *infra*, pp. 11-10 to 11-10.

2. **How to use:** In general, you will probably want to use the *LSSDIR* file to compile a list of firms that you think you may be interested in. Once you have this list, you might want to use it to select firms whose on-campus interviews you will register for, or to create a mailing list to which you can mail your resumé. Here are some thoughts and tips about how to create a list of prospects for yourself:

   a. **Geographical region:** Narrowing the pool down by ***location*** is quite easy. Use the *CITY-STATE* segment to do this. The city is fully spelled out in the *CITY-STATE* segment, and the state is searchable by its two-digit postal code. Thus to find all firms in Chicago, just search for:

   ```
   city-state(chicago)
   ```

   or to find all firms in Missouri, use:

   ```
   city-state(mo)
   ```

   You can use the **OR** connector within a segment limit to find all firms in a region. Thus if you are interested in New England, you could search for:

   ```
   city-state(ma or nh or vt or ct or me)
   ```

   b. **Specialty:** The *LSSDIR* file is especially good for finding firms that have practitioners in a particular ***specialty*** that you are interested in. This information is collected in the *PRACTICE-AREA* segment. As you can see from looking at the sample document (*supra*, p. 11-6), the information as presented has a one or two word description of the practice area, followed by a number representing the number of practitioners in that area. (These numbers, like all numbers, are for the particular office represented by the document you are looking at, not all lawyers at the firm.)

   Here are some words and phrases that I suggest you use for capturing a particular area of practice. I have compiled this list after reviewing the listings supplied in *LSSDIR* by five or six large national law firms. Each firm is allowed to characterize its areas of practice as it wishes, so there is not complete uniformity in how a particular area is described from firm to firm. For instance, the same area might be described by one firm as "corporate" and by another firm as "business" or "transactional."

admiralty or maritime	intellectual prop! or copyright! or trademark! or patent!
antitrust or trade regulation	labor
banking	litigation or appellate
bankruptcy	product liability
corporate or business or transactional	real estate
energy	securities
environmental	tax
erisa	trusts or estates or probate
finance	

The best way to use the *PRACTICE-AREA* information is by stringing together all the words or phrases that you think may summarize the area of practice you are interested in, and combining that with other selection criteria (e.g., geography). Thus to find all firms that seem to have a practice in intellectual property in Houston, you would search for:

```
practice-area(intellectual or copyright! or
  trademark! or patent!) and city-state(houston)
```

By the way, you cannot assume that merely because a particular practice area name occurs in a documents, the firm necessarily has lawyers currently practicing in that area. Often, a firm will list an area (perhaps one in which it has had past practitioners), and then put a dash in lieu of a number. Therefore, you will want to check the documents received to make sure that there really do seem to be practitioners in that area at that office of that firm. Unfortunately, there is no way to do a numerical search on a practice area. That is, there is no way to find just those firms having more than, say, 10 lawyers practicing tax law, or to find law firms for which tax law represents more than 10% of their business.

c. Size: Somewhat surprisingly, there is no direct way to find firms of a given size. This is because there is no arithmetically-searchable segment that contains the total number of lawyers (or even the total number of partners) at the firm. However, you can use the *MEN-PARTNER*, *WOMEN-PARTNER*, *MEN-ASSOC* or *WOMEN-ASSOC* segments to approximate a size-based search. In general, there are more associates at a firm than partners, and again in general, there are usually somewhat more (often nearly twice as many) male associates as female associates. A rough but possibly useful rule of thumb is that the total number of lawyers in the firm is around three times the number of male associates, so that to find, say, firms in New York with more than 100 lawyers, you could search for:

```
men-assoc > 33 and city-state(new york)
```

a search which produces 49 firms. You can also do range searching:

```
city-state(new york) and men-assoc > 10 and men-assoc < 30
```

d. Special type of lawyer: The *LSSDIR* file contains especially explicit categorization of partners and associates at a firm according to certain individual traits or status, such as race, sexual orientation or gender. (See the complete list of partner and associate categories *supra*, p. 11-8.) You can use this information to home in on firms that you think might be a comfortable place for you. Some examples:

```
(afro-am-partner > 0 or afro-am-assoc > 1) and
  city-state(seattle)
```

(produces 7 hits)

```
(gay-partner > 0 or gay-assoc > 0) and
  city-state(new york)
```

(12 hits)

By the way, the numbers retrieved by searches on the *GAY-PARTNER* and *GAY-ASSOC* segments appear to be only for lawyers who are "openly gay" (which is the description of sexual orientation used in the *FIRM-COMPOSITION* segment).

3. **Generating a mailing list:** Once you have narrowed your search so that it retrieves a set of firms that you think meets your needs, you can then generate a ***mailing list*** for that set. To do that, take the following steps:[3]

   Type:

   `address,p` [ENTER]

   This is the equivalent of a [PRINT DOC] request,[4] with the printing to be done in "ADDRESS" format.

   First, you'll be asked to choose where the download should be delivered. You'll normally select #1 ("Printed on the printer attached to this terminal or computer, after you sign off; OR Copied to a disk, after you sign off.")

   You will now be given a set of choices regarding format and selection. First, you should use the "OPT" option, and make sure that all print options (e.g., "Print Cover Page") are set to "No."

   Then, go back to the main format-choices screen (the one on which "OPT" is one of the choices), and select one of the formats. Your choice should either be "MANY" or "SEL." To select all firms that are part of your current search set, and print their names and addresses without starting a new page for each document, type "MANY." To select individual firms by their document-number, select "SEL".

   When you have finished your research, press [SIGN OFF] (Alt-F9, or type **`.so`**) as you normally would do. Then, behave as you would for any other print-out. That is, decide whether to save your search, then answer "Y" when the system asks whether you want to start document delivery. Typically, you will then tell the system to store the document to your disk rather than your printer (so that you can manipulate the names and addresses in

---

3. These instructions are also available online. When you first log in to the *LSSDIR* file, you'll see some instructions. Choose "Generating a Mailing List," which you select by entering "4."

4. See *supra*, p. 2-83 for a discussion of [PRINT DOC].

your word processor).

If you are using MS-DOS or Windows, run the LEXFORM program to manipulate your stored file.[5] When you use LEXFORM, make sure to set "Document Format Options" to "B" ("Maintain LEXIS format") rather than the usual "A" ("Automatic line wrapping by word processor"), so that you will preserve the document's original line-endings.

At this point, you should have a file looking something like this:

```
Ms. Norma F. Cirincione <END FIELD>
Director of Legal Personnel <END FIELD>
Cleary, Gottlieb, Steen & Hamilton <END FIELD>
One Liberty Plaza
New York, NY 10006 <END FIELD>
Ms. Cirincione <END FIELD>
<END RECORD>
```

You will now need to use your word-processor search-and-replace function to replace the <END FIELD> and <END RECORD> codes with your word processing application's "end of field" and "end of record" codes for the merge process. For instance, if you use Word Perfect, you should replace each <END FIELD> with a Merge-R (F9), and you should replace each <END RECORD> with a Merge-E (Shift-F9, plus the letter E). Then, you can develop a customized letter and envelope format, with which the data file you just created can be merged.

4. **Zeroing in on a firm:** So far, our discussion of *LSSDIR* has assumed that you don't have the names of firms that you think you'd be interested in, and want to use the system to locate likely candidates. But *LSSDIR* is also useful where you know of a firm that is a prospect for you, and you want to find more out about it.

   To locate a firm, you will generally want to use a combination of the *NAME* and *CITY-STATE* segments. Thus to find the Los Angeles office of Skadden, Arps et al., you could search for:

   `name(skadden and arps) and city-state(los angeles)`

   Here is a brief sampling of the many things about a firm that you can learn by inspecting the *LSSDIR* document for that firm:

   - The name and title of the person to whom you should send your resumé (in the *HIRING-ATTORNEY* segment).[6]
   - The location and staffing of other offices of that firm (in the *OTHER-OFFICES* segment).
   - The number of openings for the summer following the current school year, and information about the past three summers, all in the *OPENINGS* segment. Of particular

---

5. See *supra*, p. 2-95.

6. This person is usually not the hiring attorney, but a person holding a title such as "Director of Attorney Recruiting" or "Director of Legal Personnel." By the way, it is this person's name that you get when you request a mailing list by the procedure described earlier.

interest are the figures for how many 2Ls and 3Ls the firm hired the past summer, and whether those people had previously been summer associates at the firm. For instance, if you look at the *OPENINGS* segment for Jones, Day reprinted on p. 11-6, you can see that the firm hired 15 people as "3Ls" (that is, as starting associates following graduation), of whom 8 had previously spent a summer at the firm. This would suggest that you might still get an offer for a starting associate post even if you had not worked there the previous summer.

- The composition of the firm (in the *FIRM-COMPOSITION* segment). For instance, you can tell that 7 of the 82 partners of Jones, Day's Cleveland office are women, and 1 of the 82 is African American.
- Areas of practice (in the *PRACTICE-AREA* segment). For instance, you can tell that Jones, Day has a substantial intellectual property department (18% of the lawyers in Cleveland).
- Salaries for recently-admitted lawyers (in the *NEW-ASSOC* segment). (*Example:* First year salaries at Jones, Day for the class of 1995 were $70,000.) Also, you can find the firm's estimated average hours worked and billed for new associates (also in the *NEW-ASSOC* segment).
- Details about the summer associate program (in the *SUMMER-ASSOC* segment). (*Example:* Jones, Day pays $1,221 per week; split summers are sometimes permitted.)
- How many lawyers at the firm work part-time (in the *PART-TIME-WORK* segment).
- The number of years after law school at which an associate is considered for partnership (in the *PARTNERSHIP* segment). (*Example:* After 8.5 years at Jones, Day.) There are also detailed figures showing the number of entering associates who made partner when this waiting period had passed. (*Example:* Of 19 associates who entered Jones, Day's Cleveland office in 1986, 2 eventually made partner as of 1995.)
- A narrative description of the firm, including treatment of its structure, how it handles assignments of new associates, and representative major clients (all in the *TEXT* segment).

B. The *EMPDIR* file: There is a second file covering employment at large law firms. This is the LEXIS Employer Directory, contained in the *EMPDIR* file (*CAREER* library). Currently, *EMPDIR* covers a little over 600 law firms. Much of the information found in *EMPDIR* overlaps with that found in *LSSDIR*; however, *EMPDIR* also contains data on the firm's "hiring criteria," and in some cases more extensive data on application dates/deadlines and interview locations than *LSSDIR*.

Searching in this file is very similar to searching in *LSSDIR* file. However, the segment names are sometimes different (e.g., *EMPDIR* uses *FIRM-NAME* instead of *NAME*; *CITY* instead of *CITY-STATE*, etc.)

As with *LSSDIR*, you primarily use segment-limited searching techniques. For example, to find listings for all those firms represented in the *EMPDIR* file that are located in Chicago:

```
city(chicago)
```

Similarly, to get the listing for a particular law firm:

```
firm-name(hopkins and sutter)
```

As with *LSSDIR*, you can create a mailing list from your answer set by using the **address,p** command.[7]

C. Martindale-Hubbell® Law Directory: The largest source of information — in terms of number of firms covered — about private law firms on LEXIS is the files prepared by the Martindale-Hubbell Law Directory. In the world of practitioners, Mardindale-Hubbell is generally viewed as far-and-away the leading directory of lawyers.

The main attraction of the Martindale-Hubbell files on the LEXIS service is that they cover virtually every law firm (and, indeed, virtually every individual practitioner) in America. Basically, the Martindale-Hubbell files on the LEXIS service correspond fairly closely to the published Martindale-Hubbell Law Directory.

Therefore, the main use to which you can put the Martindale-Hubbell files in your job-hunting is to identify firms that are not among those represented in *LSSDIR*. Typically, this will be because the firm is too small to recruit annually on multiple campuses, which seems to be the criterion for a listing in *LSSDIR*. To give you some idea of the breadth of the Martindale-Hubbell universe, there are about 70,000 law firms (not counting sole practitioners) listed, compared with the 1,000 or so for *LSSDIR*.

1. **Use to get a list of firms:** To use Martindale-Hubbell to get a list of law firms, you should choose the *USPROF* file in the *CAREER* library. This is one of several Martindale-Hubbell files in the *CAREER* library. *USPROF* corresponds to the law firm listings in the fine-print pages at the front of each Martindale-Hubbell volume. A firm will have its profile represented in *USPROF* even though the firm has chosen not to purchase from Martindale-Hubbell the right to list its lawyers' biographies.[8]

   Before we go into the details of using the *USPROF* file to create a list of law firms, you should understand that this single file contains two very different types of documents in it: Individual Attorney Listing documents, and Law Firm Listing documents. An Individual Attorney Listing document, as its name suggests, covers a single lawyer, and tells you her firm name and address, date of birth, college and law school and other information. A Law Firm Listing document covers the whole firm, and tells you such things as the firm's areas of practice, the names of the lawyers in the firm, and the locations of its non-headquarters offices, if any.

   A law firm with 10 lawyers in it will therefore have only one Law Firm Listing document, but 10 Individual Attorney Listing documents. If you were to send a resumé to each "document," you would be sending 11 documents where one would probably suffice. There-

---

7. See p. 11-11 *supra* for more details.

8. You may not be aware that Martindale-Hubbell charges a law firm to have its lawyers' biographies listed. The larger-print listings, one paragraph for each lawyer in a firm, that make up most of the pages in a Martindale-Hubbell volume are thus paid advertising. These biographies are available on the LEXIS service in the *USBIO* file, discussed *infra*, p. 11-17.

fore, you need a strategy for retrieving only Law Firm Listing documents, not Individual Attorney Listing documents.

There is no easy way to cause the system to give you just Law Firm Listing documents. The best technique is probably to add the following negative segment-limitation to each search:

```
and not admitted aft 1850
```

This segment-limitation relies on the fact that an Individual Attorney Listing document contains a segment called *ADMITTED* that recites the year the individual lawyer was admitted to practice. A Law Firm Listing document, by contrast, has no *ADMITTED* segment at all, and therefore will not be retrieved by the search.

a. Segment layout: Here are the segments that you might find of interest in searching the *USPROF* file for Law Firm Listing documents:

Name of Segment	Description
NAME	Name of firm
LOCATION	Location of firm. Includes address, telephone and fax. The city and state are usually completely spelled out. The zipcode is included. The name of the county is also supplied.
PRACTICE	Areas of practice at the firm. (*Example:* "General Practice. Administrative, Corporate Financing, Real Estate, Bankruptcy...")
PERSONNEL	A listing of the names of all lawyers at the firm.
FIRM-LANGUAGE	Each language (other than English) spoken by a lawyer at the firm. (Not present in all documents.)
BRANCHES	Addresses and telephone numbers of each office of the firm.
CITY	City in which the firm is located.
STATE	State (spelled out) in which the firm is located.
COUNTY	County in which the firm is located.
CLIENTS	The names of representative clients of the firm. (Not present in all records.)

b. Selecting firms: Here are some illustrations of how you might compile a listing of firms to mail your resumé to or to investigate further:

- ***Geographically**. Example:*

```
city(white plains) and state(new york) and not
  admitted aft 1850
```

- ***By area of practice***. Use the *PRACTICE* segment for this. Thus:

```
city(detroit) and practice(environmental) and not
  admitted aft 1850
```

- ***By client***. If you have "pull" or contacts with a particular corporation, and want to locate firms that represent that corporation, you can do this with the *CLIENTS* field. You might also want to do this if you have expertise in a particular industry, which is dominated by a few large companies. Thus:

```
clients(general motors or ford or chrysler
  or toyota)
```

- ***By firm size.*** There is no way to use *USPROF* to retrieve just those firms larger than a certain size, or smaller than a certain size. Once you retrieve a particular firm's listing, you can immediately determine the size by looking at the number of names listed in the *PERSONNEL* segment, but there is no way to have the system have do the size-analysis for you.

  However, you can select based on size if you use the *USBIO* file in the *CAREER* library, rather than the *USPROF* file. A firm will be listed in *USBIO* only if it has purchased the space to list the detailed biographies of its lawyers.[9] Nearly all firms larger than about 20 lawyers have done this, but many firms smaller than that size have not. If you do want to use *USBIO* to do a selection based on firm size, use the *FIRM-SIZE* segment. Most of the other segment names in *USBIO* are the same as they are for *USPROF.* Thus to find all listings for law firms in St. Louis, Missouri with more than 30 lawyers, you would search in *USBIO* for:

```
city(st louis) and state(missouri) and
  firm-size > 30
```

c. **Mailing list:** You can approximate the effect of a mailing list by printing all of your retrieved documents in CITE format. To do this, press the [PRINT ALL] key (Shift-F4 or type **.pa**). Then, supply the format that you want the documents printed in, which will be **.ci** (for CITE format). You will then get a series of listings, with each firm's name, address and phone and fax number. There is some copyright information included in each listing; also, the information is run together, so that there is no carriage return after, say, the firm name. Therefore, even though you store this listing onto your hard disk, you will have to do some manipulation, probably by hand, in order to be able to use it to generate letters and mailing labels.

2. **Making a list of lawyers:** So far, we've assumed that what you want to compile is a list of law firms. You may, however, compile a list of ***individual lawyers***, again using the *USPROF* file (*CAREER* library). To do this, you will want to do the exact opposite of the "and not admitted aft 1850" trick that we used for finding firms. Thus for each search, in addition to whatever other selection criteria you use, you will add the fragment:

```
and admitted aft 1850
```

Some of the segments that are likely to be found in an Individual Attorney Listing docu-

9. See *supra*, p. 11-15.

ment, and not found in a Law Firm Listing document, are:

Name of Segment	Description
BORN	Birth year of lawyer (arithmetically searchable), plus city and state of birth
ADMITTED	Year and state of bar admission
COLLEGE	Name of college, and undergraduate degree (e.g., "Stanford University (A.B.)")
LAW-SCHOOL	Name of law school and degree (e.g., "University of California Boalt Hall School of Law (J.D.)")
TEXT	Text of the lawyer's biography (only exists for lawyers whose biography is printed in the paid Professional Biographies section of the Martindale Directory)
POSITION	Position held by the lawyer at the firm (e.g., "Associate" or "Member")
FIRM	Name of law firm at which the lawyer practices
PRACTICE-AREAS	Practice areas in which the lawyer concentrates (e.g., "environmental law"; "civil litigation").

a. **List of lawyers attending your school:** One good use for a list of individual attorneys is to make a list of lawyers in the region you are interested in who graduated from ***your law school***. Then, you could send your resumé to these individual lawyers, in the hopes that they will put in a good word for you with the Recruiting Coordinator or Hiring Partner. To do this, you of course use the *LAW-SCHOOL* segment. Thus:

```
city(minneapolis) and law-school(harvard)
```

b. **Year of birth:** It can also be handy to use the lawyer's year of birth. To do this, you use the *BORN* segment, together with the **BEF**, **AFT** and **IS** connectors. Thus to find all lawyers in Dallas who went to the University of Chicago Law School and were born after 1960:

```
city(dallas) and law-school(chicago)
  and born aft 1960
```

3. **In-depth research on a firm or lawyer:** Instead of using the Martindale-Hubbell files to put together a list of prospects, you can also use it to do in-depth research on a firm or lawyer that you already know you are interested in.

If the firm you are interested in has detailed biographical listings for its lawyers in the Professional Biographies section of Martindale-Hubbell (i.e., paid listings),[10] you should use the *USBIO* file in the *CAREER* library. This will give you a document for each firm corresponding to the full firm biography listings in Martindale-Hubbell. That is, you will get, in addition to things like *NAME*, *LOCATION* and *PRACTICE* segments (which have the same things in them as the comparable listings in the *USPROF* file) a *TEXT* segment, which contains the full-text biographical listings of each lawyer in the firm.

To get the listing for a firm in the *USBIO* file, use the *NAME* segment. Also, keep in mind

10. See *supra*, p. 11-14.

that, as with the *USBIO* listings, a document represents typically just a ***single office*** of the firm, not all offices combined. Thus you will want to combine *NAME* with *CITY.* For instance, to get listings for the main (New York) office of Skadden, Arps, you would search for:

```
city(new york) and name(skadden and arps)
```

If the firm you are interested in does not have detailed biographical listings in the Professional Biographies section, then you should search for it using the *USPROF* file; otherwise, you would do your search the same way (using the *NAME* and *CITY* segments) as in the above example.

To do detailed research on an ***individual lawyer***, your best bet is probably to use the *USPROF* file. Then, you can use the *NAME* field, together with the *FIRM* field. Thus:

```
name(joseph and flom) and firm(skadden and arps)
```

If you do not know the firm, you can search just on the *NAME*, or on the *NAME* plus some other attribute (perhaps *BORN*, *LAW-SCHOOL*, *CITY* or *STATE*).

By the way, essentially the same per-lawyer information is contained in the *USPROF* version as in the *USBIO* version (assuming that the lawyer works at a firm that has a listing in *USBIO*). However, the presentation of the information is a little different. In *USBIO*, the entire biography of the lawyer, including birth date, education and description of accomplishments, is all run together in the *TEXT* segment. In *USPROF*, the information is separated into discrete segments (e.g., *BORN*, *LAW-SCHOOL*, *TEXT* for the description of past position, honors, etc.). You cannot reliably search by lawyer-name in the *USBIO* file, which is why I recommend that you do lawyer-specific searches in the *USPROF* file.

D. Butterworths Law Directory: If you happen to be looking for a job in England, Northern Ireland, Scotland or Wales, you'll want to look at the Butterworths Law Directory (*CAREER* library, *BLD* file). This file covers both firms of barristers (essentially, lawyers licensed to try cases in court) and firms of solicitors (those who do not try cases).

Here are two brief examples of how you might use the *BLD* file:

- To locate law firms and individual lawyers located in Dublin and specializing in litigation, you'd enter:

```
city(dublin) and specialization(litigation)
```

- To find the listing for a particular law firm, you'd enter:

```
name(smith and jones)
```

E. Directory of Bankruptcy Attorneys: If you want to practice bankruptcy law, you'll want to consult the Directory of Bankruptcy Attorneys (*CAREER* library, *BKRDIR* file).

This file is organized by individual lawyers, not law firms. Thus if you use it to retrieve job leads, each document you retrieve will cover one lawyer (though it will list that lawyer's firm as well as the lawyer's own name). Also, there's a segment for "state," but not for "city." The state information is listed by postal abbreviation. Thus to find all bankruptcy lawyers in the state of Washington, you'd search for:

```
state(wa)
```

IV. JUDICIAL CLERKSHIPS

A. **Finding openings with *JCLERK*:** If you would like to seek a judicial clerkship, the *JCLERK* file (in the *CAREER* library) is a fabulous resource. *JCLERK* gives you detailed listings concerning clerkship openings for federal judges (District Court, Magistrate and Court of Appeals), and for state court judges sitting on the highest court of each state. The file includes a wealth of information about each judge's clerkships, including number hired, interview dates, criteria, salary, length, names and law schools of current clerks, etc.

The *JCLERK* file is sponsored by the law schools of Harvard, U. of Michigan, Stanford, Yale, Virginia, Columbia and U. of Chicago. It is based on questionnaires distributed to federal and state court judges.

The file's coverage of federal and highest-state-court judges is extensive but by no means encyclopedic. So to some extent for federal clerkships, and to a greater extent for highest-state-court clerkships, you should supplement the research you do on *JCLERK* with other sources.

1. **Segment layout:** Here is a sample document from a *JCLERK* file, showing at left the names of the segments.

JCLERK File
Sample Document-Segment Description

JUDGE-NAME	Weinstein, Jack B. - Federal Judge
COURT	U.S. DISTRICT COURT - EDNY
ADDRESS	U.S. Courthouse, 225 Cadman Plaza East Brooklyn, NY 11201
BENCH-STATUS	BENCH-STATUS: Senior
YEAR-APPOINTED	YEAR-APPOINTED: 1967
BY-PRESIDENT	BY-PRESIDENT: Johnson
PRIOR-POSITION	POSITION PRIOR TO APPT.: Professor Columbia U.
LAW-SCHOOL	LAW-SCHOOL: Columbia U.
COLLEGE	COLLEGE: Brooklyn College
HIRE-CLRK	CLERKSHIP OPENINGS HIRE-CLRK: No
CLRK-98/99	CLRK-98/99: No
CLRK-NO	CLRK-NO:
CLRK-97/98	CLRK-97/98: Yes
CLRK-NO2	CLRK-NO2: 2
CLRK-LENGTH	CLRK-LENGTH: 1 Yr.
INTERVIEW-DATE	FIRST INTERVIEW DATE 1996-97: 12/15/1995
APPL-INCLUDE (Group Segment)	APPLICATIONS SHOULD INCLUDE resumé: Yes Law School Transcript: Yes Undergraduate Transcript: No Writing Sample: YES Recommendation Letters: 2-3 Bar Required: No If Bar Required, Which State:
CRITERIA	SELECTION CRITERIA: Academic excellence, writing skills, ability to work with others, broad experience, public interest orientation.

PREFERENCES

```
SELECTION PREFERENCE: Minority and women applicants encour-
aged to apply.
```

SALARY

```
SALARY INFORMATION: JSP11
```

CONTACT

```
CONTACT: Nicholas Turner - Clerk - (718) 260-2523
```

DATA-CURRENT

```
FORM COMPLETED: 01-22-97
```

CLERK-97/98

```
                    Judicial Clerks for the 1997-98 Term
       Clerk Name              Law School            Class of
```

CLERK-96/97

```
                     Judicial Clerks for the 1996-97 Term
       Clerk Name              Law School            Class of
Turner, Nicholas               Yale                    1996
Dinnerstein, Julie             Columbia                1995
```

CLERK-95/96

```
                     Judicial Clerks for the 1995-96 Term
       Clerk Name              Law School            Class of
Stephenson, Michele            Columbia                1995
Rubin, Josh                    NYU                     1995
```

```
                 Judicial Clerk Employment Profile 1995-1998
      Total Total Total Afric.                 Native
Term  ClerksFemaleMale  Amer  Asian Hispanic Amer     Disab.
1997-98
1996-97  2     1     1     1
1995-96  2     1     1     1
```

B. How to use *JCLERK*: Here are some tips on how to search the *JCLERK* file to put together a list of clerkships that you may be interested in:

1. Geography and court-type: Most obviously, you can use the system to limit the judges you retrieve to those on a particular type of court and/or in a particular location.

To select based on the type of court (state vs. federal, or District Court vs. Court of Appeals), use the *COURT* segment. For federal judges, use the word "U.S." For District Court judges, use the word "District." For Court of Appeals judges, use the word "Appeals." Also, use the *COURT* segment — combined with the *ADDRESS* segment — to limit yourself to a state or federal court of a particular state.

Thus to find all federal District Court judges sitting in Massachusetts:

```
court(u.s. and district) and
 (court(mass!) or address(ma!))
```
[11]

For federal Court of Appeals judges sitting on the Ninth Circuit:

```
court(u.s. and appeals and ninth)
```

By the way, if you use "U.S." and "District" you will find not only federal District Court judges but also federal "Magistrate Judges." If you do not want to include Magistrate

Judges, you should add

```
and not judge-name(magistrate)
```

to your search.

Limiting yourself to state-court judges is slightly trickier. Since there is no single word that you can count on finding in, and only in, the listings of state-court judges, you should instead eliminate federal judges. Thus to find all New Jersey state-court judges:

```
court(new jersey) and not court(u.s.)
```

2. **Hiring for current year:** You can (and probably should) limit yourself to those judges who are still hiring clerks for the academic year that you are interested in. The system has segments for the current and next clerkship years (which as of this writing are *CLRK-97/98* and *CLRK-98/99*, respectively). Each of these segments contains either "yes" or "no." Thus to find all Second Circuit judges who are looking for clerks for the 98/99 year:

```
court(second and circuit and u.s.) and clrk-98/99(yes)
```

3. **Judge's or clerk's law school:** You can limit your selection according to the ***law school*** attended by either the judge, her current clerks, or both. The judge's law school is contained in the *LAW-SCHOOL* segment. Information on each clerk's law school is contained in the general information about the clerks for a year, in the segment called *CLERK-NN/NN*, where NN/NN is a year. (As of this writing, these segments are called *CLERK-95/96* and *CLERK-96/97*.)

   Thus to find those judges (federal or state, and anywhere in the country) who have hired clerks for the most recent or next term from Brooklyn Law School:

```
clerk-95/96(brooklyn) or clerk-96/97(brooklyn)
```

   Most judges list the names of the current clerks, not just their law school, so you could in theory contact a clerk to find out about his or her experiences with the judge, before deciding whether to pursue that opportunity.

4. **Length of clerkship:** Some clerkships are for one year, and others for two years. You can limit yourself to those clerkships offering the length you want by using the *CLRK-LENGTH* segment, together with the "=" connector. Thus to find only those Oklahoma clerkships lasting one year:

```
court(oklahoma) and clrk-length = 1
```

5. **Generating a mailing list:** Once you have narrowed your search so that it retrieves a set of judges that you think are worth contacting, you can then generate a ***mailing list*** for that set. To do that, first type:

11. For most judges, the *COURT* segment will contain the name of the state where the judge sits, whether she's a state or federal court judge. (Example: "U.S. District Court for the Northern District of Illinois.") However, for some judges, the *COURT* segment omits the state (e.g., plain old "U.S. District Court"). To find these judges on a per-state basis, you'll need to include the *ADDRESS* segment, which typically lists the state by its two-letter postal abbreviation.

address,p [ENTER]

Then, take the same steps as for printing a mailing list from the *LSSDIR* file, as described on p. 11-11 above.[12]

C. The Judicial Staff Directory: For additional information about federal judges, you may want to consult the Judicial Staff Directory (*CAREER* library, *JUDDIR* file). This file consists mainly of biographies of virtually every sitting federal District Court, Court of Appeals and U.S. Supreme Court judge.

1. **When to use:** The *JUDDIR* file does not have the same focus on judicial clerkships as does *JCLERK*, so it probably shouldn't be your main resource when you're trying to generate a list of likely clerkship prospects. Instead, you're best off using *JUDDIR* during your clerkship search for two main purposes:

   - You want to identify those federal judges who are not listed in *JCLERK* (because they did not fill out the *JCLERK* questionnaire form.)
   - You want to get detailed biographical information on a particular federal judge, perhaps because you'll be interviewing with him or her. The biographical section of *JUDDIR* typically gives you detailed information such as the names of the judge's spouse and children, prior professional experience, books and articles written, and other information that's hard to get any other way.

2. **Sample document:** The basic "judge" entry in *JUDDIR* consists of two significant segments, *NAME* and *BIOGRAPHY.* Here's what a typical listing looks like:

Brieant, Charles L.

BIOGRAPHY:

BIOGRAPHIES OF JUDGES AND STAFF

Brieant, Charles L., Judge, U.S. District Court for the Southern District of New York, 101 East Post Road, White Plains, NY 10601. Nominated for appointment in 1971 by President Nixon (R). Born March 13, 1923 in Ossining, NY. Married in 1948 to Virginia Elizabeth. Children: Cynthia B. Hendricks, Charles L., III, Victoria E. Misuraca and Julia W. Clavette. Education: Columbia Univ., 1947, B.A.; Columbia Law School, 1949, LL.B. Admitted to New York Bar, 1949. Military Service: entered active duty, 1943, U.S. Army Air Corps; released in 1946 after WWII service. Career Record: 1948-51, Water Commissioner, Ossining; 1952-58, Town Justice, Ossining; 1958-59, Village Attorney, Briarcliff Manor, NY; 1958-59, Special Asst. to District Atty., Westchester County, NY; 1960-63, Town Supervisor, Ossining; 1968, asst. counsel, Com. on Fire Insurance, New York State Legislature; 1970-71, County Legislator. Member: Judicial Conf. of the United States, District Judge rep., 1989-present, Chief Judge, 1986-93; New York State Bar Assn.; Westchester County Bar Assn.; Ossining Bar Assn.

   a. **Segment layout:** As you might deduce from looking at the above listing, the *NAME* segment consists solely of the judge's name, and the *BIOGRAPHY* segment includes everything else (including a repetition of the judge's name).

3. **How to use:** Here are a couple of examples of how you might use *JUDDIR*:

12. These instructions are also available online. When you first log in to the *JCLERK* file, you'll see some instructions. On the second page of instructions, choose "Generating a Mailing List," which you select by entering "3."

- You want to find all judges who sit in the Southern District of New York. Because the phrase "Southern District of New York" might occur in a judge's biographical listing even though he does not now sit in that district (e.g., his biography says that he once was "clerk to Judge Joe Smith of the Southern District of New York"), there's no way to be sure of not getting some false hits. About the best you can do is:

  ```
  biography(judge w/10 southern district w/10 new york)
  ```

  This formulation may give you some false hits, but shouldn't miss anyone.

- You want to get the listing for a particular judge. Enter:

  ```
  name(Brieant w/3 Charles)
  ```

- You want to know how many judges there are in a particular Circuit, or in a particular District within a Circuit. For this, there's a single table in *JUDDIR* that gives all the information for all Circuits. The easiest way to get this document on your screen is something like:

  ```
  stats(2nd circuit)
  ```

  The table you'll get back looks like this, in part:

CIRCUITS	Number of Authorized Judgeships	Number of Vacancies	Number of Nominations in Senate
Districts of the 2ND CIRCUIT			
Connecticut District	8.00	1	0
New York Eastern District	15.00	1	0
New York Northern District	5.00	1	0
New York Southern District	28.00	3	1
New York Western District	4.00	0	0
Vermont District	2.00	2	0
TOTAL	62.00	8	1

V. GOVERNMENT AND CORPORATE COUNSEL POSITIONS

A. Government positions: The LEXIS service gives you very good coverage of attorney positions available in the federal government, but no structured coverage of such positions in state government.[13] The three main files that you will want to look at for federal-government positions are: Federal Careers for Attorneys (file *FCA*); Federal Law Related Careers for Attorneys (file *LRCFG*); and the United States Government Manual (file *USGM*). All of these files are in the *CAREER* library.

1. Federal Careers for Attorneys: Assuming that you want to work for the federal government as a practicing lawyer, the principal file you will want to consult is Federal Careers

13. There are no files expressly devoted to state-government attorney positions. However, the *LAWENF* file, discussed *infra*, p. 11-29, lists state and local prosecutors.

for Attorneys (*FCA*), in the *CAREER* library. Each document in this file covers an agency, office or department.

The segment layout of the *FCA* file is simple. There are only four segments on which you are likely to want to search:

Name of Segment	Description
BRANCH	Name of the branch of the federal government being covered. The choices are: "Executive Branch — Executive Office of the President"; "Executive Branch — Cabinet Departments"; "Other Executive Branch Agencies and Government Corporations"; "Legislative Branch — Legal Offices"; "Legislative Branch — Congressional Committees/Subcommittees"; "Judicial Branch"; and "Legal Services Corp."
AGENCY	Name of the agency or office being covered (e.g., "Central Intelligence Agency, Office of the General Counsel")
DESCRIPTION	A narrative, often many pages long, summarizing the operations of the department, and the roles attorneys play in the department. Usually the segment includes a detailed treatment of each office or division within the department.
APPLICATION	Information about how to apply for a legal post in the department.

a. Tips on usage: Here are some tips on how to use *FCA* to find an appropriate job:

If you know the name of the agency you are interested in, use the *AGENCY* segment. Thus to see the documents summarizing legal posts at the Department of Justice, you would search for:

```
agency(justice)
```

If you don't know the department, but you know that you want to work in a certain branch or major division of government, use the *BRANCH* segment. Thus to explore jobs working for congressional committees:

```
branch(congressional)
```

(Consult the description of the *BRANCH* segment in the above listings to see the various categories used in this segment.)

If you're not sure what agency or office a particular type of post falls under, try the *DESCRIPTION* segment, which contains the narrative text describing each department. Thus if you didn't know that the U.S. Attorney's Offices are part of the Department of Justice, you could find the description of these offices by:

```
description((u.s. attorney) or (united states attorney))
```

(This will retrieve 16 documents, each corresponding to a separate agency or department. However, a quick glance in KWIC format through the documents would show you that the listings for the Justice Department were the ones you wanted.)

If you would like to look in the places where the most jobs are, here is a listing of some of the larger federal government departments (in terms of the number of lawyers they employ), together with a simple search that will get you that department's listing in *FCA*:

Name of Dept.	# of Lawyers Employed Nationwide	Suggested Search
Treasury Dept. — General Counsel	2,100	`agency(treasury and general counsel)`
Justice Dept.	7,300 (incl. 1,340 FBI Spec. Agts)	`agency(department w/3 justice)`
Justice Dept. — U.S. Attorney's Offices	4,300 Assistant U.S. Attorneys	`agency(department w/3 justice)` then `focus u.s. attorney`
Treasury Dept. — Internal Revenue Service, Office of Chief Counsel	1,620	`agency(internal revenue)`
Military Judge Advocate General Corps:		
Army JAGC	1,800	`agency(army and judge advocate)`
Navy JAGC	1,000	`agency(navy and judge advocate)`
Air Force JAGC	1,400	`agency(air force and judge advocate)`
Marine Corps JAGC	370	`agency(marine and judge advocate)`

You should be aware that there are some special application or job-commitment requirements that govern the way many federal agencies hire recent law school graduates. For instance, the only way a person without work experience (i.e., one who is about to graduate from law school) can be accepted into the Justice Department is via the department's Honor Program, which is available only to "outstanding" third-year law students (apparently, typically ones in the top one-third of their class). Or, to cite an example of a stringent job-commitment requirement, any attorney accepted by the IRS Office of Chief Counsel is expected to remain for four years.

Once you get a document describing the department you are interested in on the screen, the application procedures are summarized in either the *APPLICATION* or *DESCRIPTION* segments. To find this information, use the FOCUS feature:

```
focus (application or resume)
```

You can find additional information about some federal-government departments that hire lawyers by using a different file, the Public Interest Lawyer Directory (file *PUBINT*, in the *CAREER* library). For instance, there is a single document in *PUBINT* that covers much of the Justice Department's attorney-hiring process. See the discussion of the *PUBINT* file beginning *infra*, p. 11-30.

b. Mailing list: You can create a mailing list from the entries you've retrieved in *FCA*. To do this, follow the instructions given for mailing list generation in the discussion of *JCLERK*.[14]

2. Law Related Careers: The Law Related Careers for Attorneys in the Federal Government file (file *LRCFG* in the *CAREER* library) will help you locate jobs that do not involve the practice of law *per se*, but that have enough of a legal component that the position is likely to be attractive to one trained as a lawyer. Examples of job titles that are (or at least are considered by the *LRCFG* file to be) law-related include: "Environmental Protection Specialist"; "CIA Operations Officer"; "Employee Relations Specialist"; "Equal Employment Opportunity Specialist"; and "Internal Revenue Agent." (There are actually hundreds of titles listed, which these are only a few.)

The *LRCFG* file contains 10 overview documents which, taken together, give you a very nice summary of the federal hiring process, including such topics as "Pros and Cons of Federal Employment," "Summer Employment" and "Where to Find Information About Current Vacancies." Much of this information relates to finding a true legal position as well as a law-related one. To see all of these overview documents, search for (in the *LRCFG* file, *CAREER* library):

```
part(one)
```

Apart from these overview documents, a document in the *LRCFG* file usually covers a particular "position." Therefore, to use *LRCFG* productively, you will have to first figure out the names (or at least key words present in the names) of positions that you might be interested in. You can get a list of job titles used by most federal agencies by searching for:

```
title(job titles)
```

You can then browse through this list, to spot job titles that you think might be of interest. Then, use the three digit code next to the job title in this list, and search for it in the *DEPARTMENT* segment. Thus if you saw the title "Labor Relations Specialist" and wanted to find the document summarizing that type of position, you would write down the three digit code associated with that position (which happens to be "233") and then search for:

```
department(233)
```

This will then give you a description of posts involving Labor Relations, including a list of agencies hiring the largest number of practitioners of this specialty, as well as application and salary information for each type of post.

3. United States Government Manual: Finally, as part of your federal-government job search, you will want to take at least a quick look at the United States Government Manual

---

14. See *supra*, p. 11-22.

(in file *USGM*, in the *CAREER* library). This is the official handbook of the federal government. It gives you, for each agency, a list of the principal officials, a statement of the agency's purpose, its role in history, plus names to contact for further information.

Typically, you would only look at the Government Manual once you had become interested in employment with a particular agency. To find the description of a given agency, use the *AGENCY* segment. Thus to find out about the Environmental Protection Agency, you would search for:

```
agency(environmental protection)
```
[15]

4. **Other files:** There are four other files that might be helpful to you in your search for a government job. Because these are less directly linked to the practice of law than the files described above, I'll just give you a brief sense of what's in each file, and you can explore further on your own:

   a. **Lawyer's Plum Book:** For "plum" (i.e., relatively high-paying and important) positions in the executive branch of the federal government, consult the Lawyer's Plum Book, (library *CAREER*, file *PLUMBK*). Because this file is organized on a department-by-department basis, it's also useful to give you an overview of what each department or sub-department does.

   b. **Federal Staff Directory:** The Federal Staff Directory (library *CAREER*, file *FEDDIR*) may be useful to you in two ways:

      - If you're interested in working for a particular federal department or agency, you can get a good overview of how the agency works, together with phone numbers and addresses for it.

        For agencies that fall within the President's direct control, use the *EXEC-AGENCIES* segment. Thus:

        ```
        exec-agencies(central intelligence agency)
        ```

        will get you a description of the CIA.

        For independent agencies not within the President's direct control, use the *IND-AGENCIES* segment. Thus

        ```
        ind-agencies(federal communications comm!)
        ```

        will get you a description of the FCC.

      - If you've got a lead to a particular person who holds a federal executive-branch office, you can get a biography of him or her. Use the *NAME* segment; thus:

        ```
        name(janet w/3 reno)
        ```

   c. **Congressional Staff Directory:** If you hope to work for a Congressional Committee an individual member of Congress, consult the Congressional Staff Directory (library

15. You can create a mailing list from the entries you've retrieved in *USGM*. To do this, follow the instructions given for mailing list generation in the discussion of *JCLERK, supra*, p. 11-22.

CAREER, file CONDIR). This file gives you not only a biography of each member of Congress, but the name-by-name details of their staffs, their Committee assignments, their seniority, etc. Typically, you'll search by the member's name; thus:

```
senator(barbara w/4 boxer)
```

or

```
representative(newt! w/4 gingrich)
```

d. **Prosecutors and other law enforcement administrators:** If you're looking for a post with a prosecutor's office, or a job that's otherwise linked to law enforcement, look at the National Directory of Law Enforcement Administrators (library *CAREER*, file *LAWENF*). This directory contains names, addresses and phone numbers for such law enforcement personnel as county and district prosecutors, state correctional agencies, state criminal investigative units, chiefs of police and city sheriffs, etc.

For instance, to get the names, addresses and phone numbers of all county and district prosecutors in California, you'd enter:

```
section(prosecutor) and address(california)
```
[16]

B. **Jobs with corporations:** You can also use the LEXIS service to help you find a position as lawyer for a corporation, sometimes known as a "corporate counsel" position.

There is no file on the LEXIS service for corporate-counsel positions that lists detailed salary and hiring information. That is, there is no corporate-counsel equivalent to the private-law-firm-oriented *LSSDIR* (*supra*, p. 11-5).[17] Therefore, if you want to restrict yourself to corporations that are currently looking for attorneys, or that have summer programs, you simply cannot do this on the LEXIS service.

However, you can get a pretty good sense of which corporations have sizable legal departments by using the Corporate Law Departments listings in the online version of Martindale Hubbell. These corporate listings are in the file called *USCORP*, in the *CAREER* library (or the *MARHUB* library, if you prefer).

The layout of a record in the *USCORP* file is similar, though not identical, to the listing for a law firm in the *USBIO* file (*supra*, p. 11-17). Thus you can search on *NAME* (the name of the corporation), *TEXT* (containing the detailed biographies of each lawyer at the company), *CITY, STATE*, *COUNTY, CORP-PROFILE* (a brief profile of the corporation), and *FIRM-SIZE* (the number of attorneys in the corporation).

Typically, you will want to search on *CITY* or *STATE*, possibly combining these with a value for *FIRM-SIZE*. Thus to find all corporations in the state of Michigan with a legal department of more than five lawyers:

```
state(michigan) and firm-size > 5
```

16. You can create a mailing list from the entries you've retrieved in *LAWENF*. To do this, follow the instructions given for mailing list generation in the discussion of *LSSDIR, supra*, p. 11-11.

17. *LSSDIR* itself has a few corporate-counsel listings.

You can find the listings for a particular corporation by using the *NAME* segment. Thus to find listings for the Amway Corporation legal department:

```
name(amway)
```

If you are interested in a corporation that has multiple branches, search in all locations where you know the corporation has an office. Some corporations list all of their lawyers (regardless of location) under a single listing, usually in the corporation's headquarters city. Other corporations have a separate listing for each office where the company has lawyers. Finally, some corporations have both a whole-corporation and individual branch-office listings.

> **Important note:** The corporate law department listings in the *USCORP* file are far ***less complete*** than the law firm listings (in files *USPROF* and *USBIO*). Whereas the vast majority of firms of more than 20 lawyers purchase a biographical listing in Martindale-Hubbell (and thus appear in the *USBIO* file), most corporations apparently do not purchase a comparable listing in *USCORP* for their lawyers. For instance, I.B.M. has no listings. Therefore, you should look upon the *USCORP* listings as only a supplement to your other efforts to find corporate counsel positions. Probably the best use you can make of the *USCORP* listings is to get detailed information about a corporation once you've fixed your attention on it from other sources (e.g., job listings at your law school placement office).

VI. LEGAL AID, PUBLIC DEFENDER, AND PUBLIC-INTEREST POSITIONS

A. The *NLADA* file: If you're looking for a job as a legal-aid lawyer, public defender, or "public interest" lawyer, consult the National Directory of Legal Aid and Defenders Officers (*CAREER* library, *NLADA* file). This Directory contains addresses, contact names and titles, phone numbers, and descriptions, for the following types of organizations:

— Civil Legal Services and Legal Aid Offices

— Public Defender Offices

— State-wide Associations for Criminal Defense

— Programs for Special Needs (i.e., specialized "public interest" programs)

— Support Services

1. **Public defender positions:** Because of the peculiar structure of the *NLADA* file, there's no specialized segment you can search in to reliably get Public Defender offices and nothing else. Therefore, just search for the phrase "public defender" without specifying a segment. You'll probably want to combine this with an address. For states, use the two-letter postal code as well as the full state name. Thus:

```
public defender and address(fl or florida)
```

2. **Legal aid:** Similarly, there's no specialized segment identifying legal aid offices. (By "legal aid," I mean services devoted to fulfilling the *civil* legal needs of the poor and other

specialized groups.) The best phrase to use seems to be "civil legal services," because the compilers of the directory have used this phrase as introductory text for each legal aid officer. Again, you'll usually want to add an address qualifier. Thus:

```
civil legal services and address(ia or iowa)
```

3. **Specialized and "public interest":** The *NLADA* directory includes a number of entries for what are commonly called "public interest" groups, typically groups rendering assistance regarding a particular subject-matter speciality. For these, use of the subject-matter name will probably be your best bet. Thus plain-old:

```
immigration
```

or

```
environmental
```

each works pretty well.

a. **Special programs:** If you think you might want to work in a public-interest program devoted to a single area of speciality, but you haven't identified a particular speciality, you can browse through the various special programs by searching on:

```
program w/5 special needs
```

This works wells because the compilers of the NLADA directory seem to have identified most special-purpose programs and tagged them with the words "program for special needs." Thus there are entries for groups interested in (among other topics) womens' rights, rights of native americans, housing, juvenile and child welfare, rights of the elderly, and disabilities.

4. **Mailing list:** You can create a mailing list from the entries you've retrieved in *NLADA*. To do this, follow the instructions given for mailing list generation in the discussion of *JCLERK*.[18]

B. The *PUBINT* file: A second source of info about "public interest" jobs is the *PUBINT* file (still in the *CAREER* library). This is the "Public Interest Directory." It contains information about public interest employers who currently forecast job openings for first, second and third-year law students. It's sponsored by the placement offices of the University of Chicago and Columbia law schools, and co-sponsored by 112 additional law school placement offices.

1. **Searching *PUBINT*:** Searching the *PUBINT* file is pretty similar to searching the *NLADA* file (discussed above).

You'll find the *CITY-STATE* segment useful for narrowing things down geographically (e.g., a search on **`CITY-STATE(chicago)`** will find employers located in that city.)

You'll find the *PRACTICE-AREA* segment especially useful, if you know what social problem or area of law you're interested in. Thus:

```
PRACTICE-AREA(immigration)
```

18. See *supra*, p. 11-22.

finds 28 public-interest groups that list immigration as at least one of the practice areas they're involved in.

2. **Mailing list:** You can create a mailing list from the listings you retrieve. Follow the instructions given onscreen when you log in to *PUBINT.* (These are essentially the same as those for *JCLERK*, discussed *supra*. p. 11-19.)

VII. ADVICE TO YOUNG LAWYERS

A. The *MENTOR* file: Now for something completely different. The *MENTOR* file (*CAREER* library) contains the full text of four publications by Jay G. Foonberg, an expert on "Law Firm Marketing." These books consist of advice about how to set up your own firm, how to get clients, how to find a non-traditional job that will make use of your law degree, and similar topics.

When you log in to *MENTOR*, you'll see the following choices, each of which leads you to a book-length set of documents:

```
Choose a subject by entering an equal sign followed by the number.
          JAY G. FOONBERG PUBLICATIONS
<=1>  HOW TO START & BUILD A LAW PRACTICE
<=2>  HOW TO GET AND KEEP GOOD CLIENTS
<=3>  NON-TRADITIONAL JOBS FOR LAWYERS
<=4>  FINDING THE RIGHT LAWYER
```

The first three are the most likely to be relevant to you. Here's a thumbnail description of each:

— *How to Start and Build a Law Practice*, as its name implies, tells you how to open your own solo law practice. There are chapters on such topics as "Getting Started," "Getting Located," "Getting Equipped," "Getting Clients," "Setting Fees," and so on.

— *How to Get and Keep Good Clients* focuses on the client-getting part of developing your own practice. It contains chapters with titles like "Getting Business from Others In the Office," "Getting Work from Large Or Publicly Held Companies," "Big Firm Techniques that Can Work for a Small Firm," etc.

— *Non-Traditional Jobs Where You Can Use a Law Degree* suggests alternatives to traditional law practice. The kinds of careers the author has in mind are things like house counsel to a corporation, government service, accounting, law-firm management, labor law, and so forth.

The online version of these books is organized with LINK markers. You'll have to be patient to get these materials into an easy-to-read continuous format; LEXIS-NEXIS presents them in a way that usually requires you to jump to a different marker every couple of paragraphs or so.

B. The SOLO file: A second source of information about practice-building is the *SOLO* file (again in the *CAREER* library). This file contains the issues of *The Solo Practitioner*, a newsletter whose author says that it is "designed to assist prospective solo practitioners by giving them guidance in their decision whether to go solo." The newsletter contains guidance about marketing and psychology, advice on ethics, interviews with noted practitioners, etc. As of mid-1997, three issues have been published and are online.

Chapter 12

The LEXIS®-NEXIS® Office for Legal Education

I. THE LEXIS-NEXIS OFFICE FOR LEGAL EDUCATION GENERALLY

A. About the LEXIS-NEXIS Office for Legal Education: The LEXIS-NEXIS Office for Legal Education is a software package that enables you to read and make notes in electronic books and course materials, and to make your own electronic textual databases. It's a version of information-management technology used by many law firms. It's available for MS-Windows 3.1 and MS-Windows 95, as well as Macintosh.

1. **How to get a copy:** At least for the 1997-98 school year, LEXIS-NEXIS Office for Legal Education software is being given free to every law student at an ABA-accredited law school. Contact your school's LEXIS representative for details.

B. Folio Views software: A key component of the LEXIS-NEXIS Office for Legal Education is a software package called Folio Views®. Folio Views is an "infobase manager": it lets you create your own "infobase," which is a fully searchable text database that sits on your PC. I tell you more about Folio Views beginning on p. 12-8 below.

1. **Publications:** Just as you can make your own searchable infobase with Folio Views, so publishers can use it to create electronic books and other materials. Thus LEXIS-NEXIS now publishes a number of law-related materials in Folio Views format. You can obtain a listing of such materials in two ways:

   - It's part of the LEXIS-NEXIS Software Collection (available in diskette or CD-ROM versions), which LEXIS-NEXIS gives free to qualified law students. Contact your school's LEXIS representative for information about how to get the collection.
   - Alternatively, you can visit the LEXIS-NEXIS law school site on the Internet: http://www.lexis.com/lawschool.[1] When you are at the main screen of this site, click on "Bookstore" to get a listing of the publications that are available in Folio format.

C. Components: The LEXIS-NEXIS Office for Legal Education has several components:

- LEXIS-NEXIS Research Software. This is the core "session manager" software that lets you perform searches on the LEXIS-NEXIS online services from your PC.

1. For more about this website, see p. 11-1 above.

- The LEXIS-NEXIS Online Connection™ program. This is a program-and-toolbar combination that you can attach to any of your applications, and that lets you automatically dial up the LEXIS-NEXIS services and easily download documents into your word processor, Folio Views Infobase, or other application.
- Folio Views® Software, the package I mentioned above that lets you create your own full-text fully-searchable "infobase" of class notes, cases and other materials on your own hard disk.
- CheckCite software, a product that lets you automatically retrieve a case if you supply its citation, lets you verify the accuracy of any case citation, and more.[2]

D. Things you can do with LEXIS-NEXIS Office for Legal Education: In a recent survey, 90% of entering law students owned their own computers. If you're part of that 90%, here are some of the law-school-related things you can do with your computer and LEXIS-NEXIS Office for Legal Education:

1. **Electronic books:** As I mentioned, a number of books are now available in Folio-based electronic form, including nearly all of the ***casebooks*** published by Michie. If your professor has assigned you such a casebook, the electronic version will enhance the traditional print version and foster your critical thinking skills. You can link all class materials and information sources into one coherent picture. And you can annotate the materials, with electronic margin notes, customizable highlighting, etc.

2. **Find materials:** As you read through an electronic casebook, you'll see ***hyperlink references*** to other materials, such as cases that are mentioned in the notes but that are not included in full text in the casebook. You can then click on the hyperlink to easily and automatically ***retrieve the cited case*** from the LEXIS-NEXIS online services.

3. **Class notes:** You can put your ***class notes*** into electronic form with Folio Views. This allows you to spend less time organizing and more time thinking and learning. You can highlight key text, insert bookmarks, and attach sticky notes, all electronically.

4. **Search:** You can ***search the full text*** of the electronic casebook or of your notes, to find all occurrences of any word, phrase or combination of words and phrases. After you do your search, you can view those areas of the text that contain "hits," and organize them in any way that has meaning to you.

5. **Design outlines:** You can ***build your own course outline*** in Folio. When you do this, you can incorporate other sources, like excerpts from cases and pieces of your class notes.

6. **Insert links:** In your electronic casebook, your class notes or your course outline, you can ***insert your own hyperlinks.*** For instance, you can insert a link between something in your class notes and something in your course outline.

For the rest of this chapter, we'll review two of the components of the LEXIS-NEXIS Office for Legal Education: Online Connection and Folio Views.

2. See p. 10-2 above for further details on CheckCite.

II. THE LEXIS-NEXIS ONLINE CONNECTION PROGRAM

A. The LEXIS-NEXIS Online Connection program generally: The LEXIS-NEXIS Online Connection program is available free to all qualified law students.[3] The Online Connection gives you two main things:

- a floating ***toolbar*** that's always accessible. This toolbar lets you easily access the LEXIS-NEXIS online services, Folio Views, your word processing software, and certain of your other Windows applications.
- an easy, fill-in-the-blank way of connecting with the LEXIS-NEXIS services, fetching cases or other documents, and ***downloading*** those documents into your word processor or other application.

Please note that the following discussion of Online Connection assumes that you're using Online Connection as a standalone program. That's the way you'll be using it if you're using the LEXIS-NEXIS Session Manager Software v. 4.2 (packaged together with Folio Views software, v. 3.11), the combination that LEXIS is giving out during the 1997-98 school year. If you're using LEXIS-NEXIS Research Manager 7.0 (expected to be distributed to law students for the 1998-99 school year), the Online Connection program is not a standalone, but is instead integrated into the Research Manager.

B. The toolbar: The "LEXIS-NEXIS toolbar" is a key element of the Online Connection program. It allows you to move seamlessly between various applications to manipulate data. When you install the Online Connection as part of the Office for Legal Education, the toolbar will automatically have buttons for dialing up to LEXIS-NEXIS and for invoking Folio Views and other applications (e.g., word processing).

When you install Online Connection, the program looks for additional third-party applications on your hard disk that the program can "include" on the toolbar. By this, I mean that a button for that application gets placed on the toolbar. Then, you can start up that application just by clicking on the button. At this point, the main third-party applications that can appear on the toolbar are a number of word processors,[4] the CheckCite, CompareRite, CiteRite and FullAuthority programs,[5] two "suites" of applications,[6] and Law Schools Online.

Here's what a sample LEXIS-NEXIS toolbar might look like:[7]

---

3. The Online Connection is part of the CD-ROM given to law students at each school. A diskette version is also available. Contact your school's LEXIS representatives for information about how to get your copy.

4. The word processors now linkable in this way include Microsoft Word for Windows 2.0 and 6.0; WordPerfect for Windows 5.2, 6.0 and 6.1; and Ami Pro 3.0.

5. These four programs are discussed in Chapter 10.

6. These are Microsoft Office Manager and WordPerfect Desktop Application Director.

7. Its precise look will depend on what applications you've got installed on your system. For instance, if you had Word Perfect installed, there'd be a button for that program on the toolbar.

1. **What you do with it:** So what good's this toolbar? Well, it's a ***"floating"*** toolbar. This means that it's always on your screen, whatever application you're running. You can move it around, or make it disappear. With it, you're only one click away from starting any of the applications represented on the buttons.

C. **Connecting to LEXIS-NEXIS:** Apart from the toolbar, another function of the Online Connection program is to give you an easy way to connect with the LEXIS-NEXIS services, and to perform searches, or download cases and other materials, automatically and easily.

You can get a sense of the connection possibilities of Online Connection by looking at the following dialog box, which appears when you click the magnifying-glass button ( ) on the Online Connection program's toolbar:

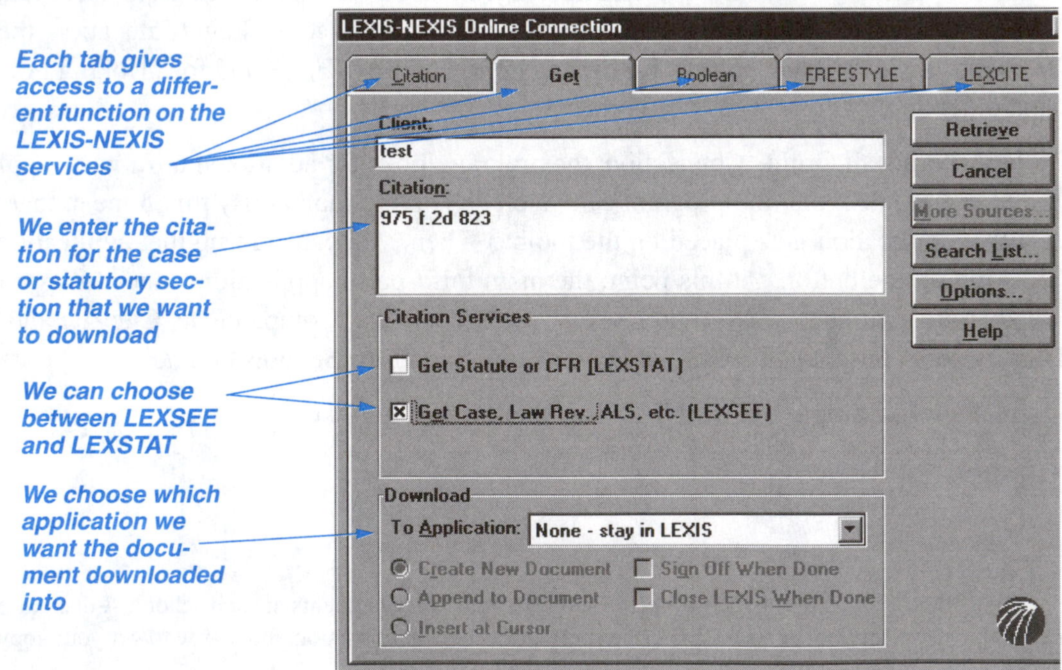

As you can see, the Online Connection gives you a choice among "Citation", "Get" (which is the tab brought to the front in the above screen-print), "Boolean," "FREESTYLE" and "LEXCITE." Each of these tabs lets you automatically carry out one or more core functions on the LEXIS service.

1. **The "Get" tab:** Using the "Get" tab shown above, for instance, we can cause the system to ***automatically download*** a case (using the LEXSEE feature) or a statutory provision (using the LEXSTAT feature). Furthermore, we can automatically insert the document into the application of our choice, typically our word processor or Folio Views.
2. **The "Citation" tab:** Using the "Citation" tab, we can cause the system to ***check any citation***, using either Auto-Cite or SHEPARD'S:

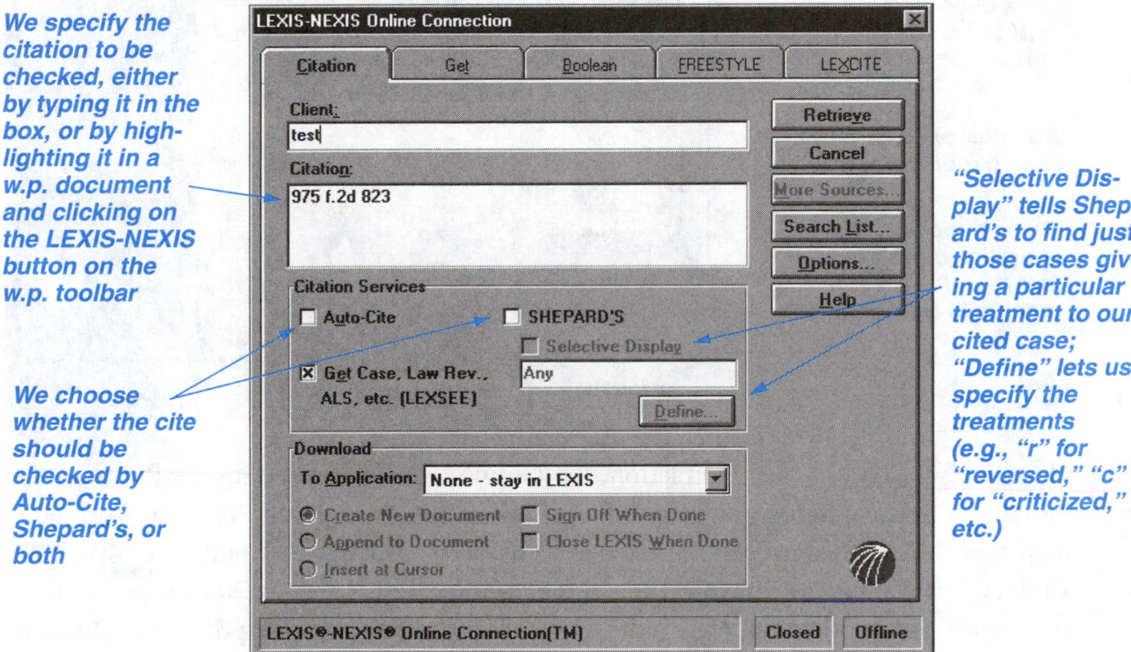

3. **The "Boolean" tab:** The "Boolean" tab lets us select a library and file, then type a Boolean search:

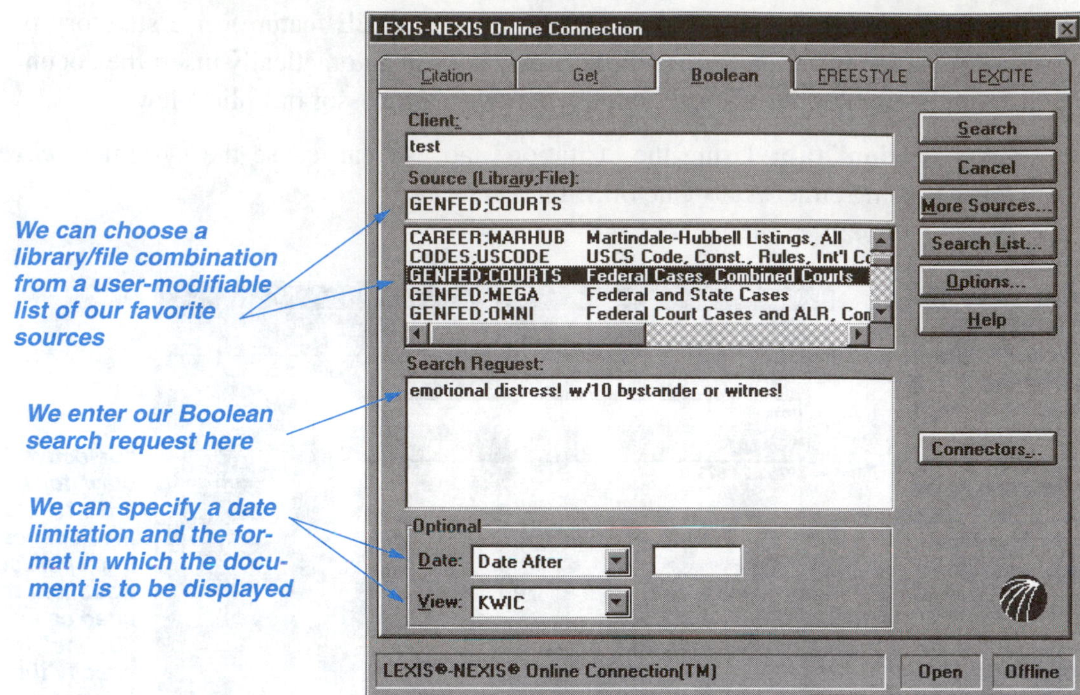

Once we've filled in the information, the Online Connection program will automatically go online, do the search and put us into the LEXIS-NEXIS Research Software with the first case displayed. At that point, we can use the "Download from LEXIS" button ( ) on the Online Connection toolbar to download the retrieved documents into our word processor or other local software application. Here's the dialog box we get when we press the "Download from LEXIS" button:

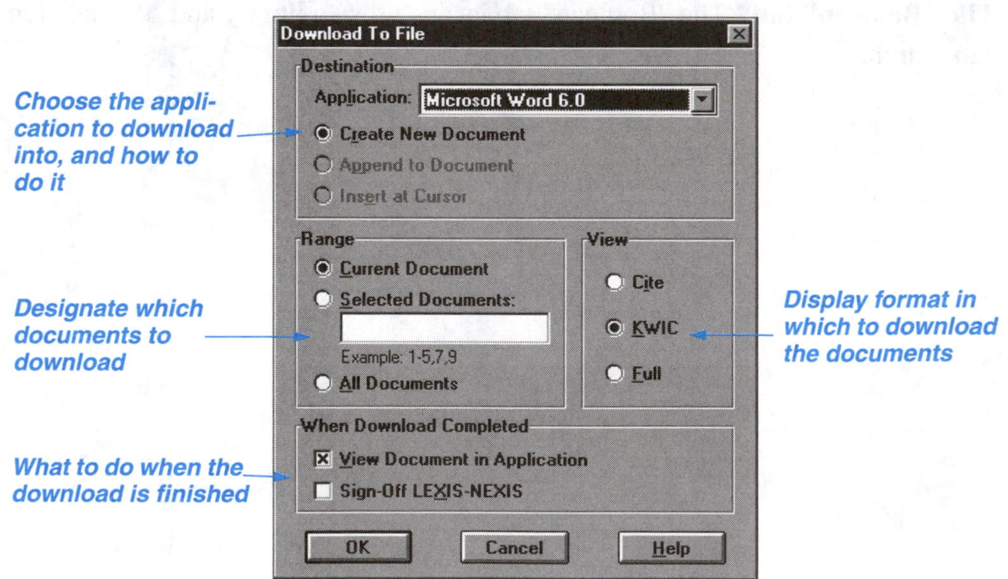

4. **The "FREESTYLE" tab:** The "FREESTYLE" tab works similarly to the "Boolean" tab, except that it lets you enter a FREESTYLE ("plain English") search, then goes online to perform that search:[8]

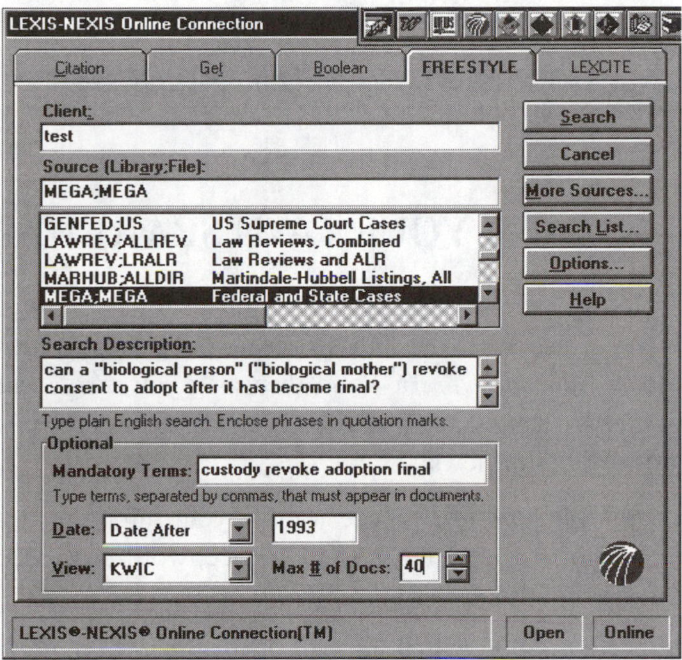

Observe that nearly all of the features of FREESTYLE, such as phrases, Mandatory terms, and number of documents to retrieve, are supported. As with the "Boolean" tab, you'll be placed in the Session Manager with the first retrieved document showing, and you can use the "Download from LEXIS" button to download all or selected documents to your local application.

5. **The "LEXCITE" tab:** The last tab is "LEXCITE," which lets you perform a LEXCITE search to retrieve all cases citing the case you specify. (LEXCITE is crucial for finding references to very recent or unpublished opinions, which could be missing from SHEPARD'S or Auto-Cite.[9])

6. **Other features:** The LEXIS-NEXIS Online Connection Program includes many other features. Here's a brief summary of a few:

   - It automatically modifies the ***toolbar*** of some of your ***third-party applications*** (e.g., MS-Word for Windows and WordPerfect for Windows), so that these toolbars include a button for connecting with the LEXIS-NEXIS services;

   - You can ***save*** selected, or all, ***search requests***, keep them as long as you want, and re-

8. Instead of hand-typing a FREESTYLE search into the "Search request" box, you can highlight a portion of text in a word-processing or Folio Views document; then, if you click the "LEXIS" button on the application's toolbar, the material you've highlighted will be automatically placed in the Online Connection program's "Search request" box, where it will serve as the FREESTYLE search request.

9. For more about LEXCITE, see p. 2-74 *supra*.

use them.

- You can ***store*** many kinds of ***default settings*** (e.g., what kind of Auto-Cite or Shepard's search to do by default; maximum size of download before the services should warn you; how many minutes of inactivity should cause the services to log you off automatically; what default local application to download to, etc.)

- You can view a ***list*** of all ***libraries and files***, and select the one you want to search in, without having to go online first.

III. Folio Views — MAKE YOUR OWN SEARCHABLE "INFOBASE"

A. About Folio Views: The LEXIS-NEXIS Office for Legal Education package includes the Folio Views Infobase Manager, v. 3.1a. Folio Views lets you ***create your own full-text-searchable infobase*** of cases, statutes, class notes and other text documents. Here are some of the things you can do with Folio Views:

- You can put ***whatever kind of text*** you want in your infobase — cases and statutory sections you've downloaded from the LEXIS service, word processor documents (e.g., class notes or home-made outline), and more.

- You can ***search*** your entire textual infobase instantly, to find all occurrences of any word, phrase or combination of words and phrases;

- You can insert ***"notes"*** wherever you want, which look like yellow sticky notes and which display extra material (like a professor's comments, or a definition) in a small popup window;

- You can insert ***"jump links"*** wherever you want, to link two pieces of the infobase together as a cross-reference. (For instance, if a case cites a statutory provision, you can insert a jump link between the citation in the case and the text of the statutory provision; then, you can click on the citation and the text of the statute will instantly appear.)

- You can quickly ***"highlight"*** any text you want, in any background color. You can use different highlighter colors to mark different kinds of text.

- You can create a ***"bookmark"*** at any point, so you can instantly find the place you've marked;

- You can add ***imported graphics*** to any point (e.g., a flow chart you've created in a drawing package);

- You can ***format your text*** as extensively as you could in any word processor, with full control over point size and type style, margins, color, and practically any other aspect of how the documents will look. You also get full control over the printing process — you can print out some or all documents, just the selected portions of documents, etc.

We can't cover all of these options in detail in this book. However, the following section outlines two common law-school scenarios, and gives you guidance on how the LEXIS-NEXIS

Office software, and Folio Views in particular, can help you in your studies.

In these instructions, I assume that the version of Folio Views you're using is 3.1. Where the way you do something is different in Views 4.0, I tell you the difference in a parenthetical note.

1. **Outlining:** Suppose you want to create a ***course outline***, and integrate it with your class notes or with outside sources like the text of cases. Here's how you'd go about this, using Folio Views software:

   a. **Create the outline in your word processor:** First, create your own outline in your word processing program from your class notes, materials obtained from professors and classmates, and cases or other materials downloaded from the LEXIS-NEXIS services. To do this, follow the steps applicable to your word processing software.

   b. **Import into Folio Views:** Next, ***import*** your outline into Folio Views:

      ① Click the ***OPEN*** button on the toolbelt running vertically at the left of the screen. (*Note:* In Folio Views version 4.0, use the FILE/IMPORT button.)

      ② Choose the correct file type from the list of import filters on the ***List of Files of Type*** drop-down list.

      ③ Type the name of the file to be imported in the ***File Name*** box.

      ④ Click ***OK***. (*Note:* If you are importing information into an existing infobase, you must choose the ***Insert at Cursor*** option before clicking OK.)

   c. **Personalize:** ***Personalize*** your outline (which is now a Folio Views infobase) with the following features:

❑ Place a BOOKMARK at significant areas:

① Position the cursor where you want to place the bookmark.

② Click ***Bookmark*** on the toolbelt, or choose ***Customize***, ***Bookmark***. (*Note:* In Folio Views 4.0, the term is ***Tools***, not *Customize*.)

③ Enter a name for the Bookmark, up to 127 characters.

④ Click ***OK***.

❑ Place STICKY NOTES in significant areas:

① Place a cursor at the point in the paragraph where you wish to attach a note.

② Choose ***Customize***, ***Note***. (*Note:* In Folio Views 4.0, the term is ***Tools***, not *Customize*.)

③ Type the desired information in the ***Note*** window.

④ When you're finished typing the note, double-click the top left corner of the ***Note*** window, or press ESC.

⑤ Choose ***Yes*** to save the note.

❑ Place HIGHLIGHTERS in the significant areas:

① Click ***Highlighter*** on the toolbelt.

② Type a name for the highlighter in the ***Highlighter Name*** box.

③ Click the ***Character*** button if you want to give the highlighter visual attributes. For example, use ***Background*** to indicate specific colors.

④ Click the ***Add*** button on the Highlighter dialog box to add the new highlighter to the ***Highlighter Name*** list.

⑤ Click the ***Close*** button.

❑ Create PROGRAM LINKS to relevant materials in other software programs:

① Select the text or object that you want to make the "launch point."

② Choose ***Customize***, ***Program Link***. (*Note:* In Folio Views 4.0, choose ***Tools***, ***Links***, ***Program***.)

③ Locate the executable file for the program you want to have launched.

④ Click ***OK***.

❑ Create JUMP LINKS between related areas of the infobase:

① Place the cursor at the location your jump link should reference.

② Choose ***Customize***, ***Jump Destination***. (*Note:* In Folio Views 4.0, choose ***Insert***, ***Jump Destination***.)

③ Type a name for the jump destination in the ***Name*** box.

④ Choose OK.

⑤ Select the text or object you want to make your "launch point."

⑥ Choose ***Customize***, ***Jump Link***. (*Note:* In Folio Views 4.0, choose ***Tools***, ***Links Jump***.)

⑦ Select your jump destination from the ***Name*** list.

⑧ Click ***OK***.

2. **Writing briefs:** LEXIS-NEXIS Office for Legal Education can help you through the whole process of ***writing a brief***, from finding relevant briefs and materials on the LEXIS-NEXIS services to organizing your information in a Folio Views infobase. Here are the steps you might take:

   a. **Open a new infobase:** First, ***open a new infobase*** in your Folio Views software program:

   ① Choose ***File***, ***New*** from the pull-down menu.

   ② Type the desired name in the ***File Name*** box (e.g., **`brief.nfo`**)

   ③ If you wish, supply any additional information in the "Infobase Information" box. (*Note:* Step 3 does not apply to v. 4.0 of Folio Views software.)

④ Click ***OK***.

b. Research your subject: Next, ***research*** your subject area in the LEXIS-NEXIS services. Pay special attention to the *BRIEFS* file in the *GENFED* library; every Supreme Court brief since 1979 can be found in this file.

c. Download: ***Download*** all relevant documents from the LEXIS-NEXIS services into a Folio Views infobase:

① When you find relevant documents, click the ***Download*** icon on the LEXIS-NEXIS toolbar.

② Select ***Views 3.1*** from the Application box.

③ Click ***Append to Document*** and select the appropriate settings if the defaults are not correct.

④ Click ***OK***. The document(s) will be downloaded through filters that will automatically append them to your existing infobase.

d. Organize: ***Organize*** the information in your infobase in a logical, coherent way. Perform a QUERY SEARCH in your infobase to identify those documents dealing with specific issues:

① Click ***Query*** on the Toolbelt, or choose ***Search, Query***. The Query Dialog Box appears.

② Type what you are looking for in the Query For box. Use proximity connectors or wildcard characters as necessary.

③ Click ***OK***.

e. Create Levels: ***Create "Levels"*** to organize issues and thus write more logical arguments:

① Choose ***Layout***, ***Level***.

② Type a name for the new level in the Level Name box. (*Note:* All levels initially belong to the "normal" level.)

③ Click the ***Character*** button if you want to give the level visual attributes.

④ Click the ***Add*** button on the level dialog box to add the new level to the Level Name list.

⑤ Click the ***Close*** button.

f. Annotate: ***Annotate*** the information in your infobase:

❑ Place STICKY NOTES in significant areas:

① Place a cursor at the point in the paragraph where you wish to attach a note.

② Choose ***Customize***, ***Note***. (*Note:* In Folio Views 4.0, the term is ***Tools***, not

Customize.)

③ Type the desired information in the ***Note*** window.

④ When you're finished typing the note, double-click the top left corner of the Note window, or press ESC.

⑤ Choose ***Yes*** to save the note.

❏ Place HIGHLIGHTERS in the significant areas:

① Click ***Highlighter*** on the toolbelt.

② Type a name for the highlighter in the ***Highlighter Name*** box.

③ Click the ***Character*** button if you want to give the highlighter visual attributes. For example, use ***Background*** to indicate specific colors.

④ Click the ***Add*** button on the Highlighter dialog box to add the new highlighter to the ***Highlighter Name*** list.

⑤ click the ***Close*** button.

g. Verify cites: ***Verify the citations*** in your brief with the CheckCite™ program.[10]

❏ CheckCite automatically checks the accuracy of your citations through SHEPARD'S, Auto-Cite, and the LEXCITE feature on the LEXIS-NEXIS services.

h. Table of Authorities: ***Create a Table of Authorities*** with the FullAuthority™ program.

❏ FullAuthority automatically generates a Table of Authorities from your brief.[11]

---

10. See p. 10-2 for more about CheckCite.

11. See p. 10-13 for more about FullAuthority.

Appendix

A Equivalents

This Appendix lists pairs of equivalents on the LEXIS® service. A search for one word of an equivalent-pair will find documents containing the other word. Note that this list is solely for the LEXIS service — the NEXIS® service has a quite different (and larger) set of equivalents, not shown here.

LEXIS Equivalents

Term	Equivalent	Term	Equivalent	Term	Equivalent
A.D.	AD	D.A.	DA	FLORIDA	FLA
A.E.C.	AEC	D.O.D.	DOD	FORTIETH	40TH
A.G.	AG	D.O.T.	DOT	FORTY	40
A.L.R.	ALR	DAKOTA	DAK	FOUR	4
A.R.R.	ARR	DECEMBER	DEC	FOURTEEN	14
AFFD.	AFF'D	DELAWARE	DEL	FOURTEENTH	14TH
AFFG	AFF'G	DIES	DIE	FOURTH	4TH
AFFIRMED	AFF'D	E.O.	EO	FRIDAY	FRI
AFFIRMING	AFF'G	E.P.T.L.	EPTL	G.C.M.	GCM
ALABAMA	ALA	EFFECTIVE	EFF	GEORGIA	GA
ALASKA	ALAS.	EIGHT	8	GOES	GO
AMENDED	AMD	EIGHTEEN	18	H.E.W.	HEW
AMENDING	AMG	EIGHTEENTH	18TH	H.U.D.	HUD
ANONYMOUS	ANON	EIGHTH	8TH	I.C.C.	ICC
APPENDICES	APPENDIX	EIGHTIETH	80TH	I.R.B.	IRB
APRIL	APR	EIGHTY	80	I.R.C.	IRC
ARIZONA	ARIZ	ELEVEN	11	I.R.S.	IRS
ARKANSAS	ARK	ELEVENTH	11TH	INDIANA	IND
AUGUST	AUG	EXHIBIT	EXH	INDICES	INDEX
AVENUE	AVE	F	FED	JANUARY	JAN
B.F.P.	BFP	F.A.A.	FAA	JULY	JUL
B.T.A.	BTA	F.A.A.A.	FAAA	JUNE	JUN
C.A.	CA	F.B.I.	FBI	KANSAS	KAN
C.B.	CB	F.C.C.	FCC	KENTUCKY	KY
C.C.A.	CCA	F.D.A.	FDA	LB	LBS
C.C.P.A.	CCPA	F.D.I.C.	FDIC	LOUISIANA	LA
C.F.R.	CFR	F.I.C.A.	FICA	M.T.	MT
C.I.A.	CIA	F.M.C.	FMC	MANUSCRIPT	MS
C.I.F.	CIF	F.O.B.	FOB	MARCH	MAR
C.O.D.	COD	F.P.C.	FPC	MARYLAND	MY
C.P.A.	CPA	F.R.	FR	MATRICES	MATRIX
C.P.L.	CPL	F.R.D.	FRD	MEMO	MEMORANDA
C.P.L.R.	CPLR	F.T.C.	FTC	MEMORANDUM	MEMORANDA
CA	CCA	FEBRUARY	FEB	MICHIGAN	MICH
CAL	CALIF	FIFTEEN	15	MIMEOGRAPH	MIM
CALIFORNIA	CALIF	FIFTEENTH	15TH	MINNESOTA	MINN
CERTIORARI	CERT	FIFTH	5TH	MISSOURI	MO
CHAPTER	CH	FIFTIETH	50TH	MONDAY	MON
CIRCUIT	CIR	FIFTY	50	MONTANA	MONT
COLORADO	COLO	FIRST	1ST	MOTION	MOT
CONNECTICUT	CONN	FIVE	5	N.A.S.A.	NASA

LEXIS Equivalents (Cont.)

Term	Equivalent
N.L.R.B.	NLRB
N.Y.	NY
NEBRASKA	NEB
NEVADA	NEV
NINE	9
NINETEEN	19
NINETEENTH	19TH
NINETIETH	90TH
NINETY	90
NINTH	9TH
NOVEMBER	NOV
O.D.	OD
O.E.O.	OEO
OCTOBER	OCT
OKLAHOMA	OKLA
ONE	1
P.L.	PL
PARAGRAPH	PARA
PENNSYLVANIA	PA
PERMANENT	PERM
POUND	LBS
R.S.	RS
REGULATION	REG
REHEADING	REH
REVD	REV'D
REVERSED	REV'D
REVERSING	REV'G
REVG	REV'G
S.C.A.	SCA
S.C.P.A.	SCPA
S.M.	SM
S.P.R.	SPR
S.S.T.	SST
SATURDAY	SAT
SEC	§
SECOND	2ND
SECTION	§
SEPTEMBER	SEPT
SEVEN	7
SEVENTEEN	17
SEVENTEENTH	17TH
SEVENTH	7TH
SEVENTIETH.	70TH
SEVENTY	70
SIX	6
SIXTEEN	16
SIXTEENTH	16TH
SIXTH	6TH
SIXTIETH	60TH
SIXTY	60
SUBDIV	SUBD
SUBDIVISION	SUBD
SUBSEC	§§
SUBSECTION	§§
SUNDAY	SUN
SUPPLEMENT	SUPP
T.C.	TC
T.C.M.	TCM
T.D.	TD
T.I.R.	TIR
TEMPORARY	TEMP
TEN	10
TENNESSEE	TENN
TENTH	10TH
TEXAS	TEX
THIRD	3RD
THIRTEEN	13
THIRTEENTH	13TH
THIRTIETH	30TH
THIRTY	30
THREE	3
THURSDAY	THUR
TITLE	TIT
TREASURY	TREA
TUESDAY	TUE
TWELFTH	12TH
TWELVE	12
TWENTIETH	20TH
TWENTY	20
TWO	2
U.C.C.	UCC
U.S.C.	USC
U.S.C.A.	USCA
U.S.C.M.A.	USCMA
VERMONT	VT
VERTICES	VERTEX
VIRGINIA	VA
VOLUME	VOL
WEDNESDAY	WED
WILLFUL	WILFUL
WISCONSIN	WIS
WYOMING	WYO

Appendix

B Noise Words

This Appendix lists words that are "noise" words on LEXIS®. That is, these words, because of the frequency with which they occur in legal writing, are not placed in the LEXIS-NEXIS master dictionary and are thus not searchable. If you include any of these words in your search request, the word will be ignored when the services processes your request.

Some of these words are not considered noise words on NEXIS because the latter has fewer searchable libraries and files and, therefore, those words occur less frequently. Words in **boldface** are searchable on NEXIS but not on LEXIS.

LEXIS-NEXIS Noise Words

ALL	HENCE	REALLY	THOSE
ALSO	HER	**SAID**	THUS
AM	HERE	SHE	TO
AN	HEREBY	**SO**	TOO
AND	HEREIN	SHOULD	UNTO
ANY	HEREOF	**SOME**	**US**
ARE	HEREON	SUCH	VERY
AS	HERETO	THAN	VIZ
AT	HEREWITH	THAT	WAS
BE	HIM	THE	WE
BECAUSE	HIS	THEIR	WERE
BEEN	HOWEVER	THEM	WHAT
COULD	I.E.	THEN	WHEN
DID	IF	THERE	WHERE
DO	INTO	THEREBY	WHEREBY
DOES	IS	THEREFORE	WHEREIN
E.G.	**IT**	THEREFROM	WHETHER
EVER	ITS	THEREIN	WHICH
FROM	ME	THEREOF	**WHO**
HAD	NOR	THEREON	WHOM
HARDLY	OF	THERETO	WHOSE
HAS	**ON**	THEREWITH	WHY
HAVE	ONTO	THESE	WITH
HAVING	OR	THEY	WOULD
HE	OUR	THIS	YOU

There are also a few noise words applicable to public records sources on the LEXIS-NEXIS services. These are:

ASSOC	CO	CORPORATION	LIMITED
ASSOCIATE	COMPANY	INC	LTD
ASSOCIATION	CORP	INCORPORATED	

Appendix C

State Code Topic Abbreviations

This Appendix shows you the abbreviation to use for each individual topic, in the five states (California, Louisiana, Maryland, New York and Texas) that require a topic when using the LEXSTAT® feature.

For example: to retrieve section 11400 of the California Education Code, you would transmit:

```
lexstat ca ed 11400
```

CALIFORNIA

Code Name	LEXSTAT Format	Code Name	LEXSTAT Format
Business & Professions	ca bus prof	Labor	ca lab
Appendix I	ca bus prof app i	Military & Veterans	ca mil vet
Appendix II	ca bus prof app ii	Penal	ca pen
Civil	ca civ	Probate	ca prob
Code of Civil Procedure	ca civ proc	Public Contract	ca pub con
Corporations	ca corp	Public Resources	ca pub res
Education	ca ed	Public Utilities	ca pub util
Elections	ca elec	Appendix A	ca pub util app a
Evidence	ca evid	Appendix B	ca pub util app b
Financial	ca fin	Revenue & Taxation	ca rev tax
Fish & Game	ca fish g	Streets & Highways	ca sts hy
Food & Agriculture	ca food agr	Unemployment Insurance	ca unemp ins
Government	ca gov		
Harbors & Navigation	ca harb nav	Uniform Commercial	ca u com
Appendix I	ca harb nav app i	Vehicle	ca veh
Appendix II	ca harb nav app ii	Water	ca wat
Health & Safety	ca health saf	Welfare & Institutions	ca wel inst
Insurance	ca ins	Uncodified Water Acts	ca uncod water deer x § x

LOUISIANA

Example: **lexstat la cjp 2**

Code Name	LEXSTAT Format	Code Name	LEXSTAT Format
Juvenile Procedure	la c.j.p. x	Criminal Procedure	la c.cr.p. x
Civil Procedure	la c.c.p. x	Revised Statutes	la rev stat x
Civil Code	la c.c. x		

MARYLAND

Example: **lexstat md rp 8a-101**

Code Name	LEXSTAT Format	Code Name	LEXSTAT Format
Agriculture	md ag	Financial Institutions	md fi
Business Occupations and Professions	md bop	Health-General	md hg
Commercial Law	md co	Health Occupations	md ho
Corporations and Assoc	md ca	Labor & Employment	md lab emp
Courts and Judicial Proc.	md cj	Natural Resources	md nr
Education	md ed	Real Property	md rp
Environment	md en	State Finance & Procurement	md st
Estates and Trusts	md et	State Government	md sg
Family Law	md fl	Tax-General	md tg
		Tax-Property	md tp
		Transportation	md tr

NEW YORK

Example: **lexstat ny real p 339-j**

Code Name	LEXSTAT Format	Code Name	LEXSTAT Format
Abandoned Property	ny aban prop	Estates, Powers and Trust Law	ny eptl
Agricultural Conservation & Adjust.	ny agr conserv adj	Executive	ny exec
Agricultural & Markets	ny agr mkts	Family Court Act	ny fam ct act
Alcoholic Bever. & Ctrl.	ny al bev	General Associations	ny gen assn
Alternative County Gov.	ny alt co gov	General Business	ny gen bus
Arts & Cultural Affairs	ny art cult affr	General City	ny gen city
Banking	ny bank	General Construction	ny gen const
Benevolent Orders	ny be ord	General Municipal	ny gen mun
Business Corporations	ny bus corp	General Obligations	ny gen oblig
Canal	ny canal	Highway	ny high
Civil Practice Law & Rules	ny cplr	Indian	ny indian
Civil Rights	ny civ rts	Insurance	ny ins
Civil Service	ny civ serv	Judiciary	ny jud
Cooperative Corporat.	ny co-op corp	Labor	ny labor
Correction	ny correc	Legislative	ny legis
County	ny county	Lien	ny lien
Court of Claims Act	ny ct c act	Local Finance	ny loc fin
Criminal Procedure	ny cpl	Mental Hygiene	ny men hyg
Debtor and Creditor	ny dr cr	Military	ny mil
Domestic Relations	ny dom rel	Multiple Dwelling	ny mult d
Economic Development	ny econ dev	Multiple Residence	ny mult r
Education	ny educ	Municipal Home Rule	ny mun h r
Election	ny elec	Navigation	ny nav
Eminent Domain Procedure Law	ny edpl	New York City Civil Court Act	ny city civ ct act
Employer's Liability	ny em liab	New York City Criminal Court Act	ny city crim ct act
Energy	ny energy	Not-for-Profit Corp. Law	ny n-pcl
Environmental Conservation Law	ny ecl	Parks, Recreation and Historic Preservat. Law	ny prhpl

NEW YORK (Cont.)

Example: `lexstat ny real p 339-j`

Partnership	ny partn	State Administrative Procedure Act	ny st adm p act
Penal	ny penal	State Finance	ny st fin
Personal Property	ny pers p	State Printing and Public Documents	ny st print
Private Housing Fin.	ny priv hous fin	Statute of Local Government	ny stat loc gov
Public Authorities	ny pub a	Surrogate's Court Procedure Act	ny scpa
Public Building	ny pub b	Tax	ny tax
Public Health	ny pub health	Town	ny town
Public Housing	ny pub house	Transportation	ny trans
Public Lands	ny pub l	Transportation Corps.	ny trans corp
Public Officers	ny pub o	Uniform City Court Act	ny ucca
Public Service	ny pub ser	Uniform Commercial Code	ny ucc
Racing, Pari-Mutual Wagering and Breed.	ny racing wagering	Uniform District Court Act	ny udca
Railroad	ny rr	Uniform Justice Court Act	ny ujca
Rapid Transit	ny rap tr	Vehical and Traffic	ny veh tr
Real Property	ny real p	Village	ny vill
Real Property Actions & Proceedings	ny rpapl	Volunteer Ambulance Workers' Benefits	ny vol amb work ben
Real Property Tax Law	ny rptl	Volunteer Firefighters' Benefits	ny vol fire ben
Religious Corporations	ny relig corp	Workers Compensation	ny work comp
Retirement and Social Security	ny retire soc sec	Unconsolidated	ny unconsol ch x § x
Rural Electric Cooperat.	ny rur el co-op		
Second Class Cities	ny sec cl cities		
Social Services	ny soc serv		
Soil & Water Conserv. Districts	ny soil w con dist		
State	ny state		

TEXAS

Example: `lexstat tx fam 1.01`

Code Name	LEXSTAT Format	Code Name	LEXSTAT Format
Agriculture	tx agric	Health & Safety	tx health & safety
Alcoholic Beverage	tx alco bev	Human Resources	tx hum res
Business and Commerce	tx bus com	Insurance	tx ins art
Business Corporation Act	tx bus corp act art	Local Government	tx local gov
Civil Practice & Remed.	tx civ prac rem	Natural Resources	tx nat res
Code of Criminal Proc.	tx code crim proc art	Parks and Wildlife	tx parks wild
Education	tx educ	Penal	tx penal
Election	tx elec	Probate	tx prob
Family	tx fam	Property	tx prop
Government	tx gov	Tax	tx tax
		Water	tx wat
		Revised Civil Statutes	tx rev civ stat

Appendix D

Law Reviews On LEXIS®-NEXIS®

Here are the law reviews available on LEXIS-NEXIS. All are to be found in the *LAWREV* library. Nearly all of journals published by law schools, but not all of the commercially-published law journals, are included in the *ALLREV* file (*LAWREV* library); those that are not should be accessed in the single-journal file listed below.

The √ symbol after a journal's name means that the publication was added to the *LAWREV* library in 1993 or later.

All journals can be accessed by use of the LEXSEE® feature, using the abbreviation shown in the table. Thus to see the article beginning on p. 1679 of vol. 100 of the *Yale Law Journal*, type:

```
lexsee 100 yale l j 1679
```

Journal Title	Filename	LEXSEE Format	Beginning Year	Beginning Volume
ADMINISTRATIVE LAW JOURNAL √	ADMLJ	ADMIN L J AM U	1993	7
AIR FORCE LAW REVIEW √	AIRFLR	A F L REV	1994	38
AKRON LAW REVIEW √	AKRONL	AKRON L REV	1994	28
ALABAMA LAW REVIEW √	ALALR	ALA L REV	1993	45
ALBANY LAW JOURNAL OF SCIENCE & TECHNOLOGY √	ALJST	ALB L J SCI & TECH	1994	4
ALBANY LAW REVIEW √	ALBLR	ALB L REV	1994	57
AMERICAN BANKRUPTCY INSTITUTE JOURNAL √	ABIJ	ABI JNL LEXIS	1994	--
AMERICAN BANKRUPTCY INSTITUTE LAW REVIEW √	ABILR	AM BANKR INST	1993	--
AMERICAN BANKRUPTCY LAW JOURNAL	AMBLJ	AM BANK L J	1982	56
AMERICAN JOURNAL OF CRIMINAL LAW √	AJCRIL	AM J CRIM L	1995	22
AMERICAN JOURNAL OF INTERNATIONAL LAW	AJIL	AJIL	1980	74
AMERICAN JOURNAL OF LAW & MEDICINE	LAWMED	AM JL MED	1982	7
AMERICAN JOURNAL OF TAX POLICY √	AMJTP	AM J OF TAX POL'Y	1994	11
AMERICAN UNIVERSITY JOURNAL OF GENDER & THE LAW √	AUJGL	AM U J GENDER & LAW	1995	3
AMERICAN UNIVERSITY JOURNAL OF INTERNATIONAL LAW AND POLICY √	AUJILP	AM U J INT'L & POL'Y	1993	8

Journal Title	Filename	LEXSEE Format	Beginning Year	Beginning Volume
AMERICAN UNIVERSITY LAW REVIEW	AMERU	AM U L REV	1982	32
ARIZONA JOURNAL OF INTERNATIONAL AND COMPARATIVE LAW √	AJICL	ARIZ J INT'L & COMP LAW	1994	11
ARIZONA LAW REVIEW √	AZLR	ARIZ L REV	1993	35
ARIZONA STATE LAW JOURNAL √	ASLJ	ARIZ ST L J	1994	26
ARKANSAS LAW REVIEW √	ARKLR	ARK L REV	1993	46
ASIAN LAW JOURNAL √	ASIAN	ASIAN L J	1995	2
BANKRUPTCY DEVELOPMENTS JOURNAL	BNKDEV	BANK DEV J	1984	1
BAYLOR LAW REVIEW √	BAYLOR	BAYLOR L REV	1993	45
BOSTON COLLEGE ENV. AFFAIRS LAW REVIEW	ENVAFF	BC ENVTL AFF L REV	1982	10
BOSTON COLLEGE INTERNATIONAL & COMPARATIVE LAW REVIEW √	BSNTIC	B C INT'L & COMP L REV	1996	19
BOSTON COLLEGE THIRD WORLD LAW JOURNAL √	BCTWLJ	BC THIRD WORLD L J	1996	16
BOSTON COLLEGE LAW REVIEW √	BCLR	BC L REV	1993	34
BOSTON UNIVERSITY INTERNATIONAL LAW JOURNAL √	BUILJ	BU INT'L L J	1994	12
BOSTON UNIVERSITY JOURNAL OF SCIENCE AND TECHNOLOGY LAW √	BUJSTL	BU J SCI & TECH L	1995	1
BOSTON UNIVERSITY LAW REVIEW	BOSULR	B UL REV	1982	62
BOSTON UNIVERSITY PUBLIC INTEREST LAW JOURNAL √	BUPILJ	BU PUB INT L J	1993	3
BRIGHAM YOUNG UNIVERSITY LAW REVIEW √	BYULR	BYUL REV	1993	1993
BROOKLYN LAW REVIEW	BRKLR	BR L REV	1982	49
BROOKLYN JOURNAL OF INTERNATIONAL LAW √	BJINTL	BROOKLYN J INT'L L	1995	21
BUFFALO LAW REVIEW √	BUFFLR	BUFFALO L REV	1994	42
BUSINESS LAWYER, THE √	BUSLAW	BUS LAW	1981	37
CALIFORNIA LAW REVIEW	CALLR	CAL L REV	1982	70
CALIFORNIA WESTERN INTERNATIONAL LAW JOURNAL √	CAWILJ	CAL W INT'L L J	1994	25
CALIFORNIA WESTERN LAW REVIEW √	CAWEST	CAL W L REV	1993	31
CAMPBELL LAW REVIEW √	CAMPLR	CAMPBELL L REV	1993	16
CANADA - U.S. LAW JOURNAL √	CUSLJ	CAN - US L J	1994	20
CAPITAL UNIVERSITY LAW REVIEW √	CAPULR	CAP U L REV	1993	25
CARDOZO ARTS & ENTERTAINMENT LAW JOURNAL √	CAELJ	CARDOZO ARTS & ENT L J	1992	11
CARDOZO LAW REVIEW √	CDZOLR	CARDOZO L REV	1993	14
CARDOZO WOMEN'S LAW JOURNAL √	CWLAWJ	CARDOZO WOMEN'S L J	1996	3
CASE WESTERN RESERVE JOURNAL OF INTERNATIONAL LAW √	CWRJIL	CASE W RES J INT'L L	1993	25

Journal Title	Filename	LEXSEE Format	Beginning Year	Beginning Volume
CASE WESTERN RESERVE LAW REVIEW	CASEWR	CASE W RES	1982	33
CATHOLIC UNIVERSITY LAW REVIEW	CATHLR	CATH UL REV	1982	32
CHICAGO-KENT LAW REVIEW	CKLR	CHI KENT L REV	1981	58
CHICAGO LEGAL FORUM √	CHIFOR	U CHI LEGAL F	1993	--
CHICANO-LATINO LAW REVIEW √	CHILAT	CHICANO-LATINO L. REV	1995	17
CLEVELAND STATE LAW REVIEW √	CSLRV	CLEV ST L REV	1993	41
CLINICAL LAW REVIEW √	CLINLR	CLINICAL L REV	1995	1
COLORADO JOURNAL OF INTERNATIONAL ENVIRONMENTAL LAW AND POLICY √	COJIEL	COLO J INT'L ENVTL L & POL'Y	1995	6
COLUMBIA BUSINESS LAW REVIEW	COLBUS	COLUM BUS L REV	1986	1
COLUMBIA HUMAN RIGHTS LAW REVIEW √	COLHRT	COLUM HUMAN RIGHTS L REV	1995	26
COLUMBIA JOURNAL OF ENVIRONMENTAL LAW √	COLJEL	COLUM J ENVTL L	1993	18
COLUMBIA JOURNAL OF LAW AND SOCIAL PROBLEMS √	CJLSP	COLUM J L & SOC PROBS	1994	28
COLUMBIA JOURNAL OF TRANS-NATIONAL LAW √	COLJTL	COLUM J TRANSNAT'L L	1995	1
COLUMBIA LAW REVIEW	COLUM	COLUM L REV	1982	82
COMPARATIVE LABOR LAW JOURNAL	COMLAB	COMP LAB L	1976	1
CONNECTICUT INSURANCE LAW JOURNAL √	CTINSL	CONN INS L J	1995	1
CONNECTICUT JOURNAL OF INTERNATIONAL LAW √	CJIL	CONN J INT'L L	1993	8
CONNECTICUT LAW REVIEW √	CONNLR	CONN L REV	1993	25
CORNELL INTERNATIONAL LAW JOURNAL √	CORINT	CORNELL INT'L L J	1993	26
CORNELL LAW REVIEW	CORLR	CORNELL L REV	1982	68
CUMBERLAND LAW REVIEW √	CUMLR	CUMB L REV	1993	24
CREIGHTON LAW REVIEW √	CRTLR	CREIGHTON L REV	1993	26
DELAWARE JOURNAL OF CORP. LAW	DELJCL	DEL J CORP L	1982	7
DENVER JOURNAL OF INTERNATIONAL LAW & POLICY √	DENINT	DENV J INT'L L & POL'Y	1995	23
DENVER UNIVERSITY LAW REVIEW √	DENLR	DENV U L REV	1993	71
DEPAUL BUSINESS LAW JOURNAL √	DBUSLJ	DEPAUL BUS L J	1993	6
DEPAUL LAW REVIEW √	DEPAUL	DEPAUL L REV	1993	43
DETROIT COLLEGE OF LAW REVIEW √	DETCLR	DET C L REV	1994	

Journal Title	Filename	LEXSEE Format	Beginning Year	Beginning Volume
DICKINSON JOURNAL OF INTERNATIONAL LAW √	DJILAW	DICK J INT'L L	1995	14
DICKINSON LAW REVIEW √	DKSNLR	DICK L REV	1993	98
DUKE ENVIRONMENTAL LAW & POLICY FORUM √	DELPF	DUKE ENV L & POL'Y F	1995	5
DUKE JOURNAL OF COMPARATIVE & INTERNATIONAL LAW √	DJCIL	DUKE J COMP & INT'L L	1993	3
DUKE JOURNAL OF GENDER LAW & POLICY √	DUKEJG	DUKE J GENDER L & POL'Y	1995	2
DUKE LAW JOURNAL	DUKELJ	DUKE L J	1982	1982
DUQUESNE LAW REVIEW √	DUQLR	DUQ L REV	1993	32
ELDER LAW JOURNAL √	ELDER	ELDER L J	1994	2
EMORY INTERNATIONAL LAW REVIEW √	EILR	EMORY INT'L L REV	1994	8
EMORY LAW JOURNAL √	EMORY	EMORY L J	V.31 #1	31
ENERGY LAW JOURNAL √	ENERLJ	ENERGY L J	1993	15
ENVIRONMENTAL LAW	ENVLAW	ENVTL L	1981	12
FEDERAL COMMUNICATIONS LAW JOURNAL	COMLAW	FED COM L J	V.34 #1	34
FLORIDA JOURNAL OF INTERNATIONAL LAW √	FLAJIL	FLA J INT'L L	1993	8
FLORIDA JOURNAL OF LAW AND PUBLIC POLICY √	JLPP	J LAW & PUB POL'Y	1993	6
FLORIDA LAW REVIEW √	FLAREV	FLA L REV	1993	45
FLORIDA STATE UNIVERSITY LAW REVIEW	FSULR	FL ST UL REV	1982	10
FOOD & DRUG LAW JOURNAL √	FADLJ	FOOD DRUG L J	1996	51
FORDHAM INTERNATIONAL LAW JOURNAL √	FILJ	FORDHAM INT'L L J	1993	16
FORDHAM IINTELLECTUAL PROPERTY, MEDIA, & ENTERTAINMENT LAW JOURNAL √	IPMELJ	FORDHAM I P, MEDIA, & ENT L J	1995	6
FORDHAM LAW REVIEW	FORDLR	FORDHAM L REV	1982	51
FORDHAM URBAN LAW JOURNAL √	FULJ	FORDHAM URB L J	1993	20
GEORGETOWN LAW JOURNAL	GEOLJ	GEO L J	1982	71
GEORGE MASON LAW REVIEW √	GMLR	GEO MASON L REV	1994	1
GEORGIA LAW REVIEW	GALREV	GA L REV	1982	17
GEO. WASH. JOURNAL INTERNATIONAL LAW & ECON. √	GWJILE	GW J INT'L L & ECON	1992	26
GEO. WASH. LAW REVIEW	GWLR	GEO WASH L REV	1982	51
GEORGIA JOURNAL OF INTERNATIONAL & COMPARATIVE LAW √	GAJICL	GA J INT'L & COMP L	1994	24
GOLDEN GATE UNIVERSITY LAW REVIEW √	GGLR	GOLDEN GATE U L REV	1993	23

Journal Title	Filename	LEXSEE Format	Beginning Year	Beginning Volume
GONZAGA LAW REVIEW √	GONLR	GONZ L REV	1995	30
HARVARD BLACKLETTER JOURNAL √	HRVBLJ	HARV BLACK-LETTER J	1993	10
HARVARD CIVIL RIGHTS/CIVIL LIBERTIES LAW REVIEW √	HRVCIV	HARV CR-CLR REV	1993	28
HARVARD ENVIRONMENTAL LAW REVIEW √	HRVELR	HARV ENVTL L REV	1994	18
HARVARD HUMAN RIGHTS JOURNAL √	HRVHRJ	HARV HM RTS J	1993	7
HARVARD INTERNATIONAL LAW JOURNAL √	HRVILJ	HARV INT'L L J	1993	34
HARVARD JOURNAL OF LAW & TECHNOLOGY	HRVTEC	HARV J LAW AND TEC	1988	1
HARVARD JOURNAL ON LEGISLATION √	HRVJL	HARV J ON LEGIS	1993	31
HARVARD WOMEN'S LAW JOURNAL √	HRVWLJ	HARV WOMEN'S L J	1993	16
HARVARD LAW REVIEW	HARV	HARV L REV	1982	96
HASTINGS LAW JOURNAL	HASTLJ	HAST L J	1982	34
HEALTH MATRIX √	HEAMAT	HEALTH MATRIX	1994	4
HOFSTRA LABOR LAW JOURNAL √	HLABLJ	HOFSTRA LAB L J	1993	11
HOFSTRA LAW REVIEW	HOFSLR	HOFSTRA L R	1982	11
HONG KONG LAW JOURNAL √	HKLJNL	HONG KONG L J	1995	25
HOUSTON JOURNAL OF INTERNATIONAL LAW √	HOUJIL	HOUS J INT'L L	1993	16
HOUSTON LAW REVIEW √	HOULR	HOUS L REV	1993	30
HOWARD LAW JOURNAL	HOWARD	HOW L J	V.25 #1	25
IDAHO LAW REVIEW √	IDALR	IDAHO L REV	1993	30
ILSA JOURNAL OF INTERNATIONAL & COMPARATIVE LAW √	ILSAIC	ILSA J INT'L & COMP L	1995	2
INDIANA JOURNAL OF GLOBAL LEGAL STUDIES √	INJGLS	IND J GLOBAL LEG STUD	1995	3
INDIANA LAW JOURNAL	INDLJ	IND L J	1982	58
INTERNATIONAL LEGAL MATERIALS √	ILM	ILM	1980	19
IOWA LAW REVIEW	IOWALR	IOWA L REV	1982	68
JOHN MARSHALL LAW REVIEW √	JMLRV	J MARSHALL L REV	1994	27
JOURNAL OF AIR LAW & COMMERCE √	JALC	J AIR L & COM	1994	59
JOURNAL OF ARTS & ENTERTAINMENT LAW √	JAELAW	J ART & ENT LAW	1994	5
JOURNAL OF CONT. HEALTH LAW & POLICY √	JCHLP	J CONTEMP H L & POL'Y	1993	9
JOURNAL OF CONTEMPORARY LAW √	JNLCON	J CONTEMP L	1993	19
JOURNAL OF CORPORATION LAW √	JCORPL	IOWA J CORP L	1993	18
JOURNAL OF CRIMINAL LAW & CRIMINOLOGY	JLCRIM	J CRIM L	1982	73
JOURNAL OF DISPUTE RESOLUTION √	JDISPR	J DISP RESOL	1995	1995

Journal Title	Filename	LEXSEE Format	Beginning Year	Beginning Volume
JOURNAL OF ENVIRONMENTAL LAW & LITIGATION √	JENV	J ENVTL L & LITIG	1995	10
JOURNAL OF INTELLECTUAL PROPERTY LAW √	JIPL	J INTELL PROP L	1994	1
JOURNAL OF INTERNATIONAL LAW & BUSINESS √	INTBUS	J INTL L BUS	1982	4
JOURNAL OF INTERNATIONAL LAW & PRACTICE √	DEJILP	D C L J INT'L & PRAC	1994	3
JOURNAL OF INTERNATIONAL LEGAL STUDIES √	JINTLS	J INT'L LEGAL STUD	1995	1
JOURNAL OF INTERNATIONAL TAXATION √	JITAX	JITAX	1990	1
JOURNAL OF LAW & COMMERCE √	JLCOMM	J L & COMM	1993	13
JOURNAL OF LAW & ECONOMICS √	JLAWEC	J OF L & ECON	1994	37
JOURNAL OF LAW & HEALTH √	JLAWH	J L & HEALTH	1993	8
JOURNAL OF LAW & POLICY √	JLPOL	J L & POL'Y	1994	2
JOURNAL OF LAW & POLITICS √	JLAWP	J L & POLI-TICS	1996	7
JOURNAL OF LAW & TECHNOLOGY (**Note:** this journal is no longer published, but the file will remain online until further notice)	LAWTEC	JL TECH	1986	1
JOURNAL OF THE LEGAL PROFESSION √	JLPROF	J LEGAL PROF	1995	19
JOURNAL OF LEGAL STUDIES √	JLGLST	J OF LEG STUD	1994	23
JOURNAL OF LEGISLATION √	JLEG	J LGIS	1993	19
JOURNAL OF PHARMACY LAW √	JPHARM	J PHARMACY & LAW	1993	2
JOURNAL OF PARTNERSHIP TAXATION √	JPTAX	J P TAX	1985	1
JOURNAL OF REAL ESTATE & TAXATION √	JRETAX	JRETAX	1985	12
JOURNAL OF TAXATION √	JTAX	JTAX	1985	62
KANSAS JOURNAL OF LAW & PUBLIC POLICY √	KSJPP	KAN J L & PUB POL'Y	1995	4
KENTUCKY LAW JOURNAL	KYLAWJ	KY L J	1983	71
LAND AND WATER LAW REVIEW √	LWLREV	LAND & WATER L REV	1995	30
LAW & INEQUALITY: JOURNAL OF THEORY AND PRACTICE √	LAWINQ	LAW & INEQ J	1993	12
LAW & PSYCHOLOGY REVIEW √	LAWPSY	LAW & PSY-CHOL. REV	1994	18
LAW LIBRARY JOURNAL √	LLIBJ	LAW LIBR J	1990	82
LOUISIANA LAW REVIEW	LOULR	LA L REV	1982	43
LOYOLA OF LOS ANGELES ENTERTAINMENT LAW JOURNAL √	LLAELJ	LOY LA ENT L J	1995	15
LOYOLA OF LOS ANGELES INTERNATIONAL & COMPARATIVE LAW JOURNAL	LICLJ	LOY L A INT'L & COMP L J	1993	16
LOYOLA OF LOS ANGELES LAW REVIEW √	LLALR	LOY LA L REV	1993	26

Journal Title	Filename	LEXSEE Format	Beginning Year	Beginning Volume
LOYOLA UNIVERSITY CHICAGO LAW JOURNAL √	LUCLJ	LOY U CHI L J	1993	25
MAINE LAW REVIEW √	MELREV	ME L REV	1993	46
MARQUETTE LAW REVIEW √	MARLR	MARQ L REV	1992	75
MARQUETTE SPORTS LAW JOURNAL √	MSPLJ	MARQ SPORTS L J	1993	3
MARYLAND JOURNAL OF CONTEMPORARY LEGAL ISSUES √	MDJCLI	MD J CONTMEP L ISSUES	1994	6
MARYLAND JOURNAL OF INTERNATIONAL LAW & TRADE √	MJIT	MD J INT'L L & TRADE	1993	17
MARYLAND LAW REVIEW	MDLREV	MD L REV	1982	42
MCGILL LAW JOURNAL √	MCGILL	MCGILL J L	1995	40
MEMPHIS STATE UNIVERSITY LAW REVIEW √	MSULR	MEM ST U L REV	1983	24
MERCER LAW REVIEW √	MERCER	MERCER L REV	1993	44
MICHIGAN JOURNAL OF GENDER & LAW √	MJGLAW	MICH J GEN-DER & L	1994	2
MICHIGAN JOURNAL OF INTERNATIONAL LAW √	MJIL	MICH J INT'L L	1993	14
MICHIGAN JOURNAL OF LAW REFORM	MIJLR	U MICH J L REF	1982	15
MICHIGAN JOURNAL OF RACE & LAW √	MIJRL	MICH J RACE & L	1996	1
MICHIGAN LAW REVIEW	MICHLR	MICH L REV	1982	81
MICHIGAN TELECOMMUNICATIONS AND TECHNOLOGY LAW REVIEW √	MTTLR	MICH TEL TECH L REV	1995	95
MILITARY LAW REVIEW	MLR	MIL L REV	1982	98
MINNESOTA JOURNAL OF GLOBAL TRADE √	MJGT	MINN J GLOBAL TRADE	1993	3
MINNESOTA LAW REVIEW	MINNLR	MINN L REV	1982	67
MISSISSIPPI LAW JOURNAL √	UMSLJ	MISS L J	1993	62
MISSOURI LAW REVIEW √	UMOLR	MO L REV	1993	58
MISSOURI (KC) LAW REVIEW √	UMKCLR	UMKC L REV	1993	61
NAVAL LAW REVIEW √	NAVYLR	NAVAL L REV	1995	42
NEBRASKA LAW REVIEW √	UNELR	NEB L REV	1992	71
NEW ENGLAND JOURNAL ON CRIMINAL & CIVIL CONFINEMENT √	NEJCCC	N E J ON CRIM & CIV C	1993	20
NEW ENGLAND LAW REVIEW √	NENGLR	NEW ENG L REV	1993	27
NEW MEXICO LAW REVIEW √	UNMLR	N M L REV	1992	23
NEW YORK LAW SCHOOL JOURNAL OF HUMAN RIGHTS √	NYJHR	NYL SCH J HUM RTS	1993	11
NEW YORK LAW SCHOOL OF INTERNATIONAL & COMPARATIVE LAW JOURNAL √	NYJICL	NYL SCH J INT'L & COMP L	1995	15
NEW YORK LAW SCHOOL LAW REVIEW √	NYLSLR	NYL SCH L REV	1992	37
NEW YORK UNIVERSITY LAW REVIEW	NYULR	NYUL REV	1982	57

Journal Title	Filename	LEXSEE Format	Beginning Year	Beginning Volume
NEW YORK UNIVERSITY TAX LAW REVIEW	NYUTAX	TAX L REV	1982	37
NORTH CAROLINA CENTRAL LAW JOURNAL √	NCCLJ	NC CENT L J	1993	20
N.C. JOURNAL OF INTERNATIONAL LAW/COMM. REG √	NCJICR	N/C J INT'L L & COMM REG	1993	18
NORTH CAROLINA LAW REVIEW	NCLR	NCL REV	1982	61
NORTH DAKOTA LAW REVIEW √	NDAKLR	N DAK L REV	1993	69
NORTHERN ILLINOIS UNIVERSITY LAW REVIEW √	NIULR	N ILL U L REV	1994	14
NORTHERN KENTUCKY LAW REVIEW	NKYLR	N KY L REV	1993	20
NORTHWESTERN UNIVERSITY LAW REVIEW	NWULR	NW U L REV	1985	80
NOTRE DAME JOURNAL OF LEGAL ETHICS & PUBLIC POLICY √	NDJELP	ND J L ETHICS & PUB POL'Y	1996	10
NOTRE DAME LAW REVIEW	NOTRE	NOTRE DAME L REV	1982	58
NOVA LAW REVIEW √	NOVALR	NOVA L REV	1995	19
OHIO NORTHERN UNIVERSITY LAW REVIEW √	ONLR	OHIO NU L REV	1993	19
OHIO STATE JOURNAL ON DISPUTE RESOLUTION √	OHSJDR	OHIO ST J ON DISP RESOL	1995	10
OHIO STATE LAW JOURNAL	OHSTLJ	OH ST L J	1982	43
OKLAHOMA LAW REVIEW √	OKLR	OKLA L REV	1992	45
OREGON LAW REVIEW √	UOLR	OR L REV	1993	72
PACE ENVIRONMENTAL LAW REVIEW √	PELR	PACE ENVTL L REV	1993	10
PACE INTERNATIONAL LAW REVIEW √	PILR	PACE INT'L L REV	1993	6
PACE LAW REVIEW √	PACELR	PACE L REV	1993	13
PACIFIC LAW JOURNAL √	PACLJ	PAC L J	1995	26
PACIFIC RIM LAW & POLICY JOURNAL √	PRLPJ	PAC RIM L & POL'Y	1996	5
PENNSYLVANIA LAW REVIEW	UPENN	U PA L REV	1982	131
PEPPERDINE LAW REVIEW √	PEPPLR	PEPP L REV	1993	20
PUGET SOUND LAW REVIEW √	PSDLR	PUGET SOUND L REV	1993	16
QUINNIPIAC LAW REVIEW (QLR) √	QUINLR	QUINNIPAC L REV	1994	14
REVIEW OF LITIGATION √	REVLIT	REV LITIG	1994	13
REVISTA JURIDICA UNIVERSIDAD DE PUERTO RICO √	RJUDPR	REV JUR U P R	1996	65
RICHMOND JOURNAL OF LAW & TECHNOLOGY √	RJOLT	RICH J L & TECH	1995	1
RUTGERS COMPUTER & TECHNOLOGY LAW JOURNAL √	RCTLJ	RUTGERS COMPUTER & TECH L J	1995	20
RUTGERS LAW JOURNAL √	RUTLJ	RUTGERS L J	1994	25
RUTGERS LAW REVIEW √	RUTLR	RUTGERS L REV	1993	45

Journal Title	Filename	LEXSEE Format	Beginning Year	Beginning Volume
SAN DIEGO JUSTICE JOURNAL √	SDJL	SAN DIEGO JUSTICE J	1994	1
SAN DIEGO LAW REVIEW √	SDLREV	SAN DIEGO L REV	1993	30
SANTA CLARA COMPUTER & HIGH TECHNOLOGY LAW JOURNAL √	CHTLJ	COMPUTER & HIGH TECH L J	1994	10
SANTA CLARA LAW REVIEW √	SCLREV	SANTA CLARA L REV	1994	34
SETON HALL CONSTITUTIONAL LAW JOURNAL √	SHCLJ	SETON HALL CONST L J	1994	5
SETON HALL JOURNAL OF SPORT LAW √	SHJSL	SETON HALL J SPORT	1993	4
SETON HALL LAW REVIEW √	SHLR	SETON HALL L REV	1993	23
SETON HALL LEGISLATIVE JOURNAL √	SHLEGJ	SETON HALL LEGIS J	1993	18
SOUTH CAROLINA ENVIRONMENTAL LAW JOURNAL √	SCELJ	SC ENVTL L J	1993	3
SOUTH CAROLINA LAW REVIEW √	SCLR	S C L REV	1993	44
SOUTH DAKOTA LAW REVIEW √	SDAKLR	S D L REV	1993	38
SOUTH TEXAS LAW REVIEW √	STEXLR	S TEX L REV	1993	35
SOUTHERN CALIFORNIA INTERDISCIPLINARY LAW JOURNAL √	SCILJ	S CAL INTER-DIS L J	1993	3
SOUTHERN CALIFORNIA REVIEW OF LAW & WOMEN'S STUDIES √	SCRLWS	S CAL REV L & WOMEN'S STUD	1994	3
SOUTHERN CAL LAW REVIEW	SOCALR	S CA LR	1982	55
SOUTHERN ILLINOIS LAW JOURNAL √	SILJ	S ILL U L J	1993	17
SOUTHERN UNIVERSITY LAW REVIEW √	SOLREV	SUL REV	1995	22
SOUTHWESTERN JOURNAL OF LAW & TRADE IN THE AMERICAS √	STRADE	SW J OF L & TRADE AM	1994	1
SOUTHERN METHODIST UNIVERSITY LAW REVIEW	SMULR	SMU L REV	1993	47
SOUTHWESTERN UNIVERSITY LAW REVIEW √	SOULR	SW U L REV	1994	24
THE SPORTS LAWYERS JOURNAL √	SLAWJ	SPORTS LAW J	1995	2
ST JOHN'S JOURNAL OF LEGAL COMMENTARY √	STJJLC	ST JOHN'S J L COMM	1993	8
ST. JOHN'S LAW REVIEW √	STJOHN	ST JOHN'S L REV	1993	67
ST. LOUIS UNIVERSITY LAW JOURNAL √	STULJ	ST. LOUIS L J	1993	37
ST LOUIS UNIVERSITY PUBLIC LAW REVIEW √	STUPLR	ST LOUIS U PUB L REV	1994	13
ST. LOUIS-WARSAW TRANSATLANTIC LAW JOURNAL √	STLWT	ST. LOUIS-WARSAW TRANS'L	1995	1995
ST. MARY'S LAW JOURNAL √	STMLJ	ST. MARY'S L J	1993	24
ST. THOMAS LAW REVIEW √	STTHLR	ST THOMAS L REV	1993	6

Journal Title	Filename	LEXSEE Format	Beginning Year	Beginning Volume
STANFORD ENVIRONMENTAL LAW JOURNAL √	SELJ	STAN ENVTL L J	1993	12
STANFORD JOURNAL OF INTERNATIONAL LAW √	STJIL	STAN J INT'L L	1993	29
STANFORD JOURNAL OF LAW, BUSI-NESS & FINANCE √	SJLBF	STAN J L BUS & FIN	1995	1
STANFORD LAW & POLICY REVIEW √	SLPR	STAN L & POL'Y REV	1994	5
STANFORD LAW REVIEW	STANLR	STAN L REV	1982	35
STETSON LAW REVIEW √	STETLR	STETSON LAW REV	1993	23
SUFFOLK TRANSNATIONAL LAW JOURNAL √	STRANS	SUFFOLK TRANSNAT'L L J	1994	27
SUFFOLK LAW REVIEW √	SUFLR	SUFFOLK U L REV	1992	26
SYRACUSE JOURNAL OF INTERNATIONAL LAW & COMMERCE √	SJILC	SYRACUSE J INT'L L & COM	1993	18
SYRACUSE LAW REVIEW √	SYLR	SYRACUSE L REV	1992	43
TEMPLE ENVIRONMENTAL LAW & TECHNOLOGY LAW JOURNAL √	TELTJ	TEMP ENVTL L & TECH J	1994	13
TEMPLE INTERNATIONAL & COMPARATIVE LAW JOURNAL √	TICLJ	TEMP INT'L & COMP L J	1993	7
TEMPLE LAW REVIEW √	TEMPLE	TEMPLE L REV	1993	66
TEMPLE POLITICAL & CIVIL RIGHTS LAW REVIEW √	TPCRLR	TEMPLE POL & CIV RTS L R	1993	21
TEXAS INTERNATIONAL LAW JOURNAL √	TEXILJ	TEX INT'L L J	1994	29
TEXAS INTELLECTUAL PROPERTY LAW JOURNAL √	TXIPLJ	TEX INTELL PROP L J	1992	1
TEXAS LAW REVIEW	TEXLR	TEX L REV	1983	62
TEXAS TECH LAW REVIEW √	TTLR	TEX TECH L REV	1993	24
TEXAS WESLEYAN LAW REVIEW √	TWLREV	TEX WES-LEYAN L REV	1995	2
THOMAS M COOLEY LAW REVIEW √	TMCLR	T M COOLEY L REV	1994	11
TRANSPORTATION LAW JOURNAL	TRANLJ	TRANS L J	1982	12
TULANE ENVIRONMENTAL LAW JOURNAL √	TELJ	TUL ENVTL L J	1992	6
TULANE JOURNAL OF INTERNATIONAL & COMPARATIVE LAW √	TJICL	TUL J INT'L & COMP L	1995	3
TULANE LAW REVIEW	TULLR	TUL L R	1982	57
TULANE MARITIME LAW JOURNAL	MARLAW	MAR LAW	1980	5
TULSA JOURNAL OF COMPARATIVE & INTERNATIONAL LAW √	TJ COMP	TULSA J COMP & INT'L L	1994	2
TULSA LAW JOURNAL √	TULSLJ	TULSA L J	1993	29
U.C. DAVIS JOURNAL OF INTERNATIONAL LAW & POLICY √	UCDAVI	U C DAVIS J INT'L L & POL'Y	1995	1

Journal Title	Filename	LEXSEE Format	Beginning Year	Beginning Volume
U.C. DAVIS LAW REVIEW √	UCDAV	U C DAVIS L REV	1993	26
UCLA JOURNAL OF ENVIRONMENTAL LAW & POLICY √	UCJELP	UCLA J ENVTL L & POL'Y	1995	13
UCLA LAW REVIEW	UCLALR	UCLA L REV	1982	30
UCLA PACIFIC BASIN LAW JOURNAL √	UCLAPB	UCLA PAC BASIN L J	1993	12
UCLA WOMEN'S LAW JOURNAL √	UCLAWJ	UCLA WOMEN'S L J	1993	4
UNITED STATES-MEXICO LAW JOURNAL √	USMLJ	US MEXICO L J	1993	1
UNIVERSITY OF ARKANSAS AT LITTLE ROCK LAW JOURNAL √	UALRLJ	U ARK LIT-TLE ROCK L J	1994	16
UNIVERSITY OF BALTIMORE INTELLECTUAL PROPERTY LAW JOURNAL √	UBIPJ	U BALT INTELL PROP J	1993	2
UNIVERSITY OF BALTIMORE LAW REVIEW √	BALTLR	U BALT L REV	1992	21
UNIVERSITY OF CHICAGO LAW REVIEW	UCHIC	U CHI L REV	1982	49
UNIVERSITY OF CHICAGO LAW SCHOOL ROUNDTABLE √	CLSRT	U CHI L SCH	1994	1
UNIVERSITY OF CINCINNATI LAW REVIEW	UCINLR	U CIN L REV	1982	51
UNIVERSITY OF COLORADO LAW REVIEW √	UCLR	U COLO L REV	1992	64
UNIVERSITY OF DAYTON LAW REVIEW √	DAYTON	DAYTON L REV	1993	18
UNIVERSITY OF DETROIT MERCY √	UDMLR	U DET MERCY L REV	1994	71
UNIVERSITY OF HAWAII LAW REVIEW √	HAWLR	U HAWAII L REV	1992	14
UNIVERSITY OF ILLINOIS LAW REVIEW	ILLREV	U ILL L REV	1982	1982
UNIVERSITY OF KANSAS LAW REVIEW √	UKLR	KAN L REV	1992	41
UNIVERSITY OF LOUISVILLE JOURNAL OF FAMILY LAW √	ULJFL	U OF LOUIS-VILLE J OF FAM L	1994	33
UNIVERSITY OF MIAMI ENTERTAINMENT & SPORTS LAW REVIEW √	UMESLR	U MIAMI ENT & SPORTS L REV	1994	10
UNIVERSITY OF MIAMI INTER-AMERICAN LAW REVIEW √	UMINT	U MIAMI INTER-AM L REV	1994	26
UNIVERSITY OF MIAMI LAW REVIEW	UMIALR	U MIAMI L REV	1981	36
UNIVERSITY OF PENNSYLVANIA JOURNAL OF INTERNATIONAL BUSINESS LAW √	JIBUSL	U PA J INT'L BUS L	1993	14
UNIVERSITY OF PITTSBURGH LAW REVIEW	PITTLR	U PITT L REV	1982	44
UNIVERSITY OF RICHMOND LAW REVIEW √	URLR	U RICH L REV	1993	28

Journal Title	Filename	LEXSEE Format	Beginning Year	Beginning Volume
UNIVERSITY OF SAN FRANCISCO LAW REVIEW √	USFLR	U SF L REV	1994	291
UNIVERSITY OF TENNESSEE LAW REVIEW	TENLR	TENN L REV	1982	50
UNIVERSITY OF TOLEDO LAW REVIEW √	UTLR	U TOL L REV	1992	24
UTAH LAW REIVEW	UTAHLR	UTAH L REV	1993	--
VALPARAISO UNIVERSITY LAW REVIEW √	VALULR	VAL U L REV	1993	28
VANDERBILT JOURNAL OF TRANSNATIONAL LAW √	VJTL	VAND J TRANSNAT'L L	1994	27
VANDERBILT LAW REVIEW	VANDLR	VAND L REV	1982	35
VILLANOVA ENVIRONMENTAL LAW JOURNAL √	VELJ	VILL ENVTL L J	1993	4
VILLANOVA SPORTS & ENTERTAINMENT LAW FORUM √	VSELF	VILL SPORTS & ENT L FORUM	1995	2
VILLANOVA LAW REVIEW √	VILLR	VILL L REV	1993	38
VIRGINIA ENVIRONMENTAL LAW JOURNAL √	VAELJ	VA ENVTL L J	1993	33
VIRGINIA JOURNAL OF INTERNATIONAL LAW √	VAJIL	VA J INT'L L	1993	33
VIRGINIA JOURNAL OF SOCIAL POLICY & THE LAW √	VAJSPL	VAJ SOC POL'Y & L	1994	2
VIRGINIA LAW REVIEW	UVA	VA L REV	1982	28
VIRGINIA TAX REVIEW	UVATAX	VA TAX REV	1981	1
WAKE FOREST LAW REVIEW √	WAKELR	WAKE FOR-EST L REV	1993	28
WASHBURN LAW JOURNAL √	WASHLJ	WASHBURN LJ	1995	35
WASHINGTON & LEE LAW REVIEW	WASLEE	WASH & LEE L REV	1992	49
WASHINGTON LAW QUARTERLY	WASHLQ	WASH U L Q	1993	71
WASHINGTON LAW REVIEW	WASHLR	WA L REV	1982	58
WASHINGTON UNIVERSITY JOURNAL OF URBAN & CONTEMPORARY LAW √	WUJUCL	WASH U J URB & CON-TEMP L	1995	48
WAYNE LAW REVIEW √	WAYNE	WAYNE L REV	1994	40
WEST VIRGINIA LAW REVIEW √	WVLR	W VA L REV	1994	96
WESTERN NEW ENGLAND LAW REVIEW √	WNELR	W NEW ENG L REV	1994	16
WESTERN STATE UNIVERSITY LAW REVIEW √	WSULR	W ST U L REV	1993	21
WHITTIER LAW REVIEW √	WHITLR	WHITTIER L REV	1993	14
WIDENER JOURNAL OF PUBLIC LAW √	WIDJPL	WIDENER J PUBLIC L	1995	4
WILLAMETTE LAW REVIEW √	WILLLR	WILLAMETTE L REV	1994	30
WILLIAM & MARY BILL OF RIGHTS JOURNAL √	WMBRJ	WM & MARY BILL OF RTS J	1993	2

Journal Title	Filename	LEXSEE Format	Beginning Year	Beginning Volume
WILLIAM & MARY LAW REVIEW	WMMARY	WM AND MARY L REV	1982	24
WILLIAM MITCHELL LAW REVIEW √	WMLREV	WM MITCH-ELL L REV	1993	19
WISCONSIN ENVIRONMENTAL LAW JOURNAL √	WELJ	WIS ENVTL L J	1994	1
WISCONSIN INTERNATIONAL LAW JOURNAL √	WISILJ	WIS INT'L L J	1993	12
WISCONSIN WOMEN'S LAW JOURNAL √	WIWLJ	WIS WOMEN'S L J	1995	10
WISCONSIN LAW REVIEW	WISLR	WIS L REV	1982	1982
YALE JOURNAL OF LAW & FEMINISM √	YALFEM	YALE J L & FEMINISM	1995	7
YALE JOURNAL OF LAW & THE HUMANITIES √	YJLHUM	YALE J L & HUMAN	1995	7
YALE JOURNAL ON REGULATION	YALEJR	YALE JR	1983	1
YALE LAW JOURNAL	YALE	YALE L J	1982	92

Cases on LEXIS®-NEXIS®

Appendix E-1 shows the LEXIS service's coverage of federal case law.

E-1
LEXIS Coverage of Federal Case Law

Name of Court	LEXIS Library & File	Description	Date Full Coverage Begins
U.S. Supreme Court	*GENFED/US*	U.S. Supreme Court Cases	1790
Combined U.S. Courts of Appeal	*GENFED/USAPP*	All federal Courts of Appeal cases in a single file	1789
Individual U.S. Courts of Appeal	*GENFED/1CIR* ; *GENFED/2CIR* ; etc.	1st Circuit cases 2nd Circuit cases etc.	1912
Combined U.S. District Courts	*GENFED/DIST*	All U.S. District Courts in a single file	1789
Individual U.S. District Courts	*GENFED/1DIST* ; *GENFED/2DIST* ; * * * *GENFED/11DIST* *GENFED/DCDIST*	Dist. Ct. cases from 1st Cir. Dist. Ct. cases from 2nd Cir. * * * Dist. Ct. cases from 11th Cir. Dist. Ct. cases from D.C. Cir.	1912

Appendix E-2 shows LEXIS's coverage of state case law.

E-2
LEXIS Coverage of State Case Law
(All files are in the MEGA Library)

State	LEXIS File	Description	Date Full Coverage Begins
Alabama	*ALA* *ALCRIM* *ALCIV* *ALAPP*	Supreme Court Court of Criminal Appeals Court of Civil Appeals Court of Appeals	1954 1969 1969 1965-69
Alaska	*ALAS* *AKAPP*	Supreme Court Court of Appeals	1959 1980
Arizona	*ARIZ* *AZAPP*	Supreme Court Court of Appeals	1898 1965
Arkansas	*ARK* *ARAPP*	Supreme Court Court of Appeals	1944 1979
California	*CAL* *CAAPP*	Supreme Court Courts of Appeals	1883 1944
Colorado	*COLO* *COAPP*	Supreme Court Court of Appeals	1864 1970
Connecticut	*CONN* *CTAPP* *CTSUPR* *CTCIR*	Supreme Court Appellate Court Superior Court & Court of Common Pleas Circuit Court	1938 1983 1961 1961-74
Delaware	*DEL* *DELCH* *DELFAM* *DESUPR*	Supreme Court Court of Chancery Family Court Superior Court	1945 1945 1979 1945
District of Columbia	*DCAPP* *DC*	Appeals Court Circuit Court	1943 1919-71
Florida	*FLA* *FLAPP*	Supreme Court District Courts of Appeals	1886 1957
Georgia	*GA* *GAAPP*	Supreme Court Court of Appeals	1937 1945
Hawaii	*HAW* *HIAPP*	Supreme Court Intermediate Court of Appeals	1959 1980
Idaho	*IDA* *IDAPP*	Supreme Court Court of Appeals	1944 1982
Illinois	*ILL* *ILAPP*	Supreme Court Appellate Court	1885 1944

E-2
LEXIS Coverage of State Case Law (Cont.)
(All files are in the MEGA Library)

State	LEXIS File	Description	Date Full Coverage Begins
Indiana	*IND* *INAPP*	Supreme Court Court of Appeals	1933 1936
Iowa	*IOWA* *IAAPP*	Supreme Court Court of Appeals	1944 1977
Kansas	*KAN* *KSAPP*	Supreme Court Court of Appeals	1945 1977
Kentucky	*KY* *KYAPP*	Supreme Court Court of Appeals	1944 1976
Louisiana	*LA* *LAAPP*	Supreme Court Court of Appeals	1887 1944
Maine	*MECTS*	Supreme Court	1965
Maryland	*MD* *MDAPP*	Court of Appeals Court of Special Appeals	1937 1967
Massachusetts	*MASS* *MAAPP*	Supreme Judicial Court Appeals Court	1899 1972
Michigan	*MICH* *MIAPP*	Supreme Court Court of Appeals	1899 1965
Minnesota	*MINN* *MNAPP*	Supreme Court Appeals Court	1898 1983
Mississippi	*MISS* *MSAPP*	Supreme Court Court of Appeals	1944 1995
Missouri	*MO* *MOAPP*	Supreme Court Court of Appeals	1924 1944
Montana	*MTCTS*	Supreme Court	1965
Nebraska	*NEB* *NEAPP*	Supreme Court Court of Appeals	1965 1992
Nevada	*NVCTS*	Supreme Court	1945
New Hampshire	*NHCTS*	Supreme Court	1965
New Jersey	*NJ* *NJSUPR* *NJMISC*	Supreme Court Superior Court Miscellaneous Courts	1899 1899 1949-83
New Mexico	*NM* *NMAPP*	Supreme Court Court of Appeals	1945 1966

E-2
LEXIS Coverage of State Case Law (Cont.)
(All files are in the MEGA Library)

State	LEXIS File	Description	Date Full Coverage Begins
New York	*NY* *APPDIV* *MS2D*	Court of Appeals Appellate Division Miscellaneous Lower Courts	1884 1912 1912
North Carolina	*NC* *NCAPP*	Supreme Court Court of Appeals	1943 1968
North Dakota	*ND* *NDAPP*	Supreme Court Court of Appeals	1929 1987
Ohio	*OHIO* *OHAPP* *OHMISC*	Supreme Court Courts of Appeals Miscellaneous Courts	1821 1913 1922
Oklahoma	*OKLA* *OKAPP* *OKCRIM*	Supreme Court Court of Appeals Court of Criminal Appeals	1943 1969 1945
Oregon	*ORE* *ORAPP*	Supreme Court Court of Appeals	1945 1969
Pennsylvania	*PA* *PASUPR* *COMMON* *PHILA*	Supreme Court Superior Court Commonwealth Court County Reporter	1885 1944 1970 1975
Rhode Island	*RICTS*	Supreme Court	1965
South Carolina	*SC* *SCAPP*	Supreme Court Court of Appeals	1965 1983
South Dakota	*SDCTS*	Supreme Court	1965
Tennessee	*TENN* *TNAPP* *TNCRIM*	Supreme Court Court of Appeals Court of Criminal Appeals	1944 1943 1967
Texas	*TEX* *TXAPP* *TXCRIM*	Supreme Court Court of Appeals and Court of Civil Appeals Court of Criminal Appeals	1886 1981 1944-81 1943
Utah	*UTAH* *UTAPP*	Supreme Court Court of Appeals	1945 1987
Vermont	*VTCTS*	Supreme Court	1965
Virginia	*VA* *VAAPP*	Supreme Court Court of Appeals	1925 1985
Virgin Islands	*VICTS*	Territorial Courts	1990
Washington	*WASH* *WAAPP*	Supreme Court Court of Appeals	1898 1969

E-2
LEXIS Coverage of State Case Law (Cont.)
(All files are in the MEGA Library)

State	LEXIS File	Description	Date Full Coverage Begins
West Virginia	*WVCTS*	Supreme Court	1965
Wisconsin	*WISC* *WIAPP*	Supreme Court Court of Appeals	1944 1978
Wyoming	*WYCTS*	Supreme Court	1959

Descriptions of Some LEXIS®-NEXIS® Files

Appendix F-1 lists and describes files found in the *MEGA*™ library.

F-1
Files in the *MEGA* Library

File Name	Description
Combined File	
MEGA	Combined federal and state case law
Chronological Groups	
1YEAR	*MEGA* file for the previous 12 months
NEWER	*MEGA* file from 1945
***MEGA* Files by Circuit**	
1MEGA	Federal case law from: - U.S. Supreme Court - First Circuit - Districts in First Circuit - State case law from Maine, Mass., New Hamp. & R.I.
2MEGA	Federal case law from: - U.S. Supreme Court - Second Circuit - Districts in Second Circuit - State case law from Conn., New York & Vermont
[and so on through *11MEGA*, plus *DCMEGA* for D.C.-related case law]	

F-1
Files in the *MEGA* Library (Cont.)

File Name	Description
***MEGA* Files by State**	
AKMEGA	Alaska state case law Federal case law from: - U.S. Supreme Court - Ninth Circuit - Federal District Court of Alas.
ALMEGA	Alabama state case law Federal case law from: - U.S. Supreme Court - Eleventh Circuit - Federal District Courts of Ala.
[and so on through all 50 states, with the form being *XXMEGA*, where *XX* is the two-digit postal abbreviation for the state]	
ST1ST, ST2ND, etc.	State cases from the First Circuit (and so on through 11th Circuit)
XXALL	Federal District and State Courts for XX, where XX is the two-digit postal abbreviation for a state, the District of Columbia, or Puerto Rico

Appendix F-2 lists and describes files found in the *GENFED* Library.

F-2
Files in the *GENFED* Library

File Name	Description
U.S. Court Files	
US	U.S. Supreme Court
USAPP	Federal Courts of Appeals
OMNI	Supreme Court, U.S. Courts of Appeals, U.S. District Courts, and various special-purpose federal courts (e.g., the U.S. Claims Court) plus ALR articles
COURTS	Same as *OMNI*, but excludes ALR articles

F-2
Files in the *GENFED* Library (Cont.)

File Name	Description
U.S. Court Files (cont.)	
SUPCIR	U.S. Supreme Court, U.S. Appeals Courts
CURRNT	All federal case law within the last 2 years
NEWER	Principally, U.S. Supreme Court, U.S. Courts of Appeals, and U.S. District Courts, all after 1955
Combined Circuit and District Files:	
1ST	U.S. Court of Appeals for First Circuit, District, and Bankruptcy Courts in the First Circuit, from 1912 forward
2ND	Same as *1ST*, but for Second Circuit
[Continues through *11TH*, as well as *CADC* for the D.C. Circuit, with varying coverage dates]	
Circuit Files:	
1CIR	U.S. Court of Appeals from the First Circuit, from 1912
2CIR	Same as *1CIR*, but for Second Circuit
[Continues through *11CIR*, plus *DCCIR* for D.C. Circuit and *CAFC* for C.A. for the Federal Circuit, and *CCPA* for Court of Customs & Patent Appeals]	
Federal District Court Files:	
DIST	All federal District Courts
1DIST	Federal District Courts from the First Circuit
2DIST	Same as *1DIST*, but for the Second Circuit
[continues through *11DIST*, plus *DCDIST* for Federal District Court of D.C.]	

Appendix F-3 lists and describes files found in the *STATES* Library.

F-3
Files in the *STATES* Library

File Name	Description
OMNI	State courts (all 50 states) & ALR Annotations
COURTS	State courts from all 50 states
HIGHCT	State courts of last resort from all 50 states
ALCTS-WYCTS	State case law from each state, the District of Columbia, and the U.S. Virgin Islands (each has its own file)
ALLCDE	State codes from all 50 states
XXCODE	State code for each state (XX is the postal abbreviation for the state)

Appendix G

LEXSEE® Citation Formats

This Appendix shows you the abbreviation to use for each type of reporter, or other source, when issuing a LEXSEE request. LEXSEE requests for most types of documents must be in the following format:

NUMBER (volume or year)	ABBREVIATION (reporter, forum, or jurisdiction)	NUMBER (page/paragraph or document number)

For instance:

```
lexsee 300 us 1
lexsee 200 f2d 132
lexsee 143 a.2d 456
```

As in the above examples, a single space is required between the first number and the abbreviation, and another space is needed between the abbreviation and the second number. Within an abbreviation, spaces, periods and case are all optional (e.g., you can use **App.Div.2d**, **AppDiv2d**, **app div 2d**, etc.)

LEXSEE formats are shown for reporters, administrative regulations, administrative decisions, and most other types of primary legal documents available on the LEXIS service. LEXSEE formats for law reviews can be found in Appendix E.

This is a partial list of LEXSEE publications. For a complete list, see the LEXSEE Publications List which should be in your school's LEXIS workroom. If your school's copy is missing, call the LEXIS Reference Hotline to find the LEXSEE citiation for the reporter you're looking for.

LEXSEE Citation Formats

Reporter, Forum or Jurisdiction	LEXSEE Abbreviation
Abbott's Admiralty Reports	**Abb. Adm.**
Abbott's U.S. Circuit & District Court Reports	**Abb.**
Action On Decisions LEXIS cite	**AOD LEXIS**
Administrative Law Journal American University	**Admin. L.J. Am. U.**
Agriculture Board of Contract Appeals LEXIS cite	**AGBCA LEXIS**
Air Force Law Review	**A.F. L. Rev.**

LEXSEE Citation Formats (Cont.)

Alabama Acts	Ala. Acts
Alabama Acts	Al. Act
Alabama Advance Legislative Service	Al. ALS
Alabama Appellate Court Opinions LEXIS cite	Ala. App. LEXIS
Alabama Appellate Court Reports	Ala. App.
Alabama Attorney General Opinions	Op. Atty Gen. Ala.
Alabama Attorney General Opinions LEXIS cite	Ala. AG LEXIS
Alabama Civil Appellate Opinions LEXIS cite	Ala. Civ. App. LEXIS
Alabama Criminal Appellate Opinions LEXIS cite	Ala. Crim. App. LEXIS
Alabama House Bill	Al. HB
Alabama House Joint Resolution	Al. HJR
Alabama House Report	Al. HR
Alabama Law Journal	Ala. L. Rev.
Alabama Lawyer, The	Ala. Lawyer
Alabama No Action LEXIS cite	Ala. Sec. No-Act. LEXIS
Alabama Public Act	Al. Pub. Act
Alabama Reports	Ala.
Alabama Securities LEXIS cite	Ala. Sec. LEXIS
Alabama Senate Bill	Al. SB
Alabama Senate Joint Resolution	Al. SJR
Alabama Senate Report	Al. SR
Alabama Supreme Court Opinions LEXIS cite	Ala. LEXIS
Alabama Tax LEXIS cite	Ala. Tax LEXIS
Alaska Advance Legislative Service	AK. ALS
Alaska Attorney General Opinions (Number)	Op. Atty Gen. Alas. No.
Alaska Attorney General Opinions LEXIS cite	Alas. AG LEXIS
Alaska Attorney General Opinions (Informal)	Op. (Inf.) Atty Gen. Alas.
Alaska Chapter	AK. Ch.
Alaska Court of Appeals LEXIS cite	Alas. App. LEXIS
Alaska House Bill	AK. HB
Alaska House Resolution	Ak. HR
Alaska Reports	Alaska
Alaska Resolve	Ak. RESOLVE
Alaska Senate Bill	AK. SB
Alaska Senate Resolution	Ak. SR
Alaska Session Laws	Alaska Sess. Laws
Alaska Supreme Court LEXIS cite	Alas. LEXIS
Alaska Tax LEXIS cite	Alas. Tax LEXIS
Albany Law Journal of Science & Technology	Alb. L.J. Sci. & Tech.

LEXSEE Citation Formats (Cont.)

Albany Law Review	Alb. L. Rev.
American Bankruptcy Institute Law Review	Am. Bankr. Inst. L. Rev.
American Bankruptcy Law Journal	Am. Bank. L.J
American Disabilities Decisions	Am. Disabilities Dec.
American Federal Tax Reporter (P-H)	A.F.T.R. (P-H)
American Federal Tax Reporter (P-H), second series	A.F.T.R.2d (P-H)
American Journal of Criminal Law	Am. J. Crim. L.
American Journal of International Law	A.J.I.L.
American Journal of Law and Medicine	Am. J. L. and Med.
American Labor Cases (P-H)	Am. Lab. Cas.
American Law Register	Am. Law Reg.
American Law Reports, 2d series	A.L.R.2d
American Law Reports, 3d series	A.L.R.3d
American Law Reports, 4th series	A.L.R.4th
American Law Reports, 5th series	A.L.R.5th
American Law Reports, Federal series	A.L.R. Fed.
American Law Reports	A.L.R.
American Maritime Cases	AMC
American University Journal of Gender and the Law	Am. U.J. Gender & Law
American University Journal of International Law and Policy	Am. U.J. Int'l L. & Pol'y
American University Law Review	Am. U.L. Rev.
Annals of Health Law	Ann. Health L.
Appeals Cases, District of Columbia	App. D.C.
Arizona 1st Special Session Chapter	Ariz. 1st Sp. Sess. Ch.
Arizona 1st Special Session House Bill	Ariz. 1st Sp. Sess. HB
Arizona 1st Special Session Senate Bill	Ariz. 1st Sp. Sess. SB
Arizona Advance Legislative Service	Ariz. ALS
Arizona Advance Reporter	Ariz. Adv. Rep.
Arizona ALS 1st Special Session	Ariz. ALS 1st Sp. Sess.
Arizona ALS 2nd Special Session	Ariz. ALS 2nd Sp. Sess
Arizona Appeals Opinions LEXIS cite	Ariz. App. LEXIS
Arizona Appeals Reports	Ariz. App.
Arizona Attorney General Opinions	Op. Atty Gen. Ariz.
Arizona Attorney General Opinions LEXIS cite	Ariz. AG LEXIS
Arizona Chapter	Ariz. Ch.

LEXSEE Citation Formats (Cont.)

Source	Citation Format
Arizona House Bill	Ariz. HB
Arizona House Concurrent Memorial	ARIZ. HCM
Arizona Journal of International and Comparative Law	Ariz. J. Int'l & Comp. Law
Arizona Law Review	Ariz. L. Rev.
Arizona Reports	Ariz.
Arizona Securities LEXIS cite	Ariz. Sec. LEXIS
Arizona Senate Bill	Ariz. SB
Arizona Session Laws	Ariz. Sess.
Arizona State Law Journal	Ariz St L.J.
Arizona Supreme Court LEXIS cite	Ariz. LEXIS
Arizona Tax LEXIS cite	Ariz. Tax LEXIS
Arkansas Acts	Ark. Acts
Arkansas Advance Legislative Service	Ark. ALS
Arkansas Advance Legislative Service (1st Extra Session)	Ark. ALS (1st Extra. Sess.)
Arkansas Advance Legislative Service (2d Extra Session)	Ark. ALS (2nd Extra. Sess.)
Arkansas Advance Legislative Service (3d Extra Session)	Ark. ALS (3rd Extra. Sess.)
Arkansas Advance Opinions	Ark. Adv. Op.
Arkansas Appellate Opinions LEXIS cite	Ark. App. LEXIS
Arkansas Appellate Reports	Ark. App.
Arkansas Attorney General Opinions	Op. Atty Gen. Ark.
Arkansas Attorney General Opinions LEXIS cite	Ark. AG LEXIS
Arkansas House Bill	Ark. HB
Arkansas Law Review	Ark. L. Rev.
Arkansas Reports	Ark.
Arkansas Senate Bills	Ark. SB
Arkansas Supreme Court Opinions LEXIS cite	Ark. LEXIS
Armed Services Board of Contract Appeals Opinions LEXIS cite	ASBCA LEXIS
Asian Law Journal	Asian L. J.
Atlantic Reporter	A.
Atlantic Reporter, 2d series	A.2d
Australia Administrative Appeals Tribunal Opinions LEXIS cite	AUST AATCT LEXIS
Australian & New Zealand Journal of Criminology	Aust. & N.Z. J. Crimnlgy
Australian Bar Review	Australian Bar Rev.
Australian Immigration Review Tribunal LEXIS cite	AUST IRTCT LEXIS
Automobile Insurance Cases (CCH)	Auto. Cas. (CCH)
Automobile Insurance Cases (CCH), 2d series	Auto. Cas. 2d (CCH)

LEXSEE Citation Formats (Cont.)

Australian Journal of Corporate Law	Aust. J. Corp. Law
Australian Journal of Family Law	Aust J. Family Law
Australian Journal of Labour Law	Aust. J. Labour Law
Australian Property Law Journal	Aust. Property L. J.
Aviation Cases (CCH)	Av. Cas. (CCH)
Baldwin's US Circuit Court Report	Baldw.
Banking Law Journal	Banking L.J.
Bankruptcy Court Decisions (CRR)	Bankr. Ct. Dec. (CRR)
Bankruptcy Court Decisions (CRR), 2d series	Bankr. Ct. Dec. 2d (CRR)
Bankruptcy Developments Journal	Bank. Dev. J.
Bankruptcy Law Reporter (CCH)	Bankr. L. Rep. (CCH)
Bankruptcy Litigation Manual	Bankr. Lit. Man.
Bankruptcy Opinions LEXIS cite	Bankr. LEXIS
Bankruptcy Reporter	Bankr.
Basic Documents of International Economic Law	B.D.I.E.L.
Basic Documents of International Economic Law LEXIS cite	BDIEL AD LEXIS
Baylor Law Review	Baylor L. Rev.
Benedict's District Court Reports (US)	Ben.
Bissell's US Circuit Reports	Biss.
Black's US Supreme Court Reports	Black
Blatchford's Prize Cases	Blatch. Prize Cas.
Blatchford's US Circuit Court Reports	Blatchf.
Board of Alien Labor Certification Appeals LEXIS cite	BALCA LEXIS
Board of Contract Appeals (CCH)	B.C.A. (CCH)
Board of Immigration Appeals LEXIS cite	BIA LEXIS
Board of Patent Appeals & Interferences LEXIS cite	Pat. App. LEXIS
Board of Tax Appeals	B.T.A.
Board of Tax Appeals LEXIS cite	BTA LEXIS
Boston College Environmental Affairs Law Review	B. C. Envtl. Aff. L. Rev
Boston College Law Review	B.C. L. Rev
Boston University International Law Journal	B.U. Int'l L.J.
Boston University Journal of Science & Technology Law	B.U. J. SCI. & TECH. L.
Boston University Law Review	B.U.L. Rev.
Boston University Public Interest Law Journal	B.U. Pub. Int. L. J.
Brigham Young University Law Review	B.Y.U.L. Rev.

LEXSEE Citation Formats (Cont.)

Brooklyn Journal of International Law	Brooklyn J. Int'l L.
Brooklyn Law Review	Brooklyn L. Rev.
Buffalo Law Review	Buffalo L. Rev
California Administrative Board Reports	Cal AB
California Advance Legislative Service	Cal ALS
California Advance Legislative Service Extra Session	Cal ALS Extra Session
California Advance Legislative Service Proposition	Cal Als Prop
California Advance Legislative Service Rules	Cal Als Rule
California Appellate Opinions LEXIS cite	Cal. App. LEXIS
California Appellate Reports, 2d series	Cal. App. 2d
California Appellate Reports, 2d series Supplement	Cal. App. 2d Supp.
California Appellate Reports, 3d series	Cal. App. 3d
California Appellate Reports, 3d series Supplement	Cal. App. 3d Supp.
California Appellate Reports, 4th series	Cal. App. 4th
California Appellate Reports, 4th series Supplement	Cal. App. 4th Supp.
California Appellate Reports, Supplement	Cal. App. Supp.
California Attorney General Opinions	Op. Atty Gen. Cal.
California Attorney General Opinions LEXIS cite	Cal. AG LEXIS
California Compensation Cases	Cal. Comp. Cas
California Daily Opinion Service	Cal. Daily Op. Service
California Department of Corporations LEXIS cite	Cal. Sec. LEXIS
California Environmental LEXIS cite	Cal. ENV LEXIS
California Franchise Tax Board & Board of Equalization LEXIS cite	Cal. Tax LEXIS
California Law Review	Calif. L. Rev.
California Public Utilities Commission LEXIS cite	Cal. PUC LEXIS
California Public Utilties Commission	CPUC
California Public Utilties Commission, 2d series	CPUC2d
California Reporter	Cal. Rptr.
California Reporter, 2d series	Cal. Rptr. 2d
California Reports	Cal.
California Reports, 2d series	Cal. 2d
California Reports, 3d series	Cal. 3d
California Reports, 3d series Special Trib Supplement	Cal. 3d (Spec Trib Supp)
California Reports, 4th series	Cal. 4th
California Senate Bills	Cal SB
California Supreme Court LEXIS cite	Cal. LEXIS
California Western International Law Journal	Cal. W. Int'l L. J.

LEXSEE Citation Formats (Cont.)

California Western Law Review	Cal. W. L. Rev.
Campbell Law Review	Campbell L. Rev.
Canada-U.S. Law Journal	Can.-U.S.L.J.
Canada Supreme Court LEXIS cite	Can. S. Ct. LEXIS
Canadian Criminal Cases	C.C.C.
Canadian Criminal Cases, 2d series	C.C.C. 2d
Canadian Criminal Cases, 3d series	C.C.C. 3d
Canadian Patent Reporter	C.P.R.
Capital University Law Review	Cap. U. L. Rev.
Cardozo Arts & Entertainment Law Journal	Cardozo Arts & Ent LJ
Cardozo Law Review	Cardozo L. Rev.
Case Western Reserve Journal of International Law	Case W. Res. J. Int'l L.
Case Western Reserve Law Review	Case W. Res.
Catholic University Law Review	Cath. U.L. Rev.
Chicago-Kent Law Review	Chi.-Kent. L. Rev.
Civil Aeronautics Board LEXIS cite	CAB LEXIS
Civil Aeronautics Board Reports	C.A.B.
Claims Court Reporter	Cl. Ct.
Cleveland State Law Review	Clev. St. L. Rev.
Clifford's US Circuit Court Reports	Cliff.
Clinical Law Review	Clinical L. Rev.
Collier Bankruptcy Cases (MB)	Collier Bankr. Cas. (MB)
Collier Bankruptcy Cases (MB)	Collier Bankr Cas 2d (MB)
Colorado 1st Extra Session House Bill	Colo. 1st Extra Sess HB
Colorado 1st Extra Session Senate Bill	Colo. 1st Extra Sess SB
Colorado 1st Extra Session Senate Bill	Colo. 1st Extra Sess. Ch.
Colorado Advance Legislative Service	Colo. ALS
Colorado ALS 1st Extra Session	Colo. Als 1st Extra Sess
Colorado Attorney General Opinions	Op. Atty Gen. Col.
Colorado Attorney General Opinions LEXIS cite	Colo. AG LEXIS
Colorado Chapter	Colo. Ch.
Colorado Court of Appeals LEXIS cite	Colo. App. LEXIS
Colorado Court of Appeals Reports	Colo. App.
Colorado House Bill	Colo. HB.

LEXSEE Citation Formats (Cont.)

Colorado Reports	Colo.
Colorado SEC LEXIS cite	Colo. Sec. LEXIS
Colorado SEC No Action LEXIS cite	Colo. Sec. No-Act. LEXIS
Colorado Senate Bill	Colo. SB
Colorado Supreme Court LEXIS cite	Colo. LEXIS
Colorado Tax LEXIS cite	Colo. Tax LEXIS
Columbia Business Law Review	COLUM. BUS. L. REV.
Columbia Journal of Environmental Law	Colum. J. Envtl. L.
Columbia Journal of Law and Social Problems	Colum. J. L. & Soc. Probs.
Columbia Journal of Transnational Law	Colum. J. Transnat'l L.
Columbia Law Review	Colum. L. Rev.
Commercial Dispute Resolution Journal	Comm. Dispute Res. J.
Commissions Decisions Patent & Trademark LEXIS cite	Commr. Pat. LEXIS
CommLaw Conspectus	CommLaw Conspectus
Commodity Futures Law Reporter (CCH)	Comm. Fut. L. Rep. (CCH)
Commodity Futures Trading Commission LEXIS cite	CFTC LEXIS
Competition & Consumer Law Journal	Comp. & Consumer L.J.
Comptroller General Decisions	Comp. Gen.
Conference Reports, House of Representatives	Conf. Rept.
Congressional Record -Digest	Cong Rec D
Congressional Record - Extension of Remarks	Cong Rec E
Congressional Record - House	Cong Rec H
Congressional Record - House (lobbying)	Cong Rec HL
Congressional Record - Senate	Cong Rec S
Connecticut Advance Legislative Service	Ct. ALS
Connecticut Appellate LEXIS cite	Conn. App. LEXIS
Connecticut Appellate Reports	Conn. App.
Connecticut Attorney General Opinions LEXIS cite	Conn. AG LEXIS
Connecticut Circuit Court Reports	Conn. Cir. Ct.
Connecticut House Bill	Ct. HB
Connecticut Insurance Law Journal	Conn. Ins. L.J.
Connecticut Journal of International Law	Conn. J. Int'l L.
Connecticut Law Journal	Conn. L.J.
Connecticut Law Review	Conn. L. Rev.
Connecticut Opinions of the Attorney General	Conn. Op. Atty Gen.

LEXSEE Citation Formats (Cont.)

Connecticut Public Act	Ct. P.A.
Connecticut Public Utilities Commission LEXIS cite	Conn. PUC LEXIS
Connecticut Reports	Conn.
Connecticut SEC LEXIS cite	Conn. Sec. LEXIS
Connecticut SEC No Action LEXIS cite	Conn. Sec. No-Act. LEXIS
Connecticut Senate Bill	Ct. SB
Connecticut Special Act	Ct. S.A.
Connecticut Superior Court LEXIS cite	Conn. Super. LEXIS
Connecticut Supplement	Conn. Supp.
Connecticut Supreme Court LEXIS cite	Conn. LEXIS
Contract Cases Federal (CCH)	Cont. Cas. Fed. (CCH)
Copyright Law Reporter (CCH)	Copy. L. Rep. (CCH)
Cornell International Law Journal	Cornell Int'l L.J.
Cornell Law Review	Cornell L. Rev.
Corps of Engineers Board of Contract Appeals LEXIS cite	Eng. BCA LEXIS
Court Martial Reports	C.M.R.
Court of Appeals, Federal Circuit	CAFC
Court of Claims	Ct. Cl.
Court of Customs & Patent Appeals Reports	C.C.P.A.
Court of International Trade	C.I.T.
Court of International Trade LEXIS cite	Ct. Intl. Trade LEXIS
Court of Military Appeals LEXIS cite	CMA LEXIS
Court of Military Review LEXIS cite	CMR LEXIS
Creighton Law Review	Creighton L. Rev.
Cumberland Law Review	Cumb. L. Rev.
Cummulative Bulletin	C.B.
Cumulative Bulletin LEXIS cite	IRB LEXIS
Curtis' US Circuit Court Decisions	Curt.
Customs Appeals Decisions	C.A.D.
Customs Bulletin & Decisions	Cust. B. & Dec.
Customs Bulletin & Decisions Number	Cust. B. & Dec. No.
Customs Bulletin LEXIS cite	CUSBUL LEXIS
Customs Court Decisions	Cust. Ct.
Daily Journal DAR (California)	Daily Journal DAR
Dallas' Reports (PA)	Dall.
Day's Reports (CT)	Day
Delaware Advance Legislative Service	Del. ALS

LEXSEE Citation Formats (Cont.)

Delaware Attorney General Delaware	Op. Atty Gen. Del.
Delaware Attorney General Opinions LEXIS cite	DE. AG LEXIS
Delaware Chancery LEXIS cite	Del. Ch. LEXIS
Delaware Chancery Reports	Del. Ch.
Delaware House Bill	Del. HB
Delaware House Joint Resolution	Del. HJR
Delaware Journal of Corporate Law	Del. J. Corp. L.
Delaware Laws	Del. Laws
Delaware Public Service Commission LEXIS cite	Del. PSC LEXIS
Delaware Reports	Del.
Delaware SEC No Action LEXIS cite	Del. Sec. No-Act. LEXIS
Delaware Senate Bills	Del. SB
Delaware Senate Joint Resolution	Del. SJR
Delaware Superior Court LEXIS cite	Del. Super. LEXIS
Delaware Supreme Court LEXIS cite	Del. LEXIS
Delaware Tax LEXIS cite	Del. Tax LEXIS
Denver Journal Of International Law & Policy	Denv. J. Int'l L. & Pol'y
Denver University Law Review	Denv. U.L. Rev.
Department of Energy Board of Contract Appeals LEXIS cite	EBCA LEXIS
Department of Labor Board of Contract Appeals LEXIS cite	DOL BCA LEXIS
Department of Transportation, Aviation LEXIS cite	DOT Av. LEXIS
Department of Transportation, Board of Contract Appeals LEXIS cite	DOT BCA LEXIS
DePaul Business Law Journal	DePaul Bus. L.J.
DePaul Law Review	DePaul L. Rev.
Detroit College of Law Review	Det C. L. Rev
Dickinson Law Review	Dick L. Rev.
District of Columbia Acts	D.C. Act
District of Columbia Advance Legislative Service	D.C. ALS
District of Columbia Appeals Court LEXIS cite	D.C. App. LEXIS
District of Columbia Laws	D.C. Law
District of Columbia Reports	D.C.
District of Columbia Statutes at Large	D.C. Stat
Dominion Law Reports, 2d series (Canada)	D.L.R. 2d
Dominion Law Reports, 3d series (Canada)	D.L.R. 3d
Dominion Law Reports, 4th series (Canada)	D.L.R. 4th
Duke Environmental Law & Policy Forum	Duke Env L & Pol'y F
Duke Journal of Comparative & International Law	Duke J Comp & Intl L
Duke Journal of Gender Law & Policy	Duke J. Gender L. & Pol'y
Duke Law Journal	Duke L.J.

LEXSEE Citation Formats (Cont.)

Duquesne Law Review	Duq. L. Rev.
Elder Law Journal	Elder L.J.
Emory International Law Review	Emory Int'l L. Rev.
Emory Law Journal	Emory L.J.
Employee Benefit Cases	E.B.C.
Employee Practice Decisions (CCH)	Empl. Prac. Dec. (CCH)
Employee Relations	Empl. Rel.
Employee Relations Appendix	Empl. Rel. Appx.
Energy Law Journal	Energy L.J.
Environmental Law	Envtl. L.
Environmental Law Reporter, Pending Litigation	ELR Pend. Lit.
Environmental Law Reporter, Regulations	ELR Reg.
Environmental Law Reporter, Statutes	ELR Stat.
Environmental Reporter Cases (BNA)	ERC (BNA)
Equal Employment Opportunity Commission LEXIS cite	EEOC LEXIS
Fair Employment Practice Cases (BNA)	Fair Empl Prac Cas (BNA)
Family Court of Australia LEXIS cite	AUST FAMCT LEXIS
Federal Appellate (Electronic cite for 6th Circuit)	FED App.
Federal Banking Law Reporter (CCH)	Fed Banking L Rep (CCH)
Federal Carrier Cases (CCH)	Fed. Carr. Cas. (CCH)
Federal Cases	F. Cas.
Federal Circuit Trade Cases	Fed. Cir. (T)
Federal Claims Court	Fed. Cl.
Federal Communications Commission	F.C.C.
Federal Communications Commission Record	FCC Rcd
Federal Communications Commission, 2d series	F.C.C.2d
Federal Communications Commission LEXIS cite	FCC LEXIS
Federal Communications Law Journal	Fed. Com. L.J.
Federal Court of Australia LEXIS cite	AUST FEDCT LEXIS
Federal Energy Regulatory Commission	F.E.R.C.
Federal Energy Regulatory Commission LEXIS cite	FERC LEXIS
Federal Labor Relations Authority Decision Number	F.L.R.A. ALJ Dec. No.
Federal Labor Relations Authority Decisions	F.L.R.A.
Federal Labor Relations Authority LEXIS cite	FLRA LEXIS
Federal Labor Relations Authority Number	FLRA No.
Federal Power Commission LEXIS cite	FPC LEXIS
Federal Power Commission Reports	F.P.C.

LEXSEE Citation Formats (Cont.)

Federal Register	FR
Federal Reporter	F.
Federal Reporter, 2d series	F.2d
Federal Reporter, 3d series	F.3d
Federal Rules Decisions	F.R.D.
Federal Rules Service (Callaghan)	Fed. R. Serv (Callaghan)
Federal Rules Service (Callaghan), 2d series	Fed R Serv 2d (Callaghan)
Federal Rules Service (Callaghan), 3d series	Fed R Serv 3d (Callaghan)
Federal Securities Law Reporter (CCH)	Fed. Sec. L. Rep. (CCH)
Federal Sentencing Reporter	Fed. Sent. R.
Federal Service Impasses Panel	F.S.I.P.
Federal Service Impasses Panel LEXIS cite	FSIP LEXIS
Federal Service Impasses Panel Number	F.S.I.P. No.
Federal Service Impasses Panel Report Number	FSIP Rep No.
Federal Supplement	F. Supp.
Federal Trade Commission Decisions	F.T.C.
Federal Trade Commission LEXIS cite	FTC LEXIS
Fire & Casualty Cases (CCH)	Fire & Casualty Cas(CCH)
Flippin's Circuit Court Reports (US)	Flip.
Florida Advance Legislative Service	Fl. ALS
Florida Appellate LEXIS cite	Fla. App. LEXIS
Florida Attorney General Opinions	Op. Atty Gen. Fla.
Florida Attorney General Opinions LEXIS cite	Fla. AG LEXIS
Florida Environmental LEXIS cite	Fla. ENV LEXIS
Florida House Bill	Fla. HB
Florida Journal of International Law	Fla. J. Int'l L.
Florida Jurisprudence	FLJ (Title) TOC 1
Florida Law Review	Fla. L. Rev.
Florida Law Weekly	Fla. Law W.
Florida Law Weekly District	Fla. Law W.D.
Florida Law Weekly Federal US Supreme Court	Fla. Law W. Fed. S
Florida Law Weekly Supreme	Fla. Law W.S.
Florida Laws Chapter	Fla. Laws ch.
Florida Public Employee Reporter (LRP)	FPER (LRP)
Florida Public Employee Reporter (LRP) LEXIS cite	FPER (LRP) LEXIS
Florida Public Service Commission	FPSC
Florida Public Utilities Commission LEXIS cite	Fla. PUC LEXIS
Florida Reports	Fla.

LEXSEE Citation Formats (Cont.)

Florida SEC LEXIS cite	Fla. Sec. LEXIS
Florida Senate Bills	Fla. SB
Florida State University Law Review	Fla. St. U.L. Rev.
Florida Supplement	Fla. Supp.
Florida Supreme Court LEXIS cite	Fla. LEXIS
Florida Tax LEXIS cite	Fla. Tax LEXIS
Fordham Environmental Law Journal	Fordham Envtl. Law J.
Fordham International Law Journal	Fordham Int'l L.J.
Fordham Law Review	Fordham L. Rev.
Fordham Urban Law Journal	Fordham Urb. L.J.
General Council Memorandum	G.C.M.
General Services Board of Contract Appeals LEXIS cite	GSBCA LEXIS
George Mason Law Review	Geo Mason L. Rev
George Washington Journal of International Law & Economics	GW J. Int'l L. & Econ.
George Washington Law Review	Geo. Wash. L. Rev.
Georgetown Law Journal	Geo. L.J.
Georgia Acts	Ga. Act
Georgia Advance Legislative Service	Ga. ALS
Georgia Advance Legislative Service Extra Session	Ga. ALS (Extra. Sess.)
Georgia Appeals LEXIS cite	Ga. App. LEXIS
Georgia Appeals Reports	Ga. App.
Georgia Attorney General Opinions	Op. Atty Gen. Ga.
Georgia Attorney General Opinions LEXIS cite	Ga. AG LEXIS
Georgia Environmental LEXIS cite	Ga. ENV LEXIS
Georgia House Bill	Ga. HB
Georgia House Bill (Extra Session)	Ga. HB (Extra. Sess.)
Georgia House Joint Resolution	Ga. HJR
Georgia House Report	Ga. HR
Georgia Journal of International & Comparative Law	Ga. J. Int'l & Comp. L.
Georgia Law Review	Ga. L. Rev.
Georgia Laws	Ga. Laws
Georgia Reports	Ga.
Georgia SEC LEXIS cite	Ga. Sec. LEXIS
Georgia Senate Bill	Ga. SB
Georgia Senate Joint Resolution	Ga. SJR
Georgia Senate Report	Ga. SR
Georgia Supreme Court LEXIS cite	Ga. LEXIS

LEXSEE Citation Formats (Cont.)

Golden Gate University Law Review	Golden Gate U.L. Rev
Gongaza Law Review	Gonz. L. Rev.
Harvard Law Review	Harv. L. Rev.
Harvard's Black Letter Journal	Harv. BlackLetter J.
Harvard's Civil Rights - Civil Liberties Law Review	Harv. C.R.-C.L. L. Rev.
Harvard's Environmental Law Review	Harv. Envtl. L. Rev.
Harvard's Human Rights Journal	Harv. Hum. Rpts. J.
Harvard's International Law Journal	Harv. Int'l L.J.
Harvard's Journal of Law and Technology	Harv. J. Law and Tec
Harvard's Journal on Legislation	Harv. J. on Legis.
Harvard's Women's Law Journal	Harv. Women's L.J.
Hastings Law Journal	Hastings L.J.
Hawaii ACTS	Hi. Act
Hawaii Advance Legislative Service	Hi. ALS
Hawaii Appellate LEXIS cite	Haw. App. LEXIS
Hawaii Appellate Reports	Haw. App.
Hawaii Attorney General Opinions	Op. Atty Gen. Hi
Hawaii Attorney General Opinions LEXIS cite	Haw. AG LEXIS
Hawaii House Bills	Hi. HB
Hawaii Law Review	Hawaii L. Rev.
Hawaii Reports	Haw.
Hawaii Senate Bills	Hi. SB
Hawaii Supreme LEXIS cite	Haw. LEXIS
Health Matrix	Health Matrix
Hempstead's Reports (US)	Hempst.
High Court of Australia LEXIS cite	AUST HIGHCT LEXIS
Hofstra Labor Law Journal	Hofstra Lab L.J.
Hofstra Law Review	Hofstra L. Rev.
Hong Kong Law Journal	Hong Kong L. J.
House of Representatives Concurrent Resolution - federal bill - unenacted version(s) of bill	H.R. Con. Res.
House of Representatives Concurrent Resolution - federal bill - enacted version of bill	Enacted H.R. Con. Res.
House of Representatives Concurrent Resolution - federal bill - tracking report	Bill Tracking H.R. Con. Res.
House of Representatives - federal bill - enacted version of bill	Enacted H.R.

LEXSEE Citation Formats (Cont.)

House of Representatives - federal bill - tracking report	Bill Tracking H.R.
House of Representatives - federal bill - unenacted version(s) of bill	H.R.
House of Representatives Joint Resolution - federal bill - enacted version of bill	Enacted H.R.J. Res.
House of Representatives Joint Resolution - federal bill - tracking report	Bill Tracking H.R.J. Res.
House of Representatives Joint Resolution - federal bill - unenacted version(s) of bill	H.R.J. Res.
House of Representatives Resolution - federal bill - enacted version of bill	Enacted H.R. Res.
House of Representatives Resolution - federal bill - tracking report	Bill Tracking H.R. Res
House of Representatives Resolution - federal bill - unenacted version(s) of bill	H.R. Res
Housing & Urban Development Board of Contract Appeals LEXIS cite	HUD BCA LEXIS
Houston Journal of International Law	Hous. J. Int'l L
Houston Law Review	Hous. L. Rev.
Houston Lawyer	Houston Lawyer
Howard Law Journal	How. L.J.
Howard's Nisi Prius (NY)	How. Pr.
Howard's Supreme Court Reports (MS)	HOW.
Idaho Advance Legislative Service	Ida. ALS
Idaho Appellate LEXIS cite	Ida. App. LEXIS
Idaho Attorney General Opinions	Op. Atty Gen. Idaho
Idaho Attorney General Opinions LEXIS cite	Ida. AG LEXIS
Idaho Chapter	Ida. Ch.
Idaho House Bills	Ida. HB
Idaho House Concurrent Resolution	Ida. HCR
Idaho House Joint Memorial	Ida. HJM
Idaho Law Review	Idaho L. Rev.
Idaho Reports	Idaho
Idaho SEC LEXIS cite	Id. Sec. LEXIS
Idaho SEC No-Action LEXIS cite	Id. Sec. No-Act. LEXIS
Idaho Senate Bills	Ida. SB
Idaho Senate Concurrent Resolution	Ida. SCR
Idaho Senate Joint Memorial	Ida. SJM
Idaho Session Laws	Idaho Sess. Laws
Idaho Supreme LEXIS cite	Ida. LEXIS
Idaho Tax LEXIS cite	Ida. Tax LEXIS
Illinois Advance Legislative Service	ILL. ALS
Illinois Appellate Court Reports	Ill. App.
Illinois Appellate Court Reports, 2d series	Ill. App. 2d
Illinois Appellate Court Reports, 3d series	Ill. App. 3d

LEXSEE Citation Formats (Cont.)

Illinois Appellate Court Reports, Appendix	Ill. App. (A)
Illinois Appellate Court Reports, Appendix, 2d series	Ill. App. 2d (A)
Illinois Appellate Court Reports, Appendix, 3d series	Ill. App. 3d (A)
Illinois Appellate LEXIS cite	Ill. App. LEXIS
Illinois Attorney General Opinions	Op. Atty Gen. Ill.
Illinois Attorney General Opinions LEXIS cite	Ill. AG LEXIS
Illinois Decisions	Ill. Dec.
Illinois Environmental LEXIS cite	Ill. ENV LEXIS
Illinois House Bills	ILL. HB
Illinois Laws	Ill. Laws
Illinois Public Act	ILL. P.A.
Illinois Public Utilities Commission LEXIS cite	Ill. PUC LEXIS
Illinois Reports	Ill.
Illinois Reports, 2d	Ill. 2d
Illinois SEC LEXIS cite	Il. Sec. LEXIS
Illinois Senate Bills	ILL. SB
Illinois Supreme LEXIS cite	Ill. LEXIS
Immigration & Nationality Decisions	I. & N. Dec.
Indiana Acts	Ind. Acts
Indiana Administrative Code	IAC
Indiana Advance Legislative Service	Ind. ALS
Indiana Appeals LEXIS cite	Ind. App. LEXIS
Indiana Attorney General Opinions	Op. Atty Gen. Ind.
Indiana Attorney General Opinions LEXIS cite	Ind. AG LEXIS
Indiana Court of Appeals Reports	Ind. App.
Indiana Decisions	Ind. Dec.
Indiana House Enacted Act	Ind. HEA
Indiana Law Journal	Ind. L.J.
Indiana Public Utilities Commission LEXIS cite	Ind. PUC LEXIS
Indiana Reports	Ind.
Indiana Sec LEXIS cite	Ind. Sec. LEXIS
Indiana Sec. No-Action LEXIS cite	Ind. Sec. No-Act. LEXIS
Indiana Supreme Court LEXIS cite	Ind. LEXIS
Indiana Tax LEXIS cite	Ind. Tax LEXIS
Individual Employment Rights Cases (BNA)	BNA IER CAS
Insurance Tax Review	Ins. Tax Rev.
Interior Board of Contract Appeals LEXIS cite	IBCA LEXIS
Interior Board of Land Appeals Decisions	IBLA
Interior Board of Land Appeals LEXIS cite	IBLA LEXIS
Interior Decisions	I.D.
Interior Decisions LEXIS cite	I.D. LEXIS
Internal Revenue Bulletin	I.R.B.

LEXSEE Citation Formats (Cont.)

International Lawyer	Int'l Law.
International Legal Materials	I.L.M.
International Trade Commission General Council Memo LEXIS cite	ITC GCM LEXIS
International Trade Commission LEXIS cite	ITC LEXIS
Interstate Commerce Commission LEXIS cite	ICC LEXIS
Interstate Commerce Commission Reports	I.C.C.
Interstate Commerce Commission Reports, 2d series	I.C.C. 2d
Interstate Commerce Commission, Valuation Reports	Val. Rep.
Iowa Acts	Iowa Acts
Iowa Advance Legislative Service	Ia. ALS
Iowa Attorney General Opinions	Op. Atty Gen. Iowa
Iowa Attorney General Opinions LEXIS cite	Iowa AG LEXIS
Iowa Court of Appeals LEXIS cite	Iowa App. LEXIS
Iowa House File	Ia. HF
Iowa House Joint Resolution	Ia. HJR
Iowa Journal of Corporation Law	Iowa J. Corp. L.
Iowa Law Review	Iowa L. Rev.
Iowa Laws	Ia. Laws
Iowa Reports	Iowa
Iowa SEC LEXIS cite	Ia. Sec. LEXIS
Iowa Senate File	Ia. SF
Iowa Senate Joint Resolution	Ia. SJR
Iowa Supreme Court LEXIS cite	owa Sup. LEXIS
Iowa Tax LEXIS cite	Iowa Tax LEXIS
IRS General Council Memorandum LEXIS cite	IRS GCM LEXIS
J.W. Wallace's United States Circuit Court	Wall. Jr.
John Marshall Law Review	J. Marshall L. Rev
Journal of Air and Commerce	J. Air L. & Com.
Journal of Art & Entertainment Law	J. Art & Ent. Law
Journal of Contemporary Health Law and Policy	J. Contemp HL & Pol'y
Journal of Contempary Law	J. Contemp. L.
Journal of Contract Law	J. Contract Law
Journal of Criminal Law	J. Crim. L.
Journal of Dispute Resolution	J. Disp. Resol.
Journal of Intellectual Property	J Intell. Prop. L.
Journal of International Law & Business	J. INTL. L. BUS.
Journal of Law & Commerce	J.L. & Com.
Journal of Law & Health	J. L. & Health
Journal of Law & Technology	J.L. & TECH.

LEXSEE Citation Formats (Cont.)

Journal of Law and Policy	J.L. & Pol'y
Journal of Law and Public Policy	J. Law & Pub Pol'y
Journal of Pharmacy & Law	J. Pharmacy & Law
Journal of the Legal Profession	J. Legal Prof.
Kansas Advance Legislative Service	Kan. ALS
Kansas Attorney General Opinions	Op. Atty Gen Kan.
Kansas Attorney General Opinions LEXIS cite	Kan. AG LEXIS
Kansas Court of Appeals LEXIS cite	Kan. App. LEXIS
Kansas Court of Appeals Reports	Kan. App.
Kansas Court of Appeals Reports, 2nd series	Kan. App. 2d
Kansas House Bill	Kan. HB
Kansas House Concurrent Resolution	Kan. HCR
Kansas Journal of Law & Public Policy	Kan. J.L. & Pub. Pol'y
Kansas Law Review	Kan. L. Rev.
Kansas Reports	Kan.
Kansas SEC No-Action LEXIS cite	Kan. Sec. No-Act. LEXIS
Kansas Securities Exchange Commission LEXIS cite	Kan. Sec. LEXIS
Kansas Senate Bill	Kan. SB
Kansas Senate Concurrent Resolution	Kan. SCR
Kansas Supreme Court LEXIS cite	Kan. LEXIS
Kansas Tax LEXIS cite	Kan. Tax LEXIS
Kentucky 1st Extra Session Chapter	Ky. 1st Extra Sess Ch.
Kentucky 1st Extra Session House Bill	Ky. 1st Extra Sess HB
Kentucky 1st Extra Session House Concurrent Resolution	Ky. 1st Extra Sess HCR
Kentucky 1st Extra Session House Joint Resolution	Ky. 1st Extra Sess HJR
Kentucky 1st Extra Session Senate Bill	Ky. 1st Extra Sess SB
Kentucky 1st Extra Session Senate Concurrent Resolution	Ky. 1st Extra Sess SCR
Kentucky 1st Session Senate Joint Resolution	Ky. 1st Extra Sess SJR
Kentucky Acts	Ky. Acts
Kentucky Advance Legislative Service	Ky. ALS
Kentucky Advance Leglisative Service 1st Extra Session	Ky. ALS 1st Extra Sess.
Kentucky Attorney General Opinions	Op. Atty Gen. Ky.
Kentucky Attorney General Opinions LEXIS cite	Op. Atty Gen. Ky. LEXIS
Kentucky Board of Tax Appeals LEXIS cite	Ky. Tax LEXIS

LEXSEE Citation Formats (Cont.)

Kentucky Chapter	Ky. Ch.
Kentucky Court of Appeals LEXIS cite	Ky. App. LEXIS
Kentucky Court of Appeals Reports	Ky. Op.
Kentucky House Bill	Ky. HB
Kentucky House Concurrent Resolution	Ky. HCR
Kentucky House Joint Resolution	Ky. HJR
Kentucky Law Journal	Ky. L.J.
Kentucky Reports	Ky.
Kentucky Resolution	Ky. Resolution
Kentucky Securites Exchange Commission LEXIS cite	Ky. Sec. LEXIS
Kentucky Senate Bill	Ky. SB
Kentucky Senate Concurrent Resolution	Ky. SCR
Kentucky Senate Joint Resolution	Ky. SJR
Kentucky Supreme Court LEXIS cite	Ky. LEXIS
Labor Arbitration Reports (BNA)	Lab. Arb. (BNA)
Labor Cases (CCH)	Lab. Cas. (CCH)
Labor Relations Reference Manual (BNA)	L.R.R.M.
Labour Arbitration Cases	L.A.C.
Land and Water Law Review	Land & Water L. Rev.
Law and Inequality: Journal of Theory and Practice	Law & Ineq.
Law & Psychology Review	Law & Psychol. Rev.
Law Library Journal	Law Libr. J.
Lawyers' Edition, Supreme Court Reports	L. Ed.
Lawyers' Edition, Supreme Court Reports, 2d	L. Ed. 2d
Life Health & Accident Insurance Cases, 2d series	Life. Cas. 2d(CCH)
Life Health & Accident Insurance Cases (CCH)	Life. Cas. (CCH)
Louisiana Acts	La. ACT
Louisiana Advance Legislative Service	La. ALS
Louisiana Annual Reports	La. Ann.
Louisiana Attorney General LEXIS cite	La. AG LEXIS
Louisiana Attorney General Opinions	Op. Atty Gen. La.
Louisiana Court of Appeals LEXIS cite	La. App. LEXIS
Louisiana Court of Appeals Reports	La. App.
Louisiana Environmental LEXIS cite	La. ENV LEXIS
Louisiana Extraordinary Session 1st Act	La. E.S. 1 ACT
Louisiana Extraordinary Session 1st House Bill	La. E.S. 1 HB
Louisiana Extraordinary Session 1st Senate Bill	La. E.S. 1 SB
Louisiana Extraordinary Session 2nd Act	La. E.S. 2 ACT
Louisiana Extraordinary Session 2nd House Bill	La. E.S. 2 HB
Louisiana House Bill	La. HB
Louisiana Law Review	La. L. Rev.

LEXSEE Citation Formats (Cont.)

Louisiana Public Service Commission LEXIS cite	La. PUC LEXIS
Louisiana Reports	La.
Louisiana Resolution	La. RESOLUTION
Louisiana Senate Bill	La. SB
Louisiana Supreme Court LEXIS cite	La. LEXIS
Louisiana Tax LEXIS cite	La. Tax LEXIS
Lowell's District Court Reports (U.S. Massachusets District)	Low.
Loyola of Los Angeles Entertainment Law Journal	Loy. L. A. Ent. L. J.
Loyola of Los Angeles International and	Loy. L.A. Int'l & Comp. L.J. Comparative Law Journal
Loyola University of Chicago Law Journal	Loy. U. Chi. L.J.
Loyola University of Los Angeles Law Review	Loy. L.A. L. Rev.
Maine Advance Legislative Service	Me. ALS
Maine Attorney General LEXIS cite	Me. AG LEXIS
Maine Attorney General Opinions	Op. Atty Gen. Me.
Maine Chapter	Me. Ch.
Maine House Proposal	Me. HP
Maine Initiated Bill	Me. IB
Maine Law Review	Me. L. Rev.
Maine Laws	Me. Laws
Maine Reports	Me.
Maine Resolution	Me. Resolution
Maine Senate Proposal	Me. SP
Maine Supreme Court LEXIS cite	Me. LEXIS
Maritime Law	Mar. Law.
Marquette Law Review	Marq. L. Rev.
Marquette Sports Law Journal	Marq. Sports L.J.
Maryland Advance Legislative Service	Md. ALS
Maryland Appellate Reports	Md. App.
Maryland Attorney General LEXIS cite	Md. AG LEXIS
Maryland Attorney General Opinions	Op. Atty Gen. Md.
Maryland Chancery	Md. Ch.
Maryland Court of Appeals LEXIS cite	Md. LEXIS
Maryland Court of Special Appeals LEXIS cite	Md. App. LEXIS
Maryland House Bill	Md. HB
Maryland Journal of Contemporary Legal Issues	Md. J. Contemp. L. Issues
Maryland Journal of International Law & Trade	Md. J. Int'l L. & Trade
Maryland Law Review	Md. L. Rev.

LEXSEE Citation Formats (Cont.)

Maryland Laws	Md. Laws
Maryland Public Service Commission	Md. P.S.C.
Maryland Public Service Commission LEXIS cite	Md. PSC LEXIS
Maryland Reports	Md.
Maryland SEC No-Action LEXIS cite	Md. Sec. No-Act. LEXIS
Maryland Senate Bill	Md. SB
Maryland Tax Court LEXIS cite	Md. Tax LEXIS
Massachusetts Advance Legislative Service	Mass. ALS
Massachusetts Advance Sheet	Mass. Adv. Sh.
Massachusetts Appellate Court Advance Sheet	Mass. App. Ct. Adv. Sh.
Massachusetts Attorney General LEXIS cite	Mass. AG LEXIS
Massachusetts Attorney General Opinions	Op. Atty Gen. Mass.
Massachusetts Court of Appeals LEXIS cite	Mass. App. LEXIS
Massachusetts Court of Appeals Reports	Mass. App. Ct.
Massachusetts House Bill	Mass. H.B.
Massachusetts Reports	Mass.
Massachusetts SEC No-Action LEXIS cite	Mass. Sec. No-Act. LEXIS
Massachusetts Securities Exchange Commission LEXIS cite	Mass. Sec. LEXIS
Massachusetts Senate Bill	Mass. S.B.
Massachusetts Supreme Judicial Court LEXIS cite	Mass. LEXIS
Massachusetts Tax Appeals LEXIS cite	Mass. Tax LEXIS
McAllister's U.S. Circuit Court Reports	McAll.
McCahon's Reports (KS)	McCahon
McGill Law Journal	McGill L.J.
Media Law Reporter (BNA)	Media L. Rep
Memphis State University Law Review	Mem. St. U.L. Rev.
Mercer Law Review	Mercer L. Rev.
Merit Systems Protection Board Decisions	M.S.P.B.
Merit Systems Protection Board LEXIS cite	MSPB LEXIS
Merit Systems Protection Review	M.S.P.R.
Michigan Advance Legislative Service	Mi. ALS
Michigan Attorney General LEXIS cite	Mich. AG LEXIS
Michigan Attorney General Opinions	Op. Atty Gen. Mich.
Michigan Bar Journal	MI Bar Jnl.
Michigan Court of Appeals LEXIS cite	Mich. App. LEXIS
Michigan Court of Appeals Reports	Mich. App.
Michigan Department of Commerce, Corporations & Securities Bureau LEXIS cite	Mich. Sec. LEXIS
Michigan Environmental LEXIS cite	Mich. ENV LEXIS

LEXSEE Citation Formats (Cont.)

Michigan House Bill	Mi. HB
Michigan Initiative	Mi. Init.
Michigan Journal of International Law	Mich. J. Int'l L.
Michigan Law Review	Mich. L. Rev.
Michigan Public Acts	Mi. P.A.
Michigan Public Employee Reporter (LRP)	MPER (LRP)
Michigan Public Employee Reporter (LRP) LEXIS cite	MPER (LRP) LEXIS
Michigan Public Service Commission LEXIS cite	Mich. PSC LEXIS
Michigan Reports	Mich.
Michigan Senate Bill	Mi. SB
Michigan Supreme Court LEXIS cite	Mich. LEXIS
Michigan Tax Tribunals LEXIS cite	Mich. Tax LEXIS
Michigan Telecommunications and Technology Law Review	Mich. Tel Tech. L.R.
Michigan Worker's Compensation Appeals Board LEXIS cite	Mich. Wrk. Comp. LEXIS
Military Justice Reporter	M.J.
Military Law Review	Mil. L. Rev.
Minnesota 1st Special Session Chapter	Minn. 1st Sp. Sess. Ch
Minnesota 1st Special Session House File Number	Minn. 1st Sp. Sess. H.F. No.
Minnesota 1st Special Session Senate File Number	Minn. 1st Sp. Sess. S.F. No.
Minnesota Advance Legislative Service	Minn. ALS
Minnesota Advance Legislative Service 1st Special Session	Minn. ALS 1st Sp. Sess.
Minnesota Attorney General LEXIS cite	Minn. AG LEXIS
Minnesota Attorney General Opinions	Op. Atty Gen Minn.
Minnesota Chapter Law	Minn. Chapter Law
Minnesota Court of Appeals LEXIS cite	Minn. App. LEXIS
Minnesota House Bill	Minn. H.B.
Minnesota House Bill Number	Minn. H.B. NO.
Minnesota House File Number	Minn. H.F. No.
Minnesota Journal of Global Trade	Minn. J. Global Trade
Minnesota Law Review	Minn. L. Rev.
Minnesota Public Utilities Commission LEXIS cite	Minn. PUC LEXIS
Minnesota Reports	Minn.
Minnesota Resolution	Minn. Resolution
Minnesota Senate Bill	Minn. S.B.
Minnesota Senate Bill Number	Minn. S.B. NO.
Minnesota Senate File Number	Minn. S.F. No.

LEXSEE Citation Formats (Cont.)

Minnesota Supreme Court LEXIS cite	Minn. LEXIS
Minnesota Tax Court LEXIS cite	Minn. Tax LEXIS
Mississippi Advance Legislative Service	Miss. ALS
Mississippi Attorney General LEXIS cite	Miss. AG LEXIS
Mississippi Attorney General Opinions	Op. Atty Gen Miss.
Mississippi House Bill	Miss. H.B.
Mississippi House Concurrent Resolution	Miss. H.C.R.
Mississippi House Joint Resolution	Miss. H.J.R.
Mississippi Law Journal	Miss. L.J.
Mississippi Laws	Miss. Laws
Mississippi Reports	Miss.
Mississippi Senate	Miss. S.B.
Mississippi Senate Concurrent Resolution	Miss. S.C.R.
Mississippi Senate Joint Resolution	Miss. S.J.R.
Mississippi Supreme Court LEXIS cite	Miss. LEXIS
Missouri Advance Legislative Service	Mo. ALS
Missouri Appeals Reports	Mo. App.
Missouri Attorney General LEXIS cite	Mo. AG LEXIS
Missouri Attorney General Opinions	Op. Atty Gen Mo.
Missouri Code of State Regulations	C.S.R.
Missouri Court of Appeals LEXIS cite	Mo. App. LEXIS
Missouri House Bill	Mo. HB
Missouri House Joint Resolution	MO. HJR
Missouri Laws	MO. LAWS
Missouri Public Service Commission (N.S.)	Mo. P.S.C. (N.S.)
Missouri Public Service Commission LEXIS cite	Mo. PSC LEXIS
Missouri Reports	Mo.
Missouri Secretary of State, Division of Securities LEXIS cite	Mo. Sec. LEXIS
Missouri Senate Bill	Mo. SB
Missouri Senate Joint Resolution	MO. SJR
Missouri State Tax & Administrative Hearing Commission LEXIS cite	Mo. Tax LEXIS
Missouri Supreme Court LEXIS cite	Mo. LEXIS
Missouri Tax Letter Rulings LEXIS cite	Mo. Tax Ltr. Rul. LEXIS
Montana Advance Legislative Service	Mt. ALS
Montana Advance Legislative Service Special Session	Mt. ALS Sp. Sess.
Montana Attorney General LEXIS cite	Mont. AG LEXIS
Montana Attorney General Opinions	Op. Atty Gen. Mont.
Montana Attorney General Opinions (Number)	Op. Atty Gen. Mont. No.
Montana Chapter	Mt. Ch.
Montana House Bill	Mt. HB

LEXSEE Citation Formats (Cont.)

Montana House Concurrent Resolution	M.T. HCR
Montana House Joint Resolution	MT HJR
Montana House Resolution	Mt. HR
Montana Reports	Mont.
Montana Resolution	M.T. Resolution
Montana Senate Bill	Mt. SB
Montana Senate Concurrent Resolution	MT SCR
Montana Senate Joint Resolution	MT SJR
Montana Senate Resolution	Mt. SR
Montana Special Session Chapter	Mt. Sp. Sess. CH
Montana Special Session House Bill	Mt. Sp. Sess. HB
Montana Special Session House Joint Resolution	Mt. Sp. Sess. HJR
Montana Special Session House Resolution	Mt. Sp. Sess. HR
Montana Special Session Senate Bill	Mt. Sp. Sess. SB
Montana Special Session Senate Joint Resolution	Mt. Sp. Sess. SJR
Montana Special Session Senate Resolution	Mt. Sp. Sess. SR
Montana State Reporter (MT)	Mont. St. Rep.
Montana State Tax Appeals Board LEXIS cite	Mont. Tax LEXIS
Montana Supreme Court LEXIS cite	Mont. LEXIS
Motor Carrier Cases, Interstate Commerce Commission Reports	M.C.C.
Motor Carrier Cases LEXIS cite	MCC LEXIS
NASA Board of Contract Appeals LEXIS cite	NASA BCA LEXIS
National Association of Insurance Commissioners Proceedings	NAIC Proc.
National Labor Relations Board	NLRB No. Number
National Labor Relations Board Decisions	NLRB Dec. (CCH)
National Labor Relations Board General Counsel Memorandum LEXIS cite	NLRB GCM LEXIS
National Labor Relations Board LEXIS cite	NLRB LEXIS
National Labor Relations Board Reports	N.L.R.B.
National Oceanic & Atmospheric Administration LEXIS cite	NOAA LEXIS
National Regulatory Commission Issuances	N.R.C.
National Transportation Safety Board Decisions	N.T.S.B.
National Transportation Safety Board LEXIS cite	NTSB LEXIS
Natural Resources Tax Review	Nat. Res. Tax Rev.
Naval Law Review	Naval L. Rev.
Nebraska Advance Legislative Service	Neb. ALS
Nebraska Appeals	Neb. App.
Nebraska Appeals LEXIS cite	Neb. App. LEXIS
Nebraska Court of Appeals Decisions	NCA

LEXSEE Citation Formats (Cont.)

Nebraska Law Review	Neb. L. Rev.
Nebraska Laws	Neb. Laws
Nebraska Legislative Bill	Neb. LB
Nebraska Legislative Resolution	Neb. LR
Nebraska Reports	Neb.
Nebraska Supreme Court LEXIS cite	Neb. LEXIS
Negligence Cases (CCH)	Neg. Cas. (CCH)
Negligence Cases 2nd (CCH)	Neg. Cas. 2d (CCH)
Nevada Advance Legislative Service	Nev. ALS
Nevada Advance Legislative Service (Special Session)	Nev. ALS (th Sp. Sess.)
Nevada Advance Opinion Number	Nev. Adv. Ops. No.
Nevada Assembly Bill	Nev. AB
Nevada Attorney General LEXIS cite	Nev. AG LEXIS
Nevada Attorney General Opinions	Op. Atty Gen. Nev.
Nevada Chapter	Nev. Ch.
Nevada House Bill	Nev. HB
Nevada Reports	Nev.
Nevada Resolution	Nev. Resolution
Nevada Senate Bill	Nev. SB
Nevada Supreme Court LEXIS cite	Nev. LEXIS
New England Journal of Criminal/Civil Confinement	N.E. J. on Crim. & Civ. C.
New England Law Review	New Eng. L. Rev.
New Hampshire Advance Legislative Service	NH ALS
New Hampshire Attorney General LEXIS cite	N.H. AG LEXIS
New Hampshire Attorney General Opinions	Op. Atty Gen N.H.
New Hampshire Board of Tax & Land Appeals LEXIS cite	N.H. Tax LEXIS
New Hampshire Chapter	NH Ch.
New Hampshire House Bill	NH HB
New Hampshire House Joint Resolution	N.H. HJR
New Hampshire Laws	NH LAWS
New Hampshire Reporter	N.H.
New Hampshire Senate Bill	NH SB
New Hampshire Senate Joint Resolution	N.H. SJR
New Hampshire Supreme Court LEXIS cite	N.H. LEXIS
New Jersey Advance Legislative Service	N.J. ALS
New Jersey Agency Reports, 2d series (Community Affairs)	N.J.A.R.2d (CAF)
New Jersey Agency Reports, 2d series (Transportation)	N.J.A.R.2d (TRP)
New Jersey Agency Reports, 2d series (Police Training Commission)	N.J.A.R.2d (PTC)

LEXSEE Citation Formats (Cont.)

New Jersey Agency Reports, 2d series (Pensions)	N.J.A.R.2d (TYP)
New Jersey Agency Reports, 2d series (Higher Education)	N.J.A.R.2d (HED)
New Jersey Agency Reports, 2d series (Casino Control Commission)	N.J.A.R.2d (CCC)
New Jersey Agency Reports, 2d series (Health)	N.J.A.R.2d (HLT)
New Jersey Agency Reports, 2d series (Insurance)	N.J.A.R.2d (INS)
New Jersey Agency Reports, 2d series (Banking)	N.J.A.R.2d (BKG)
New Jersey Agency Reports, 2d series (Racing Commission)	N.J.A.R.2d (RAC)
New Jersey Agency Reports, 2d series (Board of Regulatory Commissioners)	N.J.A.R.2d (BRC)
New Jersey Agency Reports, 2d series (Unemployment Compensation)	N.J.A.R.2d (UCC)
New Jersey Agency Reports, 2d series (Workers Compensation)	N.J.A.R.2D (WCC)
New Jersey Agency Reports, 2d series (State Department)	N.J.A.R.2d (STE)
New Jersey Agency Reports, 2d series (Real Estate Commission)	N.J.A.R.2d (REC)
New Jersey Agency Reports, 2d series (Professional Boards)	N.J.A.R.2d (BDS)
New Jersey Agency Reports, 2d series (Division of Economic Assistance)	N.J.A.R.2d (DEA)
New Jersey Agency Reports, 2d series (Education)	N.J.A.R.2d (EDU)
New Jersey Agency Reports, 2d series (Civil Service)	N.J.A.R.2d (CSV)
New Jersey Agency Reports, 2d series (Consumer Affairs)	N.J.A.R.2d (CMA)
New Jersey Agency Reports, 2d series (Alcohol Beverage Control))	N.J.A.R.2d (ABC)
New Jersey Agency Reports, 2d series (Special Education)	N.J.A.R.2d (EDS)
New Jersey Agency Reports, 2d series (Division of Medical Assistance & Health Services)	N.J.A.R.2d (DMA)
New Jersey Agency Reports, 2d series (Labor & Industry)	N.J.A.R.2d (LBR)
New Jersey Agency Reports, 2d series (Office of Administrative Law)	N.J.A.R.2d (OAL)
New Jersey Agency Reports, 2d series (Motor Vehicles)	N.J.A.R.2d (MVH)
New Jersey Agency Reports, 2d series (State Police)	N.J.A.R.2d (POL)
New Jersey Agency Reports, 2d series (Civil Rights)	N.J.A.R.2d (CRT)
New Jersey Agency Reports, 2d series (Pinelands Commission)	N.J.A.R.2d (EPC)

LEXSEE Citation Formats (Cont.)

New Jersey Agency Reports, 2d series (Environmental Protection & Energy)	N.J.A.R.2d (EPE)
New Jersey Assembly Concurrent Resolution	N.J. ACR
New Jersey Assembly Joint Resolution	N.J. AJR
New Jersey Assembly Number	N.J. A.N.
New Jersey Attorney General LEXIS cite	N.J. AG LEXIS
New Jersey Attorney General Opinions	Op. Atty Gen N.J.
New Jersey Chapter	N.J. Ch.
New Jersey Concurrent Resolution	N.J. CR
New Jersey Environmental LEXIS cite	N.J. ENV LEXIS
New Jersey Equity Reports	N.J. Eq.
New Jersey Joint Resolution	N.J. JR
New Jersey Law Reports	N.J.L.
New Jersey Laws	N.J. Laws
New Jersey Miscellaneous Reports	N.J. Misc.
New Jersey Public Employee Reporter (LRP)	NJPER (LRP)
New Jersey Public Employee Reporter (LRP) LEXIS cite	NJPER (LRP) LEXIS
New Jersey Reports	N.J.
New Jersey Senate Concurrent Resolution	N.J. SCR
New Jersey Senate Joint Resolution	N.J. SJR
New Jersey Senate Number	N.J. S.N.
New Jersey Superior Court LEXIS cite	N.J. Super. LEXIS
New Jersey Superior Court Reports	N.J. Super.
New Jersey Supreme Court LEXIS cite	N.J. LEXIS
New Jersey Tax Court LEXIS cite	N.J. Tax LEXIS
New Jersey Tax Court Reports	N.J. Tax
New Mexico Advance Legislative Service	N.M. ALS
New Mexico Attorney General LEXIS cite	N.M. AG LEXIS
New Mexico Attorney General Opinions	Op. Atty Gen. N.M.
New Mexico Chapter	N.M. Ch.
New Mexico Court of Appeals	N.M. App.
New Mexico Court of Appeals LEXIS cite	N.M. App. LEXIS
New Mexico House Bill	N.M. HB
New Mexico Law Review	N.M.L. Rev.
New Mexico Laws	N.M. Laws
New Mexico Reports	N.M.
New Mexico Senate Bill	N.M. SB
New Mexico State Bar Bulletin	N.M. St. B. Bull.
New Mexico Supreme Court LEXIS cite	N.M. LEXIS
New York Advance Legislative Service	N.Y. ALS
New York Appellate Division LEXIS cite	N.Y. App. Div. LEXIS

LEXSEE Citation Formats (Cont.)

Publication	Citation Format
New York Appellate Division Reports	A.D.
New York Appellate Division Reports, second series	A.D.2d
New York Assembly Number	N.Y. A.N.
New York Attorney General LEXIS cite	N.Y. AG LEXIS
New York Attorney General Opinions	Op. Atty Gen. N.Y.
New York Attorney General Opinions (Informal)	Op. (Inf.) Atty Gen. N.Y.
New York City Tax LEXIS cite	N.Y. City Tax LEXIS
New York Civil Court Procedures Reporter (n.s.)	
N.Y. Civ. Proc. Rep. (n.s.)	
New York Environmental LEXIS cite	N.Y. ENV LEXIS
New York Jurisprudence	NYJ (title) TOC 1
New York Law School Journal of Human Rights	N. Y. L. Sch. J. Hum. Rts.
New York Law School Journal of International & Comparative Law	N. Y. L. Sch. J. Int'l & Comp. L.
New York Law School Law Review	N. Y. L. Sch. L. Rev.
New York Laws	N.Y. LAWS
New York Miscellaneous LEXIS cite	N.Y. Misc. LEX-IS
New York Miscellaneous Reports	Misc.
New York Miscellaneous Reports, 2nd series	Misc. 2d
New York Public Service Commission	NY PSC
New York Public Service Commission LEXIS cite	N.Y. PUC LEXIS
New York Reports	N.Y.
New York Reports, 2nd series	N.Y.2d
New York Senate Number	N.Y. S.N.
New York State Comptroller Decisions	N.Y. St. Comp.
New York State Comptroller LEXIS cite	N.Y. Comp. LEX-IS
New York Supplement	N.Y.S.
New York Supplement, 2nd series	N.Y.S.2d
New York Supreme Court LEXIS cite	N.Y. LEXIS
New York Tax Commission LEXIS cite	N.Y. Tax LEXIS
New York University Law Review	N.Y.U.L. Rev.
New York University Tax Law Review	Tax L. Rev.
Newberry's District Court Admiralty Reports (U.S.)	Newb. Adm.
North Carolina Advance Legislative Service	N.C. ALS
North Carolina Attorney General LEXIS cite	N.C. AG LEXIS
North Carolina Attorney General Opinions	Op. Atty Gen. N.C.
North Carolina Central Law Journal	N.C. Cent. L.J.
North Carolina Chapter	N.C. Ch.

LEXSEE Citation Formats (Cont.)

North Carolina Court of Appeals LEXIS cite	N.C. App. LEXIS
North Carolina Court of Appeals Reports	N.C. App.
North Carolina House Bill	N.C. HB
North Carolina Journal of International Law & Commerce Regulations	N.C. J. Int'l L. & Comm. Reg.
North Carolina Law Review	N.C.L. Rev.
North Carolina Reports	N.C.
North Carolina Senate Bill	N.C. SB
North Carolina Session Laws	N.C. Sess. Laws
North Carolina Supreme Court LEXIS cite	N.C. LEXIS
North Carolina Tax LEXIS cite	N.C. Tax LEXIS
North Dakota Advance Legislative Service	N.D. ALS
North Dakota Attorney General LEXIS cite	N.D. AG LEXIS
North Dakota Attorney General Opinions	Op. Atty Gen. N.D.
North Dakota Chapter	N.D. Ch.
North Dakota Court of Appeals LEXIS cite	N.D. App. LEXIS
North Dakota House Bill	N.D. HB
North Dakota House Concurrent Resolution	N.D. HCR
North Dakota House Joint Resolution	N.D. HJR
North Dakota House Resolution	N.D. HR
North Dakota Law Review	N. Dak. L. Rev.
North Dakota Laws	N.D. Laws
North Dakota Reports	N.D.
North Dakota Resolution	ND Resolution
North Dakota Senate Bill	N.D. SB
North Dakota Senate Concurrent Resolution	N.D. SCR
North Dakota Senate Joint Resolution	N.D. SJR
North Dakota Senate Resolution	N.D. SR
North Dakota Supreme Court LEXIS cite	N.D. LEXIS
North Eastern Reporter	N.E.
North Eastern Reporter, 2nd series	N.E.2d
North Western Reporter	N.W.
North Western Reporter 2nd	N.W.2d
Northern Illinois University Law	N. Ill. U. L. Rev. Review
Northern Kentucky Law Review	N. Ky. L. Rev.
Northwestern University Law Review	Nw. U.L. Rev.
Notre Dame Journal of Legislation	J. Legis.
Notre Dame Law Review	Notre Dame L. Rev.
Nuclear Regulatory Commission LEXIS cite	NRC LEXIS
Occupational Safety & Health Cases (BNA)	OSHC (BNA)
Occupational Safety & Health Decisions (CCH)	OSHD (CCH)
Occupational Safety & Health Review Commission	OSAHRC
Occupational Safety & Health Review Commission LEXIS cite	OSAHRC LEXIS

LEXSEE Citation Formats (Cont.)

Office of Comptroller of the Currency Cumulative Bulletin LEXIS cite	OCC CB LEXIS
Office of Comptroller of the Currency Enforcement Decisions LEXIS cite	OCC Enf. Dec. LEXIS
Office of Legal Counsel LEXIS cite	OLC LEXIS
Office of the Comptroller of the Currency Letters LEXIS cite	OCC Ltr. LEXIS
Ohio Appellate Reports	Ohio App.
Ohio Appellate Reports, 2nd series	Ohio App. 2d
Ohio Appellate Reports, 3rd series	Ohio App. 3d
Ohio Attorney General LEXIS cite	Ohio AG LEXIS
Ohio Attorney General Opinions	Op. Atty Gen. Ohio
Ohio Bar Association Reports	Ohio B. Rep.
Ohio Board of Tax Appeals LEXIS cite	Ohio Tax LEXIS
Ohio Court of Appeals LEXIS cite	Ohio App. LEXIS
Ohio Environmental LEXIS cite	Ohio ENV LEXIS
Ohio House Bill	Ohio HB
Ohio House Joint Resolution	Ohio HJR
Ohio Jurisprudence	OHJ (title) TOC 1
Ohio Law Abstracts	Ohio L. Abs.
Ohio Law Reporter	Ohio L. Rep.
Ohio Miscellaneous Courts LEXIS cite	Ohio Misc. LEXIS
Ohio Miscellaneous Reports	Ohio Misc.
Ohio Miscellaneous Reports, 2nd series	Ohio Misc. 2d
Ohio Northern University Law Review	Ohio N.U.L. Rev.
Ohio Opinions	Ohio Op.
Ohio Opinions, 2nd series	Ohio Op. 2d
Ohio Opinions, 3rd series	Ohio Op. 3d
Ohio Public Employee Reporter (LRP)	OPER (LRP)
Ohio Public Employee Reporter (LRP) LEXIS cite	OPER (LRP) LEXIS
Ohio Public Utilities Commission LEXIS cite	Ohio PUC LEXIS
Ohio Reports	Ohio
Ohio Securites Exchange Commission LEXIS cite	Oh. Sec. LEXIS
Ohio Senate Bill	Ohio SB
Ohio Senate Joint Resolution	Ohio SJR
Ohio State Law Journal	Ohio St. L.J.
Ohio State Journal on Dispute Resolution	Ohio St. J. on Disp. Resol.
Ohio State Reports	Ohio St.
Ohio State Reports, 2nd series	Ohio St. 2d
Ohio State Reports, 3rd series	Ohio St. 3d
Ohio Supreme Court LEXIS cite	Ohio LEXIS
Oklahoma Advance Legislative Service	OK. ALS
Oklahoma Attorney General LEXIS cite	Okla. AG LEXIS

LEXSEE Citation Formats (Cont.)

Oklahoma Attorney General Opinions	Op. Atty Gen. Okla.
Oklahoma Bar Association Journal	O.B.A.J.
Oklahoma Chapter	OK. Ch.
Oklahoma Court of Appeals LEXIS cite	Okla. Civ. App. LEXIS
Oklahoma Court of Criminal Appeals LEXIS cite	Okla. Crim. App. LEXIS
Oklahoma House Bill	OK. HB
Oklahoma House Concurrent Resolution	OK. HCR
Oklahoma House Joint Resolution	OK. HJR
Oklahoma House Resolution	OK. HR
Oklahoma Law Review	Okla. L. Rev.
Oklahoma Reports	Okla.
Oklahoma Resolution	Ok. RESOLUTION
Oklahoma Securities Commission LEXIS cite	Okla. Sec. LEXIS
Oklahoma Senate Bill	OK. SB
Oklahoma Senate Concurrent Resolution	OK. SCR
Oklahoma Senate Joint Resolution	OK. SJR
Oklahoma Senate Resolution	OK. SR
Oklahoma Supreme Court LEXIS cite	Okla. LEXIS
Oklahoma Tax Commission LEXIS cite	Okla. Tax LEXIS
Opinions of the Office of Legal Counsel (Volume A)	Op. O.L.C. (Vol. A)
Opinions of the Office of Legal Counsel (Volume B)	Op. O.L.C. (Vol. B)
Opinions of the Office of Legal Counsel	Op. O.L.C.
Opinions of the Secretary of Public Relations	Op. Sec. P.R.
Oregon Advance Legislative Service	Ore. ALS
Oregon Attorney General LEXIS cite	Ore. AG LEXIS
Oregon Attorney General Opinions	Op. Atty Gen. Ore.
Oregon Court of Appeals LEXIS cite	Ore. App. LEXIS
Oregon Court of Appeals Reports	Ore. App.
Oregon House Bill	Ore. HB
Oregon House Concurrent Resolution	Ore. HCR
Oregon House Joint Memorial	Ore. HJM
Oregon House Joint Resolution	Ore. HJR
Oregon Law Review	Or. L. Rev.
Oregon Laws & Regulations	Ore. Laws
Oregon Reports	Ore.
Oregon Securities Commission LEXIS cite	Ore. Sec. LEXIS
Oregon Senate Bill	Ore. SB
Oregon Senate Concurrent Resolution	Ore. SCR
Oregon Senate Joint Memorial	Ore. SJM
Oregon Senate Joint Resolution	Ore. SJR

LEXSEE Citation Formats (Cont.)

Oregon State Bar Bulletin	OR St. Bar Bull.
Oregon Supreme Court LEXIS cite	Ore. LEXIS
Oregon Tax Court LEXIS cite	Ore. Tax LEXIS
Oregon Tax Reports	OTR
Pace Environmental Law Review	Pace Envtl. L. Rev
Pace International Law Review	Pace Int'l L. Rev.
Pace Law Review	Pace L. Rev.
Pacific Law Journal	Pac. L.J.
Pacific Reporter	P.
Pacific Reporter, 2nd series	P.2d
Patton, Jr. & Health Reports (VA)	P.H.
Pennsylvania Advance Legislative Service	Pa. ALS
Pennsylvania Attorney General LEXIS cite	Pa. AG LEXIS
Pennsylvania Attorney General Opinions	Op. Atty Gen. Pa.
Pennsylvania Bulletin	Pa. Bull.
Pennsylvania Commonwealth Court LEXIS cite	Pa. Commw. LEXIS
Pennsylvania Commonwealth Court Reports	Pa. Commw.
Pennsylvania Commonwealth Court Tax LEXIS cite	Pa. Tax LEXIS
Pennsylvania Environmental Hearing Board LEXIS cite	Pa. Envirn. LEXIS
Pennsylvania House Bill	Pa. HB
Pennsylvania House Concurrent Resolution	Pa. HCR
Pennsylvania House Joint Resolution	Pa. HJR
Pennsylvania Laws	Pa. Laws
Pennsylvania Public Utilities Commission	Pa. PUC
Pennsylvania Public Utilities Commission LEXIS cite	Pa. PUC LEXIS
Pennsylvania Securites Commission LEXIS cite	Pa. Sec. LEXIS
Pennsylvania Senate Bill	Pa. SB
Pennsylvania Senate Concurrent Resolution	Pa. SCR
Pennsylvania Senate Joint Resolution	Pa. SJR
Pennsylvania State Reports	Pa.
Pennsylvania Superior Court LEXIS cite	Pa. Super. LEXIS
Pennsylvania Superior Court Reports	Pa. Super.
Pennsylvania Supreme Court LEXIS cite	Pa. LEXIS
Pension Benefit Guarantee Corporation LEXIS cite	PBGC LEXIS
Pepperdine Law Review	Pepp. L. Rev.
Peter's District Court Admiralty Reports	Pet. Adm.
Peter's United States Circuit Court Reports	Pet. C.C.
Philadelphia County Reporter LEXIS cite	Phila. Cty. Rptr. LEXIS
Philadelphia Reports (PA)	Phila.

LEXSEE Citation Formats (Cont.)

Postal Service Board of Contract Appeals LEXIS cite	PSBCA LEXIS
Private Letter Ruling	PRIVATE RULING
Private Letter Ruling LEXIS cite	PRL LEXIS
Product Liability Reports (CCH)	CCH Prod. Liab. Rep.
Public Employment Reporter for California	PERC (LRP)
Public Employment Reporter for California LEXIS cite	PERC (LRP) LEXIS
Public Employment Reporter for Illinois	PERI (LRP)
Public Employment Reporter for Illinois LEXIS cite	PERI (LRP) LEXIS
Public Lands Revised	Pub. Lands Rev.
Public Laws	P.L.
Public Utilities Reports , 4th series	P.U.R.4th
Puerto Rico Act	PR ACT
Puerto Rico Advance Legislative Service	PR ALS
Puerto Rico House Bill	PR H.B.
Puerto Rico Laws	PR LAWS
Puerto Rico Senate Bill	PR S.B.
Puerto Rico Sentencias	P.R. Sent.
Puget Sound Law Review	Puget Sound L. Rev.
Quinnipiac Law Review	Quinnipiac L. Rev
Radio Regulation Reporter, 2nd series (P & F)	Rad. Reg. 2d (P & F)
Research Institute of America, Federal Tax * Each chapter is individually available through the LEXSEE feature by using the following format: reporter abbreviation, chapter number, section number, i.e. RIAFTC A 1000	RIAFTC *
Resolution Trust Corporation LEXIS cite	RTC LEXIS
Revenue Procedure	REV. PROC.
Revenue Ruling	REV. RUL.
Review of Litigation, the	Rev. Litig
Rhode Island Advance Legislative Service	R.I. ALS
Rhode Island Attorney General LEXIS cite	R.I. AG LEXIS
Rhode Island Attorney General Opinions	Op. Atty Gen R.I.
Rhode Island Bar Journal	RI Bar Jnl.
Rhode Island House Bill	R.I. HB
Rhode Island Public Chapter	R.I. Pub. Ch.
Rhode Island Public Laws	R.I. Pub. Laws
Rhode Island Reports	R.I
Rhode Island Senate Bill	R.I. SB
Rhode Island Supreme Court LEXIS cite	R.I. LEXIS
Rhode Island Tax Appeals LEXIS cite	R.I. Tax LEXIS

LEXSEE Citation Formats (Cont.)

RICO Business Dispute Guide	RICO Bus. Disp. Guide
Rutgers Computer & Technology Law Journal	Rutgers Computer & Tech. L.J.
Rutgers Law Journal	Rutgers L. J.
Rutgers Law Review	Rutgers L. Rev.
San Diego Justice Journal	San Diego Justice J.
San Diego Law Review	San Diego L. Rev.
Santa Clara Computer & High Tech. Law Journal	Computer & High Tech L. J.
Santa Clara Law Review	Santa Clara L. Rev.
Securities & Exchange Commission Decisions	S.E.C.
Securities & Exchange Commission Decisions LEXIS cite	SEC LEXIS
Securities & Exchange Commission Judicial Decisions	SEC Jud. Dec.
Securities & Exchange Commission No-Action LEXIS cite	SEC No-Act. LEXIS
Senate Concurrent Resolution - federal bill - enacted version of bill	Enacted S. Con. Res.
Senate Concurrent Resolution - federal bill - tracking report	Bill Tracking S. Con. Res.
Senate Concurrent Resolution - federal bill - unenacted version(s) of bill	S. Con. Res.
Senate - federal bill - enacted version of bill	Enacted S.
Senate - federal bill - tracking report	Bill Tracking S.
Senate - federal bill - unenacted version(s) of bill	S.
Senate Joint Resolution - federal bill - enacted version of bill	Enacted S.J. Res.
Senate Joint Resolution - federal bill - tracking report	Bill Tracking S.J. Res.
Senate Joint Resolution - federal bill - unenacted version(s) of bill	S.J. Res.
Senate Resolution - federal bill - enacted version of bill	Enacted S. Res.
Senate Resolution - federal bill - tracking report	Bill Tracking S. Res.
Senate Resolution - federal bill - unenacted version(s) of bill	S. Res.
Session Laws of Kansas	Kan. Sess. Laws
Seton Hall Journal of Sport Law	Seton Hall J. Sport L.
Seton Hall Law Review	Seton Hall L. Rev.
Seton Hall Legislative Journal	Seton Hall Legis. J
Slip opinion (Court of International Trade only)	SLIP OP.
SMU Law Review	SMU L. Rev.
South Carolina Acts and Joint Resolutions	S.C. Acts

LEXSEE Citation Formats (Cont.)

South Carolina Attorney General LEXIS cite	S.C. AG LEXIS
South Carolina Attorney General Opinions	Op. Atty Gen S.C.
South Carolina Court of Appeals LEXIS cite	S.C. App. LEXIS
South Carolina Environmental Law Journal	S.C. Envtl. L.J.
South Carolina House Bill	S.C. H.B.
South Carolina Law Review	S.C. L. Rev.
South Carolina Reports	S.C.
South Carolina Senate Bill	S.C. S.B.
South Carolina Supreme Court LEXIS cite	S.C. LEXIS
South Carolina Tax Commission LEXIS cite	S.C. Tax LEXIS
South Dakota Advance Legislative Service	S.D. ALS
South Dakota Attorney General LEXIS cite	S.D. AG LEXIS
South Dakota Attorney General Opinions	Op. Atty Gen. S.D.
South Dakota Chapter	S.D. CH
South Dakota House Bill	S.D. HB
South Dakota Law Review	S.D. L. REV.
South Dakota Laws	S.D. Laws
South Dakota Reports	S.D.
South Dakota SEC No-Action LEXIS cite	S.D. Sec. No-Act. LEXIS
South Dakota Securities Commission LEXIS cite	S.D. Sec. LEXIS
South Dakota Senate Bill	S.D. SB
South Dakota Supreme Court LEXIS cite	S.D. LEXIS
South Eastern Reporter	S.E.
South Eastern Reporter, 2nd series	S.E.2d
South Texas Law Review	S Tex. L. Rev.
South Western Reporter	S.W.
South Western Reporter, 2nd series	S.W.2d
Southern California Interdiciplinary Law Journal	S. Cal Interdis L.J.
Southern California Law Review	S. Cal. L. Rev.
Southern California Review of Law and Women's Studies	S. Cal. Rev. L. & Women's Stud.
Southern Illinois University Law Journal	S. Ill. U. L. J.
Southern Methodist University Law Review	SMU L. Rev.
Southern Reporter	So.
Southern Reporter, 2nd series	So. 2d
Southern University Law Review	S.U.L.Rev.
Southwestern Journal of Law & Trade in the Americas	Sw.J. of L.& Trade Am.
Southwestern University Law Review	Sw. U. L. Rev.
Sprague's United States District Court (Admiralty) Decisions	Sprague
St. John's Journal of Legal Community	St. John's J. L. Comm.

LEXSEE Citation Formats (Cont.)

St. John's Law Review	St. John's L. Rev.
St. Louis Law Journal	St. Louis L.J.
St. Louis University Public Law Review	St Louis U. Pub. L. Rev
St. Mary's Law Journal	St. Mary's L. J.
St. Thomas Law Review	St. Thomas L. Rev.
Stanford Environmental Law Journal	Stan. Envtl. L.J.
Stanford Journal of International Law	Stan. J Int'l L.
Stanford Journal of Law, Business & Finance	Stan. J.L. Bus. & Fin.
Stanford Law & Policy Review	Stan. L. & Pol'y Rev.
Stanford Law Review	Stan. L. Rev.
Stetson Law Review	Stetson L. Rev.
Suffolk Transnational Law Journal	Suffolk Transnat'l L. J.
Suffolk University Law Review	Suffolk U. L. Rev.
Sumner's United States Circuit Court Reports	Sumn.
Supreme Court of Australian Capital Territory Opinions LEXIS cite	AUST ACTSC LEXIS
Supreme Court of Northern Territory LEXIS cite (Australia)	AUST NTSC LEXIS
Supreme Court of South Australia LEXIS cite	AUST SASC LEXIS
Supreme Court of Tasmania LEXIS cite (Australia)	AUST TASSC LEXIS
Supreme Court Reporter	S.C. R.
Supreme Court Reporter	S. Ct.
Syracuse Journal of International Law & Commerce	Syracuse J. Int'l L. & Com.
Syracuse Law Review	Syracuse L. Rev.
Tax Court	T.C.
Tax Court Memorandum (Prentice Hall)	T.C.Mem.(P-H)
Tax Court Memorandum Decisions	T.C. Memo
Tax Court Memorandum Decisions (CCH)	T.C.M. (CCH)
Tax Court Number	T.C. No.
Technical Memorandum LEXIS cite	TM LEXIS
Temple Environmental Law & Technology Journal	Temp. Envtl. L. & Tech. J.
Temple International & Comparative Law Journal	Temp. Int'l & Comp. L.J.
Temple Law Review	Temple L. Rev.

LEXSEE Citation Formats (Cont.)

Temple Political & Civil Rights Law Review	Temple Pol & Civ Rts L R
Tennessee Advance Legislative Service	Tn. ALS
Tennessee Appeals	Tenn. App.
Tennessee Attorney General LEXIS cite	Tenn. AG LEXIS
Tennessee Attorney General Opinions	Op. Atty Gen. Tenn.
Tennessee Court of Appeals LEXIS cite	Tenn. App. LEXIS
Tennessee Court of Criminal Appeals LEXIS cite	Tenn. Crim. App. LEXIS
Tennessee House Bill	Tn. HB
Tennessee Law Review	Tenn. L. Rev.
Tennessee Public Acts	Tenn. Pub. Acts
Tennessee Public Chapter	Tn. Pub. Ch.
Tennessee Regulations LEXIS cite	Tenn. Reg. LEXIS
Tennessee Reports	Tenn.
Tennessee Senate Bill	Tn. SB
Tennessee Supreme Court LEXIS cite	Tenn. LEXIS
Texas Advance Legislative Service	Tex. ALS
Texas Attorney General LEXIS cite	Tex. AG LEXIS
Texas Attorney General Opinions	Op. Atty Gen. Tex.
Texas Chapter	Tex. Ch
Texas Comptroller LEXIS cite	Tex. Tax LEXIS
Texas Court of Appeals & Civil Appeals LEXIS cite	Tex. App. LEXIS
Texas Court of Criminal Appeals LEXIS cite	Tex. Crim. App. LEXIS
Texas Criminal Reports	Tex. Crim.
Texas General Laws	Tex. Gen. Laws
Texas House Bill	Tex. HB
Texas House Concurrent Resolution	Tex. HCR
Texas House Joint Resolution	Tex. HJR
Texas Intellectual Property Law Journal	Tex. Intell. Prop. L. J.
Texas International Law Journal	Tex Int'l L. J.
Texas Jurisprudence	TXJ (title) TOC 1
Texas Law Review	Tex. L. Rev.
Texas Public Utilities Commission Bulletins	Texas P.U.C. Bulletin
Texas Public Utilities Commission LEXIS cite	Tex. PUC LEXIS
Texas Reports	Tex.
Texas Securities Commission LEXIS cite	Tex. Sec. LEXIS
Texas Senate Bill	Tex. SB
Texas Senate Concurrent Resolution	Tex. SCR
Texas Senate Joint Resolution	Tex. SJR

LEXSEE Citation Formats (Cont.)

Texas Supreme Court Journal	Tex. Sup. J.
Texas Supreme Court LEXIS cite	Tex. LEXIS
Texas Technical Law Review	Tex. Tech L. Rev.
Texas Wesleyan Law Review	Tex. Wesleyan L. Rev.
Thomas M. Cooley Law Review	T. M. Cooley L. Rev.
Trade Cases (CCH)	Trade Cas. (CCH)
Trademark Reporter, The	TMR
Trademark Trial & Appeals Board LEXIS cite	TTAB LEXIS
Transportation Law Journal	Transp. L. J.
Treasury Decisions Under Customs & Other Laws	Treas. Dec.
Tulane Environmental Law Journal	Tul. Envtl. L.J.
Tulane Law Review	Tul. L. Rev.
Tulsa Journal of Comparative & International Law	Tulsa J. Comp. & Int'l L.
Tulsa Law Journal	Tulsa L. J.
U.C.L.A. Environmental Law & Policy	UCLA J. Envtl. L. & Pol'y
U.C.L.A. Law Review	UCLA L. Rev.
U.C.L.A. Pacific Basin Law Journal	UCLA PAC. BASIN L.J.
U.C.L.A. Women's Law Journal	UCLA Women's L.J.
U.S. Tax Court Memorandum LEXIS cite	Tax Ct. Memo LEXIS
Uniform Commercial Code Reporting Service	U.C.C. Rep. Serv. (Callaghan)
Uniform Commercial Code Reporting Service, 2nd series	U.C.C.R. Serv. 2d (Callaghan)
United States Attorney General LEXIS cite	U.S. AG LEXIS
United States Claims Court LEXIS cite	U.S. Cl. Ct. LEXIS
United States Claims LEXIS cite	U.S. Claims LEXIS
United States Comptroller General LEXIS cite	U.S. Comp. Gen. LEXIS
United States Court of Appeals	U.S. App.
United States Court of Appeals (DC)	U.S. App. D.C.
United States Court of Appeals LEXIS cite	U.S. App. LEXIS
United States Court of Claims LEXIS cite	U.S. Ct. Cl LEXIS
United States Court of Military Appeals	U.S.C.M.A.
United States District Court LEXIS cite	U.S. Dist. LEX-IS

LEXSEE Citation Formats (Cont.)

United States Land Office Decisions	Pub. Lands Dec.
United States Law Week (BNA)	U.S.L.W.
United States Patents Quarterly (BNA)	U.S.P.Q. (BNA)
United States Patents Quarterly 2nd (BNA)	U.S.P.Q.2D (BNA)
United States Reports	U.S.
United States Supreme Court LEXIS cite	U.S. LEXIS
United States Tax Cases (CCH)	U.S. Tax Cas. (CCH)
United States Tax Court LEXIS cite	U.S. Tax Ct. LEXIS
United States Veteran's Appeals LEXIS cite	U.S. Vet. App. LEXIS
University of Arkansas - Little Rock Law Journal	U. Ark. Little Rock L.J.
University of Baltimore Intellectual Property Journal	U. Balt. Intell. Prop. J.
University of Baltimore Law Review	U. Balt. L. Rev.
University of California at Davis Law Review	U.C. Davis L. Rev.
University of Chicago Law Review	U. Chi. L. Rev.
University of Chicago Law School Roundtable	U Chi L Sch Roundtable
University of Chicago Legal Forum	U Chi Legal F
University of Cincinnati Law Review	U. Cin. L. Rev.
University of Colorado Law Review	U. Colo. L. Rev.
University of Dayton Law Review	Dayton L. Rev.
University of Detroit Mercy Law Review	U. Det.. Mercy L. Rev.
University of Florida Law Review	Fla. L. Rev.
University of Illinois Law Review	U. Ill. L. Rev.
University of Louisville Journal of Family Law	U. of Louisville J. of Fam. L.
University of Miami Entertainment & Sports Law Review	U. Miami Ent. & Sports L. Rev
University of Miami Inter-American Law Review	U. Miami Inter-Am. L. Rev.
University of Miami Law Review	U. Miami L. Rev.
University of Michigan Journal of Law Reform	U. Mich. J.L. Ref.
University of Missouri at Kansas City Law Review	UMKC L. Rev.
University of Missouri Law Review	Mo. L. Rev.
University of Pennsylvania International Business Law	U. Pa. J. Int'l Bus. L.
University of Pennsylvania Journal of Internation Business Law	U. Pa. J. Int'l Bus. L.

LEXSEE Citation Formats (Cont.)

University of Pennsylvania Law Review	U. Pa. L. Rev.
University of Pittsburgh Law Review	U. Pitt. L. Rev.
University of Richmond Law Review	U. Rich. L. Rev.
University of San Francisco Law Review	U.S.F.L.
University of Toledo Law Review	U. Tol. L. Rev.
US Statutes at Large	Stat
Utah Advance Legislative Service	Ut. ALS
Utah Advance Reports	Utah Adv. Rep.
Utah Attorney General LEXIS cite	Utah AG LEXIS
Utah Attorney General Opinions	Op. Atty Gen. Utah
Utah Chapter	Ut. Ch.
Utah Court of Appeals LEXIS cite	Utah App. LEXIS
Utah House Bill	Ut. HB
Utah Law Review	Utah L. Rev.
Utah Laws	Utah Laws
Utah Reports	Utah
Utah Reports, 2nd series	Utah 2d
Utah Resolution	Ut. Resolution
Utah SEC No-Action LEXIS cite	Utah Sec. No-Act. LEXIS
Utah Securities Commission LEXIS cite	Utah Sec. LEXIS
Utah Senate Bill	Ut. SB
Utah State Tax Commission LEXIS cite	Utah Tax LEXIS
Utah Supreme Court LEXIS cite	Utah LEXIS
Valparaiso University Law Review	Val. U.L. Rev.
Vanderbilt Journal of Transnational Law	Vand. J. Transnat'l L.
Vanderbilt Law Review	Vand. L. Rev.
Vermont Act	Vt. ACT
Vermont Advance Legislative Service	Vt. ALS
Vermont Department of Taxation LEXIS cite	Vt. Tax LEXIS
Vermont House	Vt. H.
Vermont Laws	Vt Laws
Vermont Reports	Vt.
Vermont Senate	Vt. S.
Vermont Supreme Court LEXIS cite	Vt. LEXIS
Veteran's Appeals	Vet. App.
Veterans Administration Board of Contract Appeals LEXIS cite	VA BCA LEXIS
Villanova Environmental Law Journal	Vill. Envtl. L.J.
Villanova Law Review	Vill. L. Rev.
Virgin Islands Act	V.I. Act
Virgin Islands Advance Legislative Service	V.I. ALS

LEXSEE Citation Formats (Cont.)

Virgin Islands Bill	V.I. Bill
Virgin Islands LEXIS cite	V.I. LEXIS
Virgin Islands Resolution	V.I. Resolution
Virgin Islands Session Laws	V.I. SESS. LAWS
Virginia Acts	Va. Acts
Virginia Advance Legislative Service	Va. ALS
Virginia Attorney General LEXIS cite	Va. AG LEXIS
Virginia Attorney General Opinions	Op. Atty Gen. Va.
Virginia Chapter	Va. Ch.
Virginia Court of Appeals LEXIS cite	Va. App. LEXIS
Virginia Court of Appeals Reports	Va. App.
Virginia Department of Taxation LEXIS cite	Va. Tax LEXIS
Virginia Environmental Law Journal	Va. Envtl. L.J.
Virginia House Bill	Va. HB
Virginia House Joint Resolution	Va. HJR
Virginia Journal of International Law	Va. J. Int'l L.
Virginia Journal of Social Policy & the Law	Va. J. Soc. Pol'y & L.
Virginia Law Reporter	VLR
Virginia Law Review	Va. L.Rev.
Virginia Reports	Va.
Virginia Securities Commission LEXIS cite	Va. Sec. LEXIS
Virginia Senate Bill	Va. SB
Virginia Senate Joint Resolution	Va. SJR
Virginia Supreme Court LEXIS cite	Va. LEXIS
Virginia Tax Review	Va. Tax Rev.
Wage & Hour Cases (BNA)	Wage & Hour Cas. (BNA)
Wage & Hour Cases, 2nd series (BNA)	Wage & Hour Cas. 2d (BNA)
Wake Forest Law Review	Wake Forest L. Rev.
Wallace's Reports (United States)	Wall.
Ware's United States District Court Report	Ware
Washburn Law Journal	Washburn L. J.
Washington Advance Legislative Service	Wa. ALS
Washington & Lee Law Review	Wash & Lee L. Rev.
Washington Appellate Reports	Wash. App.
Washington Attorney General LEXIS cite	Wash. AG LEXIS
Washington Attorney General Opinions	Op. Atty Gen. Wash.
Washington Attorney General Opinions (number)	Op. Atty Gen. Wash. No.
Washington Board of Tax Appeals LEXIS cite	Wash. Tax LEXIS
Washington Chapter	Wa. Ch.

LEXSEE Citation Formats (Cont.)

Washington Chapter Laws	Wa. Ch. Laws
Washington Court of Appeals LEXIS cite	Wash. App. LEX-IS
Washington House Bill	Wa. HB
Washington House Joint Resolution	Wa. HJR
Washington Initiative	Wa. Init.
Washington Law Review	Wash. L. Rev.
Washington Reports	Wash.
Washington Reports, 2nd series	Wash. 2d
Washington Securities Commission LEXIS cite	Wa. Sec. LEXIS
Washington Senate Bill	Wa. SB
Washington Supreme Court LEXIS cite	Wash. LEXIS
Washington University Law Quarterly	Wash. U. L. Q.
Washington Utilities & Transportation Commission LEXIS cite	Wash. UTC LEXIS
Wayne Law Review	Wayne L. Rev
Weekly Law Bulletin (OH)	Weekly L. Bull.
West Virginia Acts	W. Va. Acts
West Virginia Advance Legislative Service	W.V. ALS
West Virginia Attorney General LEXIS cite	W. Va. AG LEXIS
West Virginia Attorney General Opinions	Op. Atty Gen. W.Va.
West Virginia Chapter	W.V. Ch.
West Virginia House Bill	W.V. HB
West Virginia House Joint Resolution	W.V. HJR
West Virginia House Resolution	W.V. HR
West Virginia Law Review	W. Va. L. Rev
West Virginia Reports	W. Va.
West Virginia Senate Bill	W.V. SB
West Virginia Senate Joint Resolution	W.V. SJR
West Virginia Senate Resolution	W.V. SR
West Virginia Supreme Court LEXIS cite	W. Va. LEXIS
West Virginia Tax LEXIS cite	W. Va. Tax LEXIS
Western Law Journal (OH)	West. Law J.
Western New England Law Review	W New Eng. L. Rev
Western State University Law Review	W. St. U. L. Rev.
Wheeler's Criminal Cases	Wheeler Cr.
Whittier Law Review	Whittier L. Rev.
Willamette Law Review	Willamette L. Rev
William & Mary Bill of Rights Journal	Wm. & Mary Bill of Rts. J.
William & Mary Law Review	Wm and Mary L. Rev.

LEXSEE Citation Formats (Cont.)

William & Mary Review of Virginia Law	Wm. & Mary Rev. Va. L.
William Mitchell Law Review	Wm. Mitchell L. Rev.
Wisconsin Act	Wis. Act
Wisconsin Advance Legislative Service	Wis. ALS
Wisconsin Assembly Bill	Wis. AB
Wisconsin Assembly Joint Resolution	Wis. AJR
Wisconsin Attorney General LEXIS cite	Wisc. AG LEXIS
Wisconsin Attorney General Opinions	Op. Atty Gen. Wis.
Wisconsin Court of Appeals LEXIS cite	Wisc. App. LEXIS
Wisconsin Court of Appeals Reports	Wis. App.
Wisconsin Environmental Law Journal	Wis. Envtl. L. J.
Wisconsin Joint Resolution	Wis. Joint Res
Wisconsin Law Review	Wis. L. Rev.
Wisconsin Laws	Wis. Laws
Wisconsin Public Utilities Commission LEXIS cite	Wisc. PUC LEXIS
Wisconsin Reports	Wis.
Wisconsin Reports, 2nd series	Wis. 2d
Wisconsin Securities Commission LEXIS cite	Wisc. Sec. LEXIS
Wisconsin Senate Bill	Wis. SB
Wisconsin Senate Joint Resolution	Wis. SJR
Wisconsin Supreme Court LEXIS cite	Wisc. LEXIS
Wisconsin Tax Appeals Commission LEXIS cite	Wisc. Tax LEXIS
Wisconsin Women's Law Journal	Wis. Women's L.J.
Wood's United States Circuit Court Reports	Woods
Woolworth's Circuit Court Reports	Wool.
Wyoming Advance Legislative Service	Wy. ALS
Wyoming Attorney General LEXIS cite	Wyo. AG LEXIS
Wyoming Attorney General Opinions	Op. Atty Gen. Wyo.
Wyoming Chapter	Wy. Ch.
Wyoming Enrolled Act	Wy. EA
Wyoming House Bill	Wy. HB
Wyoming House File	Wy. HF
Wyoming No-Action LEXIS cite	Wy. No-Act. LEXIS
Wyoming Reports	Wyo.
Wyoming Securities Commission LEXIS cite	Wy. Sec. LEXIS
Wyoming Senate Bill	Wy. SB
Wyoming Senate File	Wy. SF
Wyoming Session Laws	Wyo. Sess. Laws
Wyoming Supreme Court LEXIS cite	Wyo. LEXIS

LEXSEE Citation Formats (Cont.)

Wyoming Tax Commission LEXIS cite	Wyo. Tax LEXIS
Yale Journal of Law & the Humanities	Yale J. L. & Human
Yale Journal on Regulations	Yale J. on Reg.
Yale Law & Policy Review	Yale L. & Pol'y Rev.
Yale Law Journal	Yale L.J

Appendix H

Statutes on LEXIS®-NEXIS®

This Appendix shows you, for each state, the name of the file (in library *CODES*) containing the Code for the state, the format for performing a LEXSTAT® request on a section of that Code, and the name of the file containing the state's Advance Legislative Service.

The LEXSTAT feature lets you view the full text of a statute section at any point in your research, by transmitting **lexstat** followed by the citation of the code section you want to see. For example:

```
lexstat fl code 61.044
```

For five states (California, Louisiana, Maryland, New York and Texas), your LEXSTAT request must include the abbreviation for the particular code title or section you wish to retrieve, for example:

```
lexstat ca civ proc code 1281
```

State	Code File Name	LEXSTAT Format	ALS File Name
Alabama	ALCODE	al code 1270	ALALS
Alaska	AKCODE	ak code 09.20.010	AKALS
Arizona	AZCODE	az code 36-2152	AZALS
Arkansas*	ARCODE	ar code 9309	ARALS
California	CACODE	ca gov 20022	CAALS
Colorado	COCODE	co code 12G105	COALS
Connecticut	CTCODE	ct code 5-275	CTALS
Delaware*	DECODE	31 de code 309	DEALS
D.C.*	DCCODE	dc code 6-3401	DCALS
Florida	FLCODE	fl code 520.74	FLALS
Georgia*	GACODE	ga code 19-2-1	GAALS
Hawaii*	HICODE	hi code 91-14	HIALS
Idaho	IDCODE	id code 9-203	IDALS
Illinois	ILCODE	625 ilcs 5/6-601	ILALS
Indiana*	INCODE	in code 4-36	INALS
Iowa	IACODE	ia code 422.12	IAALS
Kansas*	KSCODE	ks code 60-2414	KSALS
Kentucky*	KYCODE	ky code 158.035	KYALS
Louisiana	LACODE	la code 17:283	LAALS
Maine	MECODE	25 me code 2003	MEALS

State	Code File Name	LEXSTAT Format	ALS File Name
Maryland*	MDCODE	md rp 8a-201	MDALS
Massachusetts	MACODE	ma code 209a 3	MAALS
Michigan	MICODE	mi code 287.706	MIALS
Minnesota	MNCODE	mn code 120.062	MNALS
Mississippi*	MSCODE	ms code 43!105	MSALS
Missouri	MOCODE	mo code 197.200	MOALS
Montana*	MTCODE	mt code 331301	MTALS
Nebraska	NECODE	ne code 30-2806	NEALS
Nevada*	NVCODE	nv code 268.096	NVALS
New Hampshire*	NHCODE	nh code 188-e:5	NHALS
New Jersey	NJCODE	nj code 54a:2-1	NJALS
New Mexico*	NMCODE	nm code 61-6-1	NMALS
New York	NYCODE'	ny gen mun 370	NYALS
North Carolina	NCCODE	nc code 105-273	NCALS
North Dakota	NDCODE	nd code 206	NDALS
Ohio*	OHCODE	oh code 4582.30	OHALS
Oklahoma	OKCODE	43a ok code 3-302	OKALS
Oregon	ORCODE	or code 1.001	ORALS
Pennsylvania	PACODE	18 pa code 3204	PAALS
Puerto Rico*	PRCODE	27 pr code 1101	PRALS
Rhode Island	RICODE	ri code 3-5-11	RIALS
South Carolina	SCCODE	sc code 1-7-80	SCALS
South Dakota	SDCODE	sd code 42-7-48	SDALS
Tennessee*	TNCODE	tn code 56%1601	TNALS
Texas	TXCODE	tx fam 3.581	TXALS
Utah*	UTCODE	ut code 26-25a-101	UTALS
Vermont*	VTCODE	22 vt code 454	VTALS
Virginia	VACODE	va code 8.01-229	VAALS
Virgin Islands	VICODE	16 vi code 91	VIALS
Washington	WACODE	wa code 13.32a.020	WAALS
West Virginia	WVCODE	wv code 46a-2-128	WVALS
Wisconsin	WICODE	wi code 77.67	WIALS
Wyoming	WYCODE	wy code 31-2-205	WYALS
United States	USCODE	5 uscs 5901	PUBLAW
Code of Federal Regulations	CFR	10 cfr 580.03	——

* States marked with a single asterisk offer annotated statutes.

The statutes of the states of Louisiana, Maine, New Jersey, Oklahoma, Pennsylvania and Texas have been added to the LEXIS service by LEXIS-NEXIS, a division of Reed Elsevier Inc., and are being made available under license from West Publishing Company.

Index

LEXIS-NEXIS for Law Students

B

C

I

J

K

L

M

N

O

P

Q

R

T

Law In A Flash Flashcards

Flashcards

Civil Procedure 1 ◆	$16.95
Civil Procedure 2 ◆	16.95
Constitutional Law ▲	16.95
Contracts ◆▲	16.95
Corporations	16.95
Criminal Law ◆▲	16.95
Criminal Procedure ▲	16.95
Evidence ▲	16.95
Future Interests ▲	16.95
Professional Responsibility (953 cards)	32.95
Real Property ◆▲	16.95
Sales (UCC Art.2) ▲	16.95
Torts ◆▲	16.95
Wills & Trusts	16.95

Flashcard Sets

First Year Law Set (includes all sets marked ◆ *plus* the book Strategies & Tactics for First Year Law.)	95.00
Multistate Bar Review Set (includes all sets marked ▲ *plus* the book Strategies & Tactics for MBE)	165.00
Professional Responsibility Set (includes the *Professional Responsibility* flashcards *plus* the book Strategies & Tactics for the MPRE)	45.00

Law In A Flash Software

(for Windows® 3.1 and Windows® 95 only)

Law In A Flash Interactive Software combines the best features of our flashcards with the power of the computer. Just some of the great features:

- Contains the complete text of the corresponding *Law In A Flash* printed flashcards
- Side-by-side comparison of your own answer to the card's preformulated answer
- Fully customizable, savable sessions – pick which topics to review and in what order
- Mark cards for further review or printing
- Score your answers, to help you spot those topics in which you need further review

Every *Law In A Flash* title and set is available as software.

Requirements: 386, 486, or Pentium-based computer running Windows® 3.1 or Windows® 95; 8 megabytes RAM (16MB recommended); 3.5" high-density floppy drive; 3MB free space per title; Windows-supported mouse and printer (optional)

Individual titles	$19.95
Professional Responsibility (covers 953 cards)	34.95
First Year Law Set*	115.00
Multistate Bar Review Set*	195.00
Professional Responsibility/MPRE Set*	49.95

* These software sets contain the same titles as printed card sets *plus* the corresponding *Strategies & Tactics* books (see below).

Strategies & Tactics Series

Strategies & Tactics for the MBE

Packed with the most valuable advice you can find on how to successfully attack the MBE. Each MBE subject is covered, including Criminal Procedure (part of Criminal Law), Future Interests (part of Real Property), and Sales (part of Contracts). The book contains 350 actual past MBE questions broken down by subject, plus a full-length 200-question practice MBE. Each question has a ***fully-detailed answer*** which describes in detail not only why the correct answer is correct, but why each of the wrong answer choices is wrong.

☛ Covers all the new MBE specifications tested on and after July, 1997.

Each title *$34.95*

Strategies & Tactics for First Year Law

A complete guide to your first year of law school, from the first day of class to studying for exams. Packed with the inside information that will help you survive what most consider the worst year of law school and come out on top.

☛ Completely revised for 1997.

$12.95

Strategies & Tactics for the MPRE

Packed with exam tactics that help lead you to the right answers and expert advice on spotting and avoiding the traps set by the Bar Examiners. Contains actual questions from past MPRE's, with detailed answers.

$19.95